THE JOURNAL OF GEORGE FOX

THE JOURNAL OF
GEORGE FOX

A REVISED EDITION BY
JOHN L. NICKALLS

WITH AN EPILOGUE BY
HENRY J. CADBURY
AND
AN INTRODUCTION BY
GEOFFREY F. NUTTALL

PHILADELPHIA
RELIGIOUS SOCIETY OF FRIENDS
1985

ISBN 0941308-05-7

Published by
Philadelphia Yearly Meeting
of the Religious Society of Friends
with permission of
London Yearly Meeting
of the Religious Society of Friends
1985

First printed, being published by the Syndics of the
Cambridge University Press 1952
Reprinted by London Yearly Meeting with minor corrections 1975

Library of Congress Catalog Card Number 85-080 620

Obtainable from Friends Book Store
156 North 15th Street
Philadelphia, PA 19102

CONTENTS

THE JOURNAL

INTRODUCTION:
GEORGE FOX AND HIS JOURNAL

BY GEOFFREY F. NUTTALL, D.D.

'THE power of the Lord was over all.' If George Fox's personality is to be expressed in a single phrase, then this is it. Throughout his life Fox walked cheerfully over the world in the power of the Lord, finding it, as William Penn was to say of him, a match for every service or occasion.

One immediate and obvious effect was that he was fearless. 'I never feared death nor sufferings in my life.' 'One of the parliament men told me they must have me to Smithfield to burn me as they did the martyrs, but I told him I was over their fires and feared them not.' Nor was this a vain boast, either in the sense that it was an idle threat or in the sense that he would retract if suffering came. At Lichfield, where to Fox's vision the market place was like a pool of blood, Edward Wightman was burned for blasphemy only a few years before Fox was born; nor would Wightman have been the last, had Archbishop Laud had his way. Witches, moreover, were burned till a much later period, and by some Fox was said to be a witch. Nor was persecution long in coming. By 1659, a bare twelve years from the beginning of Fox's ministry, twenty-one Quakers are known to have died in prison or as a consequence of ill usage.

Of these sufferings, rough handling and imprisonment alike, Fox bore a full share, and never shrank from them. When a man came with a naked sword and set it to Fox's side, 'I looked up at him in his face and said to him, "Alack for thee, it's no more to me than a straw."'

Not for nothing was his mother of the stock of the martyrs. In prison, like Paul and Silas, he would sing in the Lord's power, and sing till the fiddler who had been brought into the dungeon to drown him was drowned himself and silenced. When the news reached Fox that at Evesham stocks had been set up against his coming, to Evesham at once he went. On another occasion, when he had been banished from Perth, 'it was upon me from the Lord to go back again . . . and so set the power of God over them'. To our sophisticated detachment such behaviour seems to have more than a touch of exhibitionism; but it bore a witness which was unmistakable. It also set a noble example. At Reading and elsewhere this was reproduced even by the children, who, when their parents were all in prison, themselves kept up the meeting for worship. In Penn's words: 'We are the people above all others that must stand in the gap.' And as in the beginnings of Christianity, such courage proved powerful in convincing others. 'Many turned Quakers', says Richard Baxter, 'because the Quakers kept their meetings openly, and went to prison for it cheerfully.'

Together with this physical courage, as will already be clear, went moral firmness and fidelity to truth. In the writings of the early Quakers, who sometimes called themselves Friends in Truth, truth is a word which recurs constantly, and with a meaning which goes far beyond mere truthfulness, high though Friends rated this. 'The truth can live in the gaols,' wrote Fox from one of them.[1] The connotation of the word is emotional and moral rather than intellectual. For Fox as for Isaac Watts, because for the Hebrew poets who inspired them, 'Thy truth for ever firmly stood, and shall from age to age endure.' It is natural that a life devoted to truth should itself bear something of this steadfastness. Fox's father did not become a Quaker but he knew his son's quality here. On one occasion, after a dispute between Fox and some ministers of religion, Fox writes that his father

[1] G. Fox, *Epistles* (1698), p. 199.

'thwacked his cane on the ground, and said, "Well", said he, "I see he that will but stand to the truth it will carry him out."' It had always been so. When Fox was still a child, it was a common saying among people that knew him, 'If George says "Verily", there is no altering him.' So it remained. 'If formal etiquette expected him to say to a man what he very well knew was not true, then he resolved to have nothing more to do with formal etiquette till the end of the world!'[1]

The kind of situation into which Fox was brought by this resolve may be illustrated from the story of his imprisonment at Launceston. He was taking exercise in the castle green when Peter Ceely, the Justice of the Peace who had arrested him, came by. Ceely doffed his hat, and said, 'How do you, Mr. Fox? Your servant, Sir.' 'Major Ceely', replied Fox, 'take heed of hypocrisy and a rotten heart, for when came I to be thy master and thee my servant? Do servants use to cast their masters into prison?'

In the trial which followed, Fox requested the judge to let his mittimus be read.

> The judge said it should not. I said it ought to be, seeing it concerned my life and liberty. And the judge said again it should not be read. And I said, 'It ought to be read; and if I have done any thing worthy of death or bonds, let all the country know of it.' So I spoke unto one of my fellow prisoners, 'Thou hast a copy of it. Read it up,' said I. 'But it shall not be read', said the judge. 'Gaoler, take him away. I will see whether he or I shall be master.' So they did and after a while they called for me again, and I still cried to have my mittimus read up, for that signified my crime. And then I bid William Salt read it up again, and he read it up, and the judge and justices and whole court were silent, for the people were mighty willing to hear it (pp. 246-7).

In the end Fox got his way. He almost always did. What could one do against a spirit so indomitable? Fox was always determined to have justice. It was part of his

[1] R. M. Jones, *George Fox—Seeker and Friend*, p. 200.

fidelity to truth. 'I desire nothing but law and justice at thy hands,' he told a judge once; 'for I do not look for mercy'. For the same reason, he could not agree to be released from prison on a pardon. He had not done wrong, and he could not pretend that he had.

Courage and moral strength are always impressive, and especially so when combined. In Fox's case they were accompanied by a distinctive attitude to persecutors, or, perhaps it would be truer to say, to some of them. Towards officials, such as 'priests' (as he called all ordained clergymen and ministers) and Justices of the Peace, he was commonly resentful and sharp of tongue. In his eyes religion and justice were but mocked by them: they were not living according to what they professed. Towards publicans and sinners, on the other hand, he often showed a remarkable forbearance. To a drunken fellow-prisoner in Scarborough Castle, who had challenged him to a fight, Fox said, 'I was come to answer him, with my hands in my pockets, and . . . there was my hair and my back, and what a shame it was for him to challenge a man whose principle he knew was not to strike; . . . and one of the officers said, "You are a happy man that can bear such things."' Nor was this an isolated case. On an earlier occasion, in London, Fox heard a rude Irish colonel threatening to kill all the Quakers; so he went to him and said, '"Here is gospel for thee, here is my hair, and here is my cheek, and here are my shoulders", and turned them to him . . . and the truth came so over him that he grew loving.'

Fox's explicit equation here of the gospel with behaviour, and with behaviour of a certain kind, is worth noting. It is characteristic of him, and is a key to much in Quakerism. It is also worth noting that he later records of the man who had challenged him to fight, 'the Lord soon cut him off in his wickedness'. This is one of several similar observations. Fox's evident satisfaction in thus recording what he believed to be the Lord's judgments reveals a certain hardness in him and has sometimes disturbed readers who have failed to perceive his intense devotion to justice. It is more to the point to remark that he could behave towards a man with forbearance and could yet record the man's bad end; for it is typical of a realism in him which is often apparent. On another occasion, when he was in court, he observed, as he puts it, that 'the power of darkness riz up in them like a mountain'. Nevertheless, he looked the judge in the face, 'and the witness started up in him and made him blush'. Fox is peculiarly sensitive, that is to say, to the evil in men *and* to the good in them; and he can be sensitive to both at one and the same time.

'And the truth came so over him that he grew loving.' We are still in the context of the Lord's power coming over all. The phrase shows, further, the motive of Fox's forbearance. Outwardly, his behaviour can sometimes appear mere passiveness, as when, on being attacked by a rude wicked man, 'I stood stiff and still and let him strike.' But the motive is through the power of the Lord to win men, and in particular to win them to be loving. Now most men, rude wicked men anyway, are not in a way of loving. 'We love, because he first loved us,' Fox read in his New Testament. Ideally, therefore, his forbearance was an endeavour to express a spirit of love through which others' hearts might grow gentle. He was human, and did not always love his persecutors; that he ever did so is sufficiently remarkable. At Ulverston, in 1652, he was beaten with stakes and clubs till he had fallen unconscious. When he recovered, 'I lay a little still, and the power of the Lord sprang through me, and the eternal refreshings refreshed me, that I stood up again in the eternal power of God and stretched out my arms amongst them all, and said again with a loud voice, "Strike again, here is my arms and my head and my cheeks." . . . and I was in the love of God to them all that had persecuted me.' It is a striking scene, and vital for gauging the quality of the man.

Who was this man? and why was he so bitterly persecuted? As for who he was, the answer is short. He was a nobody: a weaver's son from an utterly undistinguished village in Leicestershire; with how little schooling can be seen at a glance from the big, bold scrawl and erratic spelling in what few scraps of his handwriting are still preserved. The reason why he was persecuted is more complicated; but in a word it was because he was a revolutionary, and a revolutionary in religion at a time when religion dominated men's minds. *Primitive Christianity Revived* was the title which William Penn gave to one of his books, and nothing expresses better what Fox was after. His was not the first but the last of a series of endeavours in this direction, and because it was the last it was both the most extreme and the most keenly resented by those who were concerned for reformation but were satisfied with the limits already reached. Fox was in no way peculiar, for instance, in belittling university education as equipment for the ministry. In 1653 alarm was felt in more than one quarter lest Parliament should destroy the universities altogether; and a majority of the members were for abolishing the payment of tithes in support of the ministry. Fox was not only steadfast in bearing testimony against the system of tithes, he wanted to abolish a paid ministry altogether; for he could find none in the New Testament. Oaths, likewise, were forbidden in the New Testament; then they were forbidden to Christians still; and if oaths in a court of law were an accepted foundation of contemporary society, so much the worse for contemporary society.

It is thus not surprising that Quakers were said to be against both magistracy and ministry, and were feared; or that, because they were feared, they were persecuted. Fox says himself that his purpose was 'to bring people off from all the world's religions, which are vain'. Men's fears might not have come to anything, had he remained an isolated figure with no following, like many another harmless fanatic of the time. But Fox quickly became the leader of a widespread, closely-knit community devoted to him personally and in sympathy with his revolutionary outlook; and of this the authorities were fully aware.

He began, however, alone; and he had a right to be proud of this. As the Quaker movement grew, it owed much to other leaders also: in particular to James Nayler, a man of temperament more ethereal than Fox always understood, and to the fervent and lion-hearted woman whom eventually Fox married, Margaret Fell. It is true that Fox sometimes unduly magnified his own share in the convincing of others, of whom Nayler was one. But nothing can rob him of the glory of having founded Quakerism, and of having done so alone, by the sheer force of personality and of faith in his mission. Like Paul, he was anxious to claim independence of others in the discovery of his message; and in fact no substantial dependence has been established. For centuries weavers had borne a name for independence and radicalism in religion. In Leicestershire Lollard traditions had lingered since Wycliffe was Rector of Lutterworth, not so far from Fenny Drayton, where Fox was born. To the atmosphere of his own time he owed more than he knew or would allow. To all intents and purposes, nevertheless, Fox was, what Penn calls him, 'an original, being no man's copy'; and in this lay much of his strength. If, as a Quaker historian observes, Friends have been ready 'to step out as pioneers of worthy causes without waiting to make sure of any large band of followers',[1] they have themselves but followed where Fox led. To refer this, with Carlyle, to his 'enormous sacred Self-confidence'[2] is to miss the mark. It is truer, as well as kinder, to see in him something larger, something nearer to what Godwin calls 'that generous confidence which, in a great soul, is never extinguished'.[3]

[1] A. N. Brayshaw, *The Quakers: their Story and Message*, p. 194.

[2] *Letters and Speeches of Oliver Cromwell*, ed. T. Carlyle (Everyman edn.), iii, 341.

[3] William Godwin, of Mary Wollstonecraft, in *Memoirs of Mary Wollstonecraft* (Constable's Miscellany), p. 101.

'All must first know the voice crying in the wilderness, in their hearts.' In this characteristic utterance of Fox we may see an accepted expression of genius, namely, the assumption that what is true for oneself is true also for others, and for all others; its universalizing. We may also see something more. The Reformation principles of justification by faith and of the priesthood of all believers had already introduced a universalizing element into religion; but it was possible for this to become but a theory of universalism, held only by the few who had the wit, and the desire, to theorize. Experience, however, is open to all to share; and in treating his own experience as possible for all Fox also provided a surer basis for the universalizing element in Reformed religion.

What, then, was it which was distinctive about his own experience? Something like this. With the recovery of the Bible in the vernacular, Christians had come to hear the voice of God speaking not only to the prophets and apostles of old but through these to themselves. The word of the Lord endureth for ever, and what was written in Scripture was found to possess contemporary significance and power, and to provide a message which could be preached to others with conviction. 'You will say, Christ saith this, and the apostles say this; but what canst thou say?' These words of Fox proved effective in convincing Margaret Fell, but many were asking questions of this kind besides Fox. Fox, however, went further. He held, with Oliver Cromwell, that God speaks without a written word sometimes, yet according to it. He urged men to attend to the words of the Spirit of Christ still speaking within their hearts, 'Christ within you, the hope of glory.' He argued, moreover, that, unless men first did this, they could not hope to read Scripture with any genuine understanding. 'They could not know the spiritual meaning of Moses', the prophets', and John's words, nor see their path and travels, much less see through them and to the end of them into the kingdom, unless they had the Spirit and light of Jesus.' This is a position familiar to most of us to-day, but it was very far from familiar then. Fox also held that by hearkening to the voice of the living Christ latter-day Christians, and all Christians, might live in the power of Christ's endless life as Christ's first disciples had done; and, furthermore, that Christ's power could transport men, even in this life, into paradise, such a paradise as Adam and Eve knew before they fell, thus giving men triumph over their sinful propensities. This proved more than most men could accept, or can; but we can see its place in the context of the power of the Lord being over all.

On the relation of the voice, or the light, of Christ within the heart to the figure of Jesus of Nazareth, Fox did not succeed in satisfying the theologians of his day; but then they rarely satisfied one another. Later Quaker history, it is true, shows that they were not altogether astray in fearing a divorce here rather than an association of some kind. For Fox himself, however, there was the closest association, in whatever terms it was to be expressed. His principle of loving forbearance, to take a single but telling instance, was clearly influenced as much by the example of Jesus in the Gospels as by any inward voice. No one, in fact, knew his Bible better than Fox did, or could quote it in argument more devastatingly. His use of Scripture, together with the nature of the books and passages from which he quotes, or which affect his imagery, most frequently, remains an inviting field for research.

Later Quaker devotion, again, shows a tendency so to concentrate on the light within that in meetings for worship at some periods prayer, in the normal sense of prayer addressed outside oneself, prayer which can thus be expressed vocally, fell into relative desuetude. This also was in no way true of Fox. Fox knew how, as well as when, to be silent, how ' to famish them from words ', as he puts it; but normally he was as great in prayer as in preaching, so great that Penn says he excelled here above all. ' The most awful, living, reverent frame I ever felt or beheld,

I must say, was his in prayer. And truly it was a testimony (that) he knew and lived nearer to the Lord than other men.' George Fox's Lord was no mere light within.

Nevertheless, the light was there, shining steadily and welcomingly, the light of Christ; and it was to this that Fox pointed men unwearyingly. 'Mind that which is pure in you to guide you to God', he would say.[1] Even in childhood, he tells us, he had been taught how to walk to be kept pure; and he had kept his childhood's vow not to be wanton when he grew to manhood. Here again he universalized his own experience. If he could be kept pure, so could others. He claimed no special grace for himself, no gift that was not for all men to receive who would. Nor did he pretend that it was possible to live in purity without persistent watchfulness, in utter dependence on the power of God. That which was pure had to be minded. 'Friend', he wrote to Oliver Cromwell's favourite daughter, Lady Claypole, 'Be still and cool in thy own mind and spirit from thy own thoughts, and then thou wilt feel the principle of God to turn thy mind to the Lord God, whereby thou wilt receive his strength and power from whence life comes to allay all tempests, blusterings and storms.' Later in the same letter he writes:

> What the light doth make manifest and discover, temptations, confusions, distractions, distempers, do not look at the temptations, confusions, corruptions, but at the light which discovers them, that makes them manifest; and with the same light you will feel over them, to receive power to stand against them . . . For looking down at sin, and corruption, and distraction, you are swallowed up in it; but looking at the light which discovers them, you will see over them. That will give victory; and you will find grace and strength: and there is the first step of peace (pp. 347-8 post).

His letter, Fox says, settled and stayed Lady Claypole's mind for the present, and proved useful for the settling of others' minds also. Yet in a day when, in Fox's quaint

[1] G. Fox, *Epistles* (1698), p. 9.

phrase, popular preachers would 'roar up for sin, in their pulpits', it sounded strange teaching; as to many weighed down with the world's evil it still sounds strange. It is, indeed, a teaching which, unless Fox's Christian presuppositions are realized and accepted, can easily bring a man into peril and has often done so: the peril, for instance, of being more like the Pharisee than the publican. Yet Fox was not wrong in finding in his New Testament the promise that over Christians sin should not have dominion. That he took this promise seriously and claimed its fulfilment in experience shows him entirely in character. The Lord's power was over all, sin included.

Had he not held this conviction so strongly, he would never have had the heart to go through either with his forbearance to those who persecuted him, or, more particularly, with his refusal to take up arms. For himself, he had early 'come into the covenant of peace which was before wars and strifes were', as he told those who pressed him to fight for Parliament in the Civil Wars. He had found what it meant to live 'in the virtue of that life and power that took away the occasion of all wars'. But he was far too shrewd an observer of his fellow men to suppose that this was true generally. Nothing could be further from the truth than to see Fox's testimony against taking part in war as idealistic and up in the air. It was exactly the opposite. Fox moved constantly among rude and wicked men, and was keenly sensitive to the evil in them, to the lust, as he found it called in the New Testament, from which all wars arose. His object was to overcome this lust by going among men in the power of the Lord and behaving towards them in the way '*the most likely* to reach to the inward witness and so change the evil mind into the right mind'.[1] It was essentially a missionary gospel which he preached, the gospel of Christ's power to meet evil and to overcome it; and it had its origin and seal in his own experience. There before starting out on his ministry, he had seen an ocean of darkness and death,

[1] A. N. Brayshaw, *op. cit.*, p. 131.

but also an infinite ocean of light and love, which flowed over the ocean of darkness. What he now sought was to be the Lord's instrument in bringing about a similar vision and a similar triumph in the lives of others. And with this we are back at the courage and fidelity and forbearance which first attracted us in him.

But Fox not only lived a remarkable life, he was also the author of a remarkable *Journal*. It is not a journal at all in the strict sense of an account written, if not daily, at least shortly after each incident described, when the future is still dark. It is, rather, an autobiography or book of memoirs, written in retrospect in order to illustrate the power of the Lord as shown in his servant's 'Sufferings and Passages', as earlier, briefer accounts by other Quakers were often entitled.[1] Also, although we possess the original manuscript of the *Journal*, it is not in Fox's hand. It was not written by Fox but dictated, and was taken down mainly by his stepson-in-law, Thomas Lower. This makes the effectiveness with which it conveys his personality the more remarkable. Even so, it was not given to the world in its original form until the present century. Fox did not issue it during his lifetime but left instructions for its publication after his death. When he died, it was nearly twenty years after he had composed the *Journal* and more than fifty since the incidents recounted in its earlier sections. Toleration had come, and the missionary exaltation of Quakerism had grown cooler. Consequently, it was thought wise not only to omit or tone down many passages which to a politer age might seem wild or fanatical, but also to smooth out Fox's rugged style and occasionally outlandish vocabulary. This was a pity, though one can see broadly why it was done. A detailed study of the alterations made, and of the additions and omissions, with the reasons for them, so far as these can be ascertained,

[1] A brief narrative by Fox himself bearing a similar title is still extant. It brings his story only to the year 1653 and adds nothing substantial to the *Journal*. See the *Bulletin* of the Friends Historical Association, Philadelphia, xxxix, 1 (Spring, 1950), pp. 27-31.

is another subject demanding research. It would throw light on the aesthetic as well as the ethical canons of editing in the 1690's.

Not that Fox was a man of one book only. Although he composed no other work of comparable length, he published within his lifetime some two hundred tracts and other writings, while the number of unpublished papers by him, now often lost but known from a manuscript catalogue in a contemporary hand, runs into thousands. Many of his earlier published pamphlets have never been reprinted, or much regarded even by his biographers. Though ephemeral in the sense that they were essentially tracts for the times, they deserve attention: their systematic study would throw light on the times as well as on Fox. Some of them, mainly those with an interest primarily homiletic rather than social or political, were gathered together after Fox's death and republished in a single volume entitled *Gospel-Truth Demonstrated.* This was preceded by a collected volume of some four hundred of his *Epistles*, most of which were written to groups of Friends or others and are in the nature of exhortations or warnings rather than personal letters. In this country *Gospel-Truth Demonstrated* has never been re-issued; nor have the *Epistles*, though there is a modern anthology of selections from them.[1] Only the *Journal* has been continually republished, till by 1891 it was in its eighth edition. With its appearance twenty years later as first taken down by Thomas Lower,[2] fresh interest was aroused and has been maintained. The nature and purpose of the present edition is explained in the Editor's preface.

Fox might not have been altogether pleased, had he foreseen the reasons for which his *Journal* would come to be valued; for it now interests, even delights, readers who have little or no sympathy with his faith in the power

[1] *A Day-Book of Counsel and Comfort from the Epistles of George Fox*, ed. L. V. Hodgkin, Macmillan, 1937.

[2] *The Journal of George Fox*, ed. N. Penney, Cambridge University Press, 1911.

of the Lord. Fox lived in an age when literary self-expression could still be direct and naïve: the sophistication and self-consciousness of the following century were not yet felt. In his *Journal*, like Bunyan in *Grace Abounding*, and Baxter in his autobiography, Fox is so absorbed in the spiritual purpose of his narration that he does not stop to think whether he is giving himself away, or to add touches of artistry with the purpose of bringing out how things should have happened or even of heightening the effect of things as they were. Things as they were were quite sufficiently remarkable; and in any case his devotion to truth demanded a straight narrative. That this did not result in a bald narrative is one of the mysteries of creative writing. All we can say is that Fox's personality was so well integrated, so dominant and pervasive, that what he dictated was, like himself, alive.

Nor is it only himself that he reveals so ingenuously. He had the skill to sketch many a character or situation in a few short vivid phrases. Take this paragraph, which follows closely on the scene of violence at Ulverston, when, though mazed with the blows he had received, he was in the love of God to all his persecutors.

> And so I was moved of the Lord to come up again through them and up into Ulverston market, and there meets me a man with a sword, a soldier. 'Sir', said he, 'I am your servant, I am ashamed that you should be thus abused, for you are a man,' said he. He was grieved and said he would assist me in what he could, and I told him that it was no matter, the Lord's power was over all (p. 128-9).

The conversation here is highly characteristic. These are real people, speaking naturally.

> As soon as I came to the door, a young woman came to the door. 'What! Is it you?' said she as though she had seen me before, 'Come in,' said she: for the Lord's power bowed their hearts (p. 73).

Or again:

> And it being in the evening there being a company of serving

men and wild fellows, they met me and encompassed me about and had an intent to have done me some mischief. And it being dark, I asked, ' What ! are you highwaymen ? ' (p. 278).

The syntax is loose; but one can see and hear, almost feel, it as it happens.

Or take Fox's description of the situation which brought about his being belaboured so roughly at Ulverston: the picture of the minister who was ' blustering on in his preaching ', when ' of a sudden all the people in the steeplehouse were in an outrage and an uproar '; so that ' people tumbled over their seats for fear . . . and the blood ran down several people so as I never saw the like in my life, as I looked at them when they were dragging me along '.

This last phrase explains something of the *Journal's* power. Fox possessed the detachment to look at men. He had need to do so, it is true. At Aberystwyth ' I turned but my back from the man that was giving oats to my horse, and I looked back again and he was filling his pockets with the provender that was given to my horse '. Fox looked at men, and he remembered what he saw. Small wonder that men cried ' Look at his eyes ! ' and ' Don't pierce me so with thy eyes ! Keep thy eyes off me ! ' He looked at them, and knew what was in them. Sometimes he saw them not only as they were but as they would be. ' As I parted from him ', he says of James Nayler in 1655, ' I cast my eyes upon him, and a fear struck in me concerning him.' Within a year Nayler had run out into imaginations, as Fox calls it, and had brought shame upon Friends generally.

Fox was thus not only always minding a light within. He was also, as Penn says of him, a discerner of others' spirits. That he should have been given to visions more generally is hardly surprising. Such visions as, on various occasions, he had of ' a bear and two great mastiff dogs, that I should pass by them and they should do me no hurt ', of ' a desperate creature like a wild horse or colt that was coming to destroy me: but I got victory over it ', of ' a black coffin, but I passed over it ', of ' an ugly slubbering hound ', are all presumably to be regarded as but the projections into concrete symbols of a presentiment of danger which often came to him and seldom without cause. He had, however, at least one vision of a more meditative kind, his account of which contains some exquisite dream-language, especially in its closing sentences.

And I had a vision about the time that I was in this travail and sufferings, that I was walking in the fields, and many Friends were with me, and I bid them dig in the earth, and they did and I went down. And there was a mighty vault top-full of people kept under the earth, rocks and stones. So I bid them break open the earth and let all the people out, and they did, and all the people came forth to liberty; and it was a mighty place.

And when they had done I went on and bid them dig again. They did, and there was a mighty vault full of people, and I bid them throw it down and let all the people out, and so they did.

And I went on again, and bid them dig again, and Friends said unto me, ' George, thou finds out all things,' and so there they digged, and I went down, and went along the vault; and there sat a woman in white looking at time how it passed away. And there followed me a woman down in the vault, in which vault was the treasure; and so she laid her hand on the treasure on my left hand and then time whisked on apace; but I clapped my hand upon her, and said, ' Touch not the treasure.'

And then time passed not so swift (p. 578).

Something of Fox's secret is in this passage. Much, no doubt, cannot be explained. The whole passage was omitted from the *Journal* as first published. The self-satisfaction of ' George, thou finds out all things ', as well as the visionary nature of the whole, were not welcomed in 1700. To-day, perhaps, we are more ready to understand. ' There is no great leadership where there is not a mystic. Nothing splendid has ever been achieved except by those who dared to believe that something inside themselves was superior to circumstances, and in the pursuit of the great secret the follower finds that detachment which to the world around savours of mystery.'[1]

This vision of Fox's may well throw light upon his mental processes generally. At least we may say that attention to the eye of faith, looking on the things which are not seen but eternal, is likely to foster insight and intuition more at large. 'The strength of her mind lay in intuition,' wrote William Godwin of Mary Wollstonecraft; 'she was often right, by this means only, in matters of mere speculation. . . . She adopted one opinion, and rejected another, spontaneously, by a sort of tact.' To compare George Fox with Mary Wollstonecraft may seem fanciful, but the passage is suggestive; as are the words with which Godwin continues: 'In a robust and unwavering judgment of this sort, there is a kind of witchcraft; when it decides justly, it produces a responsive vibration in every ingenuous mind.'[2]

May we not have here something that explains George Fox's leadership? For not his least remarkable faculty was his ability to draw men to himself and to claim their entire and life-long devotion. That he could do this is, at the same time, the best evidence that he was no mere visionary. He also possessed a robust common sense and had considerable organizing powers. If the Society of Friends has had a continuing existence, while other bands of Commonwealth enthusiasts were forgotten before the century was out, it owes this in no small measure to the system of monthly and quarterly meetings for business which Fox established. His shrewdness, not to say his humour, may be illustrated from the occasion when he was sent up to London after being tried at Lancaster. First he persuaded the authorities at Lancaster to save themselves the expense of sending the gaoler and bailiffs with him as guards, and to trust him to travel with one or two of his own friends only. Then, when he appeared in London

[1] Professor John Fraser, on 'The Influence of Lister's Work on Surgery', in *Joseph, Baron Lister*, ed. A. Logan Turner, 1927, p. 105.

[2] W. Godwin, *op. cit.*, p. 125.

on the charge of plotting to imbrue the whole nation in blood, he said, 'I had need to have had two or three troops of horse to have come along with me if such things could be proved,' and was soon set free.

Yet more than shrewdness and common sense are needed to win men as Fox could win them. Despite the central place in his life of forbearance to enemies, it is all too easy to miss his tenderness and gentleness. His courage is more evident; but his tender side was equally essential to his make-up. The scene in which the Lord Protector catched him by the hand and said, with tears in his eyes, 'Come again to my house', says something for Fox as well as for Cromwell. Soldiers, too, 'took me by the hand very friendly, and said they would have me alongst with them'. 'Nathaniel', said Fox to a minister with whom he had been disputing, 'give me thy hand'; for, he added, he would not quench the least measure of God in any, much less put out his starlight. It was the same with Quaker meetings for worship. Fox had no greater praise for a meeting for worship than to call it a tender broken meeting; and if any, in bubbling forth a few words of ministry, should go beyond their measure, he bade Friends bear it: 'that is the tender'.

So it was that the men and women whom he gathered round him not only believed in him but loved him. One Friend, John Banks, who had a withered arm, dreamed one night that he was with 'dear George Fox', and felt such faith in Fox that he believed Fox could heal his arm; he accordingly sought Fox out, and received the healing he desired. However the 'miracle', as Fox would have called it, is to be interpreted, and many similar incidents are recorded during his life,[1] the story says much for the relation between the two men. 'George', wrote another Friend when in prison at Lancaster, 'sometimes when I think on thee, the power rises and warms my heart. Bonds and fetters (are) ready to burst asunder, for it is not possible

[1] See *George Fox's 'Book of Miracles'*, ed. H. J. Cadbury, Cambridge University Press, 1948.

that they can hold me.'[1] Robert Widders, the writer of this letter, was a husbandman; John Banks was a glover; not many mighty, not many noble, were called. But when they were, their relation to Fox was just the same. It was so, for instance, with William Penn, the courtier of gentle birth who became the founder of Pennsylvania. In the whole of Penn's carefully balanced character-sketch of Fox printed in his preface to the first edition of Fox's *Journal*, a sketch which is still the best and which has continually been drawn on in the present study, nothing is more moving than the start of affection with which it closes. 'I have done', Penn writes, 'as to this part of my Preface, when I have left this short epitaph to his name: "Many sons have done virtuously in this day; but, dear George, thou excellest them all."'

Out of the strong came forth sweetness. By few has Samson's riddle been better resolved.

[1] Swarthmore MSS. (Friends House), iv, 41.

Extracts from

WILLIAM PENN'S PREFACE

to the Original Edition of

George Fox's Journal, 1694

GEORGE FOX was born in Leicestershire in the year 1624. He descended of honest and sufficient parents, who endeavoured to bring him up, as they did the rest of their children, in the way and worship of the nation; especially his mother, who was a woman accomplished above most of her degree in the place where she lived. But from a child he appeared of another frame of mind than the rest of his brethren; being more religious, inward, still, solid and observing beyond his years, as the answers he would give and the questions he would put upon occasion manifested, to the astonishment of those that heard him, especially in divine things.

His mother taking notice of his singular temper, and the gravity, wisdom, and piety that very early shined through him, refusing childish and vain sports and company when very young, she was tender and indulgent over him, so that from her he met with little difficulty. As to his employment, he was brought up in country business; and as he took most delight in sheep, so he was very skilful in them; an employment that very well suited his mind in several respects, both for its innocency and solitude, and was a just figure of his after ministry and service.

I shall not break in upon his own account, which is by much the best that can be given, and therefore desire, what I can, to avoid saying anything of what is said already as to the particular passages of his coming forth. But in general, when he was somewhat above twenty, he left his friends, and visited the most retired and religious people in those parts; and some few there were in this nation, who waited for the consolation of Israel night and day; as Zacharias, Anna, and good old Simeon did of old time. To these he was sent, and these he sought out in the neighbouring countries, and among them he sojourned till his more ample ministry came upon him. At this time he taught, and was an example of, silence, endeavouring to bring them from self-performances, testifying and turning to the light of Christ within them, and encouraging them to wait in patience to feel the power of it to stir in their hearts, that their knowledge and worship of God might stand in the power of an endless life, which was to be found in the Light, as it was obeyed in the manifestation of it in man. For in the Word was life, and that life is the Light of men. Life in the Word, Light in men, and life in men as the Light is obeyed; the Children of the Light living by the life of the Word, by which the Word begets them again to God, which is the regeneration and new birth, without which there is no coming unto the Kingdom of God; and which, whoever comes to, is greater than John; that is, than John's dispensation, which was not that of the kingdom, but the consummation of the legal, and forerunning of the gospel times. Accordingly, several meetings were gathered in those parts, and thus his time was employed for some years.

In 1652, he being in his usual retirement to the Lord, upon a very high mountain in some of the hither parts of Yorkshire,[1] as I take it, his mind exercised towards the Lord, he had a vision of the great work of God in the earth, and of the way that he was to go forth to begin it. He saw people as thick as motes in the sun, that should in time be brought home to the Lord, that there might be but one shepherd and one sheepfold in all the earth. There his eye was directed northward, beholding a great people that should receive him and his message in those parts. Upon this mountain he was moved of the Lord to sound out his great and notable day, as if he had been in a great

[1] Pendle Hill is in Lancashire.

auditory, and from thence went forth, as the Lord had shown him; and in every place where he came, if not before he came to it, he had his particular exercise and service shown to him, so that the Lord was his leader indeed; for it was not in vain that he travailed, God in most places sealing his commission with the convincement of some of all sorts, as well publicans as sober professors of religion.

Some of the first and most eminent of them, which are at rest, were Richard Farnsworth, James Nayler, William Dewsbury, Francis Howgill, Edward Burrough, John Camm, John Audland, Richard Hubberthorn, Thomas Taylor, John Aldam, Thomas Holme, Alexander Parker, William Simpson, William Caton, John Stubbs, Robert Widders, John Burnyeat, Robert Lodge, Thomas Salthouse, and many more worthies, that cannot be well here named, together with divers yet living of the first and great convincement, who after the knowledge of God's purging judgments in themselves, and some time in waiting in silence upon him, to feel and receive power from on high to speak in his name, which none else rightly can, though they may use the same words, felt the divine motions and were frequently drawn forth, especially to visit the public assemblies to reprove, inform and exhort them, sometimes in markets, fairs, streets, and by the highway-side, calling people to repentance and to turn to the Lord with their hearts as well as their mouths, directing them to the Light of Christ within them to see and examine and consider their ways by, and to eschew the evil and do the good and acceptable will of God. And they suffered great hardships for their love and good-will, being often stocked, stoned, beaten, whipt and imprisoned, though honest men and of good report where they lived, that had left wives and children and houses and lands to visit them with a living call to repentance. And though the priests generally set themselves to oppose them and write against them, and insinuated most false and scandalous stories to defame them, stirring up the magistrates to suppress them, especially in those northern parts, yet God was pleased so to fill them with his living power and give them such an open door of utterance in his service, that there was a mighty convincement over those parts.

And through the tender and singular indulgence of Judge Bradshaw and Judge Fell, who were wont to go that circuit, in the infancy of things, the priests were never able to gain the point they laboured for, which was to have proceeded to blood, and if possible, Herod like, by a cruel exercise of the civil power, to have cut them off and rooted them out of the country; especially Judge Fell, who was not only a check to their rage but finally countenanced this people; for his wife receiving the Truth with the first, it had that influence upon his spirit, being a just and wise man, and seeing in his own wife and family a full confutation to all the popular clamours against the way of Truth, that he covered them what he could, and freely opened his doors, and gave up his house to his wife and her friends, not valuing the reproach of ignorant or evil minded people, which I here mention to his and her honour, and which will be, I believe, an honour and a blessing to such of their name and family as shall be found in that tenderness, humility, love and zeal for the truth and people of the Lord.

That house was for some years at first, till the Truth had opened its way in the southern part of this island, an eminent receptacle of this people. Others of good note and substance in those northern countries had also opened their houses with their hearts, to the many publishers that in a short time the Lord had raised to declare his salvation to the people, and where meetings of the Lord's messengers were frequently held, to communicate their services and exercises and comfort and edify one another in their blessed ministry.

I return to this excellent man. For his personal qualities both natural, moral and divine as they appeared in his converse with brethren and in the church of God, take as follows:

He was a man that God endued with a clear and wonderful

depth, a discerner of others' spirits, and very much a master of his own. And though the side of his understanding which lay next to the world, and especially the expression of it, might sound uncouth and unfashionable to nice ears, his matter was nevertheless very profound; and would not only bear to be often considered but the more it was so the more weighty and instructing it appeared. And abruptly and brokenly as sometimes his sentences would fall from him about divine things, it is well known they were often as texts to many fairer declarations. And indeed it showed, beyond all contradiction, that God sent him, that no arts or parts had any share in his matter or manner of his ministry; and that so many great, excellent, and necessary truths as he came forth to preach to mankind had therefore nothing of man's wit or wisdom to recommend them; so that as to man he was an original, being no man's copy. And his ministry and writings show they are from one that was not taught of man, nor had learned what he said by study. Nor were they notional or speculative, but sensible and practical truths, tending to conversion and regeneration and the setting up of the kingdom of God in the hearts of men; and the way of it was his work.

From the clearness of the principle, the power and efficacy of it, in the exemplary sobriety, plainness, zeal, steadiness, humility, gravity, punctuality, charity, and circumspect care in the government of Church affairs, which shined in his and their life and testimony that God employed in this work, it greatly confirmed me that it was of God, and engaged my soul in a deep love, fear, reverence and thankfulness for his love and mercy therein to mankind; in which mind I remain, and shall, I hope, to the end of my days.

In his testimony or ministry, he much laboured to open Truth to the people's understandings, and to bottom them upon the principle, and principal, Christ Jesus, the Light of the world, that by bringing them to something that was of God in themselves, they might the better know and judge of him and themselves.

He had an extraordinary gift in opening the Scriptures.

He would go to the marrow of things, and show the mind, harmony, and fulfilling of them with much plainness and to great comfort and edification.

The mystery of the first and second Adam, of the fall and restoration, of the law and gospel, of shadows and substance, of the servant's and son's state, and the fulfilling of the Scriptures in Christ, and by Christ the true Light, in all that are his through the obedience of faith, were much of the substance and drift of his testimonies. In all which he was witnessed to be of God, being sensibly felt to speak that which he had received of Christ, and which was his own experience, in that which never errs nor fails.

But above all he excelled in prayer. The inwardness and weight of his spirit, the reverence and solemnity of his address and behaviour, and the fewness and fullness of his words, have often struck even strangers with admiration, as they used to reach others with consolation. The most awful, living, reverent frame I ever felt or beheld, I must say, was his in prayer. And truly it was a testimony that he knew and lived nearer to the Lord than other men; for they that know him most will see most reason to approach him with reverence and fear.

He was of an innocent life, no busy-body, nor self-seeker, neither touchy nor critical; what fell from him was very inoffensive, if not very edifying. So meek, contented, modest, easy, steady, tender, it was a pleasure to be in his company. He exercised no authority but over evil, and that everywhere and in all, but with love, compassion, and long-suffering, a most merciful man, as ready to forgive as unapt to take or give an offence. Thousands can truly say he was of an excellent spirit and savour among them, and because thereof, the most excellent spirits loved him with an unfeigned and unfading love.

He was an incessant labourer; for in his younger time, before his many great and deep sufferings and travels had enfeebled his body for itinerant services, he laboured much in the word, and doctrine and discipline, in England, Scotland and Ireland, turning many to God, and confirming those that were convinced of the Truth, and settling good order as to church affairs among them. And towards the conclusion of his travelling services, between the years '71 and '77, he visited the churches of Christ in the plantations in America, and in the United Provinces and Germany, to the convincement and consolation of many. After that time he chiefly resided in and about the city of London; and besides the services of his ministry, which were frequent and serviceable, he writ much both to them that are within and those that are without the communion. But the care he took of the affairs of the church in general was very great.

He was often where the records of the affairs of the church are kept and where the letters from the many Meetings of God's people over all the world, where settled, come upon occasions; which letters he had read to him, and communicated them to the meeting that is weekly[1] held there for such services; and he would be sure to stir them up to discharge them, especially in suffering cases, showing great sympathy and compassion upon all such occasions, carefully looking into the respective cases, and endeavouring speedy relief, according to the nature of them. So that the churches, and any of the suffering members thereof, were sure not to be forgotten or delayed in their desires, if he were there.

As he was unwearied, so he was undaunted in his services for God and his people; he was no more to be moved to fear than to wrath. His behaviour at Derby, Lichfield, Appleby, before Oliver Cromwell, at Launceston, Scarborough, Worcester, and Westminster Hall, with many other places and exercises, did abundantly evidence it to his enemies as well as his friends.

But, as in the primitive times some rose up against the blessed apostles of our Lord Jesus Christ even from among those that they had turned to the hope of the gospel, and who became their greatest trouble, so this man of God had his share of suffering from some that were convinced

[1] 'The Meeting for Sufferings', now held monthly.

by him, who through prejudice or mistake ran against him, as one that sought dominion over conscience, because he pressed, by his presence or epistles, a ready and zealous compliance with such good and wholesome things as tended to an orderly conversation about the affairs of the church, and in their walking before men. That which contributed much to this ill work was, in some, a begrudging of this meek man the love and esteem he had and deserved in the hearts of the people, and weakness in others that were taken with their groundless suggestions of imposition and blind obedience.

They would have had every man independent, that as he had the principle in himself, he should only stand and fall to that and nobody else, not considering that the principle is one in all. And though the measure of light or grace might differ, yet the nature of it was the same, and being so, they struck at the spiritual unity which a people guided by the same principle are naturally led into. So that what is an evil to one, is so to all, and what is virtuous, honest and of good report to one, is so to all, from the sense and savour of the one universal principle which is common to all, the root of all true Christian fellowship and that spirit into which the people of God drink and come to be spiritually minded, and of one heart and one soul.

Some weakly mistook good order in the government of church affairs, for discipline in worship, and that it was so pressed or recommended by him and other brethren. And they were ready to reflect the same things that dissenters had very reasonably objected upon the national churches that have coercively pressed conformity to their respective creeds and worships. Whereas these things related wholly to conversation and the outward and (I may say) civil part of the church, that men should walk up to the principles of their belief, and not be wanting in care and charity. But though some have stumbled and fallen through mistakes, and an unreasonable obstinacy, even to a prejudice, yet blessed be God the generality have returned to their first love.

In all these occasions, though there was no person the discontented struck so sharply at as this good man, he bore all their weakness and prejudice, and returned not reflection for reflection but forgave them their weak and bitter speeches, praying for them that they might have a sense of their hurt, see the subtilty of the enemy to rend and divide, and return into their first love that thought no ill.

And truly, I must say, that though God had visibly clothed him with a divine preference and authority, and indeed his very presence expressed a religious majesty, yet he never abused it; but held his place in the Church of God with great meekness and a most engaging humility and moderation. For upon all occasions, like his blessed Master, he was a servant to all; holding and exercising his eldership in the invisible power that had gathered them, with reverence to the Head, and care over the body; and was received only in that spirit and power of Christ, as the first and chief elder in this age; who, as he was therefore worthy of double honour, so for the same reason it was given by the faithful of this day; because his authority was inward and not outward, and that he got it and kept it by the love of God and power of an endless life.

I write my knowledge and not report; and my witness is true, having been with him for weeks and months together on divers occasions, and those of the nearest and most exercising nature, and that by night and by day, by sea and by land, in this and in foreign countries; and I can say I never saw him out of his place, or not a match for every service or occasion.

For in all things he acquitted himself like a man, yea, a strong man, a new and heavenly-minded man, a divine and a naturalist, and all of God Almighty's making. I have been surprised at his questions and answers in natural things; that whilst he was ignorant of useless and sophistical science, he had in him the foundation of useful and commendable knowledge, and cherished it everywhere. Civil beyond all forms of breeding, in his behaviour; very temperate, eating little and sleeping less, though a bulky person.

Thus he lived and sojourned among us; and as he lived, so he died; feeling the same eternal power, that had raised and preserved him, in his last moments. So full of assurance was he that he triumphed over death; and so even to the last, as if death were hardly worth notice or a mention; recommending to some with him the despatch and dispersion of an epistle just before written to the churches of Christ throughout the world, and his own books; but, above all, Friends, and of all Friends, those in Ireland and America, twice over saying, 'Mind poor Friends in Ireland and America.' And to some that came in and inquired how he found himself, he answered, 'Never heed, the Lord's power is over all weakness and death; the Seed reigns, blessed be the Lord'; which was about four or five hours before his departure out of this world.

He was at the great meeting near Lombard Street on the First day of the week, and it was the Third day following, about ten at night, when he left us, being at the house of Henry Gouldney in the same court. In a good old age he went, after having lived to see his children's children to many generations in the Truth. He had the comfort of a short illness, and the blessing of a clear sense to the last; and we may truly say, with a man of God of old, that 'being dead, he yet speaketh'; and though absent in body, he is present in spirit; neither time nor place being able to interrupt the communion of saints, or dissolve the fellowships of the spirits of the just. His works praise him, because they are to the praise of him that worked by him; for which his memorial is and shall be blessed.

I have done when I have left this short epitaph to his name. *Many sons have done virtuously in this day, but dear George thou excellest them all.*

William Penn

PREFACE

By The Editor

THIS new edition of George Fox's Journal is designed to replace for the general reader the text prepared by Thomas Ellwood, which was first published in 1694 and has been many times reprinted without substantial alterations, in England until 1902, and in America until 1892.

These editions are listed in an appendix to the 1902 issue of the eighth (Bicentenary) edition published in London.

The following brief particulars of some of the principal MSS. still extant, and of Ellwood's edition, will help to explain the differences between the present edition and those which have gone before it.

George Fox, through most of his life, did not keep a journal in the ordinary sense of a nearly contemporary day-to-day record. It was also Fox's habit to dictate, in preference to writing himself, if there was an amanuensis at hand.

In 1675, or possibly beginning in 1674, Fox dictated to Thomas Lower, his stepson-in-law, an autobiography down to the year of writing. This is now called the *Spence MS.* Interspersed through the narrative, and now bound with it, are numerous letters, pastoral epistles, and other papers. After the end of the autobiography are a number of notes on early Quaker history, and various testamentary instructions. The *Spence MS.* has been published *verbatim* and *literatim* under the title *The Journal of George Fox*, by Cambridge University Press, 1911, 2 volumes, with an introduction by T. Edmund Harvey and full editorial notes by Norman Penney. It is referred to as the *Cambridge Journal.* This MS. was at one time thought to be the one called by Fox the *Great Journal*; but Henry J. Cadbury, in his *Annual Catalogue of George Fox's Papers* (1939), has shown that the *Great Journal* was another rather similar MS., now lost.

The following MSS. are of more limited scope, but valuably supplement the *Spence MS.*

When in prison at Lancaster in 1664, Fox wrote or dictated detailed accounts of a number of experiences at various times between 1647 and the time of writing. They are chiefly ' sufferings for preaching the truth '. The MS. preserved is either the original dictated by Fox, or a contemporary copy. This MS., known as *The Short Journal*, has been published *verbatim* and *literatim* under that title by Cambridge University Press, 1925, with an introduction by T. Edmund Harvey and full editorial notes by Norman Penney. It is referred to as the *Short Journal.*

It is not strictly a journal, nor is it continuous enough to be called an autobiography. But its reporting is ten years nearer in time to the events described than is the *Spence MS.*; and it contains many vivid touches omitted from the later account. Presumably Fox used it to help his recollection when he was dictating his autobiography. The *Cambridge* and the *Short* Journals, reproducing the MSS. exactly, and with their valuable introductions and full notes, remain of the first importance for the fullest study of Fox.

There are several seventeenth-century copies of the Journal of Fox's Irish travels. One is included in the *Spence* MS. and printed in *Camb. Jnl.* It was not, like the rest of the autobiography, dictated in 1675, but is a running account written during Fox's journey in Ireland in 1669. It opens with a passage by one of Fox's companions, referring to Fox in the third person, but most of it is by Fox himself, probably dictated to the same companion. Other copies are in *Epistles and Queries* (George Fox's Papers Xx), *G.F.'s Epistles* (George Fox's Papers Z), and in *Ecroyd MS.* (see *J.F.H.S.*, xiv, 81 ff.).

In the *Spence MS.* the journeys to, in, and from America and the West Indies are left by the autobiographer to be covered by then existing diaries and letters, some of which are no longer extant. For the voyage from England to Barbados we depend upon the detailed log of a fellow-passenger, John Hull. A seventeenth-century MS. copy of this is in *Epistles and Queries*, mentioned just above, and is printed in *Camb. Jnl.* For the sojourn in Barbados we depend upon letters by Fox and others.

The journeys from Barbados onwards until arrival home in England were recorded almost from day to day. Out of this period of a year and a half, about a year was spent in strenuous and hazardous travel on the American mainland. For eleven months of this we have the original diaries.

Of all the MSS. about Fox's life, these *American Diaries* are, I believe, those most truly to be described as a journal by George Fox. The little home-made pocket notebooks, written beside camp-fires and in the log-cabins of pioneers in the wilderness, are perhaps the only MSS., dictated as diaries from day to day by Fox himself, of which the originals survive. The substance of their story, except for the first seven weeks, is to be found in the *Spence MS.* and is printed in *Camb. Jnl.* The two original diaries are preserved among the MS. records of Friends at Bristol. They have been used in the present edition and are here given in full. For further details, see editorial paragraphs on pp. 608-9, 639, 655. Other seventeenth-century MS. copies of the *American Diaries* are in the Bodleian Library, in a handwriting thought to be that of Thomas Ellwood, and in the *Ecroyd MS.* See Bibliography, p. xvi f. post, for ownership of the various MSS.

Thomas Ellwood worked on the instructions of the Second-day Morning Meeting, a committee of the Society of Friends in London, and in accord with the desire of Fox that his life and writings should be published. The *Journal* which Ellwood prepared was a composite work, presenting a continuous account of

Fox's life in the form of an autobiography, in a more uniform, more polished, and more cautious style in many places than the various MSS. which have been mentioned. Some passages he considerably abbreviated. Ellwood worked with more freedom than would to-day be approved, putting passages into autobiographical form from other sources, but he was an able and a careful editor. He also adapted or omitted many of Fox's own vigorous phrases, his picturesque details, his apparent overvaluation of praise, claims to psychic powers, and matter thought liable to cause political or theological protest, besides doubtful or unverifiable statements.[1] Moreover, after the end of the true autobiography, he compiled an autobiographical narrative for the last fifteen years of Fox's life. It is based upon information in diaries kept for, but not by, Fox; and it is heavily loaded with pastoral and doctrinal papers and letters. Three of these diaries are printed in the same volume as the *Short Journal* described above.

The different character and quality of the later sources mark off Ellwood's narrative of the last years, from Fox's own work, and it has not been included here. The present text ends with the end of the autobiographical portion of the *Spence MS.*, in 1675; and the last fifteen years of Fox's life are covered by a chapter written for this volume by Henry J. Cadbury.

As to the narrative, the present edition is as complete as Ellwood's within the same period. And it expresses the story in Fox's own words in preference to Ellwood's more polished presentation of it. In a few cases I have adopted Ellwood's account of an incident as clearer than that available in the MS.

[1] Fox's report of Justice Clarke's words about Ellen Fretwell's being an instrument of the Devil, and of the judgment upon him, was objected to. An amended leaf (pp. 309-10) was circulated to purchasers of the 1694 edition, omitting the justice's name, his remarks about Ellen Fretwell, as well as the sentences referred to in my footnote on p. 509 post. Few purchasers seem to have substituted the altered leaf. The omissions were maintained in subsequent editions.

The main source has been the *Spence MS.* as printed in the *Cambridge Journal.* Matter supplementing the MS., taken from Ellwood's edition, has been enclosed within angular brackets, ⟨ ⟩, without reference to its position in the source, to which the year and the context are sufficient guide. The most important passage from Ellwood to be used is that which opens the book, and which, except for short interpolations, provides the narrative down to 1650, near the foot of p. 49 of the present edition. This long passage from Ellwood is necessary because no MS. source survives for most of it; the first sixteen pages of the *Spence MS.* are lacking. *Short Journal* has provided down to 1664 many vivid details and some whole incidents. These passages occasionally replace an inferior account in *Camb. Jnl.* Passages from *S.J.* are marked at the beginning and end with footnote references. Where such a footnote begins with ' Cf.' the passage indicated contains a number of borrowings from *S.J.*, which are not individually marked.

A few sources other than *Cambridge Journal*, Ellwood, and *Short Journal* have been drawn upon. These additional sources are identified either by footnotes or by editorial paragraphs placed within square brackets [ ]. The most notable instances are the *American Diaries* and a number of letters from Fox to his wife which have not been printed in previous editions of the Journal.

Not all the controversial or pastoral papers and similar documents inserted in the Ellwood editions have been used; in so far as they have a biographical interest they have been retained. Doctrinal papers have been abbreviated to give the most essential points, unless their importance seemed to warrant printing the whole. Many papers of protest and remonstrance have been omitted. In each case a footnote directs to where the full text can be found in the first edition, 1694, and in the eighth (Bicentenary) edition. The year and the context provide an easy guide to finding them in any full edition. If some other text of a document has been used instead of the text in Ellwood's edition, the reference to the source used has been placed first.

Inserted documents not of a narrative kind, and several passages of discourse have been printed in smaller type.

The pagination of the 1694 edition contains several irregularities, requiring partial description here to clarify the footnote references to that edition. About 90 page-numbers were used twice. At the first use, from p. 201 onwards, they carry an asterisk. Where (2) is added to the page-number in my footnotes, the reference is to the page-number occurring a second time, and without *. These follow the first use, in a second series, and the pagination is thereafter regular.

Documents in *Cambridge Journal* not previously printed have not been used again here unless they seemed to me to contribute substantially to the narrative.

Where Ellwood's narrative was built up from matter taken out of letters in the *Spence MS.*, the letters themselves or parts of them have as a rule been printed in preference to Ellwood's compilation from them. William Penn's fine estimate of Fox's character, written for the first edition, again prefaces the *Journal.*

In transcribing the text for the present edition the punctuation and spelling, including personal names, have been modernized, and many capital letters occurring in the sources have been dispensed with. Simple grammatical errors, which often occur, such as the use of singular verb after plural subject, have been corrected. Some slight obscurities due to faulty construction have been left. The forms of place-names have been modernized, usually in the text if the change is slight, by footnote if it is considerable.

Obsolete words and obsolete meanings have been explained in footnotes, in more cases than some readers will think necessary. A number of archaic forms and usages have been retained as showing how Fox spoke, since nearly all the narrative was dictated by him. He often used *after* where we should say *afterwards*; this has usually been made clearer by the use of a comma. He often said *I riz* (sometimes written *risse*), but here uniformly printed *riz*, meaning 'I rose'; and *run* for *ran* will also be found. *Naked,* meaning unarmed, is a reminder of how recently in Fox's time arms naturally included armour.

Readers who are puzzled by the system of dating used, may find the following explanation useful.

Dates which appear in the sources are given in the form in which they occur, viz. the Old Style or Julian calendar in use in seventeenth-century England. Their modern equivalents in our New Style or Gregorian calendar adopted in 1752, are added in [ ] immediately after each date. The apparent discrepancy is greater than might be expected in those documents which were dated in the Quaker manner, i.e. by the number of the month instead of the name, as explained below. Dates added editorially are in modern style only.

By the Julian calendar which continued in use in England until the end of 1751, the year began with 25th March. Documents dated from 1st January to 24th March, therefore, may easily be misread by a year. The Gregorian calendar, beginning the year with 1st January, had been in use in the rest of western Europe since 1582. Many people, therefore, in writing dates in January, February and March, gave also the New Style year as well, as e.g. 1st February, 1660/1; the second year gives us the historical date.

Quaker dating introduces a further complication. The Society of Friends from its beginning called the months by numbers, refusing to use their ' heathen ' names. Until 1752, therefore, First Month means March, and Twelfth Month February. But in accord with the Old Style calendar the first 24 days of First Month, March, were in the old year, and as a rule were dated so, though in a few instances the whole of First Month was dated with the new year. With the adoption of the New Style calendar in 1752 the Quaker numbering of months was revised and January (instead of March) became First Month. By way of example, the following table expresses the months from December, 1689, until March, 1691, according to the various styles.

DECEMBER, 1689, TO MARCH, 1691, EXPRESSED ACCORDING TO OLD STYLE AND NEW STYLE

OLD STYLE			NEW STYLE	
Months by Numbers	*Years*	*Months by Names* (Historical Dating)	*Years*	*Months by Numbers*
Tenth	1689	December	1689	Twelfth
Eleventh		January	1690	First
Twelfth		February		Second
First 1-24	1689	March 1-24		Third
First 25-31	1690	March 25-31		Third
Second		April		Fourth
Third		May		Fifth
Fourth		June		Sixth
Fifth		July		Seventh
Sixth		August		Eighth
Seventh		September		Ninth
Eighth		October		Tenth
Ninth		November		Eleventh
Tenth		December	1690	Twelfth
Eleventh		January	1691	First
Twelfth		February		Second
First 1-24	1690	March 1-24		Third
First 25-31	1691	March 25-31		Third

In preparing the text, the unpublished draft for a new edition which Norman Penney left at his death has been invaluable to me; and I have used it extensively, and also many of his footnotes identifying persons who were not followers of Fox.

To more helpers than I can here name I should like to accord my grateful thanks, but especially to the following:

Henry J. Cadbury and Geoffrey F. Nuttall have read my MS.; T. Edmund Harvey has read some portions of it; and all three have given valuable advice and help, resulting in improvement of the text and notes. Henry J. Cadbury has also kindly contributed the chapter on George Fox's later years, and Geoffrey F. Nuttall the Introduction. Nina Saxon Snell has been so good as to undertake the index; and my wife has given me valuable help with proof reading.

I should also like to thank Isabel Grubb for information respecting places mentioned in Fox's Irish travels, Russell Mortimer for details about seventeenth-century Bristol, George Dott of the Royal Scottish Geographical Society for help over some obscure Scottish place names, and G. P. B. Naish of the National Maritime Museum, Greenwich, for guidance as to the probable tonnages of the two ships in which Fox crossed the Atlantic ocean in 1671 and 1673; in the absence of actual record it can be no more than a well-based guess. To Muriel Hicks, assistant librarian at Friends House, I am deeply indebted for her carrying so large a share of the regular work of the library for several years past, as well as for occasional consultation of sources.

Thanks are also tendered to the following who have very kindly allowed the MSS. belonging to them to be used in preparing the present edition: Bristol Friends for the original MS. diaries of Fox's American travels; Brindley Marten for a seventeenth-century copy of the same diaries; L. Violet Holdsworth for the letter from George Fox to Margaret Fox, printed on p. 686, which was a gift to her father, Dr. Thomas Hodgkin; and to the University Press, Cambridge, for kindly allowing me to use the printed text of the MSS. as they appear in the *Cambridge Journal* and the *Short Journal*. If there is any other material used for which permission should have been asked, the omission is unwitting and my apologies are offered to the owners of it.

This edition has been undertaken on the initiative of the Library Committee of the Society of Friends in London.

Its preparation and its publication at a price which makes it available to a wide circle, have been made possible by support from the funds of a number of bodies of Friends which, jointly, and in about equal shares as between England and America, have borne the cost, viz. The Yearly Meeting Fund of Friends in Great Britain, the Readership Committee of Woodbrooke College, Birmingham, whose grant of a fellowship enabled me to complete the text; and in America, funds connected with Philadelphia (Arch Street) Yearly Meeting, Philadelphia (Race Street) Yearly Meeting, New York Yearly Meeting, and the Five Years Meeting.

A text so intricately composed from diverse sources will no doubt be found to contain faults. For these the editor must accept responsibility. The present edition provides Fox's own story in his own words and style. It is presented with the needs of the modern reader in view, and with the design that it may serve the author's purpose better in this day than the former standard editions, which made Fox's Journal known as one of the great religious autobiographies in the English language.

J.L.N.

Library of the Society of Friends,
Friends House, Euston Road, London, N.W.1.

BIBLIOGRAPHY

MANUSCRIPTS

Abraham MS. A volume of early Quaker MSS. at Friends House, London. Described in *J.F.H.S.*, xi, 145-90.

Bodleian MSS. A seventeenth-century copy of the Journal of Fox's travels in America. MS. Add. A. 95, in the Bodleian Library, Oxford. Printed in *J.F.H.S.*, ix, 5-39.

Bristol MSS. V. 'Letters and Papers of George Fox and other Early Friends', a volume in the records of the Society of Friends in Bristol. See *J.F.H.S.*, ix, 189-98. See also Preface, p. ix ante.

Ecroyd MS. A seventeenth-century copy of the journals of Fox in Ireland and in America, with letters. Described in *J.F.H.S.*, xiv, 81 ff. Now in the possession of Brindley Martin.

Epistles and Queries of G.F.'s (Fox Papers Xx). A MS. volume at Friends House, London. Described in *Ann. Cata.*, see below.

Fox Papers marked with letters (R, X, Xx, etc.). Various MSS. by Fox, at Friends House, London. Described in *Ann. Cata.*, see below.

Gibson MSS. A collection of miscellaneous Quaker MSS. in 10 volumes at Friends House, London.

Portfolio 9, Portfolio 10, etc. A varied collection of MSS. in 42 volumes, formerly loose in Portfolios, at Friends House, London.

Records of Friends Sufferings. MS. volumes recording persecutions; at Friends House, London.

Short Journal. At Friends House, London. See Preface, p. viii ante.

Spence MSS. At Friends House, London. See Preface, pp. vii-viii ante.

Swarthmore MSS. A collection of about 1,400 early Quaker letters in 7 volumes, at Friends House, London.

PRINTED WORKS

Ann. Cata. Annual Catalogue of George Fox's Papers. Edited by Henry J. Cadbury. Philadelphia and London, 1939.

Beginnings. Beginnings of Quakerism. By William C. Braithwaite. London, 1912.

Bicent. The Journal of George Fox. 8th, Bicentenary ed. London, 1891, reprinted 1901 and 1902. 2 vols.

Bulletin F.H.A. *Bulletin of the Friends Historical Association.* Philadelphia, 1907. In progress.

C.R. *Calamy Revised.* A revision of Calamy's 'Account' of the ministers and others ejected in 1660. By A. G. Matthews. Oxford, 1934.

Camb. Jnl. *The Journal of George Fox.* Edited by Norman Penney. Cambridge, 1911. 2 vols.

Ellwood. *The Journal of George Fox.* London, 1694. The pagination of this volume contains various irregularities, see Preface, p. xii ante.

F.P.T. *First Publishers of Truth.* Early records of the introduction of Quakerism into the counties of England and Wales. Edited by Norman Penney. London, 1907.

George Fox's Book of Miracles. By Henry J. Cadbury. Cambridge, 1948.

J.F.H.S. *Journal of the Friends' Historical Society.* London, 1903. In progress.

Letters of Early Friends. Edited by A. R. Barclay. London, 1841.

Quakers in Wales. By T. Mardy Rees. Carmarthen, 1925.

S.J. *Short and Itinerary Journals of George Fox.* Edited by Norman Penney. Cambridge, 1925.

Smith. *A Descriptive Catalogue of Friends Books . . . from their first rise . . .* By Joseph Smith. London, 1867. 2 vols. This is the standard bibliography of two centuries of Quakerism.

Also his *Bibliotheca Anti-Quakeriana.* London, 1873.

Sufferings. *A Collection of the Sufferings of the Quakers.* By Joseph Besse. London, 1753. 2 vols.

W.R. *Walker Revised.* A revision of Walker's 'Sufferings of the Clergy, 1642-1660'. By A. G. Matthews. Oxford, 1948.

See also the Bibliographical Note to 'George Fox's Later Years', by Henry J. Cadbury, p. 713 post.

THE JOURNAL

CHAPTER I

[1]⟨THAT all may know the dealings of the Lord with me, and the various exercises, trials, and troubles through which he led me in order to prepare and fit me for the work unto which he had appointed me, and may thereby be drawn to admire and glorify his infinite wisdom and goodness, I think fit (before I proceed to set forth my public travels in the service of Truth), briefly to mention how it was with me in my youth, and how the work of the Lord was begun and gradually carried on in me, even from my childhood.

I was born in the month called July in the year 1624, at Drayton-in-the-Clay[2] in Leicestershire. My father's name was Christopher Fox; he was by profession a weaver, an honest man, and there was a Seed of God in him. The neighbours called him 'Righteous Christer'. My mother was an upright woman; her maiden name was Mary Lago, of the family of the Lagos and of the stock of the martyrs.

In my very young years I had a gravity and stayedness of mind and spirit not usual in children, insomuch that, when I have seen old men carry themselves lightly and wantonly towards each other, I have had a dislike thereof risen in my heart, and have said within myself, 'If ever I come to be a man, surely I should not do so nor be so wanton.'

When I came to eleven years of age, I knew pureness and righteousness; for while I was a child I was taught how to walk to be kept pure. The Lord taught me to be

[1] ⟨ ⟩ These brackets indicate matter taken from the first (Ellwood's) edition, 1694. The various sources are explained in the editorial preface. The passage here begun ends on p. 20.

[2] Now Fenny Drayton.

faithful in all things, and to act faithfully two ways, viz. inwardly to God and outwardly to man, and to keep to 'yea' and 'nay' in all things. For the Lord showed me that though the people of the world have mouths full of deceit and changeable words, yet I was to keep to 'yea' and 'nay' in all things; and that my words should be few and savoury, seasoned with grace; and that I might not eat and drink to make myself wanton but for health, using the creatures in their service, as servants in their places, to the glory of him that hath created them; they being in their covenant, and I being brought up into the covenant, as sanctified by the Word which was in the beginning, by which all things are upheld; wherein is unity with the creation.

But people being strangers to the covenant of life with God, they eat and drink to make themselves wanton with the creatures, devouring them upon their own lusts, and living in all filthiness, loving foul ways and devouring the creation; and all this in the world, in the pollutions thereof, without God; and therefore I was to shun all such.

Afterwards, as I grew up, my relations thought to have me a priest,[1] but others persuaded to the contrary; whereupon I was put to a man,[2] a shoemaker by trade, and that dealt in wool, and used grazing, and sold cattle; and a great deal went through my hands. While I was with him, he was blessed; but after I left him he broke, and came to nothing. I never wronged man or woman in all that time, for the Lord's power was with me and over me, to preserve me. While I was in that service, I used in my dealings the word 'verily', and it was a common saying among people that knew me, 'If George says "Verily" there is no altering him.' When boys and rude people would laugh at me, I let them alone and went my way, but people had generally a love to me for my innocency and honesty.

When I came towards nineteen years of age, I being

[1] Fox applied the term priest to all professional preachers, ministers and clergy, irrespective of the particular sect to which they belonged.

[2] Probably George Gee of Mancetter, a neighbouring village.

upon business at a fair,[1] one of my cousins, whose name was Bradford, being a professor[2] and having another professor with him, came to me and asked me to drink part of a jug of beer with them, and I, being thirsty, went in with them, for I loved any that had a sense of good, or that did seek after the Lord. And when we had drunk a glass apiece, they began to drink healths and called for more drink, agreeing together that he that would not drink should pay all. I was grieved that any that made profession of religion should offer to do so. They grieved me very much, having never had such a thing put to me before by any sort of people; wherefore I rose up to be gone, and putting my hand into my pocket I took out a groat and laid it down upon the table before them and said, 'If it be so, I'll leave you.' So I went away; and when I had done what business I had to do, I returned home, but did not go to bed that night, nor could not sleep, but sometimes walked up and down, and sometimes prayed and cried to the Lord, who said unto me, 'Thou seest how young people go together into vanity and old people into the earth; and thou must forsake all, both young and old, and keep out of all, and be as a stranger unto all.'

Then, at the command of God, on the 9th day of the Seventh Month [September],[3] 1643, I left my relations and brake off all familiarity or fellowship with young or old. And I passed to Lutterworth, where I stayed some time; and from thence I went to Northampton, where also I made some stay, then passed from thence to Newport Pagnell in Buckinghamshire, where, after I had stayed awhile, I went unto Barnet, and came thither in the Fourth Month, called June, in the year 1644. And as I thus travelled through the countries,[4] professors took notice

[1] At Atherstone, near Drayton.

[2] That is, one who makes profession of religious faith.

[3] It is to be noted in reading dates in these pages that, previous to the reform of the Calendar in 1752, March was the First Month of the year.

[4] Fox uses *country* both in its indefinite sense and instead of *county*.

of me and sought to be acquainted with me, but I was afraid of them for I was sensible they did not possess what they professed.

Now during the time that I was at Barnet a strong temptation to despair came upon me. And then I saw how Christ was tempted, and mighty troubles I was in. And sometimes I kept myself retired in my chamber, and often walked solitary in the Chase there, to wait upon the Lord. And I wondered why these things should come to me; and I looked upon myself and said, 'Was I ever so before?' Then I thought, because I had forsaken my relations I had done amiss against them; so I was brought to call to mind all my time that I had spent and to consider whether I had wronged any. But temptations grew more and more and I was tempted almost to despair, and when Satan could not effect his design upon me that way, then he laid snares for me and baits to draw me to commit some sin, whereby he might take advantage to bring me to despair. I was about twenty years of age when these exercises came upon me, and some years I continued in that condition, in great trouble; and fain I would have put it from me. And I went to many a priest to look for comfort but found no comfort from them.

From Barnet I went to London, where I took a lodging, and was under great misery and trouble there, for I looked upon the great professors of the city of London, and I saw all was dark and under the chain of darkness. And I had an uncle there, one Pickering, a Baptist (and they were tender then), yet I could not impart my mind to him nor join with them, for I saw all, young and old, where they were. Some tender people would have had me stay, but I was fearful, and returned homewards into Leicestershire again, having a regard upon my mind unto my parents and relations, lest I should grieve them, who, I understood, were troubled at my absence.

When I was come down into Leicestershire, my relations would have had me married, but I told them I was but a lad, and I must get wisdom. Others would have had me into the auxiliary band among the soldiery, but I refused; and I was grieved that they proffered such things to me, being a tender youth. Then I went to Coventry, where I took a chamber for a while at a professor's house till people began to be acquainted with me, for there were many tender people in that town.

And after some time I went into my own country again, and was there about a year, in great sorrows and troubles, and walked many nights by myself. Then the priest of Drayton, the town of my birth, whose name was Nathaniel Stephens, would come often to me, and I went often to him, and another priest sometimes would come with him; and they would have given place to me to hear me, and I would ask them questions and reason with them. And this priest Stephens asked me a question, why Christ cried out upon the Cross, 'My God, my God, why has thou forsaken me?' and why he said, 'If it be possible, let this cup pass from me, yet not my will but thine be done'? And I told him at that time the sins of all mankind were upon him, and their iniquities and transgressions with which he was wounded, which he was to bear, and to be an offering for them as he was man, but died not as he was God; and so, in that he died for all men, and tasted death for every man, he was an offering for the sins of the whole world. This I spoke, being at that time in a measure sensible of Christ's sufferings, and what he went through. And the priest said it was a very good, full answer, and such an one as he had not heard. And at that time he would applaud and speak highly of me to others; and what I said in discourse to him on the week-days that he would preach of on the First-days, for which I did not like him. And this priest afterwards became my great persecutor.

After this I went to another ancient priest[1] at Mancetter in Warwickshire and reasoned with him about the ground of despair and temptations, but he was ignorant of my condition; and he bid me take tobacco and sing psalms.

[1] Richard Abel.

Tobacco was a thing I did not love and psalms I was not in an estate to sing; I could not sing. Then he bid me come again and he would tell me many things, but when I came again he was angry and pettish, for my former words had displeased him. And he told my troubles and sorrows and griefs to his servants, so that it got among the milk-lasses, which grieved me that I should open my mind to such an one. I saw they were all miserable comforters; and this brought my troubles more upon me.

Then I heard of a priest living about Tamworth, who was accounted an experienced man, and I went seven miles to him; but I found him but like an empty, hollow cask. Then I heard of one called Doctor Cradock, of Coventry, and I went to him, and I asked him the ground of temptations and despair and how troubles came to be wrought in man. He asked me who were Christ's father and mother. I told him Mary was his mother, and that he was supposed to be the son of Joseph, but he was the Son of God. Now, as we were talking together in his garden, the alley being narrow, I chanced, in turning, to set my foot on the side of a bed, at which the man was in such a rage as if his house had been on fire. And thus all our discourse was lost, and I went away in sorrow, worse than I was when I came. I thought them miserable comforters, and I saw they were all as nothing to me, for they could not reach my condition.

After this I went to another, one Macham,[1] a priest in high account. And he would needs give me some physic and I was to have been let blood, but they could not get one drop of blood from me, either in arms or head, though they endeavoured it, my body being, as it were, dried up with sorrows, grief, and troubles, which were so great upon me that I could have wished I had never been born to see vanity and wickedness, or that I had been born blind, that I might never have seen wickedness nor vanity, and deaf, that I might never have heard vain and wicked words, or the Lord's name blasphemed.

[1] John Machen, Prebendary of Lichfield (*J.F.H.S.*, ii 9).

And when the time called Christmas came, while others were feasting and sporting themselves, I would have gone and looked out poor widows from house to house, and have given them some money. And when I was invited to marriages, as I sometimes was, I would go to none at all, but the next day, or soon after, I would go and visit them, and if they were poor, I gave them some money; for I had wherewith both to keep myself from being chargeable to others, and to administer something to the necessities of others.

About the beginning of the year 1646, as I was going to Coventry, and entering towards the gate, a consideration arose in me, how it was said that all Christians are believers, both Protestants and Papists; and the Lord opened to me that, if all were believers, then they were all born of God and passed from death to life, and that none were true believers but such; and though others said they were believers, yet they were not. At another time, as I was walking in a field on a First-day morning, the Lord opened unto me that being bred at Oxford or Cambridge was not enough to fit and qualify men to be ministers of Christ; and I stranged[1] at it because it was the common belief of people. But I saw clearly, as the Lord opened it to me, and was satisfied, and admired the goodness of the Lord who had opened this thing unto me that morning, which struck at Priest Stephens's ministry, namely, that to be bred at Oxford or Cambridge was not enough to make a man fit to be a minister of Christ. So that which opened in me, I saw, struck at the priest's ministry.

But my relations were much troubled at me that I would not go with them to hear the priest, for I would get into the orchard or the fields, with my Bible by myself. And I told them, 'Did not the apostle say to believers that they needed no man to teach them, but as the anointing teacheth them?' And though they knew this was Scripture and that it was true, yet they would be grieved because I could not be subject in this matter to go to hear the priest with

[1] i.e. thought it strange.

them. For I saw that a true believer was another thing than they looked upon it to be. And I saw that being bred at Oxford or Cambridge did not qualify or fit a man to be a minister of Christ; and what then should I follow such for? So neither them nor any of the Dissenting people could I join with, but was as a stranger to all, relying wholly upon the Lord Jesus Christ.

At another time it was opened in me that God, who made the world, did not dwell in temples made with hands. This, at the first, seemed a strange word because both priests and people use to call their temples or churches, dreadful places, and holy ground, and the temples of God. But the Lord showed me, so that I did see clearly, that he did not dwell in these temples which men had commanded and set up, but in people's hearts; for both Stephen and the Apostle Paul bore testimony that he did not dwell in temples made with hands, not even in that which he had once commanded to be built, since he put an end to it; but that his people were his temple, and he dwelt in them. This opened in me as I walked in the fields to my relations' house. And when I came there, they told me that Nathaniel Stephens the priest had been there, and told them he was afraid of me for going after new lights. And I smiled in myself, knowing what the Lord had opened in me concerning him and his brethren, but I told not my relations, who, though they saw beyond the priests, yet they went to hear them, and were grieved because I would not go also. But I brought them Scriptures, and told them there was an anointing within man to teach him, and that the Lord would teach his people himself. And I had great openings concerning the things written in the Revelations; and when I spoke of them, the priests and professors would say that was a sealed-up book, and would have kept me out of it, but I told them Christ could open the seals, and that they were the nearest things to us, for the Epistles were written to the saints that lived in former ages, but the Revelations were written of things to come.

After this, I met with a sort of people that held women

have no souls, adding in a light manner, no more than a goose. But I reproved them and told them that was not right, for Mary said, 'My soul doth magnify the Lord, and my spirit hath rejoiced in God my Saviour.'

And removing again to another place, I came among a people that relied much on dreams. And I told them, except they could distinguish between dream and dream, they would mash or confound all together; for there were three sorts of dreams; for multitude of business sometimes caused dreams; and there were whisperings of Satan in man in the night-season; and there were speakings of God to man in dreams. But these people came out of these things, and at last became Friends.

Now though I had great openings, yet great trouble and temptation came many times upon me, so that when it was day I wished for night, and when it was night I wished for day; and by reason of the openings I had in my troubles, I could say as David said, 'Day unto day uttereth speech, and night unto night showeth knowledge.' And when I had openings, they answered one another and answered the Scriptures, for I had great openings of the Scriptures; and when I was in troubles, one trouble also answered to another.

About the beginning of the year 1647, I was moved of the Lord to go into Derbyshire, where I met with some friendly people, and had many discourses with them. Then passing further into the Peak country, I met with more friendly people, and with some in empty, high notions. And travelling on through some parts of Leicestershire and into Nottinghamshire, there I met with a tender people, and a very tender woman whose name was Elizabeth Hooton; and with these I had some meetings and discourses. But my troubles continued, and I was often under great temptations; and I fasted much, and walked abroad in solitary places many days, and often took my Bible and went and sat in hollow trees and lonesome places till night came on; and frequently in the night walked mournfully about by myself, for I was a man of sorrows in the times of the first workings of the Lord in me.

Now during all this time I was never joined in profession of religion with any, but gave up myself to the Lord, having forsaken all evil company, and taken leave of father and mother and all other relations, and travelled up and down as a stranger in the earth, which way the Lord inclined my heart, taking a chamber to myself in the town where I came, and tarrying sometimes a month, sometimes more, sometimes less in a place. For I durst not stay long in any place, being afraid both of professor and profane, lest, being a tender young man, I should be hurt by conversing much with either. For which reason I kept myself much as a stranger, seeking heavenly wisdom and getting knowledge from the Lord, and was brought off from outward things to rely wholly on the Lord alone. And though my exercises and troubles were very great, yet were they not so continual but that I had some intermissions, and was sometimes brought into such an heavenly joy that I thought I had been in Abraham's bosom. As I cannot declare the misery I was in, it was so great and heavy upon me, so neither can I set forth the mercies of God unto me in all my misery. Oh, the everlasting love of God to my soul when I was in great distress ! When my troubles and torments were great, then was his love exceeding great. Thou, Lord, makest a fruitful field a barren wilderness, and a barren wilderness a fruitful field; thou bringest down and settest up; thou killest and makest alive; all honour and glory be to thee, O Lord of glory ! The knowledge of thee in the spirit is life, but that knowledge which is fleshly works death. And while there is this knowledge in the flesh, deceit and self-will conform to anything, and will say, 'Yes, yes', to that it doth not know. The knowledge which the world hath of what the prophets and apostles spake is a fleshly knowledge; and the apostates from the life in which the prophets and apostles were, have gotten their words, the Holy Scriptures, in a form, but not in their life nor spirit that gave them forth. And so they all lie in confusion and are making provision for the flesh, to fulfil the lusts thereof, but not to fulfil the law and command of Christ in his power and spirit; for that, they say, they cannot do, but to fulfil the lusts of the flesh, that they can do with delight.

Now after I had received that opening from the Lord that to be bred at Oxford or Cambridge was not sufficient to fit a man to be a minister of Christ, I regarded the priests less, and looked more after the dissenting people. And among them I saw there was some tenderness, and many of them came afterwards to be convinced, for they had some openings. But as I had forsaken all the priests, so I left the separate preachers also, and those called the most experienced people; for I saw there was none among them all that could speak to my condition. And when all my hopes in them and in all men were gone, so that I had nothing outwardly to help me, nor could tell what to do, then, Oh then, I heard a voice which said, ‘There is one, even Christ Jesus, that can speak to thy condition’, and when I heard it my heart did leap for joy. Then the Lord did let me see why there was none upon the earth that could speak to my condition, namely, that I might give him all the glory; for all are concluded under sin, and shut up in unbelief as I had been, that Jesus Christ might have the pre-eminence, who enlightens, and gives grace, and faith, and power. Thus, when God doth work who shall let[1] it? And this I knew experimentally.

My desires after the Lord grew stronger, and zeal in the pure knowledge of God and of Christ alone, without the help of any man, book, or writing. For though I read the Scriptures that spoke of Christ and of God, yet I knew him not but by revelation, as he who hath the key did open, and as the Father of life drew me to his Son by his spirit. And then the Lord did gently lead me along, and did let me see his love, which was endless and eternal, and surpasseth all the knowledge that men have in the natural state, or can get by history or books; and that love let

[1] Prevent.

me see myself as I was without him. And I was afraid of all company, for I saw them perfectly where they were, through the love of God which let me see myself. I had not fellowship with any people, priests, or professors, nor any sort of separated people, but with Christ, who hath the key, and opened the door of light and life unto me. And I was afraid of all carnal talk and talkers, for I could see nothing but corruptions, and the life lay under the burden of corruptions. And when I myself was in the deep, under all shut up, I could not believe that I should ever overcome; my troubles, my sorrows, and my temptations were so great, that I thought many times I should have despaired, I was so tempted. But when Christ opened to me how he was tempted by the same Devil, and had overcome him and bruised his head, and that through him and his power, light, grace and spirit, I should overcome also, I had confidence in him. So he it was that opened to me when I was shut up and had not hope nor faith. Christ it was who had enlightened me, that gave me his light to believe in, and gave me hope, which is himself, revealed himself in me, and gave me his spirit and gave me his grace, which I found sufficient in the deeps and in weakness. Thus, in the deepest miseries, and in greatest sorrows and temptations, that many times beset me, the Lord in his mercy did keep me.

And I found that there were two thirsts in me, the one after the creatures, to have gotten help and strength there, and the other after the Lord the creator and his Son Jesus Christ. And I saw all the world could do me no good. If I had had a king's diet, palace, and attendance, all would have been as nothing, for nothing gave me comfort but the Lord by his power. And I saw professors, priests, and people were whole and at ease in that condition which was my misery, and they loved that which I would have been rid of. But the Lord did stay my desires upon himself from whom my help came, and my care was cast upon him alone. Therefore, all wait patiently upon the Lord, whatsoever condition you be in; wait in the grace and truth that comes by Jesus; for if ye so do, there is a promise to you, and the Lord God will fulfil it in you. And blessed are all they indeed that do hunger and thirst after righteousness; they shall be satisfied with it. I have found it so, praised be the Lord who filleth with it, and satisfieth the desires of the hungry soul. O let the house of the spiritual Israel say, 'His mercy endureth for ever.' It is the great love of God to make a wilderness of that which is pleasant to the outward eye and fleshly mind; and to make a fruitful field of a barren wilderness. This is the great work of God. But while people's minds do run in the earthly, after the creatures and changeable things, and changeable ways and religions, and changeable, uncertain teachers, their minds are in bondage. And they are brittle and changeable, and tossed up and down with windy doctrines and thoughts, and notions and things, their minds being from the unchangeable truth in the inward parts, the light of Jesus Christ, which would keep their minds to the unchangeable, who is the way to the Father, who in all my troubles did preserve me by his spirit and power. Praised be his holy name for ever.

Again I heard a voice which did say, 'Thou Serpent, thou dost seek to destroy the life but canst not, for the sword which keepeth the tree of life shall destroy thee.' So Christ, the Word of God, that bruised the head of the Serpent the destroyer, preserved me, my inward mind being joined to his good Seed, that bruised the head of this Serpent the destroyer. And this inward life did spring up in me, to answer all the opposing professors and priests, and did bring in Scriptures to my memory to refute them with.

At another time I saw the great love of God, and I was filled with admiration at the infiniteness of it; and then I saw what was cast out from God, and what entered into God's kingdom, and how by Jesus, the opener of the door by his heavenly key, the entrance was given. And I saw death, how it had passed upon all men and oppressed the Seed of God in man and in me, and how I in the Seed came forth, and what the promise was to. Yet it was so with me that there seemed to be two pleading in me; and questionings arose in my mind about gifts and prophecies, and I was tempted again to despair, as if I had sinned against the Holy Ghost. And I was in great perplexity and trouble for many days, yet I gave up myself to the Lord still.

And one day when I had been walking solitarily abroad and was come home, I was taken up in the love of God, so that I could not but admire the greatness of his love. And while I was in that condition it was opened unto me by the eternal Light and power, and I therein saw clearly that all was done and to be done in and by Christ, and how he conquers and destroys this tempter, the Devil and all his works, and is atop of him, and that all these troubles were good for me, and temptations for the trial of my faith which Christ had given me. And the Lord opened me that I saw through all these troubles and temptations. My living faith was raised, that I saw all was done by Christ, the life, and my belief was in him. And when at any time my condition was veiled, my secret belief was stayed firm, and hope underneath held me, as an anchor in the bottom of the sea, and anchored my immortal soul to its Bishop, causing it to swim above the sea, the world where all the raging waves, foul weather, tempests, and temptations are. But oh, then did I see my troubles, trials, and temptations more than ever I had done! As the Light appeared, all appeared that is out of the Light, darkness, death, temptations, the unrighteous, the ungodly; all was manifest and seen in the Light.

Then after this there did a pure fire appear in me; then I saw how he sat as a refiner's fire and as the fuller's soap; and then the spiritual discerning came into me, by which I did discern my own thoughts, groans and sighs, and what it was that did veil me, and what it was that did open me. And that which could not abide in the patience nor endure the fire, in the Light I found to be the groans of the flesh (that could not give up to the will of God), which had veiled me, and that could not be patient in all trials, troubles and anguishes and perplexities, and could not give up self to die by the Cross, the power of God, that the living and quickened might follow him; and that that which would cloud and veil from the presence of Christ, that which the sword of the Spirit cuts down and which must die, might not be kept alive. And I discerned the groans of the spirit, which did open me, and made intercession to God, in which spirit is the true waiting upon God for the redemption of the body and of the whole creation. And by this true spirit, in which the true sighing is, I saw over the false sighings and groanings. And by this invisible spirit I discerned all the false hearing and the false seeing, and the false smelling which was atop, above the Spirit, quenching and grieving it; and that all they that were there were in confusion and deceit, where the false asking and praying is, in deceit, and atop in that nature and tongue that takes God's holy name in vain, and wallows in the Egyptian sea, and asketh but hath not. For they hate his light and resist the Holy Ghost, and turn the grace into wantonness, and rebel against the Spirit, and are erred from the faith they should ask in, and from the spirit they should pray by. He that knoweth these things in the true spirit, can witness them. The divine light of Christ manifesteth all things; and the spiritual fire trieth all things, and severeth all things. Several things did I then see as the Lord opened them to me, for he showed me that which can live in his holy refining fire, and that can live to God under his law. And he made me sensible how the law and the prophets were until John and how the least in the everlasting kingdom of God is greater than John.

The pure and perfect law of God is over the flesh to keep it and its works, which are not perfect, under, by the perfect law; and the law of God that is perfect answers the perfect principle of God in every one. And this law the Jews and the prophets and John were to perform and do. None knows the giver of this law but by the spirit of God, neither can any truly read it or hear its voice but by the spirit of

God. He that can receive it let him. John, who was the greatest prophet that was born of a woman, did bear witness to the light, which Christ the great heavenly prophet hath enlightened every man that cometh into the world withal, that they might believe in it, and become the children of light, and so have the light of life, and not come into condemnation. For the true belief stands in the light that condemns all evil and the Devil, who is the prince of darkness, who would draw out of the light into condemnation. And they that walk in this light come to the mountain of the house of God established above all mountains, and to God's teaching, who will teach them his ways. These things were opened to me in the light.

And I saw the mountains burning up and the rubbish, and the rough and crooked ways and places made smooth and plain that the Lord might come into his tabernacle. These things are to be found in man's heart. But to speak of these things being within seemed strange to the rough and crooked and mountainous ones. Yet the Lord said, 'O Earth, hear the word of the Lord!' The law of the Spirit crosseth the fleshly mind, spirit and will, which lives in disobedience, and doth not keep within the law of the Spirit. I saw this law was the pure love of God which was upon me, and which I must go through, though I was troubled while I was under it; for I could not be dead to the law but through the law which did judge and condemn that which is to be condemned. I saw many talked of the law, who had never known the law to be their schoolmaster; and many talked of the Gospel of Christ, who had never known life and immortality brought to light in them by it. You that have been under that schoolmaster, and the condemnation of it, know these things; for through the Lord in that day opened these things unto me in secret, they have since been published by his eternal spirit, as on the house-top. And as you are brought into the law, and through the law to be dead to it, and witness the righteousness of the law fulfilled in you, ye will afterwards come to know what it is to be brought into the faith, and through faith from under the law. And abiding in the faith which Christ is the author of, ye will have peace and access to God. But if ye look out from the faith, and from that which would keep you in the victory, and look after fleshly things or words, ye will be brought into bondage to the flesh again, and to the law which takes hold upon the flesh and sin and worketh wrath, and the works of the flesh will appear again. The law of God takes hold upon the law of sin and death; but the law of faith, or the law of the Spirit of life, which is the love of God, and which comes by Jesus (who is the end of the law for righteousness' sake), this makes free from the law of sin and death. This law of life fleshly-minded men do not know; yet they will tempt you, to draw you from the Spirit into the flesh, and so into bondage.

Therefore ye, who know the love of God, and the law of his Spirit, and the freedom that is in Jesus Christ, stand fast in him, in that divine faith which he is the author of in you; and be not entangled with the yoke of bondage. For the ministry of Christ Jesus and his teaching bringeth into liberty and freedom; but the ministry that is of man and by man, and which stands in the will of man, bringeth into bondage, and under the shadow of death and darkness. And therefore none can be a minister of Christ Jesus but in the eternal Spirit, which was before the Scriptures were given forth; for if they have not his spirit, they are none of his. Though they may have his light to condemn them that hate it, yet they can never bring any into unity and fellowship in the Spirit, except they be in it. For the Seed of God is a burdensome stone to the selfish, fleshly, earthly will which reigns in its own knowledge and understanding, that must perish, and in its wisdom, that is devilish. And the Spirit of God is grieved and vexed and quenched with that which brings into the fleshly bondage, and that which wars against the spirit of God must be mortified by it. For the flesh lusteth against the spirit, and the spirit against the flesh, and these are contrary the one to the other. The flesh would have its liberty, and the spirit would have its liberty; but the spirit is to have its liberty and not the flesh. If therefore ye quench the spirit, and join to the flesh, and be servants of it, then ye are judged and tormented by the spirit; but if ye join to the spirit and serve God in it, ye have liberty and victory over the flesh and its works. Therefore keep in the daily cross, the power of God, by which ye may witness all that to be crucified which is contrary to the will of God, and which shall not come into his kingdom.

These things are here mentioned and opened for information, exhortation and comfort to others, as the Lord opened them unto me in that day. And in that day I wondered that the children of Israel should murmur for water and victuals, for I could have fasted long without murmuring or minding victuals. But I was judged sometimes, that I was not contented to be sometimes without the water and bread of life, that I might learn to know how to want and how to abound.

And I heard of a woman in Lancashire that had fasted two and twenty days, and I travelled to see her; but when I came to her I saw that she was under a temptation. And when I had spoken to her what I had from the Lord, I left her, her father being one high in profession. And passing on, I went among the professors at Dukinfield and Manchester, where I stayed a while and declared Truth among them. And there were some convinced, who received the Lord's teaching, by which they were confirmed and stood in the Truth. But the professors were in a rage, all pleading for sin and imperfection, and could not endure to hear talk of perfection, and of an holy and sinless life. But the Lord's power was over all; though they were chained under darkness and sin, which they pleaded for, and quenched the tender thing in them.

About this time there was a great meeting of the Baptists, at Broughton,[1] in Leicestershire, with some that had separated from them; and people of other notions went thither, and I went also. Not many of the Baptists came, but abundance of other people were there. And the Lord

[1] Probably Broughton-Astley.

opened my mouth, and his everlasting Truth was declared amongst them, and the power of the Lord was over them all. For in that day the Lord's power began to spring, and I had great openings in the Scriptures. And several were convinced in those parts, and were turned from darkness to light, and from the power of Satan unto God, and his power they did receive and by it many were raised up to praise God. And when I reasoned with professors and other people, some were convinced and did stand.

Yet I was under great temptations sometimes, and my inward sufferings were heavy; but I could find none to open my condition to but the Lord alone, unto whom I cried night and day. And I went back into Nottinghamshire, and there the Lord shewed me that the natures of those things which were hurtful without were within, in the hearts and minds of wicked men. The natures of dogs, swine, vipers, of Sodom and Egypt, Pharaoh, Cain, Ishmael, Esau, etc. The natures of these I saw within, though people had been looking without. And I cried to the Lord, saying, 'Why should I be thus, seeing I was never addicted to commit those evils?' And the Lord answered that it was needful I should have a sense of all conditions, how else should I speak to all conditions; and in this I saw the infinite love of God. I saw also that there was an ocean of darkness and death, but an infinite ocean of light and love, which flowed over the ocean of darkness. And in that also I saw the infinite love of God; and I had great openings.

And as I was walking by the steeplehouse side, in the town of Mansfield, the Lord said unto me, 'That which people do trample upon must be thy food.' And as the Lord spoke he opened it to me how that people and professors did trample upon the life, even the life of Christ was trampled upon; and they fed upon words, and fed one another with words, but trampled upon the life, and trampled underfoot the blood of the Son of God, which blood was my life, and they lived in their airy notions, talking of him. It seemed strange to me at the first that

I should feed on that which the high professors trampled upon, but the Lord opened it clearly to me by his eternal spirit and power.〉

[a]In Mansfield there came a priest who was looked upon to be above others, and all that professed themselves above the priests went to hear him and cried him up. I was against their going, and spoke to them against their going, and asked them if they had not a teacher within them: the anointing to teach them, and why would they go out to man. And then when they were gone to hear him, I was in sore travail, and it came upon me that I was moved to go to the steeplehouse[1] to tell the people and the priest, and to bid them to cease from man whose breath was in their nostrils, and to tell them where their teacher was, within them, the spirit and the light of Jesus, and how God that made the world doth not dwell in temples made with hands. And many other things concerning the Truth I spake to them. And they were pretty moderate to hear the Truth, whereby, after, many were wrought upon.[a] 〈Then came people from far and near to see me; and I was fearful of being drawn out by them, yet I was made to speak and open things to them.

There was one Brown, who had great prophecies and sights upon his death-bed of me. And he spoke openly of what I should be made instrumental by the Lord to bring forth. And of others he spake that they should come to nothing, which was fulfilled on some, that then were something in show. And when this man was buried, a great work of the Lord fell upon me, to the admiration of many, who thought I had been dead, and many came to see me, for about fourteen days' time. For I was very much altered in countenance and person as if my body had been new moulded or changed. And while I was in that condition, I had a sense and discerning given me by the Lord, through which I saw plainly that when many people

[1] Fox's use of 'steeplehouse' and 'church' are explained on p. 93-4 in the paragraph about Ulrome.

[a]. . . . . .[a] *S.J.*, p. 1.

talked of God and of Christ, etc., the Serpent spoke in them; but this was hard to be borne. Yet the work of the Lord went on in some, and my sorrows and troubles began to wear off and tears of joy dropped from me, so that I could have wept night and day with tears of joy to the Lord, in humility and brokenness of heart. And I saw into that which was without end, and things which cannot be uttered, and of the greatness and infiniteness of the love of God, which cannot be expressed by words. For I had been brought through the very ocean of darkness and death, and through the power and over the power of Satan, by the eternal glorious power of Christ. Even through that darkness was I brought, which covered-over all the world, and which chained down all, and shut up all in the death. And the same eternal power of God, which brought me through these things, was that which afterwards shook the nations, priests, professors, and people. Then could I say I had been in spiritual Babylon, Sodom, Egypt, and the grave; but by the eternal power of God I was come out of it, and was brought over it and the power of it, into the power of Christ. And I saw the harvest white, and the Seed of God lying thick in the ground, as ever did wheat that was sown outwardly, and none to gather it; and for this I mourned with tears.

And a report went abroad of me that I was a young man that had a discerning spirit; whereupon many came to me from far and near, professors, priests, and people. And the Lord's power brake forth; and I had great openings, and prophecies, and spake unto them of the things of God, and they heard with attention and silence, and went away, and spread the fame thereof. Then came the tempter, and set upon me again, charging me that I had sinned against the Holy Ghost, but I could not tell in what. And then Paul's condition came before me, how, after he had been taken up into the third heaven and seen things not lawful to be uttered, a messenger of Satan was sent to buffet him again. Thus, by the power of Christ, I got over that temptation also.

CHAPTER II

IN the year 1648, as I was sitting in a Friend's house in Nottinghamshire (for by this time the power of God had opened the hearts of some to receive the word of life and reconciliation), I saw there was a great crack to go throughout the earth, and a great smoke to go as the crack went; and that after the crack there should be a great shaking. This was the earth in people's hearts, which was to be shaken before the Seed of God was raised out of the earth. And it was so; for the Lord's power began to shake them, and great meetings we began to have, and a mighty power and work of God there was amongst people, to the astonishment of both people and priests.

And there was a meeting of priests and professors at a justice's house, and I went among them. And there they discoursed how Paul said he had not known sin, but by the law, which said, 'Thou shalt not lust': and they held that to be spoken of the outward law. But I told them Paul spake that after he was convinced; for he had the outward law before, and was bred up in it, when he was in the lust of persecution; but this was the law of God in his mind, which he served, and which the law in his members warred against; for that which he thought had been life to him proved death. So the more sober of the priests and professors yielded, and consented that it was not the outward law, but the inward, which showed the inward lust which Paul spake of after he was convinced. For the outward law took hold upon the outward action, but the inward law upon the inward lust.

After this I went again to Mansfield, where was a great meeting of professors and people, and I was moved to pray, and the Lord's power was so great that the house seemed to be shaken. When I had done, some of the professors said it was now as in the days of the apostles, when the house was shaken where they were. After I had prayed, one of the professors would pray, which brought deadness and a veil over them. And others of the professors were grieved at him and told him it was a temptation upon him. Then he came to me, and desired that I would pray again, but I could not pray in man's will.

Soon after there was another great meeting of professors, and a captain, whose name was Amor Stoddard, came in. And they were discoursing of the blood of Christ; and as they were discoursing of it, I saw, through the immediate opening of the invisible Spirit, the blood of Christ. And I cried out among them, and said, ' Do ye not see the blood of Christ ? see it in your hearts, to sprinkle your hearts and consciences from dead works to serve the living God ? ' for I saw it, the blood of the New Covenant, how it came into the heart. This startled the professors, who would have the blood only without them and not in them. But Captain Stoddard was reached, and said, ' Let the youth speak; hear the youth speak ', when he saw they endeavoured to bear me down with many words.

There was also a company of priests, that were looked upon to be tender. One of their names was Kellet; and several people that were tender went to hear them. And I was moved to go after them, and bid them mind the Lord's teaching in their inward parts. That priest Kellet was against parsonages then, but afterwards he got a great one, and turned a persecutor.

Now, after I had had some service in these parts, I went through Derbyshire into my own country, Leicestershire, again, and several tender people were convinced. And passing thence, I met with a great company of professors in Warwickshire, who were praying and expounding the Scriptures in the fields. And they gave the Bible to me, and I opened it on the fifth of Matthew, where Christ expounded the law; and I opened the inward state to them and the outward state; and they fell into a fierce contention, and so parted: but the Lord's power got ground.

[a]In Leicestershire, as I was passing through the fields, I was moved to go to Leicester, and when I came there I heard of a great meeting for a dispute and that there were many to preach,[a] Presbyterians, Independents, Baptists, and Common-prayer-men. The meeting was in a steeplehouse; and I was moved to go among them. And I heard their discourse and reasonings, some being in pews and the priest in the pulpit, abundance of people being gathered together. At last one woman asked a question out of Peter, what that birth was, viz. a being 'born again of incorruptible seed, by the Word of God, that liveth and abideth for ever'. And the priest said to her, 'I permit not a woman to speak in the church'; though he had before given liberty for any to speak. Whereupon I was rapt up, as in a rapture, in the Lord's power; and I stepped up in a place and asked the priest, 'Dost thou call this place a church? Or dost thou call this mixed multitude a church?' For the woman asking a question, he ought to have answered it, having given liberty for any to speak. But he did not answer me neither, but asked me what a church was. I told him the Church was the pillar and ground of Truth, made up of living stones, living members, a spiritual household which Christ was the head of, but he was not the head of a mixed multitude, or of an old house made up of lime, stones, and wood.

[a]Then I spoke how that the Church was in God the Father of our Lord Jesus Christ, and what the woman was that was not to speak, and what the woman was that might prophesy and speak; and it broke them all to pieces and confused them, and they all turned against me into jangling.[a]

The priest came down out of his pulpit, and others out of their pews, and the dispute[1] there was marred. But I went to a great inn, and there disputed the thing with the priests and professors of all sorts, and they were all on a

[1] i.e. a properly conducted argument, not a mere wrangle.

[a]......[a] Cf. *S.J.*, p. 3.

fire. But I maintained the true Church, and the true head thereof, over the heads of them all, till they all gave out and fled away. And there was one man that seemed loving, and appeared for a while to join with me, but he soon turned against me, and joined with a priest in pleading for infants' baptism, though he himself had been a Baptist before, and so left me alone. Howbeit, there were several convinced that day; and the woman that asked the question aforesaid was convinced, and her family; and the Lord's power and glory shined over all.

After this I returned into Nottinghamshire again, and went into the Vale of Beavor.[1] And as I went, I preached repentance to the people; and there were many convinced in the Vale of Beavor, in many towns, for I stayed some weeks amongst them. And one morning, as I was sitting by the fire, a great cloud came over me, and a temptation beset me; but I sat still. And it was said, 'All things come by nature'; and the elements and stars came over me so that I was in a manner quite clouded with it. But inasmuch as I sat, still and silent, the people of the house perceived nothing. And as I sat still under it and let it alone, a living hope arose in me, and a true voice, which said, 'There is a living God who made all things.' And immediately the cloud and temptation vanished away, and life rose over it all, and my heart was glad, and I praised the living God.

And after some time, I met with some people who had such a notion that there was no God but that all things came by nature. And I had great dispute with them and overturned them and made some of them confess that there was a living God. Then I saw that it was good that I had gone through that exercise. And we had great meetings in those parts, for the power of the Lord broke through in that side of the country.

And returning into Nottinghamshire I found there a company of shattered Baptists, and others; and the Lord's power wrought mightily and gathered many of them.

[1] i.e. Belvoir.

Then afterwards I went to Mansfield and thereaway, where the Lord's power was wonderfully manifested both at Mansfield and other towns thereabouts. And in Derbyshire the mighty power of God wrought in a wonderful manner. At Eaton, a town near Derby, there was a meeting of Friends, where there was such a mighty power of God that they were greatly shaken, and many mouths were opened in the power of the Lord God. And many were moved by the Lord to go to steeplehouses, to the priests and to the people, to declare the everlasting Truth unto them.

And at a certain time, when I was at Mansfield, there was a sitting of the justices about hiring of servants; and it was upon me from the Lord to go and speak to the justices that they should not oppress the servants in their wages. So I walked towards the inn where they sat[1] but finding a company of fiddlers there, I did not go in but thought to come in the morning, when I might have a more serious opportunity to discourse with them, not thinking that a seasonable time. But when I came again in the morning, they were gone, and I was struck even blind that I could not see. And I inquired of the innkeeper where the justices were to sit that day and he told me at a town eight miles off. My sight began to come to me again, and I went and ran thitherward as fast as I could. And then I was come to the house where they were, and many servants with them, I exhorted the justices not to oppress the servants in their wages, but to do that which was right and just to them; and I exhorted the servants to do their duties, and serve honestly, etc. And they all received my exhortation kindly, for I was moved of the Lord therein.

Moreover, I was moved to go to several courts and steeplehouses at Mansfield and other places to warn them to leave off oppression and oaths, and to turn from deceit and to turn to the Lord, and do justly. Particularly at Mansfield, after I had been at a court there, I was moved to go and speak to one of the wickedest men in the country,

[1] The Bowl in Hand.

one who was a common drunkard, a noted whore-master, and a rhyme-maker; and I reproved him in the dread of the mighty God for his evil courses. And when I had done speaking and left him, he came after me, and told me that he was so smitten when I spoke to him, that he had scarce any strength left in him. So this man was convinced, and turned from his wickedness, and remained an honest, sober man, to the astonishment of the people who had known him before.

Thus the work of the Lord went forward, and many were turned from the darkness to the light within the compass of these three years, 1646, 1647, and 1648. And divers meetings of Friends, in several places, were then gathered to God's teaching, by his light, spirit, and power; for the Lord's power brake forth more and more wonderfully.

Now was I come up in spirit through the flaming sword into the paradise of God. All things were new, and all the creation gave another smell unto me than before, beyond what words can utter. I knew nothing but pureness, and innocency, and righteousness, being renewed up into the image of God by Christ Jesus, so that I say I was come up to the state of Adam which he was in before he fell. The creation was opened to me, and it was showed me how all things had their names given them according to their nature and virtue. And I was at a stand in my mind whether I should practise physic for the good of mankind, seeing the nature and virtues of the creatures were so opened to me by the Lord. But I was immediately taken up in spirit, to see into another or more steadfast state than Adam's in innocency, even into a state in Christ Jesus, that should never fall. And the Lord showed me that such as were faithful to him in the power and light of Christ, should come up into that state in which Adam was before he fell, in which the admirable works of the creation, and the virtues thereof, may be known, through the openings of that divine Word of wisdom and power by which they were made. Great things did the Lord lead me into, and wonderful depths were opened unto me, beyond what can by words be declared; but as people come into subjection to the spirit of God, and grow up in the image and power of the Almighty, they may receive the Word of wisdom, that opens all things, and come to know the hidden unity in the Eternal Being.

Thus travelled I on in the Lord's service, as the Lord led me. And when I came to Nottingham, the mighty power of God was there among Friends. From thence I went to Clawson in Leicestershire, in the Vale of Beavor, and the mighty power of God was there also in several towns and villages where Friends were gathered. While I was there, the Lord opened to me three things relating to those three great professions in the world, physic, divinity (so called), and law. And he showed me that the physicians were out of the wisdom of God by which the creatures were made, and so knew not the virtues of the creatures, because they were out of the Word of wisdom by which they were made. And he showed me that the priests were out of the true faith which Christ is the author of, the faith which purifies and gives victory and brings people to have access to God, by which they please God, which mystery of faith is held in a pure conscience. He showed me also, that the lawyers were out of the equity and out of the true justice, and out of the law of God, which went over the first transgression and over all sin, and answered the spirit of God that was grieved and transgressed in man. And that these three, the physicians, the priests, and the lawyers, ruled the world out of the wisdom, out of the faith and out of the equity and law of God, the one pretending the cure of the body, the other the cure of the soul, and the third the property of the people. But I saw they were all out, out of the wisdom, out of the faith, out of the equity and perfect law of God.

And as the Lord opened these things unto me, I felt his power went forth over all, by which all might be reformed, if they would receive and bow unto it. The priests might be reformed and brought into the true faith which was the gift of God. The lawyers might be reformed and brought into the law of God which answers that of God (that is transgressed) in every one, and brings to love one's neighbour as himself. This lets man see if he wrongs his neighbour he wrongs himself; and this teaches him to do unto others as he would they should do unto him. The physicians might be reformed, and brought into the wisdom of God by which all things were made and created; that they might receive a right knowledge of the creatures and understand the virtues of them, which the Word of wisdom, by which they were made and are upheld, hath given them. Abundance was opened concerning these things; how all lay out of the wisdom of God, and out of the righteousness and holiness that man at the first was made in. But as all believe in the light and walk in the light, which Christ hath enlightened every man that cometh into the world withal, and so become children of the light, and of the day of Christ; in his day all things are seen, visible and invisible, by the divine light of Christ, the spiritual, heavenly man, by whom all things were made and created.

Then I saw concerning the priests, that although they stood in the deceit, and acted by the dark power, which both they and their people were kept under, yet they were not the greatest deceivers spoken of in the Scriptures; for these were not come so far as many of them had come. But the Lord opened to me who the greatest deceivers were, and how far they might come; even such as came as far as Cain, to hear the voice of God; and such as came out of Egypt, and through the Red Sea, and to praise God on the banks of the sea-shore; such as could speak by experience of God's miracles and wonders; such as were come as far as Korah and Dathan and their company; such as came as far as Balaam, who could speak the word of the Lord, who heard his voice and knew it, and knew his spirit and could see the star of Jacob and the goodliness of Israel's tent; the second birth, which no enchantment could prevail against. These that could speak so much of their experiences of God, and yet turned from the Spirit and the Word, and went into the gainsaying, these were, and would be, the great deceivers far beyond the priests. Likewise among the Christians, such as should preach in Christ's name, and should work miracles, cast out devils, and go as far as a Cain, a Korah, and a Balaam, in the Gospel times, these were and would be the great deceivers. They that could speak some experiences of Christ and God, but lived not in the life, these were they that led the world after them, who got the form of godliness, but denied the power; who inwardly ravened from the Spirit, and brought people into the form, but persecuted them that were in the power, as Cain did; and ran greedily after the error of Balaam through covetousness, loving the wages of unrighteousness as Balaam did. These followers of Cain, Korah, and Balaam have brought the world, since the apostles' days, to be like a sea. And such as these, I saw might deceive now, as they had in former ages; but it is impossible for them to deceive the elect, who were chosen in Christ, who was before the world began, and before the deceiver was, though others may be deceived in their openings and prophecies, not keeping their minds to the Lord Jesus Christ who doth open and reveal to his.

And I saw the state of those, both priests and people, who in reading the Scriptures, cry out much against Cain, Esau, and Judas, and other wicked men of former times, mentioned in the Holy Scriptures; but do not see the nature of Cain, of Esau, of Judas, and those others, in themselves. And these said it was they, they, they, that were the bad people; putting it off from themselves: but when some of these came, with the light and spirit of Truth, to see into themselves, then they came to say, 'I, I, I, it is I myself that have been the Ishmael, and the Esau', etc. For then they came to see the nature of wild Ishmael in themselves, the nature of Cain, of Esau, of Korah, of Balaam and of the son of perdition in themselves, sitting above all that is called God in them.

So I saw it was the fallen man that was got up into the Scriptures and was finding fault with those before-mentioned, and, with the backsliding Jews, calling them the sturdy oaks and tall cedars and fat bulls of Bashan, wild heifers, vipers, serpents, etc., and charging them that it was they that closed their eyes and stopped their ears and hardened their hearts, and were dull of hearing, that it was they that hated the light and rebelled against it, and that quenched the Spirit, and vexed, and grieved it, and walked despitefully against the spirit of grace, and turned the grace of God into wantonness, and that it was they that resisted the Holy Ghost, and they that got the form of godliness, and turned against the power, and that they were the inwardly ravening wolves, that had got the sheep's clothing, and that they were the wells without water, and clouds without rain, and trees without fruit, etc. But when these, who were so much taken up with finding fault with others, and thought themselves clear from these things, came to look into themselves, and with the light of Christ throughly to search themselves, they might see enough of this in themselves; and then the cry could not be, it is he, or they, as before, but I and we are found in these conditions.

I saw also how people read the Scriptures without a right sense of them, and without duly applying them to their own states. For, when they read that death reigned from Adam to Moses, that the law and the prophets were until John, and that the least in the kingdom is greater than John, they read these things without them and applied them to others without them, and the things were true of others without them, but they did not turn in to find the truth of these things in themselves. But as these things came to be opened in me, I saw death reigned over them from Adam to Moses, from the entrance into transgression till they came to the ministration of condemnation, which restrains people from sin that brings death. Then, when the ministration of Moses is passed through, the ministry of the prophets comes to be read and understood, which reaches through the figures, types and shadows unto John, the greatest prophet born of woman; whose ministration prepares the way of the Lord by bringing down the exalted mountains and making straight paths. And as this ministration is passed through, an entrance comes to be known into the everlasting kingdom.

So I saw plainly that none could read Moses aright without Moses' spirit, by which Moses saw how man was in the image of God in Paradise, and how he fell, and how death came over him, and how all men have been under this death. I saw how Moses received the pure law that went over all transgressors, and how the clean beasts which were figures and types were offered up, when the people were come into the righteous law that went over the first transgression. And both Moses and the prophets saw through the types and figures and beyond them, and saw Christ the great prophet that was to come to fulfil them.

And I saw that none could read John's words aright and with a true understanding of them, but in and with the same divine Spirit by which John spoke them, and by his burning, shining light, which is sent from God. For by that Spirit their crooked natures might be made straight, and their rough natures smooth, and the exacter and violent doer in them might be thrown out, and they that had been hypocrites might come to bring forth fruits meet for repentance, and their mountain of sin and earthliness might be laid low in them, and their valley exalted in them, that there might be a way prepared for the Lord in them; and then the least in the kingdom is greater than John. But all must first know the voice crying in the wilderness, in their hearts, which through transgression were become as a wilderness. Thus I saw it was an easy matter to say death reigned from Adam to Moses, and that the law and the prophets were until John, and that the least in the kingdom is greater than John; but none could know death reigned from Adam to Moses, etc., but by the same Holy Spirit which Moses, and the prophets, and John were in. They could not know the spiritual meaning of Moses', the prophets', and John's words, nor see their path and travels, much less see through them and to the end of them into the kingdom, unless they had the Spirit and the light of Jesus; nor could they know the words of Christ and of his apostles without his Spirit. But as man comes through by the Spirit and power of God to Christ who fulfils the types, figures, shadows, promises, and prophecies that were of him, and is led by the Holy Ghost into the truth and substance of the Scriptures, sitting down in him who is the author and end of them, then are they read and understood with profit and great delight.

Moreover the Lord God let me see, when I was brought up into his image in righteousness and holiness, and into the paradise of God, the state how Adam was made a living soul, and also the stature of Christ, the mystery, that had been hid from ages and generations, which things are hard to be uttered and cannot be borne by many. For, of all the sects in Christendom (so called) that I discoursed withal, I found none that could bear to be told that any should come to Adam's perfection, into that image of God and righteousness and holiness that Adam was in before he fell, to be so clear and pure without sin, as he was. Therefore how should they be able to bear being told that any should grow up to the measure of the stature of the fulness of Christ, when they cannot bear to hear that any should come, whilst upon earth, into the same power and Spirit that the prophets and apostles were in ? Though it be a certain truth, that none can understand their writings aright without the same Spirit by which they were written.

Now the Lord God hath opened to me by his invisible power how that every man was enlightened by the divine light of Christ; and I saw it shine through all, and that they that believed in it came out of condemnation and came to the light of life and became the children of it, but they that hated it, and did not believe in it, were condemned by it, though they made a profession of Christ. This I saw in the pure openings of the Light without the help of any man, neither did I then know where to find it in the Scriptures; though afterwards, searching the Scriptures, I found it. For I saw in that Light and Spirit which was before Scripture was given forth, and which led the holy men of God to give them forth, that all must come to that Spirit, if they would know God, or Christ, or the Scriptures aright, which they that gave them forth were led and taught by.

But I observed a dulness and drowsy heaviness upon people, which I wondered at, for sometimes when I would set myself to sleep, my mind went over all to the beginning, in that which is from everlasting to everlasting. I saw death was to pass over this sleepy, heavy state, and I told people they must come to witness death to that sleepy, heavy nature, and a cross to it in the power of God, that their minds and hearts might be on things above.

And on a certain time, as I was walking in the fields, the Lord said unto me, ‘ Thy name is written in the Lamb’s book of life, which was before the foundation of the world ’; and as the Lord spoke it I believed, and saw it in the new birth. Then, some time after, the Lord commanded me to go abroad into the world, which was like a briery, thorny wilderness, and when I came in the Lord’s mighty power with the word of life into the world, the world swelled and made a noise like the great raging waves of the sea. Priests and professors, magistrates and people, were all like a sea, when I came to proclaim the day of the Lord amongst them and to preach repentance to them.

Now I was sent to turn people from darkness to the light that they might receive Christ Jesus, for to as many as should receive him in his light, I saw that he would give power to become the sons of God, which I had obtained by receiving Christ. And I was to direct people to the Spirit that gave forth the Scriptures, by which they might be led into all Truth, and so up to Christ and God, as they had been who gave them forth. And I was to turn them to the grace of God, and to the Truth in the heart, which came by Jesus, that by this grace they might be taught, which would bring them into salvation, that their hearts might be established by it, and their words might be seasoned, and all might come to know their salvation nigh. For I saw that Christ had died for all men, and was a propitiation for all, and had enlightened all men and women with his divine and saving light, and that none could be a true believer but who believed in it. I saw that the grace of God, which brings salvation, had appeared to all men, and that the manifestation of the Spirit of God was given to every man to profit withal. These things I did not see by the help of man, nor by the letter, though they are written in the letter, but I saw them in the light of the Lord Jesus Christ, and by his immediate Spirit and power, as did the holy men of God, by whom the Holy Scriptures were written. Yet I had no slight esteem of the Holy Scriptures, but they were very precious to me, for I was in that spirit by which they were given forth, and what the Lord opened in me I afterwards found was agreeable to them. I could speak much of these things and many volumes might be written, but all would prove too short to set forth the infinite love, wisdom, and power of God, in preparing, fitting, and furnishing me for the service he had appointed me to; letting me see the depths of Satan on the one hand, and opening to me, on the other hand, the divine mysteries of his own everlasting kingdom.

Now, when the Lord God and his son, Jesus Christ,

did send me forth into the world, to preach his everlasting gospel and kingdom, I was glad that I was commanded to turn people to that inward light, spirit, and grace, by which all might know their salvation, and their way to God; even that divine Spirit which would lead them into all Truth and which I infallibly knew would never deceive any. But with and by this divine power and spirit of God, and the light of Jesus, I was to bring people off from all their own ways to Christ, the new and living way, and from their churches, which men had made and gathered, to the Church in God, the general assembly written in heaven, which Christ is the head of, and off from the world's teachers made by men, to learn of Christ, who is the way, the truth, and the life, of whom the Father said, ‘ This is my beloved Son, hear ye him ’; and off from all the world's worships, to know the spirit of Truth in the inward parts, and to be led thereby, that in it they might worship the Father of spirits, who seeks such to worship him, which spirit they that worshipped not in knew not what they worshipped.

And I was to bring people off from all the world's religions, which are vain, that they might know the pure religion, and might visit the fatherless, the widows and the strangers, and keep themselves from the spots of the world. And then there would not be so many beggars, the sight of whom often grieved my heart, to see so much hard-heartedness amongst them that professed the name of Christ. And I was to bring them off from all the world's fellowships, and prayings, and singings, which stood in forms without power, that their fellowships might be in the Holy Ghost, and in the eternal Spirit of God; that they might pray in the Holy Ghost, and sing in the spirit and with the grace that comes by Jesus, making melody in their hearts to the Lord who hath sent his beloved Son to be their Saviour, and caused his heavenly sun to shine upon all the world, and through them all, and his heavenly rain to fall upon the just and the unjust (as his outward rain doth fall, and his outward sun doth shine on all), which is God's unspeakable love to the world.

And I was to bring people off from Jewish ceremonies, and from heathenish fables, and from men's inventions and windy doctrines, by which they blowed the people about this way and the other way, from sect to sect; and all their beggarly rudiments, with their schools and colleges for making ministers of Christ, who are indeed ministers of their own making but not of Christ's; and from all their images and crosses, and sprinkling of infants, with all their holy days (so called) and all their vain traditions, which they had gotten up since the apostles' days, which the Lord's power was against, and in the dread and authority thereof I was moved to declare against them all, and against all that preached and not freely, as being such as had not received freely from Christ.

Moreover when the Lord sent me forth into the world, he forbade me to put off my hat to any, high or low; and I was required to 'thee' and 'thou' all men and women, without any respect to rich or poor, great or small. And as I travelled up and down, I was not to bid people 'good morrow' or 'good evening', neither might I bow or scrape with my leg to any one; and this made the sects and professions to rage. But the Lord's power carried me over all to his glory, and many came to be turned to God in a little time, for the heavenly day of the Lord sprang from on high, and brake forth apace, by the light of which many came to see where they were.

But oh, the rage that then was in the priests, magistrates, professors, and people of all sorts, but especially in priests and professors! for, though 'thou' to a single person was according to their own learning, their accidence and grammar rules, and according to the Bible, yet they could not bear to hear it, and the hat-honour, because I could not put off my hat to them, it set them all into a rage. But the Lord showed me that it was an honour below, which he would lay in the dust and stain it, an honour which proud flesh looked for, but sought not the honour which came from God only, that it was an honour invented by men in the Fall, and in the alienation from God, who were offended if it were not given them, and yet would be looked upon as saints, church-members, and great Christians. But Christ saith, ‘ How can ye believe, who receive honour one of another, and seek not the honour that cometh from God only ? ’ ‘ And I ’, saith Christ, ‘ receive not honour of men ’: showing that men have an honour, which men will receive and give, but Christ will have none of it. This is the honour which Christ will not receive, and which must be laid in the dust. Oh, the rage and scorn, the heat and fury that arose ! Oh, the blows, punchings, beatings, and imprisonments that we underwent for not putting off our hats to men ! For that soon tried all men's patience and sobriety, what it was. Some had their hats violently plucked off and thrown away so that they quite lost them. The bad language and evil usage we received on this account are hard to be expressed, besides the danger we were sometimes in of losing our lives for this matter, and that, by the great professors of Christianity, who thereby discovered that they were not true believers. And though it was but a small thing in the eye of man, yet a wonderful confusion it brought among all professors and priests. But, blessed be the Lord, many came to see the vanity of that custom of putting off the hat to men, and felt the weight of Truth's testimony against it.

About this time I was sorely exercised in going to their courts to cry for justice, and in speaking and writing to judges and justices to do justly, and in warning such as kept public houses for entertainment that they should not let people have more drink than would do them good, and in testifying against their wakes or feasts, their May-games, sports, plays, and shows, which trained up people to vanity and looseness, and led them from the fear of God, and the days they had set forth for holy-days were usually the times wherein they most dishonoured God by these things. In fairs also, and in markets, I was made to declare against their deceitful merchandise and cheating and cozening, warning all to deal justly, to speak the truth, to let their 'yea' be 'yea', and their 'nay' be 'nay'; and to do unto others as they would have others do unto them, and forewarning them of the great and terrible day of the Lord which would come upon them all. I was moved also to cry against all sorts of music, and against the mountebanks playing tricks on their stages, for they burdened the pure life, and stirred up people's minds to vanity.

I was much exercised too, with school-masters and school-mistresses, warning them to teach their children sobriety in the fear of the Lord, that they might not be nursed and trained up in lightness, vanity, and wantonness. Likewise I was made to warn masters and mistresses, fathers and mothers in private families, to take care that their children and servants might be trained up in the fear of the Lord; and that they themselves should be therein examples and patterns of sobriety and virtue to them. For I saw that as the Jews were to teach their children the law of God and the old covenant, and to train them up in it, and their servants, yea the very strangers were to keep the Sabbath amongst them, and be circumcised, before they might eat of their sacrifices, so all Christians, and all that made a profession of Christianity, ought to train up their children and servants in the new covenant of light, Christ Jesus, who is God's salvation to the ends of the earth, that all may know their salvation. And they ought to train them up in the law of life, the law of the Spirit, the law of love and of faith, that they might be made free from the law of sin and death. And all Christians ought to be circumcised by the Spirit, which puts off the body of the sins of the flesh, that they may come to eat of the heavenly sacrifice, Christ Jesus, that true spiritual food, which none can rightly feed upon but they that are circumcised by the Spirit. Likewise, I was exercised about the star-gazers, who drew people's minds from Christ, the bright and the morning star, and from the sun of righteousness, by whom the sun, and moon, and stars, and all things else were made, who is the wisdom of God, and from whom the right knowledge of all things is received.

But the black earthly spirit of the priests wounded my life; and when I heard the bell toll to call people together to the steeplehouse, it struck at my life, for it was just like a market-bell to gather people together that the priest might set forth his ware to sale. Oh, the vast sums of money that are gotten by the trade they make of selling the Scriptures, and by their preaching, from the highest bishop to the lowest priest! What one trade else in the world is comparable to it, notwithstanding the Scriptures were given forth freely, and Christ commanded his ministers to preach freely, and the prophets and apostles denounced judgement against all covetous hirelings and diviners for money. But in this free spirit of the Lord Jesus was I sent forth to declare the word of life and reconciliation freely, that all might come up to Christ, who gives freely, and who renews up into the image of God which man and woman were in before they fell, that they might sit down in heavenly places in Christ Jesus.〉

CHAPTER III

[a]Now as I passed to Nottingham 〈on a First-day in the morning with Friends to a meeting,〉 when I came on top of a hill, as I looked upon the town the great steeplehouse struck at my life when I spied it, a great idol and idolatrous temple.[a] 〈And the Lord said unto me, 'Thou must go cry against yonder great idol, and against the worshippers therein.' So I said nothing of this to the Friends that were with me, but went on with them to the meeting, where the mighty power of the Lord God was amongst us, in which I left Friends sitting in the meeting, and I went away to the steeplehouse.[1] And when I came there, all the people looked like fallow ground, and the priest, like a great lump of earth, stood in his pulpit

[1] Church of St. Mary, Nicholas Folkingham, incumbent.
[a] . . . . . .[a] *S.J.*, p. 1.

above. He took for his text these words of Peter, 'We have also a more sure word of prophecy, whereunto ye do well that ye take heed, as unto a light that shineth in a dark place, until the day dawn, and the day-star arise in your hearts.' And he told the people that the Scriptures were the touchstone and judge by which they were to try all doctrines, religions, and opinions, and to end controversy. Now the Lord's power was so mighty upon me, and so strong in me, that I could not hold, but was made to cry out and say, 'Oh, no, it is not the Scriptures', and [b]was commanded to tell them God did not dwell in temples made with hands.[b] But I told them what it was, namely, the Holy Spirit, by which the holy men of God gave forth the Scriptures, whereby opinions, religions, and judgements were to be tried; for it led into all Truth, and so gave the knowledge of all Truth. For the Jews had the Scriptures, and yet resisted the Holy Ghost, and rejected Christ the bright morning star, and they persecuted Christ and his apostles, and took upon them to try their doctrines by the Scriptures, but erred in judgement, and did not try them aright, because they tried without the Holy Ghost. Now as I spoke thus amongst them, the officers came and took me away and put me into prison, a pitiful stinking place, [c]where the wind brought all the stench of the house of office in the place, where the stench of the place was in my throat and head many days after.[c]

But that day the Lord's power sounded so in their ears that they were amazed at the voice, and could not get it out of their ears for some time after, they were so reached by the Lord's power in the steeplehouse. At night they took me out of prison and had me before the mayor,[1] aldermen and sheriffs of the town; and when I was brought before them, the mayor was in a peevish, fretful temper,

[1] William Nix was mayor and John Reckless and Richard Watkinson sheriffs.

[b]......[b] *Short Account*, MS. Portfolio 36.172. See *Bulletin F.H.A.*, Vol. 39, p. 27.

[c]......[c] *S.J.*, p. 2.

but the Lord's power allayed him. Then they examined me at large, and I told them how the Lord had moved me to come. Then after some discourse between them and me, they sent me back to prison. But some time after, the head sheriff, whose name was John Reckless, sent for me to his house. And when I came in, his wife met me in the hall, and said, 'Salvation is come to our house.' And she took me by the hand, and was much wrought upon by the power of the Lord God, and her husband; [d]and all their family were wrought upon by the power of the Lord, and they believed in the Truth; and this was the first day of the week.[d] And I lodged at the sheriff's house, and great meetings we had in his house. And some persons of considerable condition in the world came to them, and the Lord's power appeared eminently amongst them. And this sheriff sent for the other sheriff, and for a woman they had had dealings with in the way of trade; and he told her before the other sheriff, that they had wronged her in their dealings with her (for the other sheriff and he were partners), and that they ought to make her restitution. This he spoke cheerfully; but the other sheriff denied it, and the woman said she knew nothing of it. But the friendly sheriff said it was so, and that the other knew it well enough; and then, having discovered the matter, and acknowledged the wrong done by them, he made restitution to the woman, and exhorted the other sheriff to do the like.

The Lord's power was with this friendly sheriff, and wrought a mighty change in him, and great openings he had. The next market-day, [d]being the seventh day of the week,[d] as he was walking with me in the chamber, in his slippers, he said, 'I must go into the market and preach repentance to the people'; and accordingly he went, in his slippers, into the market, and into several streets, and preached repentance to the people, very many being wrought upon. Several others also in the town were moved to speak to the mayor and magistrates, and to the people, exhorting them

[d]. . . . . [d] *S.J.*, p. 2.

to repent. Hereupon the magistrates grew very angry, and sent for me from the sheriff's house, and committed me to the common prison. When the Assize came on, there was one moved to come and offer up himself for me, body for body, yea, life also. But when I should have been brought before the judge, the sheriff's man being somewhat long in fetching me to the Sessions-house, the judge was risen before I came. At which I understood the judge was somewhat offended and said he would have admonished the youth if he had been brought before him; for I was then imprisoned by the name of a youth. So I was returned to prison again, and put into the common gaol. And the Lord's power was great among Friends; but the people began to be very rude; wherefore the governor of the castle[1] sent down soldiers and dispersed them; and after that they were quiet. But both priests and people were astonished at the wonderful power that broke forth; and several of the priests were made tender, and some did confess to the power of the Lord.〉

[e]When I was a prisoner in the same place there came a woman to me to the prison and two with her and said that she had been possessed two and thirty years. And the priests had kept her and had kept fasting days about her, and could not do her any good, and she said the Lord said unto her, 'Arise, for I have a sanctified people; haste and go to them, for thy redemption draweth nigh.' And when I came out of prison I bade Friends have her to Mansfield. At that time our meetings were disturbed by wild people, and both they and the professors and priests said that we were false prophets and deceivers, and that there was witchcraft amongst us. The poor woman would make such a noise in roaring, and sometimes lying along upon her belly upon the ground with her spirit and roaring and voice, that it would set all Friends in a heat and sweat. And I said, 'All Friends, keep to your own, lest that which is in her get into you', and so she affrighted the world from our meetings.

[1] Colonel John Hutchinson (1615-1664).

Then they said if that were cast out of her while she were with us, and were made well, then they would say that we were of God. This said the world, and I had said before that she should be set free.

Then it was upon me that we should have a meeting at Skegby at Elizabeth Hooton's[1] house; and we had her there. And there were many Friends almost overcome by her with the stink that came out of her; roaring and tumbling on the ground, and the same day she was worse than ever she was. Another day we met about her, and about the first hour the Life rose in Friends and said it was done. She rose up, and her countenance changed and became white; and before it was wan and earthly; and she sat down at my thigh as I was sitting, and lifted up her hands and said, 'Ten thousand praise the Lord', and did not know where she was, and so she was well; and we kept her about a fortnight in the sight of the world and she wrought and did things, and then we sent her away to her friends. And then the world's professors, priests, and teachers never could call us any more false prophets, deceivers, or witches after, but it did a great deal of good in the country among people in relation to the Truth and to the stopping the mouths of the world and their slanderous aspersions.[e]

⟨Now after I was set at liberty from Nottingham gaol, where I had been kept prisoner a pretty long time, I travelled as before in the work of the Lord. And coming to Mansfield-Woodhouse, there was a distracted woman under a doctor's hand, with her hair loose all about her ears. He was about to let her blood, she being first bound, and many people being about her holding her by violence; but he could get no blood from her. And I desired them to unbind her and let her alone, for they could not touch the spirit in her, by which she was tormented. So they did unbind her; and I was moved to speak to her in the name of the Lord to bid her be quiet and still, and she was

[1] Elizabeth Hooton (*c.* 1600-1672), Fox's first convert and preacher of Quakerism, died in Jamaica.

[e]. . . . . .[e] *S.J.*, pp. 2, 3.

so. The Lord's power settled her mind, and she mended and afterwards received the Truth, and continued in it to her death. And the Lord's name was honoured, to whom the glory of all his works belongs. Many great and wonderful things were wrought by the heavenly power in those days, for the Lord made bare his omnipotent arm, and manifested his power, to the astonishment of many, by the healing virtue whereof many have been delivered from great infirmities, and the devils were made subject through his name, of which particular instances might be given beyond what this unbelieving age is able to receive or bear. Blessed for ever be the name of the Lord and everlastingly honoured and over all exalted, and magnified be the arm of his glorious power, by which he hath wrought gloriously; and let the honour and praise of all his works be ascribed to him alone.

Now while I was at Mansfield-Woodhouse, I was moved to go to the steeplehouse there on a [f]First-day, out of the meeting in Mansfield, and when the priest had done[f] I declared the Truth to the priest and people. But the people fell upon me⟩ [f]with their fists, books, and without compassion or mercy beat me down in the steeplehouse and almost smothered me in it, being under them. And sorely was I bruised in the steeplehouse, and they threw me against the walls and when that they had thrust and thrown me out of the steeplehouse, when I came into the yard I fell down, being so sorely bruised and beat among them. And I got up again and then they punched and thrust and struck me up and down and they set me in the stocks and brought a whip to whip me, but did not. And as I sat in the stocks they threw stones at me, and my head, arms, breast, shoulders, back, and sides were so bruised that I was mazed and dazzled with the blows. And I was hot when they put me in the stocks.[f] ⟨After some time they had me before the magistrate, at a knight's house[1] and examined me, where were many great persons,⟩ [g]and

[1] Said to be the house of Sir John Digby, at Mansfield-Woodhouse.
[f]. . . . . .[f] *S.J.*, p. 12.

I reasoned with them of the things of God and of God and his teachings, and Christ's, and how that God that made the world did not dwell in temples made with hands; and of divers things of the Truth I spake to them, and they,[g] ⟨seeing how evilly I had been used, set me at liberty. The rude people were⟩ [g]ready to fall upon me with staves but the constable kept them off. And when they had set me at liberty, they threatened me with pistols, if ever I came again they would kill me and shoot me; and they would carry their pistols to the steeplehouse. And with threatening I was freed. And I was scarce able to go or well to stand, by reason of ill-usage. Yet with much ado I got about a mile from the town, and as I was passing along the fields Friends met me. I was so bruised that I could not turn in my bed, and bruised inwardly at my heart, but after a while the power of the Lord went through me and healed me, that I was well, glory be to the Lord for ever.[g]

⟨That day some people were convinced of the Lord's Truth and turned to his teaching, at which I rejoiced.

Then I went out of Nottinghamshire, into Leicestershire, several Friends accompanying me. And there were some Baptists in that country whom I desired to see and speak with, because they were separated from the public worship. So one Samuel Oates,[1] who was one of their chief teachers, and others of the heads of them, with several others of their company, came to meet us at Barrow; and there we discoursed with them. And one of them said that what was not of faith was sin. Whereupon I asked them what faith was, and how it was wrought in man. But they turned off from that and spoke of their baptism in water. Then I asked them whether their mountain of sin was brought down and laid low in them, and their rough and crooked ways made smooth and straight in them, for they looked upon the Scriptures as meaning outward mountains and

[1] The father of the notorious Titus Oates was Samuel Oates (1610-1683), and for a time a Baptist preacher.

[g]......[g] *S.J.*, p. 12.

ways. But I told them they must find them in their own hearts; which they seemed to wonder at. And we asked them who baptized John the Baptist, and who baptized Peter, John, and the rest of the apostles, and put them to prove by Scripture that these were baptized in water, but they were silent. Then I asked them, seeing Judas, who betrayed Christ and was called the son of perdition, had hanged himself, what son of perdition was that which Paul spoke of, that sat in the temple of God, exalted above all that is called God, and what temple of God that was in which this son of perdition sat, and whether he that betrays Christ within, in himself, be not one in nature with that Judas that betrayed Christ without. But they could not tell what to make of this, nor what to say to it. So after we had some discourse together we parted, and some of them were loving to us.

On the First-day of the week following we came to Bagworth, and〉 [h]I was moved to go from a meeting with other Friends to the steeplehouse, and some Friends they let in, and me they kept out. And they shut the doors and shut out besides many of their own people. And after they had their sermon as they call it, they opened the door, and I went in, and began to speak the Truth to them and they heard me awhile, and then they rushed me out and I spoke to them in the steeplehouse yard the Truth of God; and they had much ado to hold their hands off us. There we had good service and the Truth came over all.[h] 〈Afterwards we had a meeting in the steeplehouse yard amongst several people that were in high notions.

Passing away I heard of a people that were in prison in Coventry for religion. And as I walked towards the gaol, the word of the Lord came to me saying, ‘ My love was always to thee, and thou art in my love.’ And I was ravished with the sense of the love of God and greatly strengthened in my inward man. But when I came into the gaol, where those prisoners were, a great power of

[h]. . . . . .[h] *S.J.*, pp. 12-13.

darkness struck at me, and I sat still, having my spirit gathered into the love of God. At last these prisoners began to rant and vapour and blaspheme, at which my soul was greatly grieved. They said they were God, but another of them said, 'We could not bear such things.' So when they were calm, I stood up and asked them whether they did such things by motion, or from Scripture; and they said, 'From Scripture.' Then, a Bible lying by, I asked them for that Scripture; and they showed me that place where the sheet was let down to Peter, and it was said to him, what was sanctified he should not call common or unclean. Now when I had showed them that that Scripture made nothing for their purpose, they brought another Scripture which spoke of God's reconciling all things to himself, things in heaven and things in earth. I told them I owned that Scripture also, but showed them that that was nothing to their purpose neither. Then seeing they said they were God, I asked them, if they knew whether it would rain tomorrow. They said they could not tell. I told them God could tell. Again, I asked them if they thought they should be always in that condition, or should change, and they answered they could not tell. Then said I unto them, 'God can tell, and God doth not change. You say you are God, and yet you cannot tell whether you shall change or no.' So they were confounded, and quite brought down for the time. Then after I had reproved them for their blasphemous expressions, I went away, for I perceived they were Ranters, and I had met with none before. And I admired the goodness of the Lord in appearing so unto me before I went amongst them. Not long after this, one of these Ranters, whose name was Joseph Salmon, put forth a paper or book of recantation,[1] upon which they were set at liberty.

From Coventry I went to a place called Atherstone, and〉 [i]when I was two miles off it the bell rang upon a market day for a lecture, and it struck at my life, and I was moved to go to the steeplehouse. And when I came into it I

[1] *Heights in Depths and Depths in Heights*, 1651.

found a man speaking, and as I stood among the people the glory and life shined over all, and with it I was crowned. And when the priest had done I spoke to him and the people the truth and the light which let them see all that ever they had done, and of their teacher within them, and how the Lord was come to teach them himself, and of the Seed Christ in them; how they were to mind that, and the promise that was to the Seed of God within them, which is Christ. And they were generally pretty quiet, only some few raged, and it set them in a hurry and under a rage. Some said I was mad, and spoke to my outward relations to tie me up. And I passed away in peace in the power of the Lord God, and the Truth came over all and reached in the hearts of many people.

Then I was moved to go to Market Bosworth in Leicestershire on a lecture day, being the market day. ⟨He that preached that day was Nathaniel Stephens, who was priest of the town where I was born. He raged much⟩ when I spoke to him and the people in the steeplehouse and yard of the truth and light within them to guide them to Christ from sin.[i] ⟨And he told the people I was mad (though he had said before to one Colonel Purefoy[I] that there never was such a plant bred in England), and he bid the people they should not hear me.⟩ [j]And the clerk bid us go out of the steeplehouse, for he was to lock the door. When we were in the market place Friends asked where was the place to try the ministers but in the steeplehouse, and bid them to come forth and prove their call and ministry. But the people of the town and market fell upon us and stoned us very sore and abused us, hundreds of them with stones, a great way out of the town, that it was a wonder that we escaped with our lives; and so we passed away in the Truth of God, to the shame of both priests and professors, for there were many there; and Friends had but little harm.[j] ⟨Howbeit some people were made loving that day, and others were confirmed, seeing the rage of both

[I] George Purefoy, squire of Drayton.

[i]. . . . . .[i] Cf. *S.J.*, p. 13. [j]. . . . . .[j] Cf. *S.J.*, p. 13.

priests and professors; and some cried out that the priest durst not stand to prove his ministry.

And as I travelled through markets, fairs, and divers places, I saw death and darkness in all people, where the power of the Lord God had not shaken them. And as I was passing on in Leicestershire I came to Twycross, where there were excise-men, and I was moved of the Lord to go to them and warn them to take heed of oppressing the poor, and people were much affected with it. Now there was in that town a great man, that had long lain sick and was given over by the physicians; and some Friends in the town desired me to go to see him. And I went up to him and was moved to pray by him〉; [k]spoke to him in his bed, and the power of the Lord entered him that he was loving and tender.[k]

[k]And I left him and came down among the family in the house, and spake a few words to the people that they should fear the Lord and repent and prize their time and the like words, and there came one of his servants with a naked sword and run at me ere I was aware of him, and set it to my side, and there held it, and I looked up at him in his face and said to him, 'Alack for thee, it's no more to me than a straw.' And then he went away in a rage, with threatening words, and I passed away, and the power of the Lord came over all, and his master mended, according to my belief and faith that I had seen before. And he then turned this man away that run at me with the sword,[k] 〈and afterwards he was very loving to Friends; and when I came to that town again both he and his wife came to see me.

After this I was moved to go into Derbyshire, where the mighty power of God was among Friends. And I went to Chesterfield where one Thomas Bretland was priest. He was one that saw beyond the common sort of priests, for he had been partly convinced,〉 who was above the priests and had spoken much in behalf of Truth before he was priest there. The priest of the town being dead,

[k]......[k] *S.J.*, p. 15.

he had got the parsonage and choked himself with it. And [l]I was moved of the Lord by his power to go to the steeplehouse[l] ⟨and to speak to him and the people in the great love of God that they might come off from all men's teaching unto God's teaching, and he was not able to⟩ oppose. [l]And when I had spoken what was upon me to speak, they put me forth of the steeplehouse[l] and had me before the Mayor[1] ⟨and threatened to send me with some others to the House of Correction⟩. [l]And the Mayor had some speech with me about coming to the steeplehouse and I said to him, 'Whether it is better to obey God or man, judge ye. The apostles suffered for declaring against the temple and did bring people to Christ from the traditions.' So he caused the watchman to put us out of the town about the eleventh hour of the night.[l] The judgements of the Lord came on that priest soon after and he was cut off and died, but there were several convinced of the Lord's Truth, and the Lord's power began to spread mightily up and down in those parts.

And then that priest Stephens, of Drayton, my native place, he preached and told my relations that I was carried up with a whirlwind into heaven, and after was found full of gold and silver; and so my relations wrote a letter to me to come and show myself, and so I answered the letter, and they showed it to the priest, and the priest said, anyone might write a letter, but where was the man. So my relations did conclude it was so, for, said they, when he went from us he had a great deal of gold and silver about him, nevertheless they sent to me again. And after, I went homewards, and one or two went along with me; [m]and one said he had been a professor forty years, and he had not tasted of the love of God so much, for his heart was opened with it;[m] and we came to a town where we met many professors; and many were convinced at Kidsley Park.

[1] The Mayor of Chesterfield was Ralph Clark.

[l]. . . . . .[l] *S.J.*, pp. 3-4. [m]. . . . . .[m] *S.J.*, p. 4.

Then we passed [n]through Friends[n] to Derby and lay at a doctor's house. His wife was convinced and several in the town; and as I was walking in my chamber, the [steeplehouse] bell rung, and it struck at my life, at the very hearing of it; and I asked the woman of the house what the bell rung for, and she said there was to be a great lecture that day and abundance of the officers of the army, and priests, and preachers were to be there, and a colonel that was a preacher.[1] I was moved of the Lord to go up to them, and when they had done, I spake to them what the Lord commanded me, [n]of the Truth, and the day of the Lord, and the light within them, and the spirit to teach and lead them to God;[n] and they were pretty quiet. There came an officer to me and took me by the hand and said I must go before the magistrates, and the other two that were with me, and so when we came before them about the first hour ⟨afternoon, they asked me why we came thither. I said God moved us to do so, and I told them, 'God dwells not in temples made with hands.'⟩ I told them also all their preaching, baptism, and sacrifices would never sanctify them, and I had many words with them. And I told them they were not to dispute of God and Christ, but to obey him. The power of God was thundered among them and they flew like chaff, and they put me in and out of the room from the first hour to the ninth hour at night in examinations, having me backward and forward, and, said ⟨in a deriding manner⟩ that I was taken up in raptures, as they called it.

At last they asked me whether I was sanctified.

I said, 'Sanctified? yes', for I was in the Paradise of God.

They said, had I no sin?

'Sin?' said I, 'Christ my Saviour hath taken away my sin, and in him there is no sin.'

⟨They asked how we knew that Christ did abide in us.

I said, 'By his Spirit that he has given us.'

[1] Nathaniel Barton.

[n]. . . . .[n] *S.J.*, p. 4.

They temptingly asked if any of us were Christ.

I answered, 'Nay, we are nothing, Christ is all.'

They said, 'If a man steal is it no sin?'

I answered, 'All unrighteousness is sin.'〉

And many such like words they had with me. And so they committed me as a blasphemer and as a man that had no sin, and committed another man with me 〈to the House of Correction in Derby for six months〉; as by the mittimus may be seen:

〈To the Master of the House of Correction in Derby, greeting,

We have sent you herewithal the bodies of George Fox, late of Mansfield, in the county of Nottingham, and John Fretwell, late of Stainsby, in the county of Derby, husbandman, brought before us this present day, and charged with the avowed uttering and broaching of divers blasphemous opinions contrary to a late Act of Parliament, which, upon their examination before us, they have confessed. These are therefore to require you, forthwith upon sight hereof, to receive them, the said George Fox and John Fretwell, into your custody, and them therein safely to keep during the space of six months, without bail or mainprize, or until they shall find sufficient security to be of the good behaviour, or be thence delivered by order from ourselves. Hereof you are not to fail.

Given under our hands and seals this 30th day of October 1650.

Ger. Bennet.[1]
Nath. Barton.〉

And then many people came from far and near to see a man that had no sin; and then did the priests roar up for sin, in their pulpits, and preach up sin, that people said never was the like heard. It was all their works to plead for it.

So after some time that man that was imprisoned with me did not stand, but got in with the keeper and made way to the justice to go see his mother, and so got his liberty; and then they reported that he should say that I had

[1] Gervase Bennet (d. 1670) of Snelston.

bewitched him and deceived him. And then my spirit was doubled upon me[1] when that man was gone. And some Friends would have removed me to the Parliament, it being then in the days of the Commonwealth. Then the priests and justices and professors and keeper were all in great rage against me. The keeper watched my words and asked me questions to ensnare me, sometimes would ask me such silly questions as whether the door was latched or not—things to get something to make sin of it. But I was kept watchful and chaste, and they admired at it. And several times I had motions from the Lord to go into the town, in time of fairs and markets, to speak to the people (though I was in prison), and I would tell the keeper and ask him to let me go, and he would not; and then I said to him, 'Then let it be upon thee, the iniquity of the people be upon thee'; and the Lord said to me that I was not to be removed from that place yet, but was set as a king for the body's[2] sake, and for the true hope that doth purify and the true faith that gives the victory and the true belief that overcomes the world.

⟨Not long after my commitment, I was moved to write both to priests and magistrates of Derby.[3] And first I directed these following lines to the priests:

O Friends, I was sent unto you to tell you that, if you had received the gospel freely, you would minister it freely without money or price; but you make it a trade and sale of what the prophets and apostles have spoken; and so you corrupt the Truth. And you are the men that lead silly women captive, who are ever learning and never able to come to the knowledge of the Truth; you have a form of godliness, but you deny the power . . . You show forth the vain nature; you stand in the steps of them that crucified my Saviour and mocked him; you are their children, you show forth their fruit. They had the chief place in the assemblies and so have you; they loved to be called Rabbi, and so do you. G.F.

[1] Cf. II Kings, ii. 9.
[2] i.e. the body of believers.
[3] In full in Ellwood, p. 33; and Bicent., i, 52.

I wrote to the magistrates who committed me to this effect:

Friends, I am forced, in tender love unto your souls, to write unto you, and to beseech you to consider what you do, and what commands of God call for. He doth require justice and mercy, to break every yoke and to let the oppressed go free. But who calleth for justice or loveth mercy, or contendeth for the Truth? Is not judgement turned backward, and doth not justice stand afar off? Is not Truth silenced in the streets, or can equity enter? And do not they that depart from evil make themselves a prey? O consider what ye do in time, and take heed whom ye imprison . . .

G.F.

After I had thus far cleared my conscience to them, I waited in the holy patience, leaving the event to God in whose will I stood. And after some time I was moved to write again[1] to the justices that had committed me to prison to lay their evils before them, that they might repent. One of them that signed the mittimus, to wit Nathaniel Barton, was a colonel, a justice, and a preacher.

And as I had written unto them jointly, so, after some respite of time, I writ to each of them by himself. To Justice Bennet thus:

Friend, Thou dost profess God and Christ in words, see how thou dost follow him. To take off burdens, to visit them that be in prison, and show mercy, clothe thy own flesh, and deal thy bread to the hungry; these are God's commandments. To relieve the fatherless, and to visit the widows in their afflications, and to keep thyself unspotted of the world; this is pure religion before God. . . . His servant thou art; whom thou dost obey, whether it is of sin unto death or of obedience unto righteousness. Think upon Lazarus and Dives, the one fared sumptuously every day, the other was a beggar. See if thou be not Dives. Be not deceived, God is not mocked with vain words; 'evil communication corrupteth good manners'; awake to righteousness, and sin not.[2] G.F.

[1] Ellwood, p. 34; Bicent., i, 53.

[2] In full, Ellwood, p. 34; Bicent., i, 54.

That to justice Barton was in these words:

Friend, Thou that preachest Christ and the Scripture in words, when any come to follow that which thou hast spoken of, and to live the life of the Scriptures, then they that speak the Scriptures, but do not lead their lives according thereunto, persecute them that do. Mind the prophets, and Jesus Christ and his apostles, and all the holy men of God. What they spoke was from the life; but they that had not the life, but the words, persecuted and imprisoned them that lived the life, which they had backslidden from. G.F.

And it was upon me to write to the mayor of Derby[1] also; who, though he did not sign the mittimus, had a hand with the rest in sending me to prison, and to him I writ in this manner:

Friend, Thou art set in place to do justice; but, in imprisoning my body, thou hast done contrary to justice, according to your own law. Oh, take heed of pleasing men more than God, for that is the way of the scribes and pharisees, they sought the praise of men more than God. Remember who said, 'I was a stranger, and ye took me not in; I was in prison and ye visited me not.' O friend, thy envy is not against me, but against the power of Truth. I had no envy to you, but love. Oh, take heed of oppression, 'for the day of the Lord is coming, that shall burn as an oven; and all the proud and all that do wickedly shall be as stubble; and the day that cometh shall burn them all up, saith the Lord of Hosts; it shall leave them neither root nor branch '.[2] . . .

I writ also unto the court at Derby.[3]

To the ringers who used to ring the bells in the steeple-house in Derby I sent these few lines:⟩

To the ringers of St. Peters (so called) 1650.

Friends, Oh, take heed of pleasures, and prize your time now while you have it, and do not spend it in pleasures nor carelessness. The time will come that you will say you had time,

[1] Noah Bullock.

[2] In full, Ellwood, p. 35-6; Bicent., i, 55. A version, signed Elizabeth Hooton, is in Swarthmore MSS., ii, 43.

[3] Ellwood, p. 36; Bicent., i, 55-6.

when it is past. Oh, look at the love of God now, while you have time; for it bringeth to loathe all vanities and worldly pleasures. Oh, consider; time is precious ! Fear God and rejoice in him who hath made heaven and earth.[1]

G.F.

And when professors came to me to dispute and discourse, I would feel them, before they came to plead for sin and imperfection. And I asked them whether they believed. And they said ' Yes '.

Then I asked them, ' In whom ? '

And they said, ' In Christ.'

And I said to them, ' If you believe, you are passed from death to life and so from the sin that bringeth death.' They said they believed no such thing that any could be free from sin while upon the earth. Then I bid them keep from babbling about the Scriptures, which were holy men's words, ' whilst you plead for unholiness '.

And then, it may be, another company of professors would come, and they also would be pleading for sin. And I would ask them whether they had hope.

And they would say, ' Yes; God forbid else but that we should have hope.' And I asked them, ' What hope is it, does it purify you as he is pure, Christ in you the hope of glory ? ' And they could not endure to hear of purity, or being made pure here.

Then I bid them keep from talking of the Scriptures, ' the holy men's words, for the holy men pleaded for holiness in heart and life and conversation here; and you plead for impurity and sin which is of the Devil, what have you to do with the holy men's words ? '

And then, it may be, another company would come, that would be talking of the Scriptures and pleading for sin.

And I would ask them, ' Have you any faith ? ' And they would say, ' Yes ', and that they were Christians.

And I said, ' What faith is it ? Will it give victory

[1] MS. Epistles and Queries of George Fox (Xx), p. 265; Ellwood, p. 36; Bicent., i, 56.

over sin and over the Devil, and purify your hearts, and bring you to have access to God again and to please God, which faith is held in a pure conscience?' And they could not endure to talk of purity or victory over sin and the Devil here upon the earth. Then I bid them give over talking and babbling of the Scriptures that were given forth by holy men, as they were moved by the Holy Ghost.

The keeper[1] being a great professor was in a mighty rage against me, yet it pleased the Lord to strike him. So one day as I was walking in my chamber I heard a doleful noise, and I made a stand, and he was speaking to his wife how that he saw the day of judgement, and he saw George there and was afraid of him because that he had done him so much wrong, and spoke so much against him to professors, and justices, and the priests, and in taverns and alehouses. So, toward evening he came trembling up into my chamber and said to me, 'I have been as a lion against you, but now I come like a lamb, and come like the gaoler in the Acts that came to Paul and Silas, trembling.' And he desired that he might lodge with me, and I told him I was in his power and he might do what he would, and he said, nay, he would have my leave, and he could desire to be always with me, but not to have me as a prisoner, and said that he had been plagued and his house was plagued, for my sake, like Pharaoh's and Abimelech's concerning Abraham and Isaac, and so I suffered him to lodge with me. Then he told me all his heart, and believed what I said to be true of the true faith, and hope, etc., and wondered that the other man did not stand to his principle, that was put into prison with me, and said he was a knave and I was an honest man; and the [other] °poor man was in trouble a great while before he returned to the power of God again.°

And so the keeper confessed all to me, how that when I had the several motions from the Lord to go out and speak to people and he would not let me go, and when I laid it

[1] Thomas Sharman.

°......° *S.J.*, p. 5.

upon him, he was distracted and amazed for an hour afterward, and was much troubled and in such a condition for a time that one might have killed him with a crab,[1] as he said. So ⟨when the morning came⟩ he went to the justices and told them he and his house had been plagued for my sake, and the justices said that the plagues were on them too for keeping me in prison. This was Justice Bennet of Derby that first called us Quakers because we bid them tremble at the word of God, and this was in the year 1650. And the justices gave leave that I should have liberty to go a mile. And I perceived their end, and I told the gaoler that if they would set me how far a mile was, I might walk in it sometimes, but it's like they thought I would go away. I told them I was not of that spirit; and the gaoler confessed it after, that they did it with that intent to have me gone away to ease the plague from them, and they said I was an honest man.

And this gaoler had a sister that was a tender young woman; and she came up into my chamber to visit me and went down and told them what an innocent people we were, and did none any hurt but did good unto all, and to them that hated us, and desired them to be tender towards us. And a little after, she died.

⟨Now it came upon me to write a paper, to be spread abroad. And it was as followeth:

The Lord doth show unto man his thoughts, and discovereth all the secret workings in man. A man may be brought to see his evil thoughts and running mind and vain imaginations, and may strive to keep them down, and to keep his mind in, but cannot overcome them nor keep his mind within to the Lord. Now in this state and condition, submit to the spirit of the Lord, that shows them, and that will bring to wait upon the Lord, and he that hath discovered them will destroy them. Therefore stand in the faith of the Lord Jesus Christ, who is the author of the true faith, and mind him; for he will discover the root of lusts, and evil thoughts, and vain imaginations, and how they are begotten, conceived, and bred, and then how they are brought

[1] i.e. apple, cf. p. 108.

forth, and how every evil member doth work. He will discover every principle from its own nature and root.

So mind the faith of Christ, and the anointing which is in you to be taught by it, which will discover all workings in you, and as he teacheth you, so obey and forsake, else you will not grow up in the faith, nor in the life of Christ, where the love of God is received. Now love begetteth love, its own nature and image: and when mercy and truth do meet, what joy there is ! Mercy doth triumph in judgement; and love and mercy do bear the judgement of the world in patience. That which cannot bear the world's judgement is not the love of God, for love beareth all things and is above the world's judgement, for the world's judgement is but foolishness . . . The fleshly mind doth mind the flesh, and talketh fleshly. Its knowledge is fleshly and not spiritual, but savours of death and not of the spirit of life. Now some men have the nature of swine wallowing in the mire, and some men have the nature of dogs to bite both the sheep and one another; and some men have the nature of lions, to tear, devour, and destroy. And some men have the nature of wolves, to tear and devour the lambs and sheep of Christ; and some men have the nature of the Serpent (that old adversary), to sting, envenom, and poison. 'He that hath an ear to hear, let him hear', and learn these things within himself. And some men have the natures of other beasts and creatures, minding nothing but earthly and visible things, and feeding without the fear of God. Some men have the nature of an horse, to praunce and vapour in their strength, and to be swift in doing evil; and some men have the nature of tall, sturdy oaks, to flourish and spread in wisdom and strength, who are strong in evil, which must perish and come to the fire. Thus the evil is but one in all, but worketh many ways; and whatsoever a man's or woman's nature is addicted to that is outward, the Evil One will fit him with that, and will please his nature and appetite to keep his mind in his inventions, and in the creatures, from the Creator.

Oh, therefore let not the mind go forth from God ! for if it do, it will be stained, and venomed, and corrupted ! And if the mind go forth from the Lord it is hard to bring it in again; therefore take heed of the enemy, and keep in the faith of Christ. Oh, therefore mind that which is eternal and invisible, and him who is the Creator and mover of all things ! for the things that are made are not made of things that do appear; for the visible covereth the invisible sight in you. But as the

Lord who is invisible doth open you by his invisible power and spirit, and brings down the carnal mind in you, so the invisible and immortal things are brought to light in you. Oh, therefore, you that know the light walk in the light ! for there are children of darkness, that will talk of the light and of the truth, and not walk in it. But the children of the light love the light, and walk in the light, but the children of darkness walk in darkness, and hate the light; and in them the earthly lusts and the carnal mind choke the Seed of faith; and that bringeth oppression on the Seed, and death over them. Oh, therefore, mind the pure spirit of the everlasting God ! which will teach you to use the creatures in their right place, and which judgeth the evil . . . So to live and walk in the spirit of God is joy, and peace, and life; but the mind going forth into the creatures, or into any visible things from the Lord, this bringeth death.

Now when the mind is got into the flesh and into death, then the accuser gets within, and the law of sin and death gets into the flesh. And then the life suffers under the law of sin and death; and then there is straitness and failings. For then the good is shut up, and then the self-righteousness is set a-top. And then man doth work in the outward law, and he cannot justify himself by the law but is condemned by the Light; for he cannot get out of that state but by abiding in the Light, and resting in the mercy of God, and believing in him, from whom all mercy doth flow. For there is peace in resting in the Lord Jesus . . . G.F.[1]

I writ another paper[2] also, much about the same time, and sent it forth amongst the convinced people. But many that had been convinced of the Truth turned aside, because of the persecution that arose; whereupon I writ a few lines[3] for the comfort and encouragement of the faithful.〉

And when I was in the House of Correction my relations came to me and were much troubled that I should be in prison, for they looked upon it to be a great shame to them

[1] In full, Ellwood (ed., 1694), p. 38; Bicent., i, 58-61.
[2] Printed, Ellwood, pp. 40-1; Bicent., i, 61.
[3] Printed, Ellwood, pp. 40-1; Bicent., i, 61-2.

for me to be in gaol.[1] It was a strange thing to be imprisoned then for religion. They went to the justice that cast me into prison, and would have been bound in one hundred pounds; and others in Derby, fifty pounds apiece, that I might have gone home with them and that I should come no more amongst them to declare against the priests. They had me up before the justice with them; and because I would not have them to be bound, for I was innocent from any ill behaviour and had spoken the word of life and Truth unto them, Justice Bennet got up into a rage; and as I was kneeling down to pray to the Lord to forgive him, he ran upon me with both his hands and struck me, and cried, ‘ Away with him gaoler. Take him away gaoler.’ And some thought I was mad because I stood for purity, perfection, and righteousness.

⟨After I had been before the justices, and they had required sureties for my good behaviour (which I could not consent should be given, to blemish my innocency), it came upon me to write to the justices again.[2] Some little time after, I wrote to them again, thus:

Friends,

Would ye have me bound to my good behaviour from drunkenness, or swearing, or adultery, and the like? The Lord hath redeemed me from all these things; and the love of God hath brought me to loathe all wantonness, blessed be his name! They who are drunkards and fighters and swearers have their liberty without bonds; and you lay your law upon me, whom neither you, nor any other can justly accuse of these things; praised be the Lord! I can look at no man for my liberty, but to the Lord alone, who hath all men's hearts in his hand.

And after some time, not finding my spirit clear of them, I writ to them again, as followeth:

[1] In the MS. (*Camb. Jnl.*, i, 10, 13) there are two references to a visit from relations, which probably relate to the same visit. They are here combined. The first reference, which is short and without detail is, in Ellwood ed., made into a second visit, introduced by these words, *After it was bruited abroad that I was in Derby dungeon, my relations came to see me again* . . . Ellwood, 41, 46; Bicent., i, 62, 69.

[2] Printed, Ellwood, p. 41; Bicent., i, 62-3.

Friends,

Had you known who sent me to you, ye would have received me; for the Lord sent me to warn you of the woes that are coming upon you; and to bid you look at the Lord and not at man. But when I told you my experience, what the Lord had done for me, then your hearts were hardened, and you sent me to prison, where you have kept me many weeks. If the love of God had broke your hearts, then would ye see what ye have done; ye would not have imprisoned me had not my Father suffered you; and by his power I shall be loosed, for he openeth and shutteth; to him be all glory! In what have I misbehaved myself, that any should be bound for me? All men's words will do me no good, not their bonds neither, to keep my heart if I have not a guide within, to keep me in the upright life of God . . .[1]

I was moved also to write again to the priests of Derby.[2]

Thus having cleared my conscience to the priests, it was not long before a concern came upon me again to write to the Justices.[3]

Besides this, I writ to Colonel Barton who was both a justice and a preacher.[4]〉

And many times when they were setting me at liberty, was I moved of the Lord God to write to them, and then their rages would be up and they would keep me in prison again.

One time whilst I was in gaol there was a conjurer brought to prison and he threatened how he would talk with me and what he would do to me—a wicked ungodly man, but he had never power to open his mouth unto me. And one time the gaoler and he fell out and he threatened the gaoler to raise the Devil to break his house down and made the gaoler afraid; and I was moved of the Lord to go in his power and thresh him in it, and to say, 'Come, let's see what thou canst do'; and bid him do his worst; and told him the Devil was raised high enough in him

[1] In full, Ellwood, p. 42; Bicent., i, 63.
[2] Ellwood ed., p. 43; Bicent., i, 64.
[3] Ellwood, p. 43; Bicent., i, 64.
[4] Ellwood, p. 44; Bicent., i, 65.

already; but the power of the Lord chained him, and he slunk away and went from me.

And when I had liberty I went into the market and streets and warned people to repentance, and so returned to prison again. I was allowed a mile to walk out by myself.

And there came one Rice Jones a soldier, of Nottingham, that had been a Baptist, and several others with him, who were going to Worcester fight. Says he to me, 'Thy faith stands in a man that died at Jerusalem and there was never any such thing.' I said unto him, <'How!> Did not Christ suffer without the gates at Jerusalem through the professing Jews, and chief priests, and Pilate?' and he denied it that ever Christ suffered there outwardly. Then I asked him whether there were not chief priests and Jews, and Pilate there outwardly. Then he said I was a chief priest; and I told him if he did confess there was a chief priest and Jews there outwardly, then he must needs confess that Christ was persecuted and suffered there outwardly under them. Which as to the priests outwardly being there he would not deny, and said he would say little to that. And < yet> from this man and his company was the slander raised upon us that the Quakers should deny Christ that died and suffered at Jerusalem, which was all utterly false, and never the least thought of it in our hearts. And also he said that never any of the prophets, nor apostles, nor holy men of God suffered anything outwardly, but all their sufferings were inwardly. And I instanced to him many of the prophets and apostles, how they suffered and by whom they suffered. So I brought the power of the Lord over his imaginations and whimsies; and he went his ways.

And there came another company that pretended they were triers of spirits; and I asked them a question, what was the first step to peace, and what was it by which a man might see his salvation; and they were up in the air and said I was mad. So such came to try spirits as did not know themselves nor their own spirits. And daily trials and disputes had I with professors of all sorts.

And there were several sorts of religions in prison; and

on the First-days when I got out I would go and visit them in their meetings in the prison.

And when I was in the House of Correction, there came a trooper to me and said, as he was sitting in the steeplehouse hearing the priest he was in an exceeding great trouble, and the voice of the Lord came to him saying, 'What, dost not thou know that my servant is in prison? Go to him for directions.' And he came, and I spake to his condition and opened his understanding, and settled his mind in the light and spirit of God in himself; and I told him, that which showed him his sin and troubled him, for it would show him his salvation; for he that shows a man his sins is he that takes it away. So the Lord's power opened to him, so that he began to have great understanding of the Lord's Truth and mercies, and began to speak boldly in his quarters amongst the soldiers and others concerning Truth. The Scriptures were very much opened to him so that he said that his two Colonels, Nathaniel Barton and Thomas Saunders, were as blind as Nebuchadnezzar to cast me, the servant of the Lord, into prison. For this they began also to have a spite and malice against him, that when he came to Worcester fight, and the two armies lay one nigh the other, and two came out of the King's army and challenged two out of the Parliament army to fight with them, his two Colonels made choice of him and another to go and fight with them. And they went forth to them, and his companion was killed; and after, he drove the two within musket shot of the town and never fired his own pistol at them. This he told me out of his own mouth; but when the fight was over he saw the deceit and hypocrisy of the officers and he laid down his arms and saw to the end of fighting, and how the Lord had miraculously preserved him.

My time being nearly out of being committed six months to the House of Correction, they filled the House of Correction with persons that they had taken up to be soldiers:[1]

[1] During April, 1651, the Commonwealth forces were actively strengthened, following the discovery of a Royalist plot.

and then they would have had me to be captain of them to go forth to Worcester fight and the soldiers cried they would have none but me. So the keeper of the House of Correction was commanded to bring me up before the Commissioners and soldiers in the market place; and there they proffered me that preferment because of my virtue,[1] as they said, with many other compliments, and asked me if I would not take up arms for the Commonwealth against the King. But I told them I lived in the virtue of that life and power that took away the occasion of all wars, and I knew from whence all wars did rise, from the lust according to James's doctrine.[2] Still they courted me to accept of their offer and thought that I did but compliment with them. But I told them I was come into the covenant of peace which was before wars and strifes were. And they said they offered it in love and kindness to me because of my virtue, and such like ⟨flattering words they used⟩, and I told them if that were their love and kindness I trampled it under my feet. ⟨Then their rage got up and⟩ they said, 'Take him away gaoler, and cast him into the dungeon amongst the rogues and felons'; which they then did and put me into the dungeon amongst thirty felons in a lousy, stinking [p]low place in the ground[p] without any bed. Here they kept me ⟨a close prisoner⟩ almost a half year, unless it were at times; and sometimes they would let me walk in the garden, for they had a belief of me that I would not go away.

And in this time I was exceeding much oppressed with judges and magistrates and courts, and was moved to write to the judges concerning their putting men to death for cattle and for money and small things, several times, how contrary to the law of God it was. One time, I was under great sufferings ⟨in my spirit⟩ through it, ⟨and under the very sense of death;⟩ but when I came out of it, ⟨standing in the will of God a heavenly breathing arose in my soul to

[1] Meaning *valour*. Fox puns in reply, meaning "in reliance upon".

[2] James, iv. 1.

[p]......[p] *S.J.*, p. 5.

the Lord. Then did I see⟩ the heavens opened and the glory of God shined over all. Two men suffered for small things, and I was moved to admonish them for their theft and encourage them concerning their suffering, it being contrary to the law of God; and a little after they had suffered their spirits appeared to me as I was walking, and I saw the men were well.

⟨So I wrote to the judges as followeth:⟩

I am moved to write unto you to take heed of putting men to death for stealing cattle or money, etc.: for the thieves in the old time were to make restitution; and if they had not wherewith, they were to be sold for their theft. Mind the laws of God in the Scriptures and the Spirit that gave them forth and let them be your rule in executing judgement; and show mercy, that you receive mercy from God, the judge of all. And take heed of gifts and rewards, and of pride, for God doth forbid them, and they do blind the eyes of the wise. I do not write to give liberty to sin, God hath forbidden it; but that you should judge according to his laws, and show mercy, for he delighteth in true judgement and in mercy. I beseech you to mind these things, and prize your time now you have it, and fear God and serve him, for he is a consuming fire.

And there was a young woman that was to be put to death for robbing her master; and judgement was given and a grave made for her and she carried to execution. I was made to write to the judge and to the jury about her, and when she came there ⟨though they had her upon the ladder with a cloth bound over her face, ready to be turned off, yet⟩ they had not power to hang her (as by the paper which I sent to be read at the gallows may be seen), but she was brought back again. And they came with great rage against me into the prison. Afterwards ⟨in the prison⟩ this young woman came to be convinced of God's everlasting Truth.

And I also writ to the judges what a sore thing it was that prisoners should lie so long in gaol, and how that they learned badness one of another in talking of their bad deeds, and therefore speedy justice should have been done. For

I was a tender youth and dwelt in the fear of God. I was grieved to hear their bad language and was made often to reprove them for their words and bad carriage each towards other.

And so people did admire that I should be so preserved and kept, for they could never catch a word nor action for almost a whole year from me, to make anything of; for the Lord's infinite power upheld and preserved me all the time. But many turned off, that had been convinced, because of the persecution.

⟨So Worcester fight came on, and Justice Bennet sent the constables to press me for a soldier, seeing I would not accept of a command.[1] I told them I was brought off from outward wars. They came down again to give me press-money but I would take none. Then I was brought up to Sergeant Hole's, kept there awhile, and then taken down again. After a while at night the constables fetched me up again and brought me before the Commissioners, and they said I should go for a soldier, but I told them that I was dead to it. They said I was alive. I told them, 'Where envy and hatred are there is confusion.' They offered me money twice, but I would not take it. Then they were wroth, and I was committed close prisoner without bail or mainprize. Thereupon I writ to them again, directing my letter to Colonel Barton, who was a preacher, and the rest that were concerned in my commitment.[2]

Now when they had gotten me into Derby dungeon, it was the belief and saying of people that I should never come out: but I had faith in God, and believed I should be delivered in his time; for the Lord had said to me before, that I was not to be removed from that place yet, being set there for a service which he had for me to do.⟩

And one time, him that should have been the lieutenant

[1] Cromwell's army passed near Derby towards the end of August, 1651, gathering reinforcements everywhere, as it hurried south to intercept the Royalist Scottish army at Worcester on 3rd September.

[2] Ellwood, p. 49; Bicent., i, 73.

but refused it, they cast into prison also; and the gaoler's wife said she would let him go out to walk with me in the backside. As I walked a little before him I heard the hedge crack, and I stepped back to him and asked him why he would offer to do so, and so brought him in. So he went forth no more with me; but when he walked forth by himself he ran away, but they fetched him again soon after.

⟨About this time I was moved to give forth the following lines to go amongst the convinced and tender people, to manifest the deceits of the world, and how the priests have deceived the people:

To all you that love the Lord Jesus Christ with a pure and naked heart, and the generation of the righteous:

Christ was ever hated; and the righteous for his sake. Mind who they were that did ever hate them; he that was born after the flesh did persecute him that was born after the spirit; and so it is now. And mind who were the chiefest against Christ; even the great, learned men, the heads of the people, rulers, and teachers, that professed the law and the prophets, and looked for Christ. They looked for an outwardly glorious Christ to hold up their outward glory; but Christ spake against the works of the world, and against the priests, and scribes, and Pharisees, and their hypocritical profession. He that is a stranger to Christ is an hireling; but the servants of Jesus Christ are freemen . . . [1]

Again a concern came upon me to write to the magistrates of Derby; which I did as followeth:⟩

Dear Friends,

I desire you to consider in time whom you do imprison; for the magistrate is set for the punishment of evil doers, but the praise of them that do well. But when the Lord doth send his messengers unto you to warn you of the woes that will come on you, except you repent, then you persecute them, and put them in prison, and say, 'We have a law, and by our law we may do it.' For you indeed justify yourselves before men. But God knoweth your hearts; for he will not be worshipped with your forms and professions, and shows of religion. But

[1] In full, Ellwood, pp. 50-1; Bicent., i, 73-5.

consider, ye that talk of God, what part of you is brought into him, for they are his children that do his will . . . I desire you to consider how it is written, that when the church is come together into one place they may all prophesy one by one, that all may hear and all may learn, and all may be comforted; and if anything be revealed to another that sitteth by, let the first hold his peace. But in your assembly it is not so; but he that teaches for hire must speak, and none must contradict him. Again, it was to the apostles, that after the reading of the law and the prophets, the rulers sent unto them, 'Men and brethren, if ye have any word of exhortation for the people say on.' I desire you to consider in silence, and strive not against the Lord; for he is stronger than you all. Though you refuse to let his people go and hold them fast for a time, yet, when the Lord cometh, he will make known who are his . . .[1]

⟨Great was the exercise and travail in spirit that I went under during my imprisonment here because of the wickedness that was in this town.⟩ And a great judgment was upon the town, and I saw the power of God went away from them, as the waters ran from the town dam when the flood gates were up, for they were an hardened people; and yet there were some convinced. ⟨And I mourned over them; and it came upon me to give forth the following lines as a lamentation for them:

O Derby ! as the waters run away when the floodgates are up, so doth the visitation of God's love pass away from thee, O Derby ! Therefore look where thou art, and how thou art grounded; and consider, before thou art utterly forsaken. The Lord moved me twice before I came to cry against the deceits and vanities that are in thee, and to warn all to look at the Lord, and not at man . . . it doth break my heart to see how God is dishonoured in thee, O Derby ![2]

Now after that I had seen the visitation of God's love pass away from this place, I knew that my imprisonment here would not continue long; but I saw that when the Lord should bring me forth, it would be as the letting of a

[1] In full, Swarthmore MSS., vii, 94; Ellwood, p. 51; Bicent., i, 75-6.
[2] In full, Ellwood, p. 52; Bicent., i, 76.

lion out of a den amongst the wild beasts of the forest. For all professions stood in a beastly spirit and nature, pleading for sin, and for the body and of sin and imperfection as long as they lived. And they all kicked and yelled, and roared, and raged, and ran against the life and spirit which gave forth the Scriptures, which they professed in words. And so it was.

They could not agree what to do with me⟩; and sometime they would have me up before the Parliament, and another time they would have banished me to Ireland. At first they called me a deceiver and seducer and a blasphemer; and then when God brought his plagues upon them they said I was an honest and virtuous man. But their good report and bad report, their well or ill speaking was nothing to me; for the one did not lift me up, nor the other cast me down, praised be the Lord.

⟨At length they were made to turn me out of gaol about the beginning of winter in the year 1651⟩, qwho had been kept a year, within three weeks, in four prisons, the House of Correction, and at the town prison and the county gaol and dungeon, and then in the high gaol where I was kept till I was set freely at liberty. And this was in the month called October,[1] in the Commonwealth's days. And then the light and truth and glory of the Lord flowed and spread abroad.q

CHAPTER IV

AND when I came out of Derby prison I came near Burton upon Trent where some were convinced, and so to Bushel[2]-House where I had a meeting. And I went up into the country where there were friendly people. But there was a raging, wicked professor had an intent to have done me a mischief, but the Lord prevented him.

[1] About 8th October, 1651.
[2] Probably Bishop Hill, a farm at Hanbury.
q. . . . . .q Cf. *S.J.*, p. 5.

So I passed through the country, where I had meetings and the Lord's power and spirit accompanied me, and I came into Leicestershire towards my own country (where the priests reported I was taken up above the clouds and after found again full of gold and silver) that they might see their lies. This was priest Stevens aforesaid that had said to Colonel Purefoy that never such a plant was bred in England.

And as I was one time walking in a close with several Friends I lifted up my head and I espied three steeplehouse spires. They struck at my life and I asked Friends what they were, and they said, Lichfield. The word of the Lord came to me thither I might go, ⟨so, being come to the house we were going to⟩ I bid friends that were with me walk into the house from me; and they did and as soon as they were gone (for I said nothing to them whither I would go) I went over hedge and ditch till I came within a mile of Lichfield. When I came into a great field where there were shepherds keeping their sheep, I was commanded of the Lord to pull off my shoes of a sudden; and I stood still, and the word of the Lord was like a fire in me; and being winter, I untied my shoes and put them off; and when I had done I was commanded to give them to the shepherds and was to charge them to let no one have them except they paid for them. And the poor shepherds trembled and were astonished.

So I went about a mile till I came into the town, and as soon as I came within the town the word of the Lord came unto me again to cry, 'Woe unto the bloody city of Lichfield!'; so I went up and down the streets crying, 'Woe unto the bloody city of Lichfield!' Being market day I went into the market place and went up and down in several places of it and made stands, crying, 'Woe unto the bloody city of Lichfield!', and no one touched me nor laid hands on me. As I went down the town there ran like a channel of blood down the streets, and the market place was like a pool of blood.

And so at last some friends and friendly people came to

me and said, 'Alack George! where are thy shoes?' and I told them it was no matter; so when I had declared what was upon me and cleared myself, I came out of the town in peace about a mile to the shepherds: and there I went to them and took my shoes and gave them some money, but the fire of the Lord was so in my feet and all over me that I did not matter to put my shoes on any more and was at a stand whether I should or no till I felt freedom from the Lord so to do.

And so at last I came to a ditch and washed my feet and put on my shoes; and when I had done, I considered why I should go and cry against that city and call it a bloody city; for though the Parliament had the minster one while and the King another while, and much blood had been shed in the town, yet that could not be charged upon the town. But as I went through the town there ran like a channel of blood down the streets and the market place was like a pool of blood; this I saw as I went through it crying, 'Woe to the bloody city of Lichfield.'

But after, I came to see that there were a thousand martyrs in Lichfield in the Emperor Diocletian's time. And so I must go in my stockings through the channel of their blood in their market place. So I might raise up the blood of those martyrs that had been shed and lay cold in their streets, which had been shed above a thousand years before. So the sense of this blood was upon me, for which I obeyed the word of the Lord. And the ancient records will testify how many of the Christian Britons suffered there.

And much more might I write of this thing and of the sense of the blood of the martyrs that hath been slain in this nation both in and under the ten persecutions and since, for the name of Christ's sake. But I leave it to the Lord and his book, out of which all shall be judged; for his book is a true record, and his Spirit is a true register, or recorder. And then I passed up and down and had meetings amongst friendly people in several places. And my relations were offended at me.

After some time I came into Nottinghamshire again to Mansfield and Derbyshire, visiting friends. Then passing into Yorkshire I preached repentance, through Doncaster and several other places, and then came to Balby; where Richard Farnsworth was convinced and several others.[1] So I passed through the countries to several places, preaching repentance and the word of life to them, and went into the country about Wakefield where James Nayler lived, where he and Thomas Goodaire and William Dewsbury and many more were convinced.[2]

From thence I passed through the country towards Captain Pursloe's by Selby.[3] And one, John Leek there, had been to visit me in Derby prison, being convinced. And I had a horse, but was fain to leave my horse, not knowing what to do with him, for I was moved to go to many great houses to admonish them and to exhort them to turn to the Lord.

And so as I passed on I was moved of the Lord to go to Beverley steeplehouse, a great professing place, on the seventh day at night, and being very wet, I went to an inn; and as soon as I came to the door, a young woman came to the door. 'What! is it you?' said she as though she had seen me before, 'Come in', said she: for the Lord's power bowed their hearts. So I refreshed myself and went to bed, and the next morning my clothes were sore wet.

[1] Viz. Thomas Killam (d. 1690), John Killam, Thomas Aldam (*c.* 1616-1660), all early publishers of Quakerism. W. Dewsbury, *Works*, 1688, p. (ix).

[2] This was at Lieut. Roper's house, believed to be at Stanley. There, writes Fox (Dewsbury, *Works*, 1688, p. (x)), James Nayler came to see him and was convinced after some discussion; and after one evening meeting, 'it being a moonshine night I walked into the field and William Dewsbury and his wife came to me into the field and confessed to the Truth and received it.' Both Nayler (*c.* 1618-1660) and Dewsbury (1621-1688) were leaders in the first spread of Quakerism. Nayler, through a dangerous extravagance, was barbarously punished by Parliament for blasphemy, and estranged from Friends, but was later re-united. Dewsbury spent nearly twenty years in prisons.

[3] Probably Richard Pursglove of Cranswick.

In the morning I paid for what I had and went up to the steeplehouse, and there was a man preaching.[1] And when he had done, I was moved to speak to him and the people in the mighty power of God, [a]of the truth of God and the day of the Lord, and the Light of Christ within them, and of the spirit, and of God's teaching by the spirit, and that God that made the world did not dwell in the temples made with hands.[a] The power of the Lord was so strong as it struck a mighty dread amongst the people. The Mayor came down to me and took me by the hand and reasoned moderately with me, but they none of them had any power to meddle with me, [a]they were in an amazement[a] and so I passed away out of the town.[2] In the afternoon, about two miles off, I went to another steeplehouse, and when the priest had done, I was moved to speak to him and the people very largely, and showed them the way of life and truth, and the way of reprobation and election; and how that they should find Esau and Ishmael in themselves though they found so much fault of them without them. The priest said he was but a child and could not dispute with me: I told him I did not come to dispute but to hold forth the word of life and truth unto them, that they might all know the one Seed which the promise of God was to, both in the male and female. And the people were very loving and they would have had me come again in the week day and preach amongst them: but I directed them to their teacher Christ Jesus, and so passed away.

I came to an inn where they were loath to receive me unless I would go first to a constable, which was the custom of their country. I was not free so to do, but told them I was an innocent man and should lie out rather, so at last they received me, and I stayed there all night.

The next day I came to Cranswick to Captain Pursloe's.

[1] John Pomroy, lecturer at Beverley.

[2] *A Short Account*, MS. Portfolio 36.172, see *Bulletin F.H.A.*, Vol. 39, p. 27, adds that he ' refreshed himself with some hips and hawes that he got about the hedges '.

[a]......[a] *S.J.*, p. 6.

And he went with me to Justice Hotham's,[1] a pretty tender man, that had some experience of God's working in his heart. After that I had some discourse with him of the things of God, he took me into his closet, and said he had known that principle this ten year, and he was glad that the Lord did now publish it abroad to people. And so after a while there came in a priest with whom I had some discourse concerning the Truth, but his mouth was quickly stopped, for he was nothing but a notion⟨ist, and not in possession of what he talked of.⟩

And after a while there came in a great woman of Beverley, that had some business with Justice Hotham. And she said unto him that the last sabbath day (as she called it) there was an angel or spirit came into the body of the church (meaning the steeplehouse), and spoke strange things, and the wonderful things of God, to the astonishment of all that were in the steeplehouse; and when he had done it he passed away; and that they did not know whence he came nor whither it went; but it astonished all the priests, and professors, and magistrates of the town. And Justice Hotham gave me this relation, but I said nothing to him till the woman was gone. And when she was gone I gave him a full relation how I had been at Beverley steeplehouse and had spoken to the priest and people the last First-day, which was the day she spoke of it to him.

And there were some great high priests and other doctors in the country that Justice Hotham had acquaintance with and would fain have them speak with me, and said he would send for them under pretence it was a patient at his house that wanted physic; but I told him it was no matter for sending for them upon that account, and that he should not do so.

So when the next First-day came Justice Hotham walked out with me into the fields, and then, Captain Pursloe coming up after us, Justice Hotham left us and went home and Captain Pursloe went into the steeplehouse with me.

[1] Durant Hotham (1619-1691), of Winthorpe in Lockington parish.

⟨And when the priests had done⟩ [b]I had a brave service with the priests and people, and the Truth came over all in laying open the false teachers and priests, and the Truth and the true teachers, and the light and the spirit of Christ in them, and that God that made the world dwelt not in temples made with hands, but their bodies were the temples of the Holy Ghost.[b] And some then received the Truth at that place and were convinced, and stand to this day and have a fine meeting thereaways.

And in the afternoon I went to the great high priest, their doctor, that Justice Hotham said he would send for to speak with me, to the steeplehouse three miles off, where he preached, and sat me down in the steeplehouse till the priest had done. And he took a text, which was, 'Ho, every one that thirsteth, let him come freely, without money and without price.' And so I was moved of the Lord God to say unto him, 'Come down, thou deceiver and hireling, for dost thou bid people come freely and take of the water of life freely, and yet thou takest three hundred pounds off them for preaching the Scriptures to them. Mayest thou not blush for shame? Did the prophet Isaiah and Christ so do that spoke those words and gave them forth freely? Did not Christ command his ministers, "Freely you have received, freely give"?' And so the priest, like a man amazed, packed away; and this was the man Justice Hotham would have sent for to have spoken with me, as aforesaid. And so after the priest had left his flock, I had as much time as I could desire to speak to the people, and I directed them to the grace of God that would teach them and bring them salvation, and directed them from darkness to the light and to the spirit of God their free teacher.

And after, at night, I came to Justice Hotham's house, and when I came in, he took me in his arms and said his house was my house, and he was exceeding glad at the work of the Lord and his power.

And when I turned back again to Hotham's house he

[b]. . . . . .[b] *S.J.*, p. 8.

told me what reasonings he had in himself concerning his not going with me to the steeplehouse; for if he had gone to the steeplehouse with me, the officers would have put me to him, and then he should have been so put to it and he should not have known what to have done. And when Captain Pursloe came up he was glad that he was come to go with me, though neither of them was dressed, nor had their bands about their necks. It was a strange thing then to see a man come into the steeplehouse without a band; yet Captain Pursloe went in without his band; the Lord's power·and truth so affected him, he minded not such things.

And afterwards I passed away through the country [c]northwards and there were no Friends; and sometimes I lay out all night though in the winter-season, and at night I came in my travels to a house, being weary,[c] and there was a rude company of people and I asked the woman if she had any meat; and she was something strange because I said 'thee' and 'thou' to her; I asked her if she had any milk but she denied it, and I asked her if she had any cream, though I did not greatly like such meat but only to try her, and she denied it also. And there stood a churn in her house; and a little boy put his hand into the churn [c]in which there was a great deal of cream, and plucked it down before my face, and it did run like a pool in the floor of the house[c] and so it manifested the woman to be a liar. The woman was amazed and took the child and whipped it sorely, and blessed herself; but I reproved her for her lying and deceit. So I walked out of her house after the Lord God had manifested her deceit and perverseness, and came to a stack of hay and lay in the haystack all night in the snow and rain, being but three days before the time called Christmas.

And so the next day I came into York[1] where there were several people that were very tender; and upon the First-day I was commanded of the Lord to go to the great minster

[1] 23rd December, 1651.
[c]. . . . . .[c] *S.J.*, p. 16.

and speak to priest Bowles[1] and all his hearers in their great cathedral; and so when the priest had done I told them and him I had something from the Lord God to speak to the priest and people. 'Then say on quickly' says a professor, for it was very cold weather of frost and snow. And so I told them this was the word of the Lord God unto them: that they lived in words but that God Almighty looked for fruits amongst them: so as soon as the words were out of my mouth they hurried me out and threw me down the stairs, but I got up again without any hurt and I went to my lodging again. Several were convinced there, for the very groans of the weight and oppression that was upon the spirit of God in me would open people, and strike at them, and make them confess that my very groans did reach to them, for my life was burdened with their profession without possession and words without fruit. And so I passed out of York, after several had received the Truth and were convinced of God's Truth and his teaching.

And I saw towards Cleveland that there was a people that had tasted of the power of God: and I saw then there was a Seed in that country and that God had humble people there.

And that night I passed on and a Papist overtook me and told me of his religion and of their meetings, and I let him speak all that was in his mind. That night I stayed at an ale house, and the next morning I was moved of the Lord to speak the word of the Lord to him, and I went to his house and declared against his religion and all their ways. I told him that God was come to teach his people himself; and this put the Papist in such a rage that he could not endure to stay in his own house.

And the next day I came to Burraby,[2] and there was a priest and several friendly people that met together and the people were convinced and have stood ever since, and there

[1] Edward Bowles, M.A. (1613-1662), Presbyterian.
[2] Probably Borrowby, north of Thirsk.

is a great meeting in that town. The priest was made to confess to Truth, though he came not into it.

And the next day I passed to Cleveland amongst those people that had tasted of the power of God, but were all shattered to pieces and the heads of them turned Ranters. Now they had had great meetings, so I told them after that they had had such meetings they did not wait upon God to feel his power to gather their minds together to feel his presence and power and therein to sit to wait upon him, for they had spoken themselves dry and had spent their portions and not lived in that which they spake, and now they were dry. They had some kind of meetings but took tobacco and drank ale in them and so grew light and loose.

But my message unto them was from the Lord that they might all come together again and wait to feel the Lord's power and spirit in themselves to gather them to Christ and to be taught of him who says, 'Learn of me.' For after, when they had declared that which the Lord had opened to them, then the people were to receive it, and the speakers and they were to live in that themselves. But when they had no more to declare but to go to seek forms without life, that made themselves dry and barren and the people also. Thence came all their loss, for the Lord would renew his mercies and his strength if they would wait upon him. But the heads of them all came to nothing; but most of the people came to be convinced and received God's everlasting Truth, and stand a meeting to this day and sit under the Lord Jesus Christ's teaching, their Saviour.

And so, upon the First-day after, the word of the Lord came to me to go to the steeplehouse; and so when the priest had done, I spake the Truth to him and the people and directed them to their teacher Christ Jesus, their free teacher that bought them. And so the priest came to me, with whom I had a little discourse, but he was soon stopped and silent, after which I passed away, having had several meetings amongst those people.

[d]And I was moved to go to Stokesly steeplehouse, and

when the priest had done I spoke to him as I was moved and to the people the Truth of God, and they were moderate and I let them see their true teacher, and how that their teacher was found in the steps of the false teachers, and how the Lord was come to teach his people himself, and the light which Christ did enlighten withal they might come to in themselves, and so by it come to Christ; so when we were gone out of the steeplehouse into the street, the priest sent for me to his house, and I sent to him and bad him come into the street among the people to try his ministry and himself, and it was in the snow in the winter, and he did not come, and so I passed away in the Truth that reacheth in all hearts.[d]

After this I passed through the country to a market town, where I met with many professors with whom I had a great deal of reasoning; and I asked them many questions and they were made to confess they had never such deep questions asked in their lives. It being very deep snow, I passed through the country to a place called Staithes, where I met with many professors and Ranters. Great meetings I had amongst them, and a great convincement there was. One old man, about a hundred years old, and a chief constable, and a priest, one Philip Scafe,[1] received the Truth, that since is become a pretty minister of God's free gospel.

And then I went to the steeplehouse, where was a high priest, that did much oppress the people with tithes. And when I spoke unto him, he fled away after I had laid his oppressing of the people upon him. For if the people went a hundred miles off a-fishing, he would make them pay the tithe money, though they catched the fish at such a distance and carried the fish to Yarmouth to sell. And the chief of the parish were very light and vain, so after I spoke the word of life to them I slighted their light spirits, seeing they did not receive it. But the word of the Lord stuck with some of them so that at night some of the heads of

[1] Philip Scafe or Scarth (d. 1693), minister at Robin Hood's Bay.

[d]......[d] *S.J.*, p. 9.

the parish came to me and were most of them convinced and satisfied, and confessed to Truth. So the Truth began to spread up and down the country and great meetings we had, that the priest began to rage, and the Ranters began to be stirred. They sent to me that they would have a dispute with me, both the oppressing priest and the leader of all the Ranters, and a day was set, and the Ranter, ⟨whose name was Thomas Bushel⟩ came and his company, and another priest, Levens[e], a Scot, but not the oppressing priest of Staithes. And the priest that was convinced and a great number of people met, and so when we were set, the Ranter said to me that he had a vision of me: that I was sitting in a great chair, and that he was to come and put off his hat and bow down to the ground before me, and so he did; and many other flattering words he said. When he had done I told him it was his own figure: and said unto him, 'Repent, thou beast.' He said it was jealousy in me to say so. Then I asked him the ground of jealousy and how it came to be bred in man, and the nature of a heathen, what made it, and how that was bred in man; for I saw him directly in that nature of the beast, and therefore I would have known from him how that came to be bred in him. So I told him he should give me an account of things done in the body before we came to discourse of things done out of the body. So I stopped up his mouth that he could say no more and all his fellow Ranters were stopped up, for he was the head of them.

Then I called for the oppressing high priest but he came not but only the Scottish priest aforesaid: and his mouth was stopped presently with a very few words, as being out of the life of what he did profess.

And then I laid the Ranters, ranking them with the old Ranters in Sodom; and all the priests I manifested to be amongst all their fellow hirelings and bearing rule amongst people by their means, seeking for their gain from their quarter, and teaching for their gain and filthy lucre, and divining for money; and so brought all the

[e] *S.J.*, p. 8.

prophets and Christ and the apostles over the heads of them and showed them how they (to wit, the prophets, Christ, and the apostles) had discovered them by their marks and fruits. And so I directed people to their teacher, Christ Jesus their saviour, when these mountains were laid low, and so did set up Christ in the hearts of his people.

And so all was quiet and their mouths stopped: though it broiled within, but the life had stopped it up that it could not break out.

After the meeting was done this Scotch priest desired me to walk with him a-top of the cliffs, so I took William Ratcliffe,[f] his brother-in-law, alongst with me, which was in some measure convinced, and told him, ' It may be he will report, after I am gone, that which I did not say to him ', and therefore I desired to have some friendly man by to hear what we did say. So as I went he asked me concerning the light of Christ and what the soul was, and I answered him fully. So he went away and meeting with the other priest, Philip Scafe, that was convinced, in madness brake his cane upon the ground, and said if ever he met me or saw me again he would have my life or I should have his; he would give his head if I was not knocked down within a month. So Friends perceived his intent was when he desired to have walked with me alone, either to have thrust me down over cliff or to have stabbed me: and when that was frustrated that made him rage and mad. For before this came to pass, I being one day at his house, I saw a dog-like nature in him; and I was moved to tell him he was a dog, and so his nature showed itself: but I feared not his prophesies nor his threats. But I feared God Almighty, though many weak Friends feared much that this priest would have done me some mischief or have set on others. But after some years this Scottish priest and his wife came to be convinced and I was at their house about twelve years after this.

After this there came another high priest to me which was reputed above all in the country; and so as I was

[f] *S.J.*, p. 8.

speaking in the meeting that the Gospel was the power of God and how it brought life and immortality to light in men, and turning people from the darkness to the light, this high priest said the Gospel was mortal. But I told him the true minister said the Gospel was the power of God and how could he make the power of God mortal. Upon that the other priest, Philip Scafe, that was convinced and had felt the power of God which was immortal, took him up and reproved him. So a great dispute the convinced priest and the high priest had, the convinced priest holding that the Gospel was immortal, and the other high priest held that it was mortal. But the Lord's power stopped his mouth, and these things mightily convinced the people to see the darkness that was in the high priest and the light that was in the other convinced priest.

But people generally waited to see the fulfilling of the other Scottish priest's prophecy that I should be knocked down before the month's end. Some were afraid, but I bid them fear God and not man, for I was not afraid of him.

And then there was another priest sent to have a dispute with me [g]under a cover, hearing I was to go out of the country,[g] and Friends went with me up to the house where he was, and when we came there he went out of the house and hid him under a hedge. When they went to look for him they found him, but could not get him to me. And I went to a steeplehouse hard by, and the priest and people were in a great rage. This priest had threatened Friends what he would do, but when I came there he would not stand, but fled, the Lord's power so came over him and them.

⟨Yea, the Lord's everlasting power was over the world and did reach to the hearts of people, and made both priests and professors tremble. It shook the earthly and airy spirit, in which they held their profession of religion and worship, so that it was a dreadful thing unto them, when it was told them, 'The man in leathern breeches is come.'[1] At the

[1] Fox wore a suit of leather, doublet and breeches.

[g]......[g] *S.J.*, p. 8.

hearing thereof the priests, in many places, would get out of the way, they were so struck with the dread of the eternal power of God; and fear surprised the hypocrites.〉

So we passed away to Whitby and Scarborough where we had some service for the Lord, and there are become large meetings there since; and from thence I passed over the Wolds to Malton where we had great meetings, and at the town's end thereabouts.

〈At one town,〉 a priest challenged to dispute with me. The Lord's power seized upon the people, and one, who had been a wild, drunken man, was reached therewith, so as he came as lowly as a lamb; though he and his companions had before sent for drink of purpose to make the rude people drunk 〈that they might abuse us〉; but the Lord confounded them all. And so I went to meet the priest aforesaid, but he would not come forth, the Lord confounded him and them all. And I was moved to go to a steeplehouse there and the Lord's power came over them all.

And the First-day there came one of the highest Independent professors, a woman, that said before she was convinced that she could willingly have gone to the hanging of me. And she was confounded and convinced and stands a Friend to this day.

And so I turned to Malton again; and very great meetings there were, and several people would have come but they durst not for their relations (for it was a strange thing then to preach in houses and not to go to church as they called it); and much desired I was to go to their steeplehouses. There was a high priest kept a lecture there, and another priest had written to me and invited me to his steeplehouse, calling me his brother. So I went into the steeplehouse, and there were not passing eleven hearers; and the priest was preaching to them, but after it was known in the town that I was in the steeplehouse, it was presently filled with people. And when the chief priest had done (there being two priests in the steeplehouse), the priest that had been preaching sent the priest that sent the letter to me, to have me come and go up into the pulpit; and I sent back word unto him that I need not go up into it. Then he sent me word again he desired me to go up into it for it was a better place and there I might be seen of the people. And I sent him word again I could be seen and heard well enough there, for I came not to hold up those places nor their maintenance and trade. Then they began to be in a rage and said the false prophets should come in the last times, because I would not go up into their pulpit.

And it grieved many of the people to hear them say so. [h]And because I would not some of the people began to call me a deliverer and there began to be a tumult, upon which I started up and desired all to be quiet, and stepped up in a high seat, and cried for audience,[h] and declared unto them the marks of the false prophets and how they were come. And I set the true prophets, Christ and the apostles, over them and showed them how these were out of the steps of ⟨the true prophets and of Christ and his apostles,⟩ and then directed all people to their teacher, Christ Jesus, who would turn them from the darkness to the light, and opening the Scriptures to them, and bringing them to the Spirit of God in themselves, by which they might know ⟨who were the false prophets⟩ and so had a large time amongst them and parted in peace.

⟨Now the Lord had showed me, while I was in Derby prison, that I should speak in steeplehouses to gather people from thence; and a concern sometimes would come upon my mind about the pulpits that the priests lolled in. For the steeplehouses and pulpits were offensive to my mind, because both priests and people called them ‘ the house of God ’, and idolized them, reckoning that God dwelt there in the outward house. Whereas they should have looked for God and Christ to dwell in their hearts, and their bodies to be made the temples of God; for the apostle said, ‘ God dwelleth not in temples made with hands ’: but by reason of the people’s idolizing those places, it was counted an heinous thing to declare against them.

[h]......[h] Cf. *S.J.*, p. 10.

And after some time I went into the country to Pickering where the Justices kept their Sessions in the steeplehouse, Justice Robinson[1] being chief. I kept a meeting in the schoolhouse at the same time, and abundance of priests and professors came to it asking questions, and were answered to their satisfaction; and four chief constables and abundance of others were convinced that day. And so news was carried in to Justice Robinson that his priest was overthrown and convinced, that he had a love unto more than all the priests.

And so after the meeting was done we went to an inn, and many priests came in and Robinson's priest would have paid for my dinner, and would have wiped my shoes, but I charged Friends that no such thing should be done. But he offered to Friends that I should have his steeplehouse to preach in if I would come; but I denied it, and told him and the people that I came to bring them off from such things to Christ. And so the next morning, I went up with the four chief constables, and some others, to see Justice Robinson; and he met me at his chamber door; and I told him I could not honour him with man's honour, and he said he did not look for it. So I went into his chamber and told him the state of the false prophets and of the true prophets, Christ and the apostles, and set them over the other and directed his mind to Christ his teacher, and opened to him the parables, and how election and reprobation stood, and that election stood in the second birth and reprobation stood in the first, and what the promise of God was to, and what the judgement of God was to: and he confessed all. And he was so opened with the Truth that one other justice opposing a little he informed him.

And so at my parting he said it was very well that I did exercise that gift which God had given to me. And he called the chief constables aside and would have given them some money to have given me, saying he would not have me be at any charge in their country; and the chief

[1] Luke Robinson, M.P., of Thornton Riseborough.

constables told him that they themselves could not get me to take any money. So they refused his money and accepted of his love and kindness.

And from thence I passed up into the country with the priest aforesaid that called me brother (in whose school house I had declared ⟨at Pickering⟩); and as we passed through the country and came into a town to bait, the bells rang, and so I asked them what the bells rang for and they said for me to go and preach in the steeplehouse.

And so, as I walked up to the steeplehouse, the people were gathered about the steeplehouse yard; and the old priest would have had me to have gone into the steeplehouse and I said, nay, it was no matter; but it was something strange to people that I would not go into the house of God, as they called it.

So I ⟨stood up in the steeplehouse yard and⟩ declared to the people.

I came not to hold up their idols, temple, nor tithes, nor priests, but to declare against them; and opened to the people all their traditions, and that that piece of ground was no more holy than another piece of ground. ⟨I showed them that the apostles' going into the Jews' synagogues and temples, which God had commanded, was to bring people off from that temple and those synagogues, and from the offerings, and tithes, and covetous priests of that time; and that such as came to be convinced of the Truth, and converted to it and believed in Jesus Christ, whom the apostles preached, met together afterwards in dwelling-houses; and that all who preach Christ, the word of life, ought to preach freely, as the apostles did, and as he had commanded. So I was sent of the Lord God of Heaven and earth to preach freely, and to bring people off from these outward temples made with hands, which God dwelleth not in, that they might know their bodies to become the temples of God and of Christ; and to draw people off from all their superstitious ceremonies, and Jewish and heathenish customs, traditions, and doctrines of men; and from all the world's hireling teachers, that take tithes and great wages, preaching for hire and divining for money, whom God and Christ never sent, as themselves confess when they say they never heard God's voice nor Christ's voice. Therefore I exhorted the people to come off from all these things, and directed them to the spirit and grace of God in themselves, and to the light of Jesus in their own hearts, that they might come to know Christ, their free teacher, to bring them salvation, and to open the Scriptures to them.

Thus the Lord gave me a good opportunity amongst them to open things largely unto them. All was quiet, and many were convinced; blessed be the Lord.⟩

[i]Some places where the priests were paid, they fled away from the town when as I came to it; and the people would break open the doors if I would go into the steeplehouse, if the churchwardens would not open it. But I would not let them, but spake to them in the yards or any where, the Truth of God, and in love it was received; and many justices were loving in Yorkshire, and the Truth spread.[i]

And then I passed on where there was another great meeting and this old priest went along with me, and there came all sorts of professors to it purposely to dispute. And I sat of a haystack and spoke nothing for some hours for I was to famish them from words. So the professors spake ⟨ever and anon⟩ to this old priest and asked him several times when I would speak and begin; and he bid them wait and told them that the people waited upon Christ a long while before he spoke. And at last I was moved of the Lord to speak, and they were all reached by the Lord's power and word of life, and there was a general convincement amongst them.

And from thence I passed along with the old priest and several others. And as we were going some people called to the old priest and said, ' Mr. Boys, we owe you twenty shillings for tithe; come and take it.' And the old priest threw up his hands to them and said he had enough, he would have none of it; they might keep it, and praised the Lord he had enough.

And so we passed on to this old priest's steeplehouse in the moors, and when we came to it the old priest went before me and held open the pulpit door; and I forbade him and

[i]......[i] *S.J.*, p. 14.

told him I should not go into it. The steeplehouse was exceeding much painted,[1] and I told him and the people that the painted beast had a painted house and opened to him the ground of all those houses and their superstition and their ways, and the end of the apostles going into the temple and synagogues, which God had commanded, which was not to hold them up but to bring them to Christ, the substance. So was my end of coming there, not to hold up these temples, priests, and tithes, which God had never commanded, but to bring them off all these things to Christ the substance; and so showed them the true worship which Christ had set up, and ⟨distinguished⟩ Christ the true way from all the false ways; and opened the parables to them, turning them from the darkness to the light that with it they might see themselves and their sins and Christ, their saviour that saves them from their sins.

And so after we passed away to one Burdett's[2] house where we had a great meeting. And this old priest accompanied me and left his steeplehouse, for he had been looked upon as a great high priest above Common Prayer Men and Presbyters and Independents: and many times before he was convinced he would have gone into their steeplehouses to have preached and they would complain to Justice Hotham of him. He would bid them distrain his horse for travelling on the First-days, for Hotham spoke that to put them off with, for they knew he used none but travelled on foot. So at last he would get into the steeplehouse and get into the pulpit, and after the psalm was sung, up would Boys start to preach, for he had been a zealous man in his way before he was convinced. I had several discourses with him before he came to be convinced, and one day I asked him a question which was: what it was that Christ put his sheep forth from, that heard his voice and followed him, for them that was unput-forth by Christ could not hear his voice; which set the man so that he could not answer it—with other suchlike questions.

[1] Probably Pickering where there are noted frescoes.

[2] Burdett lived at Egton Bridge.

And after this I came up through the country towards Cranswick to Captain Pursloe and Justice Hotham's. Justice Hotham was glad that the Lord's power and truth was spread and so many had received it, and that Justice Robinson was so civil. And moreover he said, if God had not raised up this principle of light and life, the nation had been overspread with Ranterism and all the justices in the nation could not stop it with all their laws, because they would have said as they said and done as they commanded them and yet kept their principle still. But this principle of Truth overthrows the root and ground of their principle, and overthrows their principle, which they could not have done with all their laws, as he said, and he was glad the Lord had raised up this principle of life and Truth.

And from thence I passed up into Holderness [j]towards the land's end;[j] and came to a justice's house, one Pearson, where there was a very tender woman that believed in the Truth and said she could have left all and followed me. And from thence I passed to Ulrome to George Hartas's[1] where many of that town were convinced. And on the First-day I was moved to go into the steeplehouse. The priest had got another priest to help him and a many professors and contenders was gathered, but the Lord's power was over all and a great deal of good service I had for the Lord. The priests fled away, and some of those great professors were convinced, and stood, honest, faithful men, men of account ⟨in that place⟩.

And from thence I passed up in the country and had some service in the towns at night amongst people and the next day Friends and friendly people left me and I passed alone, [k]and as I went I spoke through the towns and by the sea side and to people in the fields, of the day of the Lord that was coming upon all ungodliness and unrighteousness, and how that Christ was come to teach his people himself, and[k] warning them to repent. And so I turned into a

[1] This was in March, 1652.

[j]......[j] *S.J.*, p. 6. [k]......[k] *S.J.*, p. 6.

town towards night, called Patrington; and as I was going along the town, preaching and speaking, I warned the priest that was in the street and people to repent and turn to the Lord. [1]Some heard and others said that I was mad,[1] and it grew dark before I came to the end of the town. And a great deal of people gathered about me and I declared the Truth and the word of life to them. And after, I went to an inn and desired them to let me have a lodging and they would not; and I desired them to let me have a little meat and milk and I would pay them for it, but they would not. So I walked out of the town and a company of fellows followed me and asked me what news, and I bid them repent and fear the Lord, [1]and prize their time, for I saw their question was tempting.[1]

And after I was passed a pretty way out of the town I came to another house and desired them to let me have a little meat and drink and lodging for my money, but they would not neither but denied me. And I came to another house and desired the same, but they refused me also; and then it grew so dark that I could not see the highway; but I discovered a ditch and got a little water and refreshed myself and got over the ditch and sat amongst the furze bushes, being weary with travelling, till it was day.

And at break of day I got up and passed on in the fields, [1]when I could see my way,[1] and there came a man with a great pike and went along with me to a town. He raised the town and the constable and chief constable upon me, before the sun was up, [1]having a warrant that they had made at Patrington;[1] and so I declared God's everlasting Truth amongst them and warned them to repent, and that the day of the Lord was coming upon all sin and wickedness. And they seized me with watch-bills and pikes and staves and halberds, and guarded me back again to Patrington, about three miles, and when I came there all the town was up in an uproar, and the priest and constables ⟨were consulting together⟩, and so I had an opportunity to declare the words

[1]. . . . . .[1] *S.J.*, pp. 6, 7.

of life and Truth amongst them again, and warned them to repent. And at last a professor, a tender man, called me to his house, and I took a little bread and milk, having not eaten before for some days. Then they guarded me about nine miles to a justice, and when I was come near his door there came a man riding after me and asked whether I was the man that was apprehended. And I asked him wherefore he asked, and he said, 'For no hurt', and I told him I was, and he rid away to the justice before me. And before I was brought in before him, the guard said it was well if the justice was not drunk before we came to him for he used to be drunk very early. And when I was brought before him [m]he bad me put off my hat, and I took it off in my hand, and said to him, 'Doth this trouble thee?' And I put it on again;[m] and I said 'thou' to him, and he asked the man ⟨that rid thither before me⟩ whether I was not mazed or fond. And he said, no, it was my principle. So I warned him to repent and come to the light that Christ had enlightened him withal, that with it he might see all his evil words and actions that he had done and acted, and his ungodly ways he had walked in, and ungodly words he had spoken, and so return to Christ Jesus whilst he had time, and whilst he had time to prize it: and then said he, 'Ay, ay; the Light that is spoken of in the third of John.' And I desired him that he would obey it and mind it, for I laid my hand upon him and admonished him, and he was brought down by the power of the Lord, and all the watchmen stood amazed. So after, he took me into a little parlour with the other man and desired to see what I had in my pockets of letters or intelligence, and I plucked out my linen and showed him I had no letters: so he said, 'He is not a vagrant by his linen.'

So he set me at liberty and I went back again to Patrington with the man aforesaid, who lived at Patrington, that asked whether I was the man that was apprehended, and when I came there he would have had me have a meeting at the

[m]......[m] *S.J.*, p. 7.

cross, but I said it was no matter, his house would serve. He desired I would go and lie down upon a bed or in the bed, for they had got a report that I would not lie in any bed; that he and his wife might say they had seen me lie in a bed or upon a bed; because at that time I lay many times without doors.

So on the First-day I had a great meeting there at his house. And I went out of the meeting, and said nothing to any one, and went to the steeplehouse and declared the Truth to both priest and people; and the people did not molest me so I brought the power of God over them and came again to the meeting, where there were many that were convinced of the Lord's everlasting Truth and stand to this day. And they were exceeding sorry and grieved that they should not receive me nor give me lodging ⟨when I was there before⟩.

So I passed through the country to the farthest land in that country, warning people to repent both in towns and country, and directed them to their teacher Christ Jesus. And on the First-day I came to one Colonel Overton's[1] house and had a great meeting of the prime of the people of that country; which were generally convinced and received the Truth and the word of life. Many things were opened to them of the Scriptures that they never heard in their lives; and so many were convinced and settled in God's truth.

And so I came to Patrington again and visited those Friends that were convinced; and they informed me how that a tailor and some wild blades had made that warrant to carry me before that justice. So the tailor came to ask me forgiveness, fearing I would trouble them; and the constables were afraid lest I should trouble them; but I forgave them and warned them to mend their lives and turn to the Lord.

And when I was at Ulrome before in the steeplehouse, there came a professor and gave me a push in the breast in the steeplehouse and bid me get out of the church.

[1] Robert Overton was imbued with Fifth Monarchism.

' Alack, poor man ', said I, ' dost thou call the steeplehouse the church ? the church is the people whom God has purchased with his blood, and not the house.' And Justice Hotham, hearing of the abuse of this man unto me, sent a warrant for him and bound him over to the Sessions: he was so affected with the truth and zealous to keep the peace of the country. And he had asked me before whether any people had meddled with me or abused me, but I was not to tell him any thing but was to forgive all.

And I went to several great houses warning them to repent and some received me lovingly and some slighted me. And so I passed through the country and at night came to another town and desired lodging and meat and I would pay for it. They would not let me lodge except I would go to the constable, which was the custom, they said, of all lodgers at inns if strangers; so I told them I should not go, for I was an innocent man, and that custom was for suspicious persons, but I was innocent, and if they would let me have lodging and meat I would pay for it. And so I warned them to repent and declared unto them the day of their visitation and salvation and turned them to the light of Christ and spirit of God, and so passed away, and the people was something tendered and troubled afterwards. And when it grew dark I spied a haystack and sat under it all night till morning.

And the next day I passed into Hull and admonished and warned people as I went of their salvation and to turn to Christ Jesus. And at night I got lodging, but was very sore with travelling a-foot so far.

CHAPTER V

AND so after, I passed through the country and came to Balby; and so visited Friends up and down in those parts, and then passed into the edge of Nottinghamshire and visited Friends there.

[a]I was moved to go from a meeting in Nottinghamshire to a steeplehouse, and when the priest had done, I spake to him and the people; and the priest went away, but the people stayed and heard the Truth declared to them till it was within the night; and I was moved to kneel down in the steeplehouse and pray among the people; and there came a woman behind me and kissed the crown of my head when I was praying in the dark; and she was one of the world. And there combined together a company of men to hale me out, and they did, but it was well and the Truth came over all for there were many then that had a love to the Truth, and it made them to love it the more. We had a meeting in that town, and so I passed away in the truth of God and that was over all.[a] And on the First-day I went to a steeplehouse this side of Trent, and in the afternoon I went to another on the other side of Trent, declaring to them the word of life and bringing them to their teacher, Christ Jesus, who was their saviour and died for them, that they might hear him. And so I went into the country and had several meetings up and down thereaways, and came to a place where there came a great man, and a priest, and many professors, but the Lord's truth came over them all, and they went their ways, and so I went into the meeting, and there came a man that had been at a meeting, and he raised an accusation and made a noise up and down the country and said that I said I was Christ.

[a] . . . . . . [a] *S.J.*, p. 15.

And I went to Gainsborough, and there, a Friend having been speaking in the market, the market and town were all in an uproar. And I went into a friendly man's house and the people rushed into it and it was filled with professors and disputers. And so this false accuser came in before them all, and the rude people, and accused me openly before all the people, that I said I was Christ and had brought a-many witnesses to prove it; and so set a rage in the people that they had much to do to keep their hands off me. And in the eternal power of God I was moved of the Lord God to stand up atop of the table and tell them that Christ was in them except they were reprobates; and it was the eternal power of Christ and Christ that spake in me that time to them. And generally with one consent all the people did acknowledge the thing, and gave testimony to it, and confessed to it—yea, even the very professors and all them that were in a rage against me—and I said that if the power of God and the Seed spoke in man or woman it was Christ. And so I called him Judas, and all were satisfied except himself, and a professor, and his own false witnesses. So I told him again that he was Judas and that it was the word of the Lord and of Christ to him, and Judas's end should be his. And so the Lord's power came over all and all the people parted in peace, but this Judas went away and hanged himself shortly after, and a stake was driven into his grave.

And after, the wicked priest went and raised a slander upon us and said that a Quaker had hanged himself in Lincolnshire and had a stake driven through him. This they printed to the nation, adding sin unto sin, which the Truth was clear of; for he was no more a Quaker than the priest that printed it.[1]

And so I passed out of the country in the Lord's power, and came into Yorkshire again. But many were convinced of the Lord's everlasting Truth and settled therein in Lincolnshire, and received the Lord's teaching and Gospel.

[1] Probably Cotten Crosland, of Ackworth, near Pontefract, Yorks.; see Gilpin: *The Quakers Shaken*, 1653.

And after this I went to Warmsworth steeplehouse in Yorkshire in the forenoon, [b]and some friends followed me. And they shut the door and kept me out. After a while they let in Thomas Aldam to his seat and then shut it again. And the priest said he would catechise him and fell upon him asking him questions. And at last they opened the door and I went in; and as soon as I came in, he lost his matter and stopped his preaching and said, 'What come you hither for?' And he asked again the same question; and he asked, 'What have you to say, what have you to say?' He was in such a maze, he cried, 'Come, come, I will prove them false prophets, in Matthew 7 and 24.' But he was so confounded he could not find the chapter, but fell asking me questions again, what we came hither for. And I stood still all this while, not making any disturbance among them, and at last I said, 'Seeing here are so many questions asked, I may answer them.' And then I began to speak forth the Truth amongst them, and of the false prophets and how he was in the steps of them, and I held forth Christ. And as soon as I began, the people violently rushed upon me and thrust me out of the steeplehouse again and locked the door on me. And I stayed in the steeplehouse yard till they came forth, and as soon as they had done and were come forth I began to speak to the priest and people the Truth, and how he was in the footsteps of the Pharisees. And the priest shook me and the people run upon me and beat me sore with their crab-tree staves and threw clods and stones at me and threw me about.[b] But I warned them and him of the day of the Lord, and turned them to Christ and to repent. But I received not much hurt, for the Lord's power was over them all.

And so after, I went to another steeplehouse in the afternoon, but the priest had done before I came there and so I did admonish them, and turned them to their teacher, Christ Jesus; and after returned back again to Balby, and went to Doncaster, where formerly I had preached repentance unto them on a market day, which

[b]. . . . . .[b] Cf. *S.J.*, p. 11.

had made a great noise and a dread in the country. And on the First-day I went to the steeplehouse and after the priest had done I spoke to him and the people what the Lord God commanded me, and they were in a great rage and hurried me out and threw me down the stairs, and haled me before the mayor and magistrates. A great examination I had and a great deal of work with them, and they threatened my life if ever I came there again, and that they would leave me to the mercy of the people, [c]my blood be upon my own head.[c] Nevertheless, I declared Truth unto them and turned them from the darkness to the light of Christ, whether they would hear or forbear, and how that God and Christ was come to teach his people himself. And after a while they put me out amongst the rude multitude, and some Friends were with me. They threw stones at us down the streets; and there was an innkeeper that was a bailiff came and took us into his house; and they broke his head that the blood run down his face with the stones that they threw at us, [d]and he was Lot, I told him, that ventured himself and took us into his house from the rude multitude; and we stayed there awhile in his house and showed the people the priests' fruits; and about his house the rude people waited, then we went to Balby about a mile off and the rude people stoned us down the lane, a great way out of the town,[d] but, blessed be the Lord, we did not receive much hurt.

And the next First-day I went to Tickhill and there the Friends of that side gathered together and there was a meeting; and a mighty brokenness with the power of God there was amongst the people. [e]And when Friends were in the meeting and fresh and full of the power of God I was moved to go to the steeplehouse, and the priest[1] had done. And he and most of the heads of the parish were got up into the chancel, and I went up among them. And when I began to speak, they fell upon me, and the clerk up with his Bible as I was speaking and hit me in the face

[1] John Gosfield.

[c]. . . . . .[c] *S.J.*, p. 10. [d]. . . . . .[d] Cf. *S.J.*, p. 10.

that my face gushed out with blood, and it run off me in the steeplehouse. And then they cried, 'Take him out of the church', and they punched me and thrust me out and beat me sore with books, fists and sticks, and threw me over a hedge into a close and there beat me and then threw me over again. And then they beat me into a house, punching me through the entry, and there I lost my hat and never had it again, and after dragged me into the street, stoning and beating me along, sorely blooded and bruised. And the priest beheld a great part of this his people's doings.[e]

And so after a while I got into the meeting again amongst Friends, and the priest and people coming by the Friend's house, I went forth with Friends into the yard and there I spoke to the priest and people, [f]they being in the street and I in the Friend's yard on a wall. My spirit was revived again by the power of God; for, through their bruising, beating, blooding, stoning, and throwing me down, I was almost mazed and my body sore bruised, but by the power of the Lord I was refreshed again, to him be the glory.[f] And the priest scoffed at us and called us Quakers; but I declared to them the word of life and showed to them the fruits of their teachers and how they dishonoured Christianity. And the Lord's power was so over them all, and the word of life was declared in so much power and dread to them, that the priest fell a-trembling himself, so that one said unto him, 'Look how the priest trembles and shakes, he is turned a Quaker also.'

And Friends were very much abused that day by the priest and his people. The justices hearing of it, two or three of them came and sat to hear and examine the business; and he that had shed my blood was afraid of having his hand cut off for striking me in the steeplehouse, but I forgave him and did not appear against him. So I came without my hat to Balby, about seven or eight miles.

⟨Great rage got up in priests and people, and in some of the magistrates of the West Riding of Yorkshire⟩;

[e]. . . . . .[e] Cf. *S.J.*, pp. 10, 11. [f]. . . . . .[f] *S.J.*, pp. 10, 11.

the priest of Warmsworth[1] procured a warrant for me and Thomas Aldam from the justices, and it was to be executed in all the West Riding of Yorkshire. I had a vision of a [g]man and a[g] bear and two great mastiff dogs; that I should pass by them and they should do me no hurt and so I did, [g]and they smiled upon me.[g] The constable took Thomas Aldam with the warrant and carried him to York,[2] and I went with Thomas Aldam towards York twenty miles, and he had the warrant for me in his pocket but he said he saw me before but he was loath to trouble men that were strangers, but Thomas Aldam was his neighbour; [h]he desired me that I should not tell any one that he saw me, and I told him I could not lie and so we parted.[h] So the Lord's power restrained him that he was not able to meddle with me till we came to Lieutenant Roper's, where we had a great meeting of many considerable men. The Truth was wonderfully declared amongst them and the Scriptures and Christ's words and the parables were opened unto them and the state of the church in the apostles' days and the apostacy since; and the Truth was mightily opened to them that those great men did generally confess and believe that this Truth must go over the whole world.

And there were James Nayler, Thomas Goodaire and William Dewsbury that had been convinced the year before and Richard Farnsworth and the constable aforesaid, and Thomas Aldam stayed the meeting and afterwards went towards York prison, [i]where they kept him two years,[i] but did not meddle with me.

And so I went to Wakefield; and there on the First-day after, I went to a steeplehouse where James Nayler had been a member of an Independent church.[3] And when I came in, when the priest[4] had done, the people bid me come up

[1] Thomas Rookby.
[2] Aldam's imprisonment began in May, 1652.
[3] Woodchurch (West Ardsley).
[4] Christopher Marshall (1614-1673), ejected minister.
[g]......[g] *S.J.*, p. 11. [h]......[h] *S.J.*, pp. 11, 12.
[i]......[i] *S.J.*, p. 12.

to the priest and when I came up [j]to the pulpit[j] and began to declare the word of life to him and showed them the deceit of the priest, they rushed me out, of a sudden, at the other door, and fell a-punching and beating of me, and called, ' Let us have him to the stocks '; but the Lord's power was over them and they were not suffered to put me in. [k]And this was the greatest professor in Yorkshire.[k]

And so I passed away to the meeting where were a great many professors and friendly people gathered and a great convincement there was that day, and people satisfied with the Lord's teaching which they were turned to. ⟨Here we got some lodging for⟩ we had lain out, four of us, under a hedge the night before, for there were few Friends to receive us there.

And this priest's name was Christopher Marshall, whom the Lord not long after cut off in his wickedness.[1] And James Nayler was a member of his church, whom he excommunicated not long after. And he raised a-many wicked slanders upon me, that I carried bottles and that I made people drink of my bottles, and that made them to follow me, and that I rid of a great black horse, and that I was seen in one country upon my black horse in one hour and in the same hour in another country three score miles off, and that I would give a fellow money to follow me when I was on my black horse. And with these hellish lies he fed his people to make them speak evil of the Truth which was in Jesus, that I had declared amongst them; for I went on foot and had no horse at that time, ⟨which the people generally knew⟩. But by his lies he preached many of his hearers away from him, and the Lord's power came over them all and delivered us out of their hands.

And the same day Richard Farnsworth went to another high priest's steeplehouse to declare unto them the word of Truth and a great service he had amongst them, that the

[1] He died in 1673.

[j]. . . . . .[j] *S.J.*, p. 9. [k]. . . . . .[k] *S.J.*, p. 9.

people said we made more noise in the country than the coming up of the Scotch Army,[1] the Lord's power was so mighty over all.

After this I came to a place called High Town [Liversedge], where there was a woman had been convinced a little before, and so we went to her house and had a meeting. The townspeople riz and we declared the Truth to them and the world of life and had some service with them for the Lord; and they passed away peaceably. But there was a widow woman, one Green, in the town, who went to a great man, called a gentleman, who ⟨was reported to have⟩ killed two men and a woman, and informed him against us, though he was no officer. The next morning we drew up some queries to send to the priest, and when we had done, just as we were passing away, the townspeople came up running and some friendly people and told us that this murdering man was sharpening a crook to pluck us out of the house, and pike to stab us; and was coming up with his sword by his side, but we were passing away and so missed him, [1]but we were gone hardly a quarter of an hour[1] when he came to the house, and people concluded, if we had not been gone he would have murdered some of us.

And so that night we lay in a wood, it being exceeding rainy, and we were much wet; in the morning I was moved to come back to the town again, and they gave us a full relation of this wicked man. So we passed away to Bradford, and there we came to a house where we met Richard Farnsworth, from whom we had parted before. And so when we came in they set us on meat, and as I was going to sup of their posset, the word of the Lord came to me, 'Eat not thy bread with such as has an evil eye.' And I got up from the table and ate nothing. The woman was a Baptist; and after I had admonished her and the family

[1] This doubtless refers to the march into England of the Scots under Prince Charles in 1651, which ended in the battle of Worcester on 3rd September.

[1]. . . . . .[1] *S.J.*, p. 15.

of the house to turn to the Lord Jesus Christ and hearken to him their teacher I passed away.

And so we passed through the country preaching repentance to the people and came into a market town in Derbyshire on the market day, and there was a lecture. And I went into the steeplehouse where there was a many priests and professors and people. The priest took his text out of Jeremiah 5, the latter part of the chapter, 'My people love to have it so.' [m]And when the priest had done I spake to him and the people of the Truth and the light and the day of the Lord, and of God's work in them, and the Truth in them, and the Spirit and the teacher within them, and of their teachers without them and how that the priest had[m] left out the other part of the verse, 'The prophets prophesy falsely and the priests bear rule by their means, and my people love to have it so.' [m]And when I told the priest of his wronging the Scriptures and that he did not speak it all, for if he had it had been his own condition, he fled away, and the people fell upon us and put us out, and so we passed away in the Truth.[m] At night we came to a country house; and there being no alehouse near they desired us to stay there all night, where we had a good service for the Lord, declaring his Truth amongst them; for the Lord had said unto me if I did but set up one in the same spirit that the prophets and apostles were in that gave forth the Scriptures, he or she should shake all the country in their profession ten miles about them; and if they did own God and Christ and his prophets and apostles, they must own him or her. For all people had the Scriptures, but were not in that same light and power, and spirit that they were in that gave forth the Scriptures and so they neither knew God, nor Christ, nor the prophets, nor the apostles, nor Scriptures, neither had they unity one with another being out of the power and spirit of God.

And the next day we passed on, warning people as we met them of the day of the Lord that was coming upon them. As we went I spied a great high hill called Pendle

[m]. . . . . .[m] *S.J.*, p. 14.

Hill, and I went on the top of it with much ado, it was so steep; but I was moved of the Lord to go atop of it; and when I came atop of it I saw Lancashire sea; and there atop of the hill I was moved to sound the day of the Lord;[1] and the Lord let me see a-top of the hill in what places he had a great people ⟨to be gathered. As I went down,⟩ on the hill side I found a spring of water and refreshed myself, for I had eaten little and drunk little for several days.

And so at night we came to an alehouse and stayed all night and declared much to the man of the house, and writ a paper to the priests and professors concerning the day of the Lord and how Christ was come to teach people himself by his power and spirit and to bring them off all the world's ways and teachers to his own free teaching, who had bought them and was the Saviour. And the man of the house did spread the paper up and down and was mightily affected with Truth. And the Lord opened to me at that place, and let me see a great people in white raiment by a river's side[2] coming to the Lord, and the place was near John Blaykling's where Richard Robinson lived.[3]

And the next day we passed on [n]among the fell countries[n] and at night we got a little ferns or brackens and lay upon a common and the next morning went to a town where Richard Farnsworth[4] parted with me and I was alone again.

So I came up Wensleydale; and at the market town in that dale[5] there was a lecture on the market day. I went into the steeplehouse, and after the priest had done I declared the day of the Lord to the priest and people,

[1] Cf Joel 2: 1-2. For another use of the phrase see p. 302.

[2] The river Rawthey, close to its confluence with the Lune. *S.J.* p. 16 has "by a river that parted two counties".

[3] John Blaykling (1625-1705) of Draw-well farm, Richard Robinson (d. 1673) of Brigflatts, both near Sedbergh, N.W. Yorkshire.

[4] Of Tickhill, Yorks., d. 1666.

[5] Askrigg: wrongly identified as Hawes by some editors.

[o]and bid them repent and take heed of deceitful merchandise;[o] and turned them from the darkness to the light and from the power of Satan unto God, that they might come to God and Christ's teaching freely. I declared freely and largely the word of life to the people and had not much persecution, and afterwards passed up the dales warning people to fear God and declaring his Truth to them [o]through all the towns as I went. And people took me for a mad man and distracted, and some followed me and questioned with me and were astonished,[o] and at last I came to a great house where there was a schoolmaster, and they got me into the house; and I declared the Truth to them, asking them questions about their religion and worship, and they had me into a parlor and locked me in and said I was a young man that was mad and was got away from my relations and they would keep me till they could send to my relations. [p]But they being astonished at my answers and the Truth I spoke to them I convinced them of that, and they let me forth and would have had me to have stayed all night, but I was not to stay but admonished them and turned them to the light of Christ by which they might come to see their salvation, and so passed away and wandered in the night.

And at last I came to a little alehouse ⟨upon a common⟩ where there were some fellows drinking. And I walked up and down in the house and after a time they began to drink to me. I would not drink with them and I spoke to them the Truth, warning them of the mighty day of the Lord that was coming and bid them take heed of that which showed them sin and evil in their hearts, upon which one rose against me with a club. And they held one another and then they were quiet. I was walking out as to have lien all night out doors, and he that would have struck me followed me,[p] with a batch of knives by his side, under pretence that he would have whispered with me. But I kept him off and warned him to repent. So the Lord preserved me by his power from him, and he went into the

[o]......[o] *S.J.*, p. 17. [p]......[p] Cf. *S.J.*, p. 17.

house again. [q]And I was moved to go into the house again and so staid there all night.[q] The next morning I passed away and came through other dales and warned and exhorted people to repent and turn to the Lord, and several were convinced. I came to one house, to a kinsman of John Blaykling and he would have given me money but [q]I was moved to shake my hand at it[q] and would not receive it.

So I came through the dales to a man's house, one Tennant,[1] and I was moved to speak to the family, and as I was turning away from them I was moved to turn again and to declare God's everlasting Truth to him and he was convinced, and his family, and lived and died in the Truth. And after this I went into Dent where many were convinced also. So I came to Major Bousfield's in Garsdale where he and several more received me, and some were convinced and stand to this day. And I passed through Grisedale and several other of those dales, where some were convinced.

And from Major Bousfield's I came to Richard Robinson's; and as I was passing along the way I asked a man, which was Richard Robinson's; he asked me from whence I came and I told him, 'From the Lord', and when I came to Richard Robinson's I declared the everlasting Truth to him [q]and he was convinced.[q] And yet a dark jealousy riz up in him, after I was gone to bed, that I might be somebody that was come to rob his house, and he locked all his doors fast.

And the next day, being the First-day I went to a Separate meeting[2] at Justice Benson's,[3] where the people were generally convinced; this was the place that I had seen a people coming forth in white raiment. A mighty meeting there was and is to this day, near Sedbergh, which I gathered in the name of Jesus.

[1] James Tennant (d. 1674) of Scarhouse in Langstrothdale.

[2] That is, a meeting of separated people, or Seekers.

[3] Gervase Benson (d. 1679) lived at Borrats, at Sedbergh. The meeting was held at his house on Whit Sunday the 6th June, 1652.

[q]......[q] *S.J.*, p. 17.

And in the week[1] there was a great fair at Sedbergh for hiring servants [r]and many young people came to be hired.[r] I went to the fair and declared through the fair the day of the Lord, and after I had done I went into the steeplehouse yard [r]and got up by a tree,[r] and most of the people of the fair came to me, and abundance of priests and professors. There I declared the everlasting Truth of the Lord and the word of life for several hours, and that the Lord Christ Jesus was come to teach his people himself and bring them off all the world's ways and teachers to Christ, their way to God; and I laid open all their teachers and set up the true teacher, Christ Jesus; and how they were judged by the prophets, Christ, and the apostles; and to bring them off the temples made with hands, that they themselves might know they were the temples of God. And never a priest had power to open his mouth. But at last a captain said, why would I not go into the church, for that was a fit place to preach in. I said unto him I denied their church [r]for the church was in God as in 1 Thess. I. 1.[r] There stood up a Separate preacher, one Francis Howgill,[2] that had not seen me before, and he began to dispute with the captain, but he held his peace. Then said Francis Howgill, 'This man speaks with authority and not as the scribes.' So I opened to the people that the ground and house was no holier than another place, and that the house was not the church, but the people which Christ is the head of: and so, after a while that I had made a stand amongst the people, the priests came up to me and I warned them to repent. [r]And when I was passing away a priest said to the people that I was distracted; his mouth being stopped by the power of God for opposing, that was only his cover to the people,[r] and so they turned away, but many people were glad at the hearing of the Truth declared unto them that day, which they received gladly.

[1] Wednesday, 9th June.

[2] Francis Howgill (1618-1669) of Grayrigg, Westmorland, early publisher of Quakerism, d. in Appleby gaol.

[r]. . . . . .[r] *S.J.*, p. 18.

So I passed away and I came into a house;[1] and there came in one Captain Ward[2] and he said, my very eyes pierced through him, and he was convinced of God's everlasting Truth and lived and died in it.

And the next First-day I came to Firbank Chapel[3] [s]where there was a great meeting of the sober people of the country,[s] where Francis Howgill and John Audland[4] had been preaching in the morning; and John Blaykling and some moderate people came to me and desired me not to reprove them publicly for they were not parish teachers but pretty sober men, but I would not tell them whether I would or no though I had little in me to declare publicly against them, I told them they must leave me to the Lord's movings. The chapel was full of people and many could not get in and Francis Howgill said he thought I looked into the chapel (but I did not) and that I might have killed him with a crab-apple, the Lord's power had so surprised him.

So they had quickly done with their preaching to the people at that time and they, and the people, went to their dinners; and abundance stayed till they came again. I went to a brook and got me a little water, and so I came and sat me down a-top of a rock,[5] for the word of the Lord came to me I must go and set down upon the rock in the mountain even as Christ had done before. In the afternoon the people gathered about me with several Separate teachers, where it was judged there were above a thousand people; and all those several Separate teachers were convinced of God's everlasting Truth that day; amongst whom I declared freely and largely God's everlasting Truth and word of

[1] Thomas Blaykling's at Draw-well.

[2] Henry Ward (d. 1674), of Sunnybank, Grayrigg.

[3] Between Kendal and Sedbergh. A modern building stands lower down the Fell.

[4] Audland (1630-1664), with John Camm carried Quakerism to Bristol.

[5] A rock at the top of Firbank Fell is still known as 'Fox's Pulpit', and now bears an inscription.

[s]. . . . . .[s] *S.J.*, p. 18.

life about three hours; and there were many old people that went into the Chapel, and looked out of the windows and thought it a strange thing to see a man to preach on a hill or mountain and not in their church (as they called it).

I was made to open to the people that the steeplehouse and that ground on which it stood were no more holy than that mountain, and those temples and 'dreadful houses of God', (as they called them) were not set up by the command of God nor Christ; nor their priests as Aaron's priesthood; nor their tithes as theirs was. But Christ was come, who ended the temple, and the priests, and the tithes, and Christ said, 'Learn of me', and God said, 'This is my beloved Son, hear ye him.' For the Lord had sent me with his everlasting gospel to preach, and his word of life to bring them off all those temples, tithes, priests and rudiments of the world, that had gotten up since the apostles' days, and had been set up by such who had erred from the spirit and power the apostles were in; so that they might all come to know Christ their teacher, their counsellor, their shepherd to feed them, and their bishop to oversee them and their prophet to open to them, and to know their bodies to be the temples of God and Christ for them to dwell in.

And so I opened the prophets and the figures and shadows and turned them to Christ the substance, and then opened the parables of Christ and the things that had been hid from the beginning, and showed them the estate of the Epistles how they were written to the elect; and the state of the apostacy that has been since the apostles' days, and how the priests have got the Scriptures and are not in that spirit which gave them forth; who make a trade of their words and have put them into chapter and verse; and how that the teachers and priests now are found in the steps both of the false prophets, chief priests, scribes, and Pharisees, such as both the prophets, Christ, and his apostles cried against, and so are judged by the prophets', Christ's and the apostles' spirit; and all that were in it could not own them. And so turning the people to the spirit of God, and from the darkness to the light that they might believe in it and become children of the light, and turning them from the power of Satan which they had been under to God, and that with the spirit of Truth they might be led into all the Truth of the prophets', Christ's and the apostles' words.

And so after the meeting was done I passed away to John Audland's[1] and there came John Story to me, and lighted his pipe of tobacco, and, said he, 'Will you take a pipe of tobacco', saying, 'Come, all is ours'; and I looked upon him to be a forward, bold lad. Tobacco I did not take, but it came into my mind that the lad might think I had not unity with the creation, for I saw he had a flashy, empty notion of religion; so I took his pipe and put it to my mouth and gave it to him again to stop him lest his rude tongue should say I had not unity with the creation.

And from thence I came to Preston Patrick Chapel where there was a great meeting appointed.[2] I went into it and had a large meeting amongst the people, and declared the word of life and the everlasting Truth to them, and showed them that the end of my coming into that place was not to hold it up no more than the apostles going into the Jewish synagogues and temple and Diana's was, but to bring them off all such things as they did: for the apostles brought the saints off the ⟨Jewish⟩ temple and Aaron's priesthood and told them that their bodies were the temples of God and that Christ was their teacher; and after, they met in houses.

And so from thence I came to Kendal where a meeting was appointed in the town hall; and when I had declared the Truth and word of life to them, and showed them how they might know Christ and the Scriptures, and what would be their teacher and what would be their condemnation, I passed away after I had stayed awhile in the town, and several were convinced there. One Cocks met me in the street and would have given me a roll of tobacco, for people were much given to smoking tobacco, so I accepted of his love, but denied it.

And from thence I came to Underbarrow to one Miles Bateman's and as I came on the way several people came along with me, and great disputing I had with them,

[1] At Crosslands.

[2] Wednesday, 16th June, 1652.

especially with Edward Burrough,[1] and at night the priest came and a many professors to Miles Bateman's and a great deal of disputing I had with them. Supper being provided for the priest and the rest, I was not to eat with them, but told them if they would appoint a meeting the next day at the steeplehouse and acquaint the people with it I might meet with them. A great deal of reasoning they had about it, and some were for it and some were against it.

And in the morning I walked out after I had told them concerning the meeting, and they were in much reasoning and doubting of it and me, and as I was walking upon the top of the bank there came several poor people, travellers, that I saw were in necessity; and they gave them nothing but said they were cheats. But when they were gone in to their breakfast it grieved me to see such hard-heartedness amongst professors that I ran after the poor people a matter of a quarter of a mile and gave them some money. ⟨Meanwhile, some that were in the house⟩ came out again, and seeing me a quarter of a mile off they said I could not have gone so far in such an instant except I had wings; and then the meeting was like to have been stopped, they were so filled with strange thoughts, and that quite put the meeting out of their minds and they were against it; for they could not believe I could have gone so far in such a short space. And then there came Miles and Stephen Hubbersty, more simple hearted men, and they would have the meeting. I told them I ran after those poor people to give them some money and I was grieved at their hard-heartedness that gave them nothing.

So I went to the chapel at Underbarrow; the priest came and a great meeting there was and after a while the priest fled away. Many of Crook and Underbarrow were convinced that day and received the word of life and stand to this day under Christ's teaching. And after I had

[1] Edward Burrough (1634-1662), a leading preacher of Quakerism, especially in London, died in Newgate gaol.

declared the Truth to them some hours and the meeting was done, the chief constable and some other professors fell a-reasoning with me in the steeplehouse yard; and I took a Bible and showed and opened to them the Scriptures, and showed them chapter and verse and dealt with them as one would deal with a child in swaddling clothes. They that were in the light of Christ and spirit of God did know when I spoke Scripture, though I did not mention chapter and verse after the priest's form unto them. And from thence I passed to his house with an old man, James Dickinson,[1] that was convinced of the Truth that day, and died in the Truth. And from thence I came to James Taylor's of Newton in Cartmel in Lancashire, where there were many professors which received Truth; and on the First-day[2] I went to one priest Camelford's[3] chapel [t]at Staveley,[t] and after he had done I began to speak the word of life to them. Camelford was in such a rage, and such a fret and so peevish that he had not patience to hear. [t]All was on a fire,[t] and the rude multitude struck me, and punched me, and took me and threw me headlong over the stone wall of the graveyard, but, blessed be the Lord, his power preserved me. The kirk-warden was one John Knipe, whom the Lord after cut off, who threw me down headlong over the wall. And there was a youth in the chapel that was writing after the priest; and I was moved to speak to him and he came to be convinced and became a fine minister of the Gospel, whose name was John Braithwaite.

And so I went up to an alehouse where many people resorted betwixt the times of their ⟨morning and afternoon⟩ preaching, and had a great deal of reasoning with them and showed unto them how that God was come to teach his people himself and to bring them off such teachers as were judged by the prophets, Christ, and the apostles; and

[1] James Dickinson lived at Crosthwaite in Westmorland.

[2] Sunday, 20th June, 1652.

[3] Gabriel Camelford (d. *c.* 1680).

[t]. . . . . .[t] *S.J.*, p. 19.

many received the word of life that time and stand to this day.

And the afternoon I went about two or three miles to another steeplehouse or chapel called Lindale, and when the priest had done I spoke to him and the people what the Lord commanded me. There were great opposers but they after came to be convinced; and after I came to one Captain Sandys,[1] who with his wife, if they could have had the world and Truth ⟨together⟩ they would have received it; but they were hypocrites and he a very chaffy light man, the way was too straight for them. And when I had admonished him of his lightness and of his jesting, how it was not seemly for a great professor as he was, he answered and said he had a son on his death-bed who did also reprove and warn him of it; but he neither obeyed the admonishment of his son nor of the spirit of God in himself.

And from thence I came to Ulverston and so to Swarthmoor to Judge Fell's.[2]

And there came up priest Lampitt[3] of Ulverston who I perceived had been and was still a Ranter in his mind, [u]and had liberty to do anything,[u] and I had a great deal of reasoning with him for he would talk of high notions and perfection and thereby deceived the people. He would have owned me but I could not own him nor join with him, he was so full of filth. For he said he was above John and made as though he knew all things, but I told him how that death reigned from Adam to Moses, and he was under that death and knew not Moses, for Moses saw the paradise of God; he neither knew Moses nor the prophets nor John, for that crooked nature stood in him and the rough, and the mountain of sin and corruptions. And

[1] Adam Sandys lived at Bouth, near Ulverston.

[2] Thomas Fell (1598-1658) of Swarthmoor Hall, Ulverston, Chancellor of the Duchy of Lancaster. Fox arrived late in June, 1652.

[3] William Lampitt (d. 1677). Curate of Ulverston.

[u] . . . . . . [u] *S.J.*, p. 19.

the way was not prepared in him for the Lord. He confessed he had been under a cross in things but now he could sing psalms and do anything; and I told him now he could see a thief and join hand in hand with him, and he could not preach Moses, nor the prophets, nor Christ, nor John, except he was in the same spirit as they were in.

And so Margaret Fell[1] had been abroad, and at night when she came home her children told her that priest Lampitt and I disagreed; and it struck something at her because she was in a profession with him, though he hid his dirty actions from them. So at night we had a great deal of reasoning and I declared the Truth to her and her family.

And the next day Lampitt came again and I had a great deal of discourse with him before Margaret Fell, who soon then discerned the priest clearly, and a convincement came upon her and her family of the Lord's Truth. And there was a humiliation day shortly after, within a day or two, kept at Ulverston, and Margaret Fell asked me to go to the steeplehouse with her, for she was not wholely come off, I said, 'I must do as I am ordered by the Lord', so I left her and walked into the fields, and then the word of the Lord came to me to go to the steeplehouse after them and when I came the priest Lampitt was singing with his people. His spirit and his stuff was so foul that I was moved of the Lord to speak to him and the people after they had done singing; and the word of the Lord was to them, he was not a Jew that is one outward, but he was a Jew that is one inward, whose praise was not of men but of God. ⟨Then I showed them⟩ that God was come to teach his people by his spirit and to bring them off all their old ways, religions, churches, and worship, for all their religions, and worship, and ways were but talking of other men's words, for they were out of

[1] Margaret Fell (1614-1702), wife of Judge Thomas Fell. Her home now became the cradle of the new movement and she its nursing mother. In 1669 she married George Fox.

the life and spirit that they were in that gave them forth.

One Justice Sawrey cried out, ' Take him away '; and Judge Fell's wife said to the officers, ' Let him alone, why may not he speak as well as any other '; and Lampitt said for deceit, ' Let him speak ', and so at last when I had declared a pretty while, Justice John Sawrey, a rotten professor who was very full of hypocrisy, and deceit, and envy, caused me to be put out of the steeplehouse. I spoke to the people in the steeplehouse yard, and after came up to Swarthmoor Hall. Upon the First-day after I was moved to go to Aldingham steeplehouse and when the priest had done I spoke to the priest, but he got away, and I declared to the [v]people the Gospel, the Truth, the light of Jesus Christ in their own hearts, which he had enlightened them that they might all come to, that let them see all that ever they had done, and said, and acted, and that would be their teacher when they were about their labours. The priest told me Matthew, Mark, Luke and John were the Gospel, I told him the Gospel was the power of God.[v]

I passed to Rampside and there was a chapel in which one Thomas Lawson used to preach,[1] that was a high priest. He very lovingly spoke in the morning to his people of my coming in the afternoon, and when I was come all the country gathered thereaways. So I saw there was no place more convenient to declare to the people there than in the chapel, and so I went into the chapel and all was quiet; and the priest, Thomas Lawson, went not up into his pulpit but left all to me, and the everlasting Truth was largely declared that day which reached and entered into the hearts of people; and the everlasting day of the eternal God was proclaimed and all were quiet and received the Truth in the love of it. This priest came to be convinced and stands in Truth, and grew in the wisdom of God

[1] Rector of Rampside, d. 1691, noted botanist, afterwards became a Quaker schoolmaster.

[v]......[v] *S.J.*, pp. 19, 20.

mightily and remains to this day mighty serviceable in his place. He threw off his preaching for hire and his chapel and came to preach the Lord Jesus and his kingdom freely. And after that some rude people thought to have done him a mischief and cast scandals upon him but he was carried over all.

And after I returned back to Swarthmoor again and the next First-day I went to Dalton steeplehouse, and after the priest had done I declared the word of life to the people, turning them from darkness to light and from the power of Satan to God, and bringing them off their superstitious ways and their teachers made of man, to Christ their way and to be taught of him. [w]The people grew brutish and fell of ringing the bells, but the Truth came over all.[w]

And from thence I went into the Island of Walney and after the priest[1] had done I spoke to him. He got away and I spoke to the people the Truth as it was in Jesus. But the people being something rude, [w]after a while we passed away, and in the afternoon we went up again;[w] and we went to look for the priest at his house, and he would not be seen but the people said he went to hide himself in the haymow; and they went to look for him there but could not find him. And then they said he was gone to hide himself amongst the standing corn, [w]hearing we were coming,[w] but after they had looked for him there they could not find him there neither. So I came to James Lancaster's[2] who was convinced in that island, and from there I returned to Swarthmoor again, where the Lord's power seized upon Margaret Fell and her daughter Sarah and several of them.

Then I went to Baycliff where Leonard Fell was convinced, and he became a good minister, and several others were convinced there and came into Truth. The people

[1] Mr. Soutweeke was minister of Walney Island between 1649 and 1657.

[2] James Lancaster lived at North Scale in the northern part of the island.

[w]. . . . . .[w] *S.J.*, p. 20.

could not tell how to dispute, as they said, but would fain have put on some other to hold a talk with me; but I bid them fear the Lord and not in a light way to hold a talk of the Lord's words but practise them.

As I was walking I heard old people and workpeople to say, ' He is such a man as never was, he knows people's thoughts ', for I turned them to the divine light of Christ and his spirit that let them see all their thoughts, words, and actions, that were evil, that they had thought ⟨or spoken⟩, or acted; with which light they might see their sins and with the same light they might see their saviour, Christ Jesus, to save them from their sins, and that there was their first step to peace—to stand still in the light that showed their sin and transgressions and showed them how they were strangers to the covenant of promise, without God in the world, and in the Fall of old Adam, and in the darkness and death; and with the same light they may see Christ that died for them, who is their way to God and their redeemer and saviour.

And after this I went to a chapel beyond Gleaston which was built but never priest had preached in it,[1] where all the country up and down came; and a quiet, peaceable meeting it was, where the word of life was declared amongst them and many were convinced about Gleaston. From thence I returned to Swarthmoor again. And after I had stayed there a few days and most of all the family were convinced I went from thence back again into Westmorland.

And priest Lampitt had been amongst the professors at Kendal side and mightily had incensed them against me and told them I held many strange things. So I met with them that he had incensed and sat up all night with them at James Dickinson's house[2] and answered all their objections. Then they were thoroughly satisfied both with the Truth that I had declared, and dissatisfied with Lampitt's lies that he had divulged, so that he clearly lost the best of his

[1] A place called Dendron. The chapel was built in 1642, but not in regular use till long after the time of Fox's visit.

[2] At Crosthwaite.

hearers and followers and they came to see his deceit and to forsake him.

And so I passed on to John Audland's and Gervase Benson's and had great meetings amongst those people that were convinced before, and to John Blaykling's and Richard Robinson's and had mighty great meetings there, and so up towards Grisedale.

And after this Judge Fell was come home, and Margaret sent for me to return thither, and so I came through the country back to Swarthmoor again; and the priests and professors, and that ⟨envious⟩ Justice Sawrey, had incensed Judge Fell and Captain Sandys much against the Truth with their lies; and after dinner I answered him all his objections and satisfied him by Scripture so as he was thoroughly satisfied and convinced in his judgment. And he said, 'Art thou that George Fox that Justice Luke Robinson spoke so much in commendation of amongst many of the Parliament men ? ' for he had said that all the priests and professors in the nation were nothing to him. And I told him I had been with Justice Robinson and Justice Hotham in Yorkshire who were very loving and civil to me and were convinced in their judgments by the spirit of God ⟨that the principle which I bare testimony to was the Truth⟩: and they did see over the priests of the nation so that they and many others now came to be wiser than their teachers, and came to be taught of God and Christ, and so outstripped their teachers. ⟨After we had discoursed a pretty time together,⟩ Judge Fell was satisfied that I was the man; and he came also to see by the spirit of God in his heart over all the priests and teachers of the world and did not go to hear them for some years before he died; for he knew it was the Truth, and that Christ was the teacher of his people and their saviour. He wished that I was awhile with Judge Bradshaw[1] to convince him. There came over to Judge Fell that Captain Sandys, a wicked man, to incense him; and he was full of envy against me and yet he could use the apostles' words and

[1] John Bradshaw (1602-1659).

say, 'Behold I make all things new.' I told him then he must have a new God for his god was his belly.

And then that envious Justice Sawrey he came to Swarthmoor also, and I told him his heart was rotten and he was full of hypocrisy to the brim. Several people came also and I discerned their conditions and spoke unto them. Richard Farnsworth and James Nayler were come to Swarthmoor also to see me and the family. (And James Nayler was under a fast fourteen days.) And Judge Fell for all their opposition, let the meeting be kept at his house, and a great meeting was settled there in the Lord's power, to the tormenting of the priests and professors (which has remained above twenty years to this day), he being satisfied of the Truth. After I had stayed awhile and the meeting was settled, I went to Underbarrow and had a great meeting there and from thence to Kellet and had a great meeting at Robert Widders's[1] and many were convinced there, where several came from Lancaster and some from York.

And there was a captain stood up after the meeting was done and asked me where my leather breeches were, and I let the man run on awhile and at last I held up my coat and said, 'Here are my leather breeches which frighten all your priests and professors.'

And Margaret Fell had a vision of a man in a white hat that should come and confound the priests, before my coming into those parts.

And a man had a vision of me that a man in leather breeches should come and confound the priests, and this man's priest was the first that was confounded and convinced. And a great dread there was amongst the priests and professors concerning the man in leather breeches.

On market day I went to Lancaster and I spoke in the market at the cross in the dreadful power of God and

[1] Robert Widders (*c.* 1615-1686) lived at Over Kellet. William Moore, priest of Kellet received twenty-one queries dated 30th August, 1652, believed to be from George Fox.

declared the day of the Lord to them and against all their deceitful merchandise, and preached righteousness and Truth which they should all walk and live in and follow after, and where they might find the spirit of God to guide them to it. Several people came to my lodging and many were convinced there and stand to this day. And a meeting there was settled in the power of God.

And on the First-day ⟨following, in the forenoon⟩ I had a great meeting in the street of soldiers and people and declared the word of life and the everlasting Truth to them, and showed them their teacher, Christ Jesus, and all the traditions that they had lived in, and all their worships and religions; and that their profession was good for nothing that lived out of the life and power of them that gave forth the Scriptures, and so turned them to the light of Christ, the heavenly man, and to the spirit of God in their own hearts and where they might find God and Christ and his kingdom and know him their teacher. And in the afternoon I went up to the steeplehouse at Lancaster, and when I had declared the Truth to both priest[1] and people and showed them the deceits they lived in and the power and spirit of God that they wanted, they haled me out and stoned me along the streets till I came to John Lawson's[2] house.

And another First-day I went to [x]Halton[x] steeplehouse by the water-side, to one priest Whitehead,[3] and [x]after the priest had done[x] declared the Truth to the priest and people in the dreadful power of God. There was a doctor came to me who was so full of envy that he said he could find it in his heart to run me through with his rapier though he was hanged for it the next day; yet this man came to be convinced ⟨so far as to be⟩ loving to Friends; and some people were convinced that way and stood faithful to God

[1] William Marshall, cf. p. 133, n. 3.

[2] John Lawson lived in Leonardgate, Lancaster.

[3] Thomas Whitehead (*c.* 1599-1679), rector of Halton on the river Lune.

[x]. . . . . .[x] *S.J.*, p. 21.

and Christ and his teaching, ⟨and a meeting was settled in the power of God⟩.

And so I returned back into Westmorland again and spoke through Kendal upon a market day. [y]I had silver in my pocket and I was moved to throw it out amongst the people as I was going up the street before I spoke, and my life was offered up amongst them, and the mighty power of the Lord was seen in preserving and the power of the Lord was so mighty and so strong that people flew like chaff before me, and ran into their houses and shops, for fear and terror took hold upon them. I was moved to open my mouth and lift up my voice aloud in the mighty power of the Lord, and to tell them the mighty day of the Lord was coming upon all deceitful merchandise and ways, and to call them all to repentance and a turning to the Lord God, and his spirit within them, for it to teach them and lead them, and tremble before the mighty God of Heaven and earth, for his mighty day was coming; and so passed through the streets. And many people took my part and several were convinced. And when I came to the town's end, I got upon a stump and spoke to the people, and so the people began to fight some for me and some against me, and I went and spoke to them and they parted again. So after a while I passed away without any harm.[y]

The First-day after, I had a mighty meeting at Miles Bateman's[1] aforesaid where many were convinced.

And I was moved to declare to the people how all people in the Fall were gone from the image of God, and righteousness, and holiness, and were as wells without the water of life, clouds without the heavenly rain, trees without the heavenly fruit, and were in the nature of beasts, and serpents, and tall cedars, and oaks, and bulls, and heifers,—so they might read this nature within, as the prophet described, to people that were out of Truth,—and how that they were in the nature of dogs and swine, biting and rending, and the nature of briars, thistles and thorns, and like the owls and dragons in the night, and like the wild asses and horses, snuffing up, and like the

[1] Miles Bateman, father and son, lived at Underbarrow.

[y]. . . . . .[y] Cf. *S.J.*, pp. 21-22.

mountains and rocks, and crooked and rough ways. So I exhorted them to read these without, and within in their nature, and to read without the wandering stars, and look within, all that were come to the bright and morning star. As their fallow ground must be ploughed up before it bore seed to them, so must the fallow ground of their heart be ploughed up before they bear seed to God. So all these names were spoken to man and woman since they fell from the image of God; and as they do come to be renewed again up into the image of God, they come out of the nature and so out of the name.

And many more things of this nature were declared to them and they turned to the light of Christ by which they were turned to Christ; by which they might see him their substance and their way, salvation, and free teacher. ⟨Many were convinced at that time.⟩

And after I had travelled up and down in those countries and had great meetings I came to Swarthmoor again, [z]over the sands.[z]

And after I had visited Friends awhile in those parts I heard of a great meeting of priests at Ulverston on a lecture day, and I went down and went into the steeplehouse in the dread and power of the Lord. When the priest had done I spoke amongst them the word of the Lord; which was as a hammer and a fire amongst them. And though Lampitt had been at variance with most of the priests before, yet against the Truth he and all joined together; and the mighty power of the Lord was so over all that priest Bennet[1] [z]spoke to me and asked me if I had the spirit of discerning, I told him I had, which made him to tremble.[z] And he said the steeplehouse shook and he was afraid and trembled and thought that the steeplehouse would fall on his head, and he went his ways out for fear, speaking a few confused words: and the mighty power [z]and dread of the Lord God came over all, that answered the witness in many; and the graves opened and the dead heard the voice of God.[z]

[1] Philip Bennet, M.A., sometime curate of Ulverston, at this time curate of Cartmel.

[z]. . . . . .[z] *S.J.*, p. 23.

Though there were a-many priests there they had no power as yet to persecute.

And after, I came up to Swarthmoor again, and there came up four or five priests, and I asked them whether any of them could say they ever had a word from the Lord to go and speak to such or such a people and none of them durst say so. But one of them burst out into a passion and said he could speak his experiences as well as I; but I told him experience was one thing but to go with a message and a word from the Lord as the prophets and the apostles had and did, and as I had done to them, this was another thing.

Could any of them say they had such a command or word from the Lord at any time? But none of them could answer to it. But I told them the false prophets and false apostles and anti-christs could use the words and speak of other men's experiences that never knew or heard the voice of God and Christ; and such as they might get the good words and experience of others. ⟨This puzzled them much and laid them open.⟩

And at another time there were several priests at Judge Fell's, and he was by; and I asked them the same question, whether ever they had heard the voice of God or Christ to bid them go to such or such a people to declare his word or message unto them, for any that could but read might declare the experiences of the prophets and apostles. Hereupon Thomas Taylor,[1] an ancient priest, did ingenuously confess before Judge Fell that he had never heard the voice of God nor Christ, to send him to any people, but he spoke his experiences, and the experiences of the saints and preached that, which did astonish Judge Fell, for he and all people did look that they were sent from God and Christ.

So Thomas Taylor came to be convinced at that time and travelled with me into Westmorland. We came to Crosland steeplehouse and there the people were gathered

[1] Thomas Taylor (*c.* 1617-1682) came from Carlton in Craven, near Skipton; early preacher of Quakerism, many times imprisoned.

and they would have had me go into the steeplehouse, and I said, 'It is no matter.' And there came another priest and a high constable; and this was the second day after Thomas Taylor was convinced; and the Lord opened his mouth there amongst the people that he began to declare how he had been before he was convinced and like the Pharisee that was converted to the kingdom he brought forth things new and old to the people and told them how the priests were out of the way. This did torment the other priests, and some little discourse I had with them, but they fled away, and a precious meeting there was. The Lord's power was over all and people were turned to God by his spirit, with which they came to know Christ, and God, and the Scriptures. And so I passed to several meetings, visiting Friends, and had mighty meetings in Westmorland.

And about this time the priests began to prophesy that within a month we should be all scattered again and come to nothing.

About this time, 1652, Christopher Taylor,[1] another minister, Thomas Taylor's brother, was convinced also of Truth; and they both became ministers of the Gospel and great sufferers they were; and they came to know the word of the Lord and were commanded to go to many steeplehouses and markets and places and preach Christ freely. Also John Audland and Francis Howgill and John Camm[2] came forth to be faithful ministers, and Edward Burrough, and Richard Hubberthorne,[3] and Miles and Stephen Hubbersty and Miles Halhead and several others, and so continued till their deaths, and multitudes were turned to the Lord.

And James Nayler travelled up and down in many places

[1] Christopher Taylor (*c.* 1620-1686), opened a school at Waltham Abbey, Essex; later emigrated to Pennsylvania.

[2] John Camm (1605-1657), early publisher of Quakerism, especially in Bristol.

[3] Richard Hubberthorne (1628-1662), a leading preacher of Quakerism, especially in Norwich and London.

amongst the people that were convinced. At last he and Francis Howgill were cast into Appleby gaol by the malicious priests and magistrates. And Francis Howgill and Edward Burrough died prisoners for the Lord's Truth.

After a time I returned into Lancashire again and went to Ulverston, and though Lampitt had preached and said that there was a people that did own the teachings of God, and that men and women should come to declare the Gospel, after it came to be fulfilled he persecuted it and them. I went to Lampitt's house where there was abundance of priests and professors gathered after their lecture, and there I had great disputings with them concerning Christ and the Scriptures, for they were loath to let that trade go down which they made of Christ's and the apostles' and prophets' words; but the Lord's power went over the heads of them all and his word of life was held forth, though many of them were exceeding devilish and envious. Yet after this many priests and professors came to me from far and nigh, of whom the simple-minded and innocent were satisfied and went away refreshed, but the fat and full were fed with judgment and sent empty away. And that was the word of the Lord to be divided to them. Then Lampitt began to rage when meetings were set up and we met in houses, and he said we forsook the temple and went to Jeroboam's calf's houses; so that many professors began to see how he was degenerated from that which he formerly held and preached.

And it was declared both to professors, priests, and people how that their houses called churches were more like Jeroboam's calf-houses ⟨even the old mass-houses⟩ which they had set up in the dark times of popery which they still held up, which God never commanded; for that temple which God had commanded at Jerusalem Christ came to end. And they that believed in him, their bodies came to be the temples of God and Christ and the Holy Ghost, for them to dwell in them and walk in them. All such were gathered into the name of Jesus, whose name was above every name, and there was no salvation by any other name under the whole heaven but by the name of Jesus. And these met together in several dwelling-houses which were not called the temple nor the church, but their bodies were the temples of God and the believers were the Church which Christ was the head of. So Christ was not called the head of an old house which was made by men's hands, neither did he come to purchase and sanctify and redeem with his blood an old house which they called their church, but the people which he is the head of.

A great deal of work had I with priests and people with their old mass-houses which they called their churches, which were made by men's hands; for the priests had persuaded people that it was the house of God, and the apostle said Christ purchased his Church with his own blood, and Christ calls his Church his spouse, and his bride, the Lamb's wife. So this title Church and spouse was not given to an old house but to his Church that was his people and true believers, and the apostle saith, ' Whose house we are.' So the people are God's house and dwelling.

And after this, of a lecture day, I was moved to go again to Ulverston steeplehouse where there was abundance of professors, and priests, [aa]and friendly people to hear me, and queried if I would be there.[aa]

And I went up to Lampitt who was blustering on in his preaching: and one John Sawrey,[1] called a Justice of peace, came to me after the Lord had opened my mouth to speak, [bb]and took me by the hand, and asked me if I would speak, and I said, ' Yes.'[bb] And he said if I would speak according to the Scriptures I should speak and I stranged at him for speaking so to me, ⟨for I did speak according to the Scriptures⟩. And I told him I would speak according to the Scriptures and bring the Scriptures to prove what I had to say, for I had some thing to speak to Lampitt and them; and then this Sawrey said I should not speak, contradicting his own saying where he said I should speak if I

[1] Of Plumpton Hall, Ulverston, a member of the Nominated Parliament, 1653, a Baptist.

[aa]......[aa] *S.J.*, p. 23. [bb]......[bb] *S.J.*, p. 23.

would speak according to Scriptures. [cc]Then the rude people said to the Justice, ' Give him us ! ' and he did. So of a sudden all the people in the steeplehouse were in an outrage and an uproar, that they fell upon me in the steeplehouse before his face, with staves and fists and books, and knocked me down and kicked me and trampled upon me. And many people tumbled over their seats for fear and were knocked down, and the Justice and the priests among them. And at last the Justice said among the rude people, ' Give him me ! ' and he came and took me from amongst the people again and led me out of the steeplehouse and put me into the hands of four officers and constables, and bid them whip me and put me out of the town. And they led me about a quarter of a mile, some taking hold by my collar and some by the arms and shoulders and shook me by the head, and some by the hands, and dragged me through mire and dirt and water.[cc] And many friendly people that were come to the market, and some into the steeplehouse to hear me, many of them they knocked down, and broke their heads also. And the blood ran down several people so as I never saw the like in my life, as I looked at them when they were dragging me along. And Judge Fell's son running after to see what they would do with me, they threw him into a ditch of water and cried, ' Knock out the teeth of his head ! ' And some got staves and some got hedge stakes and some got holme bushes and some got willows.

And when they had led me to the common moss, and a multitude of people following, the [cc]constables took me and gave me a wisk over the shoulders with their willow rods, and so thrust me amongst the rude multitude which then fell upon me with their hedge stakes and clubs and staves and beat me as hard as ever they could strike on my head and arms and shoulders, and it was a great while before they beat me down and mazed me, and at last I fell down upon the wet common. There I lay a pretty space,[cc] and when I recovered myself again, and saw myself lying on a

[cc]......[cc] Cf. *S.J.*, p. 24.

watery common and all the people standing about me, I lay a little still, and the power of the Lord sprang through me, and the eternal refreshings refreshed me, that I stood up again in the eternal power of God and stretched out my arms amongst them all, and said again with a loud voice, 'Strike again, here is my arms and my head and my cheeks.' And there was a mason, a rude fellow, a professor called, he gave me a blow with all his might just a-top of my hand, as it was stretched out, with his walking rule-staff. And my hand and arm was so numbed and bruised that I could not draw it in unto me again [dd]but it stood out as it was. Then the people cried out, 'He hath spoiled his hand, for ever having any use of it more.' The skin was struck off my hand and a little blood came,[dd] and I looked at it in the love of God, and I was in the love of God to them all that had persecuted me.

And after a while the Lord's power sprang through me again, and through my hand and arm, that in a minute I recovered my hand and arm and strength in the face and sight of them all [ee]and it was as well as it was before, and I had never another blow afterward.[ee]

And then they began to fall out amongst themselves, and some of them came to me and said if I would give them money they would secure me from the rest; [ee]but I denied it, and[ee] was moved of the Lord to declare unto them the word of life, and showed them their false Christianity, and the fruits of their priests, and how they were more like heathens and the Jews and not like Christians. [ee]And they said if I came into the town again they would kill me.[ee]

And so I was moved of the Lord to come up again through them and up into Ulverston market, and there meets me a man with a sword, a soldier.[1] 'Sir', said he, 'I am your servant, I am ashamed that you should be thus abused, for you are a man', said he. He was grieved and said he would assist me in what he could, and I

[1] Leonard Pearson. *J.F.H.S.*, xxxi.
[dd]......[dd] Cf. *S.J.*, p. 24. [ee]......[ee] *S.J.*, p. 24.

told him that it was no matter, the Lord's power was over all.

And so as I walked through the people in the market there was none of them had power to touch me. And this man with his sword was walking after me and some of the market people [ff]were striking up of Friends' heels[ff] in the market and I turned me about and I saw the soldier amongst them with his naked rapier; and I run amongst them and catched hold of his hand that his rapier was in and bid him put up his sword again if he would come along with me, ⟨for I was willing to draw him out from the company, lest some mischief should be done⟩.

And so he came to the town's end with me. So I came up to Swarthmoor again and there they were dressing the heads and hands of Friends and friendly people that were broken that day by the professors and hearers of Priest Lampitt. And my body and arms were yellow, black, and blue with the blows and bruises that I received amongst them that day.

And within a few days after, seven men fell upon this soldier aforesaid and beat him cruelly because he had taken my part; for it was the custom of this country to run twenty or forty people upon one man. They fell so upon Friends in many places that they could hardly pass the highways, stoning and beating and breaking their heads.

And then the priests began to prophesy again that within a half year we should be all put down and gone.

And about a fortnight after, I went into Walney Island and James Nayler went with me and we stayed over night at a little town on this side called Cocken,[1] and had a meeting where there was one convinced. [gg]And in the evening there came a man who bound himself with an oath that he would shoot me with a pistol, many people being in the fold.[2] And the people of the house went forth.

[1] Near Barrow in Furness.

[2] i.e. yard.

[ff]. . . . . .[ff] *S.J.*, p. 25.

And after a while I walked forth, the power of the Lord was so mighty to the chaining of them in the yard that the man of the house, being a professor, was so tormented and terrified that he went into a cellar to his prayers. And after, I went into the house when Truth was come over them. And there was a raw man of the house, seeing the Truth had come over, he fell to speaking and let up their spirits. And so I walked out of the house into the yard again and fell a-speaking; and then the fellow drew his pistol. And he snapped his pistol at me but it would not go off, though he struck fire. And some held him and some carried me away, and so through the power of the Lord God I escaped.[gg] So the Lord's power came over them all, though there was a great rage in the country. And the next morning I went over in a boat to James Lancaster's, [hh]he being a Friend. But his wife, being an enemy to Truth, had gathered about forty rude fellows, fishermen and the like,[hh] <for the people had persuaded James Lancaster's wife that I had bewitched her husband, and they had promised her that if she would let them know when I came hither, they would be my death>. So as soon as I came to land they rushed out with staves, clubs and fishing poles and fell upon me with them, beating and punching and thrust me backward to the sea. And when they had thrust me almost into the sea, I saw they would have knocked me down there in the sea [hh]and thought to have sunk me down into the water.[hh] So I stood up and thrust up into the middle of them again. But they all laid at me again and knocked me down and mazed me. And when I was down and came to myself I looked up and I saw James Lancaster's wife throwing stones at my face and James Lancaster her husband was lying [hh]over my shoulders[hh] to save the blows and stones. I could hardly tell whether my head was cloven to pieces it was so bruised; nevertheless I was raised up by the power of God. Then

[gg]......[gg] Cf. *S.J.*, p. 25; *Camb. Jnl.*, i, 60; *A Short Account*, Portfolio 36.172. See *Bulletin F.H.A.*, Vol. 39, p. 27.
[hh]......[hh] *S.J.*, pp. 25, 26.

they beat me down into the boat, and James Lancaster came into the boat to me and carried me over the water. ⟨But while we were on the water within their reach they struck at us with long poles and threw stones after us.⟩ We saw afterwards they were beating James Nayler, for while they were beating of me he walked up into a field and they never minded him till I was gone, and then they fell upon him and all their cry was ' Kill him, kill him '. Then James Lancaster went back again to look after James Nayler. And when I came on the other side of the water to the town [ii]where the man had bound himself with an oath to shoot me,[ii] all the town rose up with pitch-forks, staffs and flails and muck-hooks to keep me out of the town, and cried, ' Kill him, knock him in the head, bring the cart and carry him away to the grave-yard.' [ii]But they did not, but[ii] guarded me with all those weapons a pretty way off out of the town, [ii]but did not much abuse me and after a while left me.[ii] So I was alone and came to a ditch of water and washed me, for [ii]I was very dirty and wet and much bruised.[ii] So I walked a matter of three miles [jj]from that place where I washed me[jj] to Thomas Hutton's house at Rampside, where Thomas Lawson the priest lodged, that was convinced. And I could hardly speak to them when I came in I was so bruised, and I told them where I left James Nayler and they went and took each of them a horse and went and brought him thither that night. [jj]And I desired to have a little beer and I should go to bed, but when I was in bed I could turn me no more than a sucking child, I was so bruised,[jj] and the next day Margaret Fell hearing of it at Swarthmoor sent a horse for me, and as I was riding the horse knocked his foot against a stone and stumbled that it shook me and so pained me as it seemed worse to me than all my blows, my body was so tortured. So I came to Swarthmoor; and my body was exceedingly bruised.

And Justice Sawrey and Justice Thompson[1] of Lancaster

[1] George Toulnson (d. 1655), ex-Mayor.

[ii] . . . . . . [ii] *S.J.*, p. 26. [jj] . . . . . . [jj] *S.J.*, p. 26.

granted forth a warrant for me, but Judge Fell, coming home, they did not serve it upon me, for he was out of the country all this time that I was thus abused and cruelly used.

And so he sent forth warrants into Walney[1] to the constables to apprehend all those riotous persons, and some of them fled the country, and destruction is come upon many of them since. James Lancaster's wife came after to be convinced and many of those bitter persecutors also; judgments of God fell upon some of the persecutors.

And Judge Fell asked me to give him a relation of my persecution and I told him they could do not otherwise, they were in such a spirit; and they manifested their priests' fruits and profession and religion. So he told his wife that I made nothing of it and spoke as a man that had not been concerned; for the Lord's power healed me again.

I went to Yealand [kk]and had a great meeting of Friends in the evening at Silverdale where there came a priest with a pistol[kk] in his hand under a pretence to light a pipe of tobacco, [kk]but his intent was to have done a mischief with his pistol to me, he being a desperate fellow.[kk] The maid told her master and he clapped his hands a both sides the door posts and told him he should not come in there, and looking up he spied a great company of men over the wall, one with a musket and others with stakes. But the Lord God prevented their bloody design, that they went their ways and did no harm.

[1] Judge Fell's warrant was dated 3rd November, 1652.
[kk]. . . . . .[kk] *S.J.*, p. 22.

CHAPTER VI

AND after this I went to Lancaster[1] with Judge Fell to the Sessions where John Sawrey aforesaid, and Justice Thompson had given forth a warrant to apprehend me.

So I appeared at the Sessions upon the hearing of it, but was never apprehended by it. And there I met Colonel West,[2] another justice.

As I was going along to Lancaster with Judge Fell he said to me he had never such a matter brought before him before, and he could not tell well what to do in the business. Then I said unto him, when Paul was brought before the rulers, and the Jews and priests came down to accuse him and laid many false charges against him, Paul stood still all that while; and when they had done, the governor Festus and King Agrippa beckoned to him to speak for himself, which Paul did and cleared himself of all those false accusations. So he might do by me.

So when they were set in their Sessions there appeared against me forty priests; and they chose one priest Marshall[3] of Lancaster to be their orator, for two priests' sons and a priest had sworn against me that I had spoken blasphemy. They heard all that the priests could say and charge against me, and their orator sat by and explained their sayings. And when they had examined one of them upon his oath, then they examined another, and he was so confounded that he could not answer directly but said the other could say it, which made the Justices say, 'Have you sworn it upon your oath and now say that he can say it? It seems you did not hear those words spoken yourself though you have sworn to it'; and so these witnesses were confounded amongst themselves.

[1] On 18th October, 1652.
[2] William West, a member of the Nominated or Little Parliament.
[3] Dr. William Marshall, later a physician in London.

The charges against George Fox and his answers thereto.

1. *That he did affirm that he had the divinity essentially in him.*

Answer. For the word essentially, it is an expression of their own, but that the saints are the temples of God and God doth dwell in them, that I witness and the Scripture doth witness, and if God doth dwell in them the divinity dwelleth in them and the Scripture saith the saints shall be made partakers of the divine nature, this I witness. (2 Cor. vi. 15; Eph. iv. 6; 2 Pet. i. 4.)

2. *Both baptism and the Lord's Supper are unlawful.*

Answer. As for the word unlawful, it was not spoken by me, but the sprinkling of infants I deny, and there is no Scripture that speaketh of a sacrament; but the baptism that is in Christ with one spirit into one body, that I confess; and the bread that the saints break is the body of Christ and the cup that they drink is the blood of Jesus Christ, this I witness. (Gal. iii. 27; John vi. 13-58; 2 Cor. x. 16.)

3. *He did dissuade men from reading the Scriptures telling them it was carnal.*

Answer. For dissuading men from reading the Scriptures, it is false, for they were given to be read as they are and not to be made a trade upon. But the letter is carnal and killeth, but that which gave it forth is spiritual and eternal and giveth life. This I witness. (2 Cor. iii. 6.)

4. *That he was equal with God.*

Answer. That was not so spoken, but he that sanctifieth and they that are sanctified are all of one in the Father and the Son, and that ye are the sons of God. The Father and the Son are one, and we of his flesh and of his bone; this the Scripture doth witness. (Heb. ii. 11; Eph. v. 31.)

5. *That God taught deceit.*

Answer. That is false, and never was so spoken by me.

6. *That the Scriptures were anti-christ.*

Answer. That is false and was never spoken by me; but they which profess the Scripture's spirit and live not in the life and power of them, as they did which gave them forth, that I witness to be anti-christ.

7. *That he was the judge of the world.*

Answer. The saints shall judge the world, the Scripture doth witness, whereof I am one, and I witness the Scripture fulfilled. (1 Cor. vi. 2, 3.)

8. *That he was as upright as Christ.*

Answer. Those words were not so spoken by me, but as he is, so are we in this present world, and that the saints are made the righteousness of God; that the saints are one in the Father and the Son; that we shall be like him; that all teaching which is given forth by Christ is to bring the saints to perfection, even to the measure, stature, and fullness of Christ, this the Scripture doth witness, and this I do witness to be fulfilled. (1 John iii. 2; iv. 17; Eph. iv. 1-13.)

When once you deny the Truth then you are given over to believe lies and speak evil of them which live in the Truth, and your lies and envying lie upon them the righteous, you whose minds are envious and sow the seed of envy and make others envious. Oh, therefore, tremble before the Lord ye hypocrites, and mind the light of God in you, which shows you the deceit of your hearts, and obey that. Disobeying your teacher is your condemnation. Hating that light, you hate Christ.

And so I cleared all these things which they charged against me as aforesaid, and several other people that were at the meeting when they said I spoke those words they charged against me, they witnessed that the oath they had taken was altogether false and that no words like those they had sworn against me were spoken by me at that meeting. For indeed there was at that meeting most of the serious men of that side of the country at that time, who were at the Sessions and had heard me at the meeting aforesaid and at other meetings.

And Colonel West stood up who had long been weak, and blessed the Lord and said he never saw so many sober people and good faces together all the days of his life. He said that the Lord had healed him that day, [a]for he had been sick,[a] and he said, 'George, if thou hast anything to say to the people, thou mayest freely declare it in the open Sessions.' So I was moved of the Lord to speak, and as soon as I began, priest Marshall, their orator, goes his ways. And this I was moved to declare, that the Scriptures were given forth by the spirit of God and all people must first come to the spirit of God in themselves by which they might know God and Christ, of whom the prophets and the apostles learnt; and by the same spirit they might know the holy Scriptures and the spirit which was in them that gave them forth; so that spirit of God must be in them that come to know them again, by which spirit they might have fellowship with the Son and the Father and with the Scriptures and one with another, and without it they cannot know neither God, nor Christ, nor the Scriptures, nor have fellowship one with another.

And I had no sooner spoken these words but six priests that stood behind my back burst out into a passion, and there was one priest Jaques[1] said that the letter and the spirit were inseparable. And I said, 'If so, then every one that has the letter has the spirit and they may then buy the spirit with the letter of the Scriptures.'

Upon this, Judge Fell and Colonel West reproved the priests, seeing their darkness, and told them that then they might carry the spirit in their pockets as they did the Scriptures, and then all the priests rushed out in a rage against the justices because they could not have their bloody ends upon me, seeing they were so confounded. ⟨So the justices, seeing the witnesses did not agree, and that they were brought to answer the priests' envy, and that all

[1] John Jacques, vicar of Bolton-le-Sands.

[a]. . . . . .[a] *S.J.*, p. 27.

their evidence was not sufficient to make good their charge against me, discharged me.⟩ Then Judge Fell spoke to Justices Sawrey and Thompson and superseded their warrant and showed them the errors of it. [b]Judge Fell was made very serviceable to Truth, for his understanding being open; and most of his family came into the Truth.[b]

And multitudes of people praised God that day for it was a joyful day. There was Justice Benson of Westmorland who was convinced, and Mayor Rippon[1] who was mayor of the town of Lancaster who was convinced also. It was a day of everlasting salvation to hundreds of people, for the Lord Jesus Christ the way and free teacher was set up and his everlasting Gospel and word of life was preached over the heads of the priests and such money-preachers.

So the Sessions broke up and several friendly people and professors spoke to the priests in their inns and the streets. The Lord that day opened abundance of mouths to speak his word of life unto them, and they fell like an old rotten house. And the cry was amongst all people far and nigh that the Quakers had got the day and the priests were fallen.

And many were made ministers of the everlasting word of life and of the Gospel at that time, and they preached it freely. And Thomas Briggs was convinced that day and declared against his priest Jaques. For before that time he had discoursed with a Friend concerning Truth; which Friend, one John Lawson held perfection, and Thomas Briggs said unto him, 'Dost thou hold perfection?' and he up with his hand and would have struck the Friend a box on the ear. But at this day, Thomas Briggs came to be convinced, and became a faithful minister of the Gospel, and stands to this day.

⟨When the Sessions were over, James Nayler, who was present, gave a brief account of the proceedings in a letter to Friends, which is here added.

[1] Thomas Rippon, mayor in 1653 and 1654.

[b]. . . . . .[b] *S.J.*, p. 27.

Dear Friends and Brethren in the Lord Jesus Christ,

My dear love unto you all . . . the Lord doth much manifest his love and power in these parts. On the second day of last week, my brother George and I were at Lancaster; there were abundance of Friends from all parts, and a great sort which sided with the priests, giving out that they now hoped to see a stop put to that great work which had gone on so fast, and with such power that their kingdom is much shaken. We were called before Judge Fell, Colonel West, Judge Sawrey, etc., to answer what was charged against George. There were three witnesses to eight particulars, but they were much confused in themselves; which gave much light unto the Truth, whereby the justices did plainly see that it was envy; and they divers times told them so. One of the witnesses was a young priest, who confessed he had not meddled, had not another priest sent for him and set him on work. The other witnesses were two priests' sons. It was proved there by many that heard one of them say that if he had power he would make George deny his profession, and that he would take away his life. This was a single witness to one of the greatest untruths that was charged against George; and the justices told him that they saw, because he could not take away his life, he went about to take away his liberty . . . The justices, Judge Fell and Colonel West, were much convinced of the Truth, and did set up justice and equity; and have much silenced the rage of the people. Many bitter spirits were at Lancaster to see the event, but went home and cried the priests had lost the day . . .

There was a warrant against us at Appleby, but Justice Benson told them it was not according to law, and so it ceased. As I hear, he is a faithful man to the Truth. The priests began to preach against the justices, and said they were not to meddle in these things, but to end controversy between neighbour and neighbour. They are not pleased with the law because it is not in the statute to imprison us, as the priests that pleaded against us said . . . J.N.

Written from Kellet, 30th of 8th mo. [October], 1652.[1]〉

And I was in a fast this time and I was not to eat until this work of God was accomplished. So the Lord's power was wonderfully set over all and gave me dominion over all to his glory, and his Gospel was freely preached

[1] In full, Ellwood, pp. 90-92; *Bicent.*, i, 140-42.

that day over the heads of forty hireling priests. I stayed two or three days in Lancaster afterwards and had some meetings; but the rude and baser sort of people plotted together to have drawn me out of the house and to have thrown me over Lancaster bridge, but the Lord prevented them. And then they invented another stratagem. After a meeting was done in Lancaster, they brought down a distracted man in his waistcoat and another man in his waistcoat with a bundle of birchen rods bound together like besoms for them to have whipped me with them. But I was moved to speak to them in the Lord's mighty power which chained him and them, which brought him like a lamb. And I bid him throw his rods into the fire and burn them and he did so and I made him confess to the Truth and the light of Christ Jesus. So the Lord's power came over all, so as we parted in love and peace.

And when the priests had been in a rage against me at Lancaster, they had drawn up several petitions both in Westmorland and Lancashire to send to the Parliament, as you may see in the book entitled *Truth's Defence*, and the answer to the Westmorland petitions in *Saul's Errand to Damascus with his Packet of Letters*. [c]We got the petition and answered it and sent it to the Parliament before theirs was sent up. And the priests, when the time came they should have sent theirs up, did not send it up because it would cost so much money.[c][1]

But when the priests saw that they were overthrown at the Sessions at Lancaster, as aforesaid, some of the priests and envious justices informed the Judge Wyndham[2] against me, and in the open Court the judge made a speech against me at Lancaster Assizes. Colonel West being Clerk of the Assizes, the judge commanded him to grant out a warrant for me, and he spoke to the judge boldly of my innocency. The judge commanded him again either to write a warrant or go off his seat, and he told the

[1] Petition printed in Besse: *Sufferings*, 1753, i, p. 301.
[2] Probably Sir Hugh Wyndham (1603-1684).
[c]. . . . . .[c] *S.J.*, p. 27.

judge plainly he would not do it, he should do it himself if he would, and he would offer up all his estate and his body for me. So he stopped the judge, [d]which was of great service and came over the country,[d] and the Lord's power came over all and stopped the envy both in priests and justices.

The same night, I came into Lancaster at the Assizes and hearing of a warrant that was to be granted out for me, I judged it better to proffer myself, than for them to seek me. I went to Judge Fell's and Colonel West's chambers. And as soon as I came in they smiled at me, and Colonel West said, What, was I come into the dragon's mouth! So I walked up and down the town and no one questioned me nor meddled with me and I stayed there till the judge went out of town.

And thus the Lord's blessed power that is over all carried me over all and gave me dominion over all in his glorious work and service for his great name's sake.

And this persecuting John Sawrey at last was drowned; and the vengeance of God overtook the other justice, Thompson, that he was struck with the dead palsy upon the Bench and carried away off his seat and died.

And from Lancaster I returned to Robert Widders's,[1] and from thence I went to Thomas Leaper's[1] to a meeting of Friends in the evening. [e]And all the time of the meeting I felt swords and pistols about me lying in wait not far off, and was looking when they should come in.[e] And after the meeting was done, which was a very blessed meeting, I walked out afoot to Robert Widders's and I was no sooner gone but there came in a company of disguised men with naked swords and pistols cutting and hacking amongst the people of the house and put out all the candles. The people held up stools and chairs before them to save themselves. And after a while they drove all the people of the house out in the night and searched and looked for me,

[1] Robert Widders lived at Over Kellet, Thomas Leaper at Capernwray, both near Carnforth.

[d]......[d] *S.J.*, p. 72. [e]......[e] *S.J.*, p. 22.

who was the only person they looked for, and lay in wait in the highways by which I should have gone if I had ridden to Robert Widders's. So when I came to Robert Widders's some Friends came from the town where Thomas Leaper lived and gave us the relation of this; they were afraid they should come to search Robert Widders's house also for me to do me a mischief, but they came not.

Friends perceived they were some of them Frenchmen and Sir Robert Bindloss's[1] servants: for some of them said in their nation they used to tie the Protestants to trees and whip them and destroy them: these men used often to abuse Friends in their meetings and going from their meetings; for they took Richard Hubberthorne and several others out of the meeting and carried them a good way off into the fields and there bound them and left them bound in the winter season. And one of his servants came to Francis Fleming's[2] house and thrust his naked rapier in at his door and at his windows. And there came a cousin of Fleming's with a cudgel in his hand (who was no Friend) and bid him put up his rapier, but he would not, but vapored with it at him and was rude; and he up with his staff and knocked him down so as he made him sprawl on the ground and he took his rapier from him. Had it not been for Friends he would have run him through with it, and so Friends preserved his life that would have destroyed theirs.

From Robert Widders's I went to see Justice West, and Richard Hubberthorne went with me. We rid up the Sands[3] where never no man rid before, a very dangerous place, and swimmed over the water, not knowing the way nor the danger of the Sands, and came to West's house. And when we were come in he said to us, 'Did you not see two men riding over the sands? I shall have their clothes

[1] Sir Robert Bindloss (d. 1688), J.P., of Borwick Hall, Carnforth, baronet.

[2] There was a Francis Fleming (d. 1694) of Newton.

[3] The Sands stretched from Hest Bank, near Lancester to Ulverston, fourteen miles, uncovered at low water.

anon, for I am the coroner; they cannot escape drowning.' And we told him that we were the men; and he was astonished at it and wondered how we escaped drowning.

And then the priests and professors raised a report and a slander upon me that neither water could drown me nor could they draw blood of me, and that surely I was a witch. For when they beat me with great staves they did not much draw my blood but bruised my head and body. And thus the Lord's power carried me over their bloody murderous spirits, in whom the ground of witchcraft was, that kept them from God and Christ. But all these slanders were nothing to me as knowing that their forefathers, the apostate Jews, called the master of the house Beelzebub, and these apostate Christians from the life and power of God could do no less to his seed, so it was no strange thing for them to say so of the members of Christ who were heirs of him.

And about this time Richard Hubberthorne was in a great fast, and after was very weak; insomuch as people thought he was dead and it was reported that he was dead; and several Friends were sent for, and before they got to him the Lord's power had so raised him up that they met him with a bottle going for water to drink; so that Friends did admire at the wonderful power and work of God therein.

So I came back to Swarthmoor and visited Friends thataways, and brought the Lord's power over all the persecutors.

⟨I was moved to write several letters[1] to the magistrates, priests, and professors thereabouts who had raised persecution, to Justice John Sawrey, William Lampitt, priest of Ulverston, Priest Tatham,[2] and Adam Sandys, a chief hearer and follower of Lampitt.

It was upon me also to send this warning to the people of Ulverston in general.⟩

O People consider, who be within the parish of Ulverston; I was moved of the Lord to come into your public place to speak

[1] Ellwood, pp. 94-96, 99-101; *Bicent.* ed., i, 147-150, 153-155.

[2] Richard Tatham, vicar of Heversham.

among you to the directing of your minds to God, being sent of the Lord that you might know where you might find your teacher; that your minds might be stayed alone upon God, and you might not gad abroad without you for a teacher: for the Lord God alone will teach his people; and he is coming to teach them, and to gather his people from idols' temples and the customary worships, which all the world is trained up in. God hath given to every one of you a measure according to your ability, liars, drunkards, whoremongers, and thieves and who follow filthy pleasures, you have all this measure in you. This is the measure of the spirit of God that shows you sin, and shows you evil, and shows you deceit; which lets you see lying is sin, theft, drunkenness, and uncleanness, all these to be the works of darkness. Therefore mind your measure, for nothing that is unclean shall enter into the kingdom of God . . .

Therefore love the light which Christ hath enlightened you withal who saith, 'I am the light of the world', and doth enlighten every one that comes into the world. One, he loves the light and brings his works to the light, and there is no occasion at all of stumbling; and the other, he hates the light because his deeds are evil and the light will reprove him . . . And this light will teach thee, if thou lovest it, it will teach thee holiness and righteousness, without which none shall see God; but hating this light, it is your condemnation . . . The Lord is coming to teach his people himself, and gather his from hirelings and such as seek for their gain from their quarter, and from such as bear rule, by their means. The Lord is opening the eyes of foolish people that they shall see such as bear rule over them . . . Therefore to the light in you I speak, that when the book of conscience is opened then shall you witness me and you all judged out of it. So God Almighty direct your minds who love honesty and sincerity, that you may receive mercy in the time of need. Your teacher is within you; look not forth; it will teach you lying in bed, going abroad, to shun all occasion of sin and evil.

G.F.[1]

I writ also to those that most constantly followed William Lampitt the priest:

. . . To the light in all your consciences I do speak, which Christ Jesus doth enlighten you withal. It will show you time you have

[1] In full, *Camb. Jnl.*, i, 99-101; Ellwood, pp. 96-8; Bicent., i, 150-2.

spent and all your evil deeds you have done in that time, who follow such a teacher that acts contrary to this light and leads you into the ditch; and when you are all in the ditch together, teacher and people . . . remember you were warned in your life time. And if ever your eyes come to see repentance and own the light of Jesus Christ in you, you will witness me a friend of your souls and eternal good. Then will you own your condemnation; and that you must all own before you come into the new world where there is no end, but you that hate the light, whose deeds be evil, this light is your condemnation. When your condemnation is come upon you remember you were warned; and if you love this light, it will teach you, walking up and down and lying in bed, and never let you speak a vain word; but loving it you love Christ and hating the light there is the condemnation of you all. To you this is the word of God, from under it you can never pass, and never escape the terror of the Lord, in the state you are in, who hate the light.

G.F.[1]

⟨I writ also to Leonard Burton, priest of Sedbergh, much to the same purpose, he being in the same evil ground, nature, and practice which the other priests were in. Many other epistles also, and papers I writ about this time, as the Lord moved me thereunto, which I sent among the priests, professors, and people of all sorts, for the laying their evil ways open before them, that they might see and forsake them; opening the way of Truth unto them that they might come to walk therein, which are too many and large to be inserted in this place.⟩

After this I went into Westmorland, where a company of men laid wait for me with pikes and staves at a bridge, and they lighted on some Friends and missed me. But after, they came to the meeting with their pikes and staves; but Justice Benson being there and many considerable people, they were prevented from doing that mischief they intended, the Lord's power stopped them, so that they went away and did no hurt but raged much.

And so I came to Grayrigg where the priest[2] came to the

[1] In full, Ellwood, pp. 98-9; Bicent., i, 152-3.

[2] Richard Stookes.

meeting at Alexander Dixon's house,[1] which priest was a Baptist and a parish priest; and the Lord confounded him with his power. Some of his people stood upon the side of the house and tumbled down some milking pails, the house being so crammed; but after a while the priest and his company went away, being confounded, and raised a slander and said the Devil frightened him and took a side of the house down where we were in the meeting; which was all lies, but such as served the priests' and professors' turn to feed upon; and they printed it in a book.

And another time this priest came to another meeting a-top of the hill, and fell a-jangling. First he said the Scriptures were the word of God, and I told him they were the words of God but not Christ the Word. And I bid him prove it by Scripture, what he said; and then he said it was not the Scripture, and so set his foot upon the Bible and said it was but copies bound up together. And a great deal of unsavoury words came from him not worth mentioning. So we had a blessed meeting afterwards; the Lord's power and presence was felt amongst us; and he went his ways. Then after, he sent me a challenge to meet him at Kendal, and I sent him word I would meet him in his own parish, he need not go as far as Kendal. So we set the hour and met, and abundance of rude people were gathered to it, and some of his members, baptized people. They intended to have done mischief that day but God prevented them. And when we met I declared the day of the Lord to them and turned them to Christ Jesus; and he out with his Bible and said it was the word of God. I told him it was the words of God but not God the Word; his answer was he would prove the Scriptures to be the God before all the people. So I had a man that could write to take down both what he said and what I said as may be larger seen in my book of letters. But when he had spoken a great while he could not prove it; for I kept him to the Scripture for chapter and verse for it.

[1] Thursgill.

And in keeping him to prove that one error he had asserted, he ran into twenty. And the people gnashed their teeth and said he would have me anon. Thus the Baptist priest toiled till he sweated, and broiled himself and his company, all being full of wrath; and I heaped his assertions on the head of him and them all, so that at last they went away confounded and could prove nothing that they asserted. For I told them what the Scriptures said themselves, that they were the words of God but Christ was the Word. And so the Lord's power came over all and confounded their mischief which they intended against me. Friends were established in Christ, and the people that were his followers saw the folly of their teacher.

And after this I came through the country ⟨into Lancashire again⟩ visiting Friends. Priest Bennett of Cartmel had sent a challenge to dispute with me, and upon the First-day I came to his steeplehouse and there found him preaching. And when he had done I spoke to him and his people, but the priest would not stand to trial but went his ways: and a great deal of discourse I had with the people; and when I came forth into the steeplehouse yard and was discoursing with the professors and declaring of the Truth unto them, one of them sets his foot behind me and two of them run against my breast and threw me down against a grave stone, wickedly and maliciously seeking to have spoiled me, but I got up again and was moved of the Lord to speak to them. And there was one Richard Roper, one of the bitterest professors the priest had, was very fierce and zealous in his contention; and so I went up to the priest's house and a-many people followed after me and I desired him to come forth, seeing he had challenged me, but he would not at all come out or be seen. And this Roper after came to be convinced of God's eternal Truth, and became a fine minister and continued faithful to his death. So the Lord's power came over them all, which was very great.

⟨It was about the beginning of the year 1653, when⟩ I came to Swarthmoor again and went to a meeting at

Gleaston.[1] And there was another professor, and he challenged a dispute but I went to the house where he was and called him forth but he durst not meddle; so the Lord's power came over him also.

And so after a while I visited many meetings in Lancashire, ⟨and so came back to Swarthmoor again⟩.

And then James Milner and Richard Myers went out into imaginations. And a company followed them. And I was in a fast about ten days, ⟨my spirit being greatly exercised on Truth's account⟩. And as Judge Fell and Colonel Benson were in Swarthmoor Hall talking of the news in the News Book, of the Parliament, etc., I was moved to tell them that before that day fortnight the Long Parliament should be broken up and the Speaker plucked out of his chair. And that day fortnight Colonel Benson came again and was speaking to Judge Fell and said that now he saw that George was a true prophet; for Oliver had broken up the Parliament by that time.[2] And many openings I had of several things which would be too large to utter.

And James Milner and some of his company had true openings at the first; but after, got up into pride and so run out. And they sent for me and I was moved of the Lord to show them their goings forth. And they came to see their folly and condemned it; and they came in again and died in Truth.

And after, I went to a meeting at Arnside where there was a-many people; and I was moved of the Lord to say to Richard Myers amongst all the people, ' Prophet Myers, stand up upon thy legs ', for he was sitting down. And he stood up and stretched out his arm which had been lame a long time, and said, ' Be it known unto you all people and to all nations that this day I am healed ! ' And after the meeting was done, his father and mother could hardly believe it was made whole, and had him

[1] Fox wrote a paper there on 6th January, 1653.

[2] The Long Parliament which first met on 3rd November, 1640, was broken up on 20th April, 1653.

into an house and took off his doublet, and then they saw it was true. And he came to Swarthmoor meeting and there declared how the Lord had healed him. And after the Lord commanded him to go to York with a message from him, but he disobeyed the Lord; and the Lord struck him again so as he died about three quarters of a year after.

And great threatenings there were in Cumberland that if ever I came there they would take away my life; but when I heard of it I went into Cumberland to one Miles Wennington into the same parish but they had not power to touch me.

And also about this time Anthony Pearson, a great persecutor of Friends, was convinced at Appleby,[1] over whose head they carried a sword when he went to the Bench. And coming over to Swarthmoor, I being at Colonel West's they sent for me and Colonel West said, 'Go, George, for it may be of great service to the man'; and the Lord's power reached him. About this time the Lord opened several mouths to declare the Truth to priests and peoples so that several were cast into prison.

And after this I went again into Cumberland [f]where I saw the sparks of life rise before I came into it, and a multitude of people the Lord had there.[f] Anthony Pearson and his wife and several Friends went alongst with me to Bootle. Anthony Pearson went on to Carlisle Sessions for he was a Justice of the Peace in three counties.

And upon the First-day I went into the steeplehouse. And [f]the priest of the parish hearing of my coming, he had got another that came from London, to help him, and so I was moved to speak in his time, he uttered such wicked things, and therefore for the Truth's sake I was moved to speak to him if I had been imprisoned for it. So they hailed me out and people were mighty rude, and struck and beat me in the steeplehouse yard and one gave me a great blow upon the wrist with a great hedgestake,[f] with his full strength so that people thought he had broken my hand to pieces. [g]Yet I felt no harm; the power of the Lord

[1] About the beginning of 1654.

[f]. . . . . .[f] *S.J.*, p. 27.

bare all off. And the constable being a sober man rescued me out of their hands and would have set the fellow that struck me into the stocks but the rude people rescued him out of his hands.[g] The constable went a little way with us to keep the rude multitude off us; [g]and I told him he might go a little way on with us[g] to Joseph Nicholson's house [h]where we lodged; there lay a company of rude people by the way to have done us a mischief.

And in the afternoon I was moved to come up again to the market cross, and there sat me down with my friends about me. At last Friends were all moved to go into the steeplehouse, and then it came to me that I might go in.[h] And the priest had got another high priest that came from London to help him. [i]And so when I came in the priest was preaching, and all the Scriptures that he spake were of false prophets, and deceivers, and anti-Christs, and he brought them and threw them upon us. I sat me down and heard till he had done, though several Friends spoke to him in his time. So when he had done I began to speak to him, and he and the people began to be rude, and the constable stood up and charged them to keep peace 'in the name of the Commonwealth', and all was quiet. I took his Scriptures that he spoke of false prophets and anti-Christs, and deceivers, and threw them back upon him, and let him see that he was in the very steps of them.[i] But the priest began to rage and said I must not speak there. And then I told him he had his hour glass by which he had preached, and having done, the time was free for me as well as for him, for he was but a stranger. [j]And he accused me that I had broken the law in speaking to him in his time in the morning, and I told him he had broken the law then, in speaking in my time. So I called all people to the true teacher, out of the hirelings such as teach for the fleece and make a prey upon the people, for the Lord was come to teach his people himself by his spirit, and Christ saith,

[g]......[g] *S.J.*, p. 27. [h]......[h] *S.J.*, pp. 27, 28.
[i]......[i] *S.J.*, p. 28.

'Learn of me; I am the way' which doth enlighten every man that cometh into the world, that all through him might believe; and so to learn of him who had enlightened them, who was the Light, so we [j]had a brave meeting in the steeplehouse.[j] And all was quiet whilst I declared the Truth and the word of life to the people and I directed them to Christ their teacher. So when I had done I came forth; and both the priests were in such a fret and rage that they foamed at the mouth for anger against me. But the Lord's power came over them all.

<The priest of the place made an oration to the people in the steeplehouse yard, and said, 'This man hath gotten all the honest men and women in Lancashire to him; and now', he said, 'he comes here to do the same.' Then I said unto him, 'What wilt thou have left, and what have the priests left them, but such as themselves? For if it be the honest that receive the Truth and are turned to Christ, then it must be the dishonest that follow thee and such as thou art.' Some also of the priest's people began to plead for their priest and for tithes, but I told them it were better for them to plead for Christ, who had ended the tithing priesthood and tithes, and had sent forth his ministers to give freely as they had received freely.

So the Lord's power came over them all, and put them to silence, and restrained the rude people, that they could not do the mischief they intended. And when I came down again to Joseph Nicholson's house, I saw a great hole in my coat, which was cut with a knife, but it was not cut through my doublet, for the Lord had prevented their mischief.> And the next day there was a rude wicked man would have done violence to a Friend, but the Lord's power stopped him.

And I was moved to send James Lancaster to appoint a meeting at one of John Wilkinson's steeplehouses near Cockermouth, who had three parishes[1] under him and was

[1] Brigham (p. 154 post) and probably Mosser Chapel and Greysouthen.

[j]......[j] *S.J.*, p. 28.

a priest in great repute and esteem. So I stayed at Bootle in Millom till he came back again.

And some of the gentry in that country had made a plot against me; and as I was in the field they came to the house where I came from. They lighted on James Lancaster but did not much abuse him. But they came to Joseph Nicholson's house, and [k]a little boy with a rapier, and they came into the house where I was; I was just gone out of it into the fields, though I saw them when I was in the fields, but they came not to me, and they had intended to have set the boy on to have done mischief and to have murdered; but the Lord's hand prevented them and stopped them; and though others came to do us a mischief, one held another, and so through the power of the Lord we passed over them.[k] And they not finding me in the house, after a while they went their ways. And so I walked up and down in the fields that night and did not go to bed, as very often I used to do.

The next morning we passed away; and the next day we came to the steeplehouse where James Lancaster had appointed the meeting; and there were a dozen soldiers and their wives who were come from Carlisle. [l]People having notice of it, and not having seen me before, all the country people came in like as to a horse fair, and there came above a thousand people there.[l] I, lying short of the place at a house, sent all Friends before me. And there were some wicked women in a field hard by the house, and I saw they were witches, and I was moved to go ⟨out of my way into the fields⟩ unto them and declare unto them their conditions and that they were in the spirit of witch-craft.

And then I walked down towards the steeplehouse where I found James Lancaster speaking under a yew tree, and it was full of people so that I feared they would break it down. And I looked up and down for a place to stand upon to speak unto the people for they lay like people

[k] . . . . . . [k] *S.J.*, p. 28. [l] . . . . . . [l] *S.J.*, p. 29.

at a leaguer[1] all up and down; and after a while when I was discovered, and I saw that there was no place convenient to speak to the people from, a professor came to me and asked me whether I would go into the church [m]as he called it,[m] and I told him yes, [m]though I told him I denied all such places.[m]

So the people rushed in, and when I came the pulpit and the house were so full of people that I had much ado to get in; and they that could not get in stood about the walls. And when the people were settled I stood up ⟨on a seat⟩ and the Lord opened my mouth

to declare his everlasting Truth and his everlasting day, and to lay open all their teachers and their rudiments, traditions, and inventions that they had been in, in the night of apostacy, since the apostles' day; and to turn them to Christ their teacher; and to set up and direct them to his worship, and where to find the spirit and Truth that they might worship God in; and opened Christ's parables to them, and directed them to the spirit of God in them that would open the Scriptures and parables to them; and how all might come to know their Saviour and sit under his teaching, and come to be heirs of the kingdom of God, turning them from the darkness to the light, and the power of Satan unto God, so that every one might come to know who their teacher was, Christ Jesus and the Lord God, as the prophets and the apostles and the true Church did, and so to know both God and Christ's voice by which they might see all the false shepherds and teachers they had been under and see the true shepherd, priest, bishop, and prophet, Christ Jesus whom God commanded them to hear. And largely did I declare the word of life to them for about three hours time and all was still, and quiet, and satisfied.

And after I had more fully declared the word of life to them than is here mentioned I walked forth from amongst the people and the people passed away mightily satisfied. Anthony Pearson was at the meeting who was come from the Sessions. And there was a professor, following of me

[1] A military camp, or a besieging force.
[m]......[m] *S.J.*, p. 29.

and praising and commending of me, and his words were like a thistle to me and [n]his spirit was like a steeple,[n] and at last I turned about and bid him fear the Lord. There were four priests gathered together who came after the meeting was done; and one Priest Larkham[1] said, ' Sir, why do you judge so ? ' said he, ' you must not judge '. And I turned to him and said, ' Friend, dost not thou discern an exhortation from a judgment, for I admonished him to fear God and dost thou say I judge him ? ' And so I manifested him in discourse with him to be amongst the false prophets and covetous hirelings; and he and the two priests got soon away, and several people were moved to speak to them.

And then John Wilkinson[2] that was priest of that parish and two other parishes in Cumberland, when they were gone began to dispute against his own conscience several hours till generally the people turned against him. And he thought to have tired me out, but the Lord's power tired him out, and the Lord's Truth came over all and many hundreds were convinced that day and received the Lord Jesus Christ's free teaching with gladness. And many stand to this day and have died in the Truth under Christ's teaching.

The soldiers were convinced and their wives, and continued with me till the First-day. On the First-day I went to Cockermouth steeplehouse in [n]the forenoon[n] where the priest Larkham, that first opposed me as aforesaid, lived; and when the priest had done I began to speak and the people began to be rude, but the soldiers told them we had broken no law and then they were quiet. So I began to speak to the priest and laid him open amongst the false prophets and hirelings, at which word the priest got his ways and said, ' He calls me hireling ', which was true enough for all the people knew it.

[1] George Larkham (*c.* 1629-1700). Independent minister of Cockermouth.

[2] See also p. 315, post.

[n]. . . . . .[n] *S.J.*, p. 29.

And some of the great men of the town came to me and said, 'Sir, we have no learned men to dispute with you.' I told them I came not to dispute but to declare the way of salvation and the way of everlasting life, and so I declared largely the way of life and Truth to them and directed them to their teacher that had died for them and had bought them with his blood. And when I had done I passed away about two miles to ⟨Brigham⟩ another great steeplehouse of Wilkinson's that stood in a field, and the people were mightily affected and would have put my horse in the steeplehouse yard, but I said, 'No, the priest claims that. Carry him to an inn.'

And when I came into the steeplehouse yard I saw people coming as to a fair; and abundance were already gathered in the lanes and about the steeplehouse. Being hot and very thirsty I spied a brook and went down about a quarter of a mile and got a little water to drink and refreshed myself. And as I came up again I met the priest Wilkinson and as I was going by him, 'Sir', said he, 'will you preach to day? If you will', says he, 'I will not oppose you, not in word or thought'; but I said, 'Oppose it if thou wilt I have something to speak to the people. Thou carried thyself foolishly the other day and spakest against thy conscience and reason, so as thy hearers cried out against thee.' So I went away and left him, for he saw it was in vain to oppose, the people were so affected with the Lord's Truth. So I came into the steeplehouse yard; and not seeing any convenient place to speak over to the people, a professor came again and asked if I would not go into the church as he called it. And °it being hot without, and there being no place to command a people thereabouts,° I saw that would be the convenientest place to speak unto the people from, so I went in and stood up in a seat after the people were settled. The priest came in but did not go up into his pulpit. So I declared God's everlasting Truth and word of life for about three hours to the people and all was quiet and peaceable, [p]not a

°......° *S.J.*, p. 30.

word was uttered either in or out of the steeplehouse in opposition.[p]

And I brought them all to the spirit of God in themselves, by which they might know God and Christ and the Scriptures and to have heavenly fellowship in the spirit; and showed them how every one that comes into the world was enlightened by Christ the life, with which light they might see their sins and Christ their saviour, who was come to save them from their sin; with which light they might see their priest that died for them, their shepherd to feed them, and their great prophet to open to them. So with the light of Christ they might see Christ always present with them who was the author of their faith and the finisher thereof. So, opening the first covenant, I showed them the types and the substance, and bringing them to Christ the second covenant, and how they had been in the night of apostacy since the apostles' days, but now the everlasting Gospel was preached again that brought life and immortality to light, and the day of the Lord was come, and Christ was come to teach his people himself [q]and how them might find their teacher within, when they were in their labours and in their beds.[q]

And many hundreds were convinced that day, ⟨and some of them praised God and said, 'Now we know the first step to peace.'

The preacher also said privately to some of his hearers that I had broken them and overthrown them.⟩ And after, I went to a village and many people accompanied me; and as I was sitting in a house full of people and declaring the word of life unto them I cast my eye upon an unclean woman and told her she was a witch. And I was moved in the Lord's power to speak sharply to her and so she went out of the room; and people told me that I had discovered a great thing, for all the country looked upon her to be a witch. ⟨The Lord had given me a spirit of discerning by which I many times saw the states and conditions of people, and would try their spirits.⟩

And also at another time there came in such an one into Swarthmoor Hall in the meeting time, and I was moved

[p]......[p] *S.J.*, p. 30. [q]......[q] *S.J.*, p. 31.

to speak sharply to her and told her she was a witch also, and the people confessed to the same thing and said all the country looked upon her to be such an one also.

And there came in ⟨also at another time a⟩ woman and stood a little off from me and I cast my eye upon her; and I said she had been an harlot, for I perfectly saw the condition and life of the woman. The woman answered and said that many could tell her of her outward sins but none could tell her of her inward, but I told her her heart was not right before the Lord, and from the inward came the outward. Afterwards this woman came to be convinced of God's Truth, and remained a Friend.

So from that village we came up to Thomas Bewley's house[1] near Caldbeck; but when night came I walked out and lay out all night. And from thence, having some service there for the Lord, I passed to a market town, named Wigton, where I had a meeting at the cross and all was pretty quiet; and when I had declared the Truth unto them and turned them to Christ their teacher we passed away and had another meeting upon the borders in the steeple-house yard, where many professors and contenders came, but the Lord's power was over all. But after the word of life was declared some received the Truth there and at the market town aforesaid.

CHAPTER VII

AND from thence we passed into Carlisle City and on Seventh-day, the market day, I went up into the market to the cross. The magistrates had threatened and sent their sergeants. And the magistrates' wives said that if I came there they would pluck the hair off my head, and that the sergeants should take me up. Nevertheless I obeyed the Lord God and went [a]and stood a-top

[1] Thomas Bewley lived at Haltcliffe Hall. The visit took place toward the end of July, 1653.

of the cross in the middle of the market and there declared unto them that the day of the Lord was coming upon all their deceitful ways and doings and deceitful merchandise, and that they were to lay away all cozening and cheating and keep to 'yea' and 'nay', and speak the truth one to another, and spoke the Truth to them as I passed along the streets. So I set the Truth and the power of God over them. And a multitude of people followed me, and the people being throng, the sergeants could not get to me, 〈nor the magistrates wives come at me〉. So I passed away quietly after I had declared the word of life to the people. And there was a Friend led me to his own house, and many people and soldiers came to me, and some Baptists that were bitter contenders, so that one of their deacons, an old man,[a] cried out, the Lord's power being over them. And I set my eyes upon him and spoke sharply to him in the power of the Lord; and he cried, 'Don't pierce me so with thy eyes, keep thy eyes off me.'

And the pastor of the Baptists, a lieutenant, came to me to the abbey with most of his hearers, where I had a meeting and declared the word of life amongst them, and many of the Baptists and soldiers were convinced. And after the meeting was done the pastor, [b]with a rapier in his hand,[b] came and asked me what must be damned, being a high notionist and a flashy man. And I was moved of a sudden to tell him, that which spoke in him was to be damned, which stopped the pastor's mouth, and the witness of God was raised up in him. And I opened to him the state of election and reprobation, so that he said he never heard the like in his life. 〈He also came afterwards to be convinced.〉

And after, I went up to the castle amongst the soldiers. And they beat a drum and called them together and I turned them to the Lord Jesus Christ their teacher, and warned them of doing violence to any man, and that they might show forth a Christian's life, and turned them from the darkness to the light and from the power of Satan unto

[a]. . . . . .[a] Cf. *S.J.*, pp. 31, 32. [b]. . . . . .[b] *S.J.*, p. 32.

God. And I let them see what was their teacher and what would be their condemnation; and had no opposition but from the sergeants who afterwards came to be convinced.

And on the First-day after, I went into the steeplehouse,[1] and after the priest had done I spoke the truth to them and declared the word of life amongst the people. The magistrates desired me to go my ways and desired me not to speak; and the priest got away, but I still declared; and told them I came to speak the word of life and salvation from the Lord amongst them. A dreadful power of the Lord there was amongst them in the steeplehouse that the people trembled and shook: and they thought the very steeplehouse shook and thought it would have fallen down. The magistrates' wives were in a rage and tore and rent to have been at me, but the soldiers and friendly people stood thick about me. At last the rude people of the city rose and came with staves into the steeplehouse and cried, 'Down with these round-headed rogues', and threw stones, but the governor sent a file or two of musketeers into the steeplehouse and commanded the other soldiers all out, [c]that were with me, which had been convinced, and which kept the rude people off me. Then when the soldiers came to call away the other soldiers, they plucked me down and would not let me stay amongst the rude multitude,[c] and took me by the hand very friendly and said they would have me alongst with them then; and so when we were in the street all the town was of an uproar, [c]and stones flew about and cudgels, in the steeplehouse and about it, and without in the streets, and swords were drawn.[c] And the governor came down to appease the people and, for standing by and for me against the townspeople, some of the soldiers were cast into prison. [d]And there came the same lieutenant, the pastor of the Baptists, that came before with his rapier in his hand, and took me out of the crowd into his own house, where there was a Baptists' meeting.

[1] The Cathedral Church of St. Mary, Carlisle.

[c]......[c] Cf. *S.J.*, p. 32.

And so in the afternoon he offered up his meeting to declare the Truth among them,[d] and there Friends came also and we had a very quiet meeting and they heard the word of life gladly and received it.

And the next day I went to a Baptist's house, and the officers and justices and magistrates of the town were gathered together at the hall; and they granted a warrant for me and sent for me, and I went up to the town hall to them where a-many was gathered. And many rude people there were that had sworn strange things against me: and a great deal of discourse I had with them, and showed them the fruits of their priest's preaching, and how void they were of Christianity, though such great professors, but without possession ⟨for they were Independents and Presbyterians⟩.

And one sware one thing and one sware another thing against me.

[e]They asked me if I were the son of God.

I said, 'Yes.'

They asked me if I had seen God's face.

I said, 'Yes.'

They asked me whether I had the spirit of discerning.

I said, 'Yes', I discerned him that spoke to me.

They asked me whether the Scripture was the word of God.

I said, God was the Word and the Scriptures were writings; and the Word was before writings were, which Word did fulfil them.[e]

And so after a long examination they sent me to prison,[1] ⟨as a blasphemer, a heretic, and a seducer, though they could not justly charge any such thing against me.⟩

And the two gaolers were like two bear-herds. And when the head gaoler had me up into a great chamber and told me I should have what I would in that room, I told him he should not expect any money from me, and that I would

[1] The imprisonment began 1st August, 1653, and lasted seven weeks.

[d]......[d] *S.J.*, p. 32. [e]......[e] *S.J.*, p. 33.

not lie in none of his beds nor eat none of his victuals. [f]And so I sat up all night.[f] And then he put me into another room where I got a thing to lie on after a while.

And the Assizes came on and all the news and cry in the country was that I was to be hanged, and the High Sheriff said, one Sir Wilfrid Lawson, that he would guard me to my execution, and stirred them much up to take away my life. They were all in a black, dark rage, and they set three musketeers upon me—one at my chamber door, another at the stairs foot, and another at the street doors, and would let none come at me except one to bring me some necessary things. And at nights they would let up priests; about 10 o'clock at night they would bring in droves of them and exceeding rude and devilish they were, [f]when they could get no hold of my words; for the truth did convince them and was like a fire upon their heads and in their hearts.[f] But the Lord in his power gave me dominion over them all, and I let them see both their fruits and their spirits. [f]And there came most of the gentry of the country to dispute.[f] And great ladies and countesses came to see a man that they said was to die; and the priests would temptingly ask, What, must I die for their sins ?, which manifested that they were in the nature of them that crucified him that died for the sins of the world. And there was a company of bitter Scottish priests and Presbyterians, made up of envy and malice, who were not fit to speak of the things of God, they were so foul-mouthed. Many priests that came to me would be asking questions and saying the Scriptures were the Word, and I asked them how many gods there were, and they said, 'One.' I asked them whether God was not the Word, and they would say, 'Yes.' And so I let them see how they did confound themselves; for there was not a prisoner but was able to confute them. And so, when they were contriving, both judge, sheriff and justices, of putting me to death, the judge's clerk started a question to them that confounded

[f]. . . . . .[f] *S.J.*, p. 33.

them all, after which they had not power to call me out before the judges. ⟨Anthony Pearson, being then in Carlisle, and perceiving that they did not intend to bring me, as was expected, upon my trial, wrote a letter: *To the Judges of Assize and Jail-delivery for the Northern Parts sitting at Carlisle.*

. . . I am moved to lay before you the condition of George Fox, whom the magistrates of this city have cast into prison for words that he is accused to have spoken, which they call blasphemy. He was sent to the gaol till he should be delivered by due course of law; and it was expected he should have been proceeded against . . . at this Assize. . . . To my knowledge, he utterly abhors and detests every particular, which, by the Act against blasphemous opinions, is appointed to be punished . . .

Though he be committed, judgement is not given against him, nor have his accusers been face to face to affirm before him what they have informed against him, nor was he heard as to the particulars of their accusations, nor doth it appear that any word they charge against him is within the Act. Indeed I could not yet so much as see the information, no, not in court, though I desired it. . . . That his friends may not speak with him I know no law nor reason for. I do therefore claim for him a due and lawful hearing, and that he may have a copy of his charge, and freedom to answer for himself, and that rather before you than to be left to the rulers of this town who are not competent judges of blasphemy . . .

Anthony Pearson.[1]

But not withstanding this letter, the judges were resolved not to suffer me to be brought before them; but reviling and scoffing at me behind my back left me to the magistrates of the town, giving them what encouragement they could to exercise their cruelty upon me. Whereupon (though I had been kept up so close in the gaoler's house that Friends were not suffered to visit me, and Justice Benson and Justice Pearson were denied to see me) the next day, after the judges were gone out of town, an order was sent to the jailer⟩ that I should be put in the dungeon amongst

1 In full, Ellwood, p. 111; Bicent., i, 170.

the moss-troopers, and so they did; where men and women were put together and never a house of office, in a nasty and very uncivil manner which was a shame to Christianity. And the prisoners were exceeding lousy; [g]and there was one woman almost eaten to death with lice.[g] But the prisoners were made all of them very loving to me, and some of them were convinced, as the publicans and harlots of old were, so that they were able to confound a priest that might come to the gates to dispute. And Justice Benson's wife was moved of the Lord to come and visit me and to eat no meat but what she ate with me at the bars of the dungeon window, a good, honest woman, who after was imprisoned herself at York for speaking to a priest, when she was great with child, and had a child in prison.[1] She continued a good Friend till she died.

⟨Now when I saw that I was not like to be brought forth to a public hearing and trial, though I had before answered in writing the particular matters charged against me at the time of my first examination and commitment, I was moved to send forth a paper, as a public challenge to all those that did belie the Truth and me behind my back, to come forth and make good their charge.[2]

And much about the same time I writ also to the justices at Carlisle, that had cast me into prison, and that persecuted Friends at the instigation of the priests for tithes, expostulating the matter with them thus:⟩

Friends, Thomas Craister and Cuthbert Studholm.

Your noise is come up to London, what havoc, what imprisonment, is come up before the sober people. What imprisonment, what bridling, what making havoc and spoiling the goods of people have you made within these few years; unlike men, as though you had never read Scripture, to be men that minded them. Is this the end of Carlisle's religion ? Is this the end of your ministry ? And is this the end of your church Christianity profession ? You have shamed it by your folly and madness

[1] Immanuel Benson, b. 2nd February, 1654.

[2] Ellwood, p. 113; Bicent., i, 173.

[g]. . . . . .[g] *S.J.*, p. 33.

and blind zeal . . . And the everlasting gospel shall be preached again, which is the power of God, to all nations and kindreds and tongues in this the Lamb's day, which you shall appear before to judgement, and you have no way to escape. The first and the last, the beginning and the ending, the Alpha and Omega, He hath appeared, that was dead, is alive again, and lives for evermore.[1]

⟨I mentioned before that Gervase Benson and Anthony Pearson, though they had been justices of the peace, were not permitted to come to me in the prison, whereupon they jointly wrote a letter to the magistrates, priests, and people at Carlisle, concerning my imprisonment.⟩[2]

And whilst I was in the dungeon a little boy, one James Parnell, about 15 years old came to me, and he was convinced and came to be a very fine minister of the word of life and turned many to Christ.

At last he was imprisoned himself in Colchester and the gaoler was cruel with him and made him climb up and down for his victuals into a place called Little Ease or The Oven, where they kept him, and he fell down, the rope breaking, and broke his head so as he died[3] and then the wicked Independent priests made a book of it[4] and said he fasted himself to death, which was all lies.

But I continued in the dungeon amongst the prisoners; and the Little Parliament,[5] hearing that a young man was to die for religion at Carlisle, they writ down to the sheriff and magistrates. But it came after I was set at liberty. But the gaoler continued so exceeding cruel that he beat Friends and friendly people that did but come to the window to look in upon me, exceedingly, with great cudgels, as if he had been beating a pack of wool. And I could get up

[1] In full, *Camb. Jnl.*, i, 121-4; Ellwood, pp. 114-16; Bicent., i, 174-7.

[2] Ellwood, pp. 116, 117; Bicent., i, 177-8.

[3] Parnell d. 10th April, 1656.

[4] Glisson, et al.: *Relation of the Death of James Parnel*, 1656; reply: *The Lamb's Defence against Lies*, 1656.

[5] The Little or Barebones Parliament met 4th July, 1653, and ended 12th December, 1653.

to the grate where sometimes I took my meat, and the gaoler was offended and came in a rage with his great staff. And he fell a-beating of me though I was not at the window at that time, and cried, ' Come out of the window ', though I was far enough off it; and as he struck me I was made to sing in the Lord's power, and that made him rage the more. Then he fetched a fiddler[1] and brought him into the dungeon and set him to play [h]thinking to cross me;[h] and when he played I was moved in the everlasting power of the Lord God to sing; and my voice drowned them and struck them and confounded them [h]and made the fiddler sigh and give over his fiddling; and so he passed away with shame.[h]

And the governor and Justice Anthony Pearson came down; and it was such an ill savour and a shame to the magistrates that the gaoler should do such things that they called for the gaolers into the dungeon; and they came down into the dungeon to me, and they bid the gaolers find sureties for the good behaviour and so they put the under-gaoler into the dungeon with me amongst the moss-troopers,[2] who had been such a cruel fellow.

So after a while I was set at liberty by the justices and the Lord's power came over them all. And the Lord cut off two of those persecuting justices at Carlisle, and the other, after a time, was turned out of his place and went out of the town.

CHAPTER VIII

THEN after a time I went to Thomas Bewley's and there came a Baptist teacher to oppose me, who was convinced. And Robert Widders, being with me, was moved to go to Caldbeck steeplehouse, and the Baptist teacher went alongst with him, the same day, and they

[1] They beat Fox because he would not dance. See letter T. Rawlinson to M. Fell, 11th September, 1653; *Camb. Jnl.*, i, 121.

[2] i.e. Border marauders: cf also p. 162.

[h]. . . . . .[h] *S.J.*, p. 33.

almost killed Robert Widders and took the Baptist's sword from him and beat him sorely. And they sent Robert Widders to Carlisle gaol, and the Baptist aforesaid had the inheritance of an impropriation, but he went home and gave it up. And William Dewsbury went to another steeplehouse hard by, and they almost killed him, they beat him so. But the Lord's power was over all and healed them again, and Robert Widders after a while was set at liberty also.

So I went into the country and had mighty meetings, and the everlasting Gospel and the word of the Lord flourished, and thousands were turned to the Lord Jesus Christ and to his teaching, and several that took tithes as impropriators denied the receiving of them any longer, and delivered them up to the parishioners. So I came up into Westmorland and at Strickland Head I had a large meeting, and at other places, where a Justice of Peace out of Bishoprick,[1] one Henry Draper,[2] came up and a-many contenders. That day many Friends went to the steeple-houses to declare the Truth to the priests and people and the Lord's power was over all.

⟨The priests and magistrates were in a great rage against me in Westmorland and had a warrant to apprehend me, which they renewed from time to time for a long time, yet the Lord did not suffer them to serve it upon me.⟩

And so I came through Friends, visiting the meetings, till I came to Swarthmoor again, and then I heard that the Baptists and professors in Scotland had sent to me to have a dispute; and I sent to them that I would meet them in Cumberland at Thomas Bewley's where I went, but none came.

And another time as we were passing from a meeting and going through Wigton on a market day there was a guard set with pitch forks. Although there were some of

[1] i.e. Durham.

[2] Henry Draper, a justice of the peace, lived at Headlam in South Durham.

their neighbours with us they kept us out of the town and would not let us pass through the town, under a pretence of preventing the sickness, when there was no occasion for any such thing. So they fell upon us and had like to have spoiled us and our horses, but the Lord did prevent them that they did not much hurt, and so we passed away. And another time as I was passing betwixt old Thomas Bewley's and John Slee's[1] some rude fellows lay in wait in a lane and exceedingly stoned and abused us; but at the last, through the Lord's power we got through them and had not much hurt. But this was the fruits of the priests' teaching which shamed Christianity.

And after I had visited that country and Friends I went through the countries into Bishoprick and had large meetings and had a very large meeting at Justice Pearson's house where many were convinced.[2]

So I passed through Northumberland to Derwentwater[3] where there were great meetings, and the priests threatened to come but none came; and the everlasting word of life was freely preached and freely received, and many hundreds were turned to Christ their teacher.

And there came many to dispute in Northumberland, and pleaded against perfection. But I declared unto them that Adam and Eve were perfect before they fell, and all that God made was perfect, and the imperfection came by the Devil and the Fall. And Christ that came to destroy the Devil said, 'Be ye perfect.' But one of the professors said that Job said, 'What ! shall mortal man be more pure than his maker? The heavens are not clear in his sight. God charged his angels with folly.' But I showed him his mistake, that it was not Job which said so, but those which contended against Job. For Job stood for perfection and his integrity; and they were called miserable comforters. And they said the outward body was the body of death and sin. But I let them see their mistakes, and how that

[1] John Slee lived at Grisdale Howe in the barony of Greystoke.
[2] About March, 1654.
[3] The upper reaches of the river Derwent, also called Darren.

Adam and Eve had a body before the body of death and sin got into them. And man and woman would have a body when the body of sin and death was put off again; when they were renewed up into the image of God again by Christ Jesus, that they were in before they fell.

So ⟨they ceased at that time from opposing further,⟩ and many glorious meetings we had in the Lord's power.

And so we passed to Hexham, where we had a great meeting a-top of a hill, where the priest[1] came not, though he had threatened. And all was quiet, and the everlasting day and renowned Truth of the everlasting God was sounded over those dark countries and his Son set over all. And now that the day was come that all that had made a profession of the Son of God, they might receive him, and as many as did receive him to them he would give power to become the sons of God as he had done to me; and that he that had the Son of God he had life eternal and he that had not the Son of God, let him profess all the Scriptures from Genesis to the Revelation, he had not life.

And after that all were turned to the light of Christ by which they might see him and receive him and know where their teacher was, and the everlasting Truth largely declared, we passed away through Hexham peaceably and so came into Gilsland where some in that country were very thievish; where a Friend spied the priest and went to speak to him. He came down to our inn and the town's people came about us, and so the priest said he would prove us deceivers out of the Bible, but could find no Scripture for his purpose; so he went into the inn and after a while came out and brought ⟨some broken sentences of Scripture that mention⟩ 'the doctrines and commandments of men, touch them not and taste them not for they perish with the using': which, poor man, was his own condition; for we were

[1] The lecturer at this time was Thomas Tillam, Baptist, and anti-Quaker writer.

persecuted because we would not taste nor touch nor handle their doctrines which we knew perished with the using.

So I asked what he called the steeplehouse. 'Oh,' said he, 'the dreadful house of God, the temple of God', and I let him and the poor dark people see that their bodies should be the temples of God; and Christ never commanded these temples, but had ended that temple at Jerusalem which God had commanded. So the priest got away, and afterwards the people began to tell us that they feared we would take their purses or steal their horses; and judged us like themselves who are naturally given to thieving.

And the next day we came through that country into Cumberland again where we had a general meeting of many thousands of people a-top of a hill, ⟨near Langlands⟩. Heavenly and glorious it was and the glory of the Lord did shine over all, and there were as many as one could well speak over, there was such a multitude. Their eyes were kept to Christ their teacher and they came to sit under their vine, that afterwards a Friend in the ministry, Francis Howgill, went amongst them, and when he was moved to stand up amongst them he saw they had no need of words for they was all sitting down under their teacher Christ Jesus; so he was moved to sit down again amongst them without speaking anything.

So great a convincement there was in Cumberland, Bishoprick, Northumberland, Yorkshire, Westmorland and Lancashire, and the plants of God grew and flourished so by heavenly rain, and God's glory shined upon them, that many mouths the Lord opened to his praise, yea to babes and sucklings he ordained strength.

[a]In Bishoprick there were few steeplehouses but Friends were moved to go to them. Nay I may say few in England but Friends were moved to go to them and warn them of the mighty day of the Lord, to tell them where their true teacher was. And a great people was convinced.[a]

[a]......[a] *S.J.*, p. 34.

And the priests and the professors, they prophesied mightily against us about this time. For before, they prophesied we should all be knocked down within a month, as aforesaid. Then after, they prophesied within half a year; and their prophecies not coming to pass, they prophesied that we would eat one another out. For many times after the meetings, many tender people had a great way to go, and the houses not having beds, they stayed at the houses and lay in the hay mows. And Cain's fear possessed them, that when we had eaten one another out, we should all come to be maintained of the parishes ere long and that they would be troubled with us. But after this when they saw that the Lord blessed and increased Friends, as he did Abraham, both in the field and in the basket, and at their goings forth and comings in, risings up and lyings down, and that all things began to be blest unto them, then they saw the failings of all these their prophecies and that it was in vain to curse where God had blessed.

But at the first convincement, when Friends could not put off their hats to people nor say 'you' to a particular, but 'thee' and 'thou'; and could not bow nor use the world's salutations, nor fashions, nor customs, many Friends, being tradesmen of several sorts lost their custom at the first; for the people would not trade with them nor trust them, and for a time Friends that were tradesmen could hardly get enough money to buy bread. But afterwards people came to see Friends' honesty and truthfulness and 'yea' and 'nay' at a word in their dealing, and their lives and conversations did preach and reach to the witness of God in all people, and they knew and saw that, for conscience sake towards God, they would not cozen and cheat them, and at last that they might send any child and be as well used as themselves, at any of their shops.

So then things altered so that all the enquiry was, where was a draper or shopkeeper or tailor or shoemaker or any other tradesman that was a Quaker; insomuch that Friends had double the trade, beyond any of their neighbours. And if there was any trading they had it, insomuch that then the cry of all the professors and others was ' If we let these people alone they will take the trading of the nation out of our hands '.

And this hath been the Lord's doing to his people; my desire is that all may be kept in his power and spirit faithful to God and man, first to God in obeying him in all things and secondly in doing unto all men that which is just and righteous, true and holy and honest, to all men and women in all things that they have to do with or to deal withal with them, that the Lord God may be glorified in their practising truth, holiness, godliness, and righteousness amongst them, in all their lives and conversations.

And after I was put out of Carlisle prison I was moved to go to priest Wilkinson's steeplehouse[1] again and was in the steeplehouse before him; and when he came in I was declaring the Truth to the people; and we had a meeting hard by where one Thomas Stubbs was declaring the word of life, so there were not many people in the steeplehouse; for the best and most of his hearers were turned to Christ's free teaching. The priest came in and opposed me; and there did we stay all the day, for when I began he opposed me; and so if any law was broken he brake it, for he thought to have wearied me out. And he shamed when his people were haling me out, that we might see his fruits which Christ spoke of, ' They shall hale you out of the synagogues ', and then they would leave me alone. There did he stand till it was 'most night, jangling and opposing of me, and would not go to his dinner, but at last the Lord's power and truth came so over him that he packed away with his people: and so the Lord's power and truth came over them all; and after, I went to Friends that were turned to the Lord, into their meeting. And about this time many of the steeple-houses were empty, for such multitudes of people came

[1] At Brigham.

to Christ's free teaching and knew their bodies the temples of God.

And so after the great meeting in Cumberland as aforesaid I passed out of Cumberland through the countries where I had great meetings with Friends and of the world's people; and I established them upon Christ, the rock and foundation of the true prophets and apostles, but not of the false.

And after I came out of Carlisle prison aforesaid I went into the abbey chamber; and there came in a mad woman that sometimes was very desperate, and she fell down of her knees, and cried, 'Put off your hats, for grace, grace, hangs about thy neck': and so the Lord's power run through her that she was sensible of her condition and after came and confessed it to Friends.

And I came to another place in Cumberland, where a man's wife was distracted and very desperate, attempting at times to kill her children and her husband. But I was moved of the Lord God to speak to her, and she kneeled down of her bare knees and cried and said she would walk of her bare knees if she might go with me. And the Lord's power wrought through her and she went home well.

And in Bishoprick, whilst I was there, they brought a woman tied behind a man, that could neither eat nor speak, and had been so a great while; and they brought her into the house to me to Anthony Pearson's. And I was moved of the Lord God to speak to her so that she ate and spake, and was well, and got up behind her husband without any help and went away well.

And as I came out of Cumberland one time I came to Hawkshead and lighted at a Friend's house, and there was young Margaret Fell with me and William Caton; and it being a very cold season we lighted, and the lass made us a fire, her master and dame being gone to the market. And there was a boy lying in the cradle which they rocked, about eleven years old. He was grown almost double, and I cast my eye upon the boy and seeing he was dirty,

I bid the lass wash his face and his hands and get him up and bring him unto me. So she brought him to me and I bid her take him and wash him again for she had not washed him clean, then I was moved of the Lord God to lay my hands upon him and speak to him, and so bid the lass take him again and put on his clothes, and after, we passed away.

And sometime after, I called at the house, and I met his mother but did not light. ' Oh, stay ', says she, ' and have a meeting at our house for all the country is convinced by the great miracle that was done by thee upon my son, for we had carried him to Wells and Bath, and all doctors had given him over, for his grandfather and father feared he would have died and their name have gone out, having but that son; but presently after you were gone ', says she, ' we came home and found our son playing in the streets ', therefore, said she, all the country would come to hear if I would come back again and have a meeting there. And this was about three years after that she told me of it and he was grown to be a straight, full youth then. And so the Lord have the praise.

But as we were turning from the house and coming towards Swarthmoor, we overtook many rude market people, who did stone us and abuse us. But the Lord's power carried us over them all so as we had no harm.

And there was a priest at Wrexham in Wales, one Morgan Lloyd,[1] sent two of his preachers into the north to try us and see what a manner of people we were, but they were both convinced by the power of the Lord and turned to Christ; and they stayed a time and went back again.[2] One of them stands a fine minister of Christ to this day, one John ap John,[3] but the other did not continue a Friend.

⟨Friends being now grown very numerous in the northern parts of the nation, and divers young-convinced ones coming daily in among us, I was moved of the Lord to write the

[1] Morgan Lloyd (*c.* 1619-1659).

[2] The interview took place at Swarthmoor, 21st July, 1653.

[3] See p. 297 post.

following epistle, and send it forth amongst them, stirring up the pure mind, and to raise a holy care and watchfulness in them over themselves and one another, for the honour of truth:〉

To you all, Friends everywhere scattered abroad, in the measure of the life of God wait for wisdom from God, from him from whence it comes. And all which be babes of God wait for living food from the living God, to be nourished up to eternal life from one fountain from whence life comes; that orderly and in order you may all be guided and walk, servants in your places, young men and women and rulers of families; that every one in your places may adorn the truth, every one in the measure of it.

With it let your minds be kept up to the Lord Jesus from whence it doth come, that a sweet smelling savour ye may be to God, and in wisdom and with wisdom you may all be ordered and ruled; that the crown and glory you may be, one to another in the Lord. And that no strife nor bitterness nor self-will amongst you may appear, but with the Light may be condemned, in which is the unity. And that every one in particular may see the order and ruling of their own family; that in righteousness and wisdom it may be governed, the fear and dread of the Lord in everyone's heart set; that the secrets of the Lord everyone may come to receive; that stewards of his grace ye may come to be, to dispense it to everyone as they have need, and so in savour and right discerning ye all in it may be kept; that nothing that is contrary to the pure life of God in you and amongst you may be brought forth, but with it all which is contrary may be judged, so that in light, in life, in love you may all live . . . And that none may appear in words but what they be in the life, . . . and none amongst you boast yourselves above your measure; for if ye do, out of God's kingdom ye are excluded; for there gets up the pride and strife which is contrary to the Light, which Light leads to the kingdom of God, and gives every one of you an entrance thither and to understand and know the things which belong to the kingdom of God. And there the Light and life of man every one receives, him who was before the world was, by whom it was made, who is the righteousness of God and his wisdom; to whom all glory, honour, thanks, and praise belong, who is God, blessed for ever. . . .

G.F.

This is to be sent amongst all Friends in the Truth, the flock of God, to be read at their meetings in every place where they are met together.[1]

And so when the churches were settled in the north, the Lord had raised up many and sent forth many into his vineyard to preach his everlasting Gospel, as Francis Howgill and Edward Burrough to London, John Camm and John Audland to Bristol through the countries, Richard Hubberthorne and George Whitehead[2] towards Norwich, and Thomas Holme[3] into Wales, a matter of seventy ministers did the Lord raise up and send abroad out of the north countries.

⟨The sense of their service being very weighty upon me,⟩ this following paper was given forth to Friends in the Ministry.

George Fox to Friends in the ministry, 1654.

All Friends everywhere, know the Seed of God which bruiseth the seed of the serpent, and is a-top of the seed of the serpent, which seed sins not but bruiseth the serpent's head which tempts to sin and doth sin; to which Seed God's promise is God's blessing is too, which Seed is one in the male and in the female. Where it is the head, and hath bruised the head of the other, to the beginning you are come . . .

Friends everywhere abroad scattered, know the power of God in one another and in that rejoice; for then you rejoice in the Cross of Christ, him who is not of the world, which Cross is the power of God to all them that are saved. So you that know the power and feel the power, you feel the Cross of Christ, you feel the Gospel, which is the power of God unto salvation to everyone that believeth. Now he that believes in the Light believes in the everlasting covenant, in the everlasting offering; comes to the life of the prophets and Moses, comes to see Christ the hope, the mystery, which hope perisheth not; . . . the end

[1] In full, MS. portfolio 9 (Fox papers R, 3); Ellwood, p. 122-3; Bicent., i, 187-8.

[2] George Whitehead (*c.* 1636-1723) preached Quakerism, especially in East Anglia, leading Friend in London after Fox's death.

[3] Thomas Holme (*c.* 1627-1666), preached Quakerism, especially in Wales and north-west England.

of all perishing things, the end of all changeable things, the end of the decaying covenant, the end of the prophets and Moses. Christ Jesus the son, his throne you will know, heirs with him you will be, who makes kings, and brings to know his throne and his power.

There is no justification out of the Light, out of Christ. Justification is in the Light; here is the doer of the will of God, here is the entering into the kingdom. Now believing in the Light becomes a child of the Light, and here is received the wisdom that is justified of her children. Here believing in the Light, you shall not abide in darkness, but shall have the Light of life and come every one to witness the Light that shines in your hearts. . . .

Friends, be not hasty; for he that believes in the Light makes not haste. Here the grace is received by which you come to be saved; the election is known which obtains the promise; the will is seen that wills; the mind is known that runs, which obtains not but stops and dulls. . . .

This is the word of the Lord God to you. Every one in the measure of life wait, that with it all your minds may be guided up to the Father of life, with your hearts joined together up to the Father of spirits, all to receive power from him and wisdom, that with it you may be ordered to his glory, to whom be all glory for ever. All keep in the Light and life that judgeth down that which is contrary to the Light and life. So the Lord God Almighty be with you all, and keep you, meeting everywhere, being guided with that of God. With that you may see the Lord God among you, him who lighteth every man that cometh into the world, by whom the world was made, that men that be come into the world might believe. He that doth not, the Light condemns him, he that believeth comes out of condemnation. So this Light which lighteth every man that comes into the world, which they that hate it stumble at, is the Light of men.

All Friends that speak abroad, see that it be in the life of God, for that begets to God. The fruits of that shall never wither. . . . In that wait to receive power, and the Lord God Almighty preserve you. Whereby you may come to feel the Light which comprehends time and the world and fathoms it, which believed in gives you the victory over the world. And here the power of the Lord is received, which subdues all the contrary and puts off the garments that will stain and pollute. With this life you come to reach the Light in every man, which Christ enlightens every man that cometh into the world withal. And here the things of Christ come to be known and the proof of Christ heard. Keep in the Light the covenant of peace and walk in the covenant of life. . . .

So all Friends that be to the Light turned—which cometh from him by whom the world was made, before it was made, Christ Jesus the saviour of your souls, [b]with which light you come to see him, which comes from him, with which Light you will see all sin and evil and corruption that are contrary to it[b]—stand still in the Light; you will see your salvation which is walls and bulwarks against that the Light discovers. Waiting in the Light you will receive the power of God which is the gospel of peace, that you may be shod with it, and know that in one another which raiseth up the seed of God and sets it over the world and the earth and crucifies the affections and lusts; and Truth comes to reign which is the girdle.

[b]All Friends be low, and keep in the life of God to keep you low.[b] . . .

G.F.[1]

And the priests began to be in a mighty rage at Newcastle and at Kendal: and up and down in most ⟨of the northern⟩ countries: and there was one John Gilpin that had sometimes come amongst us at Kendal who ran out ⟨from the Truth into vain imaginations⟩ and which the priests made use of at times against us, but the Lord's power confounded them all.

And about this time Oliver Protector's oath was to be tendered to the soldiers when the Long Parliament was turned out: and many of the soldiers were turned out because in obedience to Christ they could not swear, as John Stubbs[2] for one; who was convinced when I was in Carlisle prison, and who became a faithful minister and travelled much in the service of the Lord in Holland, Ireland, Scotland, Leghorn, Rome, Egypt, America; and the Lord's power preserved him over the heads of the

[1] In full, Ellwood, pp. 124-7; Bicent., i, 190-4; *Camb. Jnl.*, i, 142-7.

[2] Of Dalston, Cumberland, d. 1673.

[b]. . . . . .[b] John Rouse's MS. (Fox papers Ss, 57).

Papists though many times he was in great danger of the Inquisitions. And the rest of the soldiers that had been convinced in their judgements, coming not into obedience, they took the oath of Oliver Protector, and they went into Scotland to a garrison, and the garrison thought they had been their enemies and they shot at them and killed many of them, which was a sad judgement.

And so after I had visited the churches in the north and all were settled under God's teaching, and the glory of the Lord shined over them, I passed from Swarthmoor to Lancaster, and so through [c]many towns, and felt I answered the witness of God in all people, though I spoke not a word.[c] So I left the north fresh and green under Christ their teacher. [c]And I came up into Yorkshire,[c] visiting Friends till I came to Cinder Hill Green.[1] But before I came to Cinder Hill Green we passed through Halifax, a rude town of professors, and came to one Thomas Taylor's,[2] who had been a captain, where we met with some janglers, but the Lord's power was over all, for I travelled in the motion of God's power. [c]And commonly where I had meetings upon the First-day, the priests fled their parish, though I went not to the steeple-house.[c]

And when I came to Cinder Hill Green, there was a meeting appointed three weeks before, [c]Friends that were convinced of the Truth having notice of my coming, which was judged to be about two and a half thousand people, and all peaceable and quiet.[c] And many persons of quality were there, as, captains and other officers; and there was a general convincement.

And at night we had a great meeting again in Thomas Stacey's[3] house; for people came from far and could not soon depart. The high sheriff of the county told Captain

[1] Near Handsworth Woodhouse on the border of Yorkshire and Derby.

[2] Thomas Taylor (*c.* 1627-1684) lived at Brighouse.

[3] The Staceys were of Ballifield Hall and Cinder Hill.

[c]. . . . . .[c] *S.J.*, p. 35.

Bradford[1] that he had intended to have come up with half a dozen of his troopers to the meeting; but the Lord prevented him and stopped him.

And so I stayed some meetings thereaways; and after, passed up and down in Yorkshire as far as Holderness to the land's end that way visiting Friends and the churches of Christ which were finely settled under Christ's teaching; and came at last to Captain Bradford's house where many Ranters came from York to wrangle but they were confounded. And there came the Lady Montague, who was then convinced and lived and died in the Truth.

And there was one Rice Jones and his company who fell a-prophesying against me that then I was at the highest and that after that time I should fall down as fast; and he sent a bundle of railing papers from Nottingham ⟨to⟩ Mansfield Clawson, and the towns thereabouts full of judgings against Friends for declaring the Truth in the markets and in the steeplehouses, which I answered. But his and their prophecy came upon themselves, for soon after they fell to pieces. Many of his followers came to be Friends and stand to this day. And in the Lord's blessed power his Truth increased and has increased; and I was preserved in the everlasting Seed that never fell nor changes. And Rice Jones turned a swearer, for he took the oaths which were put to him, and disobeyed the command of Christ.

And many such false prophets have risen against me, but the Lord has blasted them and will blast all who rise against the blessed Seed and me in it. My confidence is in the Lord, that whosoever did, I saw their end and how the Lord would confound them, before the Lord sent me forth. And I came again to Thomas Taylor's within three miles of Halifax, where there was a large meeting. And there came about two hundred people from Halifax, and many rude people, and butchers. And several of them had bound themselves with an oath before they came out to have killed me; and one man of them, a butcher, had killed a

[1] Probably Captain William Bradford, who became a Friend.

man and a woman. And they came in a very rude manner and made a great disturbance in the meeting; and it being in a close, Thomas Taylor, [d]being of repute amongst men, stood upon Friends' shoulders[d] and said unto them that if they would be civil they might stay, and if not he charged them to be gone off his ground; but they were the worse and said they would make it like a common and yelled and made such a noise as if they had been come to a bear baiting, and thrust Friends up and down; and Friends being peaceable the Lord's power came over them all. Though several times they thrust me off from the place I stood on with the crowding of the people together against me, still I was moved of the Lord to stand up again as I was thrust down.

And at last I was moved of the Lord to say that if they would discourse of the things of God let them come up to me one by one; and if they had anything to say or anything to object I would answer to them one after another; and then they were all silent and had nothing to say, and the Lord's power came over them all and reached the witness of God in them that they were all bound by the power of God. And a glorious powerful meeting we had and his power went over all; and the minds of people were turned by the spirit of God in them to God, and to Christ and God their teacher, and the powerful word of life was largely declared that day so that in the life and power of God we brake up our meeting.

And those rude company went their ways to Halifax; and the people asked them why they had not killed me according to the oath they had sworn, and they maliciously said I had so bewitched them they could not do it, [d]but the press of the people was so great that they could not get at me,[d] and so the Devil was chained. Friends told me that they used to come and break stools and chairs and make fearful work, but the Lord's power had bound them. And presently after, that butcher that had killed the man and woman aforesaid and that was one of those that had

[d]......[d] *S.J.*, p. 36.

bound himself with an oath to kill me, killed another man and then he was sent to York gaol. And another of the butchers aforesaid that had sworn to kill me, that used to put his tongue out of his mouth to Friends when they went by him, he died with his tongue so swollen out of his mouth that he could not get it into his mouth again till he died. And several strange and sudden judgements came upon many of these conspirators against me which would be too large to declare. But God's vengeance from heaven came upon the bloodthirsty who sought after blood, for all such spirits I laid before the Lord and left them to him to deal with them; who is stronger than them all, in whose power I was preserved and carried on to do his work. And the Lord has raised a fine people in those parts that he hath drawn to Christ and gathered in his name; who feel Christ amongst them and sit under his teaching.

And so I passed through the countries till I came to Balby and several Friends from thence went with me into Lincolnshire where I had formerly been, and some went to the steeplehouses and some to the Separate meetings.

And there came the sheriff of Lincoln[1] and several with him to the meeting. And he made a great contention and jangling for a time, but the Lord's power struck him that he received the word of life and was convinced (and several others that did oppose). And he and his wife did abide in the Truth till they died.

And great meetings and convincements there were in those parts and many were turned to the Lord Jesus and came to sit under his teaching, and left their priests and their superstitious ways, and the day of the Lord flourished over all.

And there came one, Sir Richard Wray; and he was convinced, and his brother[2] and his brother's wife, who died in the Truth, though he afterwards run out.

[1] Robert Craven (d. 1670).

[2] Probably Sir John Wray of Glentworth, baronet, and his wife Elizabeth, widow of Sir Symonds d'Ewes. Joan Wray, wife of Christopher of Fulbeck, was a prominent Friend at this period.

And after I had visited those countries I came into Derbyshire and the sheriff of Lincoln came with me into Derbyshire where two of Judge Fell's daughters met me. And we had some opposition in one meeting but the Lord's glorious power gave me dominion over all.

And there was a company of bailiffs and serving men plotted together and came in the night and called me out, and I went out to them and some Friends with me. And they were exceeding rude and violent: and had intended to have carried me away in the night with them, and to have done me a mischief, but the Lord's power chained them and went over them so that at last they went away.

And the next day Thomas Aldam went to the knight's house, whose servants some of these men were, and laid before him the bad carriage of his servants. And the knight seemed to rebuke them and did not allow of their evil carriage towards us.

And so we came after this into Nottinghamshire to Skegby where we had a great meeting of all sorts of people and the Lord's power went over all: and all was quiet and the people were turned to the spirit of God by which they came to receive his power and to sit under Christ's teaching their saviour; and a great people the Lord had thataways.

And then I passed towards Kidsley Park, where there were a-many Ranters came: but the Lord's power stopped them.

And then I went up into the Peak country towards Thomas Hammersley's,[1] where there came all the Ranters in that country and high professors. And the Ranters opposed me and fell a-swearing, and when I reproved them for swearing then they would bring Scripture for it, and said Abraham, and Jacob, and Joseph swore, and the priests, and Moses, and the prophets swore and the angel swore. And I answered and said unto them, I confessed all these did so as the Scripture records it, but I said again to them, that Christ said, ' before Abraham was I am '; and he says,

[1] Thomas Hammersley's home was at Basford, near Leek, Staffs.

'Swear not at all.' And Christ ends the prophets and the first priesthood and Moses, and reigns over the house of Jacob and Joseph, who saith, 'Swear not at all.' And God saith, 'I bring forth my first-begotten into the world; let all the angels worship him', to wit Christ that saith, 'Swear not at all' as in Matthew v. And for men's swearing to end their strife, Christ who destroyed the Devil and his works who is the author of strife, he saith, 'Swear not at all', and God saith, 'This is my beloved Son hear ye him, in whom I am well pleased', so the Son is to be heard who forbids swearing, and the Apostle James that did hear the Son of God and preached him and followed him, he forbids all oaths as in James v.

And so the Lord's power and his Son were set over all, and the word of life was fully and richly preached and many were convinced that day.

And Thomas Hammersley, he served as foreman of a jury without swearing, and the judge did confess he had been judge so long but never heard such an upright verdict as that Quaker brought in. And much might be spoken of these things, but time would fail to declare them, but the Lord's power and truth came over all, who is worthy of all praise and glory for ever.

And after this I came through Derbyshire visiting Friends; and then came to Swannington in Leicestershire where there was a General Meeting:[1] and many Ranters came and other professors and Baptists and great janglings there had been with them and the priests in that town. And several Friends came from several parts to that meeting, as John Audland, and Francis Howgill, and Edward Pyott from Bristol, and Edward Burrough from London, and several were convinced in those parts. And the Ranters that came to the meeting made a disturbance and were very rude, but at last they were confounded and the Lord's power came over them all.

And the next day Jacob Bottomley[2] came from Leicester,

[1] About 8th to 15th January, 1655.

[2] Jacob Bauthumley.

a great Ranter, but the Lord's power stopped him and came over them all.

And there came a priest also, but he was confounded by the Lord's power; and the priests, and professors, and Ranters, and Baptists, and people were all very rude about this time, and stirred up the rude people.

And we sent to the Ranters to come forth and try their God, and there came abundance who were rude, as aforesaid, and sung and whistled and danced, but the Lord's power so confounded them that many of them came to be convinced.

And after this I came to Twycross and there came some Ranters again and they sung and danced before me, but I was moved in the dread of the Lord to speak to them and reprove them and the Lord's power came over them so as some of them were reached and convinced and received the spirit of God and are come to be a pretty people and live and walk soberly in the Truth of Christ.

And I came to Anthony Bickley's[1] in Warwickshire where there was a great meeting: and several people and Baptists came and jangled, but the Lord's power came over them, [e]and then I passed into Nottinghamshire and Lincolnshire where there were brave meetings of Friends, and Truth honourable and so passed up into Leicestershire, where there were great meetings and so went to my native town where my relations lived, at a place called Drayton-of-the-Clay. Having sent before of my coming,[e] Nathaniel Stephens, the priest, had gotten another priest and had given notice to the country: and he sent down to me that I must come up to them for they could not do any thing till I came. And I having been three years away from my relations, I knew nothing of their design and intentions, but at last I went up with several Friends into the steeple-house yard where the two priests aforesaid were; and they had gathered abundance of people.

[1] Anthony Bickley, or Brickley, lived at Baddeley Ensor, near Atherstone.

[e]. . . . . .[e] *S.J.*, p. 36.

And when I came there they would have had me go into the steeplehouse and I asked them what I should do there: and they said Nathaniel Stephens the priest could not bear the cold; and I told them he might bear it as well as me. And at last we went into a great hall, and there was Richard Farnsworth with me; and a great dispute we had with those priests concerning the practice of the priests how contrary they were to Christ and the apostles; and the priests would know where tithes were forbidden or ended. And so I showed them out of Hebrews vii, how not only tithes but the priesthood that took tithes was ended, and the law was ended and disannulled by which the priesthood and tithes were made and commanded to be paid. And then the priests stirred up the people to some lightness and rudeness.

I knew this priest from a child so I laid open his condition and the manner of his preaching and how he like the rest of the priests did apply the promises to the first birth which must die. But the promises were to the Seed; not to many seeds but the one Seed Christ who was one in male and female; for all were to be born again before they could enter into the kingdom of God. Then he said I must not judge so, but I told him, he that was spiritual judged all things; and then he confessed that that was a full Scripture, ' But neighbours ', says he, ' this is the business: George Fox is come to the light of the sun, and now he thinks to put out my starlight.'

But I said, ' Nathaniel, give me thy hand '; then I told him I would not quench the least measure of God in any, much less put out his starlight ⟨if it was true starlight—light from the Morning Star⟩; and further said if he had anything from Christ or God he ought to speak it freely and not take tithes from the people for preaching, seeing Christ commanded his ministers to give freely as they had received freely. And so I charged him to preach no more for tithes or a hire; and he plucked his hand out of my hand and said he would not yield unto that.

And so after a while the people began to be rude and vain,

so we broke up, though some were made loving to Truth that day. And I told them that I should be at the town that day seven-night again; and I went into the country and had meetings, and that day seven-night came there again, and then this priest had gotten seven or eight priests to help him, for priest Stephens had given notice on a market day at a lecture at Atherstone that there would be such a dispute and meeting with me though I knew nothing of it but only that I said I should be in town that day seven-night again. And these eight priests had gathered several hundreds of people, even all the country thereabouts; and they would have had me into the steeplehouse again but I would not go in, but got on a hill and there spoke to them and the people.

And there was Thomas Taylor with me that had been a priest and James Parnell and several other Friends: and the priests thought that day to have trampled down Truth; but the Truth came over them.

But at last they and the people were so rude, they would not stand to trial with me, but would be contending here and there a little with one Friend or other. So at last the priest brought his son and another to dispute with me, but his mouth was soon stopped; and when he could not tell how to answer he would go ask his father, but his father was confounded also when he came to answer for his son. So after they had toiled themselves they went away in a rage to the priest Stephens' house to drink. And as they went away I said, I never came to a place where so many priests together would not stand me. And after a while they and their wives came about me and laid hold of me and fawned about me and said what might I have been had it not been for Friends. And then they fell a-pushing of Friends up and down to thrust them from me, and to pluck me to them.

But at last several fellows got me up in their arms and carried me to the steeplehouse porch to carry me into the steeplehouse by force, [f]the priest following. And the door being locked, a great heap of them fell down as they were carrying of me, and I under them. Then they cried for the Clerk to come to open the door. But at last I got from under them and leaped through the bars and got back to my hill again where I spoke before, and began to speak, and they took me up again and carried me to the steeplehouse wall and set me on a base like a stool and all the priests and the people stood under; and the priests cried, 'Come, to argument, to argument.' I stood still a while and looking upon the great concourse of people[f] I said I denied all their voices, for they were the voices of the hirelings, and the stranger: and they cried, 'Prove it, prove it.' And I directed them to the tenth of John, for there they might see what Christ said of such, who said he was the true shepherd that laid down his life for his sheep, and his sheep heard his voice and followed him, but the hireling would fly when the wolf came because he was an hireling; and they were such hirelings. And then the priests plucked me off from my base again and then they eight got upon bases under the steeplehouse walls. Then I felt the mighty power of God arise over all, though the people began to be a little rude.

When I was gotten to the place where I could command the people I began to speak, and I told them if they would but give audience and hear me I would show them by the Scriptures why I denied those eight teachers or priests that stood there before me and all the hireling teachers of the world whatsoever, and I would give them Scripture for what I said.

And so both priests and people consented.

So I showed them out of the prophets Isaiah, Jeremiah, Ezekiel, Micah, Malachi, and other prophets how they were in the steps of such as God had sent his true prophets to cry against; for, said I

'You are such as bear rule by your means: and the people loved to have it so: which is a horrible filthy thing committed in the land (Jer. v.). And you are such as they that used their

[f]. . . . . .[f] Cf. *S.J.*, p. 37.

tongues and said, " Thus saith the Lord " when the Lord never spoke to them; and such as followed their own spirits and saw nothing, but spoke forth a divination of their own brain and by their lives and lightness had caused the people to err (Jer. xxiii.). And they were such as you, that sought for their gain from their quarter, that were as greedy dumb dogs that could never have enough, whom the Lord sent his prophet Isaiah to cry against (Isa. lxi.). And they were such as you, as taught for handfuls of barley and pieces of bread, that sewed pillows under people's armholes that they might lie soft in their sins (Ezek. xiii.). And they were such as you, that taught for the fleece and the wool, and made a prey of the people (Ezek. xxxiv.).

'But the Lord is gathering his sheep from their mouths and from off their barren mountains and bringing of them to Christ, the one shepherd which he has set over his flocks as in Ezekiel aforesaid.

'And they were such as you that divined for money and preached for hire, and if a man did not put into their mouths they prepared war against them as their fruits declared' (Mic. iii.).

And so I went largely through the prophets, which will be too large to repeat, and then through the New Testament of Christ and the apostles, and showed them how they were like the chief priests, and scribes, and pharisees, such as Christ cried woe against (Matt. xxiii.), and such false apostles as the true apostles cried against, as taught for filthy lucre; and such anti-Christs and deceivers as they cried against, that minded earthly things and served not the Lord Jesus Christ, but their own bellies; for they that served Christ gave freely and preached freely as he commanded them.

'And they that won't preach without hire, tithes, and outward means, serve their own bellies and not Christ; and through the good words of the Scriptures and feigned words of their own, they made merchandise of the people then', said I, 'as you do now.'

And when I had largely quoted the Scriptures and showed them how they were like pharisees, loving to be called of men 'masters', and to go in long robes and to stand praying in the synagogues and to have the uppermost rooms at feasts and the like; so when I had thrown them out in the sight of the people amongst the false prophets and scribes and pharisees and showed how such as they were judged by the prophets, Christ and the apostles, and having largely spoken to them, I turned them to the light of Christ Jesus, who enlightens every man that cometh into the world, to let them see whether these things were not true as had been spoken.

And when I spake to that of God in their consciences and the light of Christ Jesus in them, they could not abide to hear tell of that; but then a professor said, 'George, what! wilt thou never have done?' and all was quiet till he spake. And I told him I should have done presently, so after I had done and cleared myself in the Lord's power, all the priests and people stood still for a time.

And at last one of the priests said that they would read the Scriptures that I had quoted: so I told them, 'With all my heart'; and they began to read Jeremiah xxiii., and there they saw the marks of the false prophets that he cried against; and when they had read a verse or two and something more than I had quoted, I said, 'Take notice, people', and then they said, 'Hold thy tongue, George', and I then bade them read the whole chapter throughout, for it was all against them, and then they stopped and would read no further, but asked me a question. And I told them I would answer their question, the other being first granted that I had charged them with, that they were false prophets, false teachers, and anti-Christs, and deceivers, and such as the true prophets, Christ and the apostles, cried against.

And a professor said, 'Nay': and I said, 'Yea, for you leaving the matter and going to another thing seems to consent to the proof of the former charge.'

So I answered their question, which was, that those false prophets were adulterated, and whether did I judge Priest Stephens an adulterer. To which I said he was adulterated from God like those false prophets and Jews in his practice.

So they stood not to vindicate him but brake up the meeting.

The priests whispered together and then Priest Stephens came to me and desired that my natural father and brother might go aside with him and the rest of the priests to keep the people off that he might speak with me privately. But I was very loth to go aside with him: but the people cried, 'Go, George, do, George, go aside with him.' And I was afraid if I did not go they would say I was disobedient to my parents. And so I went, and the rest of the priests were to keep the people off: but the people drew close to us for they could not keep them off, the people being willing to hear.

And I asked the priest what he had to say to me and he said that if he was out of the way I should pray for him, and if I was out of the way he would pray for me; and he would give me a form of words what I should pray, but I answered him and said, 'It seems Priest Stephens does not know whether he be in the right way or no, neither doth he know whether I am in the way or no. But I know that I am in the everlasting way, Christ Jesus, which he is out of. And thou wouldst give me a form of words to pray by and yet deniest the Common Prayer. And why may I not take the Common Prayer Book to pray by as well as thy form of words? ⟨If thou wouldst have me pray for thee by a form of words⟩ is not this a denying the apostles' practise of praying by the Spirit, who said he would pray in the Spirit and Holy Ghost as it gave words and utterance?' So the people fell a-laughing and I was moved to speak to him several other words, and afterwards we all parted, I telling them I should be in the town that day seven-night again. And upon those words the priests packed away.

And many people were convinced that day and the Lord's power came over all, and whereas they thought to have confounded Truth that day, many were thereby confirmed in the Truth and came to be convinced of it and stand in it; and a great shake it was to the priests My father in the flesh thwacked his cane on the ground and said, ' Well ', said he, ' I see he that will but stand to the truth it will carry him out ', though he was a hearer and follower of the priests.

So I passed into the country and that day seven-night I came again and we had appointed a meeting at my relations' house: Priest Stephens ⟨having had notice beforehand thereof, had got another priest to him,⟩ and they had got a company of troopers, and they sent for me and I told them our meeting was appointed, and they might come to me if they would, but the priest came not, but the troopers came and a-many rude people, and this was the priests' plot, that the troopers were to take every one's name and then to command them to go home and if they would not then to carry them away with them. And when they had taken several names they came to take my name. So my relations made answer that I was at home already, and so they could not take me away that time, nevertheless they took my name; and the Lord's power came over all and they went away, both priests, professors, and troopers, vexed and crossed because they had not their ends, but several were convinced that day and admired the love and power of God.

And this was that Priest Stephens that said of me, ' Never such a plant was bred in England ', and yet afterwards he reported that I was carried up in the clouds and after found full of gold and silver; and a-many lies and reports he raised on me, but the Lord swept them all away.

And the reason I would not go into their steeplehouse was because I was to bear my testimony against it, and to bring all off such things to the spirit of God that they might know their bodies to be the temples of the Holy Ghost; and to bring them off all the hireling teachers to Christ their free teacher, that had died for them and purchased them with his blood.

And after this I went into the country and had several meetings and came to Swannington and there the soldiers came again, but the meeting was quiet and the Lord's power was over all and they did not meddle.

And after I went to Leicester, and from Leicester to Whetstone;[1] and before the meeting began there came a matter of seventeen troopers of Colonel Hacker's[2] regiment with his marshall, and they took me up[3] before the meeting, though several Friends were gathered, for there were several Friends come out of several parts; and before the meeting I told the marshall he might let all these Friends go and I would answer for them all. So the marshall took me and let the Friends all go and Alexander Parker went along with me.

So at night they had me before Colonel Hacker, and his major and captains, and a great company of them, and a great deal of discourse we had about the priests and meetings, for at this time there was a noise of a plot against Oliver Cromwell. And much reasonings I had with them about the spirit of Christ who enlighteneth every one that cometh into the world; and Colonel Hacker asked whether it was not this light of Christ that made Judas betray his master and after led him to hang himself, and I told him, 'No; that was the spirit of darkness which hated Christ and his light.' Then Colonel Hacker said that I might go home and keep at home and not go abroad to meetings, and I told him I was an innocent man from all plots and denied all such works.

Then his son Needham[4] said, 'Father, this man hath reigned too long. It's time to have him cut off.' And I asked him for what; or what had I done or whom had I wronged from a child, for I was bred and born in that country, and who could accuse me of any evil from a child.

And then Colonel Hacker asked me again if I would go home and stay at home; I told him if I should promise

[1] Whetstone, about 5 miles from Leicester.

[2] Colonel Francis Hacker (d. 1660) lived at Withcote Hall, near Oakham.

[3] On 11th February, 1655.

[4] Captain Clement Needham; "son" is unconfirmed.

him so, that would manifest that I was guilty of something, for to go home and make my home a prison; and if I went to meetings they would say I brake their order; but I told them I should go to meetings as the Lord ordered me, and therefore could not submit to that, but said we were a peaceable people.

'Well then', said Colonel Hacker, 'I will send you to-morrow by six o'clock to my Lord Protector by Captain Drury, one of his life-guard.'

So that night I was kept a prisoner at the Marshalsea, and the next morning by the sixth hour I was ready and delivered to Captain Drury. And so I desired they would let me speak with Colonel Hacker. He had me to his bed-side; and he was at me again to go home and keep no more meetings. I told him I could not submit to that but must have my liberty to serve God and go to meetings.

Then he said I must go before Oliver, Lord Protector; so I kneeled on his bed-side and desired the Lord to forgive him, for he was Pilate, though he would wash his hands; and when the day of his misery and trial should come upon him I then bid him remember what I said to him.

And this Priest Stephens aforesaid with the rest of the priests and professors had stirred him up, who had said so of me before that never such a plant was bred in England; and yet here his envy was manifested; when they could not overcome me by their disputes nor arguments, nor resist my spirit, then they got soldiers to take me up.

Now when this Colonel Hacker was in the Tower of London, a day or two before he was hanged, it was told him what he had done against the innocent, and he remembered it and confessed it to Margaret Fell and said he knew well whom she meant, and he had a trouble upon him for it. And his son ⟨who told his father⟩ I had reigned too long and would have had me cut off, could see how soon his father was cut off, who after was hanged at Tyburn when the King came in.

So I was carried up by Captain Drury aforesaid from Leicester, and when we came to Harborough he told me that if I would go home and stay a fortnight, I should have my liberty if I would not go to nor keep meetings, but I told him I could not promise any such thing. And several times upon the road did he ask and try me after the same manner, and I gave him the same answer. So he brought me to London and lodged me at the Mermaid over against the Mews at Charing Cross, and I was moved of the Lord to warn people at the inns and places as I went of the day of the Lord that was coming upon them. And William Dewsbury and Marmaduke Storr were in prison at Northampton, and he let me go and visit them. And when I was at London he left me at the Mermaid and went and told Oliver Cromwell of me.

And I gave forth a paper and bid him carry it to Oliver, which is here as followeth:

Dear Friend,

Be still, and in the counsel of God stand, and that will give thee wisdom, that thou mayest frustrate men's ends, and calm men's spirits, and crumble men under, and arise and stand up in the power of the Lord God and the Lamb's authority. And fear not the face of man but fear and dread the Lord God, then his presence and wisdom and counsel thou shalt have, to throw down the rubbish and quell all the bad spirits under thy dominion. And fear them about thee.

Live in the Lord's power and life, then to thee he will give wisdom, and the pure feeling thou wilt come into, whereby thy soul will be refreshed and it will be thy delight to do the will of God, and thy meat and drink, as thou in the pure eternal power, counsel, will, and wisdom of God dwellest. Things all will be made plain before thee, for thee and to thee, from the Lord God.

In what thou dost for the Lord God thou shalt have peace and the blessing; and in that so doing, all the sober, truehearted people will be one with thee in all travails, sorrows, and pains, in feeling. And then in that a blessing from the Lord will come upon thee, will abound in thee and cover thee as thou livest and art kept in the power and dread of the Lord God of heaven and earth, where wisdom is not wanting, nor peace lacking; but where peace is enjoyed and counsel and instruction from the Lord God are given.

And the helping arm and hand that stretcheth over all the nations in the world thou wilt feel. And with that thou wilt come to break down all men's ends, that they have to themselves, and the worships that men invent and images they have set up. For the arm of the Lord helps the righteous, by his hand he carries his lambs, which arm is turned against the wicked, stretched over them. And the hand of the Lord is against those that do evil, in which hand the soul is, which brings it into peace.

Therefore live in the power of the Lord God, and feel his hand that is stretched over the nations; for a mighty work hath the Lord to do in other nations, and their quaking and shaking is but entering. So this is the word of the Lord God to thee, and a charge to thee from the Lord God. In the presence of the Lord God, live in the power of the Lord God of heaven and earth, that will make all nations to tremble and to quake; for those are God's enemies that be out of his power and counsel.

And be thou faithful to God singly, without respecting any man's person. But respect the Lord and his work; and be obedient to his will singly without any end to thyself. Live in the pure wisdom, counsel, and instruction from God; then wilt thou see God's enemies, that live out of his wisdom, power, counsel, fall in their pits, snare themselves, fear where there is no fear, slaying themselves with their envy. And the power of the Lord will stave all the wicked off of thee as thou lives in it and art kept in it.

And this is the word of the Lord God to thee. Live in the wisdom of the life of God, that with it thou mayest be ordered to his glory, and order his creatures to his glory. And be still and silent from thy own wisdom, wit, craft, subtilty, or policy that would arise in thee, but stand single to the Lord, without any end to thyself. Then God will bless thee and prosper thee in his ways; thou wilt feel his blessing in thy generation.

And thy mind stayed upon the Lord, thou wilt be kept in perfect peace, without any intent to thyself, to the glory of God. And there wilt thou feel no want, nor never a failing, nor forsaking, but the presence of the Lord God of life with thee. For now the state of this present age is, that the Lord is bringing his people into the life the Scriptures were given forth from, in which life people shall come to have unity with God, with

Scriptures and one with another, for the establishing righteousness, truth, and peace, in which is the kingdom of God.

From a lover of thy soul and eternal good,

George Fox.

⟨During the time I was prisoner at Charing Cross⟩ abundance of professors, priests, and officers, and all sorts of people came to see me. And there came one Colonel Packer[1] and his officers to see me; and there came one Cobbe,[2] and a great company of Ranters came in that time also, and they began to call for drink and tobacco; and I desired them to forbear it in my room; if they had a mind of it they might go into another room. And one of them cried, 'All is ours', and another said, 'All is well': but I replied, 'How is all well when thou art so peevish and envious and crabbed?' for I saw he was of a peevish nature. And so I spake to their conditions, and they knew it and looked at one another wondering.

And then Colonel Packer he began to talk with a light chaffy mind of God and Christ and the Scriptures: and that was a great grief to my soul and spirit when I heard him talk so lightly, so I told him he was too light to talk of the things of God and he did not know the solidity of a man; upon which the officers raged and said would I say so to their colonel: and then Packer and the Ranters bowed and scraped one to another. This Packer was a Baptist. And it was the way of the Ranters to be so extreme in their compliments that Packer bid them give over their compliments; and I told them they were fit to go together for they were both of one spirit.

And this Colonel Packer had gotten Theobalds[3] and was made a justice of peace there, and there set up a great meeting of the Baptists in Theobalds Park. He and a company of officers had purchased it; and they were exceeding high and railed against Friends and Truth, and threatened

[1] Major William Packer.

[2] Perhaps Abiezer Coppe (1619-1672), Ranter.

[3] A mansion near Cheshunt, Herts., at one time the residence of King James I.

to apprehend me with their warrants if ever I came down there.

Some time after I was set at liberty by Oliver Crómwell, I was moved of the Lord God to go down to Theobalds and appoint a meeting hard by them, where a-many of his people came, and were convinced. And the Lord's power came over him so that he had not power to meddle with me; and several of his hearers being convinced of Christ, the way and free teacher, came off from him; that made him rage the more.

So I went to Waltham and there was a meeting, but the people were very rude and they broke the windows and gathered about the house. I went out to them with the Bible in my hand and desired them to come in, and I would show them Scripture both for our practice and principles; and showed them that their teachers were in the steps of such as the prophets, Christ and the apostles, cried against. So I turned them to the light and spirit of God in their hearts, that by it they might come to know their free teacher, the Lord Jesus Christ.

And they went away all satisfied and quieted, and from that time after they never made any disturbance; so as since there is a large meeting settled in their town which was gathered in the name of Jesus to be under Christ's free teaching.

And after, this Colonel Packer, when the King came in, lost all his offices and land which he had bought belonging to the King—he who had said that before the Quakers should have liberty he would draw his sword to bring in King Charles; but when the King was come in, he had the reward of his envy and wickedness. And thus the Lord's power wrought for his lambs and Truth; and many such as he were overthrown in their folly.

And about this time there was one Chandler,[1] a great Ranter that had been a priest, and one who had run into so much wickedness that he lay as a spectacle to all people; and he cried out that he was in Hell fire, and no one could

[1] John Chandler of Southwark.

minister any comfort to him. I was moved to bid Edward Burrough to go to him and turn him to the light of Christ and settle his mind upon Christ; and so he did, for he went forthwith and his message was effectual; and he became a very fine Friend and gave forth many books for the Truth and died in Truth.

And after a few days I was had before Oliver Cromwell by Captain Drury.

[g]Upon the Fifth-day of the First-month [5th March, 1655] Captain Drury who brought George Fox up to London by order from Colonel Hacker did come to the inn into the chamber where George Fox lay and said that it was required of George Fox from Oliver Cromwell that he would promise that he would not take up a sword against the Lord Protector or the Government as it is now; and that George Fox would write down the words in answer to that which the Protector required, and for George Fox to set his hand to it.

The Fifth-day of the First-month George Fox was moved of the Lord to give out these words following which were given to Oliver Cromwell. And George Fox was then presently[1] brought before him by Captain Drury.

George Fox to Oliver Cromwell, 1654.

I, who am of the world called George Fox, do deny that the carrying or drawing of any carnal sword against any, or against thee, Oliver Cromwell, or any man. In the presence of the Lord God I declare it.

God is my witness, by whom I am moved to give this forth for the Truth's sake, from him whom the world calls George Fox; who is the son of God who is sent to stand a witness against all violence and against all the works of darkness, and to turn people from the darkness to the light, and to bring them from the occasion of the war and from the occasion of the magistrate's sword, which is a terror to the evil doers who act contrary to the light of the Lord Jesus Christ, which is a praise to them that do

[1] i.e. *at once*.

well, a protection to them that do well and not evil. Such soldiers as are put in that place no false accusers must be, no violence must do, but be content with their wages; and the magistrate bears not the sword in vain.

From under the occasion of that sword I do seek to bring people. My weapons are not carnal but spiritual, and ' my kingdom is not of this world ', therefore with a carnal weapon I do not fight, but am from those things dead; from him who is not of the world, called of the world by the name George Fox. And this I am ready to seal with my blood.

This I am moved to give forth for the Truth's sake, who a witness stand against all unrighteousness and all ungodliness, who a sufferer am for the righteous Seed's sake, waiting for the redemption of it, who a crown that is mortal seek not, for that fadeth away, but in the light dwell, which comprehends that crown, which light is the condemnation of all such; in which light I witness the crown that is immortal, that fades not away.

From him who to all your souls is a friend, for establishing of righteousness and cleansing the land of evil doers and a witness against all wicked inventions of men and murderous plots, which answered shall be with the light in all your consciences, which makes no covenant with death, to which light in you all I speak, and am clear.

F.G.

who is of the world called George Fox, who a new name hath which the world knows not.

We are witnesses of this testimony, whose names in the flesh are called Thomas Aldam
Robert Craven.[g]

He brought me in before him before he was dressed, and one Harvey:[1] (that had come amongst Friends but was disobedient) waited upon him.

[1] Charles Harvey, groom of the bed-chamber.

[g] . . . . . . [g] Presumably the witnesses to the testimony are the authors of the introductory paragraph with its third person reference to Fox and its precise dating. The title is in Fox's own hand.

And so when I came before him[1] I was moved to say, 'Peace be on this house'; and I bid him keep in the fear of God that he might receive wisdom, that by it he might be ordered, that with it he might order all things under his hand to God's glory. And I spake much to him of Truth, ⟨and a great deal of discourse I had with him about religion, wherein he carried himself very moderately; but⟩ he said we quarrelled with the priests, whom he called ministers; and I told him I did not quarrel with them, but they quarrelled with me and my friends. And such teachers, and prophets, and shepherds, that the prophets, Christ, and the apostles declared against—if we owned the prophets, Christ, and the apostles, we could not hold them up but must declare against them by the same power and spirit. And the prophets, Christ, and the apostles declared freely; and they declared against them that did not declare freely; such as preached for filthy lucre and divined for money and preached for hire and were covetous and greedy like the dumb dogs that could never have enough; and such priests as did bear rule by their means and the people that loved to have it so. Now they that have the same spirit that Christ, and the prophets, and apostles had could not but declare against all such now as they did then. And several times he said it was very good, and truth, and I told him that all Christendom so called had the Scriptures but they wanted the power and spirit that they had that gave them forth; and therefore they were not in fellowship with the Son, nor with the Father, nor with the Scriptures, nor one with another.

And many more words I had with him. And many people began to come in, that I drew a little backward, and as I was turning he catched me by the hand and said these words with tears in his eyes, 'Come again to my house; for if thou and I were but an hour in a day together we should be nearer one to the other', and that he wished me no more ill than he did to his own soul. And I told him if he did he wronged his own soul; and so I bid him

[1] The meeting took place 6th March, 1655.

hearken to and hear God's voice that he might stand in his counsel and obey it; if he did so, that would keep him from hardness of heart, and if he did not hear God's voice his heart would be hardened. And he said it was true. So I went out, and he bid me come again. And then Captain Drury came out after me and told me his Lord Protector said I was at liberty and might go whither I would, ' And ', says he, ' my Lord says you are not a fool ', and said he never saw such a paper in his life as I had sent him before by him. ⟨Then I was brought into a great hall, where the Protector's gentlemen were to dine; and I asked them what they did bring me thither for. They said, it was by the Protector's order, that I might dine with them. I bid them let the Protector know I would not eat a bit of his bread, nor drink a sup of his drink. When he heard this,⟩ he said that there was a people risen, meaning us, that he could not win either with honour, high places, or gifts, but all other people he could. For we did not seek any of their places, gifts, nor honours, but their salvation and eternal good, both in this nation and elsewhere. ⟨But it was told him again that we had forsook our own, and were not like to look for such things from him.⟩

So I went to the inn again. And this Captain Drury was an enemy to me and Truth and opposed it; and when professors came to me and he was by, he would scoff at trembling and call us Quakers, as the Independents and Presbyterians had nicknamed us before. And he came to me one time and told me, as he was lying on his bed in the daytime to rest, he fell a-trembling, that his joints knocked together and his body shook so he could not get off the bed. He was shaken so that he had no strength left, and cried to the Lord, and he felt his power was upon him that he tumbled off the bed, and cried to the Lord and said he would never speak against the Quakers more, and such as trembled at the word of God.

And one time a company of officers desired me to pray with them and I was loath, but at last I felt the power and spirit of God; and the Lord's power did so shatter them and shake them that they wondered, though they did not live in it.

And thus the Lord God of Heaven carried me over all in his power; and set his power and truth over the nation.

⟨When I came from Whitehall to The Mermaid at Charing Cross (which had been my prison) I stayed not long there but⟩ went into the city of London and great and mighty meetings we had. Many times I could hardly go along the streets, nor hardly get to a meeting, nor from a meeting, for the tumults of people; and the Truth spread exceedingly.

And the sheriff of Lincoln,[1] and Thomas Aldam, and divers Friends came up to London, and Alexander Parker abided with me.

And I went to Whitehall and was moved to declare the day of the Lord amongst them, and how the Lord was come to teach his people himself. ⟨So I preached Truth⟩ both to the officers and such as were called Oliver's gentlemen of his guard. And there was a priest (Oliver Protector had several priests that were his newsmongers), one that opposed when I was declaring the word of the Lord amongst them, that was an envious priest, and I bid him repent. And he put it in his news-book the next week that I had been at Whitehall and had bid a godly minister repent.[2]

But when I went again I met with him and abundance that gathered about me and I silenced the priest and manifested him to be a liar in several things that he did affirm then. Also he put in the news-book that I wore silver buttons which was false, for they were but alchemy. And after, he put in his news-book that I hung ribands on people's arms which made them to follow me; which was another of his lies for I never wore nor used ribands in my life.

And three Friends went to examine this priest that gave forth this false intelligence and to know of him where he had that information, and he told them it was a woman told

[1] Robert Craven.

[2] The newsmonger-priest was Henry Walker.

him so, and when they came again he would tell them the woman's name: but when they came again, he said it was a man but would not tell them his name then, but if they would come again he would tell them his name and where he lived. But when they came again the third time he said if I would give it under my hand there was no such thing he would put it in the news-book. The Friends carried it under my hand to him but he would not put it in, but was in a rage and threatened them with the constable; and this was the deceitful doing of this forger of lies; and these lies they spread over all the nation in the news-books to render Truth odious and to put evil in people's minds against Friends and Truth, which may be seen more at large in the printed book, of clearing the slanderous lies and reports against Friends and Truth.[1]

And these priests, the newsmongers, were of the Independent sect like those in Leicestershire, but the Lord's power came over all their lies and many came to see them.

The Lord's power went over the nation insomuch that many Friends were moved to go into most parts up and down the nation about this time, and into Scotland ⟨to sound forth the everlasting Gospel⟩; and the glory of the Lord was set over all to his everlasting praise.

And a great convincement there was in London, and many in Oliver Protector's house and family.[2]

And I went to see him again but could not get to him, the officers began to be so rude.

And sometimes they would turn up my coat and see for my leather breeches and then they would be in a rage.

And the Presbyterians and Independents and Baptists were in a great rage, for many of their people came to be turned to the Lord Jesus Christ, and sat under his teaching and received his power and felt it in their hearts; and then they were moved of the Lord to declare against the rest of

[1] *A Declaration . . . against several false Reports . . . in several News-Books*, etc., 1655.

[2] Charles Harvey (for a time), Mary Saunders, Lettice Shaine, Theophilus Green, are known to have been Friends.

them. So the Lord's day was set over all. And I appointed a meeting in the fields near Acton, where the Lord's power came over all and his word of life and truth was declared freely.

About this time George Fox gave forth a paper to all professors; and to the Pope and all the Kings in Europe; and to all such as follow after the world's fashions; and to Oliver Protector and such as were to try the ministers; as are hereunto annexed.

To all Professors,

All they that professed Jesus Christ in words, and heard him not when he was come, they said he was a deceiver and a devil. The chief priests were they that called him so. The Jews said, 'He hath a devil and is mad; why do ye hear him?' And others said, 'These are not the words of him that hath a devil: can the devil open the eyes of the blind?' And the Jews doubted whether he was the Christ or no; and so all, Jews in the knowledge, in the notion, that profess a Christ without, where Christ is risen, they do not own him, but do doubt of him; the same Christ now and for ever. Jesus Christ said, 'I and my Father are one'; and then the Jews took up stones to stone him. And where Jesus Christ is now come and made manifest, the Jews in the outward, in the profession, have the same hard hearts inwardly now, that they had then; and do cast stones at him where he is risen. Jesus said, 'For which of these good works do ye stone me?' The Jews answered and said, 'For thy good works we stone thee not; but for blasphemy, and that thou being a man, makest thyself God.' Jesus answered them and said, 'Is it not written in your law, I said, Ye are gods?' (John x. 34) and the Scripture cannot be broken . . .

When Stephen confessed Jesus, the substance of all figures and types, and was brought before the chief priests to his trial, he told them, 'The Most High dwelleth not in temples made with hands'; and brought the prophet to witness, and told them they were stiff-necked, and uncircumcised hearts and resisted the Holy Ghost, as their fathers did. And Stephen was full of the Holy Ghost, and said he saw Jesus, and they run upon him and stoned him to death, calling upon the Lord.

When Paul confessed Jesus Christ and his resurrection, Festus said he was mad. And when Paul preached the resurrection, some mocked; the Jews persuaded the people, and stoned him, and drove him out of the city, and thought he had been dead. The Jews stirred up the Gentiles to make their minds evil-affected towards their brethren. The Jews stirred up the devout and honourable women, and the chief of the city, and raised up persecution against Paul and Barnabas, and expelled them out of their coasts; and there was an assault made both of the Gentiles and of the Jews, with their rulers, to use them despitefully and to stone them. And all Jews in the notion do stir up the rulers, and stir up the ignorant people, and incense them against Jesus Christ where he is risen, to stone them all with one consent. It is that the Scripture might be fulfilled and the blindness of the people might be discovered.

And the same power now is made manifest, and doth overturn the world, and did overturn the world, to the exalting of the Lord, and to the pulling down of the kingdom of Satan and of this world, and setting up of his own kingdom, to his everlasting praise . . . The priests they incense all the ignorant people for fear their trade should go down; and the professors they show forth what is in them, full of rage . . . Truth hath been talked of, but now it is possessed. Christ hath been talked of, but now he is come and is possessed. The glory hath been talked of, but now it is possessed, and the glory of man is destroyed. The Son of God hath been talked of, but now he is come, and hath given us an understanding. Unity hath been talked of, but now it is come . . . Praises, praises be to thee, whose glory now shines, whose day, which is hid from the world, hid from all wise ones and all the prudent, hid from the fowls of the air, hid from all vultures' eyes, and all venomous beasts, and all liars, and all dogs, and all swine. But to them that fear thy name the secrets of thee are made manifest, the treasures of wisdom are opened and the fulness of knowledge; for thou thyself dost make thyself manifest to thy children.[1]

To the Pope and all the Kings in Europe,
Friends,

Ye heads, and rulers, and kings, and nobles of all sorts, be not bitter, nor hasty in persecuting the lambs of Christ, neither turn yourselves against the visitations of God, and his tender

[1] In full, *Camb. Jnl.*, i, 170-4; Ellwood, pp. 141-3; Bicent., i, 216-19. But Fox's authorship of this paper is in doubt.

love and mercies from on high, who sent to visit you; lest the Lord's hand, arm, and power take swiftly hold upon you; which is now stretched over the world . . . Let this go to the kings of France, Spain, and the Pope, for them to prove all things and hold that which is good. And first to prove that they have not quenched the Spirit . . . He that feeleth the light that Christ hath enlightened him withal, he feeleth Christ in his mind, which is the power of the cross of Christ, and shall not need to have a cross of wood or stone to put him in the mind of Christ or his cross, which is the power of God.

G.F.[1]

To such as follow after the fashions of the world,

What a world is this; how doth the devil garnish himself; how obedient are the people to do his will and mind, that they are altogether carried with fooleries and vanities, both men and women, that they have lost the hidden man of the heart, and the meek and quiet spirit, which is of the Lord, of great price. They have lost the adorning of Sarah; they are putting on gold gay apparel, plaiting the hair, men and women, they are powdering it; making their backs as if it were bags of meal. And they look so strange that they cannot look at one another; they are so lifted up in pride. Pride hath so lifted them up and is flown up into their heads they snuff up, like wild asses; like Ephraim, they feed upon wind; and are gotten to be like wild heifers, who feed upon the mountains. And pride hath puffed up every one. They are out of the fear of God, men and women, young and old; one puffs up another. They are not in the fashion of the world else, they are not in esteem else, they shall not be respected else, if they have not gold and silver upon their backs, or his hair be not powdered. Or if he have a company of ribands hung about his waist, red or white or black or yellow, and about his knees, and gets a company in his hat, and powders his hair, then he is a brave man, then he is accepted, then he is no Quaker, because he has ribands on his back, and belly, and knees, and his hair powdered. This is the array of the world. But is not this the lusts of the eye, the lusts of the flesh, the pride of life ?

Likewise the women having their gold, their spots on their faces, noses, cheeks, foreheads, having their rings on their fingers, wearing gold, having their cuffs double under and about

[1] In full, *Camb. Jnl.*, i, 174-5; Ellwood, pp. 146-7; Bicent., i, 222-3.

like unto a butcher with white sleeves, having their ribands tied about their hands, and three or four gold laces about their clothes: 'This is no Quaker', say they. This is that that pleaseth the world, this array, this attire pleaseth the world, and if they cannot get these things they are perverse.

Now, are not all these that have got their ribands hung about their arms, backs, waists, knees, hats, hands, like unto fiddler's-boys and show that you are gotten into the basest contemptible life as be in the fashion of the fiddler's-boys and stage-players, and quite out of the paths and steps of solid men. Are not these the spoilers of the creation, and have the fat and the best of it, and waste and destroy it? Do not these cumber God's earth? Let that of God in all consciences answer, and who are in the wisdom, judge. And further, to get a pair of breeches like a coat, and hang them about with points and up almost to the middle, and a pair of double cuffs upon his hands, and a feather in his cap, here's a gentleman; bow before him, put off your hats, bow, get a company of fiddlers, a set of music, and women to dance. This is a brave fellow. Up in the chamber; up in the chamber without, and up in the chamber within. Are these your fine Christians? 'Yea', say they, 'They are Christians.' 'But', say the serious people, 'They are out of Christ's life, and out of the apostles' command, and out of the saints' ornament.' To see such a company as is before mentioned as are in the fashions of the world, a company of them get a couple of bowls in their hands, or tables, or shovel-board; or a horse with a company of ribands on his head, as he hath on his own, and a ring in his ear and so go to horse-racing, to spoil the creature; Oh, these are gentlemen, these are bred up gentlemen, these are brave fellows and they must have their recreation, and pleasures are lawful. And these, in their sports, set up their shouts like unto the wild asses. And they are like unto the kine or beasts, when they are put to grass, lowing when they are full. And here is the glorying of them before mentioned; but it is in the flesh, not in the Lord . . .

G.F.[1]

⟨There was about this time an Order for the Trying of Ministers and for approving, or ejecting them out of their places or benefices, whereupon I writ a paper as follows:⟩

[1] In full, *Camb. Jnl.*, i, 175-7; Ellwood, pp. 144-5; Bicent., i, 219-21.

To Oliver Cromwell and the justices to try ministers, 1654,[1]
Friends,

You that be justices, in commission to try ministers, which hath so long been in the vineyard of God, now see if they be according to the Scriptures, the prophets, Christ, and the apostles, that they disapproved . . .

See if they be not such as teach for filthy lucre, for the love of money, covetous, such as love themselves, who have the form of godliness, but deny the power; from such the apostle bids, turn away . . . Paul gave Timothy an order to try ministers, and he said, 'They must not be covetous, given to wine, nor filthy lucre, nor a novice; lest they be lifted up into pride, and fall into the condemnation of the devil' (1 Tim. iii.). And these he was to try and prove without partiality . . . Christ, when he sent forth his ministers he bade them give freely, as they had received freely; and into what city or town soever they came, enquire who were worthy and there abide; and what they 'set before you', said he, 'that eat'. And these came back again to Christ, and he asked them if they wanted anything, and they said, 'No.' They did not go to a town, and call the people together to know how much they might have by the year, as those that are apostatized do now. The apostle said, 'Have I not power to eat and to drink?' But he did not say, to take tithes, Easter-reckonings, Midsummer-dues, Augmentations, and great sums of money, but, 'Have not I power to eat and to drink?' But he did not use that power amongst the Corinthians . . . From a lover of your souls, and eternal good.

G.F.[2]

CHAPTER IX

AND after, when I had cleared myself in the city, I was moved of the Lord to go into Bedfordshire to John Crook's where there was a great meeting,[3] and people generally convinced of the Lord's truth. And John Crook told me that next day several gentlemen of the country

[1] The Triers of Ministers began work March, 1655.

[2] In full, *Camb. Jnl.*, i, 178-80; Ellwood, pp. 147-9; Bicent., i, 223-5.

[3] The meeting was held at John Crook's country house, Beckerings Park, near Ridgmont, on Sunday, 18th March, 1655.

would come to dine with him, he being a Justice of the Peace, and to discourse with me. And they came and were all convinced of God's eternal Truth. And several Friends went to the steeplehouses that day. And there was a meeting in the country which Alexander Parker went to; and towards the middle of the day, it came upon me to go, though it was several miles distant. And John Crook went with me. And when we came there, there was one Gritton[1] that had been a Baptist, but he was gotten higher than them and called himself a 'trier of spirits', and told people their fortunes, and he pretended to discover to people when their goods were stolen or houses broken up, who the persons were that did it, with which he had got into the affections of many people thataways. This man was got into the meeting and was speaking and making a hideous noise over the young convinced Friends when I came in; and he bid Alexander Parker give a reason of his hope. And because he did not speak presently to him, he cried his mouth was stopped. But Alexander Parker told him Christ was his hope.

So then this Gritton directed his speech to me for I stood still and heard him. And he spoke many things which were not Scripture, and then I asked him whether he could make those things out by Scripture which he had spoken, and he said, 'Yes, yes.'

So then I bid the people take out their Bibles to search the places he might quote for proof of his assertions, but he could not make anything good by Scripture he had said, so he fled out of the house and was ashamed. And his people were generally convinced; and his spirit was discovered and he came no more amongst them. And when his people came to be convinced of God's Truth, they gave forth a book against him and denied his spirit and false discoveries. And many were turned to Christ Jesus that day and came to sit under his teaching; so that the judges were in a great rage in Bedfordshire, and many of the magistrates, because

[1] Nicholas Greaton. See R. Farnsworth: *Witchcraft Cast Out*, 1655.

there were so many turned from the hireling priests to the Lord Jesus Christ's free teaching. But John Crook, by the power of the Lord, was kept over all, though he was turned out from being a justice.

And then at last I turned up through the country to London again, where Friends were finely established in the Truth and great comings-in there were.

And after a while I passed into Kent. At Rochester they kept a guard and there they were examining people, but the Lord's power came so over them that we passed by them and were not stopped. So I went to Cranbrook, where there was a great meeting, and several soldiers, and many were turned to the Lord that day. But after the meeting some of the soldiers were somewhat rude, but the Lord's power came over them. And near Cranbrook there was one Thomas Howsigoe,[1] that was an Independent preacher, was convinced and became a faithful minister for the Lord Jesus.

⟨Some Friends had travelled into Kent before,⟩ and about this time the priests and professors stirred up the magistrates to whip John Stubbs and William Caton at Maidstone for declaring God's Truth unto them, ⟨as may be seen at large in the journal of William Caton's life⟩. And there was one Captain Dunk[2] was convinced, and he went with me to Rye where we had a meeting. And the Major and officers and several captains came in. They took what I said in writing and I was very glad of it; and all were quiet and affected with Truth. And about this time several Friends went beyond seas to declare the everlasting Truth of God.

And after, I went to Romney, they having knowledge of my coming a pretty while before, and there was a mighty meeting of people. And Samuel Fisher was there, who was an eminent preacher among the Baptists. He had been a parish priest, and for conscience sake had laid down his parsonage worth about two hundred pounds a year. And

[1] Thomas Howsigoe (d. 1660) lived at Staplehurst.

[2] John Dunk of Romney, at whose house the meeting was held.

there was another pastor of the Baptists and abundance of their people; and many were shaken with the power of God, and the life sprang up in them. And one of the pastors of the Baptists was so amazed at the Lord's power that he bid one of our Friends that was so wrought upon, have a good conscience; and I was moved of the Lord to bid him take heed of hypocrisy and deceit, and he was silent. And a great convincement there was that day, and many were turned from the darkness to the divine light of Christ and came to see their teachers' error, and to sit under the Lord Jesus Christ's teaching, and to know him their way and their covenant of light, that God had given to be their salvation to the ends of the earth; and they were brought to the one baptism and the one baptizer, Christ Jesus.

And when the meeting was done Samuel Fisher's wife said, 'Now we may discern this day betwixt flesh and spirit, and spiritual teaching from fleshly.' And the people were mightily satisfied; and the two Baptist pastors and their company fell to reasoning amongst the people when they were gone from the meeting. But I walked away. And Samuel Fisher and divers others reasoned for the word of life that was declared that day, and the other pastor and his party reasoned against it, so it cut and divided them in sunder and cut them in the midst. And a Friend came and told me that the Baptists were disputing one with another, and he desired me to go up to them, but I bid them let them alone, for the Lord would divide them and they that reasoned for Truth would be too hard for the other, and so it was.

And Samuel Fisher denied all and came to be a faithful and free minister and preacher of Christ and his Truth and was often in prisons in England and continued till the King came in and at last died a prisoner for the Lord's Truth. And he went, being moved of the Lord to declare his word of life, to Dunkirk and to Holland, ⟨divers parts of Italy, as⟩ Leghorn, Rome; and yet the Lord preserved him and John Stubbs over their Inquisitions.

And at that time John Love was in prison in the Inquisition at Rome. And there, as it was reported by the nuns in France, they hanged him in the night-time; not that they had anything against him, but that they said he was a dangerous person and might do hurt to their religion. And then after they had hanged him they reported that he had fasted himself to death. And much might be written of these things.

And from Romney I passed to Dover, and near unto Dover there was a governor that was convinced and his wife that had been Baptists. And at Dover I had a meeting where several were convinced: and the Baptists were very much offended and envious, but the Lord's power came over all. And there Luke Howard was convinced who became a faithful minister; and so I passed to Canterbury where there were a few honest-hearted people turned to the Lord, who stand to this day, and are become a great meeting since.

And so I came to Cranbrook again, where I had a great meeting and one that was with me went to the steeplehouse and was cast into prison[1] but the Lord's power came over all and his Truth spread.

And from thence I passed into Sussex where I came to a lodge near Horsham[2] where there was a great meeting and many were convinced. And from thence I passed to Steyning where we had a meeting in the market-house, and several were convinced thataways, and the Lord's power came over all.

And several meetings I had thataways. And there was a meeting appointed at a great man's house. And he and his son went to fetch several priests that had threatened to come and dispute, but when the time came none of them would come, the Lord's power struck them. And a glorious meeting we had; and the man of the house and his son were vexed because none of the priests would come. So the hearts of people were opened by the Spirit of God,

[1] This was Henry Clark, of Bankside, Southwark.

[2] Sidgwick Lodge, home of Bryan Wilkinson.

and they were turned from the hirelings to Christ Jesus their shepherd who had purchased them without money and would feed them without money or price. And Nicholas Beard and many others were convinced that day, that came to hear the dispute. And so the Lord's power came over all and his day many came to see. And abundance of Ranters and professors there were that had been so loose in their lives that they began to be weary of it and had thought to have gone into Scotland to have lived privately, and the Lord's Truth catched them all and their understandings were opened by his light, spirit, and power, through which they came to be settled upon the Lord; and so became very good Friends in the Truth and became very sober men, that great blessing and praising the Lord there was amongst them, and admiration in the country.

And from thence I passed through the countries till I came to Reading, and there were a few that had been convinced; and on the First-day in George Lamboll's orchard almost all the whole town came together. And there came two of Judge Fell's daughters to me and George Bishop ⟨of Bristol⟩ with his sword by his side ⟨for he was a captain⟩. And a glorious meeting it was, and a great convincement of people there was that day, and people were mightily satisfied. And many Baptists and Ranters came privately after meeting, reasoning and disputing, but the Lord's power came over them all. And the Ranters pleaded that God made the devil, but I denied it and I told them I was come into the power of God and the Seed Christ which was before the devil was, and bruised the head of him, and he became a devil by going out of truth and so became a murderer and a destroyer. And so I showed them that God did not make the devil, for God is a God of Truth and made all things good and blessed them, but did not bless the devil and the devil is bad and was a liar and a murderer from the beginning and spoke of himself and not from God. So the Truth stopped them and bound them and came over all the highest notions in the nation and confounded them, for with the power of the Lord God I was manifest and sought to be manifest to the spirit of God in all, that with it (which they vexed and quenched and grieved), they might be turned to God, as many were turned to the Lord Jesus Christ by the spirit of God and to sit under the Lord Jesus Christ's teaching. And there was a great meeting settled there.

And from thence I passed up to London; and after I had stayed there a while and had large meetings I passed into Essex and came to Coggeshall where there had been lately dead a fine young man, a minister.[1] And there were about two thousand people at a meeting[2] (as it was judged) and Amor Stoddard and Richard Hubberthorne were with me, and a glorious meeting there was, and the word of life freely declared, and people were turned to the Lord Jesus Christ their teacher and saviour, their way, their truth, and their life. Several hours it lasted and after the meeting was done I walked out into the fields as I used to do. And when I was gone, two or three Justices of the Peace came riding up fiercely to me in the field, and they stopped when they came at me. And I turned and looked at them and they then turned and spoke never a word to me. And one of them said to the other, 'What, will you go away, sir ?' 'Yes ', said the other, and so they went to the house. And Friends had some books of our principles, and they bought some of the books, and went their ways; but they had mischief in their hearts, for they were a kind of Presbyterian Independent justices that had sent James Parnell to Colchester prison.

And on the sixth day I had a meeting near Colchester,[3] where the Independent teachers came and many professors; and when I had stepped down from the place where I spoke, one of the Independent teachers began to make a jangling, and Captain Stoddard being with me, said, 'Stand up again, George ', for I was going away and did not at the first

[1] James Parnell (1636-1656), Quaker martyr, died in Colchester Castle, but not until the following year.

[2] Held near the end of July, 1655.

[3] At Lexden, 29th July, 1655.

hear them. So I stood up again, and after a while the Lord's power came over them and they were confounded and the Lord's Truth came over all. And a great flock of sheep has the Lord Jesus Christ in that country that feeds in his pasture of life.

And from thence I went to a place near Colchester where the First-day we had a mighty meeting and the Lord's power came over all, and people were mightily satisfied and they were turned to the Lord Jesus Christ's free teaching, and they received it gladly: and many of these people were of the stock of the martyrs.

And as I went through Colchester I went to visit James Parnell in prison, but the cruel gaoler would hardly let us come in or stay with him.

Now the manner of his casting into prison was thus: he was at a meeting at Coggeshall aforesaid and the Independent justices and priests[1] then kept a fast-day there and they sent for James from the meeting into the steeple-house; and when he came in, under a pretence to reason with him and to dispute with him, a justice of the peace clapped him on the back and said he arrested him and so sent him to the gaol.

And there the gaoler's wife threatened to have his blood, and there they did destroy him as before is mentioned, [and] as in the book of his life and death[2] may be more fully seen.

And from thence I came to Ipswich where we had a little meeting but exceeding rude; but the Lord's power came over them and I said after the meeting if any had a desire to hear further they might come to the inn. And there came in a company of rude butchers that had abused Friends, but the Lord's power so chained them that they could not do mischief. And I writ and gave forth a paper to the town warning them of the day of the Lord and to repent of the evil they lived in, and turning them to Christ their teacher and way, and from their own hireling teachers.

[1] John Sams, Independent vicar of Coggeshall.

[2] See p. 163 ante, and in *The Lamb's Defence against Lies* . . ., 1656.

And from thence we passed to Mendlesham in Suffolk where Robert Duncon and his wife lived, where we had a large meeting that was quiet, and the Lord's power was over all.

And from thence we passed to Captain Lawrence[1] where it was judged there was above a thousand people, and a-many people of quality were there. And a great convincement there was, they being turned to Christ their way and their teacher; and they sit under him their vine to this day. And all was quiet. And there we left Amor Stoddard and some more Friends to meet us again in Huntingdonshire.

And from thence we passed about the second hour in the morning to Norwich where Christopher Atkinson that dirty man, had run out and brought dishonour upon the Lord's Truth and his name; but he was judged and denied by Friends, and he after gave forth a paper of condemnation of his sin and evil.

And so we came to Yarmouth and stayed there a while, where there was a Friend one Thomas Bond in prison for the Truth of Christ. And there we had some service for the Lord, and some were turned to the Lord in that town.

And from thence we passed to another town about twenty miles off and there were many tender people in that town, and I was moved of the Lord as I sat upon my horse to speak to the people in several places as I passed alongst.

And from thence we went about five miles to another town, and so we went to an inn and set up our horses, having travelled forty five miles that day, Richard Hubberthorne being with me. And there were some Friendly people in the town, and we had a tender, broken meeting amongst them in the Lord's power, to his praise. And we bade the hostler to have our horses ready by three of the clock in the morning for we were to ride to Lynn about thirty three miles next morning. But when we were in bed at our inn, about eleven o'clock at night came in the

[1] Captain John Lawrence of Wramplingham, near Norwich.

constable and officers with a great rabble of people into the inn, and said they were come to search for two horsemen that rid upon grey horses and in grey clothes, with a hue and cry to apprehend us, from a justice, who lived near that town about five miles off where I had spoken to the people in the street as I passed along, a house having been broken the Seventh-day at night.

And so they set a guard with forks and pikes upon us that night and made many of those friendly people to watch us with others. And we told them we were honest and innocent men and scorned and abhorred such things. And the next day we were up betimes and the constable with his guard carried us before a Justice of Peace about five miles off. And we took two or three of the sufficient men of the town with us that had been with us at Captain Lawrence's at the great meeting, and they could testify that I lay the Seventh-day and the First-day night at Captain Lawrence's. For they said the house was broken up the Seventh-day night.

Now when I was brought a prisoner to London[1] to the Mermaid and had before Oliver, this Captain Lawrence brought to me about ten Independent justices, and a great deal of discourse I had with them that grieved them, for they pleaded for imperfection and sin as long as they lived and did not like to hear of Christ's teaching his people himself, and making people as clean here whilst upon the earth as Adam and Eve were before they fell.

So they had plotted together this mischief against me in the country, and pretended and forged that a house was broken, and so sent this hue and cry after me; their malice was so against the righteous and the just. And they were vexed and troubled to hear of the great meeting at John Lawrence's aforesaid for there was a Colonel convinced there that day that lived and died in the Truth. But the constable and his guard carried Richard Hubberthorne and me to the justice about five miles off (as aforesaid), in

[1] This paragraph refers to Fox's removal to London in February, 1655; see p. 193 ante.

our way towards Lynn, who was not an Independent justice as the rest. And when we were brought before him he began to be angry because we would not put off our hats to him, and I told him I had been before the Protector and he was not offended at my hat, and why should he be offended at it who was but one of his servants. So he read the forged hue and cry for the pretended house-breaking. And the constable told him that we had good horses and if it pleased him he would carry us to Norwich Gaol.

But I told the justice that that night they pretended the house was broken I was at Captain Lawrence's and these men could testify the truth thereof; and the justice, after examination of us and them, said he was sorry he had no more against us, for he believed we were not the men that had broken the house; but we told him he ought not to be sorry for not having evil against us, but rather be glad, for to rejoice when he got evil against people for house-breaking and the like, that was not a good mind in him.

So it was a good while before he would resolve either to let us go or send us to prison, and the wicked constable stirred him up as aforesaid; but after we had admonished him to fear the Lord God in his day, and he confessed we were not the men, he let us go. And the Lord's power came over him and their snare was broken.

And after, a great people came out of that town to the Lord: where I was moved to speak to them in the street and from whence this hue and cry came.

And from thence we passed to Lynn, and came there about three o'clock in the afternoon, and set up our horses; and we lighted on Joseph Fuce who was an ensign; and we bid him speak to as many people of the town that feared God, and the officers and captains, to come together. And we had a very glorious meeting amongst them and turned them to the spirit of God by which they might know God and Christ and know the Scriptures and so to learn of God and Christ as the prophets and apostles did, and many were convinced there that day. And it became a fine meeting that sits under the Lord Jesus Christ's teaching and is come off the hirelings. And so we desired Joseph Fuce to get us the gates opened by three o'clock in the morning, it being a garrison, for we had forty miles to ride the next day.

And so about the eleventh or twelfth hour the next day we came to a town near the Isle of Ely called Sutton where Amor Stoddard and his company met us again. And a multitude of people was gathered there and there were four priests and the priest of the town,[1] and a great jangle he made, but the Lord's power so confounded him that he passed away. And the other three priests stayed, whereof one was convinced.

And one of the other two, whilst I was speaking, came to lean upon me: and I bid him sit down seeing he was so slothful. And a great convincement there was that day; and many hundreds were turned from the darkness to the light and from the power of Satan unto God, and from the spirit of error to the spirit of truth to lead them into all truth. And people came to this meeting from Huntingdon and beyond, and the mayor's wife of Cambridge,[2] and they were settled under Christ's teaching and knew him their shepherd to feed them, and they died in Truth. And a glorious meeting it was, and the word of life was freely declared and gladly received. And the meeting ended in the power of the Lord and in peace. And after it was done I walked away and desired them to give our horses some provender for we had ridden a great way, and I walked up into a garden and a Friend came to me and said several justices were come to break up the meeting; but many people were gone away, so they missed their design; and after they had stayed awhile they passed away in a fret.

And after this I passed to Cambridge that evening, and when I came into the town [a]it was all in an uproar, hearing of my coming,[a] and the scholars were up, and were exceeding rude. But I kept on my horse-back and rid through

[1] William Hunt.

[2] Samuel Spalding was mayor in 1655.

[a]. . . . . .[a] *S.J.*, p. 40.

them in the Lord's power. 'Oh!' said they, 'he shines, he glisters!' but they unhorsed Captain Amor Stoddard before he could get to the inn; and when we were in the inn they were exceeding rude in the inn, and in the courts and in the streets. The miners, and colliers, and cartmen could never be ruder.

And there John Crook met us at the inn. And the people of the house asked me what I would have for supper, as is the usual way of inns. 'Supper', said I, 'were it not that the Lord's power was over these rude scholars it looked as if they would make a supper of us and pluck us to pieces'; for they knew I was so against their trade, which they were there as apprentices to learn, the trade of preaching, that they raged as bad as ever Diana's craftsmen did against Paul.

And within night [b]an alderman who was a Friend came to the inn to us, the people thronging up into the very chamber door in the inn. And after a while, I passed through all the multitude[b] to his house. And as I walked through the streets all the town was up, but they did not know me, it was darkish. But they were in a rage not only against me, but against him also, so that he was almost afraid to walk the streets with me for the tumult. So when I came into his house we sent for all the friendly people, and had a [b]sweet heavenly[b] meeting in the power of God amongst them, and there I stayed all night.

And the next morning I ordered my horse to be ready saddled by the sixth hour in the morning and so we passed out of town, and the Lord's power came over all. And the destroyers were frustrated the next morning, for they thought I would have stayed in the town and they thought to have done us mischief. And so we passed through the countries to Bishop Stortford and there were some convinced, and so to Hertford where there are some convinced also and are become a fine meeting.

And so from thence we returned back to London, where Friends gladly received us, and the Lord's power carried us

[b]......[b] *S.J.*, p. 40.

through many snares and dangers and we had great service for the Lord. And many hundreds were turned to sit under the Lord Jesus Christ their saviour's teaching and to praise the Lord through him.

And then we stayed at London awhile visiting Friends, and the Lord's power was over all. And James Nayler was come up to London. And we had great disputes with professors of all sorts and many reproaches they cast upon Truth, and lying slanderous books they gave forth against us, but we answered them all and cleared God's Truth and set it over them all. The wicked priests, Presbyterians and Independents, raised lies upon us, as that we should carry bottles which we gave people to drink which made them follow us.[1]

And this year came out the Oath of Abjuration from Oliver Protector,[2] by which many Friends suffered. And several Friends went to speak with him but he began to harden. ⟨And sufferings increasing upon Friends by reason that envious magistrates made use of that oath as a snare to catch Friends in, who, they knew could not swear at all,⟩ thereupon a paper was given forth to the magistrates as followeth:

A Paper of George Fox's to Oliver Protector concerning his making people to suffer for not taking the Oath of Abjuration. 1655.

The magistrate is not to bear the sword in vain, which is a terror to the evil doers, but the magistrates bearing the sword in vain, are not a terror to evil doers, so they are not a praise to them that do well. So God hath raised up a people with his spirit, whom people and priests and magistrates without the fear of God scornfully call Quakers, which do cry against

[1] Ellwood editions here print a paper, *To those that made a scorn of Trembling and Quaking*, Ellwood ed., 1694, pp. 156-60; Bicent., i, 238-43. It had in fact already been published as a tract in 1654. And another entitled, *An Epistle to Churches gathered into outward forms upon the Earth*, Ellwood ed., 1694, pp. 161-3; Bicent., i, 243-6.

[2] On 26th April, 1655, a Proclamation required persons suspected to be Roman Catholics to take an oath abjuring papal authority and doctrine, upon pain of imprisonment and forfeiture of estate. This occurred at the time of Fox's visit to London, recorded on p. 209.

drunkenness, for such are they that destroy God's creatures; and do cry against oaths, for because of such the land mourns, and they we see are at liberty, to which the sword should be a terror; and for crying against such are many cast into prison . . . The royal law of Christ is trodden under foot, to do as you would be done by; so that men can profess him in words and talk, but crucify him wheresoever he appears, and cast him into prison, as the talkers of him always did in the generations and ages past.

If men fearing God and men of courage did bear the sword, and covetousness were hated, then that would be a terror to evil doers and a praise to them that do well, and not cause them to suffer. Here equity would be heard in our land, and righteousness would stand up and take place, which gives not place to the unrighteous, but judgeth it. To the measure of God in thee I speak, to consider, . . . for whom thou dost rule, that thou mayest receive power from God for him to rule, and all that is contrary to God may be with his light condemned.

From a lover of thy soul and eternal good,

G.F.[1]

⟨But sufferings and imprisonments continuing and increasing, and the Protector (under whose name they were inflicted) hardening himself against the complaints that were made unto him, I was moved to give forth the following lines amongst Friends, to bring the weight of their sufferings more heavy upon the heads of the persecutors:⟩

Who is moved by the power of the Lord to go lie in prison and offer himself to the justice for his brother or sister that lies in prison, that his brother or sister may come forth of prison, and so to lay down his life for his brother or sister ? . . . If any brother in the light . . . be moved of the Lord to go to the priest or to the justice or impropriator, to lie in prison for his brother, . . . he may cheerfully do it, and heap coals of fire upon the head of the adversaries of God. Or likewise any that suffer for the Truth by them who be in the untruth . . ., as Christ hath laid down his life for you, so lay down your lives one for another. Hence you may go over the heads of the persecutors, and reach the witness of God in them all . . . And this shall

[1] In full, *Camb. Jnl.*, i, 192-4; Ellwood, pp. 163-5; Bicent., i, 246-8.

lay a judgment upon them all for ever, and be witnesses to that in their consciences for ever.

G.F.[1]

⟨Besides this, I writ also a short epistle to Friends, as an encouragement to them in their several exercises.⟩[2]

And after a while I passed down through the countries to Bedfordshire and Northamptonshire. And at Wellingborough I had a great meeting, and the Lord's everlasting power and truth was over all. And many in that country were turned to the Lord, though a great rage was amongst the professors, but the power, and spirit, and truth of God kept Friends over the rage of people; and great spoiling of goods there was upon Friends for tithes by the Independent and Presbyterian priests and some Baptist priests that had gotten into steeplehouses, as the books of sufferings will declare. So I went into Leicestershire where Colonel Hacker said if I came down there he would imprison me again, though Oliver Protector had set me at liberty; but I came down to Whetstone where his troopers had taken me before; and Colonel Hacker's wife[3] and his marshall came to the meeting and were convinced. And the glorious, powerful day of the Lord was set over all, and many were convinced that day at that meeting, where were two Justices of Peace, Peter Price and Walter Jenkins, that came out of Wales, that were convinced and came to be ministers of Christ.

So I passed from thence to Sileby to William Smyth's where there was a great meeting and there came several Baptists; and there was one of their Baptist teachers convinced that said he had baptized thirty of a day, and came to the Lord's teaching by his spirit and power.

And I passed from thence to Drayton my native town where all the priests and professors had gathered so much against me, through which I was sent to Oliver, and never

[1] George Fox Papers (x), p. 99; also printed in Ellwood, p. 165; Bicent., i, 248, 249.

[2] Printed, Ellwood, p. 166; Bicent., i, 249.

[3] Isabel Hacker, formerly Brunts.

a priest or professor did appear. And I asked some of my relations where were all the priests and professors now, and they said that the priest of Nuneaton was dead and there were eight or nine of them seeking to get into his benefice, and, 'They will let you alone now, for they are like a company of crows, when a rotten sheep is dead, they all gather together to pluck out his puddings, and so do the priests for a fallen benefice.' And these were some of their own hearers said so of them. So they had spent their venom against me, and the Lord delivered me by his power out of their snares.

And then I went to Baddesley[1] where there was a great meeting from many parts, and many came far to it. And many were convinced and turned to the Lord, and they that were convinced came under Christ's teaching and were settled upon him, their foundation and their rock. And from thence I passed into Nottinghamshire and had large meetings there, and so into Derbyshire where the Lord's power came over all, and many were turned from the darkness to the light and from the power of Satan unto God and came to receive the Holy Ghost; and great miracles by the power of the Lord were done in many places by several.

And there James Nayler met me in Derbyshire where seven or eight priests had challenged him to a dispute. And I had a travail in my spirit for him and the Lord answered me. And I was moved to bid him go on, and that God Almighty would go with him and give him the victory in his power. And so the Lord did, that all the people saw the priests were nothing and foiled, and cried, 'A Nayler, a Nayler, hath confuted them all.' So after, he came to me again, praising the Lord.

And so the Lord's day was proclaimed and set over all: and people began to see the apostacy and slavery they had been in, under their hireling teachers for means; and they came to know their teacher the Lord Jesus who had bought

[1] Baddesley Ensor, near Atherstone. Fox was there 6th November, 1655. (*Ann. Cata.* 165A.)

them and purchased them and made their peace betwixt them and God. And Friends came out of Yorkshire to see us and were glad of the prosperity of Truth.

And after this I passed into Warwickshire through Friends, visiting their meetings, and so into Worcestershire. And I had a meeting at Birmingham as I went, where there were several convinced and turned to the Lord and stand to this day.

And I came to one Cole's[1] house in Worcestershire, near Chadwick,[2] who gave an Independent preacher a meeting place. And the Independent came to be convinced. And a great meeting it was; and the meeting place would not hold the people,[3] and many were turned to the Lord that day. And this Cole, the old man, gave the Independent preacher a hundred pounds a year when he was convinced. But after he was convinced he laid aside his preaching. And then the time of trials came, and this Independent did not stand to that which did convince him but turned back; and then the old Cole took away his hundred pounds a year from him again. And the old man died in God's Truth.

And I heard at Evesham that the magistrates there had cast several of my friends in prison. And they had heard of my coming and they made a pair of stocks a yard and a half high with a trap door to come to them. And I sent for Edward Pittway,[4] a Friend, that lived near Evesham and he came to me about fifteen miles and I asked him the truth of the thing, and he said it was so. And that night I went back again with him to Evesham; and at night we had a large precious meeting and Friends and people were refreshed with the word of life and the power of the Lord. And the next morning I got up and rid to one of the prisons and visited Friends and encouraged them; and then I rid to the other prison where there were several in prison,

[1] Anthony Cole.

[2] 3 miles from Bromsgrove.

[3] Fox preached on the hill side. (*F.P.T.*)

[4] Edward Pittway lived at Bengeworth.

and one Friend, Humphrey Smith, that had been a priest, but was become a fine minister of Christ. And as I was turned away from the prison and going out of town I espied the magistrates coming up the town to have seized on me in prison, but the Lord frustrated their intent that the innocent escaped their snare and the Lord God's blessed power came over them all.

And exceeding rude and envious were the priests and professors about this time, as the books of the sufferings of Friends at this Evesham do show it.[1]

And as I was going, Friends asked me whither I would go, and I told them to Worcester, and when we came to Worcester we went to an inn and had a precious meeting and quiet: and so as we came down the street, some of the professors fell a-discoursing with Friends and like to have made a mutiny in the city. And as we went into the inn they all cluttered in the yard, but I went down amongst them and got them quieted; and the next day I went into the town and had a great deal of discourse with some professors concerning Christ and Truth, one of which denied that Christ according to the flesh was of Abraham and that according to the spirit he was declared the son of God, unto which I answered that he was of the seed of Abraham and made of the seed of David according to the flesh; and according to the spirit declared to be the Son of God as in Romans i. And after, I writ a paper to it.

And so from thence I went to Tewkesbury. And at night I had a great meeting and there came in their priest with a great deal of rabble and rude people, and the priest boasted he would see whether he or I should have the victory. And I turned the people to the divine Light which Christ the heavenly and spiritual man had enlightened them withal; that with that Light they might see their sins and how that they were in death and darkness and without God in the world; and with the same Light they might see Christ from whence it came, their Saviour and Redeemer, who had shed his blood for them and died for them; who was

[1] *The Sufferings, Tryals and Purgings of the Saints at Evesham*, n.d.

their way to God, their truth, and life. And the priest began to rage against the Light and denied it, and so went away; for the light of Christ they could not endure to hear speak of, neither priest nor professor; and so he left his rude company amongst us. But the Lord's power came over them, though mischief was in their hearts.

And from Tewkesbury we passed back again through the country to Warwick and went to an inn; and at night had a meeting at a widow woman's house where many sober people came together. And a precious meeting we had in the Lord's power, and several were convinced and turned to the Lord and stand there to this day. And after the meeting was done, as I was walking out some of the Baptists began to jangle, and the bailiff of the town and his officers came in and said, 'What do these people here at this time of night?' And so he secured Justice John Crook, and Captain Amor Stoddard, and me, and Gerard Roberts, a merchant of London,[1] but we had leave to go to our inn, all that were strangers, and were to come forth in the morning. And the next morning there came a-many rude people into the inn and into our chambers, desperate fellows, but the Lord's power gave us dominion over them. And Gerard Roberts and John Crook went up to the bailiff to speak with him and to know what he had to say to us, and he said we might go our ways: he had little to say to us. And it lay upon me as we rid out of town to ride to his house, and Friends went with me to speak to him and to tell him how that Oliver Protector had given forth an Instrument of Government in which liberty of conscience was granted; and it was very much that he would trouble peaceable people that feared God, contrary to the Instrument of Government.

[c]And the town rose up against us in the open street,[c] and the rude people gathered about us and got stones, and one of them took hold upon my horse bridle. [d]My horse

[1] Gerard Roberts (*c.* 1621-1703), wine cooper, whose house was often a rendezvous for Quaker leaders in London.

[c]. . . . . .[c] *S.J.*, p. 41.

being a strong horse turned his head, and turned the man under his feet, so he hung upon the bridle[d] and broke it. [d]And there came another man or two to throw stones at my face; and they were stopped and were made to loose the other man's hands that hung at the horse bridle. And as we rode through the streets people fell upon us with cudgels and stones and much abused us,[d] throwing stones and striking at us. And the bailiff did not stop or so much as rebuke the rude multitude, so that it was much we were not slain in the streets among them. [d]And when we were ridden quite through the town I was moved of the Lord to go back again into the street to offer up my life among them, and said to Friends whoever found freedom might follow me,[d] and they that did not might go on to Duncow.[1] And John Crook followed me, declaring the word of life to them. [d]So I passed up the street, and people fell upon me with their cudgels and abused me and struck me and threw my horse down, yet by the power of the Lord I passed through them, and called upon the town and shop-keepers and told them of their immodest state, how they were a shame to Christians and the profession of Christianity.[d]

And from thence I passed to Coventry, and when we came there they were closed up with darkness. I went to a professor's house that I had formerly tabled at, and he was drunk. And it grieved my soul so as I did not go into any house in the town, but rid into some streets of the town and into the market place; and set the power of the Lord over the town, [d]and so passed away to Daventry, where I had some jangling with priests.[d]

And from thence I came to Duncow and there I had a meeting at night; and there were some turned to the Lord by his spirit, and many at Warwick and Tewkesbury before mentioned.

So we lay at the Duncow[2] all night and there we met

[1] Now Dunchurch.

[2] Probably the inn with the sign of the Dun Cow.

[d]......[d] *S.J.*, p. 41.

with John Camm, a faithful minister. In the morning there was gathered a rude company of priests and people; and they behaved themselves more like beasts than men, for some of them came riding a-horseback into the room where we were, but the Lord gave us dominion over them all. And we came into Leicestershire where we had a great meeting again at the place where I was taken aforesaid; and so back into Warwickshire to Baddesley.

⟨Here William Edmondson, a Friend that lived in Ireland, had some drawings upon his spirit to come over into England to see me, and by him I writ a few lines to the few Friends then convinced in the north of Ireland, as follows:

Friends,

In that which convinced you wait, that you may have that removed you are convinced of. And all my dear Friends, dwell in the life and love and power and wisdom of God, in unity one with another and with God; and the peace and wisdom of God fill your hearts, that nothing may rule in you but the life, which stands in the Lord God. G.F.

When these few lines were read among the Friends in Ireland at their meeting, the power of the Lord seized upon them all that were in the room.⟩

From Baddesley we passed to Swannington and Higham, and so through the countries into Northamptonshire and Bedfordshire, having great meetings, and many were turned to the Lord by his power and spirit.

And we were at a place called Baldock in Hertfordshire, and I said to them, 'Is there nothing in this town, no profession?' And they told me there were some Baptists and a Baptist woman sick, and John Rush went along to visit her. And when we came there were a-many people in the house that were tender about her; and they told me she was not a woman for this world, and if I had anything to comfort her concerning the world to come I might speak to her. So I was moved of the Lord God to speak to her, and the Lord raised her up that she was well, to the astonishment of the town and country. Her husband's name was Baldock.[1]

[1] Thomas Baldock.

And so we went to our inn[1] again, and there were two desperate fellows fighting so that none durst come nigh them to part them, but I was moved in the Lord's power to go to them, and when I had loosed their hands, I held one by one hand and the other by the other hand; and I showed them the evil of their doings, and convinced them, and reconciled them each to other that they were loving and very thankful, so that people admired at it.

And this Baptist woman and her husband came to be convinced; and many hundreds of people have there been at meetings at their house since, and great meetings and convincement there was up and down in those parts, of people that had received the word of life, and that are come under Christ's teaching, their saviour.

And from thence I passed through the country to Market Street[2] where God had a people, and to Albans, and so to London, where Friends were glad of the glorious prosperity of Truth and the Lord's power that delivered and carried us over all.

CHAPTER X

AFTER a while, when I had visited the meetings there and all things were well, I went out of the city. Only there was one John Toldervy run out, who had been convinced; and the priests took occasion to make a book of it with many lies to render Truth odious in people's eyes and minds, and intitled it, *The Foot out of the Snare.* This man came to see his folly and answered the priests' book[3] and manifested all their lies and folly, and came over them, and died in the Truth; and the Lord's power came over them all and his everlasting seed reigned and reigns to this day. After awhile I went out of the city and left James Nayler behind me in London. And as I parted from him

[1] Probably the George Inn, known later as the 'Quaker's Hostel'.
[2] Markyate Street.
[3] In *The Naked Truth laid open*, 1656.

I cast my eyes upon him, and a fear struck in me concerning him.

And so we came to Reigate in Surrey where we had a little meeting. They told me of one Thomas Moore, a justice of peace, that was a friendly, moderate man; so I went to his house[1] and he was convinced, and he stands a faithful Friend to this day. From thence to one Pachin's,[2] where we had a meeting; several Friends came from London thither after me, and John Bolton and his wife came a-foot some miles in frost and snow, who were moved of the Lord so to do. After we had parted from Friends we went towards Horsham Park[3] and visited Friends.

From thence we passed to Arundel and Chichester, where we had meetings. And at Chichester there were many professors came in and some janglings there were, but the Lord's power was over all. And the woman of the house where the meeting was, though she was convinced, she fell into love with one of the world who was there at that time.

And after, I took her aside and was moved to pray for her, and to speak to her; and a light thing got up in her and she slighted it. And after she married this man of the world she went distracted, for he was greatly in debt and she was greatly disappointed; I was sent for to her and the Lord was entreated, and raised her up again, and settled her mind by his power; and after, her husband died and she acknowledged the just judgments of God were come upon her for slighting my exhortations when I prayed for her.

And so we passed through the country till we came to Portsmouth. And there [a]the guard bid me stand and light off my horse, where I was never unhorsed before, and the captain of the guard proved to be a friendly man.[a] The soldiers had us to the governor's house, and after some examination the Lord's power came over them that we were

[1] Thomas Moore lived at Hartswood.

[2] Thomas Patching lived at Bonwicks Place in Ifield.

[3] The home of Bryan Wilkinson was in a park at Sidgwick Lodge, in Nuthurst parish, two miles from Horsham.

[a]. . . . . .[a] *S.J.*, p. 71.

set at liberty and had a meeting in the town. And so we passed through the countries to Ringwood, and at night we had a meeting there where several were convinced and turned to the spirit of the Lord and Christ Jesus' teaching, their saviour, and stand to this day.

And from Ringwood we came to Poole and went to an inn, and sent into the town to enquire for such as feared the Lord and who were worthy; and we had a meeting with several sober people.[1] William Bayly, a Baptist teacher, was convinced there that time. And the people received the Truth in the inward parts and were turned to the Lord Jesus Christ, their rock and foundation, teacher and saviour, and to this day continue under Christ's teaching; and there is become a great gathering in the name of Jesus of a very tender people.

And we went also to Southampton where we had a meeting and several were convinced there. And Edward Pyott passed with me all this western journey.

And from thence we came to Dorchester and we lighted at an inn that was a Baptist's house; and we sent into the town to the Baptists to let us have their meeting-house to meet in, and to invite the sober people to the meeting; but they denied us, and we sent them word again why would they deny us their synagogue. And so it was noised in the town; and we had sent them word if they would not let us come to their house they might come to our inn, or any people that feared God. And they were in a great rage, and their teacher and many of them came up and they slapped their Bibles on the table; and I asked them why they were so angry, were they angry with the Bible. And they fell into discourse about their water-baptism, and I asked them whether they could say they were sent of God to baptize people, as John was, and whether they had the same power and spirit the apostles had, and they said they had not. Then I asked them how many powers there were whether there were any more than the power of God and the power of the devil, and they said there were not.

[1] The meeting was held at the house of Walter Spurrier, Baptist.

Then I said, 'If you have not the power of God as the apostles had then you act by the power of the devil.' There were many sober people there that said, 'They have thrown themselves on their backs'; and there were many substantial people convinced that night, and a precious service we had there, for the Lord and his power came over all.

And the next morning, as we were passing away, the Baptists being in a rage began to shake the dust off their feet after us. 'What!' said I, 'In the power of darkness; we which are in the power of God shake off the dust of our feet against you.' [b]In Dorsetshire there were but few convinced and in some places none at all.[b]

So from there we came to Weymouth where we enquired after the sober people; and about eighty of them gathered together at a priest's house, all very sober people. And they received the word of life and were turned to their teacher, Christ Jesus, who had enlightened them, by which they might see their sins and see him who saved them from their sins. And a blessed meeting we had with them and they received the Truth in the love of it with gladness of heart. The meeting held for several hours. And the state of their teachers and the apostacy was opened to them and the state of the apostles and the church in their days: and the state of the law and the prophets before Christ, and how Christ came to fulfil them, and how he was their teacher in the apostles' days, and how he was come now to teach his people again himself by his power and spirit. And all was quiet and loving, and the meeting broke up peaceably. Many are added to them, and some that had been Ranters came to own the Truth and came to be very sober.

There was a captain of horse in the town that sent for me and fain would have had me stay longer in the town. But I was not to stay; so he passed out with me about seven miles, and his man and Edward Pyott were with me.

And this captain was the fattest, merriest, cheerfulest

[b]......[b] *S.J.*, p. 42.

man and the most given to laughter that ever I met with; so that I several times was moved of the Lord to speak to him in the dreadful power of the Lord. And yet still he would presently after laugh at any thing that he saw; and I still admonished him to sobriety and the fear of the Lord and sincerity. And we lay at an inn that night. And the next morning I was moved to speak to him again, and then he parted from us the next morning. But he confessed next time I saw him that the power of the Lord had so amazed him that before he got home he was serious enough and left his laughing. And the man came to be convinced, and became a serious and good man, and died in the Truth.

And from thence we passed on to Honiton, and at the inn we enquired what people there were in the town that feared the Lord, and sent for them, and so there came some Particular Baptists to us, where we had a great deal of reasoning with them. And I told them they held their doctrine of particular election in Esau's, Cain's, and Ishmael's nature and not in Jacob's, the second birth's, for they must be born again before they enter the kingdom of God. And the promise of God was to the Seed, not as many but as one, which was Christ; so the election and choice stands in Christ; and they must be such as walk in his light, grace, spirit and faith. And many more words we had with them.

So we passed from thence to Topsham and there we stayed the First-day: and the innkeeper's people were rude. And at this time Miles Halhead and Thomas Salthouse were in prison at Exeter. The next morning we gave forth some queries to the priests and professors, and some rude professors came in to us, and had we not gone when we did they had stopped us. I wore a girdle, and forgot my girdle there behind me; and I sent for it to the innkeeper and he kept it. But he was so plagued about it after, that he went and burnt it lest he should be bewitched by it, as he said, his mind was so devilish; but after he had burned it he was more tormented than before. And some were convinced, nevertheless, and there continues a meeting of good Friends ever since in that town.

And after this we passed to Totnes which was a dark town: and there we lodged all night at an inn, and there Edward Pyott was sick, but the Lord's power healed him again. And the next day we came to Kingsbridge, and went to an inn, and enquired for the sober people of the town. And there was one Nicholas Tripe and his wife, and we went down to their house and they sent for the priest, and some words we had with them but he was soon confounded and so passed away. But Tripe and his wife were convinced; and since there is a meeting of good Friends in that country.

In the evening we went to our inn, and there being many people drinking in the house, I was moved of the Lord to go amongst them and to turn them to the light which Christ, the heavenly man, had enlightened them withal; with which light they may see all their evil ways, and deeds, and words; and with the same light they may see Christ Jesus their saviour. And the innkeeper stood uneasy, seeing it hindered his guests from drinking, snatched up the candle. 'Come', says he, 'here is a light for you to go into your chamber.' So the next morning I spoke to him and told him what an uncivil thing it was for him so to do, and warned him of the day of the Lord, and so we passed away.

And the next day we came to Plymouth to an inn. And at Robert Cary's house in Plymouth we had a very precious meeting. And there was one Elizabeth Trelawney, a baronet's[1] daughter, and she came into the meeting close up to me and clapped her ear very nigh me; which after I perceived she was somewhat thick of hearing. And she was convinced. And after the meeting was done there came some jangling Baptists, but the Lord's power came over them. And this Elizabeth Trelawney came and said, 'George is over all', with a loud voice. And there was a fine meeting settled there ever since in the Lord's power and many faithful Friends there were convinced.

[1] Sir John Trelawney (1592-1664).

And from thence we passed into Cornwall, [c]a dark country, through many desperate services and great opposition, but through the power of the Lord we came over all,[c] to Menheniot parish and there came to an inn. And at night we had a meeting at Edward Hancock's.[1] And thither came Thomas Mounce[2] and a priest and a great deal of people; and we made the priest to confess that he was a minister made by the State and maintained by the State [c]and not sent by Christ.[c] And he was confounded and went his ways. But many of the people stayed and I turned them to the light of Christ by which they might see their sins and see their saviour Christ Jesus, who was their way to God and their mediator that made their peace betwixt them and God, and was their shepherd to feed them; and their prophet to teach them. And I turned them to the spirit of God in themselves, by which they might know the Scriptures and be led into all the truth of them, and with the spirit to know God; and in it to have unity one with another. And many were convinced that time there and came under Christ's teaching. And there are fine gatherings in the name of Jesus thereaways to this day.

And from thence we passed through the countries and through Penryn and came to Helston; and we could not get to the knowledge of any sober people through the badness of the innkeepers. And from thence we passed up to a village where there were some Baptists and sober people lived; and some discourse we had with them, and some were made to confess, but they stumbled at the light of Christ; and they would have had us to have stayed but we passed on from thence to Market Jew[3] and lodged at an inn. [d]When we came thither in the evening I heard one say, 'These men should be examined before they go away.' Therefore I was not to go away till I was

[1] Edward and Elizabeth Hancock lived at Menheniot.

[2] Thomas Mounce (d. 1679) lived at Halbathick, near Liskeard.

[3] Now Marazion. Market Jew denotes 'the market on the ridge of the hill'.

[c]......[c] *S.J.*, p. 42.

examined.[d] And we sent out over night to enquire for any people that feared the Lord, and the next morning the mayor and aldermen gathered together with the high sheriff of the county, and they sent first the constables to us to bid us come before them, at the town hall. And we asked them for their warrant and they said they had none. And then we told them we should not go along with them without a warrant. Then they sent their sergeants and we asked them for their warrant, and they said they had none. And they told us the mayor and aldermen stayed for us; and we told them the mayor and his company did not well to trouble us in our inn and we should not go with them except they had a warrant. And so they went their way, and then they came again and we asked them for their warrant, and then one of them plucked his mace from under his cloak. And we asked them whether it were their custom to molest and trouble strangers in their inns and lodgings. And so at last I said to Edward Pyott, 'Go thy ways, Edward, and see what ails the mayor and his company.' And a great deal of discourse he had with them, but the Lord's power gave him dominion over them all. And when we came away there came several of the officers to us, and we declared unto them the incivility and unworthiness of their carriage towards us, to the Lord's Truth and servants, thus to stop and trouble them in their inn and lodgings and what an unchristian act it was.

And there I gave forth a little paper [d]to the conditions of that dark people[d] to be sent to the seven parishes at the Land's End as followeth: how the Lord was come to teach his people himself by his own son Christ Jesus.

The mighty day of the Lord is come and coming, that all hearts shall be made manifest; the secrets of everyone's heart shall be revealed with the light of Jesus, which cometh from Jesus Christ, who lighteneth every man that cometh into the world, who saith, 'Learn of me.' And, 'This is my beloved Son, hear ye him,' saith God; that all men through him might believe and the world through him might have life.

[d]......[d] *S.J.*, p. 42.

And Christ is come to teach the second priesthood himself. And everyone that will not hear this prophet which God hath raised up, and which Moses spoke of and said, 'Like unto me will God raise you up a prophet, him shall you hear'; everyone that doth not hear this prophet is to be cut off. . . . Those that despise Moses's law died under the hand of two or three witnesses, but how much greater punishment will come upon them that neglect this great salvation, Christ Jesus. . . .

If you do this light hate, this will be your condemnation, if you do it love and come to it, you will come to Christ, which light will bring you off all the world and teachers and ways of all the deceivers in it, to learn of Christ who is the way to the Father.

George Fox[1]
Edward Pyott
William Salt.

And when we came about three or four miles out of the town towards the west, William Salt, that was with me, having a copy of the paper, gave it to Major Peter Ceely's[2] clerk[3] whom he met with, and he rides on before us to a place called St. Ives, and there showed it to his master, a justice of the peace in that county.

But when William Salt told me, [e]and as soon as he had given it, I felt we were taken as prisoners[e] above ten miles before I came to St. Ives where we were taken. [e]He should have given it to me before he gave it abroad. But I saw it would be well, for if I fell upon that bad nature I should crush it and make the good to come forth.[e]

And we rid from thence across the country till we came to Ives. Edward Pyott's horse had lost a shoe and so we stayed at Ives whilst he was shoeing his horse. And I walked down to the seaside in the meanwhile, and when I came up again all the town was up in an uproar, and they were haling Edward Pyott and William Salt before Major

[1] MS. G. Fox Papers (30 R). In full, *Camb. Jnl.*, i, 206-7; Ellwood, pp. 175, 176; Bicent., i, 266-7. The printed versions bear the name of Fox only.

[2] Of the Puritan family of St. Ives.

[3] This was John Keate, see p. 239.

[e]. . . . . .[e] *S.J.*, p. 42.

Peter Ceely, a justice aforesaid. And I followed them into the justice's house, though they did not lay hands upon me, and when we came into the house it was full of rude people so as we could not tell one from another. So I asked them whether there was not an officer amongst them to keep the people civil; and then Major Ceely said he was a magistrate; and then I told him he should show forth gravity, and sobriety, and his authority, and keep the people civil, for I never saw any people ruder. For the Indians were more like Christians than they.

And so after a while they brought forth the paper aforesaid and Major Ceely asked whether I would own it, and I said, 'Yes.' Then he tendered the Oath of Abjuration to us; and then I put my hand in my pocket and gave him the answer which was given to Oliver Protector concerning it, and then he examined us one by one. And there was a young, silly priest[1] with him that asked us many frivolous things; and at last he asked to cut my hair for it was pretty long. And I was not to cut it though many times many did rage against it. And I told them I had no pride in it, and I did not put it on. And many words we had with him as you may see in the great book of *The West answering to the North*. And at last he made a mittimus[2] and put us under a guard of soldiers: and being market day we warned the people of the day of the Lord and declared the Truth to them, though they were hard and wild like Major Ceely.

And the next day he sent us guarded with several horse with swords and pistols and they carried us to Redruth, and it being the First-day the soldiers would have carried us away, and we told them it was their sabbath and we did not use to travel on that day. And several of the townspeople gathered about us, and whilst I held the soldiers in discourse Edward Pyott spoke to the people; and after, whilst Edward Pyott held the soldiers in discourse, I spoke to the people;

[1] Probably Thomas Tregosse, nephew of Peter Ceely, or Leonard Welstead.

[2] 18th January, 1656.

and in the meantime William Salt he got out into the backside and went to the steeplehouse to speak to the priests and people; and the people were exceeding desperate and in a mighty rage against him and abused him. And then the soldiers, missing him, were also in a great rage and ready to kill us all, and many people gathered about us. And I declared the day of the Lord and the word of life to them, and in the afternoon they would needs have us away. And when we had rid to the town's end I was moved of the Lord God to come back again to speak to the old man of the house; and the soldiers took out their pistols and swore that I should not go back but I heeded them not but rid back, and they rid after me. [f]But the truth brought all under; for they rode and I rode and I discharged myself,[f] and I spoke to the old man and the people; and then returned back again with them and reproved them for being so rude and violent.

So the First-day at night we were brought to a town called Smethwick then but since Falmouth.

And there came in the chief hundred constable of the country and a-many sober people, and some of them began to enquire of us. And we told them we were prisoners and under a guard for Christ's sake. And a great deal of discourse of the things of God we had and they were very sober and very loving to us, and some of them were convinced and stand to this day.

And after the constable and people aforesaid were gone, there came in other people and they were very civil and went away very loving; and then we went to our chamber to go to bed; and about the eleventh hour Edward Pyott said, 'I will shut the door, maybe some may come and do us a mischief.' And Keate, that commanded the guard, had a purpose, as we after understood, to have done us some mischief that night, but the door being bolted they missed their design. But the next morning Keate brings in his brother[1]; a rude, wicked man, and puts him into the

[1] Keate's kinsman, one Smithwick.

[f]. . . . . .[f] *S.J.*, pp. 42, 43.

room and he himself stands without. And he walks huffing up and down the room and I bid him fear the Lord; and he comes upon me and struck me with both his hands and clapped his leg behind me and would fain have thrown me down, but he could not. But I stood stiff and still and let him strike. And I looked without and I saw this Keate looking on and seeing his brother or cousin, thus to beat and abuse me; and I said unto him, 'Keate, dost thou allow this?' and he said he did. 'Is this manly or civil', said I, 'to have us under a guard and put a man to abuse and beat us? Is this manly, civil or Christian?' So I desired one of our Friends to send for the constables, and they came; and I desired Keate to let the constables see his warrant or order by which he was to carry us; and his warrant was that he was to conduct us safe to Captain Fox,[1] the governor of Pendennis Castle, and if he was not at home to carry us to Launceston gaol. So I bid the constable keep the warrant, for Keate had broken his order concerning us. For we who were his prisoners were to be safely conducted, and yet he brought a man to beat and abuse us. And then we and the constable bid him and the rest of them to go their ways; and the constable kept the warrant and said if it cost twenty shillings in charges to carry us up they should not have it again.

And I showed the soldiers the baseness of their carriage towards us and so they walked up and down the house and were pitifully blank and down; and the constables stayed with us; and then the soldiers came, by way of entreaty, to us, and said they would be civil to us if we would go with them, and thus they continued till towards the eleventh hour of the day. And the constables went to the castle and told the officers what they had done and they very much disliked Keate's base carriage towards us. And they told the constables that Major-General Desborough[2] was coming to Bodmin, and that we should meet him, and it's like he

[1] John Fox, lieutenant-governor, 1646-1658; governor, 1658-1660.

[2] John Desborough (Disbrowe) (1608-1680) in charge, under Cromwell, of the six western counties.

would free us. The governor was not at home but was gone to meet him. And after the soldiers' entreaty and promise to be more civil, the constables gave them the order again, and we went with them; and great was the civility of the constables and that town's people towards us, who kindly did entertain us, and the Lord did reward them with his Truth, that many of them stand convinced of the Lord's everlasting Truth and are gathered in to the name of Jesus, and sit under Christ their teacher and saviour to this day.

And the next night we came to Bodmin, and as we went we met Major-General Desborough. And the captain of his troop that rid before him knew me, and said:

'Oh Mr. Fox', said he, 'What do you do here?'

And I said, 'I am a prisoner.'

'Alack, for what?' said he.

And I said, 'I was taken up as I was travelling.'

Then said he, 'I will speak to my lord and he shall set you at liberty.'

And so he came from the head of his troop and rid up to the coach, and he spoke to General Desborough; and we gave him an account how we were taken. And he began to speak against the light of Christ and I admonished him, but being a hard-hearted man he slighted us; and he told the soldiers they might carry us to Launceston and that he could not stay to talk with us, his horses would take cold. And when we came at night to Bodmin, Keate went into the inn before us and he put me into a room within the door and went his way. And when I came in, there stood a man with a naked rapier in his hand, and I turned out again and called for Keate and said unto him,

'What now, Keate? What trick hast thee played now to put me into a room where there is a man with his naked rapier? What is thy end in this?'

'Oh,' said he, 'pray hold your tongue, for if you speak to this man we cannot all rule him he is so devilish.'

'So', I said, 'dost thee put me into a room where there is such a man, with a naked rapier, that thou sayest you cannot all rule him? What an unworthy bad trick is this?'

And they put me single in this room from the rest of my friends that were fellow-prisoners with me. And so his plot was discovered, and after, we got another room where we were together all night. And in the evening we declared the Truth to the people, but they were a hardened dark people; and the soldiers were very rude and wicked unto us again and sat up drinking and roaring that night.

And the next day we came to Launceston where Keate delivered us to the gaoler.[1] Now there were no Friends nor friendly people near us then. And the town was a dark hardened town, that they made us to pay seven shillings a week for our horses and seven shillings a week for our diet a-piece. But at last several sober and friendly people came to see us and some of the town came to be convinced.

And there we lay nine weeks, under a very bad gaoler who much abused us, till the Assizes. And in that time many friendly people out of several parts of the county came to visit us and were convinced. And a great rage there was amongst professors and priests, for they said, 'They, *thee* and *thou* all people without respect, and will not doff their hats to one nor bow the knee to any man.' And this troubled them fearfully. But at the Assizes they expected we should have been all hanged. 'And then', said they, 'let's see whether they dare *thou* and *thee* and keep on their hats before the judge.' But all this was little to us, for we saw how God would stain the world's honour and glory; for we were commanded not to seek that honour nor give it but know the honour that came from God only and seek for that.

And when the Assizes came,[2] abundance of people came far and nigh to hear the trial of the Quakers, being a strange thing to them. And there was one Captain

[1] 22nd January, 1656.
[2] They began on 24th March, 1656.

Braddon[1] that had his troop of horse there, and the soldiers and the sheriff's men guarded us up the streets through the multitude of people which they had much to do to get us through them, and the chambers and windows were full of people looking out upon us. And they brought us into the court, where we stood with our hats on a pretty while, and all was quiet.

And I was moved to say: 'Peace be amongst you.'

And at last Judge Glynne,[2] the Lord Chief Justice of England, a Welshman, said to the gaoler:

'What be these you have brought here into court ?'

'Prisoners, my lord', said he.

'Why do not you put off your hats ?' said the judge.

And we said nothing.

'Put off your hats', said the judge again.

But we said nothing.

Then again the judge:

'The court commands you to put off your hats.'

And then I replied and said, 'Where did ever any magistrate, king, or judge from Moses to Daniel command any to put off their hats when they came before them into their courts amongst the Jews the people of God or amongst the heathen, or where did any of the heathen command any such thing in all their courts or their kings or judges ? Or show me where it is written or printed in any law of England where any such thing is commanded; show it me and I will put off my hat.'

And then the judge grew very angry and said, 'I do not carry my law books on my back.'

Then said I, 'Tell me where it is printed in a statute book that I may read it.'

Then said the judge, 'Take him away, prevaricator, I'll firk[3] him.'

Then they took us away and put us amongst the thieves; and presently after he calls to the gaoler, 'Bring them up again.'

1 William Braddon of Treworgie.

2 Sir John Glynne (1603-1666).

3 Firk, i.e. trounce.

'Come', said he, 'where had they hats from Moses to Daniel? Come, answer me, I have you fast now,' said he.

Then I said, 'Thou mayest read in the third of Daniel that the three children were cast into the fiery furnace by Nebuchadnezzar with their cloaks, hose, and hats on.' [g]And you may see that Nebuchadnezzar was not offended at their hats.[g]

He cried again, 'Take them away, gaoler.' So then they put us again amongst the thieves; and there we were kept a great while; and then, at last, the sheriff's men and troopers made way for us, that we were almost spent to get through the crowd of people, and so guarded us to the prison again, and a multitude of people followed us, and great disputes and discourses we had with them at the gaol. And we had some very good books to inform people of the Truth and our principles; and the judge and justices heard of it, and they sent out Captain Braddon and he came into the gaol and violently took our books from us out of Edward Pyott's hands and carried them away, so that we never got them again. And in the afternoon we were had up again by the gaoler, and sheriff's men, and troopers; and a mighty broil they had to get us through the crowd of people into the court. ⟨When we were in the court, waiting to be called⟩, I, seeing the jury and such a multitude of swearers, it grieved my life to see such as professed Christianity should so openly disobey the command of Christ Jesus and the Apostle, that I was moved of the Lord God to give forth a large paper against swearing, to the grand and petty juries, which was as followeth:

Concerning Swearing

Take heed of giving people oaths to swear, for Christ our Lord and master saith, 'Swear not at all, but let your communications be yea, yea, and nay, nay, for whatsoever is more than these cometh of evil.' And if any man was to suffer death, it must be by the hand of two or three witnesses; and the hands of the

[g]......[g] *S.J.*, p. 44.

witnesses were to be put first upon him to put him to death. And the Apostle James saith, 'My brethren, above all things swear not, neither by heaven, nor by earth, nor by any other oath, lest ye fall into condemnation.' Now you may see, those that swear fall into condemnation, and are out of Christ's and the Apostle's doctrine. Therefore, every one of you having a light from Christ, who saith, 'I am the light of the world', and doth enlighten every man that cometh into the world; who also saith, 'Learn of me', whose doctrine is not to swear; and the Apostle's doctrine is not to swear; but 'Let your yea be yea, and your nay be nay, in all your communications; for whatsoever is more, cometh of evil'. So then they that go into more than yea and nay, go into the evil, and are out of the doctrine of Christ. . . .

G.F.[1]

And when we were brought before the judge into the court the jury and the justices had presented this paper[2] unto the judge: and the judge bid the clerk give me that paper and then asked me whether that seditious paper was mine. So I told them if they would read it up that I might hear it in the open court, and if it was mine I would stand by it and own it; and they would have had me to have taken it in my hand and looked upon it. And I desired them again to read it and let all the country hear it and judge whether there was any sedition in it or no; and if there were I was willing to suffer for it.

And at last the clerk of the Assizes read it with an audible voice that all the people might hear it, and when they had done I told them it was my paper and I would own it, and so might they too, except they denied the Scripture, for was not this Scripture language, and Christ's and the Apostle's words and commands which all true Christians ought to obey? So then they left that subject; and the judge fell upon us about our hats again and bid the gaoler take them off, and he did so and gave them unto us again and after a while we put them on again. And then we asked the judge and the justices what we had lain in prison

[1] In full, Ellwood, pp. 180, 181; Bicent., i, 273-5.

[2] i.e. the paper to the Land's End Parishes, p. 236-7 ante.

for this nine weeks, seeing now they objected nothing to us but about our hats; ⟨and as for putting off our hats, I told them⟩ that was the honour which God would lay in the dust, which they made so much ado about; which men seek one of another and which is the honour of men and the mark of unbelievers; for 'How can you believe', says Christ, 'that seek honour one from another and not the honour which comes from God only', and Christ saith, 'I receive not honour of man.' And all true Christians should be of his mind.

And so the judge began to make a great speech how he represented the Lord Protector's person; and he had made him Lord Chief Justice of England and sent him to come that circuit, and so on. So we desired him then that he would do us justice for our false imprisonment that we had lain all that nine weeks wrongfully for.

And then they brought in an indictment that they had framed against us, such a strange thing full of lies that I thought it had been against some of the thieves; how that we came 'by force of arms and in a hostile manner into the court', who were brought in as aforesaid. So I told them it was all false; and still we cried for justice for our wrong imprisonment who were taken up in our journey without cause by Major Peter Ceely. And then this Ceely spoke to the judge and the court and said, 'May it please you, my lord; this man (meaning me), he went aside with me and told me how serviceable I might be for his design and that he could raise four thousand[1] men in an hour's warning and involve the nation into blood and so bring in King Charles, and I would have aided him out of the country but he would not go: and, if it please you, my lord, I have a witness to swear it.' And so he called up his witness, but the judge not being very forward to call for the witness I desired of the judge that he would be pleased to let my mittimus be read in the face of the court and country in which my crime was signified for which I was sent to prison.

The judge said it should not. I said it ought to be,

[1] MSS. vary between 400, 4,000 and 40,000.

seeing it concerned my life and liberty. And the judge said again, it should not be read.

And I said, 'It ought to be read; and if I have done anything worthy of death or bonds, let all the country know of it.'

So I spoke unto one of my fellow-prisoners, 'Thou hast a copy of it. Read it up,' said I.

'But it shall not be read,' said the judge. 'Gaoler, take him away. I will see whether he or I shall be master.' So they did, and after a while they called for me again, and I still cried to have my mittimus read up; for that signified my crime. And then I bid William Salt read it up again, and he read it up, and the judge and justices and whole court were silent, for the people were mighty willing to hear it.

The mittimus was as follows:

Peter Ceely, one of the Justices of the Peace of this County, to the Keeper of His Highness's gaol at Launceston, or his lawful Deputy in that behalf, Greeting.

I send you herewithal by the bearers hereof, the bodies of Edward Pyott of Bristol, and George Fox of Drayton-in-the-Clay, in Leicestershire, and William Salt of London, which they pretend to be the places of their habitations, who go under the notion of Quakers and acknowledge themselves to be such, who have spread several papers tending to the disturbance of the public peace, and cannot render any lawful cause of coming into these parts, being persons altogether unknown, and having no pass for their travelling up and down the country, and refusing to give sureties of their good behaviour, according to the law in that behalf provided; and refuse to take the oath of abjuration, &c. These are therefore, in the name of his Highness the Lord Protector, to will and command you, that when the bodies of the said Edward Pyott, George Fox, and William Salt, shall be unto you brought, you them receive, and in his Highness's prison aforesaid you safely keep them, until by due course of law they shall be delivered. Hereof fail you not, as you will answer the contrary at your perils.

Given under my hand and seal, at St. Ives, the eighteenth day of January, 1656.

P. Ceely.

And when it was read, 'Now', said I, 'thou sayest thou art the Chief Justice of England, and you, the rest of you that be justices, you know that if I had put in sureties ⟨I might have gone whither I pleased, and⟩ then I might have gone on with my design which Major Ceely hath charged me of; and if I spoke such words to him then judge ye whether bail or main prize ought to be taken in that case of high treason.'

And I said to Peter Ceely, 'When did I take thee aside or where? Was not thy house full of rude people and thou as rude as any of them at our examination, so that I asked for a constable or some other officer to keep the people civil? And that is not a place for thee to sit in, for accusers do not use to sit with the judges, for thou oughtest to come down and stand by me and look me in the face. And now I would ask the judge and justices this question: whether or no Major Ceely is not guilty of this treason he charges against me in concealing of it so long, or does understand his place either as a soldier or a justice of peace. For he tells you here that I went aside with him and told him what a design I had in hand, and how serviceable he might be for my design and that I could raise four thousand men in an hour's time and bring in King Charles and involve the nation into blood. And he says, moreover, "May it please you, my lord, I would fain have had him go out of the country and he would not go", and therefore he committed me to prison for want of sureties for the good behaviour as the mittimus declares here. And do not you see clearly that Major Ceely is guilty of this plot and treason, and made himself a party in it by desiring me to go out of the country and asking me bail, and charging me not with this pretended treason till now, nor discovering it. But I deny and abhor his words and am innocent of this devilish design.'

So that business fell, and the judge saw clear enough that instead of ensnaring me he had ensnared himself.

And then this Major Ceely got up again and said, 'If it please you, my lord, to hear me, this man struck me and gave me such a blow as I never had in my life '; at which I smiled in my heart, and said,

' Pray thee, Major Ceely, where did I strike thee, and who is thy witness for that ? And who was by ? '

And he said, ' In the Castle Green, and Captain Braddon was standing by when you struck me.'

' Art thou a justice of peace,' said I, ' and a major of a troop of horse, and for thee to say in the face of the court before the judge that I struck thee and gave thee such a blow as thou never had the like in thy life ? What ! Art thou not ashamed ? ' So I desired the judge to let him produce his witness for that. ' And ', I said, ' Major Ceely, thou oughtest to come down off the bench and stand by me: for it is not a place for accusers to sit there.'

But I called again for his witness and then he said Captain Braddon was his witness. So I said, ' Speak, Captain Braddon; didst thou see me give him such a blow and strike him as he says ? ' And he bowed his head to me; but I desired him to speak up if he knew any such thing, but he bowed his head again. ' Nay, speak up,' said I, ' and let the court and country hear, and let not bowing of the head serve turn. And if I have done so let me have the law inflicted upon me, for I fear not sufferings nor death itself; and I am an innocent man concerning this charge.' But Captain Braddon never testified to it.

And the judge ⟨finding those snares would not hold⟩ cried, ' Take him away gaoler,' and so he fined us twenty marks a-piece for not putting off our hats, and to be kept in prison till we paid it, and sent us back to the gaol again.

And so at night Captain Braddon came to us, and seven or eight justices of peace and they were very civil to us and they told us they did believe that neither the judge nor any there did believe any of those charges that Major Ceely had charged against me in the face of the country, but Braddon said that Major Ceely had an intent to have taken away my life if he could have got another witness. ' But ', I said, ' Captain Braddon, why didst not thou witness for me or against me, seeing Major Ceely produced thee for a witness that thou saw me strike him? And when I desired thee to speak either for me or against me according to what thou knew or saw, thou wouldst not.'

'Why', says he, 'when Major Ceely and I came by you when you were walking in the Castle Green, he doffed his hat to you and said, "How do you, Mr. Fox? Your servant, Sir." Then you said unto him, "Major Ceely, take heed of hypocrisy and a rotten heart, for when came I to be thy master and thee my servant? Do servants use to cast their masters into prison?"' And this was the great blow he meant that I gave him and struck him and that wounded him so that he complained to the judge of it in the face of the country and open court, and yet made the court to believe that I struck him outwardly with my hand. And then I did remember that they walked by us and that he spoke to me as aforesaid and I spoke those words unto him as aforesaid; which hypocrisy and rotten-heartedness he manifested openly.

So we were kept in prison and divers people came far and nigh to see us, and several people of account. It was the talk of the town and country that never men answered so as we did, and that the judge and justices were not able to answer us one word in twelve.

And then there came up Humphrey Lower, a grave, sober, ancient man, a justice of peace, to visit us. And he was very sorry we should be in prison and spoke to us and said how serviceable we might be if we were out of prison; and we reasoned with him about swearing and how they tendered the Oath of Abjuration to us because we could not swear; and no people could be serviceable to God if they disobeyed the command of Christ. And they which imprisoned us for the hat honour, which was of men, and men looked for it, prisoned the good, and vexed and grieved the spirit of God in themselves, which should turn their minds to God; and so we turned him to the spirit of God in his heart and to the light of Christ Jesus; and he was thoroughly convinced ⟨and continued so to his death,⟩ and was very serviceable unto us.

And there came one Colonel Rous,[1] a justice of peace, with a great company. And he was as full of words and talk as ever I heard a man in my life, so as there was no speaking to him; so at last I asked him, to stop him, whether he had been ever at school and knew what belonged to questions and answers.

'At school!' said he, 'Yes.'

'At school!' said the soldiers, 'Doth he say so to our Colonel that is a scholar?'

Then said I, 'If he be so, let him be still and receive answers from me to what he hath said.'

[h]And so he was desired to hold his peace, or see if he could hold his peace a little while, till Truth were spoken to him. And then the light was spoken of to him (which let him see his sinful life that he had lived in, and his words and his ways), that would be his teacher to lead him from them, if he minded it, and his condemnation if he acted against it. And if he had anything to speak he might speak.

And he was stricken dumb and his mouth was shut, and he cast his head up and down and his face swelled, and he could not speak for a good space. His face was as red as a turkey.[h] And his lips rent and he mumbled, and the people thought he would have fallen down. And I stepped to him; and he said, 'I was never so in my life before.' For the Lord's power stopped the evil power and air in him and almost choked him.

And for ever after the man was very loving to Friends and never so full of airy words after to us, though he was a man full of pride. But the Lord's power came over him and the rest that were with him. And we continued still in prison, and at last there came another officer of the army, a very malicious, bitter professor whom I knew in London, and he was so full of his airy talk also and speaking slightingly of the light of Christ, and against the Truth

[1] Probably Anthony Rous, successor to John Fox, as governor of Pendennis Castle, in 1660.

[h]......[h] *S.J.*, p. 46.

as Colonel Rous did, and the spirit of God being in men as it was in the apostles' days, till the power of God that bound the evil in him had almost choked him also as it did Colonel Rous aforesaid. He was so full of evil air that he could not speak but blubbered and stuttered. And from that time the Lord's power struck through him and came over him that he was ever after more loving to us.

And several Friends from most parts of the nation came into the country to visit us. For those were very dark countries at that time; but the Lord's light and truth shined over all and many were turned from darkness to the light and from Satan's power unto God. And many were moved to go to the steeplehouses and several were sent to prison to us; and there began to be a great convincement in the country and a great rage in the priests and professors.

⟨Now the Assize being over, and we settled in prison upon such a commitment, that we were not likely to be soon released,⟩ we brake off from the gaoler, from giving seven shillings a week for our horses and seven shillings a week a-piece for ourselves, and sent our horses into the country. And then he grew very devilish and wicked, and carried us and put us into Doomsdale,[1] a nasty stinking place where they said few people came out alive; where they used to put witches and murderers before their execution; where the prisoners' excrements had not been carried out for scores of years, as it was said. It was all like mire, and in some places at the top of the shoes in water and piss, and never a house of office in the place, nor chimney. The gaoler would not let us cleanse the place, nor let us have beds nor straw to lie on; but at night some friendly people of the town brought us a candle and a little straw, and we went to burn a little of our straw to take away the stink. The thieves were put over our heads and the head gaoler lay above with the thieves. It seems the smoke went up into the room and the gaoler was in such a rage

[1] The prisoners were put into Doomsdale on 9th April, 1656, and kept there thirteen days.

that he [i]stamped with his foot and stick[i] and took the pots of excrements of the prisoners and poured it down a hole a-top of our heads in Doomsdale, so that we were so bespattered with the excrements that we could not touch ourselves nor one another, that our stink increased upon us. He quenched our straw with it. And he called us hatchet-faced dogs and such names as we never heard in our lives. What with the stink and what with the smoke, we were like to be choked and smothered, for we had the stink under our feet before but now we had it on our backs. In this manner we stood all night for we could not sit down the place being so full of the prisoners' excrements. And a great while he kept us of this manner before he would let us cleanse it or suffer us to have any victuals in but what we got through the grate.

And at one time a lass[1] brought us a little meat and he arrested her for breaking his house, and had her into the town court for breaking the prison. And a great deal of trouble he brought the young woman to, so that we had much to do to get water, or drink, or victuals. And the noise was amongst the prisoners and people how the spirits haunted and walked in Doomsdale and how many died in it, but I told them and Friends that if all the spirits and devils in hell were there I was over them and feared no such thing, for Christ our priest would sanctify the walls and the house to us, that bruised the head of the Devil. For the priest under the law he was to cleanse the plague out of the walls of the house, which Christ our priest, ended, who sanctifies both inwardly and outwardly the walls of the house and the walls of the heart and all things to his people.

And this head gaoler had been a thief and was burnt in the hand and burnt in the shoulder; and his wife had been burnt in her hand for some wickedness; and the underkeeper[2] was burnt in the hand and in the shoulder,

[1] Susanna Kemp.
[2] Nicholas Freeleven.
[i]. . . . . .[i] *S.J.*, p. 45.

and his wife was burnt in the hand also. And Colonel Bennet,[1] a Baptist teacher, who had taken or purchased the office and gaol and land belonging to the Castle, had put them in. Such we had over us.

And we drew up our sufferings and sent them to Bodmin Sessions, and sent up a copy of that to Oliver Cromwell, Protector, how we were taken by Peter Ceely and abused by Keate that commanded the horse guard that carried us to gaol. And at the Sessions the justices gave order that Doomsdale door should be opened and that we should have liberty to cleanse it and to buy our meat in the town.

⟨Near this time⟩ we sent for a young woman, one Anne Downer,[2] from London, that could write ⟨and take things well in shorthand⟩, to get and dress our meat for us, ⟨which she was very willing to do, it being also upon her spirit to come to us in the love of God⟩, and she was very serviceable to us.

And Oliver Protector sent down an order to Captain Fox to Pendennis Castle to examine the soldiers' abusing of us and striking of me; and at that time many of the gentry of the country were at the castle, and Keate's kinsman that struck me was sent for before them and much threatened; and they told him that Mr. Fox, if he should change his principle might take the extremity of the law upon him and recover sound damages. So they threatened him for abusing the prisoners; which was of great service in the country, after which Friends might have spoken in any market or steeplehouse thereabouts and none would meddle with them.

And Hugh Peters,[3] Oliver Protector's chaplain, told him they could not do George Fox a greater service for the spreading of his principles in Cornwall than to imprison

[1] Robert Bennet (1605-1683), M.P. for Launceston, 1653, 1659.

[2] Anne Downer (1624-1686) married George Whitehead, her second husband. A testimony to her, written in Fox's hand, says: 'she came afoot above two hundred miles and lay in the town of Launceston and carried herself very wisely.'

[3] Hugh Peters (1598-1660), Independent, active in the parliamentary cause, chaplain to the Council of State, 1650, executed as a regicide.

him; and so it was of the Lord and for his service, my imprisonment in those parts. And then we had liberty to come out and to walk in the Green, and divers people came to us on the First-days and great service we had amongst them, to whom we declared the word of life, and many were turned to God here and there, up and down.

And there came an envious professor;[1] and he writ many Scripture phrases and invited the town of Launceston into the Castle Yard to read it to them; and a-many Scriptures to prove that we ought to bow and put off our hats to the people and said, ' Saul bowed to the witch of Endor.' And so when he had done we got a little liberty, whether the gaoler would or no, to speak, and showed him and the people how that Saul was gone from God and had disobeyed God, like them, when he went to the witch of Endor, and that neither the prophets, Christ, nor the apostles ever taught people to bow to the witch of Endor, nor any other, and at the last the man and his rude people went away, though some stayed with us. So we showed the people that this was not Gospel instructions, to teach people to bow to the witch of Endor. For then people began to be affected with Truth, and then the Devil began to rage, <so that we were in great danger many times.>

And there came two justices of peace out of Wales[2] to visit us, which came to be fine ministers and turned many to the spirit of God and to sit under Christ's teaching, and they suffered much imprisonment; and one of them convinced three priests, and one of them became a fine minister and stands to this day.

And there came a soldier, and one of our Friends was admonishing of him and exhorting him, and I saw him begin to draw his sword at him, and I stepped to him and told him what a shame it was to offer to draw his sword of a naked[3] man and a prisoner, and how unfit and unworthy he was to carry such a weapon, for some men would have

[1] Degorie Pearse.
[2] Probably Walter Jenkins and Peter Price. See p. 222 ante.
[3] That is, unarmed.

taken it from him if he should have offered such a thing, and have broken it to pieces; and so he was shamed with it ⟨and went his way⟩. And the Lord's power did mightily preserve us there.

And the gaoler came and told me one night about the eleventh hour at night, when he was half drunk, that he had gotten a man[1] now to dispute with me. And I felt as soon as he spoke those words there was a snare intended to my body, all that night and the next day. This was when we had leave to go a little into the town.

And the next day I lay down on a grass plot to slumber and I felt something still about my body, and I started up and struck at it in the power of the Lord: and yet still it was about my body. And I rose and walked into the Castle Green and the underkeeper told me there was a maid would speak with me at the prison. And I felt a snare in his words too and I went ⟨not into the prison, but⟩ to the grate and there I saw the ⟨man that was lately brought to prison for being a⟩ conjurer and he had a naked knife in his hand. And I spoke to him and he threatened to cut my chops as he said, but he was in the gaol and could not come at me.

And this was the gaoler's great disputant; and when I came in, the gaoler was at breakfast ⟨and had then got his conjurer out with him⟩; and I told the gaoler his plot was discovered, and he got up from the table and wrung his hands, and struck his napkin away in a rage. And I went away into the chamber and left them, for at that time we were out of Doomsdale.

But at the time that the gaoler said the dispute should be, I went into the court and walked there in the place appointed, till about the eleventh hour, and nobody came; and then I walked up into the chamber again; and I heard one call for me and I went to the stair head, and the gaoler's wife was upon the stairs, and the fortune teller was at the bottom of the stairs in a rage holding his hand behind his back.

[1] George Roach.

And I said unto him, 'Man, what hast in thy hand behind thy back? Pluck thy hand before thee, let us see thy hand and what thou hast in it.' And in a rage he took forth his hand with a naked knife in it; and then I showed the gaoler's wife the wicked design of her and her husband, which was the man they had brought to dispute of the things of God; but the Lord discovered their plot and their design. And so they both raged and he threatened; and I was moved of the Lord to speak sharply to him in the dreadful power of the Lord and the Lord's power came over him and bound him down so as he never after durst appear before me to speak unto me.

And I saw that it was the Lord alone that did preserve me out of and over their bloody hands, for the Devil had a great enmity to me, ⟨and stirred up his instruments to seek my hurt. But the Lord prevented them.

Now Edward Pyott, who before his convincement had been a captain in the army, and had a good understanding in the laws and rights of the people, being sensible of the injustice and envy of Judge Glynn to us at our trial, writ an epistle to him on behalf of us all, thus:⟩

Edward Pyott to Judge Glynn, Chief Justice of England.

Friend, We are free men of England, free born; our rights and liberties are according to law and defended by it; and therefore with thee, by whose hand we have so long suffered, and yet do suffer, let us a little plainly reason concerning thy proceedings against us, whether they have been according to law, or agreeable to thy duty and office, as chief minister of the law, or justice of England . . .

The afternoon before we were brought before thee at the Assizes at Launceston, thou didst cause divers scores of our books violently to be taken from us by armed men without due process of law; which being perused if so be anything in them might be found to lay to our charge, who were innocent, and then upon our legal issue, thou hast detained till this very day. Now our books are our goods, and our goods are our property; and our liberty it is to have and enjoy our property; and of our liberty and property the law is the defence, which saith, 'No free-man shall be disseized of his freehold, liberty, or free customs, &c., nor any way otherwise destroyed: nor we shall not pass upon him but by lawful judgment of his peers or by the law of the land.' Magna Carta, cap. 29. . . .

And these things, Friend, we have laid before thee in all plainness, to the end that with the light of Jesus Christ, who lighteth every one that cometh into the world, a measure of which thou hast received which showeth thee evil, and reproveth thee for sin, for which thou must be accountable, thou, being still and cool, mayest consider and see what thou hast done against the innocent; and shame may overtake thee, and thou turn unto the Lord, who now calleth thee to repentance through his servants, who for witnessing his living Truth in them, thou hast cast into, and yet continues under cruel bonds and sufferings.

Edward Pyott.[1]

From the Gaol in
Launceston the 14th day
of the 5th month [July] 1656.

⟨By the foregoing letter the reader may observe how contrary to law we were made to suffer; but the Lord, who saw the integrity of our hearts to him and knew the innocency of our cause, was with us in our sufferings, and bore up our spirit through, and made them easy to us, and gave us opportunities of publishing his name and Truth amongst the people.⟩ And several of the towns-people came to be convinced, and were made loving to us.

And in Cornwall, Devonshire, Dorsetshire and Somersetshire, Truth began mightily to spread. And many were turned to Christ Jesus and his free teaching. And they revived an old law made in Queen Elizabeth's time[2] against sturdy vagrants and beggars going up and down, which law they put into execution against our friends and set

[1] Abridged from a MS. copy in Friends House Library, headed in Fox's hand, *G. Fox and E. Pyott to Judge Glynn.* Printed in full, *West Answering North* (1657), pp. 16-31; Ellwood, pp. 189-200; Bicent., i, 287-300.

The pages omitted argue the illegality and injustice of the proceedings at the Assizes. The letter was delivered to Judge Glynn at the Assizes at Gloucester.

[2] 39 Eliz. cap. 4.

up watch and ward in the highways, to take up all suspicious persons, as they called it, which were the Friends that came to visit us in prison, which they only took up that they might not pass up and down in the Lord's service. And them they brought before the justices. And some clothiers and other men they whipped [j]as sturdy beggars and vagrants, which were sober people[j] ⟨of about a hundred or eighty pounds a year⟩, which they took up not above four or five miles from their families, that were going to mills with their cloth.

And when Friends were got amongst the watches it would be a fortnight or three weeks before they could get out of them again; for no sooner had one party taken them and carried them before the justices and they had discharged them, but then another would take them up and carry them before other justices, which put the country to a great deal of needless cost and charges. And that which they thought to have stopped the Truth by was the means to spread it so much the more. For then Friends were continually moved to speak to one constable and to the other officer and justice. And this caused the Truth to spread the more amongst them in all their parishes.

And as Thomas Rawlinson was coming up to visit us out of the north a constable in Devonshire took him up, and at night took twenty shillings out of his pocket. And he and many Friends were cruelly beat many times by them. And they cast him into Exeter gaol after they had robbed him.

And the mayor of Launceston[1] was a very wicked man, for he would take them up and search substantial grave women, their petticoats, and head-clothes for letters, and cast them into prison.

And there was a Friend, a young man, came to me, that came not through the town. And I drew up all the gross inhuman and unchristian actions of the mayor, for his carriage was more like a heathen than a Christian; and I

[1] Philip Pearce, in 1655-6.

[j]. . . . . .[j] *S.J.*, p. 48.

gave it the young man and bid him seal it up and go out the backside of the town and come into the town through the gates. And the young man did so, and the watchman took him up and carried him before the mayor; and he presently searched his pockets and took out that letter where he saw all his actions characterized; and from that time he meddled little more with the servants of the Lord, he was so ashamed.

And they cast Henry Polixphen into prison in Devonshire for being a Jesuit, who had been a justice of peace for the most part of forty years past. And this was the rage and fruits of the Presbyterians, Independents, and Baptists in that which they called their Gospel times, which were the times of the power of darkness.

⟨Now from the sense I had of the snare that was laid, and mischief intended, in setting up those watches at the time to stop and take up Friends, it came upon me to give forth an exhortation and warning to the magistrates.[1]

Besides this general warning, there coming to my hand a copy of a warrant issued out from the Sessions at Exeter in express terms, 'for the apprehending of all Quakers', wherein Truth and Friends were reproached and vilified, I was moved to write an answer thereunto,[2] and send it abroad, for the clearing of Truth and Friends from the slanders therein cast upon them, and to manifest the wickedness of that persecuting spirit from whence it proceeded.

When I had sent abroad the foregoing papers concerning the watches that were set up to intercept and stop Friends, a great sense came upon me of the darkness and veil that was over the priests and professors of Christianity so that I was moved to give forth an awakening warning to them.[3]⟩

So we continued in prison until the next Assizes.

And a great deal of work we had betwixt the Assizes. Several men and women were taken up by the watches and sent to prison at this time. And at the Assizes several

[1] Ellwood, p. 201*; Bicent., i, 302-4.

[2] Ellwood, pp. 203*-206*; Bicent., i, 304-8.

[3] Ellwood, pp. 207*-210*; Bicent., i, 308-13.

Friends were called before the judge and indicted; and though the gaoler brought them into the court, yet they indicted them that they came in by force of arms and in a hostile manner; and the judge fined them because they would not put off their hats. But we were never called before the judge any more; but they left us by.

And Elizabeth Trelawney[1] of Plymouth, a baronet's daughter, being convinced, the priests and other great persons and professors, her kindred, were in a great rage concerning her, ⟨and writ letters to her⟩; and being a wise and tender woman in the fear of God, she sent her letters to me. And I answered the priests; and if she could own them she might set her hand to them and give them to the priests, which she did. And she grew so in the power and spirit and wisdom of God that she could answer the wisest priest and professor of them all, and had a dominion over them all in the Truth by the power of the Lord; and she continued in Truth till she died.

⟨Now while I was in prison here the Baptists and Fifth-Monarchy-Men prophesied that this year Christ should come and reign upon earth a thousand years. And they looked upon this reign to be outward, whenas he was come inwardly in the hearts of his people to reign and rule there, these professors would not receive him there. So they failed in their prophecy and expectation, and had not the possession of him. But Christ is come and doth dwell in the hearts of his people and reigns there. And thousands, at the door of whose hearts he hath been knocking, have opened to him, and he is come in, and doth sup with them and they with him, the heavenly supper with the heavenly and spiritual man. So many of these Baptist and Monarchy people turned the greatest enemies to the possessors of Christ. But he reigns in the hearts of his saints over all their envy.⟩

And divers justices came to us at the Assizes and were pretty civil, and reasoned of the things of God pretty

[1] Daughter of Sir John Trelawney (1592-1664); she was Thomas Lower's first wife, and died before 1668.

soberly and had a pity to us. And there came Captain Fox, that was governor of Pendennis Castle, and looked me in the face and said never a word, but went his ways to his company, and said he never saw a simpler man in his life. And I called after him and said, ' Stay, man, and we will see who is the simpler man.' But he went his ways, a light, chaffy man.

And at the Assizes there came one Thomas Lower[1] to visit us, and offered to give us money, and we accepted of his love but refused his money. He asked many questions of us concerning our denying the Scriptures to be the word of God and concerning the sacraments and such like. I spoke unto him, and he said my words were as a flash of lightning, they so run through him. He received satisfaction concerning all the things he asked of us and went his ways and said he never met with such wise men in his life, for they knew the thoughts of his heart and were as the wise master-builders of the assemblies that fastened their words like nails; who after came to be convinced, and remains a Friend to this day. And he went home to his aunt Hambly's[2] ⟨where he then lived, and made report to her concerning us⟩. And hearing the sound of Truth, she and her sister Grace Billing came afterwards to visit us in prison and were convinced also, and remain to this day. They have gone through great sufferings and spoiling of goods, both he and his aunt for Truth's sake.

And Judge Haggett's wife[3] came from Bristol to visit us at the second Assizes; and she was convinced and several of her children; and her husband was very loving and serviceable to Friends and had a great love to God's people, which he retained till he died.

⟨About this time I was moved to give forth the following exhortation to Friends in the ministry:

[1] Thomas Lower (1633-1720), physician, became stepson-in-law to Fox, wrote out the greater part of the MS. of this Journal at Fox's dictation.

[2] Loveday Hambly, *née* Billing (*c.* 1604-1682), of Tregangeeves, near St. Austell.

[3] Perhaps Elizabeth Yeamans who married John Haggett of Bristol.

Friends,

In the power of life and wisdom, and dread of the Lord God of life, and heaven, and earth, dwell, that in the wisdom of God over all ye may be preserved, and be a terror to all the adversaries of God, and a dread, answering that of God in them all, spreading the Truth abroad, awakening the witness, confounding deceit, gathering up out of transgression into the life, the covenant of light and peace with God. Let all nations hear the word by sound or writing. Spare no place, spare not tongue nor pen; but be obedient to the Lord God and go through the work and be valiant for the Truth upon earth; tread and trample all that is contrary under . . . Keep in the wisdom of God that spreads over all the earth, the wisdom of the creation, that is pure. Live in it; that is the word of the Lord God to you all, do not abuse it; and keep down and low; and take heed of false joys that will change.

Bring all into the worship of God. Plough up the fallow ground . . . And none are ploughed up but he who comes to the principle of God in him which he hath transgressed. Then he doth service to God; then the planting and the watering and the increase from God cometh. So the ministers of the Spirit must minister to the spirit that is transgressed and in prison, which hath been in captivity in every one; whereby with the same spirit people must be led out of captivity up to God, the Father of spirits, and do service to him and have unity with him, with the Scriptures and one with another. And this is the word of the Lord God to you all, and a charge to you all in the presence of the living God, be patterns, be examples in all countries, places, islands, nations, wherever you come; that your carriage and life may preach among all sorts of people, and to them. Then you will come to walk cheerfully over the world, answering that of God in every one; whereby in them ye may be a blessing, and make the witness of God in them to bless you. Then to the Lord God you will be a sweet savour and a blessing.

Spare no deceit. Lay the sword upon it; go over it; keep yourselves clear of the blood of all men, either by word, or writing, or speaking. And keep yourselves clean, . . . that nothing may rule nor reign but power and life itself, and that in the wisdom of God ye may be preserved in it.

G.F.[1]〉

[1] In full, Ellwood, pp. 212*-214*, Bicent., i, 315-17.

And after <the Assizes> the sheriff and the soldiers came to guard a woman that was to be put to death, with whom we had a great deal of discourse. And one of them said wickedly that Christ was as passionate a man as any that lived upon the earth; for which we rebuked him.

And we asked the gaoler what doings there were at the Sessions, and he said, 'Small matters; only a matter of thirty for bastardy', and we thought it very strange that they that professed themselves Christians, should make small matters of such things.

And I often admonished the gaoler to sobriety: for he would abuse people that came to visit us. He had been blessed and made if he had carried himself civil but the man sought his own ruin, as after came upon him.

And Edward Pyott had a cheese sent to him from his wife from Bristol, and the gaoler took the cheese from us and carried it to the mayor to search it for treasonable letters as he said; and <though they found no treason in the cheese> they kept it.

And the next year the gaoler was turned out, and for some wickedness was cast into the gaol himself and there begged of our Friends. And for some unruliness in his carriage he was cast into Doomsdale by the succeeding gaoler, and locked up in the irons and beaten. And he bid him remember how he had abused those good men that he had wickedly, without any cause, cast into that nasty dungeon; and now he deservedly should suffer for his wickedness, and the same measure he had meted to others he should have meted out to himself. And he grew to be very poor and died in prison and his wife and family came to misery.

And not long after Judge Glynne died,[1] and Major Peter Ceely and other of the persecuting justices were turned out.

And when I was in prison in Cornwall there was a Friend went to Oliver Cromwell and offered his body to him for to go to lie in Doomsdale prison for me or in my stead, that he would take him and let me go at liberty, and it

[1] Judge Glynne, d. 1666, ten years later.

so struck him and came over him that he said to his great men and his Council, 'Which of you would do so much for me if I was in the same condition ?'

Nevertheless Oliver Cromwell did not accept the Friend's proffer, but said he could not do it, for that was contrary to law; however, the Truth came over him.

And after a time Oliver Protector sent down Major-General Desborough, pretending to set us at liberty, and he proffered us if we would say we would go home and preach no more, we should have our liberty, but we could not promise him so. ⟨Then he urged that we should promise to go home 'if the Lord permitted'. Whereupon Edward Pyott wrote him the following letter.⟩

Friend and Friends,

Much might be said as to the liberty of Englishmen to travel in any part of the nation, England being as the Englishman's house by the law, and he is to be protected in any part of it . . . And liberty of conscience is a natural right and a fundamental and the exercise of it by those who profess faith in God by Jesus Christ, is to be protected as by the Instrument of Government appears. . . . Where these rights are denied us, our liberties are infringed, which are the price of much blood and treasure in the late wars. . . . We, who were first committed, were passing homewards when we were apprehended. And as far as I know we might pass if the prison doors were commanded to be opened. Should we stay if the Lord commands us to go, or should we go if the Lord commands us to stay, . . . we should then be wanderers indeed, for such are wanderers who wander out from the will and power of God, in their own wills and earthly minds. . . . Well weigh and consider, with the just weight and just balance, that justice you may do to the just and innocent in your prison.

Edward Pyott.[1]

⟨Some time having elapsed after the foregoing was delivered him, and he not giving any order for our discharge, I also writ unto him.⟩[2]

[1] In full: *Camb. Jnl.*, i, 238-9; Ellwood, p. 215*; Bicent., i, 318-19.
[2] *Camb. Jnl.*, i, 239-41; Ellwood, pp. 216*-217*; Bicent., i, 319-21.

And he came to the Castle Green and there played at bowls with the justices and other men; and several Friends were moved to go and admonish him and them, how they took their pleasure, and imprisoned the servants of God, and yet profess themselves Christians; and how the Lord would plead with them and visit them for such things.

<And I was moved to give forth several papers as a warning unto them and unto all that so misspend their time.[1]

But notwithstanding what was writ or said to him, Major-General Desborough> went his ways but left us in prison. But after, when the King came in he was cast into prison himself.

<He left the business to Colonel Bennet who had the command of the gaol.> And after a while Colonel Bennet would have set us at liberty if we would have paid his gaoler's fees, for the business was left with him by Major-General Desborough. But we told him we could give the gaoler no fees, for we were innocent sufferers, and how could they ask fees of us who had caused us to suffer so long wrongfully.

And after a time, Colonel Bennet coming to town, he sent for us to an inn and insisted again upon fees. But at last the power of the Lord came so over him that he set us at liberty on the 9th day of the 7th month [September], 1656.[2] And we were cast into prison nine weeks before the Lent Assizes.

[1] Two papers are in Ellwood, pp. 218*-219*; Bicent., i, 324, 325.

[2] The MS. Journal and previous editions give 13th in error. See *West Answering to the North*, 1657, p. 126; Swarthmore MSS., i, 167; and G. F. Nuttall in *Friends Quarterly*, 1946, 117.

CHAPTER XI

WE got horses and rid up into the country to Humphrey Lower's.[1] And upon the road we met him, and he told us he was much troubled in his spirit concerning of us and he could not rest at home but was going to Colonel Bennet to seek for our liberty. And we told him we were set at liberty and were going to his house, and glad he was of it. And at his house we had a fine, precious meeting, and many were convinced and turned by the spirit of God to the Lord Jesus Christ's teaching. And from his house we went to Loveday Hambly's house where we had a fine large meeting. And many were convinced there also and turned to the Lord Jesus Christ their teacher. And after we had tarried there two or three days we came to Thomas Mounce's where we had a General Meeting for the whole county and Friends from Plymouth were there also, which was very large in his orchard. And the Lord's power was over all and great convincement there was in many places of the county. All their watches were down in all the country and all was plain. And the Lord did let me see before I was set at liberty that he would make all the country plain before me.

And Thomas and Ann Curtis came up to see me whilst I was in prison, and one of the aldermen of Reading who was convinced. And ⟨when Ann and the other man returned⟩, Thomas Curtis stayed behind and went into Cornwall and he did good service for the Lord there at that time.

And from Thomas Mounce's we passed to Launceston again and visited that little remnant of Friends where we had been prisoners; and the Lord's plants finely grew and were established on Christ the rock and foundation.

[1] Humphrey Lower's house was Tremeere, near St. Tudy.

And when we came to Launceston, the constable, as we were going out of town, came running to us with the cheese which they had kept from us a long while, and were tormented with it; but then, being set at liberty, we would not receive it.

From Launceston we came to Okehampton, and lay at the mayor's house, who kept an inn, and who had taken up and stopped several Friends. But he was very civil to us, and convinced in his judgment.

And from thence we came through the countries to Exeter, ⟨where many Friends were in prison, and amongst the rest James Nayler, for a little before the time we were set at liberty, James ran out into imaginations, and a company with him; and they raised up a great darkness in the nation. And he came to Bristol and made a disturbance there; and from thence he was coming to Launceston to see me, but was stopped by the way and imprisoned at Exeter.⟩

That night that we came to Exeter, I spoke with James Nayler, for I saw he was out and wrong and so was his company. Next day, being the First-day[1] we went to the prison to visit the prisoners and had a meeting with them in the prison; and I did admonish them. But James Nayler and some of them could not stay the meeting but kept on their hats when I prayed. And they were the first that gave that bad example amongst Friends. So after I had been warring with the world, now there was a wicked spirit risen up amongst Friends to war against. And there was a corporal of horse came in to the meeting there, and he was convinced; and he remains a very good Friend to this day.

And there was a tender Friend died in prison at that time[2] who was coming to visit me, whose blood lies on the heads of his persecutors.

And the next day I spoke to James Nayler again, and he slighted it and was dark and much out; nevertheless he

[1] 21st Sept., 1656.

[2] This was a woman, Jane Ingram.

would have come and kissed me, but I said, seeing he had turned against the power of God, 'It is my foot'[1] and so the Lord God moved me to slight him and to set the power of God over him. And when he was come to London his resisting the power of God in me and the Truth that was declared to him became one of his greatest burdens, but he came to see it and to condemn it and all his outgoings, and after some time he returned to Truth again as in the printed relation[2] of his repentance, condemnation, and recovery may be more fully seen.

And after, we passed from Exeter[3] through Cullompton and Taunton and visited Friends and had meetings amongst them and declared the word of life unto them. And from thence we came to Podimore, to William Beaton's, and on the First-day we had a mighty large meeting there where were several hundreds of people; and a great convincement was all up and down that country. And many meetings we had and the Lord's power was over all, and many were turned by the power and spirit of God to the Lord Jesus Christ that died for them, and to sit under his free teaching, and continue to this day.

And from thence we came to John Dandoe's[4] where we had another precious meeting: and the Lord's power was over all and many were convinced of God's eternal Truth; though there was some contention by professors and Baptists in some places, yet the Lord's power came over all.

And from thence we came to Bristol the Seventh-day night, to Edward Pyott's house,[5] and it was noised over the town that I was come; and I had never been there before. And on the First-day morning I went to the meeting in

[1] Probably meaning, *it is my foot thou shouldst kiss.*

[2] Probably, *A True Narrative of the Examination, Tryall and Sufferings of James Nayler*, 1657.

[3] On 23rd Sept.

[4] John Dandoe lived at Hallatrow, N. Somerset.

[5] Edward Pyott lived at Lower Easton, about a mile N.E. from the city.

Broadmead,[1] and a great meeting there was, and quiet. And in the afternoon notice was given of a meeting to be in the orchard.[2] A rude Baptist there was, whose name was Paul Gwin, that had made before great disturbance in the city; and the mayor ⟨it was reported⟩ encouraged him and set him on, and sometimes would give him his dinner to encourage him, that he gathered a multitude of the ruder sort of people after him, that it was thought that sometimes there would be ten thousand people at our meeting in the orchard. And as I was going along into the orchard the people told me that the rude jangling Baptist was going to the meeting. And I bid the people never heed, it was nothing to me whoever went to it.

And so when I came into the orchard I stood upon the stone that Friends used to speak on and was moved of the Lord to put off my hat and to stand a pretty while and let the people look at me, for there were many thousands of people there. And this rude Baptist began to find fault with my hair and I said nothing to him: and then he goes on into words; and at last he says, 'Ye wise men of Bristol, I strange at you that you will stand here to hear a man speak and affirm that which he cannot make good.' And as yet I had not spoken a word. Upon which the Lord opened my mouth and I asked the people whether ever they heard me speak before or ever saw me before. For what kind of man was this amongst them that should so impudently say that I had said and affirmed that which I could not make good, and yet he nor they never heard me nor saw me before. And therefore that was a lying, envious, malicious spirit that spoke in him, and it was of the Devil and not of God; and therefore I charged him in the dread and power of the Lord to be silent. And the mighty power of God came over him and all his company.

[1] A street then newly built on a field of that name, just outside and to N.E. of the old city. The site of the meeting place is believed to be that now occupied by Broadmead Baptist Chapel.

[2] The old Friary orchard, by the river Frome and near Broadmead, belonging to Dennis Hollister, a Friend.

And then a glorious peaceable meeting we had, and the word of life was divided amongst them and they were turned from the darkness to the light and to Jesus Christ, their saviour, and the Scriptures were largely opened to them and they turned to the spirit of God in themselves that would lead them into all Truth and open the Scriptures to them. And the traditions and rudiments, and ways and doctrines of men that they had been in, were opened to the people, and they turned to the light of Christ that with it they might see them, and him the way out of them.

And so for many hours did I declare the word of life amongst them in the eternal power of God that by him they might come up into the beginning and be reconciled to God. And I showed them the types and figures and shadows of Christ in the time of the law, and showed them how that Christ was come that ended the types and shadows, and tithes and oaths, and denied swearing and set up ' yea ' and ' nay ' instead of it, and a free teaching. And now he was come to teach people himself, and how that his heavenly day was springing from on high. And I was moved to pray in the mighty power of the Lord and the Lord's power came over all.

And when I had done, this fellow began to babble again, and I was moved to bid John Audland, who had been like to have been destroyed before through him, if he had any thing upon him from the Lord to speak, and he was moved to bid him repent and fear God. And his own people and followers were ashamed of him, so that he passed away and never came again to disturb the meetings. So the meeting broke up quietly and the Lord's power and glory shined over all and a blessed day it was; and the Lord had the praise.

And after, this Paul Gwin passed out of the nation. And many years after, when I came to Barbados there came this Paul Gwin to a general meeting where were many justices and a judge, one Judge Fretwell. And he fell to babbling and asked me how I spelt Cain, and whether I had the same spirit as the apostles had, and I told him,

Yes, and he then had the judge take notice of it. And I told him he that had not the same Holy Ghost as the apostles had was an unclean ghost and so he went his ways. And so from Bristol, as I said before, I returned to Edward Pyott's and there we had a great meeting. And the Lord's power and Truth spread over all and many were turned to Christ Jesus, their life and their prophet, to hear him; and their shepherd to feed them; and their bishop to oversee them. And after the meeting was done I had some reasoning with some professors but the Lord's Truth came over all.

And after this the prisoners were set at liberty at Exeter, and many of them came there to Bristol.

And from Edward Pyott's we passed to Slaughterford where we had a very large meeting, Edward Pyott and William Salt being still with me. And a great turning of people there was to the Lord Jesus Christ, their teacher, that people were glad that they came to know their way, and their free teacher, and their saviour Christ Jesus.

And from thence we passed the next First-day to Justice Nathaniel Cripps's[1] in Wiltshire where there were about two or three thousand people, and all was quiet. And the mighty power of God was manifested and people were turned to the grace and Truth that came by Jesus in their hearts, which would teach them to deny all manner of ungodliness and wordly lust and would teach them to live soberly and godly in this present world; so that every man and woman might know the grace of God which was sufficient and was saving; which had appeared to all men and would bring their salvation. So here was their teacher, the grace of God, that would teach them how to live and what to deny; that would season their words and establish their hearts and bring their salvation; and this was a free teacher to every one of them, and that they might come to be heirs of this grace and of Christ from whence it came; who ended the prophets and the priests that took tithes, and the temple. And as for the hireling priests

[1] Nathaniel Cripps lived at Tetbury.

that took tithes, and their temples (which priests were made at schools and colleges and not by Christ), with all their inventions they were to be denied, as the apostles denied the true priesthood and temple which God had commanded, ⟨after Christ had put an end thereto.⟩

And so largely the Truth and the Scriptures were opened for several hours to them, and the people turned to the spirit of God in their hearts, that by it they might be led into all Truth, and know the Scriptures, and God and Christ of whom they were learnt, and have unity one with another in the same spirit. And all people generally went away satisfied and admired and were glad that they were turned to Christ Jesus their teacher and saviour.

And the next day from thence we passed to Marlborough where we had a little meeting. And Edward Pyott went to a Baptist teacher and he reasoned with him. And as he was reasoning he felt the power of God reach into the man, and he asked him whether he did not feel the power of God reach unto him when he spoke, and he confessed it.

And the Sessions[1] being that day that we had the meeting at Marlborough, they were granting forth a warrant to send for me, and Justice Stokes[2] being at that Sessions stopped them and told them there was a meeting at his house yesterday at which were several thousands. And so the warrant was stopped and our meeting was quiet and several received Christ Jesus their teacher and the new covenant and stand in it. And from thence we came to Newbury where we had a large blessed meeting and several were convinced there. And from thence we came to Reading where we had a large and precious meeting[3] in the Lord's power amongst the plants of God, and many of the world came in and were reached, adding to that meeting. And all was quiet and the Lord's power came over all. And from Reading we passed to Kingston-upon-Thames, and a few there came in to us which were turned

[1] Tuesday, 7th Oct., 1656.
[2] Edward Stokes (*c.* 1615-1667), of Tytherton Lucas.
[3] Sunday, 12th Oct., 1656.

to the Lord Jesus Christ, but since it is become a great meeting.

And from thence we passed to London,[1] and when we came near Hyde Park we saw a great clutter of people. And we espied Oliver Protector coming in his coach, and I rid up to his coach-side. But some of his life-guard would have put me away, but he forbad them. So I rid down by his coach-side with him declaring what the Lord gave me to say unto him of his condition, and of the sufferings of Friends in the nation, and how contrary this persecution was to Christ and to the apostles and Christianity. And I rid by his coach till we came to [St.] James Park gate, and he desired me to come to his house.

And the next day one of Oliver's wife's maids, Mary Saunders, came up to me to my lodgings and said that her master came to her and said he could tell her some good news. And she asked him what it was, if it were good that was well. And he said unto her George Fox was come to town: and she said that was good news indeed but could hardly believe it: but he told her how I met him and rid from Hyde Park down to James Park with him.

So the Lord's power came over all; and Friends were glad and the Lord had the glory and the praise.

And so Edward Pyott and I went to Whitehall after a time and when we came before him there was one Dr. John Owen,[2] Vice-Chancellor of Oxford, with him: so we were moved to speak to Oliver Cromwell concerning the sufferings of Friends and laid them before him and turned him to the light of Christ who had enlightened every man that cometh into the world: and he said it was a natural light, and we showed him the contrary, and how it was divine and spiritual from Christ the spiritual and heavenly man, which was called the life in Christ, the Word and the light in us. And the power of the Lord God riz in me, and I was moved to bid him lay down his crown at the feet of Jesus. Several times I spoke to him

[1] 14th or 15th Oct., 1656.
[2] John Owen, D.D. (1616-1683).

to the same effect, and I was standing by the table; and he came and sat upon the table's side by me and said he would be as high as I was. And so he continued speaking against the light of Christ Jesus, and went his ways in a light manner and then he said to his wife and companions, 'I never parted so from them before', being judged in himself, for the Lord's power came over him.

And as Edward Pyott and I went out, many of his great persons were about us, and there was one of them[1] began to speak and discourse against the light and Truth. And I was made to slight him for his speaking so lightly of the things of God; and one told me he was the Major-General of Northamptonshire. 'What!' said I, 'our old persecutor that has persecuted and sent so many of our Friends to prison, who is a shame to Christianity and religion. I am glad I have met with thee.' So I was moved to speak sharply to him of his unchristian carriages. But he fled away, for he had been a cruel persecutor in Northamptonshire.[2]

[a]And in Oliver Cromwell's days as I was walking up by Ludgate Hill, there was a stop with coaches and cars coming from the Lord Mayor's feast.[3] And Secretary Thurloe's[4] coach was there. And as I was standing by and could not get forward nor backward, there came a man with a naked rapier out of his coach, and I looking at him to see what he would do with it, it being dark, he runs at a carman standing hard by, who was stopped also, and the carman

[1] William Butler or Boteler, Major-General of the counties of Northampton, Bedford, Rutland, and Huntingdon.

[2] The Spence MS. (*Camb. Jnl.*, i, 260, but not in other editions) here records as 'credibly reported in that country' that the Major-General's wife was thought to be with child 'but brought forth a monster' which was secretly done away with.

[3] In 1656 the Lord Mayor's inaugural banquet was on 28th Oct.

[4] John Thurloe (1616-1668), Cromwell's Secretary of State.

[a] This passage, ending at [a] on page 277, does not occur in Ellwood's edition. It is written on a separate paper, dated 1657. But Fox's presence in London in the autumn at the time of the Lord Mayor's banquet, and the 'troubles within' referring probably to the fall of James Nayler, both seem to require 1656, where it is therefore placed.

up with his sling and knocked out his brains. And the man cried out. And I bid them put him into the coach, but Thurloe would not let him be brought into the coach. Then I bid them carry him into some house and wrap him up whilst his blood was warm but he died presently. And this was the fruit of such an one who should have kept the peace, which might have cost many more lives, and his own also, but the Lord prevented it.

And we had a meeting in the Palace Yard,[1] but it was so pestered with rude priests, water-men, and lackeys, and rude professors, that sometimes there would be many hundreds about it; and we could seldom keep any glass whole in the windows, it would be so often broken down by the rude company.

And this was in the Presbyterian and Independents' anti-gospel times, who were against the gospel of peace.

And one time at the Palace Yard, as I was declaring the eternal word of life and preaching the everlasting Seed of life, and many hundreds of people were gathered, some being attentive, many of the rude ones so bespattered me with dirt and muck that my hair nor clothes could hardly be seen nor face for dirt and muck. And some outlandish[2] and other civil people were so ashamed to see what a dishonour this was to Christianity, that they began to reprove and stop the rude people and the rude ones fell upon them so that they were forced to take sanctuary in Westminster Hall and fled there for safety.

And after this our meeting broke up in the power of the Lord and not much hurt done unto us. Such disturbance we had in our meetings in the city and in many places of the country also.

And when the priests could not get down our meetings with their rude rabble, then they would write to Oliver Protector that we met to plot to bring in King Charles; and so went about to make them treasonable meetings: but the Lord did give them their portion at last as is said

[1] Probably at Stephen Hart's, New Palace Yard.

[2] i.e. foreign.

before, and his lambs and birds did escape their snares and gins. And all these things were of service for Truth for it manifested them and their fruits to sober people, and all these things did work together for good to them that feared God. For we knew that not a sparrow could fall to the ground without the will of the Father who upholds all things by his word and power, and carries his lambs in his arms and brings them to mount up, as on eagles' wings, over all their storms, and waves, and floods that they cast out against us. His name has the praise for ever, and the glory, who is worthy of all, who is the helper of his people and their rock and foundation, and with them in all their afflictions and their deliverer out of the six and seven troubles, yea, even the perfection of troubles.

And this I know by experience and therefore it is good to trust in the Lord.

For the persecutions cannot be uttered that we underwent in that time, and the troubles and sufferings and reproaches every way without, even as before I came into it my troubles within, could not be uttered. But the Lord has the praise, who is the upholder of us through all, and gives the dominion over all. For that spirit which makes the just, and the good, and Seed of God to suffer within is the same that makes to suffer without when it is cast out within. So I was not ignorant of Satan's wiles and all the sufferings without are nothing to the sufferings within. But the Lord hath given me dominion over both and doth give dominion over both to his people, and he alone is worthy of the glory and praise.[a]

And so after I had visited the meetings of Friends in London I went into Buckinghamshire and Edward Pyott with me. And several places received the Truth in that country and great meetings we had: and the Lord's power came over all.

And then I passed into Northamptonshire and Nottinghamshire and into Lincolnshire. And after I had passed to several meetings in Lincolnshire, I had a last meeting where

[a] See note [a] on page 275.

Sir Richard and Sir John Wray,[1] and their wives, were at the meeting: and she was convinced and died in the Truth; and the Lord's power came over all. And they were directed to the light of Christ within to give them the knowledge of the glory of God in the face of Christ Jesus, and to the annointing within to teach them, and to the grace of God which was sufficient to save them. And when the meeting was done we passed away. And it being in the evening there being a company of serving men and wild fellows, they met me and encompassed me about and had an intent to have done me some mischief. It being dark, I asked, 'What ! are you highway men ?' and Friends and friendly people came up to me that knew some of them; so I declared the Truth unto them and showed them their uncivil and rude carriage, and the Lord's power came over all and stopped their design, blessed be his name for ever. ⟨And then I passed into⟩ Huntingdonshire, where the mayor of Huntingdon came to visit me and was very loving, and his wife received the Truth, and into Cambridgeshire. And so we came into the Fen Country where I had many meetings and the Lord's Truth spread. ⟨And Robert Craven who had been⟩ the sheriff of Lincoln was with me and Amor Stoddard and Alexander Parker; and we went to Crowland, the sheriff of Lincoln and me, and came to an inn where the townspeople were gathered together, being half drunk, a very rude place.

And I was moved to admonish them and exhort them of the day of the Lord and to leave off their drunkenness and turn to the Lord and turned them to the light of Christ in their hearts which would let them see all their evil deeds, ways, and words. And the priest[2] was amongst them and I admonished him and bid him see the fruits of his ministry. And so as I was turning them to the Lord Jesus Christ and his teaching, the priest and his clerk were in a rage and got up the tongs and fire shovel; and had not the Lord's power preserved us, we might have been murdered amongst

[1] See note on p. 180.

[2] Richard Lee.

them; yet nevertheless some received the Lord's Truth then and stand there to this day.

And from thence we passed through the country to Boston. And most of the heads of the town came to the inn; and the people seemed to be much satisfied: but there was a raging man in the yard and the sheriff of Lincoln was moved to speak to him and said, 'Thou son of Eve! thou shamest Christianity', and some other words, and he went away quiet; and some were convinced there also.

And so we passed through the countries and had large meetings up and down, and I travelled into Yorkshire,[1] and passed over Humber out of Holderness about this time, visiting Friends: and from thence returned into Leicestershire, Staffordshire, Worcestershire, Warwickshire.

And I had a meeting at Edge Hill that was very rude, for there came Ranters, Baptists, and several sorts of rude people, for I had sent word to have a meeting there a matter of three weeks before. And I went up to it, where were many hundreds of people gathered to it and many Friends and people came far to it. And the Lord's everlasting Truth and word of life reached over all and in all, that all was chained. And many that day were turned to the Lord Jesus Christ by his power and spirit, and came to sit under his blessed, everlasting, free teaching and feeding with his eternal and heavenly food. And all was quiet and peaceable and passed away quiet, so that the people said it was a mighty powerful meeting, and the presence of the Lord God was felt by his power and spirit amongst them.

And from thence I passed to Warwick and to Baddesley, having precious meetings, and from thence into Gloucestershire, and came into Oxford, where the scholars were very rude; but the Lord's power was over them all; and great meetings we had up and down.

And from thence I came to Colonel Grimes's[2] where there was a mighty meeting, and to Justice Cripps's where there

[1] He was at Warmsworth, near Doncaster, 23rd and 25th Oct., 1656.

[2] Probably Mark Grimes, of Corse.

came another justice to the meetings that was convinced, and he lay with me.

And at Cirencester we had a meeting which since is much increased: and so we came to Evesham again where I met John Camm.

And after this time, when I was set at liberty ⟨out of Launceston gaol⟩, I was moved to go over most parts of the nation, the Truth being spread up and down over the nation. And it was the general talk of the priests and professors and other sectary preachers that the false prophets and the antichrists should come in the last days and that we were they.

And I was moved to open this through the nation, how they which said we were the false prophets, antichrists, and deceivers which should come in the last times, were themselves they.[1]

⟨Thus were the objections, which the priests and professors had raised against Friends, answered and cleared, and the stumbling blocks which they laid in the way of the weak, removed. And as things were thus opened, people came to see over them and through them, and to have their minds settled upon the Lord Jesus Christ their free teacher, which was the service for which I was moved to travel over the nation after my imprisonment in Launceston gaol.⟩

And in this year the Lord's Truth was finely planted over this nation and many thousands were turned to the Lord; and seldom under a thousand in prison in the nation for tithes and going to the steeplehouses, and for contempts and not swearing and not putting off their hats. And Oliver Protector began to harden and several Friends were turned out of their offices of justices and other offices, and out of the army.

And so after I had compassed most part of the nation, I returned to London again. ⟨Finding that evil spirit at work which had drawn James Nayler and his followers out

[1] The discourse is printed in *Camb. Jnl.*, i, 246-55, and with considerable editorial changes in Ellwood, pp. 226*-231*; Bicent., i, 336-43.

from Truth, to run Friends into heats about him, I writ a short epistle to Friends, as followeth:

To all the elect seed of God called Quakers, where the death is brought into the death, and the elder is servant to the younger, and the elect is known, which cannot be deceived, but obtains victory. This is the word of the Lord God to you all.

Go not forth to the aggravating part, to strive with it out of the power of God, lest you hurt yourselves, and run into the same nature, out of the life. For patience must get the victory and answer that of God in every one, must bring every one to it, and bring them from the contrary.

So let your moderation, and temperance, and patience be known to all men in the Seed of God. For that which reacheth to the aggravating part without life sets up the aggravating part, and breeds confusion, and hath a life in outward strife, and reacheth not to the witness of God in every one, in which they come into peace and covenant with God, and fellowship with another. Therefore that which reacheth this witness of God within, and without in others, is the life and light; which will outlast all, which is over all and will overcome all. And therefore in the Seed of life live, which bruiseth the seed of death.

G.F.

I also writ another short epistle to Friends to encourage them to keep up their meetings in the Lord's power; of which epistle a copy here followeth:

Dear Friends,

Keep your meetings in the power of the Lord, which power is over all that which is in the fall and must have an end. Therefore be wise in the wisdom of God which is from above, by which all things were made and created, that that may be justified among you, and you all kept in the solid life, which was before death was, and in the light which was before the darkness was with all its works . . . For the Gospel, being the power of God, that is pure and everlasting. Know it to be your portion, in which is stability and life and immortality, shining over that which darkens the mortal.

And so be faithful every one to God, in your measures of his power and life, that ye may answer God's love and mercy to you, as the obedient children of the Most High, dwelling in love, unity, and peace, and in innocency of heart towards one another, that God may be glorified in you, and you kept faithful witnesses for him and valiant for the Truth on earth. And so God Almighty preserve you all to his glory, that ye may all feel his blessing among you and that ye may be possessors thereof.

G.F.[1]

And inasmuch as about this time many mouths were opened in our meetings to declare the goodness of the Lord, and some that were young and tender in the Truth would sometimes utter a few words in thanksgiving and praises to God; that no disorder might arise from thence in our meetings, I was moved to write an epistle to Friends, by way of advice in that matter. And thus it was:〉

All my dear Friends in the noble Seed of God, and who have known his power, life, and presence amongst you, let it be your joy to hear or see the springs break forth in any, through which you have all unity in the same feeling, life, and power. And above all things take heed of judging, ever, any one openly in your meetings, except they be openly profane, rebellious, such as be out of the Truth; that by the power and life and wisdom you may stand over them, and by it answer the witness of God in the world, that such are none of you, whom you bear your testimony against, so that therein the Truth stand clear and single.

But such as are tender, if they should be moved to bubble forth a few words, and speak in the Seed and Lamb's power, suffer and bear that, that is, the tender. And if they should go beyond their measure, bear it in the meeting for peace sake, and order, and that the spirits of the world be not moved against you. But when the meeting is done, then if anything should be moved of anyone to speak to them between yourselves or one or two of you that feel it in the life, do it in the love and wisdom that is pure and gentle from above.

For love is that which doth edify, and bears all things, and suffers, which doth fulfil the force of the law. So in this you have order, you have edification, you have wisdom that preserves you all wise and in the patience, which takes away the occasion of stumbling the weak and occasioning the spirits of the world

[1] In full, Ellwood, p. 232*; Bicent., i, 344.

to get up. You will hear and feel and see the power of God, as your faith is all in it, preaching when you do not hear words, to bind, to chain, to limit, to frustrate, that nothing shall rise nor shall come forth, but what is in the power. And with that you will let up, and open every spring, plant, and spark, in which will be your joy and refreshment.

For now you know the power of God, which is the Cross of Christ, and are come to it, which crucifies you from the state that Adam and Eve were in in the Fall, and so from the world; by which power of God you come to see the state Adam and Eve were in before they fell . . Yea, I say and to a state higher, the Seed, Christ the second Adam, by whom all things were made . . . And the way is Christ the light, the life, the truth, and the saviour, the redeemer, the sanctifier, the justifier; and so in his power and light and life who is the way to God, conversion, regeneration, and translation are known, from death to life, darkness to light, and from the power of Satan to God again.

And these are members of the Church who know the work in the operation and feeling and come to be members one of another. They who come to the Church that is in God and Christ, must come out of the state that Adam is in, in the Fall, to know the state that he was in before he fell. And now they that live in the state that Adam is in, in the Fall, and who cannot believe of coming into the state he was in before he fell, come not to the Church in God, but are afar from that, and are not passed from death to life, and likewise are enemies to the Cross of Christ, which is the power of God . . . For all the poorness, emptiness, and barrenness is in the state that Adam is in, in the Fall, out of God's power. By which power he comes to be crucified from it, by which power he comes to be made rich again and hath strength. This power is the Cross, in which mystery of the Cross is the fellowship; and this is the Cross in which is the true and everlasting glorying, which crucifies from all other glorying.

And Friends, though you may have tasted of the power and been convinced and have felt the light, yet afterwards you may feel winter storms, tempests, and hail, and be frozen, in frost and cold and a wilderness and temptations. Be patient and still in the power and still in the light that doth convince you, to keep your minds to God; in that be quiet, that you may come to the summer, that your flight be not in the winter. For if you sit still in the patience which overcomes in the power of God, there will be no flying. For the husbandman, after he hath sown his seed, he is patient. For by the power and by the light you will come to see through and feel over winter storms, tempests, and all the coldness, barrenness, emptyness. And the same light and power will go over the tempter's head, which power and light were before he was. And so in the light standing still you will see your salvation, you will see the Lord's strength, you will feel the small rain, you will feel the fresh springs in the power and light, your minds being kept low; for that which is out of the power and light lifts up. But in the power and light you will see God revealing his secrets, inspiring, and his gifts coming unto you, through which your hearts will be filled with God's love; praise to him that lives for ever more, in which light and power his blessings are received. And so the eternal power of the Lord Jesus Christ preserve and keep you in that. And so live everyone in the power of God, that you may all come to be heirs of that and know that to be your portion, and the kingdom that hath no end, and an endless life, which the seed is heir of. And so feel that over all set, which hath the promise and blessing of God.

G.F.[1]

⟨About this time I received some lines from a high-flown professor concerning the way of Christ, to which I returned answer.[2]

Great opposition did the priests and professors make about this time against the light of Christ Jesus, denying it to be universally given, and against the pouring forth of the spirit, and sons and daughters prophesying thereby. Much they laboured to darken the minds of people that they might keep them still in a dependence on their teaching. Wherefore I was moved of the Lord to give forth a paper for the opening of the minds and understandings of people and to manifest the blindness and darkness of their teachers.[3]

And I was moved of the Lord to send for one or two out of a county to Swarthmoor and to set up the men's meetings

[1] In full, *Camb. Jnl.*, i, 222-5; Ellwood, pp. 233*-235*; Bicent., i, 344-7.

[2] Ellwood, p. 235*; Bicent., i, 347-50.

[3] Ellwood, pp. 238*-243*; Bicent., i, 350-6.

where they were not: and to settle that meeting at Skipton[1] concerning the affairs of the Church, which continued till 1660.

And at the first the North took six hundred of every sort of book that was printed, and that continued for many years till the Truth was spread over the nation; and this was settled when we first began to print. And then when the Truth was spread as aforesaid, it was left to Friends' liberty for every county to send for what they liked from all parts of the nation. But the North, at the first, bore the charges of all the printing for several years, but when the Lord's Truth spread over the nation, and people came to be turned to Christ, then they were eased.

And about this time I was moved to set up the men's Quarterly Meetings throughout the nation, though in the North they were settled before.

⟨Having stayed some time in London, and visited the meetings of Friends in and about the city, and cleared myself of what services the Lord had at that time laid upon me there⟩, I passed out of London into Kent, Surrey, and Sussex,[2] and visited Friends and had great meetings; and many times I met with jangling professors and Baptists, but the Lord's power went over all.

And before we lay the night at Farnham we had a little meeting, but the people were exceeding rude, and at last the Lord's power came over them. We went to our inn after the meeting and desired any that feared God that they might come to our inn; and there came abundance of rude people, and the magistrates of the town and some professors. And I declared the Truth unto them, and the magistrates put the rude people out of the room. And when they were gone there came up another rude company of professors and some of the heads of the town and they called for faggots[3] and drink though we forbade them; who were as rude a carriaged people as ever I met withal, but the

[1] The first General Meeting was held at Skipton in 1656.

[2] January and February, 1657.

[3] Chopped meat.

Lord's power chained them that they had not power to do us any mischief; but when they went their ways, they left all their faggots and beer that they had called for into the room for us to pay in the morning. And we showed the innkeeper what an unworthy thing it was; yet he told us we must pay it, and pay it we did. And then I was moved to write a paper to the magistrates and the heads of the town, of their rude inhuman uncivil carriage to strangers that sought their good, and to the priest to show him how he had taught his people.

And I came to Basingstoke, a very rude place where they had formerly very much abused Friends. There I had a meeting in the evening, which was quiet, for the Lord's power chained the unruly. ⟨At the close of the meeting⟩ I was moved to put off my hat and pray to the Lord to open their understandings, and then they raised a report upon me and said that I was a very good man and I put off my hat to them, and bid them good-night, which was never in my heart. And we went to an inn in Basingstoke, The George, and we sent for the innkeeper as I used to do, and he came into the room to us, a very rude man. And I began to admonish him and he called for faggots and a pint of wine and drunk it off himself, and then called for another, and then called half a dozen men up into our chamber. And I bid him go out of the chamber, and said he should not drink there, for we sent for him up to admonish him concerning his eternal good. And he was exceeding mad and rude, and drunk, but I told him the chamber was mine for the time whilst I lodged in it, and so I called for the key. So, at last, he went his ways in great rage, but in the morning would not be seen; but I told his wife of his unchristian and rude carriage towards us.

And from thence we passed through the countries till we came to Bridport and had meetings on the way. And there we came to an inn and sent into the town for such as feared God. And there came a shopkeeper and put off his hat to us, and seeing we did not again to him but said 'thee' and 'thou' to him, he said he was not of our religion; and after some discourse with him we did admonish him; and his wife was somewhat loving. Thomas Curtis was with me. And this professor went down and stirred up the priest[1] and magistrates, and he sent to us to our inn to come and speak with him, for there he said were some would speak with us at his house: and so Thomas Curtis went down, and when he came there the man had laid a snare for him and got the priests and magistrates; and they boasted mightily that they had catched George Fox, thinking I had been the man. And they were in a great rage but the Lord's power came over them, and when they perceived it was not me they let him go again.

And as we were passing out of Bridport sober people came to us and said the officers were coming up to fetch me, but the Lord's power came over them all so as they had not power to touch me; nevertheless there were some convinced in that town that time and were turned to the Lord; and they stand to this day, where there is a fine meeting. And one night we came to a place called Lyme, and we went to an inn. And the house was taken up with mountebanks,[2] and there was hardly any room for us or our horses. At night we drew up some queries:

Of the grounds of all diseases:
And whether Adam or Eve had any before they fell:
And whether there was any in the restoration by Christ Jesus again:
And whether any knew the virtue of all the creatures in the creation, whose virtue and nature was according to its first name, except they were in the wisdom of God by which they were made and created.

And many other particular queries we sent to them and told them if they would not answer them we would stick them on the cross tomorrow, and it made them very cool and low, for they could not answer them. But in the morning they reasoned a little with us but could not answer us;

[1] John Eaton was rector of Bridport.

[2] Itinerant quack doctors, hence the queries that follow.

and so we left them with some friendly people, who were convinced, to stick upon the market cross. And the Lord's power came over all, and some were turned by the light and spirit of Christ to his free teaching.

But before we came to Lyme we had been at Portsmouth and Poole where we had glorious meetings and many were turned to the Lord there. And fine meetings there are there, that stand to this day. And at Ringwood we had a large general meeting where the Lord's power was over all. And at Weymouth we had a meeting and so we passed to Dorchester.

And so we passed through the country till we came to Exeter; at the Seven Stars, at the bridge foot,[1] an inn where we had a General Meeting[2] of Friends out of Cornwall and Devonshire; and thither came Humphry Lower, Thomas Lower, and John Ellis from the Land's End; and Friends from Plymouth; Justice Henry Polixphen, Elizabeth Trelawney, and divers other Friends. Where a blessed heavenly meeting we had, and I saw and said that the Lord's power had surrounded this nation round about, as with a wall and bulwark, and his Seed reached from sea unto sea, and Friends were established in the everlasting Seed of life, Christ Jesus, their life, rock, teacher and shepherd.

CHAPTER XII

AND after the meeting was done, the next morning, Major John Blackmore sent down soldiers to apprehend me but I was gone before they came. And as I was riding up the street I saw the officers going down, so the wolf missed the lamb and the Lord's power crossed them in their design. And Friends passed away peaceably and quietly, though the soldiers examined some Friends after I was gone, what they did there; and they

[1] On the Exe-bridge, kept by 'one Morgan'.
[2] Sunday, 8th Mar., 1657.

told them they were in their inn and had occasions and business to the city; so they passed away without any farther meddling with them.

And after this I came through the country and had meetings till I came to Bristol. [Fox was at Bristol about four days and then went to London.][1]

And so I visited the meetings up and down in London; and some of them were troubled with rude people and apostates that had run out with James Nayler. And I was moved to write to Oliver Cromwell, and laid before him the sufferings of Friends in the nation and in Ireland.

And I was moved again to go and speak to Oliver Protector when there was a talk of making him King. And I met him in the Park and told him that they that would put him on an earthly crown would take away his life.

And he asked me, 'What say you?'

And I said again, they that sought to put him on a crown would take away his life, and bid him mind the crown that was immortal.

And he thanked me after I had warned him of many dangers and how he would bring a shame and a ruin upon himself and his posterity, and bid me go to his house.[2] And then I was moved to write to him and told him how he would ruin his family and posterity and bring darkness upon the nation if he did so. And several papers I was moved to write to him. [Fox then returned to Bristol and went] to the meeting there.

And after meeting was done I did not stay, not so much as to eat nor drink in the town.

And so I passed up into Wales and had a meeting at the Slow.[3] And I passed through the country to Cardiff, and

[1] Contemporary letters (see *Beginnings of Quakerism*, 438n) provide this information. This journey to London is undescribed in the Journal. Events in London during this visit are, in the MS. and in previous editions, placed as though they belong to another visit. The following paragraphs relating to them are believed to be here placed in correct chronological position.

[2] Fox saw Cromwell, 24th and 25th Mar., 1657.

[3] A farm near Caerwent about five miles west of Chepstow.

there a justice of peace[1] sent for me and said he desired half a dozen might come up with me to his house. And so I took a Friend or two and went up to him, and he and his wife received me very civilly; and the next day we had a meeting in Cardiff in the town hall and the justice aforesaid sent about seventeen of his family to the meeting. And there came some disturbers but the Lord's power was over all; and many were turned to the Lord there. And some that had run out with James Nayler did not come to the meeting; and I sent word to them that the day of their visitation was over; and they did not prosper no ways.

So we passed through the country to Swansea and passed over a passage in a boat with the high sheriff of the county, and we had a blessed meeting there and a meeting was settled in the name of Jesus, which stands to this day. And the next day I went to have spoken with the high sheriff aforesaid but he would not be spoken withal.

And from thence we went to another meeting in the country where much of the presence of the Lord was with us; and from thence we went to a great man's house, who received us very lovingly. But the next morning he would not be seen; one that came ⟨in the meantime⟩ had incensed him, that we could not get to him to speak with him, he was so changed; yet overnight was exceeding loving.

So we passed through the countries and had meetings and gathered people in the name of Christ to their teacher, till we came to Brecknock: and there we set up our horses at an inn. And there went with me Thomas Holmes and John ap John, who was moved of the Lord to speak in the streets. And I had walked out a little into the fields, but by the time I came in all the town was up in an uproar; and when I came into the inn the chamber was full of people and they were speaking in Welsh. And I desired them to speak in English and they did, and great discourse we had, and after a while they went their ways. But towards night the magistrates gathered together in the street, and a multitude of people, and they bid them shout

[1] Probably John Gawler.

and gathered up the town so that for about two hours together there was such a noise as the like we had not heard; and the magistrates set them on to shout again when they had left. And there was never such an uproar amongst Diana's handicraftsmen as there was at that time, so that if the Lord's power had not prevented them they might have plucked down the house and us to pieces. And this they did till it was within night.

[a]And they had a plot amongst them, together with the woman of the inn, after it was night, to have had us out of that room where we were, which we had taken up, into another room to have supped, a great hall. And so I looked at the room, and perceiving the plot, I bid the woman bring our meat into our own chamber, for there was a table sufficient, and we would have none if we had it not in our own room, and choose her whether she would bring it or not. At last she brought it up in a great rage. Then she wished us out of her house, and we told her we had taken a house of her and grass, and so when she could not by any means get us out, they came by flattery.[a] She would have had six men come into the room under pretence to discourse with us. But we told her that no persons should come into our room that night, neither would we go out to them. [a]So the Lord prevented their mischief for they had an intent to have murdered us.[a] And the next morning after I had given forth a paper to the town of their unchristian carriages, showing the fruits of their priests and magistrates, we passed away; and I spoke to the people as I went forth of the town how they shamed both Christianity and religion.

And from thence we passed to a great meeting in a steeplehouse yard[1] where was Walter Jenkins ⟨who had been a justice⟩ and a priest and another justice, and a blessed glorious meeting we had, and there were a-many professors; and I was moved of the Lord to open to them the Scriptures and the objections that they stuck at in their

[1] Perhaps, Pontypool in Monmouthshire.

[a]. . . . . .[a] *S.J.*, p. 50-1.

profession, for I knew them very well, and to turn them to Christ who had enlightened them, with which light they might see their saviour and sins and trespasses they had been dead in, and him that redeemed them out of it, who was their way to God, their truth and life and their priest made higher than the heavens, so that they might come to sit under his teaching. And many were convinced and settled that day and a peaceable meeting it was. And after the meeting was done I went with Justice Jenkins to the other justice's house; and he said unto me, 'You have given this day great satisfaction to the people and answered all the objections that were in their minds'; for the people had the Scriptures but they were not turned to the spirit which should let them see that which gave them forth, which is the key to open them, the spirit of God.

And from thence we passed to Pontymoil[1] to Richard Hanbury's where there was a great meeting, and there came another justice of peace and several great people to it; and their understandings were opened by the Lord's spirit and power and the light of Jesus Christ, that they came to be turned to Christ from whence it came, and a great convincement there was and a large meeting there is gathered in the name of Jesus which continues thereaways to this day.

So from thence we returned back again into England and so came to Shrewsbury, where we had a great meeting and visited Friends all up and down the countries in their meetings till we came into Cheshire to William Gandy's;[2] and there we had a meeting of about two or three thousand people; and the everlasting word of life was held forth and received that day. And a blessed meeting it was, for Friends were settled by the power of God upon Christ Jesus the rock and foundation.

And at this time there was a great drought; and after the General Meeting was ended there fell a mighty rain, and there was so much rain the next day that Friends

[1] Near Pontypool.

[2] William Gandy lived at Frandley, near Warrington. The meeting was held on 28th June.

said they believed we could not pass, the brooks and waters would be so risen; but I believed so far as they had come that day to the meetings so far they had rain. So the next day about the afternoon we came back into some parts of Wales again and there was all dust, and no rain had fallen thereabout, and it was a noted thing generally amongst people that when I came, still I brought rain, and it had been so for many years.

And when Oliver Protector gave forth a proclamation for a fast[1] throughout the nation for rain when there was such a mighty drought; as far as Truth had spread in the north there was rain enough and pleasant showers, when up in the south in places they were almost spoiled for want of rain. And I was moved to give forth an answer[2] to Oliver Protector's proclamation that if he did come to own God's truth he should have rain and that drought was a sign unto them of their barrenness of the water of life, as you may see in that book given forth in answer to his proclamation. And the like observation and expectation they have beyond the seas. When there is a drought they generally look for the Quakers' General Meetings, for then they know they shall have rain; and as they receive the Truth and become fruitful unto God, they receive from him their fruitful seasons also.

About the same time was written a paper to distinguish between true and false fasts.[3]

And so we passed up into Wales through Montgomeryshire and up into Radnorshire, where there was a meeting like a leaguer for multitude. And I walked a little off from the meeting whilst the people were a-gathering, and there came John ap John to me, a Welshman; and I bid him go up to the people, and if he had anything upon him from the Lord to speak to the people in Welsh he might, ⟨and thereby gather them more together⟩.

[1] The proclamation was dated 20th Mar., 1654.

[2] Entitled, *A Warning from the Lord to all such as hang down the head for a day.* 1654.

[3] Ellwood, pp. 248*-251*; Bicent., i, 363-7.

Then there came Morgan Watkins[1] to me, who was loving to Friends and, says he, 'The people lie like a leaguer and the gentry of the country are come in.' So I bid him go up to the meeting, for I had a great travail upon me for the salvation of the people. And so I passed up to the meeting and stood a-top of a chair about three hours and sometimes leaned my hand of a man's head, and stood a pretty while before I began to speak, and many people sat a-horseback. And at last I felt the power of the Lord went over them all and the Lord's everlasting life and truth shined over all. And the Scriptures were opened to them and their objections answered in their minds and every one of them turned to the light of Christ, the heavenly man, that with it they might all see their sins and see their saviour, their redeemer, their mediator, and feed upon him their bread from heaven. And many were turned that day to the Lord Jesus Christ and his free teaching, and all were bowed down under the power of God and parted peaceably and quietly with great satisfaction, ⟨though the multitude was so great that many sat on horseback to hear⟩. And there was a priest and his wife sat a-horseback that day and heard patiently, but made no objection. And they said they never heard such a divine in their lives, and the Scriptures so opened, and the new covenant and the old covenant and the parables and the state of the Church in the apostles' days and apostacy since, and Christ and the apostles' free teaching set a-top of all the hireling teachers and people turned to him.

And people said that they thought if I would come into the country again [b]half the country would have come in, they were so taken with the Truth[b] at that meeting, and the Lord had the praise, for many were turned to him that day and a justice of peace was convinced that came to be a fine minister since, one Peter Price.

And I came back from thence to Leominster, where there was a great meeting in a close and many hundreds of people;

[1] Of Eyton, Herefordshire.

[b]. . . . . .[b] *S.J.*, p. 51.

and there was a matter of six Separate preachers and priests. And there was one Thomas Taylor with me, who had been a priest but now was become a free minister of Christ Jesus.

And after I had stood a matter of three hours and none of the priests were able to open their mouths, the Lord's power and truth so reached them; though many times their mouths were opening to speak. And at last one priest went about a bow-shot off me and there he drew several of the people after him and fell a-preaching to them, and I kept my meeting and he kept his meeting. And at last Thomas Taylor was moved to go to him and speak to him and he gave over; and then he and the people came up to me again and the Lord's power went over them all. And at last a Baptist that was convinced said, 'Where is priest Tombes[1]? how chance he does not come out?' And this priest John Tombes was priest of Leominster.

And then some went and told the priest and up comes he with the bailiffs of the town and magistrates and officers; and when he came up they set him upon a stool over against me. And I was speaking of the heavenly divine light of Christ which he enlightens every one that cometh into the world withal, and turning them to it to give them the knowledge of the glory of God in the face of Christ Jesus their saviour.

This Priest Tombes cries out, 'That is a natural light and a made light.'

And then I desired all the people to take out their Bibles; [c]for I would make the Scriptures bend him,[c] and I asked them whether he did affirm that was a created, natural, made light that John, a man that was sent from God to bear witness to it, did speak of who said, 'In him was life', to wit the Word, 'and this life was the light of men.' John i. 4. And I asked him whether this light was that created, natural, made light he meant.

[1] John Tombes (1603-1676), learned minister and controversial writer, appointed one of the Triers of ministers, 1653.

[c]. . . . . .[c] *S.J.*, p. 55.

And he said, 'Yes.'

Then said I, 'Before I have done with thee I will make thee bend to the Scriptures. The natural, created, made light is the sun, moon, and stars and this outward light. And dost thou say that God sent John to bear witness to the sun, moon, and stars which are the made lights?'

Then said he, 'Did I say so?'

'Yes', said I, 'Thou said it was a natural, created, made light that John bare witness unto. And if thou dost not like thy words, take them again and mend them. For John came to bear witness to the light which was the life in the Word, by which all the natural lights were made and created, as sun, moon, and stars and the like. And in him, to wit, the Word, was life; and that life was the light of men.'

And then he took at it again and said, that light I spoke of was a natural, created light, and so made it worse and worse in his argument.

And so I made manifest to the people how that in the beginning was the Word and the Word was with God, and God was the Word, and all things that were made were made by him, and without him was not anything made that was made. So all natural created lights were made by Christ the Word. And Christ saith he is the light of the world, and bids them believe in the light, John xii. 36. And God saith, 'I will give thee for a light to the gentiles that thou mayest be my salvation to the ends of the earth,' Isa. xlix. 6. So Christ in his life is saving. And the Apostle said, the light that shined in their hearts was to give them the knowledge of the glory of God in the face of Jesus Christ, and that was their treasure in their earthen vessels, 2 Cor. iv. 6, 7.

'Oh,' says the people, 'He is a cunning fox.'

'Oh,' says the priest to the magistrates, 'Take him away, or else I shall not speak any more.'

'But,' said I, 'Priest Tombes, thou art not in thy pulpit now, nor in thy old mass house; thou art deceived, we are in the fields.'

And so he was shuffling to be gone. And then Thomas

Taylor stood up and <undertook to make out our principles> by Christ's parable concerning the sower, Matt. xiii.

Then cries the priest, 'Let that man speak and not the other.'

So he was let up into a little jangling till the Lord's power catched him again, being by the power of the Lord God stopped and confounded. Then a Friend stood up and told him how he had sued him for tithe eggs and Friends for tithes, for he was an Anabaptist priest, and yet had the parsonage at Leominster and had several journeymen under him. And he said he had a wife and he had a concubine, and his wife was the baptized people and his concubine was the world. But the Lord's power came over them all and his everlasting Truth was declared that day, and many were turned by it to the Lord Jesus Christ, their teacher and way to God. And of great service that meeting was in those parts. And Thomas Taylor went to the priest the next day, to reason with him, and came over him by the power of the Lord.

And so I passed through Wales and had several meetings till I came to Tenby, and when I came up the street a justice of peace came out of his house and desired me to alight and stay at his house, and I did so.

And on the First-day the mayor and his wife and several others of the heads of the town came in about the tenth hour and stayed all the meeting, and a glorious meeting it was. And John ap John[1] was with me, and he went to the steeplehouse; and the governor cast him into prison. And on the Second-day morning the governor sent one of his officers to the justice's house for me, and it grieved the mayor and the justice for they were both with me in the justice's house. So the mayor and the justice went up to the governor before me; and after, I went up with the officer; and the governor had got another justice of peace with him. And when I came in I said, 'Peace be unto this house', and before he could examine me I was moved to ask him

[1] John ap John (*c.* 1630-1697) of Trevor Issa, near Llangollen; the first Welsh Quaker. See p. 172 ante.

why he did cast my friend in prison, and he said, 'For standing with his hat on his head in the church.'

I said, 'Had not the priest two caps on his head, a black one and a white, and cut off the brims of his hat and my friend then would have but one; and the brims of the hat were only to save the rain from his neck.'

'These are frivolous things,' said he.

Said I, 'Then why dost thou cast my friend in prison for such frivolous things?'

So then he began to ask me whether I owned election and reprobation. 'Yes,' said I; 'and thou art in the reprobation.' Then he was up in a rage and said he would send me to prison till I proved it, and then I told him I would prove it quickly if he would confess truth. Then I asked him whether wrath, fury, and rage, and persecution were not in the reprobation, for he that was born of the flesh persecuted him that was born of the spirit. For Christ and his disciples never persecuted nor imprisoned any.

And so he fairly confessed that he had too much of wrath, haste, and passion in him; so I told him Esau was up in him, the first birth, and not Jacob, the second birth. So the Lord's power so reached the man, and came over him that he confessed to Truth: and the other justice came and took me by the hand. And as I was passing away I was moved to speak to the governor again, and he invited me to dinner with him and set my friend at liberty.

So I went back to the other justice's house and the mayor and his wife and the justice and his wife and diverse other Friends of the town went about half a mile with us to the water's side. And there I was moved of the Lord to kneel down with them and pray to the Lord to preserve them.

And after I had turned them to the Lord Jesus Christ their free teacher and saviour I passed away; and the Lord's power came over all, and the Lord had the glory. And there is a meeting continues in that town to this day.

And so from thence we passed through the country to Pembrokeshire. And in Pembroke town we had some service for the Lord: and from thence we passed to Haverfordwest where we had a great meeting and all was quiet and the Lord's power came over all: and many were settled in the new covenant Christ Jesus, and built upon him their rock and foundation. And they stand a precious meeting to this day. And the next day, being their fair day, we passed through their fair and sounded the day of the Lord and his everlasting Truth amongst them.

And after that we came to another county, and at noon we came into a great market town[1] and went to several inns: and yet could not get any meat for our horses, and at last we came to an inn where we did get some meat for our horses. John ap John, being with me, he spoke through the town, declaring the truth to the people, and after he came to me he said he thought all the town was as people asleep. And after a while he was moved to go again, and then the town was all in an uproar and cast him into prison. So there were several of the heads of the town and others came down to the inn where I was and said they had cast my man in prison. 'For what?' said I. They said he preached in their streets; and then I asked them, 'What did he say? Did he reprove some of the drunkards and swearers, and warn them to repent and leave off their evil doing and turn to the Lord?' And then I asked who had cast him into prison; and they said the high sheriff and the justices and the mayor. So I asked the names of them and whether they did understand themselves and whether that was their carriage to travellers that passed through their town and to strangers that did admonish them and exhort them to fear the Lord and reproved sin in their gates; so they went up again and told those officers what I said. And after a while they brought down John ap John guarded with their officers and halberts to the inn door, in order to put him out of town. I, ⟨being at the inn door,⟩ bid them take their hands off him. They said the mayor and officers had commanded to put him out of the town, and I told them I would talk with their

[1] Probably Carmarthen.

mayor and justices anon of their uncivil and unchristian carriages towards him.

So I bid John go and look after the horses and get them ready, and charged the officers not to touch him. So they went their ways after I had declared the Truth to them and showed them the fruits of their priests and the incivility and unchristian-like carriage. They were a kind of Independents, but a very wicked town, for no sooner had we turned our backs from the innkeeper, whom we bid give our horses a peck of oats, but all the oats were stolen from our horses, that we ordered him to give them.

And so after we had refreshed ourselves a little and were ready, I took horse and rid up to the inn where I heard the mayor and sheriff and officers were; and I called to speak with them, and asked them the reason wherefore they had imprisoned John ap John and kept him in prison about two or three hours; but they would not answer a word to me, but looked out at the windows upon me. And then I showed them how unchristian their carriage was to travellers and strangers, and the fruits of their teachers, and declared unto them the Truth, and warned them of the day of the Lord that was coming upon all the evil doers, and how that they all knew that there were few inns in their country; and what an unworthy thing it was to hinder us in our journey, and they would not be so served themselves. And the Lord's power came over them, they were so ashamed, but I could not get a word from them in answer. So I warned them to repent and turn to the Lord; and we passed away.

[d]When I came to Cardigan, I lodged at a justice's house and had a brave meeting at a great house in the town. So we came into Cardigan, and being upon a market-day Friends spoke in the market; and all the town was in an uproar. But we passed quietly out of the town after I had spoken the Truth among them.[d]

And at night we came to a little inn, very poor but very

[d]. . . . . .[d] *S.J.*, p. 49. The exact position of this visit in the itinerary is uncertain.

cheap, for we and our horses cost but eightpence; but the horses would as soon eat the heath on the common as their oats. And we declared unto them the Truth and sounded the day of the Lord through the countries.

And before that we came to a great town[1] and went to an inn; and Edward Edwards went into the market and declared the Truth amongst them and the people came to the inn and filled the inn yard and were exceeding rude. But a good service we had for the Lord. The life of Christianity and the power of it tormented the chaffy natures and exceedingly came over them, and some there were reached and convinced. And the Lord's power came over all, so that the magistrates were bound; they had no power to meddle with us.

And after this we passed away and came to another great town[2] on a market-day, and John ap John declared the everlasting Truth through the streets and declared the day of the Lord amongst them. And many people in the evening gathered about the inn; and many being drunk, they would fain have had us forth into the street again, but we saw their design. And I told them if there were any that feared God and desired to hear Truth, they might come into our inn or else we might have a meeting with them the next morning. And some service for the Lord we had with the people both over-night and in the morning; though the people were hard to receive the Truth, yet the seed was sown, and thataways the Lord has a people turned to himself.

And in that inn also I turned but my back from the man that was giving oats to my horse, and I looked back again and he was filling his pockets with the provender that was given to my horse, a wicked thievish people to rob the poor dumb creature of his food, of which I had rather they had robbed me.

And another time as I was riding along there was a great man overtook us in the way. And he thought to have

[1] Probably Lampeter.

[2] Probably Aberystwyth.

taken us up at the next town for highwaymen, but before we came to the town I was moved of the Lord God to speak to him; and it reached to the witness of God in the man that he was so affected that he had us to his house and entertained us very civilly: and he and his wife desired us to give them Scriptures both for our principles and for Christ's alone teaching, and against the priests. So we were glad of it and furnished him with Scriptures enough. And he laid them down and was convinced of the Truth by the spirit of God in his heart, and confirmed by the Scriptures, and after set us on in our journey.

And then we came to another town[1] and went to an inn; and came a-top of a hill which they say was two or three miles high.[2] And on this hill-side I could see a great way; and I was moved to sound the day of the Lord[3] there; and set my face several ways and told John ap John, a faithful Welsh minister, in what places God would raise up a people to set under his teaching. And those places he took notice of, and since there has a great people risen in those places.

And the same thing I have been moved to do in many other places and countries, the which have been rude places, and yet I was moved to declare the Lord had a seed in those places; and after, there has been a brave people raised up in the covenant of God and gathered in the name of Jesus, where they have salvation and free teaching.

And from that hill we came down to a place called Dolgelly, and we went to an inn. And John ap John declared through the streets, and the townspeople riz and gathered about him. And there were two Independent priests in the town and they came out. And they both of them discoursed with him. And I went up to them, and as they were speaking in Welsh I asked them what was the subject they spoke about, and asked them why they were not more moderate and spoke one by one,

[1] Probably Machynlleth.
[2] Probably Cader Idris.
[3] See p. 104, note 1.

for the things of God were weighty and they should speak them with fear and reverence. And then I bid them speak in English, and they said that the light which John came to bear witness of, which was Christ the true light which enlightens every one that cometh into the world was a created, natural, and made light.

So then I took a Bible and let them see that the made and created, natural lights were the sun, moon, and stars, and the elements; but the true light which John bore witness to was the life in Christ the Word, by which all things were made and created. And it was called the light in man and woman, which was the true light which had enlightened every man that came into the world, which was a heavenly and divine light which let them see all their evil words and deeds and their sins, and the same light would let them see Christ their saviour, from whence it came to save them from their sin and to blot it out.

So this light shone in the darkness of their hearts and the darkness could not comprehend it; but where God had commanded it to shine out of darkness, in their hearts it gave them the knowledge of the glory of God in the face of Christ Jesus their saviour. So I opened the Scripture largely to them and turned them to the spirit of God in their hearts, which would reveal the Scriptures to them and lead them into all the truth of them; and so I turned them to that which would give every one of them the knowledge of their saviour who died for them and was their way to God, and made their peace betwixt them and God. And the people generally received it and with hands lifted up blessed and praised God; and the priests were stopped and quiet all the while. So I brought them to be sober that when they spoke of the things of God and Christ their saviour they might speak them with reverence and fear.

⟨The people were attentive⟩ so I was moved to speak to John ap John to stand up and speak in Welsh to them, and he did. So the meeting broke up in peace in the street and many people accompanied us to our inn, and rejoiced in the Truth that had been declared unto them, that they were turned to that light and spirit by which they might see their sin and know salvation from it.

And when we went out of town the people were so affected they lifted up their hands and blessed the Lord for our coming. And the Lord has a great people thataways, and there is a great people gathered to the Lord Jesus Christ's free teaching and have suffered much for it thereaways.

And from thence we passed to a city like a castle, <called Carnarvon>, and we rid into it and went to an inn. And after we had set up our horses at the gates, where the stable was that belonged to the inn, and after we had refreshed ourselves, John ap John spoke through the streets <which were so straight and short that> one might stand in the middle of the town and see both the gates. And a multitude of people was gathered about him, and a priest who was as dark as dark could be <began to babble, but> his mouth was soon stopped. And I declared the word of life amongst them and turned them to the light of Christ in their hearts, that by it they might see all their ways, religions and teachers, and to come off all to Christ their way and free teacher. And some of them were rude and some were civil; and they told us how they did hear how we had been persecuted and abused in many places but they would not do so to us there. So I commended their moderation and sobriety. And I warned them of the day of the Lord that was coming upon all sin and wickedness and how that Christ was come to teach his people himself by his power and by his spirit.

So from thence we passed into Beaumaris, and went to an inn. And there was a garrison in that town. And John ap John had been formerly a Separate teacher there. And he went and spoke through the streets and they cast him into prison. And the innkeeper's wife told me that the governor and the magistrates were sending for me to send me to prison also, and I told her they had done more than they could answer already and had acted contrary to Christianity in imprisoning John for reproving sin in their gates and for declaring the Truth. And there came other friendly people and told me if I went out into the street they would imprison me also, and therefore they desired me to keep in the inn. Upon which I was moved to go and walk up and down in their streets, and told the people what an uncivil and unchristian thing they had done in casting John in prison, for they were high professors, and asked was this the entertainment they had for strangers, would they be so served themselves, had they any example from Christ or the apostles to do so, who looked upon the Scriptures to be their rule.

So after a while they set John at liberty again. And the next day, being market day, we were to cross over a great water[1] not far off. Where we were to take the boat many people out of the market drew to us, amongst whom we had good service for the Lord and declared the word of life and everlasting Truth to them, and preached the day of the Lord which was coming upon all wickedness, and turned them to the light of Christ which the heavenly man had enlightened them withal, by which they might see all their sins and false ways, religions, worships and teachers; and by the same light they might see their saviour Christ Jesus, their way to God.

So the Lord's truth was declared amongst them and Christ their teacher set over all and his power came over all. Then I bid John get his horse into the boat. But they had made a plot amongst them, for there came a company of wild gentlemen (as they called them, but we found them rude men) and they and others kept his horse out of the boat; so I came to them and showed them what an unmanly and unchristian thing it was. So ⟨as I spoke⟩ I leapt with my horse into the boat amongst them. And it being pretty deep, John could not get his horse into the boat so I told them they showed an unworthy spirit and below Christianity or humanity. Seeing I could not get John in I leapt out a-horseback again into the water and stayed with John on that side. And there we stayed

[1] Menai Straits.

from the eleventh hour to the second before the boatmen came back again to fetch us; and then we had forty-two miles to ride that evening, ⟨and by the time we had paid for our passage⟩ we had but one groat left both of us of money.

So we came on about sixteen miles and got a little hay for our horses; and after, came to an alehouse for the night, but we could not have oats nor hay there, so we travelled on all night and about four o'clock in the morning we got within six miles of Wrexham where that day we met with many Friends and had a glorious meeting[1] and large, and the Lord's everlasting power and truth came over all, where there is a meeting continues to this day. But we were very weary with travelling so hard up and down in Wales; and it was hard to get meat for our horses, or ourselves either, in many places.

And the next day we passed from thence through Denbigh[2] into Flintshire and sounded the day of the Lord through the towns and came into Wrexham at night, where many of Morgan Lloyd's people came to us. But very rude, and wild, and airy they were, and little sense of Truth they had, yet there were some convinced in the town. And the next morning there was a lady sent for me, and she had a teacher at her house. ⟨I went to her house, but found that⟩ they were both very light, airy people and were too light to receive the weighty things of God; and in her lightness she came and asked me whether she should cut my hair. And I was moved to reprove her and bid her cut down the corruptions in her with the sword of the spirit of God. So after I had admonished her we passed away; and after, she made her boast in her frothy mind that she came behind me and cut off a lock of my hair, which was a lie.

And to the town ⟨of Beaumaris⟩ that had imprisoned John ap John I writ unto the mayor and sheriff to let them see their conditions and the fruits of their Christianity and

[1] Probably Trevor, the home of John ap John, between Llangollen and Ruabon.

[2] i.e. the county, not the town.

their teachers. And after, I met with some of those justices near London, and they were ashamed of their actions. So from Wrexham we came through the country to Chester[1] and stayed a while, it being their fair time, and visited Friends.

And from Chester we came through the country to Liverpool. And there being a fair there also, a Friend was standing a-top of the cross declaring ⟨the Truth to the people⟩ as I rode through the fair; who also ⟨seeing me ride by and knowing I had appointed a meeting to be the next day upon a hill not far off,⟩ gave notice that George Fox, the servant of the Lord, would have a meeting upon such a hill. If any feared the Lord, they might come there and hear him declare the word of life to them, and this I heard him declaring as I rid by the cross.

And so from Liverpool we went that night to Richard Cubham's[2] who had been convinced but not his wife; but at that time his wife was convinced also. And the next day we went to the meeting on the top of the hill, which was very large. And some rude people with a priest's wife came and made a noise for a while; but the Lord's power came over them and the meeting was quiet. And the Lord's truth came over all and many were settled upon the rock and foundation, Christ Jesus, and under his teaching, who made their peace betwixt them and God.

And we had a meeting at Malpas where we had a few Friends and people.

And from thence we came to another place where we had another meeting, and there came a bailiff with a sword, a rude man, but the Lord's power came over all and Friends were established in the Truth.

And from thence I came to Manchester, and there came a many rude people out of the town, the Sessions being there that day. And in the meeting they threw at me coals,

[1] The MS. refers to Chester as West Chester, a name corrupted from the ancient Waste Chester.

[2] Richard and Ann Cubham lived at Bickerstaffe, near Ormskirk, Lancashire.

clots, stones, water, ⟨yet the Lord's power bore me up over them that they could not strike me down⟩. And I was moved of the Lord to stand, till at last when they could do no good with their water, stones, and dirt some ran to the Sessions and told them, upon which they sent a company of officers and plucked me down and haled me out of the meeting into the Sessions-house before the justices. And all the court was in an outrage and a noise. And I asked where were the officers or magistrates that they did not keep the people civil. 'Yes', said some of the justices, they were magistrates. And I asked them why they did not appease the people and keep them sober; for one cried, 'I will swear', and another cried, 'I will swear.'

So I declared to the justices how we were abused in our meeting by the rude people throwing stones, and clots, and water, and how I was haled out and brought out of the meeting contrary to the Instrument of Government, which was that none should be molested in their meetings that professed God and owned the Lord Jesus Christ, which I did.

And so the Truth came over them, that when one of the rude fellows cried he would swear, one of the justices said, 'What! will you swear? Hold your tongue.' So at last they bid the constable have me to my lodging and there I should be secured till tomorrow morning that they sent for me. And the people were exceeding rude, but I let them see the fruits of their teachers and how they shamed Christianity and dishonoured the name of Jesus which they professed. So the constable had me to my lodging. And at night we went to a justice's house in the town that was pretty moderate; and I had a great deal of discourse with him. And the next morning we sent to the constable to know if he had anything more to say to us, but he sent us word he had nothing to say to us, we might go where we would, so we passed out of the town. And the Lord has raised up a people to stand for his name and Truth in that town over those chaffy professors.

And so from thence we passed through the country and had many precious meetings in several places, and came to Preston and many came gazing about us. And I had a General Meeting between that and Lancaster,[1] and after, we came to Lancaster, and there met Colonel West at the inn, who was mightily glad to see me. And he told Judge Fell that I was mightily grown in the Truth; but the ground was because he was come nearer to see the Truth, and could better discern it.

And from thence we came to Robert Widders's, and on the First-day I had a General Meeting near the Sands' side, of Friends out of Westmorland and Lancashire. And the Lord's everlasting power and word of life was over all and Friends were settled upon the foundation, Christ Jesus, and under his free teaching, and many were convinced and turned to the Lord.

And the next day I came over the Sands to Swarthmoor, and Friends all thereaways were glad to see me. And I stayed there two First-days visiting Friends in their meetings. And so having travelled through every county in Wales I returned to Swarthmoor again and the Lord in his eternal power had carried me through and over all.

⟨Having got a little respite from travel I was moved to write an epistle to Friends⟩:

All Friends of the Lord everywhere, whose minds are turned in towards the Lord, take heed and hearken to the light within you, which is the light of Christ and of God; which will call your minds within, as you love it, which is abroad in the creatures. So your minds may be renewed and by it turned to God with this which is pure, to worship the living God, the Lord of Hosts over all the creatures . . . And the light of God, which calls the mind out of the creatures, turns it to God, into a being[2] of endless joy and peace. And here is always a seeing God present, who is not known to the world whose hearts are in the creatures, whose knowledge is in the flesh, whose minds are not renewed

[1] Probably Carr House, near Garstang, the home of John Moone. The meeting was known as Claughton.

[2] *being* here means dwelling.

. . . So fare you well, and God Almighty bless, and guide, and keep you in his wisdom. G.F.[1]

⟨About this time Friends that were moved of the Lord to go to the steeplehouses and markets to reprove sin and warn people of the day of the Lord, suffered much hardship from the rude people, and also from the magistrates; being commonly pulled down, buffeted, and beaten, and many times sent to prison. Wherefore I was moved to give forth the following paper, to be spread abroad amongst people, to show them how contrary they acted therein to the apostles' doctrine and practice, and to bring them to more moderation.⟩

. . . Is it not more of honour and credit to prove all things and try all things, than to pluck down in the steeple-houses, and pull off the hair of their heads, and cast into prison ? Is this an honour to your truth and gospel you profess ? Doth it not show that you be out of Truth ? . . . And doth not this show that you have not this spirit poured forth upon you, that fill the gaols with so many sons and daughters, and hold up such teachers as are made by the will of man at Oxford and Cambridge, bred up at learning ? . . .

And do not all your fruits show, in all the nation where you come, in towns, cities, villages, and countries, that you are the seedsmen made by the will of man, which to the flesh do sow, of which nothing but corruption is reaped in nations, countries, cities, and villages ? . . . And so you sow to your own, persecuting him that is born of the spirit, who sows to the spirit, who of the spirit reaps life eternal; such, you who sow to the flesh, cast into prison . . . And again, what scorn, scoffing, mocking, derision, and strife, oaths, drunkenness, uncleanness, and cursed speaking, lust, and pride are seen in the streets ! And this, we see, is fruit which is reaped of the flesh . . .

The ministers of the spirit, which sow to the spirit, of the spirit come to reap life eternal. . . . The ministers of the spirit, which be born of the spirit, sons and daughters, which have the spirit poured forth upon them, who witness the promise of God

[1] From MS. George Fox Papers (R.15); Ellwood, p. 261*; Bicent., i., 384-6.

fulfilled, preach and minister to the spirit of God in prison in every one, in the sight of God the father of spirits.

God's hand is turned against you all that have destroyed God's creatures upon your lust, that have wronged by unjust dealing, and defrauded, and have oppressed, and have respected the persons of the proud, and such as be in gay apparel, and lend not your ear to the cry of the poor . . .

Now all may read each seedsman, which hath each wisdom. He that sows to the flesh, which is of that born, hath the wisdom that is earthly, sensual, and devilish; he that sows to the spirit, a minister of the spirit, hath the wisdom from above, which is pure, which is gentle, which is easy to be entreated, the wisdom by which all things were made and created. Now is each wisdom discovered, and each seedsman; the day hath discovered it, which is the light. G.F.[1]

⟨As the foregoing paper was sent forth among the world's people to let them see from whence this imprisoning and persecuting cruelty and violent dealing sprang, so I was also moved to give forth the following epistle to Friends, to stir them up to be bold and valiant for the Truth, and to encourage them in their sufferings for it:⟩

Epistle to Friends; of Christ, he must not come into the stable but in the best room.

All Friends and brethren everywhere, now is the day of your trial, and now is the time for you to be valiant, and to see that the testimony of the Lord doth not fall. For now is the day of exercise of the gifts, of your patience, of your faith, and now is the time to be armed with patience, and with the light, and with righteousness, and with the helmet of salvation . . . For the Lord may try you as he did Job, whom he made rich, whom he made poor, and whom he made rich again; who still kept his integrity in all conditions. So learn Paul's lesson, 'in all states to be content'; and have his faith, that 'nothing is able to separate us from the love of God, which we have in Christ Jesus'. Therefore be rich in life, and in grace, which will endure, who are heirs of life and born of the womb of eternity, that noble birth that cannot stoop to the birth that is born in sin. . . .

Therefore mind him that destroys the original of sin, the Devil

[1] From MS. Portfolio 10.2. In full, Ellwood, pp. 263*-265*; Bicent., i., 386-8.

and his works, and cuts off the entail of Satan, viz. sin; who would hold by entail an inheritance of sin in men and women from generation to generation, and pleads for it by all his lawyers and counsellors. And though the law did not cut it off, nor made nothing perfect, yet Christ is come and destroys the Devil and his works, and cuts off the entail of sin. This angers all the Devil's lawyers and counsellors, that Satan shall not hold sin by entail in thy garden, in thy field, in thy temple, nor thy tabernacle. So keep thy tabernacle, that there thou mayst see the glory of the Lord appear at the door thereof. And so be faithful; for you see what the worthies and the valiants of the Lord did attain to by faith . . . So bring your deeds all to the light, which you are taught to believe in by Christ, your head, the heavenly man; and see how they are wrought in God, that he may rule and reign in you. We must not have Christ Jesus, the Lord of life, put any more in the stable amongst the horses and asses, but he must now have the best chamber, the heart, and the rude, debauched spirit must be turned out. Therefore let him reign, whose right it is, who was conceived by the Holy Ghost, by which Holy Ghost you call him Lord, in which Holy Ghost you pray, and by which Holy Ghost you have comfort and fellowship with the Son and with the Father. Therefore know the triumph in the Seed, which is first and last, the beginning and ending, the top and corner-stone; in which is my love and in which I rest. G.F.

And, Friends, be careful how that you do set your feet among the tender plants, that are springing up out of God's earth; lest you do hurt them and tread upon them, and bruise them, or crush them in God's vineyard.

Let this be read in Friends' Meetings.[1]

And after those two First-days that I tarried at Swarthmoor I passed into Westmorland, visiting the meetings there. And at John Audland's there was a General Meeting of such as were convinced of the Lord and had a belief in his everlasting Truth.

I had a vision the night before of a desperate creature like a wild horse or colt that was coming to destroy me; but I got victory over it.

[1] Swarthmore MSS., ii, 961. In full, Ellwood, pp. 265*-267* Bicent., i, 389-91.

[e]As I was passing to a meeting near Sedbergh there lay a company of men in the way at a bridge at an alehouse with weapons to have done me a mischief, but I was moved to pass over another way over a water, not knowing outwardly of them, and so some of them came to a meeting rudely, but the truth of the Lord that answers the witness of God in all people, came over all, and they passed away without doing me or Friends any hurt.

Then Friends had a meeting at John Audland's, not far off that place, the next First-day where there were about a thousand people, and most convinced of the Truth of God.[e] And in the meeting-time there came one Otway, Sir John Otway's[1] brother, with some rude fellows, with his sword or rapier and he was struck by the Lord's dreadful power before he came up to the meeting, but he came up and rid round about the meeting and would fain have gotten in to me through Friends, but they stood thick so as he could not come at me. So he rid about raging, but at last he went his way. So the meeting ended gloriously and the Lord's everlasting power came over all. And this wild man went home and became distracted and not long after died. But I sent a paper to John Blaykling to read to this man when he was in his distractions, showing him his wickedness, and he did acknowledge something of it to him.

[e]And it's large to declare the works and wonders of the Lord God and the preservation of me through all by his mighty hand and power, but I saw I was in his hand.[e]

⟨From hence I went through Kendal, where a warrant had long lain to apprehend me, and the constables seeing me, ran to fetch their warrant, as I was riding through the town, but before they could come with it I was gone past, and so escaped their hands.⟩

And after, I passed through the meetings visiting of them till I came to Strickland Head, where I had a great meeting; and most of the gentry of the country were gathered to a

[1] Sir John Otway, of Ingmire Hall, near Sedbergh.

[e]. . . . . .[e] *S.J.*, p. 35.

horse race not far off the meeting, and I was moved to declare the Truth unto them; and there was a chief constable did admonish them also, and we had our meeting quiet and the word of the Lord came over all and Friends were settled in the eternal Truth.

And from thence we passed into Cumberland and had many living precious meetings there. And from thence we travelled through to Gilsland and had a meeting there; and from thence came to Carlisle, where they used to put Friends out of the town, and there came a great flood so as they could not put us out of the town, and the First-day we had a meeting there.

And from thence we passed through the country to Abbey Holme where we had a little meeting where I told Friends long before there would be a great people come out of that place to the Lord, which has since, and there is a large meeting in those parts.

And so I passed from thence to a General Meeting at Christopher Fell's at Langlands in Cumberland, which was very large; and most of the people had so forsaken the priests that the steeplehouses in some places stood empty.

And Priest John Wilkinson, mentioned before, that had three steeplehouses, had few auditors left so that he first set up a meeting in his house and preached amongst them that were left; and then after, set up a silent meeting like Friends at which came a few, for most of his auditors were come off to Friends. At last he had not past half a dozen left; they still forsook him and came off to Friends. And at last he had so few left that he would come to Pardshaw Crag where Friends had a meeting of several hundreds of people who were all come to sit under the Lord Jesus Christ's teaching; and he would come and walk about the meeting on the First-days like a man that went about the commons to look for sheep.

And I went to this Pardshaw Crag meeting, and there was he, and three or four of his followers that were yet left behind came to the meeting, and they were all thoroughly convinced, and after the meeting was done Priest Wilkinson asked me two or three questions and I satisfied him. And from that time he came amongst Friends to their meetings, and became an able minister and freely preached the Gospel and turned many to Christ's free teaching; and he continued many years in the free ministry and preaching of the Gospel, and died in the Truth.[1]

CHAPTER XIII

⟨I HAD for some time felt drawings in my spirit to go into Scotland.⟩ And Colonel William Osburne,[2] whom I had sent to ⟨desiring him to come and meet me⟩, came out of Scotland to that meeting, and some others with him. He said he never saw such a glorious meeting in his life; and after the meeting was done I passed with him and them towards Scotland. And Robert Widders went alongst with me, a thundering man against hypocrisy and deceit and the rottenness of the priests.

The first night we came into Scotland[3] we lodged at an inn. And the innkeeper told us that there was an earl would fain see me, and had left word at his house that if ever I came to Scotland he should send me word.[4] And he said there were three drawbridges to his house, and that it would be the ninth hour before the last drawbridge was drawn. So we went down to his house being but a quarter of a mile off. He received us very lovingly; and would have gone with us on our journey, but he was pre-engaged to to go to a funeral. ⟨After we had spent some time with him, we parted very friendly, and returned to our inn.⟩ So

[1] John Wilkinson of Cumberland (d. 1675) preached Quakerism in England and Ireland. See also pp. 153 ff. ante.

[2] Supporter of Quaker cause in Edinburgh, 1653, not known of after 1658.

[3] Thursday, 10th Sept., 1657.

[4] Doubtless, Robert, second Earl of Nithsdale (d. 1667), and his castle of Caerlaverock. He was popularly called ' The Philosopher '.

from thence we passed through Dumfries to Douglas, where we met with some Friends; and thence we passed to the Heads,[1] where we had a blessed meeting in the name of Jesus, and felt him in the midst.

From thence we passed to Bedcow[2] and had a meeting, and abundance of people came to it and were convinced. From thence we passed towards the highlands to Colonel Osburne's house where we gathered up the sufferings of Friends, and the principles of the Scots priests, which may be seen in the book called *The Scotch Priests' Principles*.[3]

And from thence we came back again to Heads and Bedcow and Gartshore where the Lady Margaret Hamilton was convinced, that went up to warn Oliver Cromwell and Charles Fleetwood of the day of the Lord that was coming upon them.

And on the First-day we had a great meeting and several professors came out. And the priests had frightened people with the doctrine of election and reprobation, and said that the greatest part of men and women God had ordained for hell, let them pray, or preach, or sing, and do what they could, it was all nothing if they were ordained for hell. And God had a certain number which were elected for heaven, let them do what they would, as David an adulterer and Paul a persecutor, yet elected vessels for heaven. So the fault was not at all in the creatures less or more, but God had ordained it so.

So I was made to open to the people the folly of their priests' doctrines.

And I showed them how the priests had abused those Scriptures which they had brought and quoted to them, as in Jude and other places . . . for did not God warn Cain and Balaam and gave a promise to Cain if he did well he should be accepted . . .

For if those called Christians resist the Gospel as Korah did the law and err from the spirit of Christ as Balaam did, and if they do not well as Cain, is not here a fault, which fault is in themselves and the cause of their reprobation, and not God.

[1] A hamlet close to Strathavon, Lanarkshire.

[2] Easter Bedcow, a farm near Kirkintilloch, Dunbartonshire.

[3] By George Weare *et al.*, 1657.

And doth not Christ say, 'Go preach the gospel to all nations', which is the gospel of salvation. He would not have sent them out into all nations to preach the doctrine of salvation if the greatest part of men was ordained for hell. And was not Christ a propitiation for the sins of the whole world, for the reprobates as well as the saints, and so died for the ungodly as well as the godly: and died for all men as the apostle bore witness to, and enlightens every man that cometh into the world that through him they might all believe (2 Cor. v, 15; Rom. v, 6). And Christ bids them believe in the light and so all they that hate the light, which Christ bids all believe in, they are reprobated . . .

And therefore, all people, believe in the light as Christ commands and own the grace of God your free teacher, and it will bring you your salvation for it is sufficient.[1]

And the people were opened to see, and a spring of life riz up amongst them, and many other Scriptures were opened concerning reprobation.

And these things came to the priests' ears, and the people that sat under their dark teachings began to see light and to come into the covenant of light, that the noise that I was come there was spread all over Scotland amongst the priests. And a great cry was amongst them that all was undone and that I had spoiled all the honest men and women in England, so that the worst was left to them. And they gathered great assemblies of priests together and drew up articles to be read in their parishes in the steeplehouses and that all the people should say Amen to them, which are as followeth in part: and the rest may be seen in the book of the Scotch priests' principles.

First: Cursed is he that saith every man hath a light within him sufficient to lead him to salvation and let all the people say, Amen.

Second: Cursed is he that saith faith is without sin and let all the people say, Amen.

Third: Cursed is he that denieth the sabbath day and let all the people say, Amen.

In this last they make the people curse themselves.

[1] In full Ellwood, pp. 269*, 270*; Bicent., i, 394-6.

For upon the sabbath day, which is the seventh day of the week, which the Jews keep, which was the command of God, they kept markets and fairs, and so brought the curse upon their own heads.

And Christ saith believe in the light that ye may become children of the light, and believe and be saved and he that believeth shall have everlasting life, and he that believeth passes from death to life and is grafted into Christ. And ye do well that ye take heed unto the light that shines in the dark place until the day dawn and the day star arise in your hearts, so the light is sufficient to lead unto the day star.

And faith is the gift of God and every gift of God is pure. And faith which Christ is the author of is precious and divine without sin. And this is the faith which gives victory over sin and access to God, in which faith they please God. And they are reprobates themselves concerning this faith, and in their dead faith that charges sin upon this faith, under pain of a curse; which faith gives the victory over their curse and returns it into their own bowels.

And there was a company of Scots near Bedcow challenged a dispute with some of our Scottish Friends, for with me they would not dispute. So some of the Scottish Friends met them at the market cross. And the dispute was upon some of their principles aforesaid and the sabbath day. And a Scottish Friend, a gun-smith, overthrew them clearly, for I had gotten their principles and assertions and showed him my answers, whereby he might easily overthrow them.

<There were two Independent churches in Scotland, in one of which many were convinced; but the pastor of the other was in a great rage against Truth and Friends. They had their elders, who sometimes would exercise their gifts amongst the church-members, and would sometimes be pretty tender; but their pastor speaking so much against the Light and us, the friends of Christ, he darkened his hearers, so that they grew dark and blind and dry, and lost their tenderness. And he continued preaching against Friends, and against the light of Christ Jesus, calling it natural. At last one day in his preaching, he cursed the

Light and fell down as dead in his pulpit. The people carried him out and laid him upon a gravestone and poured strong-waters into him, which fetched him to life again; and they carried him home but he was mopish. After a while he stripped off his clothes, put on a Scottish plaid and went into the country amongst the dairy-women. And when he had stayed there about two weeks, he came home and went into the pulpit again. Whereupon the people expected some great manifestation or revelation from him, but instead thereof, he began to tell them what entertainment he had met with, how one woman gave him skimmed-milk, another gave him buttermilk and another gave him good milk, so the people were fain to take him out of the pulpit again, and carry him home. He that gave me this account was Andrew Robinson, who was one of his chief hearers, and came afterwards to be convinced and received the Truth. And he said he never heard that he recovered his senses again. By this people may see the vengeance of God which came upon him that cursed the Light, which Light is the life in Christ, the Word; and it may be a warning to all others that speak evil against the light of Christ.〉

And then the priests were in such a rage that they posted up to Edinburgh, to Oliver Cromwell's Council there, with petitions against me, and a great cry was amongst them that all was gone.

And so after that I had settled Friends upon Christ their foundation thereaways, and gathered up the principles of the Scots priests and the sufferings of Friends, I went up to Edinburgh. Several Friends were come into the nation and spread over Scotland, sounding the day of the Lord and preaching the everlasting Gospel of salvation, and turning people to Christ Jesus that died for them, their free teacher.

And as I went to Edinburgh I came by Linlithgow, and there the innkeeper's wife was blind; and she received the word of life and came under Christ Jesus her saviour's teaching; and at night there came in abundance of soldiers and officers, and much discourse we had with them, and some were rude and one of the officers said that he would obey the Turks or Pilate's command if he should command him to guard Christ to crucify him. He was so far off all tenderness or sense of the spirit of Christ, that he would rather crucify the just than suffer for or with the just; whereas many officers and magistrates lost their places before they would turn against the Lord and his just one.

And from thence we came to Edinburgh, and stayed there a while, and I went to Leith, and there a-many officers came in and their wives, and many were convinced. And there came Edward Billing's[1] wife with a great deal of coral in her hand and threw it before me on the table to see whether I would declare against it or no, but I took no notice of it but declared the Truth to her and she was reached.

And there came in a-many Baptists, very rude, but the Lord's power came over them that they went away confounded, and then there came in another sort and one of them said he would dispute with me and deny there was a God, for argument's sake. So I told him he was one of those fools that said in his heart there was no God but he should know him in the day of Judgement. So he went his ways, and a fine, precious time we had with several people of account, and the Lord's power came over all.

And Colonel Osburne was with me; and Colonel Lidcott's wife was convinced, and William Welch's wife was convinced, and several of the officers that were there were convinced at that time also.

And so after, Edward Billing's wife came to be loving.

And she and her husband were then separated one from the other. And we sent for him and he came, and the Lord's power reached unto them both and they joined together in it to live together in love and unity as man and wife.

And from thence we went to Edinburgh again; and many

[1] Edward Billing or Byllynge (*c.* 1623-1686), became part-proprietor of the colony of New Jersey. Married Lilias Hepburn.

thousands of people were gathered there, and abundance of priests, about burning of a witch. And I was moved to declare the day of the Lord amongst them and so then went from thence to the meeting, and a-many rude people and Baptists came in and there the Baptists began with their logic and syllogisms. But I was moved in the Lord's power to thresh their chaffy, light minds, and showed the people that after that manner of light discoursing they might make white black and black white, and because a cock had two legs and they had two legs therefore they were cocks, and so turn any thing into lightness: which was not the manner of Christ nor his apostles' teachings and speakings. And after they went their ways we had a blessed meeting in the Lord's power which was over all.

And then Oliver's Council sent an order to the inn where I lodged, by one of their officers, that I must appear at the Parliament house that day seven-night by eight o'clock in the morning before them at the Council table:

Thursday, 8th of October, 1657, at his Highness's Council in Scotland

Ordered,

That George Fox do appear before the Council on Tuesday, the 13th of October next, in the forenoon.

Emanuel Downing,
Clerk of the Council.

So he asked me whether I would appear or no but I would not answer him whether I would or not. And I asked him whether he had not forged it; so he said it was a real thing from the Council and he was sent as their messenger with it to give me notice.

So that day seven-night I appeared before them. And they had me up into a great room where many great persons came and looked at me. And after a while the doorkeeper came and had me in, and as I was going into the Council-chamber he took off my hat, and I asked him why he did so, who was there that I might not go in with my hat on for I had been before Oliver Cromwell with my hat on. But he took it off and hung it up and had me in before them.

And when I came before them, after I had stood awhile and they said nothing to me, I was moved of the Lord to say, 'Peace be amongst you, and wait in the fear of God that you may receive his wisdom from above, by which all things were made and created, and that with it you may all be ordered and that with it you may order all things under your hands to God's glory.'

And so standing still, they asked me what was my business of coming into that nation and I told them to visit the Seed of God which had long lain in death and bondage and to the intent that all in the nation that did profess the Scriptures of Christ, the prophets and the apostles' words, might come to the light, spirit, and power which they were in that gave them forth, so that with the spirit they might know Christ and God and the Scriptures and have fellowship with them and with the Scriptures and one with another.

And then they asked me whether I had not any outward business there. And I said nay. Then they asked me how long I should stay in the country. I told them I should say little to that, my time was not to be long, yet in my freedom I stood in the will of him that sent me.

And then they desired me to withdraw and then the doorkeeper took me by the hand and had me forth.

And presently after, they sent for me in again and told me that I must depart the nation within seven days. And I asked them for what, or what I had done, what was my transgression that they passed such a sentence upon me to depart out of the nation.

So they told me they would not dispute with me. Then I desired them to hear what I had to say to them, and they said they would not hear me. I told them Pharaoh heard Moses and Aaron and yet he was a heathen and no Christian; and Herod heard John Baptist and they should not be worse than them.

And then they cried, 'Withdraw, withdraw.' And then the doorkeeper took me by the hand and had me forth.

And after I had visited Friends in Edinburgh and thereaways I writ to the Council of their unchristian carriage to banish me who was an innocent man and sought their eternal good and salvation. And some of them were troubled, as I heard, for I showed them what an unchristian carriage it was and that they would not be so served themselves, as you may see more at large.[1]

And I saw General Monk,[2] that he was as a man that bowed under Oliver Protector and had a covering over him. And take away that covering and then he was the man as he was before; as he did fulfil it in a few years after. And they that banished me came to be banished themselves not many years after, who would not do good in the day when they had power nor suffer others that would.

And from Edinburgh I passed again to Heads and there Friends had been in great sufferings, for the Presbyterian priests had excommunicated them and given charge that none might buy or sell with them nor eat nor drink with them, so they could neither sell their commodities nor buy what they wanted. So it went very hard with some of them, for if they had bought bread or victuals of any of their neighbours, the priests threatened them so with curses that they would run and fetch it from them again.

But Colonel Ashfield[3] being a justice of peace in that country gave a stop to the priests' proceedings. And he after was convinced and had a meeting since at his house; and declared the Truth amongst them, and lived and died in it.

And so after I had visited Friends at Heads and thataways I went to Glasgow. And a meeting was appointed there; but never a one of Glasgow came to it. But as I went into the city the guard at the gates had me up before the governor, where I had a great deal of discourse with him, and he was moderate, but too light to receive the Truth; but he set me at liberty and so I passed to the meeting. And seeing none of the townspeople came out to the meeting, we declared through the town, and so passed away

1 Ellwood, pp. 274*, 275*; Bicent., i, 402, 403; *Camb. Jnl*, i, 301, 302.

2 George Monk (1608-1670), afterwards first Duke of Albemarle.

3 Colonel Richard Ashfield, governor of Glasgow.

and visited Friends in their meetings thereways and returned towards Bedcow. And several Friends went to declare Truth in their steeplehouses; and the Lord's power came over them all.

And one time as I was going to Colonel Osburne's there lay a company of rude fellows that hid themselves under the hedges and in bushes; and I espied them and asked Colonel Osburne what they were and he said, said he, 'Oh, they are thieves.'

And it was upon Robert Widders to go and speak to a priest and to admonish him, and we had left him behind us; so I said to Colonel Osburne, 'I will stay in this valley and do thee go and look after him.' And he was afraid to leave me alone whilst he went to look after Robert Widders, and I said I feared them not. There were three or four of them and I called them up to me and asked them what they hid themselves in the bushes and hedges for. So they came trembling to me for the dread of the Lord had struck them, so I admonished them to be honest and brought them to the spirit of God in their hearts that they might see what an evil it was to follow after theft and robbery. But when I first called to them to come to me they were loth to come up, but I charged them to come up to me or else it might be worse with them, so the power of the Lord came over them. So I stayed till Colonel Osburne and Robert Widders came up, for it's like had we passed away they would have robbed Robert Widders.

And we passed on to Colonel Osburne's house and declared the Truth to several people that came into his house. And after, we went amongst the clans, and they were devilish and like to have spoiled us and our horses, and ran with pitchforks at us, but through the Lord's power we escaped them.

And from thence we passed to Stirling where the soldiers took us up and had us before the main guard. And after a few words with their officers we were set at liberty, the Lord's power came over them, but no meeting could we get amongst them in the town they were so closed up in darkness. But the next morning there was a man was to run a race with a horse and most of the townspeople and officers went to see it; and so as they came back again from the race I had a brave opportunity to declare the day of the Lord and his word of life amongst them. And some confessed and some opposed; but the Lord's truth and power came over them all.

And from thence we passed through the country till we came to Burntisland, and I had a meeting at one Captain Poole's house both in the morning and in the afternoon. And whilst they went to their dinner I walked to the sea-side being not free to eat with them. And he and his wife were convinced and became fine Friends afterwards, and several officers of the army came in and received the Truth.

And from thence we passed through several other places in the country and at last we came to Johnstons[1] and there were several Baptists that were very bitter and in a rage, which came to us to dispute with us, and vain janglers and disputers they were: but ⟨when they could not prevail by disputing⟩ they went and informed the governor against us, and the next morning they raised a whole company of foot and banished me and Alexander Parker and James Lancaster and Robert Widders out of the town, [a]being taken out of a Friend's house.[a]

So we got on our horses, and when they were guarding us out of the town, James Lancaster was moved to sound and sing in the power of God, and I was moved to sound the day of the Lord and the glorious everlasting Gospel. And all the streets were up and filled with people, and the soldiers were so ashamed that they cried and said they had rather have gone to Jamaica than to guard us so. And then they set us in a boat and set us over the water with our horses, and there left us. And the ground and cause of our banishment out of this place was the Baptists, who

[1] St. Johnstown, now Perth.
[a]. . . . . .[a] *S.J.*, p. 52.

were themselves not long after banished out of the army, and the governor himself when the King came in was turned off also.

And so from thence we came to another market town[1] where Edward Billing and his wife quartered, and a-many soldiers lay there; and so we came to an inn and there desired that we might have a meeting that we might preach the everlasting Gospel amongst them. And so the soldiers and officers said we should have it in the town hall, and the Scotch magistrates, in spite, went and appointed a meeting there upon town business that day. So when the officers saw that they did it in malice, they would have us go into the town hall nevertheless, but we told them 'By no means', for then they might inform the governor against them and say that they took the town hall from them by force when they were to do their town business therein. And we told them we could go to the public cross in the market place, and then they said it was market day; and we said it was best of all for we would have all people to hear the Truth and to know our principles.

So Alexander Parker went a-top of the cross with a Bible in his hand and declared the Truth amongst the soldiers and market people, but the Scotch, being dark, carnal people, never heeded it nor hardly took notice of it. And at last I was moved of the Lord God to stand up at the cross, and commanded to declare with a loud voice the everlasting Truth and the day of the Lord that was coming upon all sin and wickedness, and they came running out of the town hall, and people gathered, so as at last we had a large meeting, for they sat but in the Court only for a colour to hinder us from having the hall.

And then the magistrates and all came out, and some heard and some walked by. So the Lord's power came over them all, and they were left without excuse, whether they would hear or forbear. And many were turned to the Lord Jesus Christ that died for them, and had enlightened them, that with his light they might see their evil deeds and their

[1] Probably Dundee.

sins, and with the same light they might see their saviour, Christ Jesus, their teacher. And if they would not receive Christ and own him, that light which came from him would be their condemnation: and there were several were loving to us; and some came to be convinced afterwards, especially the English people.

And there was a soldier there that was very envious against us and hated us very much, and spoke evil of Truth ⟨and very despitefully against the light of Christ Jesus⟩. And he was mighty zealous for the priests, and one time as he was hearing the priests, having his hat before his face whilst the priest was at prayer, one of the priest's hearers stabbed him to death, who as aforesaid was a man very envious against the light of Christ: and so came to be murdered by them whom he had so cried up, and rejected Jesus Christ to be his teacher.

And from thence we came through the country to Leith, warning and admonishing people to turn to the Lord: and when we came at Leith we went to an inn, and the innkeeper told me that the Council had granted warrants out for to apprehend me because I was not gone out of the nation after the seven days that they had ordered me to depart the nation in. And several friendly people came and declared the same. So the noise of these warrants was all over. And I told them, 'What! do you tell me of their warrants against me? If there were a cartload of them I do not heed them, for the Lord's power is over them all.' For they were now afraid to meddle with me.

So from Leith I went up to Edinburgh where they said their warrants were from their Council; and I came to the inn where I used to lodge, and went and visited Friends.

And after I had visited Friends, I desired the Friends that were with me to saddle their horses and to ride out of the town with me the next morning. And there were with me Thomas Rawlinson and Alexander Parker and Robert Widders.

And when I was out of the town they asked me whither I would go, and I told them it was upon me from the Lord to go back again yonder to Johnstons whence we had been banished, and so set the power of God over them also and his Truth. And Alexander Parker said he would go along with me. And I told the other two that they might stay at a town a matter of three miles of Edinburgh till we returned.

And so Alexander Parker and I got over the water,[1] which was about three miles over, and so rid on through the country. And in the afternoon, his horse being weak was not able to hold out with me, I put on; and just as they were upon drawing up the bridges I came into Johnstons, and the officers and soldiers never questioned me.

And so I rid up the street to Captain Davenport's house from whose house we had been banished before. And when I came there, there were a-many officers more with him in his chamber; and when I came amongst them they lifted up their hands and admired that I should come again, and I told them the Lord God had sent me amongst them again. So they went their ways.

And the Baptists and others sent me a letter by way of challenge that they would discourse with me the next day. So I sent them word I would meet them at such a house about a half mile out of the town at such an hour. So thither I went, and Captain Davenport and his son went with me; and we stayed there some hours, but never a one of them came. And then as we were looking out we espied Alexander Parker coming who had lain out that night and could not reach to the town. And when I saw him I was exceeding glad that we met again.

And so the Lord's power came over them all and they had no power to touch me, for if I had stayed in the town to discourse with them they, under pretence of discoursing with me, might have raised men to put me out of the town again and therefore it was upon me to try them out of the town.

[b]So when I was off that burden[b] I passed away, and Captain Davenport returned to the town, who afterwards

[1] The Firth of Forth.

[b]......[b] *S.J.*, p. 52.

was turned out of his place for not putting off his hat and for saying ' thou ' and ' thee ' to them, and he remains a Friend to this day.

And Alexander Parker was moved to go to the town where we had the meeting at the cross aforesaid; and I passed alone through the countries to Lieutenant Foster's quarters, where there were several other officers that were convinced.

And so from thence I came up to the town where I had left Friends; and from thence we came to Edinburgh again. And I bid Robert Widders follow me, and so in the dread and power of the Lord we came to the first two sentries; and the Lord's power came so over them that we passed by them without any examination. So we rid up the streets to the market place and by the main guard and then out at the gate by the third sentry and so clear out at the suburbs. And there we came to an inn and set up our horses on the Seventh-day.

So I saw and felt that [c]I went over their very muskets, cannons, pistols, pikes, and very sword-ends.[c] And the Lord's power and immediate hand carried us over the heads of them all.

On the First-day we went up to the meeting in Edinburgh, Friends having notice that I would be at it and there were a-many officers and soldiers, and a glorious meeting it was, and the everlasting power of God was set over the nation and his Son reigned and shined over it in his glorious power, and all was quiet and never a one meddled with me. So when meeting was done and I had visited Friends I came out of the city again to my inn. And so the Second-day we set forward through the country towards the borders of England.

And Lieutenant Foster and Lieutenant Dove and Captain Watkinson were turned out of the army for owning Truth, and several other officers and soldiers, and because they would not put off their hats to them and said ' thee ' and ' thou ' to them.

[c]......[c] *S.J.*, p. 52.

And so as we travelled along the country I espied a steeplehouse and I asked them what steeplehouse it was, and they said Dunbar, and it struck [d]at my life that I should have a meeting the next day in the steeplehouse yard. Many Friends were with me that were turned out of the army.[d] And when I came thither and had taken up our inn I walked up to the steeplehouse and a Friend or two went with me. And when I came into the steeplehouse yard there was one of the chief men of the town was walking there, and I bid the Friend go and tell him there would be a meeting of the people of God in scorn called Quakers there tomorrow about the ninth hour, and bid him give notice to the town of it. And he sent me word again that they were to have a lecture there by the ninth hour and therefore we might have our meeting by the eighth hour if we would, so I told him, with all my heart, let him so give notice.

And in the morning about the eighth hour both poor and rich came, and there was a captain lay in the town and he came up and his troopers, so that we had a brave and glorious meeting and the Lord's power was set over all. So at last the priest came, but he went into the steeplehouse, and we being in the steeplehouse yard most of the people stayed with us; and Friends' voices were so full and high in the power of God that the priest could do little in the steeplehouse, so he came out again and stood a while and after went his ways.

And I opened to the people where they might find Christ Jesus, having turned them to the light which he had enlightened them withal; that with the light they might see Christ that died for them, and turn to him their saviour and free teacher. And I let them see all the hireling teachers that they had followed, who made the Gospel chargeable, and showed them all the ways they had walked in the night of apostacy, and turned them unto Christ their way to God, and showed them the religions and worships that they had been in, which men had set up, and that

[d]......[d] *S.J.*, pp. 52-3.

they had lost Christ's which he set up in spirit and truth.

This great man of the town asked the captain leave to speak to me; and I told him he might freely if he had any thing to say, but then he was silent and said little. And so after I had turned people to the spirit of God which led the holy men of God to give forth Scriptures, I showed them that they, with that measure of the spirit, truth, grace, faith, might know it in themselves, if they came to know God and Christ or the Scriptures, and so Friends being full of the power of the Lord to speak, I stepped down and let them declare what they had to say from the Lord to the people.

And I walked a little by; and presently some professors began to jangle, and so I came again and stood up again and answered their questions; and they seemed to be satisfied (and I did so once or twice). So our meeting ended in the Lord's power, quiet and peaceable, ⟨the last meeting I had in Scotland⟩. And the Truth and the power of God was set over that nation; and many were turned to the Lord Jesus Christ by his power and spirit their saviour and teacher, who shed his blood for them, and remain to this day. And since, a great increase there is, and great there will be, in Scotland. For when first I set my horse's feet a-top of the Scottish ground I felt the Seed of God to sparkle about me like innumerable sparks of fire, though there is abundance of thick, cloddy earth of hypocrisy and falseness that is a-top, and a briary, brambly nature which is to be burnt up with God's word, and ploughed up with his spiritual plough, before God's Seed brings forth heavenly and spiritual fruit to the glory of the heavenly, glorious and omnipotent Lord God almighty. But the husbandman is to wait in patience.

And so from Dunbar we came to Berwick where we were questioned a little by the soldiers, and at night we had a little meeting and the governor was loving towards us, and the Lord's power came over all.

CHAPTER XIV

AND from thence we came to Morpeth and so through the country to Newcastle visiting Friends, where I had been once before, for the Newcastle priests had given forth many books against us: and one Thomas Ledgerd, an alderman of the town, was very envious against Truth and Friends; and he and they said the Quakers would not come into great towns but lived in the fells like butterflies. And so I went, and Anthony Pearson with me, to several of these aldermen and to this Ledgerd and desired a meeting amongst them for we were now come into their great town. But Ledgerd began to plead for the Sabbath-day, and so I told him they kept markets and fairs on it, for that day which Christians meet on now (which they call their Sabbath) was the first day of the week.

[a]And he said the Scriptures were above the spirit and were above angels and were the word of God; and I told him the Word was God and the spirit gave forth Scriptures, and that he must know in himself both the Word and spirit which reconciles to the Scriptures, to God, and to one another; and that he must know it in his heart and mouth, which divides his good words from his bad and his good thoughts from his bad.[a]

So we desired to have a meeting with them seeing they had written so many books against us, but they would not, nor would be spoken with, but this man and one other. So I told them, had they not called Friends butterflies and that they would not come into any great towns, and now we were come into their towns they would not come at us but print books against us, who were the butterflies now?

[a]. . . . . .[a] *S.J.*, p. 34.

Nevertheless we got a little meeting amongst Friends and friendly people at the Gateshead where there stands a meeting to this day in the name of Jesus.

And so as I was passing away by the market place the power of the Lord riz in me to warn them of the day of the Lord that was coming upon them. And not long after all these five priests of Newcastle and their profession were turned out when the King came in.[1]

So from thence we came through the countries and had meetings visiting Friends in Bishoprick and Northumberland. We had a fine meeting at Lieutenant Dove's where many were turned to the Lord and his teaching. And I went to visit a justice of peace there, a very sober, loving man that had confessed to Truth.

And so from thence we came to Durham, and there was a man come down from London to set up a college there to make ministers of Christ, as they said. And so I and some others went to the man and reasoned with him and let him see that was not the way to make them Christ's ministers by Hebrew, Greek, and Latin and the Seven Arts, which all were but the teachings of the natural man. For the many languages began at Babel, and to the Greeks that spoke the natural Greek, the preaching of the cross of Christ was foolishness to them; and to the Jews that spoke natural Hebrew, Christ was a stumbling block to them, and as for the Romans that had Italian and Latin, they persecuted the Christians; and Pilate, one of the Roman magistrates, could set Hebrew, Greek, and Latin a-top of Christ when he crucified him.

So he might see the many languages began at Babel and they set them a-top of Christ the Word when they crucified him. And John the divine, who preached the Word that was in the beginning, said that the beast and the whore have power over tongues and languages, and they are as waters. So here he might see the whore and the beast

[1] William Cole, William Dwant, Samuel Hammond, Richard Prideaux, Thomas Weld, co-authors of anti-Quaker works, *The Perfect Pharisee*, 1653, and *A Further Discovery*, 1654.

have power over the tongues and many languages which are in mystery Babylon, for they began at Babel; and how the persecutor of Christ Jesus set them over Christ when he crucified him, but he is risen over them all, who was before they were. And did he think to make ministers of Christ by these natural, confused languages, at Babel and in Babylon, set a-top of Christ the life, by a persecutor? Oh no! And Peter and John, that could not read letters, preached the word, Christ Jesus, which was in the beginning before Babel was. And Paul was made an apostle, not of man nor by man, neither received he the Gospel of man, but by Jesus Christ, ⟨who is the same now, and so is his Gospel, as it was at that day.⟩ The man confessed to many of these things. For we showed him further that Christ that made his ministers gave gifts unto them, and desired them to pray to the Lord of the harvest to send forth labourers. When we had thus discoursed with the man he became very loving and tender; and, after he had considered further of it, he never set up his college.[1]

And when I was in Bishoprick, Anthony Pearson came to me and had a great desire that I should go with him to see Henry Vane;[2] but I had little upon me to go at that time, and he commended him to me and said Henry Vane had much enquired after me.

And I went to Henry Draper's, and there Henry Vane's chaplain came to me and began to declare to me of the righteousness of man and self-righteousness, and the righteousness of the law.

So I made answer to him and said that I was in the righteousness of Christ before self-righteousness and the righteousness of man was, and Christ's righteousness ends the righteousness of the law.

'Oh', says his chaplain, 'take heed of blasphemy and presumption.'

[1] The attempt to establish a college at Durham failed. The present university was opened in 1833.

[2] Sir Henry Vane the younger (1613-1662), of Raby Castle, prominent Parliamentarian, mystic, executed by Charles II.

And I said unto him, 'Is not Christ the end of the law for righteousness sake ? And was not he before self-righteousness and man's righteousness or the righteousness of the law either, and will be when theirs is gone who fulfils the righteousness of the law ? And thou that callest this blasphemy and presumption knowest not what thou sayest.'

So he asked me whether I would come down to Raby Castle, and I told him I should say little to that. But the next day I went down, and they had me up into the chamber to Sir Henry Vane's wife, and after a while he came up, and one of New England's magistrates, and said he, 'Is this George Fox ? I thought he had been an elder man.'

And I was moved of the Lord to speak to him of the true light which Christ doth enlighten every man that cometh into the world withal, and he saith, 'Believe in the light that ye may become children of the light'; and how that Christ had promised to his disciples to send them the Holy Ghost, the spirit of truth, which should lead them into all truth, which we witnessed, and how that the grace of God which brought salvation had appeared unto all men and was the saints' teacher in the apostles' days and so it was now.

Then, says he, 'None of all this doth reach to my experience.'

'Nay', said I, 'then how camest thou in if thou didst not by believing in the light, as Christ commands ? And how comest thou into truth if thou hast not been led by the spirit of truth which led the disciples into all truth, which Christ promised to send them ? And how camest thou to know salvation if it be not by the grace of God which brings it, which taught the saints ? And therefore what is thy experience of and in ?'

So he began to tell me how the Word became flesh and dwelt amongst them.

'Yes', said I, 'that is true amongst the disciples, but he was revealed by the light and spirit; so thou art climbed up another way than by the door. And thou hast known something formerly, but now there is a mountain of earth and imaginations up in thee and from that rises a smoke which has darkened thy brain; and thou art not the man as thou wert formerly.'

And I declared unto him that the promise of God was unto the seed and this they might know within them; and the word became flesh, but not corrupt flesh; for Christ took not upon him the nature of angels but the seed of Abraham, so he might know that seed in himself; for who are of faith are of Abraham, and come to be flesh of Christ's flesh and bone of his bone.

And then he said that I said the seed was God; and because he said it, the New England man affirmed it also. But I said I did not say so; I said he took not upon him the nature of angels but the seed. And then he remembered my words and confessed his mistake; but he grew into a great fret and a passion so that there was no room for Truth in his heart. But I was moved of the Lord to set the Seed, Jesus Christ, over his head; and how that the seed which the promise was to, not many but one, all must feel in their own particulars.

And so I went away, and he said to some Friends afterwards that if Anthony Pearson and some others had not been with me he would have put me out of his house as a mad man. So Friends that were with me stranged to see his darkness and impatience, but the Lord's power came over all.

And I did see he was vain, and high, and proud, and conceited, and that the Lord would blast him and was against him, and he grieved the righteous life. And very high he was till the King came in. And afterwards he was beheaded. But he could hardly bear Friends without they would put off their hats to him.

⟨From Durham we went to Anthony Pearson's, and from thence into Cleveland; and so passed through Yorkshire to the further end of Holderness and had mighty meetings, the Lord's power accompanying us.

After we parted from Anthony Pearson, we went by Hull

and Pontefract, through the countries to George Watkinson's house, and visited most of the meetings all up and down in these parts, till we came to Scalehouse, and so to Swarthmoor, the everlasting power and arm of God carrying us through and preserving us.

After I had visited Friends up and down thereaways, I passed through the countries into Yorkshire again, and into Cheshire, and so into Derbyshire and Nottinghamshire. And glorious meetings we had, the Lord's presence being with us.

At Nottingham I sent to Rice Jones, desiring him to make his people acquainted that I had something to say to them from the Lord. He came and told me many of them lived in the country, and he could not tell how to send to them. I told him he might acquaint those about the town of it, and send to as many in the country as he could. So the next day we met at the castle, there being about fourscore people, to whom I declared the Truth for about the space of two hours. And the Lord's power was over them all so that they had not power to open their mouths in opposition. When I had done, one of them asked me a question, which I was loath to answer, for I saw it might lead into jangling, and I was unwilling to go into jangling, for some of the people were tender; yet I could not tell how well to escape it. Wherefore I answered the question, and was moved forthwith to speak to Rice Jones and lay before him how that he had been the man that had scattered such as had been tender and some that had been convinced, and had been led out of many vanities of the world which he had formerly judged; but now he judged the power of God in them, and they, being simple, turned to him. And so he and they were turned to be vainer than the world, for many of his followers were become the greatest football players and wrestlers in the country. So I told him it was the serpent in him that had scattered and done hurt to such as were tender towards the Lord. Nevertheless, if he did wait in the fear of God for the Seed of the woman, Christ Jesus, to bruise the serpent's head in him that had scattered and done the hurt; by the Seed Christ Jesus, he coming into him, he might come to gather them again by this heavenly Seed; though it would be a hard work for him to gather them again out of those vanities he had led them into.

At this Rice Jones said, 'Thou liest; it is not the Seed of the woman that bruises the serpent's head.'

'No ?' said I, 'what is it then ?'

'I say it is the law,' said he.

'But', said I, 'the Scripture, speaking of the Seed of the woman, saith: "It shall bruise thy head, and thou shalt bruise his heel." Now, hath the law an heel', said I, 'to be bruised ?'

Then Rice Jones and all his company were at a stand, and I was moved in the power of the Lord to speak to him, and say, 'This Seed, Christ Jesus, the Seed of the woman, which should bruise the serpent's head, shall bruise thy head, and break you all to pieces.' Thus did I leave on the heads of them the Seed, Christ. And not long after, he and his company scattered to pieces, several of whom came to be Friends, and stand to this day. For many of them had been convinced about eight years before, but had been led aside by this Rice Jones; for they denied the inward cross, the power of God, and so went into vanity.

It was about eight years since I had been formerly amongst them, in which time I was to pass over them and by them, seeing they had slighted the Lord's Truth and power, and the visitation of his love unto them. But now was the time that I was moved to go to them again, and it was of great service, for many of them were brought to the Lord Jesus Christ, and were settled upon him, sitting down under his teaching and feeding, where they were kept fresh and green; and the others that would not be gathered to him soon after withered. This was that Rice Jones that some years before had said I was then at the highest, and should fall. But, poor man, he little thought how near his own fall was.

We left Nottingham, and went into Warwickshire, and

thence passing through some parts of Northamptonshire and Leicestershire, visiting Friends, and having meetings with them as we travelled, came into Bedfordshire, where we had large gatherings in the name of Jesus.

After some time we came to John Crook's house, where a General Yearly Meeting[1] for the whole nation was appointed to be held. This meeting lasted three days, and many Friends from most parts of the nation came to it, so that the inns and towns around were filled, for [b]a matter of three or four thousand people[b] were at it. And although there was some disturbance by some rude people that had run out from Truth, yet the Lord's power came over all, and a glorious meeting it was. The everlasting Gospel was preached, and many received it, which brought life and immortality to light in them, and shined over all.

Then I was moved by the power and spirit of the Lord, to open unto them the promise of God, how that it was made to the Seed, not to seeds, as many, but to one, which Seed was Christ; and that all people, both males and females, should feel this Seed in them, which was heir of the promise; that so they might all witness Christ in them, the hope of glory, the mystery which had been hid from ages and generations, which was revealed to the apostles, and is revealed again now, after this long night of apostacy . . . Now again, the everlasting Gospel must be preached to all nations, and to every creature, that they may come into the pure religion, to worship God in the spirit and in truth, and may know Christ Jesus their way to God, and him to be the author of their faith, and may receive the Gospel from heaven, and not from men; in which Gospel, received from heaven, is the heavenly fellowship, which is a mystery to all the fellowships in the world.[2]

And after the people were turned to the divine light of Christ, and his spirit, by which they might come both to know God and Christ, and the Scriptures, and to have fellowship with them, and one with another in the same

[1] Probably at Crook's country house, Beckerings Park, near Ridgmont, Beds. Fox's discourse is dated 31st May.

[2] In full Ellwood, pp. 284*-285*; Bicent., i, 418-21.

[b]. . . . . .[b] *S.J.*, p. 54.

spirit, I was moved to declare and open many other things to those Friends who had received a part of the ministry, concerning the exercise of their spiritual gifts in the Church; which, being taken in writing by one that was present, was after this manner:〉

Friends,

Take heed of destroying that which ye have begotten . . . That which calms and cools the spirit goes over the world and brings to the Father, to inherit the life eternal, and reaches to the spirits in prison in all. In the living unmovable word of the Lord God dwell, for whosoever goes out from the pure and ministers not in that, comes to an end; though he was serviceable for a time while he lived in the thing.

Take heed of many words; what reacheth to the life settles in the life. . . . If Friends do not live in the life which they speak of, so that they answer the life in those they speak to, the other part steps in, and so there comes an acquaintance, and that comes over them.

As every one is kept in the life of God over all that is contrary, then he is in his place, he doth not lay hands on any suddenly. For if he doth he may lose his discerning, and lay hands on the wrong part and so let the deceit come near him and steal over; and it will be a hard thing for him to get it down. There is no one strikes his fellow-servant but first he is gone from the pure in his own particular. Then the Light which he is gone from, Christ, cometh and giveth him his reward. This is the state of evil servants. All the boisterous, hasty, and rash, beget nothing to God; but the life, which doth reach the life, is that which begets to God. . . .

Friends, be watchful and careful in all meetings ye come into. When a man is come newly out of the world he cometh out of the dirt. Then he must not be rash. For now when he cometh into a silent meeting, that is another state. Then he must come and feel his own spirit how it is, when he cometh to those that sit silent; for he may come in the heat of his spirit out of the world. Now the others are still and cool, and he may rather do them hurt if he get them out of the cool state into the heating state.

There is a great danger to Friends travelling abroad in the world, except a man be moved of the Lord by the power of the Lord; for then keeping in that power, he is kept in his journey and in his work. . . . Though one may have openings when he is abroad, to minister to others, yet, as for his own particular growth he must dwell in the life which doth open, and that will keep down that which would boast. . . .

Friends, come into that which is over all the spirits of the world, with that ye may see where others stand, and reach that which is of God in everyone. Here is no strife, for he that goeth into strife and into contention is from the pure spirit. . . .

Now Truth hath an honour in the hearts of people that are not Friends. Friends being kept in the Truth are kept in the honour. But if any lose the power, they lose the life, they lose their crown, their honour, they lose the cross which should crucify them. And they crucify the just, and the Lamb comes to be slain. . . . The power of the Lord hath been abused by some, and the worth of Truth hath not been minded; there hath been a trampling on, and marring with your feet, and that abuseth the power. . . .

When any shall be moved to speak in a steeplehouse or market, turn in to that which moves and be obedient to it; that which would not go must be kept down. . . . It is a mighty thing to be in the work of the ministry of the Lord God and to go forth in that. It is not as a customary preaching; but it is to bring people to the end of all outward preaching. For once ye have spoken the Truth to the people and they are come into the thing you speak of, many declarations out of the life may beget them into a form. . . .

If any have been moved to speak and have quenched that which moved them, let them not go forth afterwards into words ⟨until they feel the power arise and move them thereto again⟩. For the other part gets up, and if any go forth in that, he goeth forth in his own, and the betrayer will come in.

And all Friends, meddle not with the powers of the earth; keep out of all such things. . . . Keep out of all jangling; all that are in the law come to the Lamb's power, who is the end of the law outward. . . . Christ, who was glorified with the Father before the world began, is the end of the law. This every particular must feel in himself.[1]

More was then spoken to many of these particulars which was not taken at large as it was spoken.

[1] The discourse is here condensed and abridged, the principal omissions are marked. The fullest extant accounts, which vary somewhat, are in *Camb. Jnl.*, i, 317-23; Ellwood, pp. 285* ff.; Bicent., i, 421-7.

And after the meeting was done I was walking in John Crook's garden and there came a party of horse with a constable but Friends were mostly gone. And I heard them ask what Friends were in the house and who was there, and one of them made answer and said I was there. And the soldiers and constables said I was the man they looked for, but they never came into the garden, but went into the house. And after many words that they had with John Crook and some few Friends in the house they went away in a rage and never minded me in the garden, the Lord's power so confounded them.

And so, after, I went into the house, and Friends were very glad to see them so confounded and that I had escaped them.

And the next day I passed away, and after I had visited Friends in several places I passed to London; and thus the Lord's power came over all and Friends were settled upon the foundation Jesus Christ. And all the quickened, and those that were made alive, knew Christ Jesus and came to sit down together in him in the heavenly places.

And about this time we had a dispute with a Jesuit that came over with some of the ambassadors from Spain, for he challenged all the Quakers to dispute with them at the Earl of Newport's house.[1] And at last we sent to him that we could meet with him; and then he sent us word he would meet with twelve of the wisest learned men we had. Afterward he sent us word he would meet with but six, and after he sent word again he would have but three to come. So I bid Nicholas Bond and Edward Burrough go up and talk with him lest he put it quite off at last, for all his great boast. 'And I may walk in the yard here; and if the Earl of Newport ask for me I may come up.'

And so I bid them state this question: whether or no the church of Rome was not degenerated from the Church in the primitive times, from their life and doctrine, and the power and spirit that they were in, which they did. And the

[1] Mountjoy Blount (1597?-1666), created Earl of Newport, Isle of Wight, 1628. Newport House was in Longacre.

Jesuit affirmed that they were in the virginity and purity of it.

Then by this I was come up. And we asked him whether they had the same pouring out of the Holy Ghost as the apostles had. But that he utterly denied. Then said we, ' If you have not the same Holy Ghost and the same power and spirit as the apostles had, there is a degeneration.' And there needed little more to be said to that.

And we were to make good what we said by Scriptures on both sides.

And then I asked him what Scripture they had for setting up cloisters for nuns, and monasteries and abbeys for men, and for all their several orders. And what Scripture had they for praying by beads and to images, and for making crosses and forbidding of meats and marriages and for putting people to death for religion. Now if they were in the purity and virginity of the practice of the primitive Church, then let us see some Scriptures where ever they practised any such things.

Then said he, ' There is a written word and an unwritten word.'

Then said I, ' What dost thee call thy unwritten word ? '

' The written word ', says he, ' is the Scriptures, and the unwritten word that which the apostles spoke by word of mouth, which are all these traditions which we practise, and were their unwritten word.'

Then I bid him prove that, and he brought that Scripture where the apostle said: ' When I was with you I told you these things: ' (2 Thess. ii. 5); that is, said he, ' I told you of nunneries and monasteries and putting to death for religion and praying by beads and to images,' and all the rest of the practices of the Church of Rome, he said, were the unwritten word of the apostles, which they told then and since, and have continued unto them down along by tradition.

Then I bid him read the Scriptures again, and there he might see how he perverted the apostle's words, where he tells the Church of disorderly persons and such as did not follow the apostles, who did not work at all; and therefore he had commanded them when he was with them, in his unwritten word, that they should eat their own bread: and therefore now again in his epistle, his written word, he again commands them. (2 Thess. iii. 10-15.)

So this plainly overthrew all their invented traditions so that he had no more proof to stand by. Then I told him that was another degeneration of theirs into such inventions and traditions, which the apostles and the saints never practised.

Then he came to his sacrament and altar, and began at the paschal-lamb and the shew-bread; and Christ's saying, 'This is my body' and what the apostle said to the Corinthians; and that after the priest had consecrated the bread and the wine it was immortal and divine and he that received it received the whole Christ.

Then I followed him in the Scriptures he brought till I came to Christ's words and the apostle's, and that the apostle told the Corinthians after they had taken bread and wine in remembrance of Christ that they were reprobates if Christ was not in them. (2 Cor. xiii. 7.)

Now if that was the Christ after they had eaten it then they had Christ in them. Now if this bread and this cup was Christ's body and blood, and the apostle gave that, then how can Christ be with a body in Heaven? And Christ said, 'As often as ye eat this and drink this do it in remembrance of me'; and so did the apostle; so then it was not the body but a showing-forth his death till he come.

So, mark, here is the bread and wine to be taken in remembrance of his death till he come; so then the bread and wine cannot be he, if it is to be taken in remembrance of his death till he come.

Now Christ said, 'This is my body'; also he said, 'I am the vine, and the door and rock of ages.' Therefore, is Christ an outward rock, door, or vine?

'Oh', said the Jesuit, 'that is to be interpreted.'

'Then', said I, 'interpret also his words, "This is my body," of which he said, "Take this in remembrance of me till I come."'

Then I said unto him, seeing that he said that the bread and wine were immortal and divine and the very Christ, and that whosoever received it received the whole Christ, therefore let the Pope and some of his cardinals and Jesuits give us a meeting, and we would have a bottle of wine and a loaf of bread and we would divide the wine into basins and the loaf into two pieces. And they should consecrate which part they would, and set the consecrated and unconsecrated into a cellar; and we would have a watch set on it, on each side seven, and seven locks set upon the doors, and if the consecrated bread and wine altered not its property and the bread grew not mouldy and the wine sour, but proved divine and immortal, we would all turn to them. But if the bread grew mouldy and the wine sour and dead, then they should acknowledge their error and turn all to us.

And therefore come forth and let it be tried, for this would bring glory to God and the truth to be manifest, for much blood had been shed about these things, as in Queen Mary's days.

And then the Jesuit said, 'Take a piece of new cloth and cut it into two pieces and make two garments of it, and put one upon King David's back and another upon a beggar's, and the one garment should wear away as well as the other.'

Said I, 'Is this thy answer?'

'Yes,' said he.

'Then', said I, 'I am satisfied, for you have told people that the consecrated divided loaf and wine were immortal and divine, and now say, "It will wear away as well as the other." I must tell thee Christ remains, and is the same today as yesterday, and is the saints' heavenly food in all generations and never decays, through which they have life.' So this assertion of his proved erroneous, and he went no farther with it for all people saw his error.

Then I asked him why they did put people to death and persecute them for religion. And he said, it was not the Church did it but the magistrates.

Then I asked him whether those magistrates were not counted and called believers and Christians. And he said, 'Yes.'

'Why then', said I, 'are they not members of the Church?'

And he said, 'Yes.'

'Why then, dost thou say the Church does not persecute?' So I left it to the people to judge; and so we parted and his subtlety was comprehended by simplicity.

CHAPTER XV

⟨ABOUT this time⟩ she they called the Lady Claypole[1] was very sick and troubled in mind, and nothing could comfort her. And I was moved of the Lord to write a paper and send it to her to be read unto her.

Friend,

Be still and cool in thy own mind and spirit from thy own thoughts, and then thou wilt feel the principle of God to turn thy mind to the Lord God, whereby thou wilt receive his strength and power from whence life comes, to allay all tempests, against blusterings and storms. That is it which moulds up into patience, into innocency, into soberness, into stillness, into stayedness, into quietness, up to God, with his power. Therefore mind: that is the word of the Lord God unto thee, that the authority, and thy faith in that, to work down; for that is it which keeps peace, and brings up the witness in thee, that hath been transgressed, to feel after God, who is a God of order and peace, with his power and life. When ⟨thou art in⟩ the transgression of the life of God in the particular, the mind flies up in the air, and the creature is led into the night, and nature goes out of his course, and an old garment goes on, and an uppermost clothing, and nature leads out of his course, and so it comes to be all of a fire, in the transgression; and that defaceth the glory of the first body.

Therefore be still a while from thy own thoughts, searching, seeking, desires and imaginations, and be stayed in the principle of God in thee, to stay thy mind upon God, up to God; and thou wilt find strength from him and ⟨find him to⟩ be a present

[1] Elizabeth Cromwell (1629-1658), second daughter of the Protector, m. John Claypole.

help in time of trouble, in need, and to be a God at hand. And it will keep thee humble being come to the principle of God, which hath been transgressed; which humble, God will teach in his way, which is peace; and such he doth exalt. And now as the principle of God in thee hath been transgressed, come to it, to keep thy mind down low, up to the Lord God; and deny thyself. And from thy own will, that is, the earthly, thou must be kept. Then thou wilt feel the power of God, that will bring nature into his course, and to see the glory of the first body. And there the wisdom of God will be received, which is Christ, by which all things were made and created, in wisdom to be preserved and ordered to God's glory. There thou wilt come to receive and feel the physician of value, which clothes people in their right mind, whereby they may serve God and do his will.

For all distractions, distempers, unruliness, confusion are in the transgression; which transgression must be brought down, before the principle of God, that hath been transgressed, be lifted up: whereby the mind may be seasoned and stilled in a right understanding of the Lord, whereby his blessing enters, and is felt over all that is contrary, with the power of the Lord God, which gives dominion, which awakens the principle of God within, which gives a feeling after God. Therefore, keep in the fear of the Lord God; that is the word of the Lord God unto thee. For all these things happen to thee for thy good and your good, to make you to know your own strength and means, and to know the Lord's strength and power. Trust in him, therefore.

Let the time be sufficient that is past, who in anything hath been lifted up in transgression out of the power of the Lord; for he can bring down and abase the mighty, and lay them in the dust of the earth. Therefore, all keep low in his fear, that thereby you may receive the secret of God and his wisdom, and know the shadow of the Almighty, and sit under it in all tempests, and storms, and heats. For God is a God at hand, and the Most High he rules in the children of men. So then this is the word of the Lord God unto you all; what the light doth make manifest and discover, temptations, confusions, distractions, distempers; do not look at the temptations, confusions, corruptions, but at the light that discovers them, that makes them manifest; and with the same light you will feel over them, to receive power to stand against them. Which light discovers, the same light that lets you see sin and transgression will let you see the covenant of God, which blots out your sin and transgression, which gives victory and dominion over it, and brings into covenant with God. For looking down at sin, and corruption, and distraction, you are swallowed up in it; but looking at the light that discovers them, you will see over them. That will give victory; and you will find grace and strength; and there is the first step of peace. That will bring salvation; and see to the beginning and the glory that was with the Father before the world began; and so come to know the Seed of God, which is heir of the promise of God, and the world which hath no end; unto the power of an endless life, which power of God is immortal, which brings up the soul, which is immortal, up to the immortal God, in whom it doth rejoice. So in the name and power of the Lord Jesus Christ, strengthen thee. G.F.[1]

And she said it settled and stayed her mind for the present. And many Friends got copies of it, both in England and Ireland, to read it to distracted people; and it settled several of their minds, and they did great service with it both in England and Ireland.

⟨About this time came forth a declaration from Oliver Cromwell, the Protector, for a collection towards the relief of divers Protestant Churches, driven out of Poland; and of twenty Protestant families, driven out of the confines of Bohemia. There having been published some time before a like declaration to invite the nation to a day of solemn fasting and humiliation, in order to a contribution being made for the suffering Protestants for the valleys of Lucerne, Angrona, etc., who were persecuted by the Duke of Savoy, I was moved to write to the Protector and chief magistrates on this occasion,[2] both to show them the nature of a true fast (such as God requires and accepts), and to make them sensible of their injustice and self-condemnation,

[1] Swarthmore MSS., vii, 123; Ellwood, pp. 189(2)-190(2); Bicent., i, 432-4.

[2] The paper printed in Ellwood, pp. 191(2)-194(2); Bicent., i, 435-8, is there attributed to Fox. But in the Spence MS. (*Camb. Jnl.*, i, 335-40) it does not bear his name. It was published over Margaret Fell's name in *False Prophets*, 1655. The day appointed for the fast was 14th Jun., 1655, not 1658 as here implied.

in blaming the Papists for persecuting the Protestants abroad, while they themselves, calling themselves Protestants, were at the same time persecuting their Protestant neighbours and friends at home.⟩

And often the Parliaments and Oliver Cromwell and the Committe of Safety would proclaim fasts. And then I was moved to write to them that their fasts were like unto Jezebel's for many times when they began to proclaim fasts then there was some mischief acting against us and others. For I knew their fasts were for strife and debate and to smite with the fist of wickedness. For the New England professors before they put Friends to death, proclaimed a fast also.

And many Friends being in prisons at this time, [a]a matter of two hundred[a] were moved to go to the Parliament to offer up themselves to lie in the same dungeons where their friends lay, that they that were in prison might go forth and not perish in the stinking dungeons and gaols. And this we did in love to God and our brethren that they might not die in prison, and in love to them that cast them in, that they might not bring innocent blood upon their own heads which would cry to the Lord, and bring his wrath and vengeance and plagues upon them.

And then the Parliaments would be in a rage and sometimes send them word that they would whip them and send them home again; and many times soon after the Lord would turn them out and send them home, who had not power to do good in their day. And when the Long Parliament sat I was moved to send several papers to them and speak to them how the Lord was bringing a day of darkness upon them all that should be felt.

⟨And because the Parliament that now sat was made up mostly of high professors, who, pretending to be more religious than others, were indeed greater persecutors of them that were truly religious, I was moved to send them the following lines, as a reproof of their hypocrisy.⟩[1]

[1] Ellwood, p. 195(2); Bicent., i, 439-40.

[a]. . . . . .[a] *S.J.*, p. 54.

One time, as I was going into the country, and two Friends with me, when I was gone a little above a mile out of the city, there met me two troopers who took me and the Friends that were with me prisoners and brought us to the Mews and there kept us. They were Colonel Hacker's men, but the Lord's power was so over them that they did not take us before any officers, but shortly after set us at liberty again.

And the same day, I took boat and went to Kingston, ⟨and from thence I went afterwards to Hampton Court, to speak with the Protector about the sufferings of Friends.⟩ I met him riding into Hampton-Court Park,[1] and before I came at him he was riding in the head of his life-guard, I saw and felt a waft of death go forth against him, and he looked like a dead man. When I had spoken to him of the sufferings of Friends and warned him as I was moved to speak to him, he bid me come to his house. So I went to Kingston, and the next day went up to Hampton Court. But when I came, he was very sick, and Harvey told me, who was one of his men that waited on him, that the doctors were not willing I should come in to speak with him. So I passed away, and never saw him no more.

From Kingston I went to Isaac Penington's, ⟨in Buckinghamshire,⟩ where I had appointed a meeting, and the Lord's truth and power came over all.

And after I had visited Friends in London and in the country thereaways I went into Essex. And there I ⟨had not been long before I⟩ heard Oliver Protector was dead.[2] And then I came up to London again when Richard was made Protector.

And about this time the *Church Faith*[3] was given forth, which was made at Savoy in eleven days' time: and I got a copy of it ⟨before it was published, and writ an answer to

[1] Thomas Carlyle, in *Cromwell's Letters*, suggests Friday, 20th Aug., 1658.

[2] 3rd Sept., 1658.

[3] *A Declaration of the Faith and Order . . . in the Congregational Churches in England . . . at the Savoy, October 12th 1658*; printed in 1659.

it[1]〉. And when their book of *Church Faith* were sold up and down the streets, my answer unto it was sold also. And one of the parliament men told me they must have me to Smithfield to burn me as they did the martyrs, but I told him I was over their fires and feared them not. For had all people been without a faith this sixteen hundred years that now the priests must make them one? And did not the apostle say that Christ was the author of their faith, and finisher, and were not all people to look unto Jesus, the author and finisher of their faith, and not to the priests? And a great deal of work we had about the priests' made faith. And yet they called us house-creepers leading silly women captive, because we met in houses and would not hold up their priests and temples which they had tried and made. But I let them see how that they were they that led silly women captive and crept into houses, that kept people always learning under them, who were covetous, and who had got the form of godliness; but denied the power and spirit that the apostles were in. And so they began to creep in the apostles' days, but now they had got the magistrates on their sides who upheld all those houses that they had crept into, their temples with their tithes.

But the apostles brought people off those temples and tithes and offerings that God had 〈for a time〉 commanded. And they met in several houses, and were to preach the Gospel in all nations, which they did freely as Christ had commanded them. And so do we, that bring people off these priests, temples, and tithes, which God never commanded and to meet in houses or mountains as the saints did, which were gathered in the name of Jesus, and Christ was their prophet, priest, and shepherd.

〈There was one present with the parliament men that I discoursed with, one Major Wigan,[2] a very envious man, yet he bridled himself before the parliament men and some

[1] Fox's reply: *Something in Answer to that Book called the Church Faith.*

[2] John Wigan (d. 1665), a Baptist preacher, and a colonel of Life Guards.

others that were there in company. He took upon him to make a speech, and said Christ had taken away the guilt of sin but had left the power of sin remaining in us. I told him that was strange doctrine, for Christ came to destroy the Devil and his works and the power of sin, and so to cleanse men from sin. So Major Wigan's mouth was stopped at that time. But the next day, desiring to speak with me again, I took a Friend or two with me, and went to him. Then he vented much passion and rage, beyond the bounds of a Christian or moral man. Whereupon I was made to reprove him; and having brought the Lord's power over him and let him see what condition he was in, I left him.⟩

And after this I passed into several places of the country. And I had a meeting at Sergeant Birkett's, where there were many considerable people and some of quality, and a glorious meeting it was; and the Scriptures were opened to them and Christ set above all, so that one man amongst them admired and said, 'This man is a pearl.'

And there was great persecution about seven miles off London.[1] ⟨The rude people usually came out of several parishes⟩ so that they beat, abused, and bruised Friends exceedingly. And one day they beat and abused about eighty Friends that went out of London to a meeting, and tore their coats and cloaks off their backs and threw them into ditches and ponds, and all moiled them with dirt; and when they had so done then they said Friends looked like witches. And the next First-day after, I was moved of the Lord to go to that place though I was very weak, and when I came there I bid Friends bring a table to stand upon and set it in the close where they used to meet. So according to their wonted time and course these rude people came, and I having a Bible in my hand, I showed them theirs and their priests' and teachers' fruits and the people came to be ashamed and were quiet, and so I opened the Scriptures to them and our principles, and turned them from the darkness to the light of Christ and his spirit

[1] At Mitcham, Surrey, 17th July, 1658.

by which they might know the Scriptures and see themselves and their sins; and know their saviour, Christ Jesus: and so the meeting ended quietly and the Lord's power came over all to his glory.

And great sufferings we went through in these times of Oliver Protector and the Commonwealth, and many died in prisons. And they have thrown into our meetings wild fire and rotten eggs, and brought in drums beating, and kettles to make noises with; and the priests as rude as any, as you may see in the book of the fighting priests,[1] a list of the priests that have beat and abused Friends.

And many Friends were brought up to London prisons to be tried before the Committee; and Henry Vane being chairman he would not suffer Friends to come in, except they would put off their hats, but at last the Lord's power came over him so that through some others that persuaded him they were admitted.

For many of us were imprisoned upon contempts as they called it for not putting off our hats; so it was not a likely thing for Friends to put off their hats to him, that had so long suffered for it; but the Lord's power came over them all so that several Friends were set at liberty by them.

⟨Now inasmuch as sufferings grew very sharp, I was moved of the Lord to write a few lines and send amongst Friends, to encourage them to go on faithfully and boldly.⟩[2]

And great sufferings I had about this time; and great confusion and distraction there was amongst the powers and people.

And after a while I passed to Reading, and was under great sufferings and exercises, and in a great travail in my spirit for ten weeks time.[3] For I saw how the powers were plucking each other to pieces. And I saw how many men were destroying the simplicity and betraying the Truth. And a great deal of hypocrisy, deceit, and strife was got

[1] Perhaps, 'A Catalogue of some few of the fighting Priests' at the end of *A Word of Reproof*, by E. Billing, 1659.

[2] Ellwood, p. 198(2); Bicent., i, 444.

[3] At the house of Thomas and Ann Curtis, at the sign of the George.

uppermost in people, that they were ready to sheath their swords in one another's bowels. There was a tenderness in people formerly, but when they were got up and had killed and taken possession, they came to be the worst of men; so that we had so much to do with them about our hats, and saying 'Thou' and 'Thee' to them, that they turned their profession of patience and moderation into rage and madness, and many of them were like distracted men for this hat-honour. And this time, towards 1659, the powers had hardened themselves, persecuting Friends, and had many of them in prison, and were crucifying the Seed, Christ, both in themselves and others. And at last they fell a-biting and devouring one another until they were consumed one of another; who had turned against and judged that which God had wrought in them and showed them. So, God overthrew them, and turned them upside down, and brought the King over them; who were always complaining that the Quakers met together to bring in King Charles, whereas Friends did not concern themselves with the outward powers. But at last the Lord brought him in, and many of them ⟨when they saw he would be brought in⟩ voted at their meeting of the Parliament for the bringing in of King Charles. So with heart and voice praise the name of the Lord, to whom it doth belong being on them a-top, and over all hath the supreme. And the nations will he rock, being on them a-top.

And in my great sufferings and travails at Reading I was burdened and almost choked with their hypocrisy and treachery, and falseness, I saw God would bring that a-top of them, which they had been a-top of; and all that must be brought down to that which did convince them, before they could get over that bad spirit within and without: for it is the pure, invisible spirit, that doth and must work down all deceit in people.

So when I had travailed with the witness of God which they had quenched, and I had gotten through with it and over all that hypocrisy, and saw how that would be turned under and down, and that life would rise over it, I came to have ease, and the light, power, and spirit shined over all. And in this day many of our old envious persecutors were in great confusion.

⟨I had a sight and sense of the King's return a good while before, and so had some others.⟩ For I several times writ to Oliver Cromwell and told him, while he was persecuting God's people, those he looked upon as his enemies were preparing to come upon him. Several rash spirits would have bought Somerset House that we might have meetings in it, but I was moved of the Lord to forbid them so to do, for I did foresee the King's coming in again at that time.

For there came a woman[1] to me in the Strand that had a prophesy concerning King Charles three years before he came in, and she told me she must go to him to declare it. So I told her she should wait upon the Lord and keep it to herself, for if it should be known that she went they would look upon it to be treason. But she said she must go and tell him that he must be brought into England again. And I saw her prophecy was true ⟨and that a great stroke must come upon those in power⟩, for those that had got possession were so exceeding high and such great persecution was acted by them which called themselves saints, for they would take away from Friends their copyholds because they would not swear in their courts; and sometimes when we laid these sufferings before Oliver Cromwell he would not believe it.

And Thomas Aldam and Anthony Pearson were moved to go through all the gaols in England to get copies of Friends' commitments under the gaolers' hands and lay them upon Oliver Cromwell. And when he would not release them, Thomas Aldam was moved to take his cap off his head and rend it to pieces before him and to tell him, so should his kingdom be rent from him.[2]

Another Friend was moved to go to the Parliament that was envious against Friends and to take a pitcher in

[1] Esther Biddle (*c.* 1629-1696), wife of Thomas Biddle of London.

[2] This episode occurred in 1655.

her hand and break it to pieces, and to tell them so should they be broken to pieces, which came to pass presently after.

In the time of my travail at Reading, through my travail and sorrow I looked poor and thin; and there came a company of unclean spirits to me and told me the plagues of God were upon me. And I told them it was the same spirit, that said so to Christ. When he was stricken and smitten they hid their face from him. But when I recovered and got through my travails and sufferings, my body and face were swelled ⟨when I came abroad into the air⟩, and then the bad spirits said I was grown fat, and they envied at that also. So I said it seemed no condition nor state would please that spirit of theirs. But the Lord preserved me by his power and spirit through and over all, and in the Lord's power I came to London again.

⟨Now was there a great pudder[1] made about the image or *effigies* of Oliver Cromwell lying in state, men standing and sounding with trumpets over his image after he was dead. At this my spirit was greatly grieved, and the Lord, I found, was highly offended. Then did I write the following lines and sent among them to reprove their wickedness and warn them to repent:

> Oh friends, what are ye doing ? And what mean ye to sound before an image ? Oh, how am I grieved with your abominations ! Oh, mad people, how am I wearied ! My soul is wearied with you, saith the Lord; will I not be avenged of you, think ye, for your abominations ? . . . And how are ye turned to fooleries, which things, in times past, ye stood over ! . . . The sober people in the nations stand amazed at your doings, and are ashamed, as if ye would bring in Popery. G.F.[2]

About this time great stirs were in the nation, the minds of people being unsettled, and much plotting and contriving there was by the several factions, to carry on their several interests. And a great care being upon me lest any young or raw people, that might sometimes come amongst us,

[1] i.e. pother.
[2] In full, Ellwood, p. 200(2); Bicent., i, 447-8.

should be drawn into that snare, I was moved to give forth the following epistle as a warning unto all such:

All Friends, everywhere, keep out of plots and bustling and the arm of the flesh, for all these are amongst Adam's sons in the Fall, where they are destroying men's lives like dogs and beasts and swine, goring, rending and biting one another and destroying one another, and wrestling with flesh and blood. From whence arise wars and killing but from the lusts ? Now all this is in Adam in the Fall, out of Adam that never fell, in whom there is peace and life. Ye are called to peace, therefore follow it, and that peace is in Christ, not in Adam in the Fall. All that pretend to fight for Christ they are deceived, for his kingdom is not of this world, therefore his servants do not fight. Therefore fighters are not of Christ's kingdom, but are without Christ's kingdom; for his kingdom stands in peace and righteousness, but fighters are in the lust, and all that would destroy men's lives are not of Christ's mind, who came to save men's lives. . . . All such as pretend Christ Jesus, and confess him, and yet run into the use of carnal weapons, wrestling with flesh and blood, throw away the spiritual weapons. They that would be wrestlers with flesh and blood, throw away Christ's doctrine, and flesh is got up in them, and they are weary of their sufferings. And such as would revenge themselves be out of Christ's doctrine. And such as being stricken on the one cheek would not turn the other be out of Christ's doctrine. And such as do not love one another and love enemies, be out of Christ's doctrine. . . .

All Friends everywhere, this I charge you, which is the word of the Lord God unto you all, Live in peace, in Christ, the way of peace, and therein seek the peace of all men, and no man's hurt. As I said before, in Adam in the Fall is no peace, but in Adam out of the Fall, in him is peace: so, ye being in Adam which never fell, it is love that overcomes and not hatred with hatred, nor strife with strife. Therefore live all in the peaceable life, doing good to all men and seeking the good and welfare of all men. G.F.[1]

It was not long after this before George Booth[2] rose in arms in Cheshire and Lambert went down against him.>

[1] In full, Ellwood, pp. 200(2)-202(2); Bicent., i, 448-50.

[2] Sir George Booth was defeated by Major-General John Lambert at Nantwich, Aug., 1659.

And then Lambert was coming up from Booth's defeat, and after a while went against Monk, and a great noise and jumble there was in the nation so that people began to be very rude against Friends. At which time some foolish rash spirits that came amongst us were going to take up arms, but I was moved of the Lord to forewarn them and forbid them and they left it. And in the time of the Committee of Safety we were invited by them to take up arms and great places and commands offered us, but we denied them all. And they had a great discourse amongst them whether the Quakers should have their liberty; and it was denied by many of them. Colonel Packer said, before the Quakers should have their liberty he would draw his sword to bring in King Charles. ⟨And we declared both by word and writing, testifying that our weapons and armour were not carnal but spiritual. And lest any that came amongst us should be drawn into that snare, it came upon me from the Lord to write a few lines on that occasion, and send them forth as a caution to all amongst us, of which this is a copy.

All Friends everywhere, take heed to keep out of the powers of the earth that run into wars and fightings, which make not for peace but go from that; such will not have the kingdom. And, Friends, take heed of joining with this or the other, or meddling with any, or being busy with other men's matters; but mind the Lord, and his power, and his service. So let Friends keep out of other men's matters, and keep in that which answers the witness in them all, out of the man's matter, where they must expect wars and dishonour. And all Friends everywhere, dwell in your own, in the power of the Lord God, to keep your minds up to the Lord God, from falling down to the strength of Egypt, and going there for strength, after ye are come out of it, like the children of Israel after they were come out of outward Egypt. . . . Therefore keep in the peace, and the love and power of God, and unity and love one to another, lest any go out, . . . and so know a kingdom which hath no end, and fight for that with spiritual weapons, which take away the occasion of the carnal; and there gather men to war, as many as you can, and set up as many as you will with these weapons. G.F.[1]⟩

[1] Swarthmore MSS., ii, 103. In full, Ellwood, pp. 202(2)-203(2); Bicent., i, 450, 451.

After I had visited Friends in London, and the Lord's power was set over all I travelled into the countries again.

And I passed through the countries, as Norfolk, Suffolk, Essex, Huntingdonshire, and Cambridgeshire and had several meetings amongst Friends till I came to Norwich. And about the time called Christmas we had a meeting in Norwich; and the mayor[1] heard of it and granted forth a warrant to apprehend me. And when I came into the town I heard of the warrant and so I sent some Friends to the mayor to reason with him about it, and his answer was that the soldiers should not meet, and did we think to meet.

And he would have had us go out of the town and meet out of the town, and said the townspeople were so rude that he could hardly order them, and that our meeting would make tumults in the town. But our Friends told him we were a peaceable people, and that he ought to keep the peace, for we could not but meet to worship God as our manner was. And so he became pretty moderate and did not send his officers to the meeting.

And a large meeting it was, and abundance of rude people came with an intent to have done mischief, but the Lord's power came so over them that they were chained by it, though several priests were there, and Ranters, and professors; and one priest, Sampson Townsend,[2] stood up and cried, 'Error, blasphemy, and an ungodly meeting.' And I bade him not burden himself with that which he could not make good. So I asked him what was our error and blasphemy, for he should make good his words before I had done with him, or be shamed. And as for an ungodly meeting, I did believe that there were many people there that feared God and so it was uncivil in him to charge civil, godly people with an ungodly meeting.

So he said my error and blasphemy was because I said that people must wait upon God by his power and spirit and feel his presence when they did not speak words.

[1] The mayor of Norwich, elected in 1659, was William Davy; his predecessor was Roger Mingay.

[2] Of St. Austin's and St. Saviour's, Norwich.

Then I asked him whether the prophets and holy men of God did not hear God speak to them in their silence before they spoke forth the Scriptures, and before it was penned, written or printed.

And he said, 'Yes, David and the prophets did hear God before they did pen the Scriptures and felt his presence in silence before they spoke them forth.'

Then, said I, 'All people take notice, he said this was error and blasphemy in me to say these words and now here he hath confessed it, ⟨it is no more than the holy men of God in former times witnessed.⟩'

So I let the people see that it was the holy men of God who learnt of God that spoke forth the Scriptures as they were moved of the Holy Ghost; so they heard and learnt before they spoke them forth. And so must they all hearken and hear what the spirit saith which will lead them into all Truth, and to know God, and Christ, and the Scriptures.

Then said the priest, 'This is not that George Fox I would speak withal; this is a subtle man,' said he.

So the Lord's power came over all and all the rude people were made moderate by it and reached, and other professors cried to the priest, 'Prove their blasphemy and errors which you have spoken so much of; ⟨you have spoken much against them behind their backs,⟩ but nothing can you prove now to their faces,' said they.

And so the priest being going away I told him we had many things to charge him withal and therefore let him set his time and place to answer to them; so he did, and went his ways. And that day was a glorious day and Truth came over all and people were turned to the Lord by his power and spirit and to the Lord Jesus Christ, their free teacher, who was exalted over all.

And so as I passed away, generally people's hearts were filled with love towards us, yea, the ruder sort of them were desiring for another meeting. And the evil intentions that they had against us were thrown out of all their hearts.

And at night I passed out of town to a Friend's house

and from thence to Colonel Dennis's house where we had a great meeting.

And so we passed through the countries up and down, visiting Friends in Norfolk, Huntingdonshire, Cambridgeshire, and left George Whitehead and Richard Hubberthorne to meet the priest, who was soon confounded and down, the Lord's power so came over him.

And so after I had passed through many counties in the Lord's service and visited Friends and many were convinced, though in many places the people were rude, I returned to London again when General Monk was come to London,[1] and the gates and posts of the city were pulling down, and some of the soldiers were rude, but the Lord's power came over all. And I had a vision long before this, for I saw the city lie in heaps and the gates down; and I saw it just as it was when I saw it several years after, lying in heaps when it was burned.

⟨Divers times, both by word and writing, had I forewarned the several powers, both in Oliver's time and after, of the day of recompense that was coming upon them; but they rejecting counsel, and slighting those visitations of love to them, I was moved now, before they were quite overturned, to lay their backsliding, hypocrisy, and treacherous dealing before them.[2]⟩

CHAPTER XVI

AND great fears and troubles were in many people and a looking for the King's coming in, and that all things should be altered; but I told them the Lord's power and light was over all and shined over all, and that the fear would only take hold of the hypocrites and such as had not been faithful to God, our persecutors. For in my travail and sufferings at Reading when people were at a stand and could not tell what might come in nor

[1] Monk entered London, 3rd Feb., 1660.

[2] Ellwood, pp. 204(2)-206(2); Bicent., i, 453-5.

who might rule, I told them the Lord's power was over all, for I had travailed through it, and his day shined, whosoever should come in; and all would be well whether the King came in or no, to them that loved God and were faithful to him; and so I bid all Friends fear none but the Lord, and keep in his power that is over all.

And after I had visited Friends in the city and up and down thereaways, I passed into Surrey and Sussex, and came to a great town where there was a great meeting and several Friends from Reading. And a blessed meeting there was.

And the priest of the town was in a great rage but did not come out of his house. And as I was passing away he was making a noise and raging in his house; and we bid him come out into the street ⟨and we would discourse with him,⟩ but he would not. So the Lord's power came over all, and Friends were refreshed in the Lord's power and Truth.

And from thence I went to another market town where at night we had a precious meeting, and the fresh sense of the presence of the Lord God was felt amongst us. And so I passed through the countries, as I said before, into Hampshire, and Dorsetshire, to Poole and Ringwood, visiting Friends in the Lord's power, and had great meetings amongst them.

And at Dorchester I came to an inn where we had a great meeting at night. And many soldiers came in to the meeting and were pretty civil, but the constables and officers of the town came in under pretence to look for a Jesuit whose head was shaved. And so they would have all to put off their hats or else they would take them off to look for the Jesuit's shaven crown. And so they took off my hat (for I was the man they aimed at) and they looked narrowly but not finding any bald or shaven place on my head they went away with shame. And the soldiers and other sober people were grievously troubled at them, but it was of good service for the Lord and all things wrought together for good ⟨for it affected the people⟩. And after, we had a fine meeting, and people were turned to the Lord Jesus Christ their teacher, who would reconcile them to God who had bought them.

And in Somersetshire the Presbyterians and other professors were very wicked and often used to disturb Friends' meetings. And one time there was a wicked man whom they got to come to the meeting, and he set a bear's skin upon his back, and he would go play pranks in the Quakers' General Meeting, which he did, and stood opposite against the Friend that was speaking with his tongue lolling out of his mouth and so made sport to his wicked followers and great disturbance in the meeting. And there was a bull-baiting in the way as he returned from the meeting, and he stayed to see the bull baited; and he coming too near the bull, the bull struck his horn under his throat, and struck his tongue out of his mouth which hung lolling out of his mouth as he had used it in derision before, and struck his horn up into his brain and so swung him about upon his horn. And so he that thought to have done mischief amongst God's people was mischiefed himself.[1]

So we passed from thence through the countries, having many meetings wherein they that were convinced were established and many others added to them.

As we came through the countries we had very precious and blessed meetings amongst Friends till we came to Plymouth, and so up into Cornwall, visiting all the meetings of Friends, among whom we had many blessed meetings, till we came to the Land's End. And through all that county Thomas Lower accompanied me and brought me over Horsebridge into Devonshire again And at Land's End in Cornwall there was an honest man, a fisherman convinced, that became a faithful minister,[2] of whom I told Friends he was like Peter.

[1] The MS. by Ellis Hookes, *Records of Friends' Sufferings*, i, 358, records what is apparently the same incident as taking place at Evershot, Dorset, 29th Apr., 1657. Cf. also Besse: *Sufferings*, i, 166.

[2] Nicholas Jose, of Sennen.

⟨While I was in Cornwall, there were great shipwracks about the Land's End. Now it was the custom of that country that at such a time both rich and poor went out to get as much of the wrack as they could, not caring to save the people's lives; and in some places, they call shipwracks ' God's grace '. It grieved me to hear of such unchristian actions, considering how far they were below the heathen at Malta, who received Paul and made him a fire and were courteous towards him and them that had suffered shipwrack with him. So I was moved to write a paper and send it to all the parishes, priests and magistrates, high and low, to reprove them for such greedy actions and to warn and exhort them that, if they could help to save people's lives and preserve their ships and goods, they should use their diligence therein; and consider, if it had been their own condition, they would judge it hard if they should be upon a wrack, and people should strive to get what they could get from them, and not matter their lives.[1]

This paper had a good service among people. And Friends have endeavoured much to save the lives of the men in times of wracks, and to preserve the ships and goods for them. And when some that have suffered shipwrack have been almost dead and starved, Friends have taken them to their houses to succour them and recover them, which is an act to be practised by all true Christians.⟩

And so after, I had many precious and blessed living meetings in Cornwall; and I left all Friends in peace and quietness; and Friends were glad and refreshed who were turned to Christ, their teacher and saviour, and settled upon him their foundation. And several eminent people there were, long convinced in that county, whom neither priests nor magistrates, by spoiling goods or imprisonments, could make forsake their shepherd, the Lord Jesus Christ, that had bought them. We left them unto the Lord Jesus Christ's teaching and ordering fresh and green, and so came into Devonshire again.

[1] Ellwood, pp. 207(2)-209(2); Bicent., i, 459-61.

And after we had several meetings up and down in Devonshire we came into Somersetshire, where we had several large and peaceable meetings.

And we passed through the country visiting Friends in their meetings till we came to Bristol.[1]

And the Sixth-day before we came, the soldiers with their muskets came to the meeting, for the mayor and the commander of them had combined together to make a disturbance amongst Friends, and the soldiers were exceeding rude and beat and struck Friends with their muskets and drove them out of the orchard in a great rage and threatened what they would do if Friends came again.

And I coming to Bristol the Seventh-day after this, Friends told me what a rage there was in the town and threatenings against them by the mayor[2] and the soldiers and of their cruel carriage the day before to Friends. So I sent for several Friends as George Bishop, Thomas Gouldney, and Thomas Speed, and Edward Pyott, and I desired them to go to the mayor and officers, seeing that he and they had broken up our meetings and made such work in the town, that they would desire the mayor and aldermen that they would let them have the town hall to meet in and Friends would give them £20 a year to be distributed to the poor for the use of it as aforesaid; and when the mayor and aldermen had business they would not meet in it, but only on the First-days.

And Friends were astonished at my sayings and said the mayor and aldermen would think that they were mad: but I said nay, for they should offer them a considerable benefit to the poor. And it was upon me from the Lord to bid them go; and at last they were willing, and went in the cross to their own wills. And when they had laid the thing before the mayor it came so over him that he said for his part he could consent to it, but he was but one. But he told Friends of another great hall they might have, which Friends could not accept, being altogether

[1] March, 1660.
[2] Edward Tyson, merchant, was mayor, 1659-1660.

inconvenient, so Friends came away. And the mayor was very loving to them and they felt the Lord's power had come over all.

And when they came back I spoke to them to go also to the colonel that commanded the soldiers and lay before him the rude carriage of the soldiers, and how that they came armed amongst naked,[1] innocent people that were waiting upon and worshipping the Lord. But I could not get them to go to him.

Then the next First-day we went to the meeting in the orchard where the soldiers had broken the meeting up as aforesaid. And after I had declared the Truth a great while in the meeting there came in many rude soldiers and people, some with drawn swords; and the innkeepers had made some of them drunk, and one of them had bound himself with an oath to kill and cut down that man that spoke. So he came in through all the crowd of people to within two yards of me and stopped at those four Friends aforesaid, that should have gone to the colonel as I would have had them, and fell a-jangling with them, and of a sudden I saw his sword was put up and gone. And the Lord's power came over all and chained him and them and we had a blessed meeting and the Lord's everlasting power and presence was felt amongst us.

So upon the Second-day those four Friends aforesaid went to speak with the colonel, and the colonel sent for the soldiers and cut and slashed some of them before their faces; which when I heard, I reproved Friends for letting him do so, and reproved them for not going the Seventh-day as I would have had them, which would have prevented this cutting of the soldiers, and the trouble of them at our meeting.

And thus the Lord's power came over all those persecuting, bloody minds; and the meetings there were settled in peace for a great while after and were without disturbance.

And I had a General Meeting at Edward Pyott's near

[1] See p. 255.

Bristol where there were many thousands of people, ⟨for, beside Friends from many parts thereabouts some of⟩ the Baptist and Independent teachers came to it and all was quiet, for most of the sober people came out of Bristol to it. And the people that stayed in the city said the city looked naked, the sober people were so gone forth to this meeting. And the Lord's everlasting Seed, Christ Jesus, was set over all that day, and many glorious things and truths were opened to the people, and the Lord Jesus Christ was set up who was the end of all figures and shadows and the law and first covenant. And how that all figures and shadows were given to man after man fell; and how that all these rudiments and inventions of men were set up in Christendom not by the command of Christ, being Jewish and heathenish ceremonies, many of them; and how that all might come to receive Christ Jesus the substance by his light, spirit, grace, and faith, and live and walk in him the redeemer and saviour. And all images and likenesses man has made, either of things in heaven or in earth to himself or for himself, hath been since he lost the image and likeness of God that God made him in. But now Christ was come to redeem, translate, convert, and regenerate man all out of all these things that he hath set up in the Fall, and out of the true types, figures, and shadows, and out of death and darkness, up into the light, and life, and image, and likeness of God again as man and woman were in before they fell.

And a great deal of work we had with the priests and professors pleading for imperfection. But I did let them see how Adam and Eve were perfect before they fell, and all that God made he said that it was good, and he blessed it, and how the imperfection came by the Fall, through man and woman's hearkening to the devil that was out of Truth; and how that the law made nothing perfect but was for the bringing in of the better hope, which hope is Christ who destroys the devil and his works that made man and woman imperfect. And Christ saith, 'Be ye perfect even as my heavenly father is perfect,' for he who was perfect comes to make man and woman perfect again and bring them again to the state God made them in; so he is the maker up of the breach and the peace betwixt God and man. And therefore, ⟨that this might the better be understood by the lowest capacities,⟩ I declared unto them by way of a comparison of two old people that had their house broken down by an enemy so that they with all their children were liable to all storms and tempests, and there came some men that pretended they would build it up if they would give them so much a year, but when they had gotten their money they left their house as they found it.

And so there comes a first, second, third, fourth, fifth, and sixth with this pretence to build up the old house and get people's money, and after, cry they cannot rear up the house nor make up the breach for 'there is no perfection here', cry they; 'the house can never be perfectly built up again,' though they have taken people's money for the doing of it.

For all the sects in Christendom have pretended to build up Adam and Eve's fallen house and when they have got people's money they tell them the house cannot be perfected here: and so their house lies as it did.

But I told them Christ was come freely, who hath perfected for ever by one offering all them that are sanctified, and renews them up in the image of God, as man and woman were in before they fell; and makes man and woman's house as perfect again as God had made them at the first. And this, Christ the heavenly man has done freely. And therefore all are to look unto him, and all that have received him are to walk in him, the life, the substance, the first and the last, the rock of ages and foundation of many generations. And largely were these things and many other things opened and declared unto the people, and the word of life that does abide and live, and all were to hear and obey that did abide and live, by which all might be born again of the immortal Seed, and so to feed of the milk of the word. And a glorious meeting there was and

Friends parted in the power and spirit of the Lord in peace and in his truth that is over all.

⟨About this time the soldiers under General Monk's command were rude and troublesome at Friends' meetings in many places, whereof complaint being made to him, he gave forth the following order, which did somewhat restrain them:

St. James's, 9th of March, 1659 [1660]

I do require all officers and soldiers to forbear to disturb the peaceable meetings of the Quakers; they do nothing prejudicial to the Parliament or Commonwealth of England.

George Monk.⟩

And from Bristol I passed through the countries to Olveston and Nailsworth, and Nathaniel Cripps's where there was a large meeting and several soldiers came, but were quiet.

And so from thence we passed to Gloucester through Friends, visiting their meetings. And after we had our meeting in Gloucester which was peaceable, though the town was very rude and divided, for one part of the soldiers were for the King and another for the Parliament. And as I passed out of the town over the bridge, Edward Pyott was with me, the soldiers there said they were for the King: and after we were passed away and the soldiers understood it was me, they were in a great rage, and said had they known it had been me they would have shot me with hail shot rather than I should have escaped them; but the Lord prevented their devilish design. And so I came to Colonel Grimes's house where we had a large General Meeting, and the Lord's truth and power was set over all, and people were established upon the rock and settled under the Lord Jesus Christ's teaching.

And from thence we passed to Tewkesbury and Evesham and to Worcester and I never saw the like drunkenness as then in these towns, for they had been then choosing Parliament men.[1]

And we visited Friends in all these towns in their meetings,

[1] The Convention Parliament, elected April, 1660.

and the Lord's truth was set over all. And people were finely settled therein; and Friends praised the Lord. Nay, I saw the very earth rejoiced, though great fears were in some people and many asked me what I thought of times and things. And I said unto them, the Lord's light shined over all and his power was set over all.

So from Worcester I came through the countries to Baddesley and then went to Drayton in Leicestershire to visit my relations. There was one Burton, a justice, hearing that I had a good horse, granted out his warrant and came to search for me and my horse three or four days after I was gone; and so he lost and missed his wicked end.

Thence I passed to Twycross and Swannington and so to Derby, and visited Friends. The gaoler[1] that kept me, as aforesaid, at the House of Correction here was now convinced.

And from thence I passed into Nottinghamshire, till I came to Cinder Hill Green, visiting Friends through all these countries in their meetings. And I passed to Balby where was our Yearly Meeting. And many thousands of people and Friends were gathered there. Friends met in a great orchard of John Killam's.

I heard of a troop of horse that was sent from York, about thirty miles off, to break up our meeting and that the new militia was to join with them to break up our meeting. And I went into the meeting and stood on a great stool; and two trumpeters came up sounding their trumpets pretty close to me: and the ⟨captain of the troopers⟩ cried, ' Divide to the left hand and right hand and make way '; and they rid up to me, and I was declaring in the mighty power of the Lord the everlasting Truth and word of life. And the captain of the troop bid me come down for he was come to disperse our meeting. And I told him he and they knew that we were a peaceable people and we used to have such great meetings, and if he did question that we met in a hostile way I desired him to make search amongst us, and if he found either sword or pistol about

[1] Thomas Sharman. See p. 57-8.

any there, let us suffer. Our meeting was made acquainted a great while before, and it was of no hurt to the powers.

So he told me he must see us dispersed for he came all night of purpose to disperse us. But I told him, what honour would it be to him to ride with swords and pistols amongst so many naked[1] men and women as there were. And if he would be still and quiet our meeting might not continue passing two or three hours; and when our meeting was done, as we came peaceably and civilly together, so we should part. For he might perceive that the meeting was so large that all that country thereabouts could not entertain them but that they intended to depart towards their homes at night.

And he said he could not stay, he must disperse them before he went. So I desired him if he could not stay to let a dozen of his soldiers stay and see the order and peaceableness of our meeting; so he permitted us an hour's time and left half a dozen soldiers to stay with us. So the Friends of the house gave the soldiers that stayed and their horses meat. And the captain went away.

And the soldiers that were left told us we might stay till night if we would, so we stayed about two or three hours and had a glorious powerful meeting.

And the presence of the living God was manifest amongst us. And the Seed, Christ, was set over all; and Friends were settled upon him, the foundation, and under his glorious heavenly teaching, and were all glad and refreshed that the Lord's power had given them such dominion.

And after the meeting was done Friends passed away in peace and joy, being refreshed with the presence of the Lord.

And the militia soldiers many of them stayed also, and were very much vexed because the captain and troopers had not broken up our meeting that day, and cursed the captain and the troopers. For it was reported that they intended to have made a massacre upon us that day, and the troopers, instead of assisting them, they were rather

[1] See p. 255.

assistant to us in preventing them from doing mischief and not joining with them.

This captain was a desperate man, for he had said to me in Scotland[1] he would obey commands, if it were to crucify Christ he would do it, or the great Turk's command against the Christians, if he was under him. But it was asked of him where was then his Christianity. But the Lord's power chained them all both troopers and the militia so as they went away, not having power to hurt us. And one of the troopers said, 'Here are more people flock after him than are about my Lord Protector's court.'

And the next day we had a heavenly meeting at Warmsworth of Friends in the ministry and several others; and then Friends parted, and as they passed through the countries several were taken up, for that day that our first meeting was held Lambert was routed.[2] And it made a great blunder in the country, but Friends were not kept long in prison at that time.

And at Skegby[3] in Nottinghamshire there came several that were going to be soldiers under Lambert and would have bought my horse; and because I would not sell him to them they were in a rage against me, using many threatening words; but I told them, and writ to them, that God would confound them and scatter them. And so they were, about two or three days afterwards. So the Lord's power came over all.

And from Warmsworth aforesaid in the Lord's power I passed through the country to Burton Abbey[4] where I had a great meeting; and from thence to Thomas Taylor's[5] and to Skipton where there was a General Meeting of men Friends.

And there a Friend declared naked through the town and they had much beat him and some other Friends, who came

[1] See p. 320.

[2] Lambert was defeated on Easter Monday, 22nd Apr., 1660.

[3] Fox was at Skegby in Apl., 1660.

[4] Monk Bretton.

[5] At Carlton in Craven.

to me all bloody. And as I walked in the street there was a desperate fellow which had an intent to have done me a mischief but he was prevented and our meeting was quiet.

And at this meeting some Friends did come out of most parts of the nation, for it was about business of the church both in this nation and beyond the seas.[1] For when I was in the north, several years before, I was moved to set up that meeting, for many Friends suffered and their goods were spoiled wrongfully, contrary to the law. And so several Friends that had been justices and magistrates and that did understand the law came there and were able to inform Friends, and to gather up the sufferings that they might be laid before the justices and judges.

And justices and captains had come to break up this meeting, but when they saw Friends' books and accounts of collections concerning the poor, how that we did take care one county to help another, ⟨and to provide for our poor that none of them should be chargeable to their parishes, etc.,⟩ and took care to help Friends beyond the seas, the justices and officers were made to confess that we did their work and Friends desired them to come and sit with them then.

And so they passed away lovingly and commended Friends' practice.

And many times there would be two hundred beggars of the world there, for all the country knew we met about the poor; wherefore after the meeting was done Friends would send to the bakers and give them each a penny loaf apiece, be they as many as they would; for we were taught to do good unto all but especially to the household of faith.

And this was the last General Meeting that Friends had there; and then Friends were turned all to the Quarterly and Monthly Meetings as aforesaid, there to do their business. And many precious papers may be seen that were given forth from this Meeting, as in the books of Epistles may be seen; and the manner of their collections.

And so from thence I passed through the countries

[1] 25th Apr., 1660.

visiting Friends in their meetings till I came to Lancaster and so I passed to Robert Widders's, and from thence to Arnside where I had a General Meeting for all the Friends in those countries, as Westmorland, Cumberland, and Lancashire.

And after the meeting was done, which was peaceable and quiet, and the living presence of the Lord was amongst us, there came several rude fellows from one Middleton,[1] a great man, ⟨to make some disturbance, as it was thought,⟩ but the meeting being ended they did nothing. But one of them set upon three women, and with impudent scoffs said he would kiss one of them; and did pluck her coats loose and abuse them and wrong them.[2] The same man did abuse Friends, and would have cut Friends with an axe but that he was restrained by some of his fellows.

Another time the same knight's man, whose name is Thomas, set upon six Friends going to a meeting to wait upon the Lord at Yelland. He beat them and abused them with bruising of their faces, and shed much of their blood, and wounded them sore. And they never lifted a hand against him, but gave him their backs and cheeks.

I passed after the meeting to Robert Widders's; and Friends all passed away fresh in the life and power of Christ. The next day I came to Swarthmoor, and Francis Howgill and Thomas Curtis were with me. [a]And this was the third time I had been most part about the nation.[a]

[1] Sir George Middleton, of Leighton Hall, a justice.

[2] The account of this incident is dated 13th May, 1660.

[a]. . . . . .[a] *S.J.*, p. 56.

CHAPTER XVII

WHEN I had stayed about a month at Swarthmoor and thataways, after King Charles had come into England,[1] one called Justice Porter[2] with four or five more of the magistrates gave forth a warrant to the chief constable to apprehend me.

I felt something of darkness in the house before they came, something of a great darkness. So the next day after I had felt that, the chief constable with three or four more petty constables came to Swarthmoor pretending to search the house for arms, and they went up into some of the chambers.

I was in the parlour and Richard Richardson was with me. And Margaret Fell, unto whom some of her servants had brought word, came in and told me, and I said, 'It is a plot.' And it came upon me to go out. And I called for a friend but he did not come, so I went back again to call him and so met the constables coming down the stairs; and as I was going by them I spoke some words to them; and the chief constable stepped to me, and asked me my name, and I told him freely, and then they laid hold of me and said I was the man they looked for. And I desired to see their order, and they would not show it, though after a time they did show it, with five or six names and seals at it.

Then they led me away to Ulverston and there kept me all night at a constable's house, and set a guard of fifteen or sixteen men to watch me. And some of them sat in the chimney; they were afraid I would go up the chimney, the Lord's power so terrified them. I told them I could have

[1] The King landed 25th May, 1660.

[2] Major Henry Porter (1613-1666), constable of Lancaster Castle, sometime Mayor of Lancaster, and member of Parliament.

escaped them if I would. And so I sat up all night. They were very rude and uncivil to me and to Friends and would scarce let any come in to me and would not suffer them to bring me necessaries, but with violence thrust out Friends.

And the next morning about the sixth hour I was putting on my boots and spurs ⟨to go with them before some justice⟩ and they pulled off my spur and took my knife out of my pocket and so took me along the town with a matter of thirty horse and foot, and abundance of people; and they would not stay till my horse came down.

So I went about a quarter of a mile; and some considerable Friends and Margaret Fell and the children came towards me. And a great party of horse gathered about me and cried, 'Would they rescue him; would they rescue him?' and were mad in fury and rage. So I said to them, 'Here is my back, here is my cheek, strike on.' At which words their heat assuaged.

Then they set me upon a poor little horse with a halter upon his head; two took me by one leg and put my foot in the stirrup and two or three by the other, and set me up behind the saddle, and so led me by the halter, and I had nothing to hold by. So when they were come a pretty way out of the town they beat the poor little horse and made him kick and gallop. And I lighted off him and told them they should not abuse the creature, at which they mightily raged. And they came again and took me by the feet and set me upon the horse behind the saddle and led the horse with a halter about two miles till they came to the Carter-ford.

Then my own horse came and they let me get upon him, through the persuasion of some of their own company, and they led me through the water. The water being deep the other horse would scarce have carried me over. They pulled off the bridle and led my horse in a halter a matter of fourteen miles till I came to Lancaster.[1]

A great noise they made and very rude and wicked they

[1] The passage from the beginning of the chapter to this point draws upon *Camb. Jnl.*, i, 358, 359, 367, 368; *S.J.*, pp. 56, 57.

were. One of the constables, one Ashburner, said that he did not think a thousand men could have taken me, and one Mount, a very wicked constable, said he would have served Judge Fell so if he had a warrant for him and if he had been alive. And there was one wicked fellow kneeled down and lifted up his hands and blessed God that I was taken; and a great triumph they thought to have had. And as they led me I was moved to sing praises unto the Lord in his triumphing power over all.

When I came over the Sands I told them I had liberty to choose my justice, and might go before whom I would, but Mount and the other constables raged and said I should not.

So to Lancaster they brought me and the spirits of people being mightily up when I came in the town, I stood and looked upon them and they cried, 'Look at his eyes'; and after a while I spoke to them and they were pretty sober. And then a young man came and had me to his house. And after a while they had me to Major Porter's house, called a justice, and several others were with him.

When I came in I said, 'Peace be among you'; and I began to ask him wherefore he sent out his warrant for me, and showed him the abuse of the constables and the other officers towards me, and told him I was a peaceable man and we were a peaceable people.

And Porter asked me why I came down into the country that troublesome time. I told him, to visit my brethren.

He said we had great meetings up and down; and I told him we had so, but I said our meetings were known throughout the nation to be peaceable.

He said he might restrain me, and I asked him for what.

He would not tell me the King's secrets; he said we saw the Devil in people's faces. I told him if I saw a drunkard or a swearer or peevish, heady man I could not say I saw the Spirit of God; and I asked him if he could see the Spirit of God.

He said we cried against their ministers, and I told him while we were as Saul, sitting under the priests and running up and down with his packet of letters, we were never called pestilent fellows nor makers of sects. But when we were come to exercise our consciences towards God and man, then we were called pestilent fellows as Paul was.

He said we could lay open ourselves,[1] he was a fool to talk to me. So he told me he would not dispute with me, but he had an old clerk though he was a young justice. 'Come', says he, 'is the mittimus ready, and where is his horse, he hath a good horse I hear, have you brought his horse?' So I told him where the horse was, but he did not meddle with him. So I desired to know of him for what offence and on what order. And he said he had an order from the Sheriff of Middlesex but he would not let me have it, and said moreover a prisoner was not to see for what he was committed. I told him that was not reason, how should he make his defence then, I ought to have a copy of it. So he sent for the gaoler and commanded him to put me in the dark house and keep me a close prisoner and to let none come at me and there to keep me till delivered by the King or Parliament.[2]

As I went to the gaol the constable gave me my knife again and asked me to give it to him, and I told him, nay, he had not been so civil to me. And the under-gaoler, one Hardy, a wicked man, was exceeding rude and many times would not let me have meat but under the door, but the Lord's power was over all. And many of the world came to me in great rage and were very uncivil and rude. And one time two young priests came who were very abusive and rude; the worst of people could not be worse. And there came old Preston's wife, of Holker, and a great company with her and she used many abusive words to me and told me my tongue should be cut out and I should be hanged. But the Lord God cut her off and she died in a miserable condition.

⟨I sent Thomas Cummings and Thomas Green to the gaoler to desire a copy of my mittimus that I might know

[1] i.e. express ourselves clearly.

[2] Fox was committed 5th Jun., and finally liberated 25th Oct., 1660.

wherefore I was committed. The gaoler answered he could not give a copy of it for another had been fined for the like. But he gave them liberty to read it over, wherein it was charged against me, to the best of their remembrances, to this effect:

That I was a person suspected to be a disturber of the peace of the nation, a common enemy to His Majesty our lord the King, a chief upholder of the Quakers' sect, and that I, together with others of our fanatic opinion had of late endeavoured to raise insurrections in this part of the country to the imbrueing the nation in blood, with command to the gaoler to keep me in safe custody till I should be released by order from the King and Parliament.〉

The heads of the mittimus were answered as followeth and sent to the King.

I am a prisoner at Lancaster by Justice Porter. A copy of the mittimus I cannot get. But such like expressions are found in it which are untruths.

First, that I am suspected to be a disturber of the nation's peace, unto the King an enemy, and that I and others of my company should raise insurrections to imbrue the nation in blood.

All which is false and I do deny every word in it to be truth, for through the nation I have been tried of these things formerly. In the days of Oliver I was taken up as raising arms against him, which was false, and I was taken up to London and kept prisoner till I was brought before him, when things were cleared. And I denied drawing a carnal weapon against him or any man upon the earth, for my weapons are spiritual, that take away the occasion of war and which lead into peace.

And after that Major Ceely in Cornwall, who sent me to prison, when I was brought before the judge, said that I took him aside and told him I could raise four thousand men in one hour, which was false and a lie and was then proved so to him, for such words I never spoke to him. I never was found in any plots, nor ever took any engagement, nor never took any oath, nor never learned war postures.

So these things come from Major Porter, who is lately appointed to be a Justice, who hath wanted power formerly to exercise his cruelty against us, and are but the wickedness of the old enemy. For the peace of this nation I am not a disturber of, but seek the peace of it and of all men, and stand for all nations' and men's peace upon the earth, and wish that all nations and men knew my innocency in these things.

And whereas Major Porter saith I am a common enemy to the King, that is false; for my love is to him and all men, though they be enemies to God and to themselves and to me. And I can say it is of the Lord that the King is come in, to bring down many unrighteously set up, of which I had a sight before he came in, three years. It's much he should say I am an enemy to the King, for which I have no reason, he having done nothing against me. Yet I have been imprisoned and persecuted this eleven or twelve years by them that have been against the King's father and him, which was the party that Porter was made a major by and bore arms for, and not them that were for the King. I was never a common enemy to the King nor to any man's person upon the earth. But I am in the love that fulfils the law and thinks no evil, but loves enemies, and would have the King saved and come to the knowledge of the Truth, and brought in to the fear of the Lord, and to receive his wisdom from above by which all things were made and created, that with that wisdom he may order all things to the glory of God by whom it was created. I owe nothing to the King but love, nor to any man, and love doth not kill but fulfil the law.

He saith further: a chief upholder of the Quakers' sect. The Quakers are not a sect but are in the power of God before sects were and witness the election before the world began and come to live in the life as the prophets and apostles did, that gave forth Scriptures. Therefore are we hated by envious, wrathful, wicked, and persecuting men. But God is the upholder of us all by his mighty power from the wrath of the wicked that would swallow us up.

And Major Porter further saith that I together with others of my fanatic opinion have of late endeavoured to raise insurrections in this part of the country, to the imbrueing this nation in blood. This is false. To these things I am as a child and know nothing of them and never learned the postures of war. And my weapons are spiritual and not carnal and with carnal weapons I do not fight and my kingdom is not of this world, saith Christ. And those that follow Christ in the spirit, the captain of their salvation, deny the carnal weapons, who deny drawing any carnal weapons against the King or the Parliament or any man upon the earth. Yet we have these lies and slanders laid upon us by Porter and his company that have drawn swords against the King, we who are come to the end of the law, who love enemies and wrestle not with flesh and blood and are in that which saves men's lives. And I witness against all murderous plots and all such as would imbrue the nation in blood, which be not in peace, and I am innocent of all these things and I know them not, and it is not in my heart to have any man's life destroyed upon the earth.

And Major Porter told me he imprisoned me to prevent a danger because times were troublesome and that we had meetings by hundreds. I told him we had kept our meetings in most parts of the nation to wait upon the Lord, but neither he nor any man in the nation had any occasion to suspect me of any tumultuous meetings or to raise any tumults in the nation who am a peaceable man and desire the peace and good of all and had not gone from the place where I was apprehended passing two miles, in a month since I came into the country.

And as for *fanatic*, which is furious, foolish, mad, enraged, he might have considered himself before he spoke this, and learned the humility which goes before the honour. For we through patience and meekness have borne lies, slanders, and persecutions many years, and undergone great sufferings.

And such as report these things have striven by them to take away the life of the innocent from the earth, who wrestle with spiritual weapons and not with flesh and blood, but wrestle with the power of darkness that leads from God, who save men's lives and bring them back again to God, and are in the love that thinks no evil, but loves enemies.

Such be not in a fanatic spirit. But such as are furious, like Nebuchadnezzar, and as mad as the Jews and Saul against Christ and the apostles, are not in the love to enemies, nor in the spirit which leads from under the law, nor the love which fulfils it, but are in the fanatic spirit.

And Major Porter proffered the oath of allegiance to me to take and I told him I never took oath in my life of one side or the other, against or for myself, but did abide in Christ's doctrine, who saith ' swear not at all ', and did suffer in that. And all people that have but the least soberness in them may see this to be but malice and envy of Major Porter in prisoning and persecuting of me and laying such things to my charge up and down the country, which I am innocent of as a child. And so

I am ordered to be kept prisoner till I be delivered by order from the King or Parliament.

These things are ordered to be delivered to you, to be laid afore you to consider of, before you act anything, that you may in the wisdom of the Lord consider the intent and end of men's spirits, lest you act that thing that will bring the hand of the Lord God against you and upon you, as many have done before you that have been in authority, whom God hath overthrown, whom we trust unto and fear and cry unto day and night, who hath heard us and doth hear us and will hear us, and avenge our cause. For much innocent blood hath been shed and many have been persecuted to death by such as have been in authority before you, who turned against the just, whom the Lord hath vomited out, therefore consider with yourselves, for now you have the day.

From the innocent, a sufferer in bonds, a close prisoner in Lancaster Castle, called George Fox.

⟨Upon my being taken and forcibly carried away from Margaret Fell's house, and charged with things of so high a nature, she was concerned, as looking upon it to be an injury offered to herself. Whereupon she writ the following lines and sent them abroad, directed thus:⟩

To all Magistrates concerning the wrong taking up and imprisoning of George Fox at Lancaster.

I do inform the governors of this nation, that Henry Porter, mayor of Lancaster, sent a warrant with four constables to my house, for which he had no authority or order. And they searched my house, and apprehended a man in it, which was not guilty of the breach of any law, nor guilty of any offence to any in the nation. And after they had apprehended him and brought him before Porter, there was bail offered, what he would demand, for his appearance to answer what could be laid to his charge; but he (contrary to law, if he had taken him lawfully) denied any bail and clapped him up in close prison. After he was in prison a copy of his mittimus was demanded, which ought not to be denied to any prisoner, nor no lawful magistrate will, that so he may see what is laid to his charge. But it was denied him; a copy of it he could not have, only they were suffered to read it over. And every word that was there charged against him was utterly false; and he was not guilty of any one charge in it. This will be proved and manifested to the nation. So let the governors consider of it. I am concerned in the thing, inasmuch as he was apprehended in my house; and if he be guilty I am so too. So I desire to have this searched out. Margaret Fell.[1]

And Margaret Fell went to London and spoke with the King about my taking, and showed him the manner of it and offered up her life to the King to stand as a pledge for the peace and quietness of all Friends and for their faith. And when Margaret went to London, Justice Porter vapored that he would go and meet her in the gap.[2] But when he came before the King, he having been a zealous man for the Parliament, several spoke to him concerning the plundering of their houses, so that he soon returned again into the country.

And the gaoler was very fearful and said he was afraid Major Porter would hang him because he had not put me in the dark house. And the gaoler going to see him after he came home, he was blank and quite down, and asked how I was, and pretended a way to set me at liberty, but having overshot himself in his mittimus, that I was not to be delivered but by the King or Parliament, he had put me out of his power.

And when he was in the height of his rage and threats against me I was moved to write a letter to him seeing that he appeared so zealous for the King and thought to ingratiate himself into the King's favour by imprisoning of me. I asked him whose great buck-horns were those in his house and whence he had them and where had he that wainscot that he ceiled his house withal? Had he it not from Hornby Castle that was the King's?

And did not Major Porter say that he would neither leave them cat nor dog if they would not bring in provision to him in Lancaster Castle when he held it for the Parliament against the King, he was such a fierce rigid man?

And after he had received this letter it brought him

[1] Spence MSS., iii, 105.

[2] i.e. a breach in defences.

down, who pretended now to be so zealous for the King and yet was so fierce formerly against him, who had cast me into prison as an enemy to the King and for raising new war and imbrueing the whole nation in blood, I and my faculty, as he pretended. And yet I never had taken up arms against the King in my life, but was cast into Derby dungeon six months together because I would not take up arms against the King.

And after a time of imprisonment, Ann Curtis came down from Reading to the prison at Lancaster to visit me. And it was upon her also to go to the King; for her father,[1] that had been sheriff of Bristol, the Parliament had hanged near his own door ⟨for endeavouring to bring the King in; upon which consideration she had some hopes that the King might hear her on my behalf. Accordingly when she returned to London⟩ she and Margaret Fell went together to Whitehall to the King,[2] with the answer to my mittimus. And Ann Curtis made him to know whose daughter she was, whereupon he showed much love to her. And she said she had now a request to him. He asked her what it was. She desired of the King that I might be brought up and my accusers, and he himself might be judge in the thing. And he said he would take order with the secretary and upon his word it should be done. ⟨But when they came to the secretary for the order, he, being no friend to us, said it was not in his power, but that he must go according to law, and I must be brought up by a habeas corpus before the judges.⟩ So the secretary brought an order to Judge Mallet and sent for me up by habeas corpus. So it came down into the country to bring me up; ⟨but because it was directed to the Chancellor of Lancaster, the sheriff put it off to him; on the other hand, the chancellor would not make the warrant upon it, but said the sheriff must do that. At length both chancellor and sheriff were got together; but being both enemies to Truth, they sought occasion for delay, and found, they said, an error in the

[1] Robert Yeamans, Sheriff, 1641-42, hanged for royalist action, 1643.
[2] 17th July, 1660.

writ, which was, that being directed to the chancellor, it stated, 'George Fox in prison under *your* custody', whereas the prison I was in was not, they said, in the chancellor's custody, but in the sheriff's; so the word *your* should have been *his*. Upon this they returned the writ to London, only to have that one word altered. When it was altered, and came down again,⟩ they would have had me seal and be bound, and to have paid for sealing and for charges of carrying me up. So then I told them I would seal none, I would pay none, nor would be bound. [a]So ⟨the matter rested a while, and⟩ I was kept in prison till towards Michaelmas.[a] ⟨Meanwhile the Assize came on; inasmuch as there was a writ come down for removing me up, I was not brought before the judge.⟩ At the Assizes many people came to see me; and I was moved of the Lord God to speak out of the gaol window to them and many people stood attentive to it.

And I let them see how uncertain their religion was, how that people had been persecuted for not following the Mass, and they that did hold up the Mass cried then, it was the higher power, and people must be subject to the higher power.

And then they that held up the Common Prayer and persecuted others for not following it, they said it was the higher power. Then also that we must be subject to it. And so did the Presbyterian and Independents. They cried we must be subject to the higher power also, and submit to their *Directory* and *Church Faith*. So all cried like the Jews, 'Help, men of Israel', against the true Christians. And so people might see how uncertain they are of their religions; and so I turned them to Christ Jesus that they might be built upon him their rock and foundation that changeth not. And after I had declared much to them on this wise they all were quiet.

Afterwards I gave forth a little paper concerning true religion, and another paper against persecution.[1]

[1] Ellwood, 223(2), 224(2); Bicent., i, 481-2.
[a]. . . . . .[a] *S.J.*, p. 57.

Whilst yet I was kept in Lancaster gaol, I was moved to give forth the following paper for the staying the minds of any such as might be hurried or troubled about the change of Government:

All Friends, let the dread and majesty of God fill you. And as concerning the changing of times and Governments, let not that trouble any of you, for God hath a mighty work and hand therein. And he will yet change again until that come up which must reign; and in vain shall powers and armies withstand the Lord, for his determined work shall come to pass. But what is now come up, it is just with the Lord that it should be so, and he will be served by it. Therefore let none murmur nor distrust God; for God will provoke many to zeal against unrighteousness, and for righteousness, through things which are suffered now to work for a season. . . . G.F.[1]

⟨I was moved also to write to the King, both to exhort him to exercise mercy and forgiveness towards his enemies and to warn him to restrain the profaneness and looseness that was gotten up in the nation upon his return.⟩

King Charles, thou came not into this nation by sword, and not by victory of war, but by the power of the Lord. Now if thou do not live in it, thou wilt not prosper. . . . So hear and consider, and do good in the time, whilst thou hast power, and be merciful and forgive; and that is the way to overcome, and obtain the kingdom of Christ. G.F.[2]

After great sufferings and reproaches the sheriff sent to me that I might give in bond to appear at London according to the habeas corpus for removal of me to the King's Bench. But I sent him word I should not give him any bond, for if I was the man as they represented me and my faculty I had need of a troop or two of horse with me to guard me. And then they concluded to send me up with a party of horse; but after, when they had considered what charges it would be to them, they concluded to send me up guarded by the gaoler and some

[1] In full, Ellwood, pp. 224(2), 225(2); Bicent., i, 482-3.

[2] In full, *Camb. Jnl.*, i, 361-2; Ellwood, p. 225(2); Bicent., i, 483.

bailiffs; and after, they thought again that it would be great charges to them also, they sent for me down from the prison to the gaoler's house, and said to me if I would put in bail that I would be in London by such a day of the term, I might have leave to go up with some of my own friends.

But I told them I would neither put in any bail nor give one piece of silver to the gaoler, for I was an innocent man and they had imprisoned me wrongfully and put a false charge upon me. Nevertheless, if they would let me go up with one or two of my own friends to bear me company, I might go up and be in London such a day if the Lord did permit, and I would carry my own charge or any of my friends that went with me against myself.

So they consented and I came out of prison[1] and came to Swarthmoor, and stayed there two or three days.

And from thence I went to Lancaster and so to Preston, and had meetings amongst Friends; and so came into Cheshire to William Gandy's, where was a large meeting without doors and the Lord's everlasting seed was set over all. And Friends were turned to it who are heirs of the promise.

And from thence I passed through the countries into Staffordshire and Warwickshire till I came to Anthony Bickley's, and at Nuneaton at a priest's widow's house we had a blessed meeting and the everlasting word of life was declared to them and many settled in it.

And from thence I passed through the countries visiting the meetings of Friends; in about three weeks time ⟨from my coming out of prison⟩ I came to London; and Richard Hubberthorne was with me and Robert Widders.

And when I came to Charing Cross there were multitudes of people gathered together to the burning of the bowels of them that had been the old King's judges, that had been hanged, drawn, and quartered.

And I sent to the King that I was come up according to his order, if he would speak with me, or I might come

[1] 24th Sept., 1660.

and speak with him. And we went to Judge Mallett's[1] chamber; and he was putting on his red gown in the morning to go to sit upon some more of the King's judges; and he was very peevish and froward and said I might come another time.

And we went another time to his chamber, and when I came to him again he called for the Chief Justice of England, Lord Chief Justice Foster[2] so called, and we delivered him the charge that was against me, and they read it. And one Esquire Marsh[3] was with me, one of the King's bed-chamber men. As they read those words, that I and my faculty were raising a new war and imbrueing the kingdom into blood, and an enemy to the King, they lift up and struck their hands on the table. So I told them I was the man that charge was against. They were exceeding rough at the first; but after I had spoken to the charge and told them I was as innocent of any such thing as a new-born child, and had brought it up myself and some of my faculty came with me, and left it to them and bid them do what they would, they said they desired none of these things might be found true that were charged against me. They did not accuse me, nor had nothing against me.

And as yet they had not minded my hat, but at last, seeing my hat on, they said, 'What!' did I stand with my hat on; but I told them I did not stand so in any contempt to them; and then they commanded one to take it off. Then they called for the marshal of the King's Bench and when he came they bid him use me kindly and said, 'You must take this man and secure him, but you must let him have a chamber and not put him amongst the prisoners.' 'But', says the marshal of the King's Bench, 'my Lord, I have no chamber for to put him into, my house is so full'; so he said he could not tell where to provide a room for me but amongst the prisoners: 'But', said the judges, 'you must not put him amongst the prisoners'; but he still answered he had no other place to put me in.

1 Sir Thomas Mallett (1582-1665).
2 Sir Robert Foster (1589-1663).
3 Richard Marche (*c.* 1589-1672).

Then said Judge Foster to me, 'Will you appear tomorrow about the tenth hour at the King's Bench Bar in Westminster Hall?' For there, they said, they had more authority. And I said, 'Yes, if the Lord give me strength.' Then said Foster, 'If he says yes and promises it you may take his word.'

So I appeared at the King's Bench in Westminster Hall at the hour appointed, before the Chief Justice and two or three other judges. And Robert Widders and Richard Hubberthorne and Esquire Marsh went along with me. And [b]I was in a-top of the board where the parchments lie;[b] and Robert Widders delivered their papers to them.

And I was brought into the middle of the court; and as soon as I was come in I was moved to look about and turn towards the people. And I said, 'Peace be among you'; and the power of the Lord sprung over. The same words I was moved to speak when I came before Porter, and the second time I was with the judge before the Chief Justice, and raised up the power. And the people were very moderate and the judges very cool and loving; and a great day of the Lord's mercy it was to them.

And after I had been awhile in the court the charge against me was read openly, how that I and my faculty, as aforesaid, were raising a new war to imbrue the whole nation in blood, and an enemy to the King; and as they read it they lifted up their hands. [b]And when they had read the charge there was no accuser appeared.[b] And I stretched forth my arms and said I was the man it was laid against, and desired that I might speak for myself. And I told them I was as innocent and clean and pure as a child from these things, for I never learned the postures of war, and I loved all men; I was enemy to no man. And was it a likely thing that, had I been such a man, I should be sent up with two of my own faculty a matter of two hundred miles by the magistrates and sheriff and officers of Lancashire? Were the magistrates of Lancashire

[b]......[b] *S.J.*, p. 58.

faithful to their trust that sent up a man accused of such things with a simple countryman or two? I had need to have had two or three troops of horse to have come along with me if such things could be proved. And I asked them if that did not convince their reason.

And then after many other words which we had in soberness and peace the judge asked me whether it should be filed, or what I would do with it.

But I answered and said, 'You are judges and able to judge in this matter. Do with it what you will. I am the man these charges are against, I have brought it up myself. Do you what you will, I leave it to you.'

So Judge Twysden[1] began to speak some angry words.

And then I appealed to Chief Justice Foster and Judge Mallet that heard me overnight, who said they did not accuse me, they had nothing against me.

Then there stood up in the court Esquire Marsh of the King's bed-chamber, and said it was the King's pleasure I should be set at liberty, seeing no accuser was come up against me.

And they asked me whether I would put it to the King and Council.

And I told them, 'With all my heart.'

Then they said it should be sent to the King's Council; but mighty travails there were before the invisible power wrought through them, which brought them into soberness to clear my innocency.

⟨So they sent the sheriff's return, which he made to the writ of habeas corpus, containing the matter charged against me in the mittimus, to the King, that he might see for what I was committed.[2] So the matter was sent to the King and Council, and after it had its work through them and among them, the next day the King, by his secretary Sir Edward Nicholas,[3] sent his warrant to Judge Mallet

1 Sir Thomas Twysden (1602-1683).

2 Ellwood, pp. 228(2); Bicent., i, 487; *Camb. Jnl.*, i, 371.

3 (1593-1669), Secretary of State to Charles II.

that I should be set at full liberty,[1] and the judge gave forth a second warrant to Sir John Lenthall,[2] the Marshal of the King's Bench, that I should be set at liberty.[3]

And so I was set at liberty[4] over the heads of my persecutors by the King and his Council after I had been a prisoner somewhat more than twenty weeks⟩, and the Lord's power and truth came over all, to his everlasting praise.

And there was a company of envious, wicked spirits were troubled, that I was set at liberty, who were not of the King's party. And then fear and terror took hold of Justice Porter, that I would take advantage of the law upon him and undo him and his wife and children for my wrong imprisonment. ⟨And indeed I was put on by some in authority to make him and the rest examples⟩, but I said I should leave him to the Lord; if the Lord did forgive him, I should not trouble myself with him.

And though he was mayor of Lancaster and a justice of peace of the county: and entertained the judges at his house yet after this the Lord cut him off and his wife was cast into Lancaster prison for debt, where her husband had cast me.

And this Judge Mallett was a cruel man and not long after he died: and Judge Foster became a very bitter cruel man and persecuted and premunired Friends and the Lord cut him off also: and then there came in another Lord Chief Justice, worse than Foster for persecuting our Friends, and the Lord cut him off also.

And the Lord cut off that wicked Constable Mount, and the high constable and the other constable's wife.

[1], [3] These documents printed in Ellwood, pp. 228(2), 229(2); Bicent., i, 487-8; *Camb. Jnl.*, i, 371-2. The second is dated 25th Oct., 1660.

[2] (1625-1681) knighted by both Cromwell and Charles II. Son of Speaker William Lenthall.

[4] On 25th Oct., 1660.

CHAPTER XVIII

AND when I was set at liberty the Lord's power, truth, and life, and light shined over the nation, and that which I had travailed for in my sufferings at Reading now was come over all; and glorious great meetings we had and the everlasting Truth shined and many flocked into Truth. And the priests began to be afraid, for the Common Prayer began to be set up again. And the Presbyterians with their *Directory* and Independents with their *Church Faith* came to be laid aside.

The Independents, Baptists, and Presbyterians had a tenderness at their first rise, and cried tithes were antichristian, and were called housecreepers, but when they were got up and got many members, they began to make laws and orders and said, 'Hitherto shalt thou go.' And when they got farther into the outward power, then they all got into steeplehouses and tithes; and then these things were *jure divino* with them, and for God and the church, as though God or the Church of Christ had need of earthly tithes. But had they said they had been *jure humano* we could better have believed them.

And then they began to imprison and persecute Friends because that we would not give them tithes, and many thousands of our Friends in their days suffered imprisonments. And many thousand pounds worth of goods were taken away from them, so that they made many widows and fatherless, for many died in prison that they had caused to be cast into prison.

But when the King came in, they were, most of them, turned out of their place, both magistrates and priests (but those that conformed), and that which they had persecuted us for not conforming unto, to wit their *Church Faith* and their *Directory*, they durst not stand to themselves.

But some of them conformed to the Common Prayer: and some of their hearers said they must be content with bread made of peas if they could not get wheat bread. But God brought his judgements upon all those persecuting priests and magistrates, that when the King came in they were turned out of their places and benefices, and thus the spoilers were spoiled, though I and my friends were moved to warn Oliver Cromwell and his Parliaments and courts and magistrates and priests, of the Lord's day, long before it came upon them. And for so doing many times they would cast us in prison, and abuse us, and call us giddy-headed Quakers. But when the King came in we asked them, who were the giddy-heads now.

And many then did confess we had been true prophets to the nation; and had we cried against some priests they would have liked us, but, seeing we cried against all, they disliked us; but now they did see that those priests that were looked upon then to be the best were as bad as the worst, and this, when the judgements and day of the Lord were come upon them, some of them were made to confess.

And Richard Hubberthorne was with the King;[1] and the King said none should molest us so we lived peaceably, and promised it upon the word of a King to us and that we should make such use of his promise.

And about this time the King was willing that one sort of the dissenting people should have their liberty and that we might have it as soon as any because they were sensible of our sufferings in the former power's days. But when it was going forward, one or other dirty spirits, that seemed to be for us, put in papers and set stop to it.

And some Friends had their liberty to go into the House of Lords before them and the Bishops; so Friends had their liberty to declare their reasons why they could not pay tithes, nor swear, nor join with the other worships, nor go to the steeplehouses; and they heard them very moderately; a favour which in the other power's days we could never have.

[1] 4th June, 1660.

Though in the other power's days two women did present the testimonies of above seven thousand women's hands against tithes, and the reasons why they could not hold up the priests that took tithes now; and how that Christ had ended the Jewish priesthood, etc.; but nothing did these powers in the thing.[1]

Though Oliver Cromwell at Dunbar fight had promised to the Lord that if he gave him the victory over his enemies he would take away tithes or else let him be rolled into his grave with infamy, when the Lord had given his victory and he came to be chief, he confirmed the former laws that if people did not set forth their tithes they should pay treble, and this to be executed by two justices of peace in the country upon the oath of two witnesses.

But when the King came in they took him up and hanged him, and buried him under Tyburn, where he was rolled into his grave with infamy. And when I saw him hanging there I saw his word justly come upon him.

There were about seven hundred Friends in prison in the nation, upon contempts to Oliver's and Richard's government; and when the King came in he set them all at liberty. It was said there was something drawn up that we should have our liberty, only it wanted signing. [a]And then the Fifth-Monarchy people rose and a matter of thirty of them made an insurrection in London.[a][2] On the First-day there were glorious meetings and the Lord's truth shined over all and his power was set over all. And at midnight, soon after, the drums beat and they cried, 'Arms, arms!', [a]which caused the trained bands and soldiers to arise, both in the city and country.[a]

And I got up out of bed, and in the morning took boat and came down to Whitehall stairs and went through Whitehall; and they looked strangely upon me; and I went to the Pall Mall. And all the city and suburbs were up in

[1] The women's protest, entitled *These Several Papers . . .*, was presented to Parliament, 20th July, 1659.

[2] Begun Sunday night, 6th-7th Jan., 1661, ended 9th Jan.

[a]. . . . . .[a] *S.J.*, p. 59.

arms and exceeding rude; all people were against us and they cried, 'There is a Quaker's house, pluck it down.' And divers Friends came thither to me; and as a Friend, one Henry Fell, was going to a General Meeting at Major Beard's, the soldiers knocked him down and he had been killed if the Duke of York had not come by. And all the prisons were soon after filled with Friends [b]and many died in prison, they being so thronged up.[b] And many inns were full, both in cities, towns, and country; and it was hard for any sober people to stir for several weeks time.

And so the First-day[1] came on and Friends went to their meetings as they used to do, and many were taken prisoners. And I stayed for the meeting at Pall Mall; and on the Seventh-day night there came a party of horse where I lodged, and knocked at the door. [b]The maid asked who was there, and they said a friend. She opened the door and they rushed into the house as though they would have broken all to pieces, and ran up and down the rooms,[b] and laid hold upon me. And there was a soldier, that had been for Parliament, clapped his hand to my pocket and asked whether I had any pistols. And I told him he knew that I did not use to carry pistols, why did he ask such a question of me, who he knew was a peaceable man, and did he not know our principle, for our weapons were spiritual and our principles were peaceable.

And others ran into the chamber and found Esquire Marsh in his bed, who, having a love to me, came and lodged where I did. So they that were of the King's party said, 'Why shall we take this man away? We will let him alone.'

'Oh', say the Parliament soldiers, 'he is one of the heads and chief ring-leader.' Upon this the soldiers were taking me away. And Esquire Marsh, hearing of it, he sent for him that commanded the party of horse to let me alone, for he would see me forthcoming in the morning.

And in the morning [b]about the tenth hour[b] before they

[1] 13th Jan. On the 10th a Royal proclamation forbade meetings under pretence of worship.

[b]......[b] *S.J.*, p. 59.

could fetch me and before the meeting was gathered, there came a company of foot to the house and one of them drew out his sword and held it over my head, and I asked him wherefore he drew his sword at a naked[1] man, and so being ashamed another bid him put it up and so they carried me away prisoner to Scotland Yard, to Whitehall, before the troopers could come for me.

And several Friends were coming in to the meeting and I commended their boldness and cheerfulness, and encouraged them to persevere therein.

And when they had brought me to Whitehall, Esquire Marsh spoke to Lord Gerard;[2] and he came in and bid them set me at liberty. But before I was set at liberty I was kept there two or three hours, and the soldiers and people were exceeding rude and wild for a while. And I declared the Truth unto them and [c]had a good service among the soldiers. And when the steeplehouse preaching was done the officers came to me and asked me if I would take the oath of allegiance and I told them I never took oath in my life and so preached the Gospel unto them, which was peaceable, that they should love one another. And I asked them what they did with all their carnal weapons and swords by their sides, and when would they break them to pieces and come to the gospel of peace.[c] And there came some great persons who were very full of envy. 'What!' said they, 'Do ye let him preach? Put him in such a place where he may not stir.' And so they put me there and the soldiers watched over me. And though they could confine my body and keep that up, yet I told them they could not stop up the word of life. And some came and asked me what I was and I told them, a preacher of righteousness.

When I was set at liberty the marshal demanded fees, but I told him I could not give him any, neither was it our practice; and how could they demand fees of me who was

[1] See p. 255 n.

[2] Charles, Lord Gerard, created Earl of Macclesfield in 1679, d. 1694.

[c]......[c] *S.J.*, p. 60.

innocent; nevertheless in my own power I would give him twopence to make him and the soldiers drink; but they shouted at that and took it disdainfully, so I told them if they would not accept it, choose them, for I should give them no fees.

And so I came through the guards, and the Lord's power came over them; and after I had declared the Truth to the guard and the soldiers, I went up the streets with two Irish colonels that followed me from Whitehall, and came to an inn where there were many Friends kept in prison under a guard, and I desired these two great persons to speak to the guard to let me go in and visit my friends that were in prison there in the inn, but they would not. Nevertheless I desired the sentry to let me go up and he did so. And I looked out of the window [d]towards the house where I had been taken, where the meeting was, and saw a party of musketeers[d] going to Pall Mall to search for me there again where I used sometimes to lodge. And they sent three times while I was in that house among the prisoners; and finding me not, they then turned their faces towards the inn to bid all come out that were not prisoners; so they went out; and I asked the soldiers whether I might not stay there awhile with my Friends, and they said, 'Yes,' and so I escaped their hands again.

And towards night I was down to Pall Mall; and after I had stayed there awhile I went up into the city, and great rifling of houses there was at this time to search for people. [d]Men were all in an uproar[d] and it was hard to go up and down the streets to buy provision for their houses, either men or women, without being abused. For they dragged men and women out of their houses, and some out of their sick beds by the legs. And one man that was in a fever the soldiers dragged out of his bed to prison, and when he was brought there he died, whose name was Thomas Pachin. But I went to a private Friend's house, and Richard Hubberthorne was with me, where we drew up a declaration against plots and fightings to be presented to

[d]......[d] *S.J.*, p. 60.

the King and his Council. And when we had drawn it up and sent it to the press it was taken in the press and so we lost it.

Margaret Fell went to the King and told him what work there was in the city and nation and showed him that we were a peaceable innocent people and that we must keep our meetings as we used to do and that it concerned him to see that peace was kept, that so no blood might be shed.

And all the posts were laid open to search all letters, so that none could pass; but we heard of several thousands of our Friends that were cast into prison, and Margaret Fell carried the account to the King and Council. And the third day after we had an account of several thousands more that were cast into prison, and she went and laid them also before the King and his Council; and they wondered how we could have such intelligence, seeing they had given such strict charge for the intercepting all letters; but the Lord did so order it that we had an account as aforesaid, notwithstanding all their stoppings. And then we drew up another declaration and got it printed, and sent some of them to the King and Council. And they were sold up and down the streets and at the Exchange, ⟨which declaration is as followeth:[1]

This Declaration was given unto the King upon the 21st day of the 11th Month, 1660 [January, 1661].[2]

A Declaration from the harmless and innocent people of God, called Quakers, against all plotters and fighters in the world, for the removing the ground of jealousy and suspicion from both magistrates and people in the kingdom, concerning wars and fightings. And also something in answer to that clause of the King's late Proclamation which mentions the Quakers, to clear them from the plot and fighting which therein is mentioned, and for the clearing their innocency.

[1] Ellwood's text of this has been checked by that published in 1660, *A Declaration from the Harmless and Innocent People of God called Quakers.* It has also been slightly abridged. In full, Ellwood, 1694, pp. 233(2)-237(2); Bicent., i, 494-9.

[2] i.e. 1660 by the old calendar then in use, and hence known as the *Declaration of 1660.*

Our principle is, and our practices have always been, to seek peace and ensue it and to follow after righteousness and the knowledge of God, seeking the good and welfare and doing that which tends to the peace of all. We know that wars and fightings proceed from the lusts of men (as Jas. iv. 1-3), out of which lusts the Lord hath redeemed us, and so out of the occasion of war. The occasion of which war, and war itself (wherein envious men, who are lovers of themselves more than lovers of God, lust, kill, and desire to have men's lives or estates) ariseth from the lust. All bloody principles and practices, we, as to our own particulars, do utterly deny, with all outward wars and strife and fightings with outward weapons, for any end or under any pretence whatsoever. And this is our testimony to the whole world.

And whereas it is objected:

'But although you now say that you cannot fight nor take up arms at all, yet if the spirit do move you, then you will change your principle, and then you will sell your coat and buy a sword and fight for the kingdom of Christ.'

Answer:

As for this we say to you that Christ said to Peter, 'Put up thy sword in his place'; though he had said before, he that had no sword might sell his coat and buy one (to the fulfilling of the law and Scripture), yet after, when he had bid him put it up, he said, 'He that taketh the sword shall perish with the sword.' And further, Christ said to Peter, 'Thinkest thou, that I cannot now pray to my Father, and he shall presently give me more than twelve legions of angels?' And this might satisfy Peter, after he had put up his sword, when he said to him he that took it, should perish by it, which satisfieth us. (Luke xxii. 36; Matt. xxvi. 51-53.) And in the Revelation, it's said, 'He that kills with the sword shall perish with the sword: and here is the faith and the patience of the saints.' (Rev. xiii. 10.) And so Christ's kingdom is not of this world, therefore do not his servants fight, as he told Pilate, the magistrate who crucified him. And did they not look upon Christ as a raiser of sedition? And did not he say, 'Forgive them'? But thus it is that we are numbered amongst transgressors and numbered amongst fighters, that the Scriptures might be fulfilled.

That the spirit of Christ, by which we are guided, is not changeable, so as once to command us from a thing as evil and again to move unto it; and we do certainly know, and so testify to the world, that the spirit of Christ, which leads us into all Truth, will never move us to fight and war against any man with outward weapons, neither for the kingdom of Christ, nor for the kingdoms of this world.

First:

Because the kingdom of Christ God will exalt, according to his promise, and cause it to grow and flourish in righteousness. 'Not by might, nor by power [of outward sword], but by my spirit, saith the Lord.' (Zech. iv. 6.) So those that use any weapon to fight for Christ, or for the establishing of his kingdom or government, both the spirit, principle, and practice in that we deny.

Secondly:

And as for the kingdoms of this world, we cannot covet them, much less can we fight for them, but we do earnestly desire and wait, that by the Word of God's power and its effectual operation in the hearts of men, the kingdoms of this world may become the kingdoms of the Lord, and of his Christ, that he may rule and reign in men by his spirit and truth, that thereby all people, out of all different judgements and professions may be brought into love and unity with God, and one with another, and that they may all come to witness the prophet's words who said, 'Nation shall not lift up sword against nation, neither shall they learn war any more.' (Isa. ii. 4; Mic. iv. 3.)

So, we whom the Lord hath called into the obedience of his Truth have denied wars and fightings and cannot again any more learn it. This is a certain testimony unto all the world of the truth of our hearts in this particular, that as God persuadeth every man's heart to believe, so they may receive it. For we have not, as some others, gone about cunningly with devised fables, nor have we ever denied in practice what we have professed in principle, but in sincerity and truth and by the word of God have we laboured to be made manifest unto all men, that both we and our ways might be witnessed in the hearts of all people.

And whereas all manner of evil hath been falsely spoken of us, we hereby speak forth the plain truth of our hearts, to take away the occasion of that offence, that so we being innocent may not suffer for other men's offences, nor be made a prey upon by the wills of men for that of which we were never guilty; but in the uprightness of our hearts we may, under the power ordained of God for the punishment of evil-doers and for the praise of them that do well, live a peaceable and godly life in all godliness and honesty. For although we have always suffered, and do now more abundantly suffer, yet we know that it's for righteousness' sake; 'for all our rejoicing is this, the testimony of our consciences, that in simplicity and godly sincerity, not with fleshly wisdom but by the grace of God, we have had our conversation in the world' (2 Cor. i. 12), which for us is a witness for the convincing of our enemies. For this we can say to the whole world, we have wronged no man's person or possessions, we have used no force nor violence against any man, we have been found in no plots, nor guilty of sedition. When we have been wronged, we have not sought to revenge ourselves, we have not made resistance against authority, but wherein we could not obey for conscience' sake, we have suffered even the most of any people in the nation. We have been accounted as sheep for the slaughter, persecuted and despised, beaten, stoned, wounded, stocked, whipped, imprisoned, haled out of synagogues, cast into dungeons and noisome vaults where many have died in bonds, shut up from our friends, denied needful sustenance for many days together, with other the like cruelties.

And the cause of all this our sufferings is not for any evil, but for things relating to the worship of our God and in obedience to his requirings of us. For which cause we shall freely give up our bodies a sacrifice, rather than disobey the Lord. For we know, as the Lord hath kept us innocent, so he will plead our cause, when there is none in the earth to plead it. So we, in obedience unto his Truth, do not love our lives unto the death, that we may do his will, and wrong no man in our generation, but seek the good and peace of all men. And he that hath commanded us that we shall not swear at all (Matt. v. 34), hath also commanded us that we shall not kill (Matt. v. 21), so that we can neither kill men, nor swear for nor against them. And this is both our principle and practice, and hath been from the beginning, so that if we suffer, as suspected to take up arms or make war against any, it is without any ground from us; for it neither is, nor ever was in our hearts, since we owned the truth of God; neither shall we ever do it, because it is contrary to the spirit of Christ, his doctrine, and the practice of his apostles, even contrary to him for whom we suffer all things, and endure all things.

And whereas men come against us with clubs, staves, drawn

swords, pistols cocked, and do beat, cut, and abuse us, yet we never resisted them, but to them our hair, backs, and cheeks have been ready. It is not an honour to manhood nor to nobility to run upon harmless people who lift not up a hand against them, with arms and weapons.

Therefore consider these things ye men of understanding; for plotters, raisers of insurrections, tumultuous ones, and fighters, running with swords, clubs, staves, and pistols one against another, we say, these are of the world and this hath its foundation from this unrighteous world, from the foundation of which the Lamb hath been slain, which Lamb hath redeemed us from the unrighteous world, and we are not of it, but are heirs of a world in which there is no end and of a kingdom where no corruptible thing enters. And our weapons are spiritual and not carnal, yet mighty through God to the plucking down of the strongholds of Satan, who is author of wars, fighting, murder, and plots. And our swords are broken into ploughshares and spears into pruning-hooks, as prophesied of in Micah iv. Therefore we cannot learn war any more, neither rise up against nation or kingdom with outward weapons, though you have numbered us among the transgressors and plotters. The Lord knows our innocency herein, and will plead our cause with all men and people upon earth at the day of their judgement, when all men shall have a reward according to their works. . . .

O friends offend not the Lord and his little ones, neither afflict his people, but consider and be moderate, and do not run hastily into things, but mind and consider mercy, justice, and judgement; that is the way for you to prosper and get the favour of the Lord. Our meetings were stopped and broken up in the days of Oliver, in pretence of plotting against him; and in the days of the Parliament and Committee of Safety we were looked upon as plotters to bring in King Charles, and now we are called plotters against King Charles. Oh, that men should lose their reason and go contrary to their own conscience, knowing that we have suffered all things and have been accounted plotters all along, though we have declared against them both by word of mouth and printing, and are clear from any such things. We have suffered all along because we would not take up carnal weapons to fight withal against any, and are thus made a prey upon because we are the innocent lambs of Christ and cannot avenge ourselves. These things are left upon your hearts to consider, but we are out of all those things in the patience of the saints, and we know that as Christ said, 'He that takes the sword, shall perish with the sword.' (Matt. xxvi. 52; Rev. xiii. 10.)

This is given forth from the people called Quakers to satisfy the King and his Council, and all those that have any jealousy concerning us, that all occasion of suspicion may be taken away and our innocency cleared.

Given forth under our names, and in behalf of the whole body of the Elect People of God who are called Quakers.

George Fox	Gerrard Roberts	Henry Fell
Richard Hubberthorn	John Bolton	John Hinde
John Stubbs	Leonard Fell	John Furley Junr.
Francis Howgill	Samuel Fisher	Thomas Moore.

Postscript.—Though we are numbered with plotters in this late Proclamation and put in the midst of them and numbered amongst transgressors and so have been given up to all rude, merciless men, by which our meetings are broken up, in which we edified one another in our holy faith and prayed together to the Lord that lives for ever, yet he is our pleader for us in this day. The Lord saith, 'They that feared his name spoke often together ', as in Malachi, which were as his jewels. And for this cause and no evil doing, are we cast into holes, dungeons, houses of correction, prisons, they sparing neither old nor young, men or women, and just sold to all nations and made a prey to all nations under pretence of being plotters, so that all rude people run upon us to take possession. For which we say, 'The Lord forgive them that have thus done to us,' who doth and will enable us to suffer. And never shall we lift up a hand against any man that doth thus use us, but that the Lord may have mercy upon them, that they may consider what they have done. For how is it hardly possible for them to requite us for the wrong they have done to us, who to all nations have sounded us abroad as plotters? We who were never found plotters against any power or man upon the earth since we knew the life and power of Jesus Christ manifested in us, who hath redeemed us from the world, and all works of darkness, and plotters that be in it, by which we know our election before the world began. So we say the Lord have mercy upon our enemies and forgive them, for that they have done unto us,

Oh, do as you would be done by. And do unto all men as you would have them do unto you, for this is but the law and the prophets.

And all plots, insurrections, and riotous meetings we do deny, knowing them to be of the devil, the murderer, which we in Christ, which was before they were, triumph over. And all wars and fightings with carnal weapons we do deny, who have the sword of the spirit; and all that wrong us we leave them to the Lord. And this is to clear our innocency from that aspersion cast upon us, that we are plotters. . . .⟩

There was a great darkness both in the city and country; but this declaration of ours cleared the air and laid the darkness, and the King gave forth after this a little proclamation that no soldiers should go to search any house but with a constable.

And at the execution of these Monarchy Men they cleared us from having any hand in their plot.

And after the light had shined over all, though many thousands were imprisoned up and down the nation, all gaols being full, the King gave forth after this a declaration that Friends should be set at liberty without paying fees. And so the Truth, with great labour, travail, and care, came over all, for Margaret [Fell] and Thomas Moore went often to the King and he was tender towards them.

⟨I had a sense of the grievous sufferings of Friends, and of their innocency towards God and man, and I was moved to send the following epistle to them, as a word of consolation, and to put them upon sending up an account of their sufferings:

My Dear Friends,

In the innocent seed of God, which will plead its own innocency, who be inheritors of an everlasting kingdom that is incorruptible, and of a world and riches that fade not away, peace and mercy be multiplied amongst you in all your sufferings; who never feared them, whose backs were not unready, but your hair and cheeks prepared, that sufferings never feared, knowing it is your portion in the world, from the foundation of which the Lamb was slain, who reigns in his glory, which he had with the

Father before the world began, who is your rock in all floods and waves, upon which you can stand safe, with a cheerful countenance, beholding the Lord God of the whole earth. So in the Seed of God, which was before the unrighteous world was in which are the sufferings, live and feed; wherein is the bread of life felt, and no complaint of hunger and cold. Friends, your sufferings, all that are or have been of late in prison I would have you send up an account of them, how things are amongst you, which is to be delivered unto the King and his Council; for things are pretty well here after the storm.

G.F.

So keep the word of patience which was before the world began.

London, 28th of 11th mo. 1660 [January, 1661].[1]

Much blood was shed this year, and many of them that had been the old King's judges were hanged, drawn, and quartered. Amongst them that so suffered, Colonel Hacker was one, who sent me prisoner from Leicester to London in Oliver's time, of which an account is given before. A sad day it was, and a repaying of blood with blood. For in the time of Oliver Cromwell when several men were put to death by him, being hanged, drawn, and quartered for pretended treasons, I felt from the Lord God, that their blood would not be put up but would be required; and I said as much then to several. And now upon the King's return, several that had been against the King were put to death, as the others that were for the King had been before by Oliver. This was sad work, destroying of people, contrary to the nature of Christians who have the nature of lambs and sheep. But there was a secret hand in bringing this day upon that hypocritical generation of professors, who, being got into power, grew proud, haughty, and cruel beyond others, and persecuted the people of God without pity.〉

And in the Commonwealth's time, when Friends were under cruel persecutions and sufferings, I was moved of the

[1] Corrected by a MS. copy in Swarthmore MSS., vii, 110.

Lord to write forth a paper that Friends might draw up their sufferings and lay them before the justices at the Sessions; and if they would not do them justice, then to lay it before the judge of the Assizes; and if he would not do them justice then to lay it before the Parliament; and after, before Oliver and his Council that they might see what was done in their family; and if they would not do justice, then to lay it before the Lord who heard the cries of the oppressed and the widows and the fatherless, that they had made so. For that which we suffered for, and our goods were spoiled for, was our obedience to the Lord in his power and in his spirit; and he was able to help and to succour, for we had no helper in the earth but him. And he did hear his people and did bring an overflowing scourge over all the heads of our persecutors, that brought a quaking and a dread and a fear amongst and on them all, that had nicknamed us the Children of Light and called us in scorn Quakers. But the Lord made them quake so as many of them would have been fain to have hid themselves amongst us. And at last many of them ⟨through the distress that came upon them⟩ came to confess to the Truth.

Oh the daily reproaches and beatings in highways because we would not put off our hats, and for saying 'thou' to people; and the priests spoiling our goods because we could not put into their mouths and give them tithes, besides casting in prison as the records and books of sufferings testify, and besides the great fines in courts for not swearing. But with them for all these things the Lord God did plead. Yet some of them were so wicked when they were turned out of their place and office, as to say that if they had power they would do the same again. But old Cain's sword and arms were taken out of his hand and Judas had lost his bag. And then they complained that all these things that were come to pass were along of[1] us.

And I was moved to write to those justices and to tell

[1] i.e. owing to.

them did we ever resist them when they took our ploughs and plough-gear, our cows and horses, ⟨our corn and cattle⟩, and kettles and platters from us, and whipped us, and set us in the stocks, and cast us in prison, and all this for serving and worshipping of God in spirit and truth and because we could not conform to their religions, ⟨manners, customs, and fashions⟩. Did we ever resist them? Did we not give them our backs and our cheeks and our faces to spit on, and our hair to pluck at? And had not their priests that prompted them on to such works plucked them into the ditch? Why would they say it was along of us when it was along of their priests, their blind prophets, that followed their own spirits and could foresee nothing of those times and things that were coming upon them, which we had long forewarned them of, as Jeremiah and Christ had forewarned Jerusalem. And they thought to have ruined and undone us, but they ruined themselves. But we could praise God, notwithstanding all their plundering of us, that we had a kettle, and a platter, and a horse, and plough still. And we do know that if the Presbyterians could get but the magistrates' staff to uphold them, and Judas's bag again, they would be as bad as ever they were; but our backs and cheeks were ready as aforesaid, and we could and can turn them to all the smiters on the earth; and we did not look for any help from men, but our helper was and is the Lord.

⟨Many ways were these professors warned, by word, by writing, and by signs; but they would believe none,⟩ so the Lord God brought his judgements upon all our old persecutors. William Simpson was moved of the Lord to go, at several times, for three years, naked and barefoot before them, as a sign unto them, in markets, courts, towns, and cities, priests' houses, and great houses, and tell them so should they be all stripped naked as he was stripped naked; and sometimes to put on hair sackcloth and smut his face, and to say, so would the Lord God smut and besmear all their religion, as he was besmeared, and that they should change their coat. And much sufferings did this poor man go through and whippings with horse-whips and coach-whips, stonings, and imprisonments three years before the King came in, ⟨that they might have taken warning, but they would not, but rewarded his love with cruel usage.⟩ But the mayor of Cambridge[1] did nobly to him; he put his gown about him and took him into his house.

And there was another Friend, Robert Huntington, who was moved of the Lord to go into Carlisle steeplehouse with a white sheet about him, amongst the great Presbyterians and Independents to show unto them that the surplice was coming up again; and he put a halter upon his neck to show unto them that a halter was coming upon them; which was fulfilled upon some of our persecutors when the King came in. And Richard Sale[2] near Chester being a constable, and they sending a Friend home to his parish with a pass because he travelled up and down in the work of the gospel, was convinced by the Friend and gave him his pass and liberty, and they after cast Richard Sale into prison. Afterwards he was moved to go to the steeplehouse when they were in their lecture and carry those persecuting priests and Presbyterians a lantern and candle as a sign of their darkness. And they cruelly abused him, being dark professors, and put him in their prison called Little Ease and they squeezed and screwed up his body therein, so that not long after he died.

And priest Hughes[3] of Plymouth, ⟨a priest of great note⟩, prayed in Oliver Protector's days that God would put it into the hearts of the chief magistrates of the nation to remove this cursed toleration, and others prayed to remove this intolerable toleration. But after, when the King came in, and Hughes was turned out of his great benefice for not conforming to the Common Prayer, then a Friend of Plymouth, one John Light, met with Hughes and asked him whether he would account and call toleration

[1] Perhaps Samuel Spalding. Cf. p. 218 n.

[2] Richard Sale (otherwise Shields) of Hoole.

[3] George Hughes, B.D., vicar of St. Andrew's, Plymouth.

now cursed, and whether he would not now be glad of a toleration; but he shaked his head and passed away from him: and after, many of them ⟨that had been stiff against toleration⟩ petitioned the King for meeting places and toleration, and gave great sums for licences, too.

Thomas Budd, a priest in Somersetshire, came to be convinced of the everlasting Gospel, and forsook all his parsonage and profits and came to be imprisoned for Truth, and praemunired because he could not swear. Whilst he was a preacher for money, he was highly esteemed by the bishops; and the bishop,[1] when he went his visitation progress, having an esteem for him, told him he might get his parishioners together, and get a barrel or two of drink, and plum cakes, and make merry with his parishioners and bring them off those melancholy humours they were in. So when the bishop came that way again, he told him, 'May it please your grace, I have observed your orders.' But when he came to receive God's everlasting Truth he forsook all these vanities; and then he was sorely imprisoned and persecuted, but stood faithful in God's truth to his dying day.

⟨But to return to the present time, the latter end of 1660 and the beginning of 1661.⟩

At Pall Mall there came several great persons to the meeting there, that were reached. And there came also an ambassador of some part of Germany, and he was convinced. And he would go amongst Friends to learn to be a linen weaver, that he might teach the art of it in his own country when he came home. And I sent him into the country amongst Friends where he stayed about a month and learnt the trade and after some time he passed away, receiving the Truth and owning the Lord Jesus Christ his teacher.

And there came another ambassador with a company of Irish colonels, rude men, to Pall Mall, after the meeting was done and I was gone up into a chamber. And I

[1] William Piers (1580-1670), bishop of Bath and Wells.

heard one of them say he would kill all the Quakers and Baptists and Presbyterians and Independents and Monarchy People. So I went down to him and was moved in the power of the Lord to speak to him, and it came over him. And I told him, 'The Law said, an eye for an eye and a tooth for a tooth, but thou threatens thou wilt kill all and the Quakers ⟨though they have done thee no hurt⟩ but here is gospel for thee, here is my hair, and here is my cheek, and here are my shoulders', and turned them to him. He and his company were so amazed that they said if that was our principle, and that we were as we said, then they never saw the like in their lives. So I told him and them I was the same in life as I was in words, and the Truth came so over him that he grew loving; and the ambassador that yet stood without came in, and he was also presently convinced and loving to Friends.

And he said the colonel was such a desperate man that he feared he would have done us some mischief and therefore ⟨he durst not come in with him, but he was glad to see him so moderate, and thus the Lord's power came over them all⟩.

And at London, when there was so much breaking up of meetings after the Monarchy Men had risen, and keeping them out with soldiers, Francis Howgill and I went to Mile End [e]and soldiers had just been there and the doors were shut up. And so we went to another meeting and there the soldiers had just broken up that meeting also and Friends were gathered again. And I stayed a good while in the meeting and Friends were all refreshed and well. Then I went to another meeting and the soldiers came soon after I was gone and took Friends. Great work had the soldiers made with their swords, but the Truth came over all. And several Friends were cut and wounded abroad and in that day driven like sheep by soldiers into dungeons and bad prisons.[e]

And the next First-day we went again to Mile End but the officers had been there and would not suffer any meeting,

[e]......[e] *S.J.*, pp. 60, 61.

and as we passed away there came a company of soldiers with muskets; and when they had been at the house they followed us till we came near Ratcliff: and so we lost them in the streets and escaped their hands.

And a sad time it was of persecution, but Friends stood nobly in the Truth and valiant for the Lord's name; and at last the Truth came over all.

About this time John Love was put to death, in prison at Rome.[1] And John Perrot and Charles Bailey ran out from Truth. But I was moved to give forth a paper how the Lord would blast them all, both him and his followers, and that they should wither like grass on the house-top, and so they did. But others returned and repented.

⟨Also before this time we received account from New England that they had made a law to banish the Quakers out of their colonies, upon pain of death in case they returned; and that several Friends, so banished, returning were taken and hanged,[2] and that divers more were in prison, in danger of the like sentence. And when they were put to death, as I was in prison at Lancaster, I had a perfect sense of it, as though it had been myself, and as though the halter had been put about my neck.

But as soon as we heard of it, Edward Burrough went to the King, and told him there was a vein of innocent blood opened in his dominions, which, if it were not stopped, would overrun all. To which the King answered, 'But I will stop that vein.' Edward Burrough said, 'Then do it speedily, for we do not know how many may soon be put to death.' The King answered 'As speedily as ye will. Call', said he to some present, 'the secretary, and I will do it presently.' The secretary being called, a mandamus was forthwith granted. A day or two after, Edward Burrough going again to the King, to desire the matter might be expedited, the King said he had no occasion at

[1] This took place in 1658.

[2] William Robinson and Marmaduke Stevenson were put to death at Boston, 27th October, 1659; Mary Dyer on 1st June, 1660; William Leddra on 14th March, 1661.

present to send a ship thither, but if we would send one, we might do it as soon as we would. Edward Burrough then asked the King if it would please him to grant his deputation to one called a Quaker, to carry the mandamus to New England. He said, 'Yes, to whom ye will.' Whereupon Edward Burrough named one Samuel Shattuck, (as I remember) who, being an inhabitant of New England, was banished by their law to be hanged if he came again; and to him the deputation was granted. Then we sent for one Ralph Goldsmith, an honest Friend, who was master of a good ship, and agreed with him for £300, goods or no goods, to sail in ten days. He forthwith prepared to set sail, and, with a prosperous gale, in about six weeks time arrived before the town of Boston in New England upon a First-day morning, called Sunday. With him went many passengers, both of New and Old England, that were Friends whom the Lord did move to go to bear their testimony against those bloody persecutors, who had exceeded all the world in that age in their persecutions.

The townsmen at Boston, seeing a ship come into the bay with English colours, soon came on board, and asked for the captain. Ralph Goldsmith told them he was the commander. They asked him if he had any letters. He said, 'Yes.' They asked if he would deliver them. He said, 'No, not to-day.' So they went a-shore and reported there was a ship full of Quakers, and that Samuel Shattuck was among them, who they knew was, by their law, to be put to death for coming again after banishment; but they knew not his errand, nor his authority.

So all being kept close that day, and none of the ship's company suffered to land, next morning, Samuel Shattuck, the King's deputy, and Ralph Goldsmith, the commander of the vessel, went on shore; and sending back to the ship the men that landed them, they two went through the town to the governor John Endicott's door, and knocked. He sent out a man to know their business. They sent him word their business was from the King of England, and they would deliver their message to none but the governor himself. Thereupon they were admitted to go in, and the governor came to them, and having received the deputation and the mandamus, he laid off his hat,[1] and looked upon them. Then going out, he bid the Friends follow him. So he went to the deputy-governor, and after a short consultation, came out to the Friends, and said, 'We shall obey his Majesty's commands,'⟩ as by the order may be seen, and the relation in William Coddington's book,[2] who is governor of Rhode Island and a Friend. ⟨After this, the master gave liberty to the passengers to come on shore, and presently the noise of the business flew about the town, and the Friends of the town and the passengers of the ship met together to offer up their praises and thanksgivings to God, who had so wonderfully delivered them from the teeth of the devourer. While they were thus met, in came a poor Friend who, being sentenced by their bloody law to die, had lain some time in irons, expecting execution. This added to their joy, and caused them to lift up their hearts in high praises to God, who is worthy for ever to have the praise, the glory, and the honour; for he only is able to deliver, and to save, and to support all that sincerely put their trust in him.

Here follows a copy of the mandamus:

Charles R.

Trusty and well beloved, we greet you well. Having been informed that several of our subjects amongst you, called Quakers, have been and are imprisoned by you, whereof some have been executed, and others (as hath been represented unto us), are in danger to undergo the like, we have thought fit to signify our pleasure in that behalf for the future; and do hereby require, that if there be any of those people called Quakers amongst you, now already condemned to suffer death or other corporal punishment, or that are imprisoned, and obnoxious to the like condemnation, you are to forbear to proceed any further therein; but that you forthwith send the said persons

[1] i.e. before the King's representative.

[2] *A Demonstration of True Love*; a remonstrance against New England persecution published 1674, shortly before this narrative was written.

(whether condemned or imprisoned) over into this our kingdom of England, together with the respective crimes or offences laid to their charge; to the end such course may be taken with them here, as shall be agreeable to our laws and their demerits. And for so doing, these our letters shall be your sufficient warrant and discharge.

Given at our Court at Whitehall, the 9th day of September, 1661, in the thirteenth year of our reign.

Subscribed: To our trusty and well beloved John Endicott, Esq., and to all and every other the governour or governours of our plantations of New England, and of all the colonies thereunto belonging, that now are, or hereafter shall be: and to all and every the ministers and officers of our plantations and colonies whatsoever within the continent of New England.

By his Majesty's command
William Morris.⟩

And after this several New England magistrates came over, and one of their priests. And we had several discourses with them at several times. And they were ashamed to stand to their bloody actions of hanging and murdering our Friends the servants of the Lord. And after, I appointed another meeting with them where was Simon Bradstreet, one of their magistrates. I asked Bradstreet whether he had not a hand in putting to death those four servants of God, for being Quakers only, as they had nicknamed them. And he confessed he had at the first, from which words he could not get off, being spoken before many witnesses; and that made him the more afraid. And when I came to the meeting I asked Simon Bradstreet and the rest of New England magistrates by what law they put our Friends to death and whether they would acknowledge themselves to be subject to the laws of England, and if so by what law of England did they put them to death.

And they said they were subject to the laws of England and governed by them and they had put our Friends to death by the same law as the Jesuits were put to death in England. Then I asked them whether they did believe that those our Friends were Jesuits or Jesuitically affected, and he said nay. Then said I 'Ye have murdered them if ye have put them to death by the law that Jesuits are put to death by here in England, seeing thou sayest they were no Jesuits. For by this it plainly appears you have put them to death in your own wills without any law.' And so he and they being ensnared by their own words, he said, did we come to catch them, but I told them they had catched themselves and they might justly be questioned for their lives. And if William Robinson's father were in town he would question them and bring their lives in jeopardy. Then they began to cover it and said there was no persecution now amongst them. But the next morning we had letters from New England how our Friends were persecuted. And we went unto them again and showed them our letters, but he and the rest of them were in a pitiful fear lest some should have prosecuted them for their lives and so they got out of the city and got home to New England again.

And I went to Governor John Winthrop,[1] who said he had no hand in putting our Friends to death and persecuting of them, but was against it.

And many of the old royalists were much offended with Friends because that they would not prosecute them, but we told them we left them to the Lord, and vengeance was his and he would repay it. For these were a people that fled from the bishops into New England, which bishops made them pay but twelve pence every First-day for not coming to their worship here. And now these there fined Friends five shillings a day and spoiled the goods of such as did not pay it, and whipped and imprisoned and hanged such as would not conform to their will-worship there, as the books of Friends' sufferings in New England will largely show.[2] And since, the judgements of God have fallen heavy upon them and the Indians have been raised up and have cut off many of them. But the Lord has a great people in those countries.

[1] (1606-1676); Governor of Connecticut.

[2] Especially George Bishop's *New England Judged.*

And about this time I had a very good book taken away out of the printer's hand. It was such a useful, teaching book as hardly was ever given forth, it being the signification of names and parables and types and figures in the Scriptures. And they ⟨who took it⟩ were so affected with it that they were loath to have destroyed it and if we would have given a great sum of money for it we might have had it again and that we were loath to do.

⟨Before this, while I was a prisoner in Lancaster Castle⟩, the book called *The Battledoor* was given forth, there being above thirty languages in it, of the plural and singular language, and how that ' thee ' and ' thou ' in all languages, according to all the teaching books and the Scriptures, was ' thou ' to a single person and ' you ' to more than one. John Stubbs and Benjamin Furly took great pains in the compiling of it, which I put them upon, and some things I added to it. And some of them were given to the King and his Council, to the Bishops of Canterbury[1] and London,[2] and to the two Universities, one apiece, and many bought them up; and the King said it was the proper language of all nations. And they asked the Bishop of Canterbury what he thought of it and he was so astonished at it as he would not tell what to say to it. For it so confounded people that few after were so rugged against us for saying ' thee ' and ' thou ' to a single person, which before they were exceeding bad against us for, and in danger many times of our lives, and often beaten, for using those words to some proud men, who would say, ' Thou'st " thou " me, thou ill-bred clown ', as though their breeding lay in saying ' you ' to a singular, which was contrary to all their accidence and grammar and all their teaching books that they had taught and bred up youth by. This ' thou ' and ' thee ' was a fearful cut to proud flesh and self-honour, though they would say and give that to God and Christ which they would not receive to themselves.

⟨Now the bishops and priests being busy and eager to

[1] William Juxon (1582-1663), archbishop of Canterbury.

[2] Gilbert Sheldon (1598-1677), bishop of London.

settle up their form of worship and compel all to come to it, I was moved to give forth the following paper to open unto people the nature of the true worship which Christ set up, and which God accepts, thus:

Christ's worship is free in the Spirit to all men; and such as worship in the spirit and in the truth are they that God seeks to worship him; for he is the God of truth, and is a Spirit, and the God of the spirits of all flesh. And he hath given to all nations of men and women breath and life, to live and move and have their being in him, and hath put into them an immortal soul. So all the nations of men and women are to be temples for him to dwell in; and they that defile his temple, them will he destroy. . . .

Christ's Church was never established by blood, nor held up by prisons: neither was the foundation of it laid by carnal, weaponed men, nor is it preserved by such. But when men went from the spirit and truth, then they took up carnal weapons to maintain their outward forms, and yet cannot preserve them with their carnal weapons; for one plucketh down another's form with his outward weapons. And this work and doing hath been among the Christians in name since they lost the spirit; and spiritual weapons and the true worship, which Christ set up, that is in the spirit and in the truth. . . .

And all that say they do travail for the Seed and yet bring forth nothing but a birth of strife, contention, and confusion, their fruit shows their travail to be wrong, for by the fruit the end of every one's work is seen, of what sort it is.

G.F.〉[1]

And there were many Papists and Jesuits in this year that made a boast and said that of all the sects the Quakers were the best and most self-denying people, and it was great pity that they did not return to the holy mother Church. And so they talked and made a buzz amongst people and said they would willingly discourse with Friends.

But Friends were loth because they were Jesuits and thought it was dangerous or might be esteemed so by others.

[1] In full, Ellwood, pp. 245(2), 246(2); Bicent., i, 514-15.

But I said to Friends, 'Let us discourse with them, be they what they will.' And so a meeting was appointed at Gerard Roberts's house, and there came two like courtiers.

And so they began to ask our names, and we told them we did not ask their names but understood they were called Papists and we were called Quakers.

Then I asked them the same question as I had formerly of a Jesuit, whether the Church of Rome was not degenerated from the Church in the primitive times, from the spirit, and power and practice that they were in in the apostles' time.

And one of them being subtle said he would not answer me, and I asked him why, but he would show no reason. But the other said he would answer me. And he said they were not degenerated from the Church in the primitive times. And I asked the other whether he was of the same mind and he said yes. So I bid them repeat their words over again, that we might the better understand one another, whether the Church of Rome now was in the same purity, practice, power, and spirit that the Church was in in the apostles' times. <When they saw that we would be exact with them they flew off and> denied that, and said it was presumption for any to say they had the same power and spirit that the apostles had.

So then I showed them how different their fruits and practices were from the fruits and practices of the apostles.

And therefore for them to meddle with Christ's and the apostles' words and to make people believe they succeeded the apostles, but not in the same power and spirit that the apostles were in was all in a spirit of presumption, and rebuked by the apostles' spirit.

Then one of them got up and said, 'Ye are a company of dreamers'; 'Nay', said I, 'you are the filthy dreamers that despise the government of the spirit and the power that the apostles were in, and defile your flesh and say it is presumption for any to say they have the same power and spirit the apostles were in, and if you have not the same power and spirit, then it is manifest that you are led by another power and spirit than the apostles and Church in the primitive times.'

So I began to tell them how that evil spirit led them to pray by beads and to images, and to put people to death for religion, and to set up nunneries and friaries and monasteries.

And this practice of theirs was below the law and short of the gospel, the power of God, in which was liberty.

They ⟨were soon weary of this discourse,⟩ went their ways down the stairs and gave a charge to the Papists that they should not dispute with us, nor read none of our books for we were a subtle people.

And many other disputes we had with such like and with all the other sects, as Presbyterians, Independents, Seekers, Baptists, Episcopal men, Socinians, Brownists, Lutherans, Calvinists, Arians, Fifth-Monarchy Men, Familists, Muggletonians, Ranters.

But none of them would confess to the same power and spirit that the apostles had and were in. And so the Lord's power gave us dominion over them all.

As for the Fifth-Monarchy Men, I was moved to give forth a paper to them who looked for Christ's personal coming ⟨in an outward form and manner⟩ in 1666, and some of them did prepare themselves when it thundered and rained and thought Christ was coming to set up his kingdom; and then they thought they were to kill the whore without them. But I told them the whore was alive in them and was not burnt with God's fire, nor judged in them with the same power and spirit the apostles were in. And they looked for Christ's coming outwardly, to set up his kingdom, and their looking was like unto the Pharisees 'Lo here' and 'Lo there'; but Christ was come and had set up his kingdom above sixteen hundred years since, according to Nebuchadnezzar's dream and Daniel's prophecy, and he had dashed to pieces the four monarchies and the great image with its head of gold, and silver breast, and belly of brass, and iron legs, and feet part iron and part clay.

And they were all blown away with God's wind as the chaff in the summer threshing floor.

And when Christ was come he said his kingdom was not of this world; if it was, his servants should fight, but it was not and therefore his servants did not fight. Therefore all the Fifth-Monarchy Men, that be fighters with carnal weapons, they are none of Christ's servants, but the beast's and whore's. Christ saith, 'All power in heaven and in earth is given to me', so then his kingdom was set up and he reigns. 'And we see Jesus reign', said the Apostle; and he shall reign till all things be put under his feet, though all things are not yet put under his feet, nor subdued.

This year, 1661, many Friends went beyond the seas. John Stubbs, and Henry Fell, and Richard Scosthrop were moved to go towards China and Prester John's country,[1] but no masters of ships would carry them. At last they got a warrant from the King; but the East India Company would not obey it, nor the masters of their ships. Then they went into Holland, and would have got passage there, but no passage there could they get. And then ⟨John Stubbs and Henry Fell⟩ took shipping to go to Alexandria in Egypt, and so to go by the caravans from thence. And Daniel Baker and Richard Scosthrop took another ship to go to Smyrna; and Daniel Baker left Richard Scosthrop sick in a ship, where he died, for he went with Daniel contrary to his own freedom; and that hard-hearted man left him in his sickness; but he lost his condition. And John Stubbs and Henry Fell came to Alexandria in Egypt, but the English consul banished them from thence, though they gave forth many papers and books concerning Truth to the Turks and Grecians. They gave the book called, *The Pope's Strength Broken*, to an old friar to give to the Pope and he clapt his hand to his breast and confessed it was truth that was written therein, but if he should confess to it they would burn him. And they returned to London again. John Stubbs had a vision that the English and Dutch would fall out, who had

[1] In central Asia. After a legendary ruler of it.

joined together not to carry them, and so it came to pass soon after.

And after I had stayed a time in London I passed into Essex to Colchester, and had very large meetings, and so to Coggeshall where there was a priest convinced. And I had a meeting at his house. And so after I had visited Friends in their meetings and passed through the countries I came up to London again, where I had a great service for the Lord. And a great door was opened and many flocked into Truth and the Lord's truth spread mightily this year, though Friends had great travails and sore labours, the rude people having been so heightened with the Monarchy Men's rising before.

For we had sufferings without and sufferings within, by John Perrot and his company, ⟨who sought to set up among Friends the evil practice of keeping on the hat in time of public prayer.⟩ But I told Friends the Lord's seed reigned over all and would wear all out and so it did. ⟨And I gave forth a paper as a warning to all that were concerned in it.⟩[1]

⟨Among the troubles that Friends had from without, was one concerning Friends' marriages, which some called in question. This year there was a trial at the Assizes at Nottingham[2] concerning a Friend's marriage, which was thus:⟩ [f]Two Friends some years past were joined together in marriage. The man had an estate in land and about two years they lived together. Then the man died and the woman was with child, which in time she was delivered of and it is now living. The jury found it and presented it to be heir to the land and it was admitted. Another Friend hath lately taken the woman to wife. And since, a man that was near related after the flesh to her first husband brought his action against the Friend that last took her to wife and endeavoured to dispossess them of the inheritance and to possess himself as

[1] Ellwood, p. 249(2); Bicent., i, 519-20.

[2] The Assizes were held 8th Aug., 1661. The Friends were William Ashwell and Ann (Ridge) Ashwell and their daughter, Mary Ashwell of Coddington.

next heir to the woman's first husband.[1] And this he thought to do by endeavouring to prove the first marriage not lawful and so to make the child illegitimate and not in capacity of the heirship. The man's counsel in opening did speak unsavoury words concerning Friends saying they went together like brute beasts, with other hard words. After the counsel on both sides had pleaded it, the judge[2] took the matter in hand and opened it to the jury, saying that there was a marriage in Paradise; Adam took Eve and Eve took Adam and it was the consent of the parties that made a marriage. And as for the Quakers, he did not know their opinions, but he did not believe they went together like brute beasts as had been said, but as Christians. Therefore he did believe the marriage was lawful and the child lawful heir, and then brought a case to satisfy the jury. It was to this purpose: A man that was weak of body and kept his bed, and in that condition his desire was to take a woman to be his wife, and she declared that she took that man to be her husband. The marriage was called in question, all the bishops did conclude the marriage to be lawful, as the judge said. And so the cause was carried against the man for the child.[f]

And they began to put the Oaths of Allegiance and Supremacy to Friends as a snare to them because they could not swear and thereby they praemunired several. ⟨Therefore Friends put forth in print the grounds and reasons why they refused to swear, besides which I was moved to give forth these few lines to be given to the magistrates:

The world saith, 'Kiss the book'; but the book saith 'Kiss the Son lest he be angry.' And the Son saith, 'Swear not at all, but keep to yea and nay in all your communications, for whatsoever is more than this cometh of evil.' Again, the world saith, 'Lay your hand on the book,' but the book saith, 'Handle the word'; and the word saith, 'Handle not

[1] Thomas Ashwell, brother of William.
[2] Justice John Archer (1598-1682).
[f] . . . . . [f] Corrected by Gibson MSS., iii, 137.

the traditions,' nor the inventions, nor the rudiments of the world. And God saith, 'This is my beloved Son, hear him,' who is the life, the truth, and the light, and the way to God.

G.F.

Now there being very many Friends in prison in the nation, Richard Hubberthorne and I drew up a paper concerning them, and got it delivered to the King, that he might understand how we were dealt with by his officers. It was directed thus:⟩

Friend,

Who art the chief ruler of these dominions, here is a list of some of the sufferings of the people of God, in scorn called Quakers, that have suffered under the changeable powers before thee, of whom have been imprisoned, and suffered for conscience' sake, and bearing testimony to the truth as it is in Jesus, three thousand one hundred and seventy-three persons, and there lie yet in prison in the name of the Commonwealth that we know of, seventy-three persons. Also there have died in prison, in the Commonwealth's and Oliver's and Richard's time, in their cruel and hard imprisonments, nasty straw and dungeons, thirty-two persons. And there are imprisoned in thy name, since thy arrival, by such as thought thereby to gratify themselves to thee by so doing, three thousand and sixty eight persons. And besides, our meetings are daily broken up by men with clubs and arms, which meet peaceably, according to the people in the primitive times, and are thrown into waters and trod upon, till the very blood gush out of them, the number of which can hardly be uttered. . . .

We desire that all that are in prison may be set at liberty, and for the time to come they may not be imprisoned for conscience and the truth's sake ; and if thou question the innocency of their sufferings, let them and their accusers be brought up before thee.

Witnesses of the truth of this who are lovers of your soul and your eternal peace.

To the King

George Fox
Richard Hubberthorne.[1]

[1] In full, Ellwood, pp. 250(2), 251(2); Bicent., i, 522-3. Gibson MSS., iii, 3, has been followed.

⟨I mentioned before, how that in the year 1650,[1] I was kept prisoner six months in the House of Correction at Derby, and that the keeper of the prison, a cruel man, and one that had dealt very wickedly by me, was smitten in himself, the plagues and terrors of the Lord falling upon him because thereof. This man, being afterwards convinced of Truth, wrote me a letter thus:

Dear Friend,

Having such a convenient messenger, I could do no less than give thee an account of my present condition, remembering that to the first awakening of me to a sense of life and of the inward principle, God was pleased to make use of thee as an instrument. So that sometimes I am taken with admiration that it should come by such a means as it did, that is to say, that Providence should order thee to be my prisoner, to give me my first real sight of the Truth. It makes me many times to think of the jailer's conversion by the apostles. O happy George Fox ! that first breathed that breath of life within the walls of my habitation. Notwithstanding my outward losses are, since that time, such that I am become nothing in the world, yet I hope I shall find that all these light afflictions, which are but for a moment, will work for me a far more exceeding and eternal weight of glory. They have taken all from me, and now, instead of keeping a prison, I am rather waiting when I shall become a prisoner myself. Pray for me, that my faith fail not, but that I may hold out to the death, that I may receive a crown of life. I earnestly desire to hear from thee, and of thy condition, which would very much rejoice me. Not having else at present but my kind love unto thee, and all Christian Friends with thee, in haste, I rest,

Thine in Christ Jesus,

Thomas Sharman

Derby. 22nd of 4th mo. [June], 1662.⟩

At this time I went to one Lord D'Aubigny[2] and informed him that we had two women Friends in the Inquisition in Malta and desired him to write to the magistrates there for their release. And he promised me he would and I should

[1] See p. 52 ff.

[2] Ludovick Stuart (d, 1665).

come again in a month and he would tell me of their discharge. I went again at that time, and he thought his letters had failed, because he had no answer. And he promised me to write again, and he did so, and they were set at liberty accordingly, to wit Katharine Evans and Sarah Chevers. And great sufferings they underwent there as may be seen by the book of their sufferings there.[1]

A great deal of reasoning I had with him and he did confess that Christ had enlightened every man that cometh into the world with his spiritual light; and tasted death for every man; and that the grace of God, which brings salvation, had appeared to all men; which, if they did obey it, would teach them and bring their salvation. Then I asked him what would they, the Papists, do with all their relics and images, if they did own this light to believe in and receive this grace to teach them and bring their salvation. He said it was but policy to keep people in subjection. A great deal of discourse I had with him, who was very moderate, and I never heard a Papist confess so much. Now though several about the court began to grow loving to Friends, yet the persecution was very hot; and several Friends died in prison. Whereupon I gave forth a little paper concerning the grounds and rise of persecution.[2]

And after I had visited Friends in their meetings at London I travelled through the countries visiting Friends till I came to Bristol fair.[3] And Alexander Parker was with me and John Stubbs, and we heard that the officers would come to break up our meetings. And Alexander Parker went into the meeting at Broadmead before me, and [g]it was upon him to speak in the meeting. I bade him either go before me or after me. It was upon him to go before me and when he was speaking, I sitting by him, in come some of the officers, and after some words plucked him down, and called for the other stranger that was with him,

[1] *Short Relation of some of the Cruel Sufferings of Katharine Evans and Sarah Chevers.* 1662.

[2] Ellwood, pp. 252(2), 253(2); Bicent., i, 526.

[3] In July.

that was me. So, I sitting still, they took him away and after they had examined him and bid him appear the next day he came into the meeting again and stood up and cleared himself.[g] And after Alexander Parker was taken away I stood up in the Lord's eternal power and it came over all; and the meeting was quiet, [g]and so we parted in peace. And my friend being cast into prison fell sick, but after a great while recovered. The next day after the meeting they raised the trained band and said they would hunt me out and they would have me.[g] I stayed in Bristol all the week, where many hundreds of Friends came to visit and to see me. The Seventh-day of the week, I went to Edward Pyot's, where I lay. [h]The next First-day,[1] the trained bands being up, divers Friends came to me and said I would be taken to-day and desired me not to go to the meeting except I were eternally moved of God, for it was past their reason but I should be taken, and they would not have me taken, for they would glory too much if I were taken. And so I sent Friends away to the meeting to tell me how things were; and they came to Edward Pyot's house and told me the soldiers were come and were gone to the Baptists' meeting and the Independents, and they could know the time when to come to the Quakers.[h] But I was moved of the Lord God to go to the meeting ⟨and Edward Pyot sent his son with me to show me the way from his house by the fields. As I went I met divers Friends who came to me to prevent my going.⟩ 'Alack', said Friends, 'What! wilt thou go into the dragon's mouth?' But I bid them stand by; so I went up into the meeting and it was full. And it astonished Friends to see me come in. ⟨Margaret Thomas was speaking, and when she had done I stood up⟩[2] and declared the everlasting Truth, and when I had done I was moved to pray,

[1] 27th July, 1662.

[2] A letter of John Stubbs to Margaret Fell, Monday, 28th July, 1662, describing this great meeting, says Fox 'stepped up' and she 'immediately stopped'. (*Camb. Jnl.*, ii, 21.)

g......g *S.J.*, p. 61. h......h *S.J.*, pp. 61-2.

and when I had prayed I was moved to speak a few words. And as I was going down out of the meeting place, [i]being a mighty full, hot meeting, I was moved to go back again and speak a few words, and stood up and told them that they might see there was a God in Israel that could deliver. Friends cried as I passed away, and said, 'George, the officers are coming.' So the meeting broke up in peace, and Friends were set over all their heads, and none were taken,[i] but we passed away all clear, a meeting of about two thousand people, [i]after which they roared and raged, and spies were out to watch for me.[i] And the soldiers this time had been breaking up the Independent and Baptists' meetings, [i]and at their dinners, and examining other men,[i] so missed ours and came too late to apprehend us, for our meeting was ended before they came, [i]for it was kept till the fifth hour the day before, and their usual time was to break it up about the third hour.[i] One was heard to say to another before, 'I'll warrant we shall fetch him down and shall have him', ⟨but the Lord prevented them.⟩

⟨[j]And I went from the meeting to Joan Hiley's, and several Friends with much gladness of heart came to me. And then at night I was over the water to a fine meeting at another Friend's house when it was late; and then I came into the city. Edward was a dying man to all appearance when I came to his house; but I ordered him to take things and he was subject to me. And his ague hath left him and now he is fine and well.[j]⟩ And I stayed most part of the week in Bristol and at Edward Pyot's; and they had not power to meddle with me.

⟨Having been two First-days together at the meeting at Broadmead, and feeling my spirit clear of Bristol,⟩ on the next First-day I went into the country to a meeting. And

[i]......[i] *S.J.*, p. 62.

[j]......[j] Ellwood appears to have adapted these sentences from the long letter of John Stubbs to Margaret Fell, describing the meeting of the previous day, and has put the narrative into the first person. This change has been kept, but with less alteration of the letter, which is printed in *Camb. Jnl.*, ii, 20-2.

after the meeting was done some Friends came to me from Bristol and said the soldiers had beset the meetinghouse round at Bristol [k]and went up, there being several doors, and said they would be sure to have me. And two other Friends went up into the meeting in Bristol intending to speak. And when the soldiers missed me, in a rage they kept five hundred Friends prisoners in the meeting-place till the seventh or eighth hour at night, and they sent for their suppers into the meeting-place. Then they set them at liberty; only those two that intended to speak were kept prisoners. And they queried of them which way I was gone. The Mayor would fain have spoken with me, and said I had been too cunning for them.[k] And they were grievously tormented that they had not gotten me. But I had a vision of a great mastiff dog, that would have bitten me, but I put one hand above his jaw, and the other below, and tore his jaws to pieces. So the Lord by his power tore their power to pieces, so that I escaped them.

So I passed through the countries, visiting Friends in Wiltshire and Berkshire, till I came to London, and had great meetings and the Lord's power was over all. And a blessed time it was for the spreading of his glorious truth. And it was the immediate hand and power of the Lord that did preserve me out of their hands and over the heads of all our persecutors. And the Lord alone is worthy of all the glory, who did uphold and preserve for his name and truth's sake. So at London I stayed some time, where meetings were large and the Lord's power was over all.

And after a while when the Truth had gotten over again, I went forth into the country with John Stubbs till I came to Rutland and Leicestershire, where I visited Friends, and so came to Sileby where we had a great meeting. And we came to a place called Barnet Hills[1] where ⟨lived then one Captain Brown,[2] a Baptist. After the Act came forth

[1] Bardon Hill in Charnwood Forest.

[2] Captain Henry Brown of Barrow-on-Soar. His wife Sarah d. 1693.

[k]. . . . . .[k] *S.J.*, p. 62.

for persecution, he left his house at Barrow and took a place on these hills. And this being a free place, many, both priests and others, got thither as well as he.⟩ For his wife being convinced he was afraid she would go to meetings and be cast into prison. And so to prevent it he took this place and said his wife should not go to prison.

And when we came into his house to see his wife, I asked him how he did. 'How do I?' said he, 'The plagues and vengeance of God are to me. A runnagate, a Cain I am. God may look for a witness for me and such as me; for if all were no faithfuller than I, God would have no witness left in the earth.' The man was so plagued and judged in himself for flying and drawing his wife into that private place for fear she should be cast into prison, who would neither stand to truth himself nor suffer his wife. And in this condition he lived on bread and water and thought it was too good for him, and at last got home with his wife to his own house, to Barrow, and came to be convinced of God's eternal truth, and died in it. And he said though he had not borne a testimony in his life he would bear a testimony in his death and would be buried in his orchard, and was so, who was an example to all the flying Baptists in the time of persecution, who yet persecuted us when they had power.

And from thence we passed through the country visiting Friends till we came to Swannington in Leicestershire. Will Smith was with me, and some other Friends, but they passed away, ⟨leaving me at a Friend's house at Swannington⟩. And at night there came one Lord Beaumont[1] with a company of soldiers. And as I was sitting in the hall speaking to a widow woman and her daughter, they came slapping their swords on the doors and rushed into the house with their swords and pistols, crying, 'Put out candles and make fast the doors.' And they seized upon Friends in the house; and they asked if

[1] Thomas (d. 1702), third Viscount Beaumont of Swords in the peerage of Ireland.

there were no more about the house, and they said there was another man in the hall. And there were some Friends come out of Derbyshire and one of them was called Thomas Fawkes, and this Lord Beaumont, after he had taken all their names, bid his man set down that Friend's name aforesaid 'Thomas Fox' and he said nay, his name was Fawkes; in the meantime, the soldiers brought me in, and they asked me my name.[1]

And I told them my name was George Fox, [1]which astonished them, and I said I was innocent and pure, and known over the nation.[1]

'Aye', said he, 'you are known all the world over.'

'Yes', said I, 'for no hurt, but good.' [1]And what did they come with their pistols in that manner for, we were gentle and innocent. And he held up his pistols and said, he would make me gentle.[1]

So he put his hands into my pockets and searched them and plucked out my comb-case and then he commanded one of the officers to search them farther for letters, as he pretended.

But I told him I was no letter carrier, and asked him why would he come amongst a peaceable people with sword and pistols without a constable, for it was contrary to the King's proclamation and the late Act, for he could not say there was any meeting, I being sitting as aforesaid talking with a poor widow woman and her daughter.

And so, after much reasoning with him he was somewhat down. Yet he gave the constables charge of us that night, and set a watch of the townspeople upon us; and the next morning we were to be brought before him by them. And accordingly, in the morning, they had us up before him to his house a mile off Swannington; and there he told us how we met contrary to the Act. And I desired him to show the Act to us. Says he, 'You have it in your pocket.' Then I told him he found us in no meeting. Then he asked us whether we would take the Oath of

[1]......[1] *S.J.*, p. 63.

[1] 2nd Sept., 1662.

Allegiance and Supremacy. So I told him I never took an oath in my life nor engagement nor covenant [m]and I would not swear my coat was my own; nor swear, if a man took it off, that he took it. The standers-by said, ' Would I not do so,' and I said, ' No, but I could say he was the man,' but we kept to Christ's doctrine which commands us to keep to yea and nay in all our communications.[m] But still he would force the oath upon us. Then I desired him to show us the oath and let us see whether we were the persons the oath was to be put unto, and whether it was not for the discovery of Popish recusants.

So at last he brought down a little book. We called for the statute book, but he would not show it to us, but caused a mittimus to be made, which mentioned that we were to have a meeting. And so he delivered us to the constables to carry us to Leicester Gaol. And when the constables had us to the town again, it being busy harvest time there were few people could be got to go with us, they being loath to go with their neighbours to prison, especially in such a busy time. They would have given us our mittimus to have carried ourselves with it to the gaol, for it was usual, many times, for the constables to give Friends their own mittimus, and they went themselves with it to the gaoler; they durst trust Friends with it in most places. But we told them though our Friends had done so yet we would not take this mittimus, but some of them should go alongst with us to the gaol. So at last they hired a poor labouring man to go alongst with us, who was loath to go. And as we went we passed through the people in the fields at their harvest, and in the towns. And we declared the Truth to them with our open Bibles in our hands; and the two women they carried wheels on their laps to spin in prison. So we rid through the country to Leicester in that manner, five of us, and declared how we were the prisoners of the Lord Jesus Christ for his name and his truth sake, [m]which astonished the country people and it had an effect upon their hearts.[m]

[m]......[m] *S.J.*, pp. 63, 64.

And so we came to an inn in Leicester; and the man of the house, being in commission,[1] was grieved that we should be thus sent to prison. And he sent for some lawyers and would have taken up the mittimus ⟨and kept us in his own house⟩ and not have let us go to prison. And we told him we did accept his love; and I told Friends it would be great charges to lie at an inn; and many people and Friends would come to visit us; and it may be, after a while, he would not be able to bear it, so we were better go to prison. So the next day we came to prison in Leicester and the poor man gave the mittimus to the gaoler ⟨who had been a very wicked, cruel man.

There being six or seven Friends in prison before we came, he had taken some occasion to quarrel with them and⟩ when we came to the gaol all our Friends were cast into the dungeon amongst the felons. And there was hardly room to lie down they were so throng. And we stayed all day in the prison yard and desired the gaoler to let us have some straw, and he said we did not look like men that would lie on straw.

So there came a Friend, William Smith, to me, and ⟨he being well acquainted with the house,⟩ I asked him what rooms there were in the house and what room Friends usually had been put into before they were put into the dungeon. And I asked him whether the gaoler or his wife was master. And he answered his wife was the master, who, though she was lame and sat in her chair, ⟨not being able to go but on crutches⟩ yet she would beat her husband if he came within her reach, if he did not do as she would have him do.

So I desired him to go and speak to her, and if she would let us have a room I would give her something for it; and besides if she would let all our Friends come up out of the dungeon into their rooms as formerly and leave it to them to give her what they would, it might be better for her. So after a great deal of ado with her, at last she condescended to it. For I considered that many Friends

[1] i.e. a justice of the peace.

would come far to visit me, and if we had a room it would be better for them to come to me and I to speak to them as I had occasion to speak to them.

And so after we were come into our room they told us the gaoler would not suffer us to fetch any drink out of the town, but what beer we drank we might have from him. But I told them I would cure all that, for we would get a pail of water and a little wormwood once a day and that would serve us; so we would have none of his drink, and the water he could not deny us.

And on the First-days when six or seven Friends that were in the gaol did meet together and pray to the Lord, the gaoler would come up with his great quarter-staff and mastiff dog and pluck them down by the hair of the head, and strike them with his quarter-staff; but his mastiff dog, when he struck Friends, would take the quarter-staff out of his hand instead of falling upon Friends.

And when the First-day came, I bid one of my fellow prisoners carry down a stool and set it in the yard, and give notice to the debtors and felons there would be a meeting in the yard and any that would hear the word of the Lord they might come there. So the debtors and prisoners and we went down into the court and had a very precious meeting, and he never meddled. For I said to my fellow-prisoners if any of them had anything from the Lord to speak to the people they might, and if the gaoler came I might speak to him. And so every First-day we had a meeting there as long as we were in prison, and several came out of the city and country and were convinced, and many there received the Lord's truth and stand to this day.

And so when the Sessions came, we were had up before the justices with many more Friends that were sent to prison, to us whilst we were there, to the number of about twenty. And being brought up to the Sessions the gaoler put us in the place where the thieves were put.

And then some of the justices began to tender to us the Oaths of Allegiance and Supremacy. So I told them I never took oath in my life, and they knew we could not swear because Christ and the apostle forbade it and therefore they put it as a snare to us.

And they said we must take the oath that we might manifest our allegiance to the King, but I told them I was sent up out of that town by Colonel Hacker for going to meetings under pretence that I plotted there to bring in King Charles.

And if they could prove that after Christ and the apostle had forbade swearing, they did command to swear, then we would take these oaths; or else we were resolved to obey Christ's commands and the apostle's exhortation.

So I desired them to read the mittimus wherein it was signified that we were to have a meeting; and he that was called Lord Beaumont could not by that Act have sent us to gaol without we had been found at a meeting, and found to be such persons as the Act speaks of. [n]I called for my accusers and said Paul was brought before the judgement seat as I was, and he had his accusers face to face, but where were mine. They told me I was an enemy to the King. I told them I was cast into a dungeon fourteen years since because I would not take up arms and be a captain against the King.[n] And we therefore desired them to read the mittimus before the people, and see how wrongfully we were imprisoned, but they would not, but called a jury and indicted us for refusing to swear and take the Oaths of Allegiance and Supremacy, as aforesaid.

And there being a great concourse of people, there was one that had been an alderman spoke to the jury as they went out and bid them have a good conscience, so some of the jury, being peevish, cried to the justices there was one affronted the jury, upon which they called him up and tendered him the oath also, and he took it. And as we were standing in the place where the thieves used to stand, there was a cut-purse had his hand in several Friends' pockets; and Friends declared it to the justices and showed them the man; who was called up before them; who upon

[n]. . . . . .[n] *S.J.*, p. 64. 'Fourteen years' before the writing of the narrative, but only eleven years before this examination. See p. 65.

examination could not deny it, yet did they set him at liberty.

And so the jury came in and brought us in guilty. And so, after the justices whispered together, the court bid the gaoler take us down to prison again, but the Lord's power was over them, and his everlasting truth, which we declared boldly amongst them. °And the Sessions was just like a meeting, Truth had such an operation in people's hearts.° And most of the people followed us out, so that the cryer and bailiffs were forced to call the people back again to the court. And we declared the Truth down the streets all along till we came to the gaol, the streets being full of people.

And when we came into our chamber again ⟨after some time the gaoler came to us and⟩ desired all to go forth that were not prisoners. And when they were gone he said, 'Gentlemen, it is the court's pleasure that you should all be set at liberty, except those for tithes; and there are fees due to me, you know, but I shall leave it to you to give me what you will.'

And so we were all set at liberty.[1] And after we were set at liberty the rest passed every one into their service; and Leonard Fell being with me we two came again to Swannington. And I had a letter from him they call Lord Hastings[2] which he had writ down from London to the Sessions for them to set me at liberty; and I, being set at liberty, did not give it to the justices but carried it to him called Lord Beaumont, that sent us to prison: And he broke it open and was much troubled; but at last he came a little lower, but threatened us if we had any more meetings at Swannington he would break them up and send us to prison again. So we went to Swannington and had a meeting with some Friends that came to see us, but he came not nor sent to break it up.

[1] The detention lasted about a month.

[2] Probably Henry Hastings, Lord Loughborough, who was Lord Lieutenant of Leicestershire, 1661, is meant.

°......° *S.J.*, p. 64.

And so we passed through the countries to Warwickshire where we had brave meetings: and afore we came into Warwickshire, at a place called Twycross, where lived that great man[1] whom the Lord God had raised up from his sickness ⟨in the year 1649⟩ whose man came with a drawn sword to have done me a mischief; and he and his wife came to see me.

And I passed from thence through the countries till I came into Northamptonshire and Bedfordshire, visiting Friends till I came to London.

And after a while I passed from London into Essex and down into the east and to Norfolk and had great meetings. At Norwich, when I came to Captain Lawrence's, there was great threatening of disturbance, but the meeting was quiet. And from thence I passed to Sutton and into Cambridgeshire, and there I heard of Edward Burrough's decease.[2] And from thence I passed to Littleport and the Isle of Ely, where he that had been the mayor and his wife, and the present mayor of Cambridge's wife came to the meeting. [p]At Stoke[4] we had a great General Meeting where the soldiers intended to come, hearing of me; but by the power of the Lord they were stopped. So I passed on through Chatteris where there was a warrant out for Friends and strangers that came to the town.[p]

And so I came into Lincolnshire and into Huntingdonshire to Thomas Parnell's[3] where the mayor of Huntingdon came to see me and was very loving.

And there came one from London with a motion to me after Edward Burrough was deceased, it being a whimsy got up into her head, and an imagination got into her head because Edward Burrough was deceased, that we should be all taken away, so the power of the Lord riz in me and I was moved of the Lord to tell her that her motion was false and that she was deceived and so sent her home again.

1 Of the name Noel.

2 Edward Burrough died 14th Feb., 1663.

3 Thomas Parnell lived at King's Ripton, Hunts.

4 Perhaps Stow-cum-Quy.

p......p *S.J.*, p. 64.

⟨And I wrote the following lines for the staying and settling of Friends' minds:

Friends,

Be still and wait in your own conditions, and settled in the Seed of God that doth not change, that in that ye may feel dear Edward Burrough among you in the Seed, in which and by which he begat you to God, with whom he is: and that in the Seed ye may all see and feel him, in the which is unity in the life with him. And so enjoy him in the life that doth not change, but which is invisible.

G.F.⟩

And from thence I passed through the country till I came into the Fen Country. ⟨And while I was in that country⟩ there fell a great flood, and it was dangerous to get out.

Yet we did get out and went to Lynn where we had a blessed meeting. And the next morning after the meeting was done I went to visit some prisoners, and when I came back again I went to the inn to take my horse. And as I was riding out, the officers were come to search the inn for me, though I knew nothing of it then, and a great burden fell upon my back as I was riding out of the town till I was without their gates, not knowing that they had been searching for me, but some Friends came after me and told me that they had been searching for me in the inn as I rid out of the yard. [q]They gloried at hearing of me as though they had had me.[q] And so by the immediate hand of the Lord I escaped their cruel hands.

And so I passed through the countries visiting Friends in their meetings, till I came to London again. And Friends told me that Edward Burrough said if he had been but an hour with me he should have been well.

After a while I passed into Kent, and Thomas Briggs and John Moore went with me. ⟨We went to Ashford where we had a quiet and very blessed meeting.⟩ And we came to Cranbrook, where on First-day we had a blessed meeting and quiet. And upon the third or fourth day

[q]......[q] *S.J.*, p. 65.

after, a meeting was appointed at Tenterden, where many Friends came from several parts and a many of the world's people were there and were reached with God's truth. [r]When the meeting was almost done, some of the friends of many of the world who were there whispered to them to go out of the meeting because the soldiers were coming. But they would not go, saying they would fare as we fared.[r]

When the meeting was done I walked into the fields with Thomas Briggs and bid them get our horses ready. And I espied a captain and his company of musketeers coming to the meeting with matches lit. And he sent a company of soldiers unto me, and they brought me to their captain. [r]And when he came into the yard he called and asked which was George Fox. I told him I was the man. Then he came to me ⟨and was somewhat struck⟩ and said he would secure me and put me amongst the soldiers;[r] and would not let any of the people pass away till he had taken whom he pleased. ⟨He took Thomas Briggs and the man of the house, and many more, but the power of the Lord was mightily over him and them all. Then he came to me again and said I must go along with him to the town, and he carried himself pretty civilly, bidding the soldiers bring the rest after.

As we walked I asked him why they did thus, for I had not seen so much ado a great while, and I bid him be civil to his neighbours, who were peaceable. When we were come to the town they had us to an inn that was the gaoler's house. And after a while the mayor of the town and this captain and the lieutenant, who were justices, came together and called me up to the mayor's house and examined me, why I came thither to make a disturbance. I told them I did not come to make a disturbance, neither had I made any disturbance since I came.⟩ He said [s]there was a law which was against Quakers' meetings and made only against them.[1] I told him I knew no such law and he brought out the law that was made against

[1] The Quaker Act of May, 1662.
[r]......[r] *S.J.*, p. 65.

Quakers and others. And I told him that was against such as were a terror to the King's subjects, and were enemies and held dangerous principles. For we held Truth and our meetings were peaceable, and they knew their neighbours were peaceable people, and we loved all people and we were enemies to none. And they told me I was an enemy to the King. I told them I had been cast into Derby dungeon because I would not take up arms against him fourteen years ago, about Worcester fight, and was brought up by Colonel Hacker to London as a plotter to bring in King Charles, and kept there till I was set at liberty by Oliver the Protector. Our principles were peaceable. And they asked me whether I was imprisoned in the time of the insurrection. I said, yes, I had been imprisoned and I had been set at liberty by the King's own word before.[s] ⟨I opened the Act to them and showed them the King's late declaration, gave them the examples of other justices and told them also what the House of Lords had said of it.⟩ [t]And I spoke to them of their conditions to live in the fear of God and to be tender towards their neighbours that feared God, and mind God's wisdom by which all things were made and created, that they might come to receive it, by which they might come to order all things to God's glory.[t] And so they came to be very civil to us; and they said, if they set us at liberty we would laugh at them. We said, nay we should rather pity them; for the Act was to take hold only of such as met to plot and contrive insurrections against the King. So after a great debate they set me at liberty.

And then after, they called Thomas Briggs and John Moore and asked them from whence they came, and they told them they came along with me from London. [u]At first they demanded bond of us for our appearance at the Sessions. But we denied all, being innocent and peaceable.[u] Then they would have had us to promise them to have no more meetings in their town. And we told them we could

[s]......[s] *S.J.*, pp. 65, 66. ' Fourteen years , see p. 434 note.
[t]......[t] *S.J.*, p. 66. [u]......[u] *S.J.*, p. 66.

not do that, for by so doing we should make ourselves transgressors, which we were not. [v]And many words we had of the Truth and they were brought pretty moderate.[v] ⟨When they saw they could not bring us to their terms, they told us we would see they were civil to us, for it was the mayor's pleasure we should all be set at liberty. I told them their civility was noble.⟩ And they set at liberty the two other Friends also, and all the rest. [v]And so we passed away in the power of the Lord, which freedom was a great service to the Truth.[v]

And so from thence we passed into Sussex to Newick, which formerly had been a city,[1] where there were some Friends whom we visited. And from thence we passed through Sussex and Surrey visiting Friends and having great meetings, and all quiet and free from disturbance excepting some jangling Baptists, till we came into Hampshire. ⟨After a good meeting at Southampton we came to Poulner in the parish of Ringwood where there was a monthly meeting next day.⟩ And many Friends came early thither from Southampton and from Poole. And after I had sat a while in the morning[2] with them, I desired Friends to prepare their barn for the meeting place. The weather began to be very hot and ⟨I took a Friend and walked out with him⟩ in the back side, ⟨enquiring how the affairs of Truth stood amongst them; for many of them had been convinced by me before I was a prisoner in Cornwall⟩. [v]And one of the world came to a Friend that was with me and beckoned to him and told him the trained band was raised and was coming to break up our meeting.[v] And I asked what hour it was and he said betwixt 8 or 9 of the clock. And it would be about the eleventh hour before their meeting was gathered. [v]So our Friend desired me to walk a little aside and after a while they would be gone. And then it was about the tenth hour.[v] So I walked out of the orchard into a field. ⟨After a while the young man that spoke of the trained bands left us and

[1] *Camb. Jnl.* reads 'Newne'; Ellwood prints 'Newick' but omits 'which . . . city'. Perhaps New Romney in Kent.

[2] Sunday, 31st May, 1663. *S. J.*, p.79.

[v] . . . . [v] *S.J.* p.66

went away, and when he was gone a pretty way he stood and waved his hat. So I spoke to the other young man that was with me to go see what he ailed; and he went and came not to me again, for the soldiers were come into the orchard.⟩ [w]And they spread over it and made a great noise.[w] When I had turned up by the hedge I looked and saw soldiers all about the house and I heard them enquiring for me. But they came not out of the orchard into the close to me. ⟨Some of them as I heard afterwards saw me but had no mind to meddle.⟩ And presently they took two or three men Friends that were coming to the meeting and some they met in the lanes, and so went their ways about a mile and a half. And so it grew towards the eleventh hour and Friends then began to come in apace and a large, glorious meeting we had; and the everlasting Seed of God was set over all and the people settled in the new covenant of life and upon the foundation, Christ Jesus.

And betwixt one and two in the afternoon there came a man in gay apparel and looked into the meeting and away he went. And it came into me what he was going to do. And it came into me, 'Thou hast a mile and a half to go, and when thou comest to Ringwood thou hast the drum to beat to call the soldiers together, and so much to come back again.' So to the town he goes and tells the magistrates that they had taken two or three men and left George Fox preaching to two or three hundred people. [x]So it was a pretty while before they could come, and we had a brave meeting[x] and broke up about three at the usual time. ⟨After the meeting I spoke to the Friends of the house where this meeting was held (the woman of the house lying then dead in the house); and then some Friends had me to another Friend's house a little distance from the meeting place. After we had refreshed ourselves,⟩ and I had taken leave of Friends and walked up with my horse in my hand about a furlong, one of the Friends came to me and said the soldiers were coming up again in a great rage with their swords. I being a-horse-back passed away,

[w]. . . . . .[w] *S.J.*, p. 66. [x]. . . . . .[x] *S.J.*, p. 67.

having twenty miles to go that night to one Fry's[1] in Wiltshire, to a meeting that was to be there the next day. And as we were going one of the officers passed by us, as we heard afterward, but the Lord's power so struck him that he durst not meddle with us. [y]They took and sent to prison about sixteen, and there were enquiries made after me.[y] And also we heard the soldiers and officers and the rest of the magistrates were in such a great rage that it was judged they would have done us some mischief if they had reached us at the meeting. And the officers were mad with the soldiers that they did not seize my horse in the stable the first time they came. But the Lord in his power did deliver me, and prevented them of their mischievous ends. And the women they let go, but some men Friends they sent to Winchester prison.

[z]The persecutors were wealthy men and many did observe that the just hand of God was against them as did plainly appear by their own confession, as also by the wasting of their outward estates. John Line the constable carried these men to prison and when they were brought before the Judges of the Assizes he took a false oath against them who were innocent, for which they were fined and kept prisoners more than ten years. John Line died a sad spectacle to behold; he grievously rotted away alive, and so died his wife also, being a persecutor. He did confess that he never prospered since he laid hands on the Quakers, and wished he had never meddled with them and said he thought the hand of the Lord was against him for it.[z]

So when I came to William Fry's in Wiltshire we had a blessed meeting on the Second-day, and several prisoners had liberty of the gaoler to come to it. And the constables heard of the meeting, and other officers, and they were coming on their way to break up the meeting, and news came after them that there was a house broken by thieves,

[1] William Fry of Ashgrove, Donhead St. Mary.

[y]. . . . . .[y] *S.J.*, p. 67.

[z]. . . . . .[z] *S.J.*, p. 80, where the witnesses of these confessions are also named. John Line died in 1682.

so the constables were required and forced to go back again to look after the thieves, so that our meeting was kept in quiet and by the Lord's power we were delivered.

And from thence we passed through Wiltshire into Dorsetshire and had large great meetings. And the Lord's everlasting power carried us over all, to the sounding of his Truth and word of life; and people gladly received it.

And so we travelled through the countries visiting Friends till we came to Topsham in Devonshire, where we met Margaret Fell, Sarah and Mary Fell, and Leonard Fell, and Thomas Salthouse and some Friends with her; and we travelled some weeks eight or nine score miles a week and had meetings every day.

And from thence we passed to Totnes where we visited some Friends; and from thence we passed to Kingsbridge and so to old Henry Polixphen's, an ancient justice of peace, where we had a large meeting; and from thence this old justice passed with us to Plymouth, and from thence into Cornwall, to one Justice Porter's;[1] and so to Thomas Mounce's where we had another large meeting; and from thence to Humphrey Lower's, where we had another large meeting; and from thence to Loveday Hambly's, where we had a General Meeting for the whole county. And all was quiet.

And a little before this Joseph Hellen and George Bewley had been in those parts and had been with a Ranting woman at Looe, one Blanche Pope, under pretence to convert and convince her; but before they came from her she had bewitched them with her principles so that they seemed to be like her disciples, especially Joseph Hellen. But I was made to judge them both, to Friends and others. For she had asked them who had made the Devil, did not God, and they could not answer her. And they after asked me that question, and I told them no, for all that God made was good and was blest, so was not the Devil. And he was called a serpent before he was called a devil and an adversary. And then he had the title of Devil given to him

[1] Probably Roger Porter.

because he was a destroyer; and after, he was called a dragon. And so the Devil abode not in the Truth. So the Jews were called ' of the devil ' when they went out of the Truth, and serpents. And there is no promise of God to the Devil that ever he shall return into Truth again. But the promise of God is to man and woman, that have been deceived by him. The seed of the woman shall bruise the serpent's head and shall break his power and strength to pieces. And much more was opened concerning these things which will be too large to speak of. And Friends were satisfied and they were judged with the Truth of Christ Jesus who destroys the Devil and his works, that is out of the Truth. Christ doth that is in the Truth, and brings man and woman up again into Truth. And they never came into those parts since. But one of them, Joseph Hellen, ran quite out from Truth and was denied by Friends. ⟨But George Bewley was recovered and came afterwards to be serviceable to Truth.⟩

And from Loveday Hambly's we passed; and Thomas Lower rid with us through Cornwall, from meeting to meeting, to Francis Hodges',[1] near Falmouth and Penryn, where we had a large meeting. And from thence we passed to Helston that night, where some Friends came to visit us; and the next day we passed to Thomas Teage's,[2] where we had another large meeting; and many were convinced there.

For I was made to open the state of the Church in the primitive times and the state of the Church in the wilderness, and the state of the false Church that was got up since; and that now the everlasting Gospel was preached again over the head of the beast, whore, and false prophets, and anti-christs, which had got up since the apostles' days. And now the everlasting Gospel was received and receiving, which brought life and immortality to light that they might see over the Devil that had darkened them.

[1] Francis Hodges lived at Budock.

[2] The home of Thomas Teage was at Breage, near Helston.

And the people received the Gospel and the word of life gladly. And after meeting was done I walked out and when I was coming in again I heard a great noise in the court; and the man of the house was preaching to the tinners and to the world that it was the everlasting Truth that was declared and that there was no other truth; and the people were generally confessing to it. And a glorious, blessed meeting we had for the exalting the Lord's everlasting truth and his name.

And from thence we passed to the Land's End to John Ellis's house, where we had a precious meeting. And there was a fisherman, one Nicholas Jose, that was convinced, that spoke in meetings and declared the Truth amongst the people. And the Lord's power was over all, and I was glad that the Lord had raised up his standard in those dark parts of the nation, where there is a fine meeting of honest-hearted Friends to this day. And many are come there to sit under Christ's teaching and a great people the Lord will have in that country.

And from thence we returned to Redruth and the next day to Truro, where we had a meeting. And the next morning some of the heads of the town desired to speak with me. And I went up to them and there was Colonel Rous also; and I had a great deal of discourse with them of the things of God.

And they reasoned that the Gospel was the four books of Matthew, Mark, Luke, and John, and natural. But I told them the Gospel was the power of God, which was preached before Matthew, Mark, Luke and John ⟨or any of them⟩ were printed or written, and was preached to every creature who might never see nor hear of the four books aforesaid; so that every creature was to obey the power of God, for Christ the spiritual man, would judge the world according to the Gospel, that is according to his invisible power. And the Truth came over them. So I directed them to their teacher, the grace of God, and showed them the sufficiency of it, which would teach them how to live and what to deny, and would bring them their salvation.

And so to that grace I recommended them and left them.

And from thence we returned through the country visiting Friends, and had meetings at Humphrey Lower's again, and at Thomas Mounce's, and had a large meeting at Stoke at George Hawkins's, where Friends came from Launceston and Calstock and Quethiock and several other places. And a living, precious meeting it was, and the Lord's presence and power were richly manifested amongst us. And there I left Friends under the Lord Jesus Christ's teaching.

The priests and professors of all sorts were much against Friends' silent meetings, and sometimes the priests and professors would come to our meetings; and when they saw a hundred or two hundred people all silent, waiting upon the Lord, they would break out into a wondering and despising, and some of them would say: 'Look how these people sit mumming and dumming. What edification is here where there are no words? Come', would they say, 'let us be gone, what! should we stay here to see a people sit of this manner?' And they said they never saw the like in their lives. Then it may be some Friends have been moved to speak to them and say, 'Didst thou never see the like in thy life? Look in thy own parish and let the priest and thee see there how your people sit mumming and dumming and sleeping under your priests all their life time; who keep people always under their teaching that they may be always paying.'

And in Cornwall there was one Colonel Robinson,[1] a very wicked man, one who had forsaken the nation before the King came in, for ravishing a woman, who after the King came in was made a Justice of Peace and became a cruel persecutor of our Friends, and sent many to prison. And hearing that they had some little liberty through the favour of the gaoler to come home sometimes to visit their wives and children, at the Assizes he came and made a great complaint to the judge against the gaoler and Friends; whereupon the gaoler was fined a hundred marks and

[1] Thomas Robinson, Member of Parliament for Helston, d. 1663.

Friends were kept very strictly up for a while. And the week after he returned from the Assizes he sent to a neighbour justice to desire him to go a fanatic-hunting with him. And the day that he intended and was prepared to go a fanatic-hunting, he sent his man about with his horses, and he walked afoot from his dwelling-house to a tenement, where his cows and dairy were kept and where his servants were milking. And when he came there, he asked for his bull, and the servants said they had stopped him into the field because he was unruly amongst the cows, and hindered their milking. So he went into the field to his bull, and having formerly accustomed himself to play with the bull, he began to fence with his staff at him. And the bull snuffed at him and passed a little back from him, and then turned upon him again and fiercely run upon him, and struck his horn into his thigh and so tore up his thigh to his belly, and heaved him up upon his horns and threw him over his back. And when he fell, he gored him with his horns and would run them into the ground in his rage and violence, and roared and licked up his master's blood. And the maid-servant hearing her master cry, came running into the field; and came to the bull and took him by the horns to pull him off from her master; but the bull gently put her by with his horns, and still fell a-goring of him with his horns and licking up of his blood. And then she run and got some carpenters and other people that were at work not far off to come in and rescue her master. But they could not all beat off the bull till they brought mastiff dogs, upon which the bull fled in a great rage and fury. And after, his sister came and she said unto him, 'Alack, brother, what a heavy judgement is this that is befallen you!' And he answered, 'Ah, sister, it is a heavy judgement indeed. Pray let the bull be killed and the flesh given to the poor.' And they carried him home, but he died soon after. And the bull was grown so fierce that they were forced to shoot him with guns, for none could come near him to kill him.

And after I had cleared myself of Cornwall, I left Thomas

Lower (who came over Horsebridge into Devonshire with me) and so I and Thomas Briggs and Robert Widders came through the country to Tiverton. And it being their fair-day and many Friends being there, we had a meeting. The magistrates gathered in the streets but the Lord's power stopped them, though I saw them in the streets over against the door, but they had no power to come in to meddle with us, though they had will enough so to have done.

And after the meeting was done we passed to Cullompton and Wellington. And I left some of our Friends to have a meeting at Tiverton that night, for we had appointed a meeting five miles off, where we had a meeting at a butcher's house and a large blessed meeting it was. And people were directed to their teacher, the grace of God, that brought their salvation and settled under it; and the Lord's presence was amongst us; and we were refreshed in him in whom we laboured and travailed, and the meeting was quiet.

And there had been very great persecution in that town and country a little before, inasmuch as some Friends questioned the peaceableness of our meeting, but the Lord's power chained all, and his glory shined over all. And Friends told us how they had broken up their meetings with warrants from the justices and how that they were to carry Friends before the justices by their warrants. And Friends bid them carry them; and they said nay, they must go; and Friends said nay, that was contrary to their warrants, they must carry them. And then they were fain to hire carts and horses and wagons to carry Friends in; and they lifted them up and carried them in their wagons and carts. And when they came before a justice, who was moderate, he would, it may be, get out of the way. And then they were forced to carry them before another, so that they were almost three weeks carrying and carting Friends up and down from place to place. And then when the officers came to lay their charges upon the town, the townspeople would not pay it but made them pay it themselves, and that broke the neck of their persecution ⟨there for that time⟩.

And so in other places of the nation where their warrants were to carry them, Friends told them they would not resist them and they were forced to get wagons and carry them before the justices and to prisons, till they shamed themselves, and the Lord's Truth came over all.

And at ⟨Wellington⟩[1] about this time, the town's officers warned Friends to come to the steeplehouse, and they met together to consider of it. And the Lord moved them to go to their steeplehouse to meet in, for there also they had been carrying Friends in their wagons before the justices, till they shamed themselves. And when they came into the steeplehouse they sat all down together and waited upon the Lord in his power and spirit, and minded the Lord Jesus Christ, their teacher and saviour, and did not mind the priest. So the officers came to them to put them out of the steeplehouse, and they said nay, it was not time for them to break up their meeting yet; and so when the priest had done his stuff, they would have had Friends go home to dinner; and they told them they did not use to go to dinner but were feeding upon the bread of life. And there they sat waiting upon the Lord, enjoying his power and presence, till he ordered them to depart. And so ⟨the priest's people were⟩ offended because they could not get them to the steeplehouse, and when they were there they were offended because they could not get them out again.

And so from the meeting at Cullompton, or near it, we came to Taunton, where we had a large meeting. And the next day we came into Somersetshire to a General Meeting, which was very large, and the Lord's everlasting word of life and truth was largely declared. And all people were refreshed and settled upon Christ their rock and foundation and brought under his teaching, and all was peaceable. And about two of the clock in the night there came a company of men about the house and knocked at the doors,

[1] The manuscript says 'Wellingborough' which is probably an error.

and bid them open the doors or else they would break them down, for they wanted a man that they were come to search the house for. And I got up and saw a man with his sword by his side at the door; and they let him in, and he came into the chamber to me and looked upon me and said, 'You are not the man I look for,' so he went his ways. And thus the Lord's power came over all.

And from thence we came to Street and so to Podimore, to William Beaton's, where we had a very large General Meeting. And the Lord's everlasting Truth was fully declared, and the people refreshed thereby, and all was quiet.

And from thence we came to John Dandoe's[1] where we had another large precious meeting. And from thence we came to Bristol, where we had a large service for the Lord, and all was quiet, and where we met Margaret Fell and her daughters again. And from thence we passed up to Slaughterford in Wiltshire, where was a very large meeting in a great barn. And people were gathered up into the Lord's everlasting truth and his great name.

And so I passed into Gloucestershire and had many large meetings. [aa]And we passed into Wales to Pontymoile. And when the meeting was done, the next morning we passed early away to another meeting some ten miles off. In the middle of the meeting comes a bailiff to take up the speaker, and said they had been searching for the speaker at the house which I came from that morning and so the woman of the house took him in. So when the meeting was done I passed away; and he was in the yard and bowed to me but said nothing to me. And the country was in a great rage. And at night they came and shot off a pistol or gun against the house but did no hurt. And then I passed to Ross and had a meeting.[2] And then to Hereford,[aa] and had a meeting at the inn. And after the meeting was done I passed away; and the magistrates heard of it and came to search the house after I was gone, and were in a

[1] At Hallatrow.

[2] Referred to again, p. 516.

[aa]......[aa] *S.J.*, p. 67.

great rage that they had missed me but by the Lord's power their wicked snare was broken. And Friends were established upon Christ their foundation and rock of ages.

And from thence I passed into Wales again, into Radnorshire. [bb]And on the First-day we had a great meeting and on the Third-day we had another meeting up in Wales. And so when we came to the meeting a noise was amongst Friends that the watches were set and they had taken some Friends that were coming to the meeting; so I was moved to pass another way, and so missed them. And so after the meeting was done we passed away peaceably; and those Friends were set at liberty that were taken up by the watchmen, being neighbours.[bb] And the Lord's name and standard were set up there and many hundreds there are in Wales that are settled under Christ Jesus' teaching that has bought them.

And so, after I was clear of Wales, I came into England again, and came to a market town[1] betwixt England and Wales, where was a great fair. And several Friends being at the fair, we went to an inn where Friends came to us. And the magistrates and other officers began to gather together to consult, though it was fair time; and when we were clear, we parted from Friends and passed away, and so escaped them.

And from thence we came into Shropshire where we had a large and precious meeting; and after we had had many meetings in that country as we passed through it, we came into Warwickshire, and visited Friends there; and so passed into Derbyshire and Staffordshire visiting Friends. And at a place called Whitehough[2] we had a large, blessed meeting and all was quiet, and after the meeting was done I passed away; but when I was passed away the officers came and were in a great rage that they had missed me. So the Lord God in his power gave me dominion and

[1] Probably Knighton.

[2] Whitehough (Whitehuff) is a manorhouse in the parish of Ipstones. The Mellor family lived there at this time.

[bb]......[bb] *S.J.*, pp. 67-8.

delivered me out of their wicked hands and Friends were joyful in the Lord that I escaped them.

And so from thence we passed twenty miles after the meeting was done to Captain Lingard's[1] where we had a blessed meeting, and the Lord's presence was amongst us. And after the meeting was done we passed through the Peak Country in Derbyshire, and so came to a Friend's house. And from thence we came into Yorkshire to Cinder Hill Green, where we had a large meeting, where Margaret Fell and her daughters met me again.

And from thence we passed to Balby, where we had another meeting, and there Margaret Fell and her children parted from me and went into Bishoprick. And John Whitehead met me at Balby and several other Friends came to see me there.

And from thence we passed through the country visiting Friends till I came into Holderness, and to the farther end of Holderness, and so passed down by Scarborough and Whitby and near Malton, and to York. And the Lord's everlasting power was over all.

And from thence I passed to Borrowby where I had a glorious meeting: and at York I heard of a plot.[2]

And I was moved to declare against all plots and plotters both public and private, and gave forth a paper against plottings as followeth.[3]

And I passed into Bishoprick to one Richmond's[4] where there was a General Meeting; and the Lord's power was over all, though people were exceeding rude about that time.

And from thence I came to Henry Draper's[5] where we stayed all night. And the next morning a Friend came to

[1] Probably John Lingard, of Slack Hall, near Chapel-en-le-Frith.

[2] The Kaber Rigg Plot, feebly attempted in October, 1663, was known to the authorities in July. Increased persecution followed.

[3] This paper has already been printed on p. 357 (1659). Ellwood printed it at both places.

[4] The Richmond family lived at Heighington, Co. Durham.

[5] Draper lived at Headlam, Co. Durham.

me as I was passing away and told me that if the priests and justices, for many priests were made justices in the countries at this time, if they could light on me, they would tie me to a stake and burn me, as they said. But when I was clear of Bishoprick the Lord's power gave me dominion over all.

After this I came over Stainmore into part of Yorkshire and to Sedbergh, visiting Friends there, and so into Westmorland, visiting Friends. And from thence I came into Lancashire to Swarthmoor.

After I had stayed there a while and visited Friends I passed over the Sands to Arnside and there had a General Meeting. And there came some men towards the meeting to break it up, but the meeting was done and so I passed to Robert Widders's; and from thence I passed to Underbarrow where I had a glorious meeting and the Lord's power was set over all. And from thence I passed to Grayrigg, and visited Friends there. Thence I returned to Anne Audland's, where they would have had me to have stayed their meeting the next day, but I was much burdened in my spirit whilst I was in the house. And it was upon me to go to John Blaykling's in Sedbergh and to be at their meeting where there is a very precious people.

And on the First-day the constables came to Anne Audland's to their meeting to look for me. And so by the hand and power of the Lord I escaped their snare.

And from John Blaykling's I and Leonard Fell passed to Strickland Head, and on the First-day I went to the meeting which was on a common, and a precious meeting it was.

And at night I stayed amongst Friends, and the next day I passed into Northumberland; and after the justices heard of the meeting at Strickland Head they made search for me [cc]even under the beds,[cc] but by the hand of the Lord I escaped them again, for there were some very wicked justices there.

And so I came to Hugh Hutchinson's[1] house in

[cc]. . . . . .[cc] *S.J.*, p. 69.

[1] Hugh Hutchinson lived at Sinderhope in Allendale.

Northumberland (a Friend in the ministry) where we visited Friends thereaways.

And from thence I passed to Derwentwater where we had a glorious precious meeting. And there was an ancient woman came to me and told me her husband remembered his love to me; and she said by this token I might call him to mind for that I used to call him the hale, white, old man, and she said he was six score year old and two. And he would have come to the meeting but that his horses were all employed upon some urgent occasion. He lived some years after.

And so after I had visited Friends in those parts, and settled them upon Christ their foundation, their rock, and their teacher, I passed through Northumberland till I came into Cumberland, and came to the old Thomas Bewley's. And Friends came about me and said would I come there to go into prison, for there was great persecution in that country at the time. And I had a General Meeting at Thomas Bewley's, large and precious, and the Lord's power was over all.

And from thence I passed into the country, and so came to a man's house that had been convinced, one Fletcher.[1] And there was one Musgrove,[2] deputy governor of Carlisle, but he was not stirring. But Fletcher told me if Musgrove knew that I was there he would send me to prison, he was such a wicked man.

⟨But I stayed not there, only calling on the way to see this man.⟩ And from thence we went down to ⟨William Pearson's near Wigton⟩ where the meeting was, which was very large and precious. And there were several Friends in prison at Carlisle whom I visited with a letter; and Leonard Fell went with it.

And so from William Pearson's I passed through the countries visiting Friends till I came to Pardshaw Crag where I had a large General Meeting and all was quiet

[1] Probably Richard Fletcher.

[2] The deputy-governor may have been Christopher Musgrave, son of Sir Philip Musgrave, governor.

and peaceable, and the glorious, powerful presence of the everlasting God was with us.

⟨So eager were the magistrates to stir up persecution in those parts that⟩ at this time there was offered by some a noble, and some five shillings, a day to any men that could apprehend the speakers amongst the Quakers. But the Quarter Sessions being held at this time in that country, [dd]and great floods,[dd] these men which were so hired were gone to the Sessions to look for their wages, and so all our meetings were quiet.

And so as I passed from Pardshaw Crag towards Hugh Tickell's by Keswick we met a-many people that were coming from the Sessions. And from thence we came to Thomas Laythe's,[1] where we stayed. And Friends came there to visit us and to see us.

And from thence we came to one Francis Benson's in Westmorland, near Justice Fleming's[2] house, and there we stayed all night. And that Friend Benson told me that Justice Fleming at the Sessions at Kendal was in a great rage against Friends ⟨and me in particular⟩. And in open Sessions he bid five pounds to any man that could take me. As I came to Francis Benson's, I met one man who had this five pounds proffered him, to take me; and when I passed by him he said 'That is George Fox', but he had not power to touch me, so the Lord's power preserved me over them all.

So the wicked justices being in such a rage against me, and I often being so nigh them, it tormented them the worse.

And from thence I came to James Taylor's at Cartmel in Lancashire, where I stayed the First-day, and had a precious meeting.

[1] Thomas Laythes (*c.*1628-1701) lived at Dalehead, near Keswick.
[2] Sir Daniel Fleming (1633-1701), of Rydal Hall.
[dd]......[dd] *S.J.*, p. 68.

CHAPTER XIX

AND after the meeting was done I came over the Sands to Swarthmoor.

And when I came there they told me that Colonel Kirkby[1] had sent his lieutenant there with soldiers to search for me, who had searched both boxes and trunks for me.

And as I was lying in bed I was moved of the Lord God to go next day to Colonel Kirkby's house about five miles off to speak to him. And when I came there the Flemings and several of the gentry were gathered together at Kirkby Hall to take their leave of Colonel Kirkby, he being then going up to London to the Parliament. And they had me into the parlour amongst them, Colonel Kirkby not being at that time within, but gone forth a little way; and they said little to me ⟨nor I much to them⟩; but after a while I walked out.

And after a little time Colonel Kirkby came in, and so I told him I came to visit him, understanding that he would see me, and to know what he had to say to me or whether he had anything against me. And he said before all the gentry that were gathered together at his house that as he was a gentleman he had nothing against me, but said that Margaret Fell must not keep great meetings at her house for they met contrary to the Act.

But I told him that Act did not take hold upon us but upon such as did meet to plot and contrive and to raise insurrections against the King, and we were no such people, [a]and we had the word of the King for our meetings and his speech and declaration concerning tender consciences.[a] And he knew that those that met at Margaret Fell's house were his neighbours and a peaceable people.

[1] Richard Kirkby (*c.* 1625-1681), of Kirkby Hall in Furness.

[a]. . . . . .[a] *S.J.*, p. 69.

And so after many words he shook me by the hand and said he had nothing against me [b]and if I would stay at Swarthmoor, and not keep great meetings and not many strangers, none should meddle with me.[b] And others of them said I was a deserving man; and so we parted and I returned to Swarthmoor again.

And shortly after, he being gone for London to the Parliament, I heard overnight that there was a private meeting of the justices and deputy lieutenants at Holker Hall, at Justice Preston's; and I heard that they had granted forth a warrant to apprehend me. And so I could have gone away overnight, for I had not appointed any meeting at that time, and I had cleared myself of the north and the Lord's power was over all; but I considered there being a noise of a plot in the north, if I should go away they might fall upon poor Friends, and so if I gave up myself to be taken I should choke them and Friends should escape the better; and so I gave up myself to be taken and prepared myself against they came.[1]

And the next day a lieutenant of a foot company[2] came with his sword and pistol to take me, and I told him I knew his message and errand the night before, and so had given up myself to be taken; for if I would have escaped their imprisonment I might have been forty miles off before they came; but I was an innocent man and so mattered not what they could do unto me.

And he asked me how I did hear of it, seeing the order was made privately in a parlour. I said, it was no matter for that I did hear of it. And so I asked him to let me see his order and he laid his hand on his sword, and said I must go with him before the lieutenants to answer such questions as they should propound to me. And I told him it was but civil and reasonable for him to let me see his order, but he would not. Then I told him I was ready.

And so I went along with him, and Margaret Fell went

[1] Early in January, 1664.
[2] Thomas Fleming, by name.
[b]......[b] *S.J.*, p. 69.

along with me to Holker Hall, and when we came there there were many people gathered, and one Rawlinson[1] called a justice, and Thomas Preston of Holker; and one called Sir George Middleton, and many more that I did not know.

And one, Thomas Atkinson, a Friend of Cartmel, they brought as a witness against me, for some words that he had told to one William Knipe, who had informed them, which words were that I had written against the plotters and knocked them down, which words they could not make much of, for I told them I had heard of a plot and had written against it.

And then old Preston asked me whether I had any hand in that script.

And I asked him what he meant.

And then he said, 'In the *Battledore*.'

And I answered him, 'Yes.'

Then he asked me whether I did understand the languages.

I told him [c]sufficient for myself, and[c] if I did, I knew no law that was transgressed by it; and to understand those outward languages was no matter of salvation. And if I did understand them I judged and knocked them down again for any matter of salvation that was in them, [c]for the many tongues began but at the confusion of Babel.[c]

So he turned away and said, 'George Fox knocks down all the languages. Come', says he, 'We will examine you of higher matters.'

Then George Middleton said, 'You deny God and the Church and faith.'

And I replied, 'Nay, I own God and the true Church and the true faith, but what Church dost thou own?' For I understood he was a Papist.

Then he turned again and said, 'You are a rebel and a traitor.'

I asked him unto whom he spoke or whom did he call rebel. He was so full of envy for a long while he could not

[1] Probably Robert Rawlinson of Cark Hall.
[c]......[c] *S.J.*, p. 69.

say to whom he spoke it, but at last he said he spoke it to me.

And I struck my hand on the table and told him I had suffered more than twenty such as he or any that were there; for I had been cast into Derby dungeon for six months together, because I would not take up arms against this King at Worcester fight. And at another time I was stripped and plundered by the Parliament soldiers. And I was carried up out of my own country by Colonel Hacker before Oliver Cromwell as a plotter to bring in King Charles in 1654, and I had nothing but love and good will to the King, and desired his eternal good and welfare and all his subjects. And in the time of the Committee of Safety some proffered me a colonel's place and I denied them all and bid them live peaceable.

Then said Middleton, 'Did you ever hear the like?'

'Nay', said I, 'you may hear it again if you will. For you talk of the King, a company of you, but where were you in Oliver's days? and what did you do then for him? But I have more love to the King for his eternal good and welfare than any of you have.'

Then they asked me whether I did hear of the plot.

And I said, yes, I had heard of it.

And then they asked me how I heard of it and whom I knew in it.

I told them I heard of it through the high sheriff of Yorkshire[1] who had told Dr. Hodgson that there was a plot in the north, and that was the way I heard of it, and never heard of any such thing in the south till I came into the north. And as for knowing any in the plot, I was as a child in that for I knew none of them.

Then they asked, why should I write against it if I did not know some that were in it.

And I said, 'My reason was because you are so forward to mash the innocent and guilty together. I writ against it to clear the Truth from such things, and to stop all forward foolish spirits from running into such things. And I sent

[1] Sir Thomas Gower, Bart.

copies of it to the Lord-Lieutenants and justices in Westmorland, Cumberland, Northumberland, Bishoprick, and Yorkshire, and to you here. And I sent another copy of it to the King and his Council and it's like it is in print by this time.

⟨And one of them said, 'Oh, this man hath great power!' I said, Yes, I had power to write against plotters.⟩

Then said one of them, 'You are against the laws of the land.'

I answered, 'Nay, for I and my Friends bring all people to the Spirit of God in them to mortify the deeds of the flesh; this brings them into the well-doing which eases the magistrates who are for the punishment of the evil doers. And so people being turned to the Spirit of God which brings them to mortify the deeds of the flesh, this brings them from under the occasion of the magistrate's sword. And this must needs be one with magistracy and the law that was added because of transgression and is for the praise of them that do well. So in this we establish the law and are an ease to the magistrates, and are not against it, but stand for all good government.'

[d]Preston said he would have an Independent, a Quaker, an Anabaptist, and a Presbyterian to interpret that Scripture which said, 'Woe be to the scribes and Pharisees, hypocrites.' I told him I would do it quickly, for the Jews they had the law and would not do it. The woe was unto them. The Christians they have Christ's words, and the Apostles' which saith love enemies and love one another. Now judge yourselves in this case.[d]

Then Middleton cried, 'Bring the book, and put the Oaths of Allegiance and Supremacy to him'; though he was a Papist.

So I asked him whether he had taken the Oath of Supremacy himself, who was a swearer, and we could not swear at all because Christ forbade it, and the apostle. So they were in a great rage and cried, 'Make a mittimus.'

And some would not have had the oath put to me but

[d] . . . . . . [d] *S.J.*, pp. 69, 70.

have let me have my liberty, for this was their last snare, for they had no other way to get me into prison by; for all other things had been cleared. For this was like the Papists' sacrament and altar by which they ensnared the martyrs. So after they had tendered me the oath, and I could not take it, ⟨they were to make my mittimus to send me to Lancaster gaol, but they only engaged me to appear at the Sessions. And so after several hours with them, and many words, they dismissed me⟩. So I came to Swarthmoor again with Margaret Fell. And soon after, Colonel West came to see me, who was a justice of the peace. He told some of the justices that he would go over to see me and Margaret Fell. 'But it may be', said he to them, 'some of you will take an offence at it', which he told unto us when he came over to Swarthmoor, and much more. And I asked him what he thought they would do with me at the Sessions; and he said they would tender the oath to me again.

And whilst I was at Swarthmoor there came William Kirkby into Swarthmoor meeting with the constables. And I was sitting with Friends in the meeting; and he came in and said, 'How now, Mr. Fox, you have a fine company here.'

And I said, 'Yes; we do meet to wait upon the Lord.'

And so he began to take the names of Friends, and those that did not tell their names to him he committed to the constables' hands and sent some to prison. And the constables were unwilling to take them without a warrant from him and he threatened to set them by the heels; and a constable told him he could keep them in his presence, but after, he could not keep them without a warrant. So I told him the constable said true.

And so at the Sessions at Lancaster I appeared.[1] And there was Justice Fleming who was a justice in Westmorland and Lancashire, that had bid five pounds to any man that could apprehend me, and one Justice Spencer[2] and Colonel

[1] The Quarter Sessions, 12th Jan., 1664.

[2] The Hon. William Spencer, of Ashton Hall, near Lancaster.

West and old Justice Rawlinson, the lawyer, who gave the charge. And this Rawlinson was envious against the Truth and Friends, and the Lord's power so stopped him that I thought once he would have been choked.

And there was a great sessions [e]and when I came there they called me to the bar. And the Clerk of the Peace cried,[e] 'Silence in the court on pain of imprisonment', and all was quiet, and I said twice, 'Peace be among you.'

[e]And the chairman asked me if I knew where I was, and I told him, 'Yes', and said it might be it was the not putting off my hat that troubled him, and that was not the honour that came down from God. That was a low thing and I hoped he looked not for that. And he said he looked for that too[e] and asked wherein I showed my respect to the magistrates if I did not put off my hat, and I answered, in coming when they called me. [e]And he bid them take off my hat, which they did. And so a pretty space we looked at one another till the power of the Lord God arose over all.[e]

And then ⟨old Justice Rawlinson the chairman⟩ asked me if I did know of the plot and I told him I had heard of it in Yorkshire from a Friend that had it from the sheriff, [f]but I knew no Friend nor no one in it, which was then public. They asked me why I did not declare it to the magistrates. I said I had written to the magistrates and to the King also against plots, and we were peaceable.

Then they asked me if I did not know of a law against Quakers' meetings. I said there was a law that took hold of such that were a terror to the King's subjects and such as held dangerous principles and were enemies to the King. It was Truth that we held, and were enemies to no man but loved all men, and did not meet to terrify people. The law was good in itself that was made against those that did terrify people and were enemies to the King and held dangerous principles. They told me I had been in Westmorland. I said, 'Yes, and in Cumberland too, to declare against plots.'

[e]......[e] *S.J.*, p. 70.

They asked me if I would take the Oath of Allegiance. I told them I never took oath in my life. I could not swear this was my coat. If a man took it I could not swear he was the man. They asked me if I did own myself to be a Quaker. I told them quaking and trembling at the word of God I owned according to the Scriptures. But, for the word Quaking, it was a nickname given to us by Justice Bennett that cast me into a dungeon because I would not take up arms against the King and be a captain.[f] So Rawlinson asked me ensnaringly whether I thought it was unlawful to swear, because in the Act that was made such were liable to banishment or a great fine that said it was unlawful to swear. [f]And they gave me the Book, and I took it and was turning to a place that was against swearing, and they took it from me again and bid me say after the Clerk. So I told them, if they would prove that Christ and the apostles commanded to swear after they had forbidden it, give us Scripture for this, and we would swear. It was Christ's command that we should not swear. But if I could take any oath I would take that. I told them our allegiance did not lie in oaths but in truth and faithfulness, for they had experience enough of men's swearing first one way and then another and breaking their oaths; but our yea was our yea, and our nay was our nay.[f] And after a great deal of discourse they committed me to prison. And I had a printed paper, which I sent to the King and his Council when he came into the country, which I desired, if they had the patience, they would read, or let it be read in court, but they would not. [g]And they cried, 'Take him away, gaoler.' So I bid them take notice it was in obedience to Christ's commands that I suffered. And so I was sent to prison,[g] with several more, committed some for meetings and some for not swearing. ⟨Afterwards the justices said they had private instructions from Colonel Kirkby to prosecute me notwithstanding his fair carriage and seeming kindness to me before when he declared before many of them that he had nothing against me.⟩

[f]......[f] *S.J.*, pp. 70, 71. [g]......[g] *S.J.*, p. 71.

And the wives of several Friends came and told them if they did commit their husbands to the gaol for nothing else but for the truth of Christ and good conscience sake, they would come and bring their children to the justices for them to maintain them. And a mighty power of the Lord rose in Friends that they declared much to the justices, so that some of them were set at liberty, but some they kept in prison.

⟨Amongst those that were then in prison, there were four Friends prisoners for tithes, who were sent to prison at the suit of the Countess of Derby (so called),[1] and had lain near two years and an half. One of these, whose name was Oliver Atherton, being a man of a weakly constitution, was, through his long and hard imprisonment in a cold, raw, unwholesome place, brought so low and weak in his body, that there appeared no hopes of his recovery or life, unless he might be removed from thence. Wherefore a letter was written on behalf of the said Oliver Atherton to the said countess, and sent by his son, Godfrey Atherton, wherein were laid before her the reasons why he and the rest could not pay tithes; because, if they did, they should deny Christ come in the flesh, who by his coming had put an end to tithes, and to the priesthood to which they had been given, and to the commandment by which they had been paid under the law. And his weak condition of body was also laid before her, and the apparent likelihood of his death if she did continue to hold him there; that she might be moved to pity and compassion, and also warned not to draw the guilt of his innocent blood upon herself. When his son went to her with his father's letter a servant of hers abused him, plucked off his cap, and threw it away, and put him out of the gate. Nevertheless the letter was delivered into her own hand, but she shut out all pity and tenderness, and continued him in prison till death. When his son came back to his father in prison, and told him, as he lay on his dying bed, that the countess denied his liberty, he only said, 'She hath

[1] Charlotte (1599-1664), wife of James Stanley, seventh Earl.

been the cause of shedding much blood, but this will be the heaviest blood that ever she spilt' ; and soon after he died. Then Friends having his body delivered to them to bury, as they carried it from the prison to Ormskirk, the parish wherein he had lived, they stuck up papers upon the crosses at Garstang, Preston, and other towns, through which they passed, with this inscription:

'This is Oliver Atherton, of Ormskirk parish, persecuted to death by the Countess of Derby for good conscience sake towards God and Christ, because he could not give her tithes', etc., setting forth at large the reason of his refusing to pay tithes, the length of his imprisonment, the hardships he underwent, her hard-heartedness towards him, and the manner of his death.

After his death, Richard Cubban, another of her prisoners for tithes, writ a large letter to her, on behalf of himself and his fellow-prisoners at her suit, laying their innocency before her; and that it was not out of wilfulness, stubbornness, or covetousness, that they refused to pay her tithes, but purely in good conscience towards God and Christ; and letting her know that, if she should be suffered to keep them there till every one died, as she had done their fellow-sufferer, Oliver Atherton, they could not yield to pay her; and therefore desired her to consider their case in a Christian spirit, and not bring their blood upon herself also. But she would not show any pity or compassion towards them, who had now suffered hard imprisonment about two years and an half under her. But instead thereof she sent to the town of Garstang, and threatened to complain to the King and Council, and bring them into trouble for suffering the paper concerning Oliver Atherton's death to be stuck upon their cross. The rage that she expressed made the people take the more notice of it, and some of them said the Quakers had given her a bone to pick. But she, that regarded not the life of an innocent sufferer for Christ, lived not long after herself; for that day three weeks that Oliver Atherton's body was carried through

Ormskirk to be buried, she died, and her body was carried that day seven weeks through the same town to her burying-place. And thus the Lord pursued the hard-hearted persecutor.⟩

So I was kept in prison till the Assizes, and at the Assizes there was Judge Turner and Judge Twysden. And I was had before Judge Twysden as may be seen in the papers of the examination at large as followeth

The examination of George Fox before the Judge at Lancaster concerning the oath of Allegiance 1663[1]

Lancaster the 14th day of the first month 1663 [Mar. 1664]. George Fox was called before Judge Twysden, being a prisoner at the place aforesaid.

Judge: What ! do you come into the Court with your hat on ?

Then the gaoler took it off.

George Fox: Peace be amongst you all. The hat is not the honour that came down from God.

Judge: Will you take the oath of Allegiance, George Fox ?

G.F.: I never took an oath in my life, covenant, nor engagement.

Judge: Will you swear or no ?

G.F.: Christ commands me not to swear at all, and the Apostle James likewise. I am neither Turk nor Jew nor heathen, but a Christian, and should show forth Christianity. Do you not know that the Christians in primitive times refused swearing in the days of the ten persecutions, and some of the martyrs ⟨in Queen Mary's days⟩ because Christ and the apostles had forbidden it ? Have you not experience enough how many men at first swore for the King and then against the King ? Whether must I obey God or man, I put it to thee, so judge thee.

Judge: I will not dispute with thee, George Fox. Come, read the oath to him.

And so the oath was read.

[1] In this MS. report some speeches by Fox or references to him were written in the third person. These have been changed to first person.

Judge: Give him the Book.

And so a man that stood by me held up the Book and said, 'Lay your hands upon the Book.'

G.F.: Give me the Book in my hand (which set them all a-gazing, as a hope I would have sworn; then when I got the Book in my hand, I held it up, and said) it is commanded in this Book not to swear at all. If it be a Bible, I will prove it.

And I saw it was a Bible, and I held it up, and then they plucked it out of my hand again, and cried, 'Will you swear? will you take the oath of Allegiance, yea or nay?'

G.F.: My allegiance to the King lieth not in oaths, but in truth and faithfulness, for I honour all men, much more the King, but Christ saith I must not swear, the great prophet, the saviour of the world, and the judge of the world; and thou sayest I must swear; whether must I obey, Christ or thee? For it is in tenderness of conscience that I do not swear, in obedience to the command of Christ and the Apostle, and for his sake I suffer, and in obedience to his command do I stand this day. And we have the word of a King for tender consciences, besides his speeches and declarations at Breda. Dost thou own the King?

Judge: Yes, I own the King.

G.F.: Then why dost not thou own his speeches and declarations concerning tender conscience? (to the which he replied nothing; but I said), it is in obedience to Christ, the saviour of the world, and the judge of the world, before whose judgement seat all must be brought that I do not swear, and I am a man of a tender conscience.

And then the judge stood up.

Judge: I will not be afraid of thee, George Fox, thou speakest so loud, thy voice drowns mine and the Court's; I must call for three or four criers to drown thy voice; thou hast good lungs.

G.F.: I am a prisoner here this day for the Lord Jesus Christ's sake, that made heaven and earth, and for his sake I suffer, and for him do I stand this day; and if my voice were five times louder, yet should I sound it out, and lift it up for Christ's sake, for whose cause sake I stand this day before your judgement seat, in obedience to Christ's command, who commands not to swear, before whose judgement seat you must all be brought and give an account.

⟨Then he was moved and looked angrily at me.⟩

Judge: Sirrah, will you take the oath ?

G.F.: I am none of thy sirrahs, I am no sirrah, I am a Christian. Art thou a judge and sits there and gives names to prisoners ? It does not become either thy gray hairs or thy office. Thou ought not to give names to prisoners.

Judge: I am a Christian too.

G.F.: Then do Christian works.

Judge: Sirrah, thou thinkest to frighten me with thy words (and looked aside and said, ' I am saying so again ').

G.F.: I speak in love to thee. That doth not become a judge, thou oughtest to instruct a prisoner of the law, and the Scripture, if he were ignorant, and out of the way.

Judge: George Fox, I speak in love to thee, too.

G.F.: Love gives no names.

Judge: Wilt thou swear ? Wilt thou take the oath, yea or nay ?

G.F.: As I said before, whether must I obey God or man, judge thee. Christ commands not to swear, and if thee or you, or any minister, or priest here will prove that ever Christ or the apostles, after they had forbidden swearing, commanded they should swear, then I will swear. And several priests being there never a one appeared or offered to speak.

Judge: George Fox, will you swear or no ?

G.F.: It's in obedience to Christ's command, I do not swear; and for his sake we suffer, and you are sensible enough of swearers how they first swear one way and then another, and if I could take any oath at all upon any occasion, I should take that; but it is not denying oaths upon occasions, but all oaths according to Christ's doctrine.

Judge: I am a servant to the King, and the King sent me not to dispute, but to put his laws in execution; will you swear ? Tender the Oath of Allegiance to him.

G.F.: If thou love the King, why dost thou break his word, and not own his declarations and speeches to tender consciences from Breda ? For I am a man of a tender conscience, for in obedience to Christ's command I cannot swear.

Judge: Then you will not swear. Take him away, gaoler.

G.F.: It is for Christ's sake I cannot swear, and in obedience to his commands I suffer, and so the Lord forgive you all.

And so the mighty power of God was over all.

The 16th day of the same month, I was brought before the judge the second time, where he was a little offended at my hat; but being the last morning before he was to depart away and not many people, ⟨he made the less of it.⟩

The judge read a paper to me, which was whether I would submit, stand mute, or traverse, and so have judgement passed. He spoke both these and many more words so very fast and in haste that we could not well tell what he said.

G.F.: I desire it may be traversed and tried, that I may have the liberty.

Judge: Take him away then, I will have no more with him; take him away.

G.F.: Live in the fear of God and do justice.

Judge: Why, have I not done you justice ?

G.F.: That which thou hast done hath been against the commands of Christ.

⟨So I was taken away and had to the jail again and there kept prisoner till the next Assizes. And some time before this Assize, the oath was also tendered to Margaret Fell, who was sent to prison by Fleming and Kirkby and the old Preston, and she was again committed to prison to lie till the next Assize.

Now Justice Fleming being one of the fiercest and most violent justices in persecuting Friends, and sending his honest neighbours to prison for religion's sake; and many Friends at this time being in Lancaster jail committed by him, and some having died in prison, we that were then prisoners had it upon us to write to him as followeth:⟩

To Justice Fleming.

O Justice Fleming,

Mercy and compassion and love and kindness adorn and grace men and magistrates. O, dost thou not hear the cry of the widows, and the cry of the fatherless, who are made through persecution? Were they not driven like sheep, from constable to constable, as though they had been the greatest transgressors or malefactors in the land, which grieved and broke the hearts of many sober people, to see how their innocent neighbours and their countrymen, who were men of a peaceable carriage and honest in their lives and conversations amongst men, should be thus used and served. One more is dead whom thou sentest to prison, having five children both motherless and fatherless. Surely, how canst thou do otherwise but take care of those fatherless infants, and also for the other, for his wife and family? For is it not thy place?

Consider . . . for the Lord may do to thee as thou hast done to others and thou dost not know how soon there may be the cry of the widow and fatherless in thy own family as the cry is among thy neighbours, of the fatherless and widows that are made through thee. But the Quakers can say, 'The Lord forgive thee and lay not these things to thy charge if it be his will.'[1]

⟨Besides this, which went in the name of many, I sent him also a line subscribed by myself only, and directed:

To Daniel Fleming.

Friend,

Thou hast imprisoned the servants of the Lord without the breach of any law, therefore take heed what thou doest, for in the light of the Lord God thou art seen, lest the hand of the Lord be turned against thee. G.F.

It was not long after this ere Fleming's wife died, and left him thirteen or fourteen motherless children.⟩

[1] Abraham MSS., 8; in full Ellwood, pp. 278(2)-280(2); Bicent., ii, 30-3.

And there was also one Major Wigan a prisoner and a Baptist preacher, a very wicked man, and he boasted what he would say at the Assizes if the oath were put to him, and that he would refuse to swear. But when the oath was tendered to him he desired time to consider of it, and before the Assizes came again he got leave to go to London, but did not come down again the next Assizes, but stayed at London, and there he and his wife were cut off by the plague. The judgements of God came upon them, who had given forth a very wicked book against Friends, full of lies and blasphemies.[1]

For whilst he was in Lancaster Castle he challenged Friends to have a dispute with them and I got leave of the gaoler to go up to them.[2] And he affirmed that some men never had the spirit of God, and that the true light which enlightened every one that cometh into the world was natural.

So I told him, seeing there was liberty for any one to speak, I had something to say to him. For he affirmed, as before, that some men had not the spirit of God, and that Balaam had not the spirit of God. So I proved and affirmed that Balaam had the spirit of God and that wicked men had the spirit of God, else how could they quench it, grieve it and vex it and resist the Holy Ghost like the stiff-necked Jews.

And also I showed him that the true light which enlightened every man that cometh into the world was the life in the Word that was divine and not natural. He might as well say that the Word was natural as that the life in the Word was natural. And wicked men were enlightened by this light, else how could they hate it. And the reason why they did hate it was because their deeds were evil and they would not come to it because it reproved them, and that must needs be in them that reproved them. And that light could not be the Scriptures of the New Testament, for it was before the four Evangelists and the Epistles

[1] *Antichrist's Strongest Hold overturned*, 1665.

[2] The dispute is dated 17th Mar., 1664.

and Revelation were written. So it must be the divine light which is the life in Christ the Word, before Scriptures were written; and the grace of God which brought salvation had appeared unto all men, which taught the saints.

And they that turned it into wantonness and walked despitefully, against the spirit of grace, were the wicked. And the spirit of truth, the Holy Ghost the comforter, which leads the disciples of Christ into all truth, the same should reprove the world of sin, of righteousness and of judgement and of their unbelief. So the wicked world had it to reprove them, and the true disciples and learners of Christ, that believed in the light as Christ commands, had it to lead them. But the world did not believe in the light, though they were enlightened, but hated the light which they should believe in, and loved the darkness rather. Yet this world had a righteousness and a judgement, whom the Holy Ghost reproved for their unbelief, their righteousness, and their judgement.

So I proved here that the good and the bad were enlightened and that the grace of God had appeared unto them all, and that they had the Spirit of God, else they could not vex it and grieve it. So I told him the least babe there might see him. And there stood up one Richard Cubban and proved him an antichrist and a deceiver by Scripture. Then the gaoler had me away to the prison.

This Wigan being poor, sent into the country for the poor suffering people of God in prison, for relief for them.

So many people did give freely, thinking it had been for us, but when we came to hear of it we laid it upon him and writ into the country to let Friends and people know the truth, and that it was not usual for us to have collections made for us and how that those collections were only for Wigan and another drunken preacher of his, that would be so drunk that he lost his breeches.

And he writ a book of this dispute and put in abundance of abominable lies, and after went up to London and there the Lord cut him off in his wickedness as aforesaid, and his wife. And I was kept in prison till the next Assizes.

<After this it came upon me to write to the judges, and other magistrates, concerning their giving evil words and nick-names to such as were brought before them.[1]

Before the next Assizes came, there was a Quarter Sessions holden at Lancaster by the justices, to which though we were not brought, I put Friends upon drawing up an account of their sufferings, and laying them before the justices in their open Sessions.[2] For Friends had suffered deeply by fines and distresses, the bailiffs and officers making great havoc and spoil of their goods, but no redress was made.

And because some evil-minded magistrates would be telling us sometimes of the late plot in the north, we gave forth a paper to stop their mouths, and to clear Truth and Friends therefrom.[3]

Being now a prisoner in Lancaster Castle, a deep sense came upon me of a day of sore trial and exercise that was come and coming upon all who had been in high profession of religion; and I was moved to give forth the following paper as a warning unto such:

> Now is the day that every one's faith and love to God and Christ will be tried; and who are redeemed out of the earth, and who are in the earth, will be manifested, and who is the master they serve, and whether they will run to the mountains to cover them. . . . Therefore let not such as forsake Truth for saving the earth say that your brother priest only 'serveth not the Lord Jesus Christ, but his own belly, and mindeth earthly things', for such themselves also do the same, and hug and embrace self, and not the Lord. Now it will be made manifest, who is every one's God, Christ, and Saviour, and their love will be manifest, whether it be of the world, or the love of God. . . .
>
> G.F.[4]

I writ also another short epistle to Friends, to warn

[1] Ellwood, pp. 282(2) 285(2); Bicent., ii, 36-9.
[2] *Camb. Jnl.*, ii, 65-72.
[3] Ellwood, pp. 285(2) 287(2); Bicent., ii, 39-41.
[4] In full, Ellwood, p. 287(2); Bicent., ii, 41.

them to keep out of that spirit that wrought in John Perrot and his company against the Truth.〉[1]

And at the Assizes held at Lancaster the 29th of the 6th month [August], 1664, Judges Twysden and Turner came down again and Turner sat then upon the Crown Bench, and I was brought up before him to plead to the traverse of my indictment. And the indictment was read. I had informed myself of the errors contained in the indictment and answered and pleaded to them as may be seen in the following relation more at large.

I, George Fox, being called before the judge, was put amongst the murderers and felons, and there stood among them above two hours, people, and the justices, and judge gazing upon me. And there they tried many things before the judge. And then the judge caused me to be brought, and they called me to the bar. And then he caused the jury to be called. And he asked the justices whether they had tendered me the oath at the Sessions, and they said they had. And the judge caused the book to be given to the justices for them to swear they tendered me the oath according to the indictment, and some of them refused it. And the judge said he would do it to take away occasion, that there might be no occasion, and the justices swore that they tendered me the oath according to the indictment.

And when they and the jury were sworn, the judge asked me whether I had refused the oath, the last Assizes.

And I said that I never took oath in my life, and Christ the saviour and judge of the world saith, 'Swear not at all.'

And the judge 〈seemed not to take notice of my answer but〉 asked me whether or no I had not refused to take the oath the last Assizes.

And I said the words that I said to them were that if either priest, or teacher, or the justices could prove that after Christ and the apostles had forbidden swearing, they after commanded men should swear, I would swear.

The judge said he was not at that time to dispute whether

[1] Ellwood, pp. 287-8; Bicent., ii, 42.

it was lawful to swear, but to enquire whether I did refuse to take the oath or no.

I told him those things as concerning plots, and the Pope's and foreign power contained in the oath, I utterly denied.

The judge said I said well in that.

I said again to them, as I had said before, that if they could prove that after Christ and the apostles forbade swearing, again they commanded to swear, I would swear; but Christ and the apostle commanded not to swear, therefore I should show forth Christianity for I was a Christian.

And he asked me again whether I had denied the oath. What did I say?

I answered, 'What would you have me to say? I have told thee before what I said.'

Then the judge asked me if I would have those men to swear that I had taken the oath.

Then I answered, 'Would thou have those men to swear that I have refused to take the oath?' At this the court burst out into laughter.

I asked them if that court was a playhouse, and where was gravity and sobriety, for that did not become them.

So the indictment being read, I told the judge I had something to speak to it.

So the judge spoke to me and said he would hear from me afterwards any reasons that I could allege wherefore he should not give judgement.

Then I spoke to the jury how that they could not bring me in guilty according to the indictment, ⟨for the indictment was wrong laid and had many gross errors in it⟩, and further said, 'The oath tendered to me is not the same oath in the Act; Jury, take notice of it.'

But the judge said I must not speak to the jury, but he would speak to them, and further said, 'You refused it at the Assizes, and I can tender the oath to any man now and praemunire him for not taking it', and he said they might bring me in guilty, I denying the oath.

Then I said, 'What should you do with a form? Then you may throw your form away?' And then I told the jury that it lay upon their consciences as they would answer the Lord God before his judgement seat, before whom all must be brought. And I bid the judge do me justice, and do justice.

He spoke to the jury, and the jury brought in for the King, 'Guilty.'

So I cried all people might see how they had foresworn themselves, the justices and the jury, both, and gone contrary to their own indictment, and they had small cause to laugh as they did a little before and to say I was mad.

And the judge said he would hear me, what I could allege, before he did give judgement.

Oh, the envy and rage and malice there was against me, and lightness. But the Lord confounded it all that abundance of it was slain. So their envy and malice was wonderfully stopped. So presently ⟨they set me aside, and⟩ Margaret Fell was called, who had a great deal of good service among them. Many more words were spoken concerning the Truth. And so the court broke up near the second hour.

And in the afternoon we were brought up to have our sentence passed upon us. And Margaret Fell desired that judgement and sentence might be deferred till the next morning, and we desired nothing but law and justice at his hand, for the thieves had mercy.

And I desired the judge to send some to see my prison, being so bad they would put no creature they had in it, it was so cold and rainy; and I told him that Colonel Kirkby who was then on the bench said I should be locked up and no flesh alive should come at me.

And most of the gentry of the country were gathered together expecting to hear the sentence; but they were crossed that time.

So I was had away to my prison, and some justices, with Colonel Kirkby, went up to see it, and when they came up in it they durst hardly go in it, it was so bad with rain and wind, and the badness of the floor. And others that came up said it was a jakes-house, for I had been removed out of the prison which I was in formerly. And Colonel Kirkby said I should be removed from that place ere long to some convenienter place, and other words.

And the judge shaked his head and told them, when the sentence was given he would leave me to the favour of the gaoler. And they were all crossed in that; for Kirkby spoke to the judge in the court how I was not a fit man to be conversed with, none should converse with me. And all the noise among the people was that I should be transported.

So the next day, towards the eleventh hour, we were called forth again to hear the sentence and judgement. But Margaret Fell was called first before me to the bar; and there were some counsellors pleaded, and found many errors in her indictment and so she was put by. After, the judge acknowledged them. And then the judge asked what they could say to mine, and I was willing to let no man speak for me, but to speak to it myself. And though Margaret Fell had some that pleaded for her, yet she spoke as much herself as she would. Though they had the greatest envy against me, yet the most gross errors were found in mine.

And before I came to the bar I was moved to pray, that the Lord would confound their wickedness and envy and set his truth over all and exalt his seed. The thundering voice said, 'I have glorified thee and will glorify thee again.' And I was so filled full of glory that my head and ears were filled full of glory. And then when the trumpets sounded and judges came up again, they all appeared as dead men under me.

And after he had passed sentence upon the thieves the judge asked me what I had to say that he might not pass sentence against me. And before I brought out my reasons I stood a little while. And the judge said, 'He cannot dispute.'

So I told them I was no lawyer, but I had much to say if he would but have patience to hear me.

And then he laughed, and set others a-laughing, and said, 'Come, what have you to say? He can say nothing.'

'Yes', said I, 'I have much to say, have but thee patience to hear me.' Then I asked him whether the oath was to be tendered to the King's subjects or the subjects of foreign princes.

Then said he, 'To the subjects of this realm.'

Then I said to him, 'Look to your indictment and there you may see you have left me out as a subject, for the oath is to be tendered to the King's subjects to see how they stand in point of their loyalty to the King. And you, having taken out the word 'subject', have made me uncapable of taking the oath, having not named me as a subject, so not in a capacity of taking it, for thou grants it is not to be tendered to any but the King's subjects.'

And then they looked at the statute and the indictment and saw it was as I said. And he confessed it was an error. And so they began to be disturbed within themselves and there began to be a murmuring against the clerks, and the judge got up and began to cover the error.

Then I said I had something else to say to stop his judgement. I asked him what day of the month the oath was tendered to me at the sessions at Lancaster.

And they said, 'The eleventh day of January.'

So I asked them whether or no the last eleventh day of January, which they call Monday, the Sessions were kept at Lancaster, or whether the Sessions were not on that they call Tuesday, the twelfth. 'All people', I said, 'take your almanacs and see whether any oath was tendered to George Fox the eleventh of January, and whether the sessions were not upon the twelfth.' And the clerks and people looked at their almanacs and saw it was the twelfth.

And the judge asked whether the eleventh was not the first day of the Sessions.

And they answered, there was but one day and it was the twelfth. And the judge said it was a great mistake.

And then the justices were struck and some of them were in a rage, and could have found in their hearts to have gone off the bench, and stamped and said, 'Who has done this? Someone has done it of purpose', and, 'What clerks did it?' And a great stir was among them.

Then said I, 'Are not the justices here forsworn men in the face of the country, and perjured persons?'

And I asked them whether the last Assizes holden at Lancaster, which were the tenth of March, were the fifteenth year of the King.

And they said, Nay it was the sixteenth year of the King.

Then I said, 'Look at the indictment and see whether or no it was not the fifteenth year.' And they looked at the indictment and their almanacs and saw that they had sworn a whole year false, for he swore the court that they had tendered the oath to me such a year, according to the indictment. Then they were in a rage again and stamped.

'Now', said I, 'Is not the court here, that have sworn so against me, perjured persons, and have not you false swearing enough here, who put the oath to me that cannot swear at all because Christ forbids it?'

Then they were all of a fret, both judge and justices, and could not tell what to do. And then the judge bade them look whether Margaret Fell's was so or not, and it was not so.

Then I said, 'I have something else to say· to thee to stop thy sentence,' and I asked him whether all the oath was to be put into the indictment or no.

And he said, 'Yes.'

'Then', said I, 'Look at the indictment and the oath and there you may see a power "pretended to be derived" from Rome from the Pope left out in the indictment, which is a principal matter in the oath. And if I should take the oath according to this indictment, then I grant that a power may come from Rome and take away the King's power.'

Then the judge acknowledged this was another great error.

I said I had something farther to say to him to stop his judgement. 'Thou grants all the oath is to be put into the indictment; then read the indictment and thou wilt see these words, "his heirs and successors", left out. Was not the oath given forth in King James's reign, and was not King Charles I his heir and King Charles II their successor? Therefore, you leaving out those words "his heirs and successors", you have left out the King and his father. And is not the oath to be taken to the King? And how can I take the oath to the King when you have left him out and so made no King of him. If I take this oath it must be to you, seeing the King is left out.'

Then the judge acknowledged this also to be an error.

Then I said I had yet something farther to allege to stop his sentence.

Then said the judge, 'Nay, I have enough.'

But I said, 'If thou hast enough I desire nothing but law and justice at thy hands, for I do not look for mercy.'

Then said the judge, 'You must have justice, and you shall have law.' So the indictment was thrown out, and he said I was clear from all the former.

'Why then', said I, 'I am at liberty and free from all that ever hath been done against me in this matter.'

'Yes', said the judge, 'You are free from all that has been done against you.'

Then the people said, 'He is too cunning for them all.'

So I told them they had small cause to laugh as they had done before, for they might see how the justices and jury were forsworn men.

And he started up in a rage and said, 'I can put the oath to any man here, and I will tender you the oath again.'

I told them they had example enough for swearing and false swearing, both justices and jury, yesterday before their faces; for I saw before my eyes both justices and jury forswear themselves, who heard the indictment.

He asked me whether I would take the oath.

I bade him do me justice for my false imprisonment all this while, for I ought to be at liberty.

Then he said I was at liberty, 'But I will put the oath to you again.'

Then I turned me about and cried, 'All people take notice, this is a snare, for I ought to be set free from the gaoler and this court if I am a free man, as thou says I ought to be. And yet thou tenderest me the oath before I am at liberty. But thou ought to let me be at liberty, and then thou mightest have done thy will.' And all was mighty quiet, and all people were struck and astonished.

And he had caused the grand jury to be called, for he had called on them before when I was with him, when he saw they would be overthrown. And they would fain have been dismissed, but he told them he could not dismiss them for he had business for them and they might be ready when he called them. And I felt his intent, that if I was freed he would come on again. So I looked him in the face. And the witness started up in him and made him blush when he looked at me again. For he saw that I saw him.

So he caused the oath to be read to me, and then when the oath was read he asked me whether I would take the oath or no, the grand jury standing by.

I told him I never took oath in my life.

But he cried, 'Give him the book.' And the sheriff and the justices cried, 'Give him the book.' And then the power of darkness riz up in them like a mountain. And several clerks lift up a Bible to me.

And so, standing still, at last I said, 'If it be a Bible, give it me into my hand.'

'Yes, yes,' said the judge and justices, 'Give it to him into his hand.'

And when I had it in my hand I looked into it and said, 'I see it is a Bible, and I am glad of it.'

And he bade me swear.

Then said I, 'You have given me a book to kiss and to swear on; and the book says, "Kiss the son," and the son says, "Swear not at all"; and likewise the Apostle James.'

And as I was turning them to the places and holding up the Bible, and telling them that I said as the book said, and that it and Christ forbid swearing, I wondered that the Bible was at liberty and that they did not imprison the book that forbids to swear. So I told them, 'You may imprison the book.'

The judge said, 'But we will imprison George Fox.'

I answered, 'Nay, you may imprison the book which saith, "Swear not at all."' Then they plucked the Bible out of my hand.

And this got abroad all over the country as a byword, that the Bible should be at liberty, and I in prison who said as the book said.

Then the judge asked me whether I would take the oath and bade them give me the book again and read the oath again to me, and called me to say after the clerk.

But I told them I never took any oath, covenant, nor engagement in my life. Had they not sufficient experience how men had sworn one way and then another way, and how the justices and the court were forsworn men? My loyalty to the King lay in a 'Yea' and 'Nay' which was more than an oath, for I was a man of a tender conscience; and if they had any sense of a tender conscience they would consider this. And if the judge or justices could convince me that after Christ and the Apostle had forbidden swearing they did alter that and command men to swear, then I would swear.

Then the sheriff and the judge said the angel swore in the Revelation.

And I said, 'I bring forth my first begotten son into the world, saith God; let all the angels in heaven worship him, who saith "Swear not at all."'

And the judge said he would not dispute.

And I said if they could not convince me, let the priests stand up and do it, there being many priests there; and if they could not do it let the bishop come and do it. But never a one of the priests made any answer. So then I spake much to the jury, how that which I did was for Christ's sake, and let none of them act contrary to that of God in their consciences, for before his judgement seat they must all be brought. 'And as for all those things contained in the oath, as plots and persecuting about religion, and popery, I deny them in my heart, and shall show forth Christianity this day. It is for Christ's sake I stand. For it is *Lo tishshabiun becol dabar.*[1] And they all gazed, and there was a great calm.

And after many more words both to the judge and jury, they took me away. Then in the afternoon I was called again, where I stood amongst the thieves a pretty while with my hat on, and at last the gaoler took it off. When I was called to the bar the jury brought in the new bill found against me, for not taking the oath.

And the judge asked what I could say for myself.

I bade them read the indictment, I would not answer to that I did not hear.

And as they read, the judge bade them take heed it was not false again. And they read it so mazedly that I did hardly understand what they said. And the judge asked me what I would plead, 'Guilty' or 'Not guilty'

And I said at once, hearing over a paper at a great distance from me I could not answer. But if they would give me a copy of it and time to consider of it I might answer; for the last I had but lately, and never heard it read but once over, and then in the court.

At this they were at a stand, till the judge asked me, what time I would have.

'Till the next Assizes,' I said.

And then he asked me again what I would plead.

I told him I was not guilty at all of the matter and manner, and should traverse it, and so they entered it.

And those things contained in the oath, I said, I utterly denied them in my heart, and I never took oath in my life, and if I could take any I would take that.

And the judge said that I said well, and said the King was sworn, the Parliament was sworn, and he and the

[1] Transliterated Hebrew for 'Ye shall not swear by anything'.

justices were sworn, and the law was preserved by oaths.

I told them they had sufficient experience of men's swearing. And had they not read the *Book of Martyrs*, how many of the martyrs suffered because they could not swear, both in the ten persecutions[1] and in Bonner's days ?[2] To deny swearing in obedience to Christ's commands was no new thing.

I said to him, ' Our Yea is yea, and our Nay, nay. If we transgress our Yea and Nay, let us suffer as they do that break an oath. This we sent to the King, who said it was reasonable.'

The judge said, ' I would the law were otherwise.' And after more words he said, ' All the world cannot convince you.'

' Is it likely ', I said, ' the world should convince ? The whole world lies in wickedness. Christ is from heaven and his doctrine heavenly.'

Then the judge bid the gaoler take me away, and I was had away to my chamber and they passed away from the court. And the Truth and power of the Lord God was glorious over all. And many spirits were crossed grievously in their envy and malice. And Margaret Fell they praemunired, and he passed sentence upon her.

There were many things spoken both to judge, jury, and people which were too large to mention.

And so they committed me again to close prison. And Colonel Kirkby gave order to the gaoler that no flesh alive must come at me for I was not fit to be discoursed with by men.

So I was put up in a smoky tower where the smoke of the other rooms came up and stood as a dew upon the walls, where it rained in also upon my bed and the smoke was so thick as I could hardly see a candle sometimes, and many

[1] The ten great persecutions, from Nero, A.D. 64, to Diocletian, A.D. 302.

[2] Edmund Bonner, Bishop of London in the Marian persecution, 1555-1558.

times I was locked under three locks; and the under-gaoler would hardly come up to unlock one of the upper doors; the smoke was so thick that I was almost smothered with smoke and so starved with cold and rain that my body was almost numbed, and my body swelled with the cold.

And many times when I went to stop out the rain off me in the cold winter season, my shift would be as wet as muck with rain that came in upon me. And as fast as I stopped it the wind, being high and fierce, would blow it out again; and in this manner did I lie all that long cold winter till the next Assizes.

The 16th day of the month called March, 1665, the Lent Assizes began at Lancaster, and Twysden and Turner came down again. Twysden sat upon the Crown bench and upon the 22nd of the same month I was called before him, and they read the indictment and called a jury and swore them.

First the clerk asked me if I had anything to allege against any of the jury.

I told them I knew none of them; then they swore three men how that the oath was proffered to me the last Assizes.

The judge said, 'Come, come, it was not done in a corner.' And then he asked me what I had said, or whether I had taken the oath the last Assizes.

I told him what I said, namely that they gave me the book to swear on and the book saith, 'Swear not at all', and if they could prove that, after Christ Jesus and the Apostle had denied that men should swear, they had commanded that they should swear, I would swear. Those were my words that I had said, and my allegiance lay in truth and faithfulness and not in swearing. For they had example enough how the justices and jury forsware themselves the last Assizes, 'and so in that should all your allegiance lie if you did well', and I did not deny swearing upon some account and own it upon another account but because Christ said I should not swear at all.

So the judge said he would not dispute with me but in point of law.

And I had informed myself of the errors that were in this indictment also. Though at the Assizes before, Judge Turner said to the court, 'I pray see that all the oath be in the indictment and that the word "subject" and the day of the month and the year of the King be in, for it is a shame that so many errors should be seen and found in the face of the country.' So when they read this second indictment and the oath, he tried it and the rest of them and therefore they thought that all was safe and well. But they had made for all this as many errors in this indictment as in the other and left out the word 'subject' and the day of the month also <and several material words of the oath. Surely the hand of the Lord was in it to confound their mischievous work against me and to blind them therein.>

'Then', I said, 'I have something to speak to the jury concerning the indictment.' But he would not suffer anything to be spoken to the jury, I must speak to him. And then I asked him whether the oath was to be tendered to all the King's subjects.

And he said, 'Yes.'

'Then', said I, 'look to your indictment and there you may see they have left me out as a subject in this second indictment. So it doth not concern me and the court is to take no notice of it.'

Then cried Twysden, 'Take him away, gaoler.' So I was hurried away. And the gaoler and all people looked when I should be brought out again, but they never brought me forth to the court any more. And when I was taken away the judge asked whether they were agreed, and the jury said 'For the King' and so the judge said no more. And many errors I had to speak of in the indictment but I was called no more. And I heard that they themselves had the indictment amongst them and they saw they were at a loss in the thing and had the worst on it. And the judge had sworn the court that the oath was put to me at the last Assizes there, such a day, and had he let me plead to my indictment I could have proved the court forsworn men again. I heard they had sent the indictment to London to see if it would stand, and they were informed it would not stand. So they would not let me plead to it. Nevertheless they reckoned me as a praemunired person, ⟨though I was never brought to hear the sentence, or knew of it, which was very illegal. For they ought not only to have had me present to hear the sentence given, but also to have asked me first, what I could say why sentence should not be given against me. But he knew I had so much to say that they could not give sentence if they heard it.⟩ And I grew, through smothering in a cold and smoky prison, very weak; but the Lord's power was over all ⟨and supported me through all, and enabled me to do service for him and for his Truth and people, as the place would admit.⟩

And when I was in prison at Lancaster, there was a great noise of the Turk spreading over Christendom, and a great fear in Christendom. And as I was walking in my prison chamber, I saw the Lord's power turn against him, that he was turning back again. And within a month after, the news-book came down, wherein it was mentioned that they had given him a defeat. And this I declared to some, what the Lord had let me see, when there were such fears of his overspreading Christendom. And another time, as I was walking in my chamber, with my eye to the Lord, I saw the angel of the Lord with a glittering drawn sword southward, and as though the Court had been all of a fire; and not long after, the wars began with Holland and the sickness began, and the Lord's sword was drawn.

⟨While I was in Lancaster prison I answered several books, as the *Mass*, and the *Common Prayer*, and the *Directory*, and the *Church Faith*; which are the four chief religions that are got up since the apostles' days. And there being several Friends in prison at Lancaster and other prisons for not paying tithes, I was moved to give forth the following lines to the world concerning tithes.

In the time of the law, they that did not bring their tithes into the store-house, they robbed God, and then there was not meat in their house. Therefore the Lord commanded them to bring them into his house, that there might be meat in the store-house, which was to fill the fatherless, stranger, and widow. But these priests, who are counterfeits, who take people's tithes now by a law, are from the beast, and if any will not pay them they prison them or make them pay treble. So these rob the poor people, and rob the fatherless; and the stranger and the widow are not filled, so their cry is gone up to Heaven against these . . . As there are many now in prison at Lancaster, and in other places, by a national law, the like whereof was never done by the law of God which was delivered to Moses. . . . And there be many which be prisoners at Kendal because they cannot pay tithes, as Captain Ward and Thomas Robertson, and the widow Garland who hath many small children, and these suffer because they cannot pay tithes. . . . But where the Gospel is received indeed, strife and contention are ended, and oppression is taken off. . . . G.F.[1]

After the Assizes at Lancaster were over Colonel Kirkby and some others of the justices were very uneasy with my being at Lancaster, for I had galled them sore at my trials there, and they laboured much to get me removed to some remote place.〉 Colonel Kirkby threatened I should be sent far enough, and beyond sea. And about six weeks after the Assizes,[2] they got an order from the King and Council for removal of me from Lancaster, and with it they brought a letter from the Earl of Anglesey[3] that, if those things were found true against me that I was charged withal, I deserved neither clemency nor mercy. And the greatest matter they had against me was because I could not disobey the command of Christ, and swear.

And the undersheriff and the head sheriff's man and some bailiffs came and fetched me 〈out of the castle〉 when I was not able to go or stand, and had me out of that smoky prison, being very weak, and had me down to the gaoler's house, where was William Kirkby,[4] a justice, and the under-sheriff and several others. And so they called for wine

[1] In full, Ellwood, pp. 295, 296; Bicent., ii, 54, 55.

[2] i.e. about the first week in May, 1665.

[3] Arthur Annesley (1614-1686), created Earl of Anglesey in 1661.

[4] Brother of Colonel Richard Kirkby.

to give me, but I told them I would have none of their wine.

And then they cried, 'Bring out the horses.'

Then I desired them to show me a copy of their order, if they intended to remove me, but they would show me none but their swords. Then I told them there was no sentence passed upon me nor I was not praemunired <that I knew of,> and therefore was not made the King's prisoner but the sheriff's; and they and all the country knew that my indictment was not fully pleaded unto, nor the errors allowed which were sufficient to have quashed the indictment, though they had kept me from one Assize to the other to that end to try me. And they and all the country knew that there was no sentence passed upon me of praemunire, and therefore, as before said, they could not make me the King's prisoner but the sheriff's till I had pleaded and answered to my indictment, and therefore, as I said before, I desired to see their order.

But they haled me out and lifted me up on to one of the sheriff's horses; and when I was in the street (the townspeople being all up in the streets) I told the officers that I had neither received of them civility, sobriety, humanity, nor Christianity. And so they hurried me away about fourteen miles to Bentham in Yorkshire. And I was very weak and hardly able to sit on horseback, and my clothes smelt so of smoke that they were loathsome to myself.

And the wicked gaoler, one Hunter,[1] a young man, he would come behind and give the horse a whip and make him skip and leap <that I, being weak, had much ado to sit him>; and then he would come and look me in the face and say, 'How do you, Mr. Fox?' But I told him it was not civil in him to do so. But the Lord cut him off soon after.

And at last they missed and lost their way. But when we came to Bentham, there met us a-many troopers and a marshal; and many of the gentry of the country were come in and abundance of people to stare at me. And being

[1] Randolph Hunter, 'deputy-gaoler'.

very weak, I desired them to let me lie of a bed, which the soldiers permitted me. So they went into a room and left a guard upon me and gave the marshal and the soldiers their order. And after they had stayed there a while, they pressed horses and raised the bailiff of the hundred, and the constables and others, and so had me to Giggleswick that night. And an exceeding weak man I was. And there they raised the constables with their clog shoes, who sat drinking all night in the room by me so as I could not get much rest.

And the next day we came to a market town, where there were several Friends came to see me, where Robert Widders came to me, and several Friends upon the road.

And the next night I asked the soldiers whither they intended to carry me, and whither I was to be sent and some of them said beyond sea, and others of them to Tynemouth Castle; and a great fear there was amongst the soldiers lest some should rescue me out of their hands, but that fear was needless.

And the next night we came to York, and the marshal put me up in a chamber, a great room, where there came most part of two troops to see me. And one of them, being an envious man, hearing that I was praemunired, asked of me whether my estate was copyhold or free land. ⟨I took no notice of his question.⟩

But I was moved to declare the word of life to the soldiers and many of them were very loving. And at night the Lord Frescheville,[1] that commanded the horse, came to me and was very civil and very loving, and I was made to declare many things unto him of Truth and of the reason of my imprisonment.

And so after they had stayed at York two days, I was sent by the marshal and four or five soldiers to Scarborough Castle, who were very civil men and carried themselves very lovingly to me. And as we went we baited at Malton, where they permitted Friends to come and visit me. And when we came to an inn at Scarborough they sent for the

[1] John, Baron Frescheville, was governor of York.

governor, and he sent for half a dozen soldiers and set them upon me to be my guard that night. And the next day they conducted me up into the castle, and there put me into a room and set a sentry on me, and I being weak and ready to faint, they let me go a little into the air with the sentry.

And after, they removed me out of that room where there was another prisoner, and put me in an open room, where I bestowed a matter of fifty shillings to keep the rain out of it, and from smoking. And when I had done they removed me out of that and put me into another worse room, where I had no chimney nor fire hearth. ⟨And the room being to the sea-side, and lying much open, the wind drove in the rain forcibly; so that the water came over my bed and ran about the room, that I was fain to skim it up with a platter. And when my clothes were wet, I had no fire to dry them; so that my body was numbed with cold, and my fingers swelled, that one was grown as big as two. And though I was at some charge on this room also yet I could not keep out the wind and rain.⟩

And whilst I was there that space at Scarborough many great persons came to see me. And there came one Sir Francis Cobb[1] and the governor Sir Jordan Crosland[2] came with him; and I desired the governor to go into my room and see what a room I had. And I had got a little fire made in it and it smoked so that they could not find the way out of it, and he being a Papist I told him that was his purgatory, where they had put me into. This was the former room that they removed me out of after I had bestowed that cost upon it.

And few Friends would they let come at me, nay many times not so much as to bring me a little meat; but I was forced to hire one of the world the first quarter, and sometimes the soldiers would take it from her, and then she would fight with them for it. Then I hired a soldier to fetch me

[1] *c.* 1606-1675, High Sheriff of Yorkshire.

[2] Sir Jordan Crosland (*c.* 1620-1670), governor of Scarborough Castle, 1660-1670; Member of Parliament for Scarborough, 1661.

water and bread, and something to make a fire when I was in a room where a fire could be made. A threepenny loaf served me three weeks and sometimes longer ⟨and most of my drink was water with wormwood steeped in it⟩. One time when it was very cold weather I had gotten a little elecampane[1] beer, for I had taken a great cold. And I heard one of the soldiers say to the others they would go play a pretty trick, for they would send for me up to the deputy governor, which they did, and in the meantime they would drink my strong beer out, which they did. And after, one of the officers came to me in a jeer and asked me for some strong beer, but I told them they had played their pretty trick and so took no farther notice of their wickedness. And if a Friend came up into the castle about business, if he looked but at me they would rage at him. So I was as a man buried alive, for many Friends came from far to see me but were not suffered to come at me.

⟨But inasmuch as they kept me so very strait, I spake to the keepers of the castle to this effect: 'I did not know till I was removed from Lancaster Castle, and brought prisoner to this castle of Scarborough, that I was convicted of a praemunire, for the judge did not give sentence upon me at the Assizes in open court. But seeing I am now a prisoner here, if I may not have my liberty and enlargement, let my friends and acquaintance have their liberty to come and visit me, as Paul's friends had among the Romans, who were not Christians but heathens. For Paul's friends had their liberty, and all that would, might come to him, and he had his liberty to preach to them in his hired house; but I cannot have liberty to go into the town, nor for my friends to come to me here. So you that go under the name of Christians, are worse in this respect than those heathens were.'⟩

And there were two bad prisoners that often would drink with the officers and soldiers, and because I would not sit and drink with them they made them worse against me. One time when they were almost drunk, one of them,

[1] A plant used as a stomachic or tonic medicine.

Will Wilkinson ⟨a Presbyterian who had been a captain⟩ came and challenged me to fight with him. And they were both full of beer, and when one would be at me the other withheld him, and when the other would be at me, then the other would withhold him. And the next morning when they were more sober I told him that challenged me I was come to answer him, with my hands in my pockets, and ⟨reaching my head towards him, said⟩ there was my hair and my back, and what a shame it was for him to challenge a man whose principle he knew was not to strike; he should have challenged some of the soldiers that might have answered him again. ⟨But he skipped away and went into another room, at which the soldiers fell a-laughing,⟩ and one of the officers said, 'You are a happy man that can bear such things.' ⟨After a while he took the oath, gave bond, and got out of prison⟩ and the Lord soon cut him off in his wickedness.

And Joblin,[1] the gaoler of Durham, who was prisoner with me in Scarborough Castle, and had often incensed the governor and officers against me, which would be too large to speak of, he got out of prison. But the Lord cut him off in his wickedness soon after. And the judgements of God pursued several other envious persons against me.

There were great imprisonments in this and the former year ⟨while I was prisoner at Lancaster and Scarborough⟩, and several were banished. And many were crowded into Newgate and other prisons where the sickness[2] was, and many Friends died in prison.

Many were banished and several were set on shipboard by the King's order. And some masters ⟨of ships would not carry them but⟩ set them ashore again. And some were sent to Barbadoes and Jamaica and to Nevis, and the Lord there blessed them. And one master of a ship which carried Friends, who kept Friends under decks, though the sickness

[1] John Joblin was one of the militant Baptists of this period. The warrant committing him to Scarborough Castle was dated Whitehall, 30th Nov., 1664.

[2] The plague of 1665.

was amongst them and many died of it, was so plagued for his wickedness that he lost most of his seamen also with the plague, and lay for several months crossed with contrary winds, though other ships passed out and went their voyages. And at last he arrived in the Sound at Plymouth and there the governor and magistrates would not suffer him nor none of his men to come ashore, though he wanted many necessaries for his voyage. But Friends went to the ship's side, and carried necessaries to the ship for Friends. Thomas Lower, Arthur Cotton, and John Light of Plymouth and other Friends went with it to them.

And so the master being sore crossed, and plagued, and vexed, he cursed them that put him upon this freight; and hoped he should not go far before he was taken. And within a little time that the vessel went forth of the Sound of Plymouth, she was taken by a Dutch man-of-war and carried into Holland; and the banished Friends were sent into England by the States of Holland with a let-pass and certificate ⟨that they had not made an escape but were sent back by them.⟩

And at last the Lord's power came over all and many of our persecutors were ashamed and confounded. And largely I might write of these things, but the books of sufferings testify of it more at large.

And they set a marshal over us to get money, but I was not to give him a farthing. So at last he was taken off again. And often they threatened to hang me over the wall and the officers often in their rage would bid the soldiers shoot me and run me through, and the deputy governor said ⟨that the King, knowing I had a great interest in the people, had sent me thither, that⟩ if any stir was in the nation they might hang me over the walls ⟨to keep the people down⟩. So I told him, if that was it they looked for I was ready, being innocent of all stirrings and plottings, and I never feared death nor sufferings in my life. So that stopped them from threatening me any more. ⟨There being, a while after, a marriage at a Papist's house, a great many of them were met together; and they talked much then of hanging me.⟩

There came another great company of Papists; and they affirmed the Pope was infallible and had stood infallible ever since Peter's time. But I told them and showed them out of Eusebius that one of the Bishops of Rome, Marcellinus by name, denied the faith and sacrificed to idols and therefore he was not infallible; and if they were in the infallible Spirit they need not have gaols, swords, and staves, racks, and tortures, fires and faggots, whips, and gallows to hold up their religion, and to destroy men's lives. For if they were in the infallible Spirit they would preserve men's lives, and use none but spiritual weapons.

Then I told them there was a woman in Kent that had been a Papist and had brought several to that religion. And after she came to be convinced of God's Truth and turned by it to Christ her saviour, she admonished the Papists to the same. And one of them, being a tailor, who was working at her house, ⟨she opened to him the falseness of the Popish religion and endeavoured to draw him from it to the Truth.⟩ As she was admonishing of him, he drew his knife at her and got betwixt her and the door. And I asked the woman what he would have done with his knife, and she said he would have stabbed her. And she ⟨spoke boldly to him and⟩ bid him put up his knife for she knew his principle. 'Stab thee ?' said I. 'What would he stab thee for ? Thy religion ?' 'Yes', said she, 'It is the principle of the Papists. If any turn from their religion, it is their principle to kill them ⟨if they can.' This story I told them, of⟩ one that had been one of them, that had forsaken their principles and had discovered their practices, and they did not deny it, but said, 'What ! would you declare this abroad ?' and I told them, 'Yes, such things ought to be declared abroad', how contrary to true Christianity it was. And they went away in a rage.

And there was another Papist that came to discourse with me, and he said all the patriarchs were in hell, from the creation till Christ came; and when Christ suffered he went into hell, and the Devil said to him, 'What comest thou hither for, to break open our strongholds?' And Christ said, 'To fetch them all out.' And so, he said, Christ was three days and three nights in hell, to bring them out. I told him that was false, for Christ said to the thief, 'This day shalt thou be with me in Paradise.' And Enoch and Elijah were translated into Heaven. And Abraham was in Heaven, for the Scripture saith Lazarus was in his bosom. And Moses and Elias were with Christ upon the Mount before he suffered. So that stopped the Papist's mouth ⟨and put him to a stand.⟩

And then there came one Dr. Wittie,[1] which was esteemed a great doctor of physic, and Lord Fauconberg[2] and the governor of Tynemouth Castle,[3] and several knights. ⟨I being called to them, this⟩ Wittie took up the discourse and asked me what I was in prison for. And I said because I would not disobey the command of Christ and swear. So he said I ought to swear my allegiance to the King. And he was a great Presbyterian. And I asked him whether he had not sworn against the King and House of Lords, and taken the Scotch Covenant, and now had he not sworn for the King, and what was his swearing good for. And my allegiance did not consist in swearing but in truth and faithfulness.

And so after many more words with them, after a while I was had away to my prison. And this Wittie boasted in the town among his patients that he had conquered me. And I told Sir Jordan Crosland it was a small boast in him to say he had conquered a bound man; and desired him to bid him come to me again when he came to the castle.

And he came again with a matter of sixteen or seventeen great persons ⟨and then he ran himself worse on ground than before⟩. He affirmed before them all that Christ had not enlightened every man that cometh into the world

[1] Robert Wittie, of Hull, and later of York.
[2] Thomas Belasyse (1627-1700), second Viscount Fauconberg.
[3] Colonel Edward Villiers.

and that the grace of God had not appeared unto all men, that brought salvation, and that Christ had not died for all men.

Then I asked him what sort of men were those that Christ had not enlightened, and his grace had not appeared to them, and that he had not died for.

And he said, 'He did not die for adulterers and idolaters and wicked men.'

Then I asked him again whether adulterers and idolaters and wicked men were not sinners, and whether Christ did not die for sinners, and came not to call sinners to repentance.

And he said, 'Yes.'

'So', said I, 'Thou hast stopped thy own mouth.' For I proved that the grace of God had appeared unto all men though some turned it into wantonness and walked despitefully against it, and that Christ had enlightened all men, though some hated it. And several of the people confessed that it was true. And he went away in a great rage, and came no more at me.

And another time the governor brought a priest but his mouth was soon stopped. And another time after, he brought two or three Parliament men; and they asked me whether I did own ministers and bishops. And I told them, Yes, such as Christ sent forth who said, 'Freely you have received, freely give,' and such as were qualified and were in the same power and spirit that they were in in the apostles' days. But such teachers and bishops as theirs were, that would go no farther than they had a great benefice, I did not own, for they were not like the apostles. For Christ saith to his ministers, 'Go ye into all nations and preach the Gospel.'

'And you Parliament men, that keep your priests and bishops in such great fat benefices, you have spoiled them all. For do ye think they will go into all nations to preach the gospel, or will go any farther than they have a great fat benefice? Judge yourselves.'

Then there came a great company with the old Lord

Fairfax's widow[1] and a priest. And I was made to speak to them the Truth.

The priest asked me why we said 'thee' and 'thou' to people, ⟨for he counted us but fools and idiots for speaking so⟩. And I asked him whether they that translated the Scriptures and made the grammar and accidence were fools and idiots, that left it so translated to us, as 'thee' and 'thou' to a singular and 'you' to a plural. And if they were fools and idiots then why had not they, which looked upon themselves as wise men that could not bear 'thee' and 'thou' to a singular, altered both the grammar, accidence, and Bible, and made it plural instead of singular? But if they were wise men that had so translated it, then were not they fools and idiots that did not practise it? And was it not wrong in them to be offended at us that did practise it, and call us fools and idiots? So many of them were pretty loving and tender, and acknowledged to Truth and would have given me money but I would not receive it.

And after this came Dr. Cradock with three priests more and the governor and a great company with them, and his lady[2] and another lady. And he asked me what I was in prison for; and I told him, for obeying the command of Christ and the apostle in not swearing, and if he, ⟨being both a doctor and⟩ a justice of the peace, could convince me that after Christ and the Apostle had forbidden swearing that then they commanded people to swear, I might then swear, as I had said to the judge at Lancaster, and here was the Bible. And I bid him show me.

Then he said, 'It is written "You shall swear in truth and righteousness."'

I told him I did commend him that he had brought Scripture, and I did believe I could bring as many instances in the Old Testament as he, and it may be more too, but what *you* was this: was it *you* Jews or *you* Gentiles that this

1 This was, apparently, Rhoda, second wife of Ferdinando, second Baron Fairfax.

2 Sir J. Crosland married Bridget, daughter of John Fleming, of Rydal.

command was to, for he knew that we were gentiles by nature. And where did God ever give a command to the Gentiles to swear, but to the Jews ? And so was this *you* to *you* Jews or *you* Gentiles or *you* Christians after Christ came in the gospel times ?

And unto this he would not answer, but at the last one of the priests answered, that were with him, and said it was to the Jews that this command was, to swear in truth and righteousness.

Then Dr. Cradock he confessed it was so. 'Indeed', says he, 'In the gospel times every thing was to be established out of the mouth of two or three witnesses, for there was to be no swearing then.'

Then said I, 'Why dost thou force oaths upon Christians contrary to thy own knowledge in the gospel times ? And why dost thou excommunicate my friends ?' For he had excommunicated abundance both in Yorkshire and Lancashire.

And he said, 'For not coming to the church.'

Then I said, 'You left us above twenty years ago, when we were but young lads and lasses, to the Presbyterians, Independents, and Baptists, who made spoil of our goods and persecuted us because we would not follow them. And if you would have kept your principles alive you should have sent some of your epistles and gospels and homilies and evening songs to the old men that knew your principles, and to the young men that knew little of your principles <that we might have known them>, and not have fled away from us and left us to the Presbyterians, Independents, and Baptists. For they and we might have turned Turks or Jews for any collects or homilies or epistles we had from you all this while. For Paul wrote epistles to the saints, though he was in prison.

'And so thou hast excommunicated us, both old and young, that is you have put us out of your church before you have got us into your church and brought us to know your principles; and this is madness, to put us out before we be brought in. Now had you brought us into your church, and after, if we had done some bad thing, then to put us out had been something like a ground for excommunication. But what dost thou call the church ?'

'Why ', says he, 'That which you call the steeplehouse.'

Then I asked him whether Christ shed his blood for the steeplehouse and purchased and sanctified the steeplehouse with his blood, for the Church was Christ's wife and bride and he was head of the Church. And 'Thinkest thou the steeplehouse is Christ's bride and wife: and that he is the head of that old house, or of the people ?'

'Nay ', says he, 'Christ is the head of the people and they are the Church, and not the steeplehouse.'

Then I said, 'But you have given that title *church* to an old house which belongs to the people and you have taught people to believe so.'

Then I asked him why he persecuted Friends concerning their not paying tithes, and whether God did ever give a command to the Gentiles that they should pay tithes, and whether Christ had not ended the Levitical priesthood that took tithes, and whether Christ that sent forth his disciples to preach had not commanded them to preach freely as he had given to them freely, and whether all the ministers of Christ were not bound to observe this command of Christ.

And he said he would not dispute that, but ⟨presently turned to another matter and⟩ said, 'You marry, but I know not how.'

Then I said unto him, 'It may be so ', but why did he not come and see. Then he threatened how he had and would use his power against us. But I bid him take heed for he was an old man. Then I asked him where did ever any priest from Genesis to the Revelation marry any. If he could show me any instance we would come to them to marry us.

'For thou hast excommunicated one of my friends two years after he was dead, about it. And why dost not excommunicate Isaac and Jacob, and Boaz, and Ruth, and Christ and his disciples for going to a marriage ? Why dost thou not use thy power against them; for we do not read that they were ever married by the priests; but they took one another in the assemblies of the righteous, in the presence of God and his people; and so do we. And we have all the holy men and women of our side, that the Scripture speaks of in this practice.'

So after a while he passed away with his company. And many such-like disputes and discourses I had with several sorts of people, which would be too long and tedious to relate here.

But at last the governor came under some trouble having sent out a privateer who had taken some ships that were not enemies' ships but their friends and so came under trouble, ⟨after which he grew somewhat more friendly to me⟩.

And I desired him when he came to London, he being a Parliament man, that he would speak to Esquire Marsh and to Sir Francis Cobb and some others, and tell them that I was a prisoner, and for what, and how long I had lain in prison, ⟨and he did so⟩.

And when he came down again he told me that Esquire Marsh, that was one of the King's esquires of his body, said he would go one hundred miles barefoot for my liberty, he knew me so well, and that several others spoke well of me. So the governor was very loving to me.

And after a while John Whitehead brought an order from the King for my release.

For ⟨after I had lain prisoner above a year in Scarborough Castle,⟩ I sent a letter to the King, concerning my imprisonment, and bad usage in prison; and that I was informed, no one could deliver me but he.[1]

[h]The order that is now carried down to get him released was obtained after this manner. John Whitehead and I drew up a short relation of George Fox his sufferings, and

[1] Ellwood editions attribute the release to the efforts described in the following paragraph, which is part of a letter from Ellis Hookes to Margaret Fell, London, 14th August, 1666, preserved in the MS. Journal. Ellwood, however, put it into the first person, as though recorded by Fox himself in his Journal.

Esquire Marsh went with them to the Master of Requests; and by much solicitation an order was obtained by the Master of Requests, Sir John Birkenhead, to release him. . . . The order runs thus: That the King, being certainly informed that George Fox is a man against all plotting and fighting, and one that is ready at all times to discover plots rather than to make them, and was an instrument of discovering a plot in Yorkshire, orders that he should be discharged of his imprisonment, giving security for to live peaceable.[h]

So the governor received the order, and the officers gathered together, and discharged me ⟨without requiring bonds or sureties for my peaceable living, being satisfied that I was a man of a peaceable life⟩, and gave me a certificate as followeth.

Permit the bearer hereof, George Fox, late a prisoner in Scarborough Castle and now discharged by his Majesty's order, quietly to pass about his lawful occasions, without any molestation.

Given under my hand at Scarborough Castle this first day of September, 1666. J. Crosland,

Governor of Scarborough Castle.

And I would have given the governor something for his civility but he would not receive anything, and said, whatever good he could do to my friends he would do it and never do them any hurt; and so he remained to do till he died.

And when the mayor of the town sent to him for soldiers to break up Friends Meetings, if he sent any down he would charge them not to meddle, but remained loving till he died.

And then the officers and soldiers were mightily changed and respective.[1] And said, 'He is as stiff as a tree and as pure as a bell, for we could never stir him.'

[1] i.e. attentive and courteous.

[h]. . . . . .[h] *Camb. Jnl.*, ii, 103; Ellwood, pp. 304, 305; Bicent., ii, 69, 70.

The first day I came out of that prison the fire broke out in London, that consumed most part of the city in three days time. And then I saw the Lord God was true and just in his word that he had showed me before in Lancaster Gaol. <The people of London were forewarned of this fire>; yet few people laid it to heart but grew rather more wicked and higher in pride.

We had a Friend[1] that was moved to come out of Huntingdonshire before the fire, and to scatter his money up and down the streets, and to turn his horse loose in the streets and to untie his breeches' knees, and let his stockings fall, and to unbutton his doublet, and to tell the people so should they run up and down scattering their money and their goods half undressed like mad people, as he gave them a sign. And so they did when the fire broke out and the city was burning.

And thus the Lord has exercised his prophets and people and servants by his power, and showed them signs of his judgements. And some they beat and evilly entreated and imprisoned, both in the other power's days and since. But the Lord is just, and happy are they that obey his word.

And many have been moved to go naked in their streets as signs of their nakedness. And many men and women have been moved to go naked and in sackcloth, in the other power's days and since, as signs of their nakedness from the image of God and righteousness and holiness, and how that God would strip them and make them bare and naked as they were. But, instead of considering of it, they have many times whipped them and imprisoned them or abused them.

And in Oliver Protector's days many were moved to go, some to the great Turk and to Jerusalem, and to the Pope, to warn them of the day of the Lord and to preach his everlasting gospel. And much trials and sufferings they went through, but the Lord's power did uphold all the faithful, yea even to death. And in his days the priests put up several petitions to Oliver, and his son Richard,

[1] Thomas Ibbott, of Hemingford, Hunts.

and to the parliaments and judges and justices and the Sessions, against us, stuffed full of lies and vilifying words and slanders. But through the Lord's power we got them and answered them all; and we cleared the Lord's truth and ourselves of them.

But Oh, the body of darkness that rose up against the Truth, who made lies their refuge. But the Lord swept them away, and in his power and truth, light and life, hedged his lambs about and did preserve them as on eagles' wings. And therefore I and we had great encouragement to trust to the Lord, whom we did see by his power and spirit how he did overturn and bring all the confederates and counsels and darkness that was hatched against the Truth and his people to nought, and by the same Truth gave his people dominion that in it they might serve him.

And many sad judgements came upon all my old persecutors in Lancashire, as may be seen in this following list. He that fetched me to Holker Hall, one Thomas Fleming a servant to Colonel Kirkby ⟨wasted his estate and soon after fled into Ireland.⟩ And old Thomas Preston, then high sheriff, his wife and son and daughter are since dead. And Rawlinson and Sir George Middleton, justices that bound me over to the Sessions, are both since dead. And the justices on the bench at the Sessions were Fleming and Rawlinson and Spencer and Colonel West and Matthew West of Borwick, and Porter; Porter and Rawlinson and both the Wests are since dead. And this Justice Fleming imprisoned two Friends to death, Samuel Sands and one Parkamoore, who left several fatherless children, after which Fleming's wife died and left him thirteen or fourteen motherless children.[1] And a consumption came upon Spencer's estate, and Colonel Kirkby wasted away all his estate and buried three wives.

And Richard Dodgson the chief constable died soon after, and George Mount the petty constable; and John

[1] Samuel Sands died in 1663. Sir Daniel Fleming's wife died 13th April, 1675; i.e. these "sad judgements" connect events separated by many years.

Ashburnham buried his wife soon after, who scolded much at me in her house. Also Will Knipe the witness against me soon after died. And the gaoler, one Hunter, that abused me in Lancaster prison, he was cut off in his young days. And the under-sheriff that carried me from Lancaster prison towards Scarborough till he met the soldiers aforesaid at Bentham in Yorkshire, I heard that he was dead also.

When I came into the country again[1] all these aforesaid were dead and ruined in their estates and several others of our persecutors whom the Lord blasted and ruined; and though I did not seek to execute the law upon them for their acting contrary to their own laws against me, yet the Lord had executed his vengeance upon them.

CHAPTER XX

AND after I came forth of Scarborough Castle I went about three miles unto a large General Meeting, and all was quiet; which meeting was at a Friend's house that had been a chief constable. And, on the Fourth-day after, I came into Scarborough town and had a large meeting at Peter Hodgson's house; and there came a lady unto it and several great persons, and the lady came to me and said I spoke against the priests. And I told her such as the prophets and Christ declared against I did declare against now.

There was a young man convinced in Scarborough town whilst I was in prison, the bailiff's son; and he came to dispute and spoke Hebrew to me and I spoke in Welsh to him and bid him fear God, who after became a pretty Friend.

And after I had visited Friends at Whitby I passed to Bridlington[2] where I had another meeting, and from thence

[1] i.e. in 1675. Cf. the previous footnote.
[2] Then called Burlington.

to Ulrome where I had another meeting, and from thence to Marmaduke Storr's[1] where we had a large meeting at a constable's house on whom the Lord had wrought a great miracle, as in the book of miracles may be seen.[2]

And there was a great marriage of two Friends the next day. And there came some hundreds of beggars. And Friends refreshed them instead of the rich. And in the meeting before the marriage I was moved to open to the people the state of our marriages, how the people of God took one another in the assemblies of the elders, and how God did join man and woman together before the Fall. And man had joined in the Fall but it was God's joining again in the restoration, and never from Genesis to the Revelation did ever any priests marry any, as may be read in the Scriptures. And then I showed them the duty of man and wife how they should serve God, being heirs of life and grace together.

And from thence I passed to Grace Barwick's[3] where I had a General Meeting which was very large. And so came through the Wolds to one Shipton's,[4] where I had a large meeting also.

And from thence I went to a priest's house, whose wife was convinced and mighty loving and glad to see me. This priest had said formerly ⟨in the year 1651, that if ever he met me again⟩ he would have my life or I should have his, and he would give his head if I was not knocked down in a month's time, who was now very loving and convinced of God's eternal truth.

And from thence I passed towards the sea where several Friends came to visit me, and one Philip Scafe, that had been formerly a priest but was convinced and was now become a preacher of Christ freely, and so continues.

And from thence I passed to see an old man that was

[1] Marmaduke Storr, farmer, of Owstwick.

[2] See *George Fox's Book of Miracles*, edited by Henry J. Cadbury. Cambridge University Press, 1948.

[3] Grace, widow of Robert Barwick, lived at Kelk.

[4] Richard Shipton built Lythe Hall near Whitby in 1660.

convinced who was above a hundred years old; and from thence I passed to a Friend's house where I had a great meeting and all was quiet.

So I passed through the country till I came near Malton where I had a large meeting, and near Hull also I had a large meeting. And from thence I came to a place called Howden Dyke. And as I came into the town the watchmen questioned me and them with me, and would have had us before the magistrates; but, having no warrant, they went away in a rage and said they would search for us. But I went to the Lady Montague's house where I lodged all night and Friends came to see me there. ⟨Next morning, being up betimes, I walked out into the orchard, and saw a man about sunrising go into the house in a great cloak. He stayed not long but came soon out again and went away, not seeing me. I felt something strike at my life; and went into the house, where I found the maid-servant affrighted and trembling. She told me that man had a naked rapier under his cloak. By which I perceived he came with an intent to have done mischief, but the Lord prevented him.⟩

From thence I passed through the country visiting Friends till I came to York, where we had a large meeting and I went to visit Justice Robinson, an ancient Justice of Peace that had been very loving to me and Friends at the beginning. And there was a priest with him, who told me it was said of us that we loved none but ourselves. But I told him we loved all mankind as they were God's creation and as they were children of Adam and Eve by generation, and we loved the brotherhood in the Holy Ghost. So after many more words with him, who was very loving, we passed away.

And I had given forth a book about this time entitled *Fear God and Honour the King*, ⟨in which I showed⟩ that none could fear God and honour the King but who departed from sin and evil, which book did mightily affect the soldiers and people.

And after I had visited Friends at York, I passed towards

a market town. And there was a justice riding before us. And the watchmen questioned him, and perceiving he was a justice they let him pass and so we escaped also. At this town[1] we had a great meeting at one George Watkinson's house, who formerly had been a justice. And a glorious blessed meeting it was, and very large, and the Seed of life was set over all.

Thence we passed to Thomas Taylor's[2] who had formerly been a captain, where we had a precious meeting. And there was a knight lived hard by that threatened me and said that if the King set me at liberty he would send me to prison again the next day. But the Lord's power stopped him and our meeting was quiet.

And from thence I passed through the country visiting Friends till I came to Cinder Hill Green,[3] where I had a large General Meeting. And the priest heard of it and he sent the constables to the justices and they brought a warrant, and rid their horses so hard that they had almost spoiled them. But the meeting was ended before I heard of them. And as I was going out of the house, a Friend came to me and told me they were searching another house for me. And as I was going along through the closes, I met the constables and warders and the justices' clerk. And I went through them and they looked at me. And so I went to the house that they had been searching. And thus the devil and the priests lost their design, and the Lord's power gave me dominion over them and bound them. Praised be his name for ever. And Friends all parted and escaped them and so they went away as they came, for the Lord God had frustrated their design.

And from thence I went into Derbyshire, where I had a large meeting. And some Friends were afraid of the constables coming in, for they had had great persecution in those parts.

And there was a justice of peace had taken away much

[1] Belgrave House, Gracious Street; sometimes wrongly identified as Scotton.

[2] Thomas Taylor lived at Brighouse.

[3] Near Woodhouse.

of Friends' goods. And one Ellen Fretwell had made her appeal to the Sessions. And the rest of the justices granted her her goods again, and spoke to the persecuting justice that he should not do so any more. And then she was moved to speak to that justice and to warn him, and he bid her come and sit down on the bench. 'Aye', said she, 'if I may do justice to the country I will sit down with you.' 'No', said he, 'then you shall not'; but bid her get out of the court. Then she was moved of the Lord to turn again and say that she should be there when he should not. And after the Sessions were done he got amongst some of his persecuting companions, and said that they would get some more goods of Friends if the Devil did not raise up that woman to hinder them. So he went home and drove away her brother's oxen for going to meetings.

And so another woman Friend of Chesterfield, Susan Frith, was moved of the Lord to tell him that if he continued on in his persecuting, the Lord would execute his plagues upon him.

And so this justice whose name was Clarke[1] went home and fell distracted. And they tied him in ropes but he gnawed them to pieces; and he had like to have worried his maid, <for he fell upon her and bit her>. And they were fain to put an iron instrument into his mouth to wrest his teeth out of her flesh. And so he died distracted in chains; which relation I had from Ellen Fretwell's own mouth.

Thence I passed into Nottinghamshire and had a large meeting at Skegby; from thence I went to Mansfield, where likewise I had a meeting; thence to another town where there was a fair where I saw and met with many Friends.

And from thence I passed to Nottingham through the Forest in a mighty thundering and rainy day, where many trees were blown up by the roots and some people that came from the market killed. But the Lord's power preserved us. And on the First-day I had a large meeting in Nottingham.

[1] Justice Godfrey Clarke lived near Chesterfield. Bicent. and some copies of Ellwood, omit the next two sentences. See p. x ante.

And all was brought under their teacher, the grace of God, which brought their salvation. And I established them upon the rock and foundation, Christ Jesus. And after the meeting was done I came to visit the sheriff[1] who had been convinced formerly about 1649, whose prisoner I then was. And all was quiet. And from thence I passed into Leicestershire to Sileby, where we had a large blessed meeting; and I went to Leicester to visit the prisoners there.

And from thence I came to John Penford's[2] where we had a General Meeting, large and precious. And from thence I passed through the country visiting Friends and my relations till I came into Warwickshire, and to Warwick where I visited the prisoners. And from thence I passed to Baddesley, where I had a precious meeting; and so I passed through Northamptonshire and Bedfordshire and Buckinghamshire and Oxfordshire visiting Friends. And in Oxfordshire the Devil had laid a snare for me, but the Lord brake it. And his power came over all, and his blessed truth increased.

And so after I had passed through many countries and had large meetings, visiting Friends and my relations, I came at last to London.

But I was so weak with lying about three years in cruel and hard imprisonments, my joints and my body were so <stiff and> benumbed that I could hardly get on my horse. Neither could I well bend my knees, nor hardly endure fire nor eat warm meat: I had been so long kept from it.

And so after I had visited Friends' meetings in London, which were large and precious, I walked into the ruins of the city that was burnt, which I saw lying according as the word of the Lord came to me concerning it several years before.

And after I had visited Friends a time in London I went into the countries again and had large meetings through the countries as at Reading and Kingston and in Wiltshire,

[1] John Reckless. See p. 40 ante.

[2] John Penford lived at Kirby Muxloe, near Leicester.

till I came to Bristol, and had many a large meeting at Bristol it being their fair-time.[1] And Thomas Lower came up hither out of Cornwall to see me; and Friends from several parts of the nation. And after I was clear of Bristol, I passed up to Justice Nathaniel Cripps's[2] and so through the countries till I came to London again, and had large meetings and all was quiet. Blessed be the Lord.

And though I was very weak, yet I travelled up and down in the service of the Lord.

And about this time John Swinton, and some other Scotch Friends, and some others had run out from Truth, and the Lord's power came over them so as they were made to condemn and tear all their papers of controversies to pieces. And several meetings we had and the Lord's everlasting power was over all and judgement was set. And whole days we sat, wherein many condemned their former lives and runnings out, as may be seen in the Book of Condemnations at that time, wherein the Lord's power was wonderfully manifested. Several that had run out with John Perrot and others, came in, and condemned that spirit that led them to keep on their hats when Friends prayed, and said it was of the Devil, and said that Friends were more righteous than they, and that if Friends had not stood they had been gone, and fallen into perdition. And thus the Lord's power came over all.

And then I was moved of the Lord God to set up and establish five Monthly Meetings of men and women in the city of London, besides the Women's Meeting and the Quarterly Meeting, to admonish, and exhort ⟨such as walked disorderly or carelessly, and not according to Truth⟩; and to take care of God's glory.

And the Lord opened to me and let me see what I must do, and how I must order and establish the Men's and Women's Monthly and Quarterly Meetings in all the nation, and write to other nations, where I came not, to do the same.

[1] Bristol winter fair, 1667; it began 25th January.

[2] At Tetbury, Wilts.

And whereas they had had only Quarterly Meetings, now Truth was spread and Friends were grown popular[1] that now I must set up the Monthly Meetings in the nations.

And so after things were well settled in London, and the Lord's Truth and power and seed and life reigned and shined over all in the city, then I passed forth into the countries[2] and settled the Monthly Meetings in Essex, Norfolk, and Suffolk. And Thomas Dry went along with me. And from thence, after I had visited the meetings in that country and set up the Monthly Meetings there, I had a Men's Monthly Meeting also at a priest's house that had been convinced. And from thence we passed into Huntingdonshire, where we had very large blessed meetings though there was some opposition. But the Lord's power came over all and the Monthly Men's Meetings were established there also.

And from thence we passed into Bedfordshire, where we had some opposition, but the Lord's power came over it all. And from thence we passed into Nottinghamshire. And after the Monthly Meetings were settled we had many precious meetings in those countries.

And from thence we passed into Lincolnshire. And on the day called Christmas Day [1667], at his house who had been formerly the sheriff of Lincoln,[3] we had some men Friends of all the meetings in the county, and all was quiet. And after the meeting was done we passed away from thence to a Friend's house, and I was very weak, and they threatened to come and break up our meeting but the Lord's power chained them, blessed be his name, and our meeting was quiet. And after the meeting was done I went to visit William Smith[4] who was very sick and weak at that time. And the constables and bailiffs had seized upon all Will Smith's goods, to the very bed he

[1] i.e. numerous.
[2] Late summer, 1667.
[3] Robert Craven.
[4] William Smith lived at Besthorpe, Notts.

lay upon, for Truth's sake, and they watched his corn and his beasts, that none might carry his goods and corn away.

And he that was formerly the sheriff of Lincoln was with me; and from thence we passed over Trent into Nottinghamshire again, where we had some from all the meetings in that county together, and our meeting was very glorious and peaceable, and many precious meetings we had in that county.

From thence we passed into Leicestershire and so into Warwickshire where many blessed meetings we had and the order of the Gospel was set up and the Men's Monthly Meetings were established in all those countries.

And from thence we passed into Derbyshire where we had several large blessed meetings and in many places we were threatened but escaped by the power of the Lord.

And from thence we passed into Staffordshire over the Peak hills, which were very cold, it being snow and frost. And I was so exceeding weak I was hardly able to get off or on my horse back. And at Thomas Hammersley's[1] we had a General Men's Meeting where all things were settled in the gospel order and the Monthly Meetings were established also.

And from thence we passed into Cheshire where we had several blessed meetings, a General Men's Meeting, where all the Monthly Meetings were settled according to the gospel order in the power of God. And after the meeting was done I passed away. And the justices heard of it after it was done, and were very much troubled that they had not come and broken it up and taken me; but the Lord prevented them.

And so after I had cleared myself there in the Lord's service, I passed into Lancashire to William Barnes's near Warrington,[2] where there met me some of most of the meetings in that county. And there also all the Monthly Meetings were established in the gospel order.

[1] At Basford, near Leek.

[2] William Barnes lived at Brook House, Great Sankey.

And I sent papers into Westmorland by Leonard Fell and Robert Widders, and into Bishoprick, Cleveland, and Northumberland, and into Cumberland and Scotland, for them to settle the Monthly Meetings in the Lord's power, which they did.

And so the Lord's power came over all, and all the heirs of it came to inherit it, for the authority of our meetings is the power of God, the Gospel which brings life and immortality to light, that they may see over the Devil that has darkened them, and that all the heirs of the Gospel might walk according to the Gospel, and glorify God with their bodies, souls, and spirits, which are the Lord's. And so the order of the glorious heavenly Gospel is not of man nor by man.

And from Lancashire I passed into Cheshire, and Margaret Fell, being a prisoner at Lancaster, got leave to come up to the meeting and went with me to Jane Milner's in Cheshire, and so passed back again.

And so out of Cheshire I passed into Shropshire, and from thence into Wales, into Denbighshire and Montgomeryshire and had a large General Men's Meeting at Charles Lloyd's,[1] where some opposers came in, but the Lord's power was over all.

And from thence we passed to Merionethshire where we had several blessed meetings. And from thence we passed to the seaside where we had a blessed meeting, and so passed through several counties and had many large meetings, and Friends were established upon Christ their foundation.

And from thence we returned into Shropshire again, and having settled the Monthly Meetings in the power of God both in Wales and Shropshire, and those other counties, we came into Worcestershire.

And after we had had many meetings up and down in that country amongst Friends, we had a General Men's Meeting at Pershore at Henry Gibbs's house where we settled all the Monthly Meetings in the gospel order. And the Sessions being in town that day Friends were very much

[1] At Dolobran, the seat of the Lloyd family for many generations.

concerned lest they should send some officers to break up our meeting but the Lord's power chained them all, so that our meeting was quiet, through which power we had dominion. And after the meeting was done I passed away and had several meetings in that country amongst Friends, and came to Worcester. It being their fair-time,[1] we had a precious meeting, and after I was gone out of town there was one Major Wilde, a wicked persecuting man, and some of his soldiers enquired after me, but I passed away to Droitwich and left Friends settled in good order.

And from thence we came to Shrewsbury, where we had a precious meeting, and the mayor and his officers, hearing of my being in town, they met together to consult what to do against me; for they said the great Quaker of England was come to town and therefore they took counsel together to imprison me, but some of them opposed it, so the Lord confounded them. And from thence we passed into Radnorshire where we had many precious meetings and we settled the Monthly Meetings.

And as we came forth of the country at a market town we stayed a while, and a justice's clerk and some others combined together to do us some mischief in the road. And they overtook us, but meeting many market people they were somewhat hindered of their design. But they lit on two of our company that rid behind us, and one of them drew out his sword and cut Richard Moore of Shrewsbury, a doctor of physic, and the other came galloping after me and another Friend that was with me, and rid into a brook, the bridge being narrow, to get before us, so that his horse fell into a deep hole in the water. And I saw their design and stopped and desired Friends to be patient and give them no occasion. And Richard Moore came up to us, and another Friend that knew their names, and so we rid along the road. And there we met another man drunk, who was afoot with a naked rapier in his hand. And in a bottom we met two men and two women, one of which men had his thumb cut off by this man that we met with a

[1] A toll-free market was held on 9th Feb., 1668.

naked rapier in his hand who would have ravished the young woman. And he went to rescue her and had his thumb cut off. And the other of the two was her father. This foot-man that had the naked rapier in his hand, that would have ravished the maid, had a horse a pretty way behind, following of him. And I rid after the horse and catched him and brought him to the man that had been wounded by him, and bid him carry the horse to the next justice of the peace, and by that means they might find out and pursue the man.

So upon this I writ a letter to the justices and to the judge of the Assizes which were then at hand, and I employed some Friends to carry it to the justices of peace first. And the justice rebuked his clerk and the others for abusing and disturbing us upon the highway, and they made entreaty to Friends not to appear against them at the Assizes, which Friends granted, which thing did a great deal of good in the country and stopped many rude people in the country that had used to abuse Friends formerly.

And so we passed into Herefordshire where we had several blessed meetings; and we had a General Men's Meeting also where all the Monthly Meetings were established.

And from thence we passed into Monmouthshire where I had several blessed meetings. And at Walter Jenkins's,[1] we had a large meeting and there were four priests convinced.

And at another meeting before this[2] there came into his house to the meeting the bailiff of the hundred, almost drunk, and he was to take up the speakers, he said. But the Lord's power chained him, and a mighty power of God there was in the meeting, though he raged. So after the meeting was done I stayed awhile and he stayed there and I spoke to him, and so passed away. And the country was in a great rage. And at night some rude people came

[1] At Llanvihangel Ystern Llewern, about five miles west of Monmouth.

[2] In 1663, see p. 450.

and shot a musket against the house but did no hurt. And thus the Lord's power came over all and we escaped them and went to Ross that night and had a meeting there at James Merrick's.

And so we came into Gloucestershire, where we had a General Men's Meeting at Justice Cripps's house, and settled all the Monthly Meetings in the Lord's everlasting power, and exhorted all the heirs of the power of God to take their possession of the Gospel, for that was the authority of their meetings. And after the meeting in Gloucestershire at Nathaniel Cripps's was ended, there was a justice of peace heard of it and was in a great rage that he had not come and broke up the meeting, but the Lord disappointed him.

And so after we had many blessed meetings up and down in that country, we came to Bristol,[1] and, after we had had several powerful meetings, we settled the Men's Monthly Meeting there and the Women's Meeting.

And as I was lying in my bed the word of the Lord came to me that I must go back to London. And Alexander Parker and several others came to me the next morning, and I asked them what they felt. And they asked me what was upon me, and I told them I felt I must return to London, and they said it was upon them the same. And so we gave up to return to London, for which way the Lord moved us and led us we went in his power.

And about this time there was a proclamation against meetings. And as we came through Herefordshire there was a great meeting of the Presbyterians, and they had engaged themselves to stand and give up all ⟨rather than forsake their meetings⟩ but when they heard of this proclamation the people came, but the priest was gone. And then they met in Leominster privately, and the bailiff came in and took them. But they had provided bread, and cheese, and drink in readiness that if the officers came there, they would put up their Bibles and fall upon their cold meat. And the bailiff told them the bread and cheese

[1] At the end of March, 1668.

should not cover them and he said he would have the speakers. And then they cried what would become then of their wives and children. But he took away their speakers and kept them awhile. And this bailiff told our Friend Peter Young that they were the veriest hypocrites that ever made a profession.

And before this there was one Pocock at London, that married Lady Darcy,[1] which Lady Darcy was convinced. And this Pocock was a trier of the priests, and he used to call our Friends house-creepers. And I coming into his house his lady said unto me, 'I have something to speak to thee against my husband.'

'Nay', said I, 'Thou must not speak against thy husband.'

'Yes', said she, 'But I must. The last First-day, he and his priests, the Presbyterians, met, and they had candles and tobacco pipes and bread and cheese and cold meat at table. And if the officers had come in then they had agreed to leave their preaching and praying and fall to their cold meat.'

And I said unto him, 'Is not this a shame on you that persecuted and imprisoned us and spoiled our goods because we would not follow you and be of your religion, and called us house-creepers, and now you dare not stand to your own religion yourselves? Did you ever find our meetings stuffed with bread and cheese and tobacco pipes? Or did you ever read in the Scriptures of any such practices among the saints?'

'Why', said the old Pocock, the trier of the priests, 'We must be as wise as serpents,' said he.

Then said I, 'This is indeed the serpent's wisdom; and who would have ever thought that you Presbyterians and Independents that persecuted and imprisoned and spoiled the goods of others and whipped such as would not follow your religion, now dare not stand to your own but cover it with tobacco pipes, flagons of drink, cold meat, bread, and cheese?' And this was a common practice amongst

[1] Ellwood has Abigail Darcy.

them in many places in this time of persecution, to use such deceitful covers for their worship.

And so, as I said before, we passed from Bristol into Wiltshire and established the Men's Monthly Meetings in the Lord's power there, and so passed through the countries, visiting Friends, till we came to London.

And after we had visited Friends in that city and had stayed there a while, I was moved to exhort them to bring all their marriages into the Men's and Women's Meetings, that they might lay them before the faithful there. For many had gone together contrary to their relations; and sometimes young, raw people that came among us had mixed with the world, and widows had married and had not made provision for their children before marriage again.

For I had given forth a paper about 1653 concerning of marriages, when Truth was little spread over the nation, that they might lay it before the faithful and then publish it in the market, or before the justices, and in the end of the meeting. And when all things were found clear, and they free from all other and their relations satisfied, then they might appoint a meeting of purpose for the taking of one another, and not under twelve faithful witnesses.

And these things not being observed it was therefore ordered by the same power and spirit of God that marriages might be laid before the Men's Monthly and Quarterly Meetings, or as the meetings were then established, so that they might see their relations were satisfied and that they were clear from all others, and that widows had made provision for their first husband's children before they married again. So that all things might be kept clean and pure and done in righteousness to the glory of God. And afterwards it was ordered if they came out of another county or nation they must bring a certificate from the Men's and Women's Meetings they belonged unto to the Men's and Women's Meetings where they took their wife or husband.

And so after these things, with many other services for

God, were set in order and settled in the churches in the city, I passed out of London into the countries again.

And I went into Hertfordshire and settled there the Men's Monthly Meetings; and after I had visited Friends there I went to Baldock where I had a great meeting of many hundreds of people of many sorts. Then I came to Waltham and established a school there ⟨for teaching of boys⟩, and ordered a women's school to be set up at Shacklewell to instruct young lasses and maidens in whatsoever things were civil and useful in the creation.

And after I had several precious meetings in the country I came to London again; and after I had stayed there in the Lord's service and work awhile I passed into Buckinghamshire where I had many precious meetings. And ⟨at John Brown's at Weston Turville, near Aylesbury,⟩ I had some of all the men Friends of each meeting and I established the Men's Monthly Meetings amongst them also in the order of the Gospel, the power of God. And the power of the Lord confirmed it in all that felt it. And they came to see and feel that the power of God was the authority of their meetings.

And after I had settled the Monthly Meetings there, in the order of the Gospel and upon the foundation Christ Jesus, I passed into Oxfordshire, where we had some of all the meetings together; and there, at ⟨North Newton near Banbury,⟩ at Nathaniel Ball's, who was a Friend in the ministry, we settled the Monthly Meetings in the power of the Lord, and Friends were very glad of them; for all came into possession, ⟨into their services in the Church⟩, and to take care of God's glory. And from thence we passed through the countries, visiting the Friends, till we came into Gloucestershire and through that country, visiting Friends, till we came into Monmouthshire to one Richard Hamborough's,[1] where we had some of all the meetings. And there we, in the Lord's power, settled the Monthly Meetings that all in it might take care of God's glory and admonish and exhort such as did not walk as

[1] Richard Hanbury, of Pontymoile.

became the Gospel so that it made a great cry in the country, insomuch as the very justices said, never such a man came into their country that reconciled neighbour to neighbour and husband to wife, and turned many people from their loose lives. And indeed these meetings did make a great reformation amongst people.

And from thence we passed through the country after we had visited Friends. And Richard Hamborough and his wife accompanied us a day's journey through the hills. And we came to a widow woman's house and there we stayed all night. And from thence we passed over the hills[1] declaring the Truth to people and visiting Friends, and came to another widow woman's house where we had a meeting. But the woman could not speak one word of English but praised the Lord that he should send me over those hills to come and visit them.

And from thence we passed through the country, till we came to Swansea. There on the First-day, we had a General Meeting, large and precious, and the Lord's presence was amongst us; and on a week-day after, beyond Swansea, we had a General Men's Meeting from Tenby, Swansea, Haverfordwest, and many other places where the Monthly Meetings were settled in the gospel order. And all received the power of the Lord; and the Lord's Truth was over all.

And from thence we passed up to Swansea, and so to Mumbles, thinking to get over the water there into Cornwall, but the master deceived us; who, after he had promised us, would not carry us. And from thence we passed unto another ⟨place where there was a⟩ passage-boat and after we had got in our horses, there were some rude gentry threatened to pistol the master of the boat ⟨if he took us in⟩; and he, being afraid, turned the horses out again. And so we saw little hopes of our getting over thataways, so we came back again into the country, and stayed up all night, and did not go to bed. And in the morning, about two

[1] "Over the hills" is said to refer to the place named Quakers Yard. (T. Mardy Rees: *The Quakers in Wales.*)

of the clock, we travelled through the country, and came near Cardiff where we stayed all night. And the next day we came to a place called Newport; and it being market day, Friends and a justice's son's wife came to see us. And after we had visited Friends we passed away.

⟨Beyond this market town we⟩ overtook a man, or rather he waylaid us, who rid along with us and began to examine us and asked many questions of us. And at last, meeting with two great men's pages, he stopped us in the highway, and I heard him tell them that they would take us up and stop us. And he galloped on and we rid after him, being in our way; and when he would have stopped us I told him he ought not to stop us in the King's highway for it was as free for us as for them.

And I perceived he intended to stop us at Shipton[1] in Wales, on our way as we were to pass through, it being a garrison town. Thither he galloped before us. So when he left us I was moved to exhort him to fear the Lord.

And when we came to Shipton, John ap John being with me, it was the market day, so we walked our horses down the hill into the town, and meeting several Friends they would have had us to have gone into an inn, but we were not to go into any inn but walked through the town over the bridge, and then we were out of their country. Thus the Lord's everlasting arm and power preserved us and carried us over in his work and service and labour.

And then on the First-day we had a large General Meeting in the Forest of Dean, and all was quiet. Then, next day, we passed over the water and came to a Friend's house, and from thence we came to Olveston and visited Friends; and so we passed over the water again to William Yeamans's house at Irbs Court[2] in Somersetshire. And there we passed down to a meeting at Portishead where several Bristol Friends came to us and visited us.

And from thence we passed up into the country, where

[1] Probably Chepstow.

[2] Probably Jubbs Court, five miles from Bristol. Wm. Yeamans (1639-1674), merchant of Bristol, was son in law to Margaret Fell.

we had several large meetings, and the Lord's living presence was with us in his labour and travail.

And we came to a place near Minehead where we had a General Meeting of the men Friends in Somersetshire. And there came also a cheat, who some friendly people would have had me to have taken alongst with me. And I bid them bring him to me and see whether he could look me in the face, for I saw he was a cheat. And some Friends were thinking I was hard-hearted because I would not let him go alongst with me. And when they brought him to me, he was not able to look me in the face, but looked hither and thither; for he had cheated a priest, pretending he was a minister, and got his suit and went away with it.

And after, he had like to have cheated those Friends that would have had me to take him alongst with me; but he was discovered and had his reward.

After the meeting we passed to Minehead, where there are several Friends. ⟨There we tarried that night. And in the night I had an exercise upon me, from a sense I had of a dark spirit that was working and striving to get up and to disturb the Church of Christ. Whereupon next morning I was moved to write a few lines[1] to Friends as a warning thereof.⟩

And several of them accompanied us the next day as far as Devonshire, to Barnstaple and Appledore where we had a meeting.

And this Barnstaple had been a bloody, persecuting town. For there were two men Friends that had been a great while at sea and were coming home to visit their relations, whereof one had a wife and children. The mayor sent for them under pretence to discourse with them, and put the Oath of Allegiance and Supremacy to them and ⟨because they could not swear⟩ sent them to Exeter gaol. And there Judge Archer praemunired them. And one of them died in prison. And I was moved to write a letter, one to Judge Archer, and another to the mayor of

[1] Printed, Ellwood, p. 318; Bicent., ii, 93. Dated 22nd June, 1668.

Barnstaple and laid their wicked and unchristian actions upon their heads, and that the blood of this man would be required at their hands.

And the next day we passed through the country till we came to Humphrey Lower's, where we had a very precious meeting. And from thence we passed to Truro, and so through the countries, visiting Friends, till we came to the Land's End. And so came up by the south, visiting Friends. And at Tregangeeves, at Loveday Hambly's, we had a General Meeting for all the county, where we settled the Monthly Meeting in the Lord's power. And several were brought to condemn things and came in again that had been out.

And so after we had visited the meetings in Cornwall and were clear of it, we came into Devonshire, and came to Plymouth and had a meeting there amongst Friends.

And from thence we passed to Richard Brown's and from thence into the South Hams to the widow Phillips,[1] where we had some of all the men Friends together, and there settled the Men's Monthly Meetings in the heavenly order of the Gospel, the power of God, which answered the power of God in all. And there was a great noise of a troop of horse coming to disturb our meeting; for the servant in the house was a wicked man; but the Lord's power prevented and bound them; and by it we came over all. And after the meeting was done and all things were settled we came to Kingsbridge and visited Friends thereaways.

And from thence we passed, having left Friends well settled in the power of God in those parts, through the country to Topsham, and so from thence to Membury, and had many meetings in the countries, visiting Friends, till we came to Ilchester in Somersetshire, where we had a General Men's Meeting, and there settled the Monthly Meetings for that county in the Lord's everlasting power,

[1] Elizabeth Phillips, of Baston (Batten) in the parish of West Alvington. 'South Hams' means the part of Devon south of Dartmoor, especially about Kingsbridge and Salcombe.

the order of the Gospel, the power of God before the Devil was.

And after the Meetings were settled and Friends comforted in the Lord's power and established upon Christ their rock and foundation, we passed to Podimore, to William Beaton's, where we had a blessed meeting, and all was quiet though the constables had formerly threatened.

And after we had visited most of the meetings in Somersetshire, we passed into Dorsetshire to one Harris his house,[1] where we had a large Men's Meeting, and there all the Men's Monthly Meetings were settled in the glorious order of the Gospel, and that all in the power of God might seek that which was lost, and bring again that which was driven away, and might cherish the good and reprove the evil. And after, we visited the Meetings of Friends through the countries, till we came to Southampton, where we had a large meeting on the First-day. And from thence we went to one Captain Reeves where the General Men's Meeting of Hampshire was appointed. And some of all the county came to it, and a blessed meeting we had. And the Men's Monthly Meetings were settled in the order of the Gospel, which had brought life and immortality to light in them.

And there came a rude company ⟨that had run into Ranterism, who⟩ had much opposed our meetings. And I went to the house where they lived together ⟨hard by the place where our meeting was⟩. I heard that one of them, Rose Atkins, had lain with a man, and I told the man of the house of it, and he said why did I make so strange of it, and another of them said it was for to stumble me. But I told them their wickedness should not stumble me for I was above it, and said, 'What! do you keep a bawdy house here?' The man that had lain with that Rose told me of it, and had declared his wickedness at the market cross and gloried in it.

After, they went up and down the country till at last they were cast into Winchester gaol. And this Rose had

[1] George Harris, Senr., lived at Ryme Intrinseca, near Yeovil.

like to have cut a child's throat ⟨as we were informed⟩, and he that went for her husband did stab the gaoler, but not mortal, and after they were out of prison he hanged himself. Now these people had prophesied in London when the city was fired, that the rest of London should be burned within fourteen days. And they much disturbed our meetings.

I was moved of the Lord to tell them that the plagues and judgements of God would come upon them and overtake them.

And they being Ranters, the people of the world said they were Quakers. So I was moved of the Lord to give forth a paper to the justices and people of Hampshire to clear ourselves and Truth of them.

And so after we had settled the Men's Monthly Meetings in those parts and visited Friends and the Lord's power was over all, we passed to a town where we had a meeting with Friends. And from thence we came to Farnham, where we met many Friends, it being market day. And we had many precious meetings up and down that country.

And Friends in these countries had been sorely plundered, and their goods much spoiled for tithes and going to meetings; but the Lord's power preserved us and them.

And so we passed into Surrey where we had a General Men's Meeting at a Friend's house, whom they had scarcely left cow, or horse, or swine, they had so plundered him. And we settled the Men's Monthly Meetings. And the constables threatened to come and break up our meeting, but the Lord's power stopped them.

And after we had visited Friends in that country and had many large, precious meetings amongst them, we passed into Sussex, to Richard Bax's[1] where we had a General Men's Meeting[2] and several Friends from London to visit us.

And there we had a blessed meeting and settled the Men's Monthly Meetings in the Lord's eternal power

[1] At Capel in Surrey.

[2] 9th Sept., 1668.

and Gospel of salvation; and all in it to keep the order of the Gospel. And after we had settled the meetings we passed away. And the meetings were quiet, though at times there was much threatening.

And we had several large meetings in that county: though Friends were in great sufferings and many in prison.

And I was sent for to a Friend that was sick, and to see a Friend that was prisoner, and there was danger of my being apprehended. But I went in the faith and God's power, and the Lord in it did give me dominion.

And from thence I passed through the country, visiting Friends till I came into Kent; and after I had visited a-many meetings there, we had a General Meeting at a Friend's house of some of all the men Friends from most of the Meetings in that county. And the Men's Monthly Meetings were settled in the power of God, and established in the order of the Gospel, for all the heirs of it to take their possession. And Friends, in the power of God, were joyful of the order and of the settlement in the order of the Gospel which is not of man nor by man.

And so after, I passed away visiting Friends in their meetings up and down in Kent. And when I had cleared myself of the Lord's service in Kent I came up to London. And thus the Men's Monthly Meetings were settled through the nation, having before settled the Quarterly Meetings.

And I had been in Berkshire before, where most of the eminent Friends of that county were in prison. And I informed them concerning the Men's Monthly Meetings, and they were settled.

And I sent papers over into Ireland by faithful Friends, and into Scotland, and Holland, and Barbados, and America, for Friends to settle their Men's Monthly Meetings in those countries also; for they had their General Quarterly Meetings before. But now Truth increased, they should settle their Men's Monthly Meetings in the power and spirit of God that did first convince them.

[1]Now since these meetings have been so settled the Lord has opened many mouths and many have blessed the Lord that ever the Lord God did send me to set them up. Yea with tears they have praised the Lord. For now all come to have a care of God's glory and honour, and that his name be not blasphemed which they do profess, and to see that all do walk in the Truth and righteousness, and walk in holiness which becomes the house of God, and that all come to order their conversations aright, that they may come to see the salvation of God, and that all that do profess, profess no more than they do possess; and to see that all do not only hear the word but do it, . . .[2]

And every man and woman that be heirs of the Gospel, they are heirs of this authority, and the power of God which was before the Devil was, which is not of man nor by man . . .[3]

And they shall see the government of Christ who has all power in heaven and earth given to him, and to the increase of his glorious, righteous, holy, just government there is no end. But his government and his order will remain; and he who is the author of it, is the first and last, the beginning and ending, and over all the foundation of God which stands sure, Christ Jesus, the Amen.

And so after I had settled the Monthly Meetings throughout the nation, I stayed in London a time and visited Friends' meetings.

And after a while I went to visit Esquire Marsh. And he was at dinner, and he sent for me up. * And there were several great persons at dinner with him and he would have had me sit down with him to dinner but I was not free. And he said to a great Papist then there, 'Here is a Quaker which you have not seen before.'

And the Papist asked me whether I did own the christening of children.

And I told him there was no Scripture for any such practice.

[1], [2], [3] In full, *Camb. Jnl.*, ii, 127, 128; Ellwood, pp. 321, 322; Bicent., ii, 98, 99.

'What!' said he, 'not for christening children?'

And I said, 'Nay', but if he meant the one baptism with the spirit into one body, that we owned, but to throw a little water in a child's face and say it was baptised (or christened) there was no Scripture for that.

Then he asked me whether I did own the catholic faith.

I said, 'Yes.' But neither the Pope nor the Papists were in that catholic faith, for the true catholic faith works by love and purifies the heart; and if they were in that faith that gives victory, by which they might have access to God, they would not tell people of a purgatory after they were dead. So I would prove that neither Pope nor Papists that held up purgatory were in the true faith, for the true, precious, and divine faith, which Christ is the author of gives victory over the Devil and sin that had separated man and woman from God.

And if they were in the true faith they would never make racks, and prisons, gaols, and fires to persecute and force others that were not of their faith, for this was not the practice of the true faith of Christ that was witnessed and enjoyed by the apostles and primitive Church; neither had they any such command from Christ and the apostles. But it was the practice of the faithless Jews and heathen so to do.

And I said unto him, 'Seeing thou art a great and leading man amongst the Papists and hast been taught and bred up under the Pope; and seeing thou says there is no salvation but in your Church, I have two questions to ask thee. The first is: What is it that doth bring salvation to your Church?'

He answered, 'A good life.'

'And nothing else?' said I.

'Yes', said he, 'good works.'

'And is this it that brings salvation in your Church—a good life and good works? Is this your doctrine and principle?'

'Yes', said he.

Then I said, 'Neither the Papists, Pope, nor thou dost know what it is that brings salvation.'

Then he asked me what brought salvation in our Church. I told him, 'The same that brought salvation to the Church in the apostles' days, the same brought salvation to us and not another, which is the grace of God which brings salvation, which hath appeared unto all men; which taught the saints and teaches us then and now. And this grace is it which brings salvation, which teaches to live godlily, righteously, and soberly, and to deny ungodliness and worldly lusts. So it is not good works, nor good life, that brings salvation but the grace.

'What!' said the Papist, 'doth this grace that brings salvation appear unto all men?'

'Yes,' said I.

'But I deny that,' said the Papist.

Then I said, 'I know ye Papists will deny that, and therefore ye are sect-makers and are not in the universal faith, grace, and truth, as the apostles were.'

⟨Then he spoke to me about the Mother Church. And I told him⟩ often the several sorts of sects in Christendom would accuse us and say we forsake our Mother Church.

And one while, the Papists would be charging of us for forsaking the Mother Church, who would say that Rome was the only Mother Church.

And another while, the Episcopalians; and they would be charging of us for forsaking the old Protestant religion, and they would say theirs was the reformed Mother Church.

And then again the Presbyterians and Independents; they would be accusing of us for forsaking of them, and they would say theirs was the right reformed Church.

And unto them all I answered that if we could own any outward city or place to be the Mother Church or any outward profession, we would own outward Jerusalem; where Christ and the Apostle preached and suffered and . . .[1] where the first great conversion to Christianity was. . . .[2] This title Mother has been given to places

[1], [2] Discourse in full, *Camb. Jnl.*, i, 131, 132; Ellwood, pp. 323, 324; Bicent., ii, 101, 102.

and sects amongst the degenerate Christians since the apostles' days.

But the Apostle said, 'Jerusalem that is above is the mother of us all.' So we say still that 'Jerusalem which is above is the mother of us all', and cannot own any other, neither outward Jerusalem, nor Rome, nor any sect of people for our mother, but Jerusalem, which is above, which is free, the mother of us all that are born again. . . .[1] And I say that all who are born again of the immortal Seed by the word of God that lives, and abides, and endures for ever, feed upon the milk of the word, the breasts of life, and grow by it in life, and cannot acknowledge any other to be their mother but Jerusalem which is above.

'Oh', says Esquire Marsh to the Papist, 'you do not know this man, if he would but come to the church now and then, he would be the bravest man that ever was.'

And so after many words with them I went aside with Esquire Marsh into another room for he was a justice of peace at Limehouse, and being a courtier the other justices put off the management of matters more upon him.

⟨Now he told me he was in a strait.⟩ And he said unto me, 'You cannot swear, and so also say the Independent and Baptists and Monarchy people, that they cannot swear; therefore how shall I know how to distinguish betwixt you and them seeing they and you all say it is for conscience sake you cannot swear?'

Then I said, 'I will show thee how to distinguish. These thou speaks of can and do swear in some cases; but we cannot in any case. For if a man should take their cows or horses, if thou shouldst ask them whether they would swear they were theirs, they would readily do it. But if thou try our Friends, they cannot swear for their own goods, so when thou puttest the Oath of Allegiance to them, ask whether they can swear in any case, or for their

[1] Discourse in full, *Camb. Jnl.*, i, 131, 132; Ellwood, pp. 323, 324; Bicent., ii, 101, 102.

cow or their horse; which they cannot do ⟨though they can bear witness to the Truth.⟩

'For there was a thief stole two beasts from a Friend in Berkshire, which thief was taken and cast into prison. And the Friend appeared against him at the Assizes; and some people told the judge that the Friend that prosecuted was a Quaker and would not swear. And before he heard what he would say, "Is he a Quaker?" said the judge, "and won't he swear; then put the Oaths of Allegiance and Supremacy to him." So they cast the Friend into prison and praemunired him and let the thief go at liberty that had stolen his goods.'

Then said Esquire Marsh, 'That judge was a wicked man.'

'So', then I said, 'thou must see that if we could swear in any case, we would take the Oath of Allegiance to the King who is to preserve the laws, which laws preserve every man in his estate. But they can swear for their own ends, or that such a man stole from them, to bring him to the law to preserve a part of their estates, and yet they will not take an oath to the King who is to preserve them in their whole estates and bodies also. So thou mayest easily distinguish, and put a difference betwixt us and other people.'

So this Marsh was after very serviceable to Friends in this and other matters, for he stopped several Friends and others from being praemunired in those parts where he was a justice. And in the time of the late Act for persecution several Friends were brought before him and many of them he set at liberty, and some he sent to prison for an hour or two or a night. But at last he went to the King and told him he had sent to prison some of us contrary to his conscience and he could do so no more. And he took lodgings near James's Park and removed himself and family from Limehouse. And he told the King that ⟨if he would be pleased to⟩ give liberty of conscience, that would knock down all at one blow; for then none could have any pretence ⟨to be uneasy⟩; and he was a very serviceable man to Truth and Friends in his day.

We had great service at London this year, and the Lord's truth came over all. And a meeting was set up of condemnation and that if any one had any thing to say they might come and testify unto the Truth. ⟨Many that had been out of Truth came in again, confessing and condemning their former outgoings.⟩ And John Swinton came in this year.

And Margaret Fell came up to London.

After I had stayed a while in London, I visited Friends up and down in the country in Sussex and Surrey.

John Swinton and Leonard Fell travelled with me down into the country, and we visited Friends till we came to Warwick where there were many Friends in prison. And we had a meeting in the town; and after, I passed from thence to Birmingham and Baddesley and John Swinton and another Friend passed to Leicester.

And I had a large meeting at Baddesley and passed thence through the country visiting Friends till I came to Nottingham, where, on the First-day, we had a precious meeting, but not without danger of being apprehended, the constables having threatened to take up Friends about that time.

And from thence I passed through the country till I came to Balby in Yorkshire, visiting Friends, and from thence I came to York at the time of the Assizes; at which time the Quarterly Meeting was at York. And they had seven Monthly Meetings in Yorkshire and they were desirous to have me come down that they might have seven more Monthly Meetings set up, for Truth was much spread in that country. And so whereas they had but seven Monthly Meetings before, now they have fourteen Monthly Meetings in that country; and a blessed meeting we had.

And there I met with Justice Hotham, a well-wisher to Friends and one that had been tender unto me at the first.

And after that I had finished my service for the Lord in York I passed up into the country; and a great burden fell upon me as I went ⟨but I did not presently know the reason of it⟩. And I came to a meeting on the First-day at Richard Shipton's: which was very large. And there was a priest sent to a justice and got a warrant, and came to another meeting he heard I was to be at, and he did much beat and abuse Friends and haled some of them before a justice of peace. But not finding me there they set Friends at liberty again.[1]

And after the foresaid meeting was done I passed through the countries visiting Friends to Whitby and Scarborough. And when I came into Scarborough the governor heard that I was come to town and sent to me by one of his soldiers, and said surely I would not be so unkind as not to come to see him and his wife. So after meeting was done I went up to visit him and he was very courteous and loving.

And so after I had visited most of the meetings in Yorkshire and up to the Wolds and Holderness, I passed through the country till I came to Henry Jackson's[2] where I had a great meeting, and to Thomas Taylor's, and to Eldroth to John Moore's where Sarah Fell and Susannah Fell met me. And not far off there was Colonel Kirkby, sick of the gout, who had threatened that if I ever came near he would send me to prison again and had bid forty pounds to any man that could take me. And we had a very large meeting at this Eldroth and the Lord's power and presence were amongst us.

And after the meeting was done I passed through the countries till I came into Staffordshire and so into Cheshire where we had many large and precious meetings.

In Cheshire one Sir Geoffrey Shakerley that had been a cruel persecutor of Friends lit upon a young man about eighteen or nineteen years old that had been at mill with a loaded horse or two. And the young man could not get the loaded horses soon enough out of his way, upon which he beat him with his cane, and the young man took it out of his hand and laid it down by him; and then he

[1] Ellwood, p. 326, and Bicent., ii, 105, here print a letter from Isaac Lindley to George Fox describing the incident.

[2] Henry Jackson lived at Mealhill, Hepworth, Yorkshire. About 1682 he built Totties Hall, Wooldale.

took out his pistols, and the young man took them out of his hands also, and laid them down by him, the way being narrow; and then he drew his rapier at him, and he took it out of his hand also, and laid it down by him.

And he called to his man who was a little behind him (they were both full of drink), and said, 'This Quaker hath disarmed me'; and his man would have had the Friend give him his weapons again, which he was loth to do lest he should do mischief with them. And so at last the man desired the Friend to give him the arms again, and the Friend said if he would promise to keep them from his master that he might not do mischief with them, he would deliver them to him.

So Shakerley sent away his man to fetch the constable and to bring a book to tender the Oaths of Allegiance and Supremacy to him. And he sat on his horse's back and kept the young man's horses loaded all the while till his man came back again.

So when his man came back again, he told his master he could not find the constables. And they were poor people and he could not get a Bible.

Then after the Friend gave his man his master's weapons, they went both away to look for a constable. And his man was more civil than his master, and bid the Friend stay at a smith's shop a while till they were gone and passed away. And so the Friend stayed there a while, and seeing they came not, he passed away over a common with his loaded horses; and there Shakerley, after he had ridden up and down for a constable a long while and could not find any, espying of him, he followed the young man to the town. And there came the priest and constable to him, and there Shakerley would make a mittimus to send him to gaol for disarming him.

And then the constable and the priest dissuaded him to send him forthwith, seeing the Friend was in his old clothes. And the priest said that his father was a very honest man, though his father was the veriest drunkard in the town, and used to beat his son in his drunkenness;

and his son had been used to disarm his father of his weapons in his drunkenness, which made him so expert in that work. But after this, Shakerley rode away and gave no mittimus to the constable. But it made such a noise in the country that Friends persuaded the young man to go up to London to live, to put him out of this Shakerley's way. And this relation I had from William Gandy's own mouth.

And from William Gandy's I came to Warrington, and from thence to William Barnes's[1] where we had a very large meeting two miles of Warrington.

And Colonel Kirkby was again at Warrington, who had threatened as aforesaid, and was breaking up the meetings, but the Lord's power prevented him and stopped him.

CHAPTER XXI

⟨Now I was moved of the Lord to go over into Ireland, to visit the Seed of God in that nation.⟩ From Warrington we passed to near Liverpool, where we waited for shipping and wind to pass for Ireland. And when the wind presented, we took shipping,[2] to wit, myself, Robert Lodge, James Lancaster, Thomas Briggs, and John Stubbs; and the Lord's eternal power was with us, as you may see in our journal as followeth, more at large.

[3]He waited several days for wind, and sent James Lancaster to take passage for four or five men, not mattering to have noise made of his own name, because Colonel Kirkby of Lancaster had said he would give forty pounds and ride his horse forty miles to take him, and that he had

[1] Great Sankey.

[2] In May, 1669.

[3] Several passages in the Irish Journal (i.e. to page 550) refer to George Fox in the third person; they have been retained in their original form.

gotten an order from the King; and this was his enmity to Truth, as several told him. And where he was to take shipping was in the county where this Kirkby lived. And James Lancaster brought news that the ship was ready, and would take George Fox in at Black Rock. And going afoot a great way, he was well nigh sweltered, and he being come, and the ship not there, he went to the town where he took shipping, and George Fox said to the rest of the company, 'Come, ye will triumph in the Lord, for ye will have fair wind, and weather.' And many passengers being in the ship, many were sick and cast down about them, but none of these five that went with George Fox were sick. Many of the passengers and the master of the ship were very loving, and being on the First-day at sea, George Fox was moved to declare something to them. The master of the ship said, 'Come, here are things that you never heard in your lives.'

And so when we came near to Dublin, we took boat, all being well, and four times we passed through the custom officers, yet ourselves without searching, some of them being so envious they could not look at us, knowing what we were. When we came on shore, the earth and the very air smelt with the corruption of the nation and gave another smell than England to me, with the corruption and the blood and the massacres and the foulness that ascended.

So we wandered from betwixt the eighth and ninth hour in the morning to the second hour and could not find Friends; we took up an inn and sent out to enquire, and so when we had found Friends, they were very joyful of seeing us, receiving us with great joy. So we stayed the weekly meeting, which there was a great one; and the power and life of God appeared in it. And afterwards we passed to a Province Meeting which lasted two days, a Men's Meeting about the poor, and another General Meeting, and a mighty power of the Lord appeared, and Truth was very precious, and Friends were much refreshed.

And from thence we passed twenty-four miles to another

place where we had a very good refreshing meeting, at which, after it was done, some of the Papists that were there were angry and raged very much. And hearing of it, G.F. sent for one of them, being a schoolmaster, and he would not come to him. Then G.F. gave forth a challenge to him, and his friars and monks, priests, and Jesuits, and the Pope himself, to come forth and try their God and their Christ, that they had made of bread and wine.

But no answer could he get from the papist Jesuits to try their God, and their Christ, which they had made of bread and wine; so he told them, they were worse than the priests of Baal, for Baal's priest tried their wooden god which they had made, but they durst not try their bread and wine God, and Baal's priest and people did not eat their god as they did, and then make another.

And from thence we went to New Garden, where there was a great meeting, and all along through meetings, which would be too large to write, until we came to Bandon Bridge, and the land's end, and a mighty power of the Lord was in the meetings and people taken with Truth and refreshed.

And so coming to a town, the time they call Whit Sunday[1] holy days, the Irish people had been at their Mass, the streets being full of them. G.F. called for their Jesuits and priests, and the people asked what he would do with them, and he said two-pennyworth of Mass for his horse, and he would give any of them two pence for their labours; and so he said, the candles had a Mass, and the Lambs had a Mass, why might not his horse have a Mass, as well as they, he was a good creature. And so in many towns, and cities, he called for the same, and the Papists said, 'Why do you meddle with our religion?'

And at Bandon, the provost or mayor's wife,[2] being convinced, desired her husband to come to the meeting. And he answered her and said that for her life she should not make known that G.F. was in town at a meeting.

[1] 30th May, 1669.

[2] John Poole was provost in 1669.

And the mayor of Cork was very envious against the Truth and Friends, having many in prison.

As G.F. was in Bandon getting up and dressing himself in the morning, there appeared a very ugly-visaged man, black and dark, and G.F. struck at him in the power of God, and with his horse rode over him, and his horse put his foot on the side of his cheek. And this was as he was dressing of himself. And he went down the stairs and told a Friend that was with him that the command of the Lord was to him that he must ride through Cork. But G.F. bade him tell no creature. So as he was going, some that rode with him expected him to ride another way, for Friends' desire was that he might not ride through, for there were then four warrants out against him from the mayor, he having the President's[1] letter, by which his warrant reached over the Province.

And so G.F. passing near Cork, and Friends perceiving that he would go through the town, several asked him to go to their houses, but he saw that if he alighted to their houses, he sunk into a fire; but he kept on his horse, which was the command of God, and he rid pure and clear over, for the word was to him that his horse was fittest for them, and was to be next them. And so the Friends asked him to go the backside the town, and he said, nay, his way was through the streets. And they told him the way was so slippery in the height of the market, that he could not go, and his horse could not stand, and he said that was but little, and so he called to them that rode with him, which of them would ride through the town with him, and all the rest stay behind. So there was one Paul Morris[2] rode along with him; so he bid him ride either afore him or aside him to guide him through to the market place and through the market, and so by the mayor's door that had given forth the warrants. And he, ⟨seeing him ride by,⟩ said: 'There goes George Fox.' So there the vision came to be fulfilled, and he had no power.

[1] The President of Munster was Murrough O'Brien, Earl of Inchiquin.

[2] Paul Morris lived near Rosscarbery.

But oh ! what a fire there was in the hearts and spirits of people. When he rode through the town, he being generally known, they looked and peeped.

And when I came near the prison, the prisoners saw me, and knew me, and trembled, for fear lest I should be taken. So I passed through the next sentinel and came over the bridge; and I asked Paul that was with me whether there was a Friend's house thereabouts, and he guided me to a Friend's house, and I alighted, and Friends when I came in were telling me what rage there was in the town, and how many warrants to take me.

And after a little while I went to another room to speak with some Friends, and so sitting with them a while, I felt the evil spirit in the town, in a great rage against me, and so I rose up and struck at it in the power of God. And immediately some Friends came in and told me that it was all over the town amongst the magistrates that I was in the town, and so I said, 'Let the Devil do his worst.' And after a while I called for my coat and my horse, and a Friend to guide me to the inn, for I was only to alight and stay; and many would have gone with me, but I called one aside, and he said he would go. So when I had gone a little way I asked him where the stable was, where my horse was, he said he had caused my horse to be brought to meet me on the top of the hill. And being hot he took my coat, and so we crossed over the great road, and went a middle way. And I looked over my horse's neck, when he came to me, and I espied five or six horsemen who went to a house after they had a council; and they came together again, and had another council, and two of them galloped back again, and two went one way, and the rest along the road. So I said, 'Yonder be scouts after me.' And when I came to the road on the top of the hill I espied two horsemen in the great road I passed over; I said, 'Yonder be the scouts again in the other road.' So we passed in our way, with a Friend that was a steward to a justice, and Paul that went through the town with me, about ten miles.

And at night some Friends from Cork came to tell what news there was, who next morning told us, that they were in a pitiful rage, that they had missed me and were ready to eat their own flesh. The next day I rode to a place where there were a few Friends, being the First-day; and the next day, having ridden a matter of sixteen miles, we were come again within twenty miles of Cork,[1] and baiting at an inn, there came in a man, in a little poor room next unto us. And Friends were speaking together; and feeling somewhat strike at my life, I asked them and the tapster, who was in the next room. He said, 'A gentleman.' I stayed there about two hours; we paid our reckoning and went out to our horses, and this man, coming out after us, stared upon us, and asked which way we were going, being a man of Cork. And he sang and went into the house as if he had got his prize. And the inn-keeper came also, looking most strangely upon us. So we got on our horse backs and rode away, and when we had ridden several miles further, we parted, and some went to the city of Limerick, and I went to one Abel's,[2] where the meeting was, and Friends came to the meeting. And a brave meeting there was, in the power of God; and after the meeting was done, Friends told me they had the manner of my hair and my clothes, ⟨my hat and my horse,⟩ where that man was in the inn, and at the town where he came that night, and where they came from; and I going there escaped.

Now the Province of Munster's Meeting (to which General Meeting Cork belongs) and Men's Meeting were over, wherein the power of the Lord was so great that Friends in the power and spirit of the Lord brake out into singing, many together with an audible voice making melody in their hearts; at this time I was moved to declare to Friends there in the ministry.[3]

So I passed to another province, and went to the General

[1] Probably Mallow.
[2] Probably Richard Abell who lived near Limerick.
[3] Discourse in full, Ellwood, pp. 329, 330; Bicent., ii, 111, 112.

Meeting, and Men's Meeting, which lasted two days, where there was horse and foot like a fair. From thence I passed to other meetings, where the power of the Lord God and his spirit was wonderfully manifested, to the refreshing of Friends, and from thence to the Foxe's country, who claimed kindred, but I told them my kindred were they that stood in the life and power of God. And there was a good meeting of Friends and many of the world came in as in most places, which set the justices and Papists on afire, and the Jesuits sware in some of our faces, did we come to spread our principles in that nation, they swore we should not do it, and yet they durst not dispute with us, or answer to try their God.

And from thence I passed northward, a matter of thirty-six or thirty-eight miles off [from] that place, where we had a very good meeting among Friends and the world, and from thence a matter of thirty-six miles further. And lying at a Friend's house, I felt the evil spirit to work again to purpose, being always on my watch. I saw, as it were, a grim, black fellow, who was fettering of my legs with a cord, that I had much ado to preserve my feet from him.

And that day I went to the meeting, and when I came to it the meeting was pretty well gathered, and I took a Friend of Ireland, and said: 'Let us walk a little into the garden', and when we came into the garden, I felt the power of darkness strongly working against me, and I said unto him, 'Look what is in the meeting; for I feel the power of darkness at work strongly'; and so he went, and came again, being sensible of my feelings, for he persuaded me not to come into the meeting before he went in. I told him it was their desire, and I said I thought to reserve myself for a Province Meeting where all met together. And when he came back from the meeting, he said: 'The Devil's messenger is come; he is staring up and down in the meeting', and so he and another desired me again not to come into the meeting. So I said again to him, 'Go to the Devil's messenger, and enquire of him his intent.' He came again and told me that this messenger of the

Devil said he had several writs for to take Friends. He was a Papist and a bailiff. He was as bad a man as any in the country. So when Friends had done speaking this man went away, and so I went up to the meeting. And they that were out came in again and we had a fine meeting afterwards.

And when I had done, I took my horse and rid about nine miles. And as I was going, many being with me, I bade them either go before or keep after. And as one was passing along the priest's man stood in the way with a pike to take such a man as he was, and questioned where he had been. This man that went before rid to acquaint us of being stopped, but missed us. And G.F. coming, by the power of the Lord went over[1] him. A priest to whom this man belonged (who is made a justice and hath given over his twattling tub),[2] had sent in the morning a little way, over hedge and ditch, to the bailiff's house with a special warrant, having my hair, my clothes, my person, and my horse writ in it. And with it this bailiff came to the meeting. And he had three fellows in the next garden to me to assist him, when he had taken me, and the justice-priest, and two priests more on the top of a hill, a quarter of a mile from the meeting, at the Friend's house where I stood in the garden. I thought at first they were three shades of trees, but at last I perceived they were three black coats who were peeping, and so the priest thought all sure, and thought the meeting long, and told Friends' children that the Quakers would preach themselves hungry, and so went into the Friend's house to get some drink, and having his bailiffs and his men in another road, they thought to have me sure in their fetters.

And so, when I was in the power of God over all, at night the priest sent to the bailiff to know why he did not bring me, and the bailiff said there was no such person as was prescribed in the warrant, for he had looked over all the meeting. And then the justice-priest came to the Friend's house and

[1] i.e. overcame.

[2] Slang for a pulpit.

asked him whether George Fox was not there, and the Friend said that he was there, and spake thereto. Then the priest and the bailiff fell a-knocking, and a-jangling. Thus the Devil was foiled and with his darkness could not comprehend the light. And it was strange to me how they got news of my passing almost an hundred miles to that meeting, but when some Friends questioned of his knowledge, he said, he had a letter from London, before my coming to Ireland. And it may be seen what Judases there be to betray Truth. Then I passed over the water, where so many were drowned in the massacre.[1]

And on the First-day was the General Meeting of the Province,[2] like a fair, abundance of Friends and the world. And on the Second-day was the Men's Meeting. And so at the latter end of the meeting came several into the meeting one after another, and one I felt was a spy, and he went his ways; but the meeting was quiet. And a mighty convincement was that day, and a mighty power of God was there. And the justice-priest questioned some sober people that were at the meeting, and threatened them in a rage, and they told him they would go every day if they could hear George Fox.

Then I passed away from that place to visit some other Friends in my way, and came to a market town, where there were more Friends. When I alighted I was pitifully burdened with the wicked spirit, and having not slept the night before. There a couple of ladies came in with their attendants twice to look at me, my name being over the town. They had inquired whether such a man was not come to town, and that still more struck at my life. And the Friends that were with me asked me twice to put the horse to grass, and I forbade them as feeling the darkness; and I asked them whether they had not a backside to walk in, and so they led me into the backside. And when I had walked a turn or two there came in two men.

[1] The river Bann at Portadown, where many lost their lives in 1641 during Irish resistance to English rule.

[2] Probably at Lurgan.

I asked them what they were. They that were with me answered, one was a captain that was at the meeting the other day, and the other a Friend, and so the Friend took me aside, and said he had something to speak to me. He said that the justices were met together, and had given order to the bailiffs to take me in that town. And so after a while I took leave of Friends, and bid the man that was with me to bring out the horses, so we got on horseback. And we passed towards the next county to a meeting which was near a knight's house. And so next day we came to the place of meeting, where we had a brave meeting in the power of God. Oh, the brokenness and life that flowed ! And when the meeting was done I passed twelve miles further, and then the knight did rage that I should have a meeting so near him, who had sent a private letter to the justice of the other county. So the power of God made them all to rage together, and then I passed many miles farther.

Then I came back again to the Grange, where we had a great meeting, and quiet. From thence we passed almost thirty miles farther, where we had another meeting where the Scots raged, and I felt the wicked spirit extremely mad, for some Friends thought officers would come in. But the power of God had great dominion.

And after meeting, we passed several miles farther, and when we came within two miles of a town, we saw four men, and I told them they were Friends, for I felt their spirits, and some of them had come thirty-two miles to bring me news that the justice-priest had got the judge's warrant of the Assizes to go over all his circuit, which reached nigh a hundred miles, as far up as Drogheda, and in it was [mentioned] my hat, and my hair, and my clothes, and my horse. 'Well', said I, 'if they be politic they will lay all the post towns and places where Friends live.' So I went into the town with the man of the town, for that was in the same province and circuit. And Friends came in to me, but I could neither eat nor sleep. I bid the rest go to their inns, and I said, 'Let the Devil do his worst, and this town is blessed. But nevertheless be ready in the morning by two of the clock, for I shall stay of none of you.' For this many times was our usual hour though we were up till eleven.

So I passed along taking one with me, letting the rest come after, and our road was within a stone's cast of that knight that sent a private letter to take me. And so the Friend said, 'George, we will not bait in the town, for the bishop and his deacon live in the town',[1] who had his hand in the pursuit against me. And when we were alighted and looked out at the window, I espied Friends coming up; and one of them alighted and bade the rest ride on. 'Alack', said he, 'the bishop lives here, and the deacon in the next house.' So I said, 'Never heed, the power of the Lord God is over them,' and in little time, we passed away and overtook the rest, and baited again.

Again we passed on our journey, and next morning when we went to go away from our inn (I inquired overnight what time the post came in and they said the next morning by six), as I was going out in the yard, he blew his post horn, and it struck at my life, and I said, 'Go on, they have letters to open', so we came to another county, whence I sent the postmaster a good letter, and a papist challenge to stick on his cross, instead of taking of me.

And then we passed another road farther into the country, for I had cleared all the meetings in the north, excepting one or two before me, before the judge's warrant came out. And there was a Scots sheriff down in the north, who said, the officers, if they could but take that old Jesuit, they would quickly knock all the others down presently. And I felt their rage so against me that I felt my body as cut into pieces and yet I was well. The nation swarmed with Jesuits; and the Jesuits, Protestants, and Presbyterian priests, joined all in a rage against me; but the power of the Lord God was over them all.

And so I passed into the country, and came through Friends near Drogheda into the judge's circuit where the

[1] Perhaps (but not necessarily) Armagh.

former warrants reached, and I had a meeting, where some Friends were afraid but all was quiet, and a fine meeting we had. And so, by the power of the Lord, I passed through that judge's circuit. And after the meeting was done, we passed ten miles, and came to an inn. And there, all night, I could not sleep for tories,[1] I was so troubled about them. At last I passed through a very dangerous river, and saw them on the other side, and smiled at them that I had escaped them.

And the next morning we passed on to a Friend's house where there were some Friends; and it was in another judge's circuit, who was a very bad judge. We visited Friends there, it being but a little mile off the place and town where the judges sat that day. And Friends said that if the judges knew that I was in the country, they would send for me; and my way was to pass through a dangerous river,[2] which I had seen before, which lay by the town's side. And the tories which I saw before were these judges; for though there were tories up in several places of the nation, none hurt me but the judges, justices, and priests.

Then I came to an inn, and the next day to Dublin and lodged near Lazy Hill.[3] There was no small joy amongst Friends that I had passed over the nation. But some Friends had a tender fear, because my name had made such a noise in the nation, and a great meeting in the power of God had we there, though some when the meeting was done were afraid, that the officers would come in, but the power of the Lord God was over all.

And the next day many Friends passed away, and fain would have me out of the city, but I was moved to stay the First-day's meeting before I went out, which was a very great meeting, and so went to the men's meeting, and women's meeting, and all was clear at Dublin.

[1] Dispossessed Irishmen seeking by robbery and murder to regain the lands which had been taken from them, described by their dispossessors as Irish brigands.

[2] The Boyne at Drogheda.

[3] Originally Lazars Hill, after an ancient leper hospital.

And I arose early in the morning to go to the General Meeting, and the men's meeting, and the National Meeting about the sufferings, where some might see more into things than others, there being some out of every meeting. When we parted, oh, the tenderness, and brokenness, and life, and power, that was manifested there and in that nation ! Only I resolved with myself to lay apart a week to answer several papers and writings, from monks, friars, and protestant priests. So when I had cleared all I came to Dublin again, for we did believe that after the great meeting was done, the wind would turn. And I went out and told James Lancaster, 'the wind is for us now all the business in the nation is over', for it was against us in the morning. Then I sent James afore to take shipping, and next day the ship was ready. He met a man, a soldier, by the way that was troubled that he was not at the great meeting, telling that he heard of such a man as was never heard to come out of England; Truth had such a savour amongst all people.

So we got our horses and our things on board and ourselves in the afternoon. And there accompanied us the best part of an hundred Friends to the ship, and when we were gone three or four miles upon the sea, there came in boats, which was very dangerous, eminent Friends and friendly people only moved by their love to see me. But I felt the power of darkness twenty miles afterwards as I was at sea.

And when I was just going to a great boat, some questioned one of the boats, and I bad them put off the boat to the sea from the land. And the other boat came after at last. And Friends in the power of the Lord God, came over them all, and how glad were Friends in the power of God and his life is beyond all words to utter, admiring the love of God, and his mighty power, life, and Seed.

So all passed away, save two Friends, Thomas Holmes, and a Friend of Dublin, who would see us over the water and came over the water into England with us.[1] In the

[1] In August, 1669.

night-time a mighty storm arose, that was almost ready to rend all to pieces. It rained and blew (I was fain to watch the winds as I had watched the tory priests). And I saw the power of God went over the winds; he had them in his fist, his power bound them.

And we, being two nights on the sea (and many passengers with us were sick and some Friends also, but it would not make me sick, though I had hardly slept three nights before I came to sea) the same power of the Lord God which carried me over brought me back again and gave me dominion over all in the life and power. And James Lancaster, Thomas Briggs, Robert Lodge, and all came over with me, only I left John Stubbs behind.

And a good, weighty people there is, and true, and tender, and sensible of the power of the Lord God, and his truth in that nation, worthy to be visited; and very good order they have in their meetings, and they stand up for righteousness and holiness, that dams up the way of wickedness. Oh, the sufferings, and trials gone through, by reason of the bad spirits! The Lord have the glory, whose power went over them, like a tide that covers the earth; and never a hat-man[1] or bad spirit opposed me in the nation, but Robert Cook and another foolish lad with him at Cork, were exceeding envious, beyond the bounds of civility, humanity, or Christianity, but the Seed and power of the Lord God reigns over all, blessed be his name for ever.

And a gallant visitation they had, and there is a gallant spirit in them, worthy to be visited. Many things more might I write too large to mention, but so much I thought good to signify to Friends and brethren, that they may rejoice in the power and Seed of God.

And at James Hutchinson's in Ireland there came a-many great persons and they would discourse with me about election and reprobation.

So I told them, as for our principle of truth it was too high for them, though they judged it foolish, but I would

[1] A small faction of Friends who wished to keep their hats on in prayer.

discourse with them, as a man, of election and reprobation by way of history.

[1]You say God hath ordained the greatest part of men for Hell, and they were ordained so before the world began, and your proof is in Jude, and you say Esau was reprobate and the Egyptians and the stock of Ham.

Now Christ saith to his disciples, Go, teach all nations and go into all nations to preach the Gospel. Now were they not to go to Ham's stock and Esau's stock? For did not Christ die for all the stock of Esau and Egypt and Ham? And God would have all men to be saved, mark, all men, then the stock of Esau and of Ham also, . . . and he that believes is saved and he that does not is condemned already. So the condemnation comes by unbelief. . . . And so the election and choice stands in Christ, and he that believes is saved and he that believes not is condemned already. . . .

And much more I told them I could declare of these things; and they confessed they never heard so much before.

And when I came to Liverpool we went to the mayor's house who kept an inn,[2] into his parlour where were many officers and magistrates. And I walked out again and they called in James Lancaster and asked whether that was not George Fox and he said, 'Yes'; but they had not power to meddle with me: and after I had stayed about a quarter of an hour in the house we went about a mile out of the town to a Friend's house and stayed a while.

And when G.F. was come to Liverpool the master of the ship raised a scandal: that he stayed all night at Liverpool drinking, and this he reported when he came to Dublin. Friends hearing of it, two of whom were eminent men and came over with him, knew that he did not stay above a quarter of an hour in that town. So they made him to repent of his slander, and as he came back from Dublin, his ship was cast away, and so the just judgements of God overtook him.

[1] Discourse in full, *Camb. Jnl.*, ii, 149-51; Ellwood, p. 330-31; Bicent., ii, 112-13.

[2] The mayor for the year 1668-9 was Lord Strange. It seems unlikely that he kept an inn.

From the Friend's house we went to Richard Johnson's.[1] And the next day we passed to William Barnes his house, and from thence to William Gandy's, visiting Friends and had many precious meetings in Lancashire and Cheshire; and so from thence we came to Thomas Hammersley's; and from thence to Whitehough, where a captain threatened to come and break up the meeting, but the Lord's power stopped him.

And from thence we passed through the countries, visiting Friends in their meetings, till we came to Nailsworth in Gloucestershire; and there it was noised all over the country by the Presbyterians that George Fox was turned a Presbyterian. And they prepared him a pulpit and set it in a yard, and there would be a thousand people they said that would come to hear him, the next day being the First-day. Then I said, 'This is strange that such a report should be of me.' And as we came farther, to other Friends' houses, we met with the same report.

And then we came farther where Friends' meeting place was, and there we stayed all night and there was the same report also. And we came by the yard where we saw the pulpit erected. And on the next day, being First-day, there was a very large meeting of many hundreds of people and the Lord's power and presence was amongst us.

And there was one John Fox a Presbyterian, whose name they gave out was George Fox.

And the people hearing that I was so near, they having heard this John Fox the forenoon, in the afternoon there came several hundreds of his people to the meeting where I was; and I turned them to the grace of God which would teach them and bring their salvation. And so people generally saw and were ashamed of the forgery of the Presbyterians, and the Lord's power and truth came over all.

And about this time whilst I was in Leicestershire this John Fox aforesaid ⟨who had formerly been priest of Marshfield⟩ did preach in a steeplehouse sometimes in Wiltshire by leave of a Common Prayer priest. And at

[1] Richard Johnson lived at Ormskirk, Lancs.

last he and the other priest aforesaid fell out. And a great tumult was in the steeplehouse betwixt the Presbyterians and the Episcopal men; the Common Prayer book was cut to pieces ⟨and some treasonable words spoken by some of the followers of John Fox⟩.

And the Episcopal men sent up to the Parliament and petitioned the Parliament against the said John Fox, but instead of mentioning his name, John Fox, some Presbyterians got his name changed and put in George Fox, the Quaker, ⟨when I was above two hundred miles from the place where this bustle happened⟩. And in their petition they mention that the people should cry, ' No king but George Fox.' And this was put in the News Book that was sent over all the nation. But Friends got a certificate under some of the Parliament men's hands as aforesaid to clear George Fox from that abuse and how that it was John Fox the Presbyterian priest and not George Fox the Quaker.[1]

And the Presbyterians deceitfully would come and ask Friends where was George Fox now; and we would have the Parliament men to put the certificate into the Gazette to clear me but they would not; but the Lord's power came over them all. Though from this ground some of the members in Parliament took an occasion to move in the Parliament House for the bringing forth of the last Act against seditious conventicles, as they called it, which after a little while came forth.

And this John Fox was a wicked man that came to a Friend's house who with his wife had been one of the chief of his hearers. And he said he would rather have lost all his hearers than have lost them.

But they told him they could not profit under his ministry and that he had walked in the steps of the false prophets, preaching for hire and filthy lucre, ⟨telling him Christ said, ' Freely ye have received, freely give ', and therefore he

[1] The Certificates dated 8th and 9th April, 1670, were signed by Sir Gilbert Talbot, M.P. for Plymouth, and Sir Winston Churchill, M.P. for Weymouth and Melcombe Regis. Printed in *Jnl. Friends Hist. Soc.*, ix, 155.

should not take money of people for preaching⟩. And they told him that times were hard.

Then said this John Fox, ‘ God bless preaching for that brings in money, let times go how they will; and fill my belly with good victuals and call me false prophet or what you will and kick me about the house when you have done.’

A woman that had the impropriation of the tithes of the parish asked counsel of ⟨a company of Presbyterian priests⟩ what to do against our Friend, seeing she as impropriator took the tithes of the parish, but this Friend had refused to pay any. So she asked their counsel and advice what to do with him. And they gave counsel to her to send in reapers and cut down and carry away all his corn, which she did and undid this poor man. And this relation I had from the man and woman's own mouth who lived near Sodbury in Gloucestershire, whom these priests and this woman had served so.

Thomas Atkins and his wife who lived not far from Nailsworth, a shopkeeper, told me there was a separate meeting of the Presbyterians, and they took an oath of their people that they should neither buy, or sell, or eat, or drink with Friends. And the eminentest woman amongst them fell sick and fell into a benumbed condition so as she could neither stir hand or foot; and all the doctors could do her no good. And at last there came two or three women to Thomas Atkins's wife into her shop, pretending to buy something of her. And she showed them things they asked for; and so they did confess in discourse with her that they had taken an oath as aforesaid. But the occasion of their coming was concerning this woman that lay in that misery, to desire some help and advice from her as to her recovery. And she asked them how they could dispense with their oath, and they said they must be forced to break it. So Thomas Atkins's wife took the woman in hand and cured her.

And so the Lord broke the wicked bonds of the Presbyterians asunder that they had ensnared their people with. And much might be written of these things.

⟨And after I had cleared myself of the Lord's service thataways, I passed away.⟩ And from thence we came through the country and had many precious meetings till we came to Bristol where I had many precious meetings. When I came to Bristol a letter met me there from John Stubbs in Ireland.

And there Margaret Fell and her daughters and sons-in-law met me, where we were married. ⟨Margaret Fell was come to visit her daughter Yeamans.

I had seen from the Lord a considerable time before that I should take Margaret Fell to be my wife. And when I first mentioned it to her she felt the answer of life from God thereunto. But though the Lord had opened this thing unto me, yet I had not received a command from the Lord for the accomplishment of it then. Wherefore I let the thing rest, and went on in the work and service of the Lord as before, according as the Lord led me, travelling up and down in this nation and through the nation of Ireland. But now, after I was come back from Ireland and was come to Bristol and found Margaret Fell there, it opened in me from the Lord that the thing should be now accomplished.

And after we had discoursed the thing together I told her if she also was satisfied with the accomplishing of it now she should first send for her children, which she did. And when the rest of her daughters were come⟩ I was moved to ask the children ⟨and her sons-in-law⟩ whether they were all satisfied and whether Margaret had answered them according to her husband's will to her children, she being a widow, and if her husband had left anything to her for the assistance of her children, in which if she married they might suffer loss, whether she had answered them in lieu of that and all other things. And the children made answer and said she had doubled it, and would not have me to speak of those things. ⟨I told them I was plain and would have all things done plainly, for I sought not any outward advantage to myself.⟩

And so when I had thus acquainted the children with it,

and when it had been laid before several meetings both of the men and women, assembled together for that purpose, and all were satisfied,[1] there was a large meeting appointed of purpose ⟨in the meeting house at Broad Mead in Bristol, the Lord joining us together in the honourable marriage in the everlasting covenant and immortal Seed of life,⟩ where there were several large testimonies borne by Friends.[2] ⟨Then was a certificate, relating both the proceedings and the marriage, openly read and signed by the relations and by most of the ancient Friends of that city, besides many other Friends from divers parts of the nation.⟩

And before we were married I was moved to write forth a paper to all the meetings in England both of men and woman and elsewhere, for all meetings of Friends which were begotten to the Lord were but as one meeting to me.

After this I stayed in Bristol about a week and then passed with Margaret into the country to Olveston, where Margaret passed homewards towards the north and I passed on in the work of the Lord into Wiltshire, where I had many large and precious meetings.

And from thence I passed into Berkshire, where I had many large precious meetings, and so from thence till I came into Oxfordshire and Buckinghamshire, where I had many precious meetings all along till I came to London.

⟨In London, it came upon me to write to Friends throughout the nation, about putting out poor children to trades. Wherefore I sent the following epistle to the Quarterly Meetings of Friends in all counties:⟩

London. 1st of 11th mo. 1669 [Jan., 1670].

My dear Friends,

Every Quarterly Meeting to make enquiry through all the Monthly Meetings and other meetings, to know all Friends that be poor, widows or others, that have children fit to set forth apprentices, so that once a quarter you may set forth an apprentice in your Quarterly Meeting. And so you may set

[1] Accounts of these meetings are in a MS. at Friends House, London.

[2] 27th Oct., 1669.

forth four in a year, as needs, and sometimes more, as there is occasion. And this apprentice when he comes out of his time may help his father or mother and rear up the family that is decayed. And in this doing all their poor Friends shall come to live comfortably as men. For being done in the Quarterly Meeting you will have knowledge through all the county, in all their Monthly and particular meetings, of masters that be fit for them, and for such trades as their parents desire, or you desire, or as the children are most inclinable to. And so to be placed and put forth as you order from the Quarterly Meeting to Friends, they may be preserved in the Truth. And by this in the wisdom of God you will preserve Friends' children in the Truth.

You will take off a continual maintenance. . . . For in the country you know that you may set forth an apprentice for a little to several trades, as bricklayers, and masons and carpenters, wheelwrights, ploughwrights, tailors, tanners, curriers, blacksmiths, shoemakers, nailers, butchers, weavers of linen and woollen, of stuffs and serges, and several other trades. . . . Whereby they that are decaying in their families, in seven years time they be rearing them up, and preserving of them. So you may have a stock in your Quarterly Meetings for the same purpose. And all that is given by any that do decease, except it be given to some particular or some particular meeting, may be brought up to the public stock for that same purpose. . . . For in several counties the same is practised. And some Quarterly Meetings do set forth two apprentices and sometimes they set forth children of the world that are laid upon the parish, and when they come to Friend's houses they have gathered money to set them forth to apprentices. And they have come to be Friends. And some they have set forth four or five or six years, according to their capacity. And some they have set forth longer that have been younger. In all these things the wisdom of God will teach you, by which you may come to help the children of poor Friends, that they may come to rear up their families and preserve them in the fear of God. So no more but my love in the everlasting Seed, by which you will have wisdom, to order all things to the glory of God. G.F.[1]

[1] Abridged from a MS. in George Fox, *Epistles and Queries* (Fox papers, Xx, p. 115); also printed, with adaptations, Ellwood, p. 335; Bicent., ii, 119, 120.

And so after I had stayed awhile in London and visited Friends and the Lord's power was over all, I passed down into Essex and Hertfordshire where I had many precious meetings. And from Hertfordshire I passed into Cambridgeshire and Huntingdonshire and Leicestershire and Warwickshire and Derbyshire and so through the countries visiting the Friends and had many large and precious meetings among them.

And there was one Walter Newton, a neighbour to my relations, who had been an ancient Puritan, said unto me he heard I was married, and asked the reason. And I told him, as a testimony, that all might come up into the marriage as was in the beginning, and as a testimony that all might come up out of the wilderness to the marriage of the Lamb. And he said he thought marriage was only for the procreation of children, and I told him I never thought of any such thing but only in obedience to the power of the Lord. And I judged such things below me, though I saw such things and established marriages; but I looked on it as below me. And though I saw such a thing in the Seed yet I had no command to such a thing till a half year before, though people had long talked of it, and there was some jumble in some minds about it, but the Lord's power came over all and laid all their spirits; and some after confessed it.

And whilst I was in the country I heard that Margaret was haled out of her house and carried to Lancaster prison again, an order being gotten from the King and Council to fetch her back into prison again upon her old praemunire, though she was discharged from that imprisonment by an order from the King and his Council the year before.

〈As soon as I was got to London, I hastened Thomas Lower's wife Mary, and Sarah Fell (two of my wife's daughters) to the King, to acquaint him how their mother was dealt with, and see if they could get a full discharge for her that she might enjoy her estate and liberty without molestation. This was somewhat difficult at first to get, but by diligent attendance on it they at length〉 got an order from the King that their mother should not be molested nor disquieted in the enjoyment of her estate nor house. The King commanded Sir John Otway to signify his mind by letter into the country, to the sheriff and others concerned, which he did. And after this Thomas Lower and his wife passed towards Bristol and from thence to Cornwall; and Sarah Fell and John Rous and his wife passed down into the north and brought the King's letter with them ⟨to Lancaster. And by them I wrote to my wife as followeth:

My dear heart in the truth and life, that changeth not, it was upon me that Mary Lower and Sarah should go to the King concerning thy imprisonment, and to Kirkby, that the power of the Lord might appear over them all in thy deliverance. They went, and then they thought to have come down; but it was upon me to stay them a little longer, that they might follow the business till it was effected; which it now is, and is here sent down. The late declaration of mine hath been very serviceable, people being generally satisfied with it. So no more, but my love in the holy Seed. G.F.

The declaration, here mentioned, was a printed sheet, writ upon occasion of a new persecution stirred up. For a fresh storm was risen, occasioned (as it was thought) by that tumultuous meeting in a steeplehouse in Wiltshire or Gloucestershire, mentioned a little before.⟩[1]

After I had been in the country, as I came up the streets in London the drums beat for every household to send forth a soldier into the trained bands, to be in readiness, the Act against seditious conventicles being then come into force,[2] ⟨and was turned upon us who of all people were free from sedition and tumult. Whereupon I writ the declaration before mentioned, showing from the preamble and terms of the said Act, that we were not such a people, nor our meetings such meetings as were described in that Act.[3]

1 See p. 551-2 ante.

2 The second Conventicle Act came into force 10th May, 1670.

3 *A Declaration from the People of God, called Quakers, against all Seditious Conventicles.*

I writ also another short paper on the occasion of that Act against meetings, opening our case to the magistrates, as follows:

O Friends, consider this Act, which limits us to five, that but five may meet. Is this to do as ye would be done by? Would ye be so served yourselves? We own Christ Jesus as well as you, his coming, death, and resurrection, and if we be contrary-minded to you in some things, is not this the apostle's exhortation to wait till God hath revealed it? Doth not he say, 'What is not of faith, is sin'? And seeing we have not faith in things which ye would have us to do, would it not be sin in us if we should do contrary to our faith? And why should any man have power over any other man's faith, seeing Christ is the author of it? When the apostles did preach in the name of Jesus and great multitudes heard them, and the rulers forbade them to speak any more in that name, did not they bid them judge whether it were better to obey God or man? Would not this Act have taken hold of the twelve apostles, and seventy disciples, for they met often together? And if there had been any Act or a law made then, that not above five should have met with Christ, would not that have been a hindering of him from meeting with his disciples? And do ye think that he, who is the wisdom of God, or his disciples would have obeyed it? If such a law had been made in the apostles' days, that not above five might have met together, who had been different-minded from either the Jews or the Gentiles, do ye think the Churches of Christ at Corinth, Philippi, Ephesus, Thessalonica, or the rest of the gathered Churches, would have obeyed it? O therefore consider, for we are Christians, and partake of the nature and life of Christ. And strive not to limit the Holy One; for God's power cannot be limited, and is not to be quenched. And do unto all men as ye would have them do unto you, for that is the law and the prophets. This is from those who wish you all well, and desire your everlasting good and prosperity, who are called Quakers, who seek the peace and good of all people, though they do afflict us, and cause us to suffer. G.F.

Now as I had endeavoured to soften the magistrates, and to take off the sharpness of their edge in the execution of the Act, so it was upon me to write a few lines to Friends to strengthen and encourage them to stand fast in their testimony, and bear, with Christian patience and content, the suffering that was coming upon them. This I did in the following epistle.

All my dear Friends,

Keep in the faith in God above all outward things, and in his power, that hath given you dominion over all. The same power and God is the same with you to deliver you as formerly; and God and his power is the same, and his Seed is over all, and before all, and will be, when that which makes to suffer is gone. . . .

Friends, the Lord hath blessed you in outward things; and now the Lord may try you, whether your minds be in outward things or with the Lord that gave you them? . . . And let not any one's Delilah shave his head, lest he lose his strength; neither rest in its lap, lest the Philistines be upon you. For your rest is in Christ Jesus; therefore rest not in anything else.

London, 12th of 2nd mo. [April], 1670. G.F.〉[1]

CHAPTER XXII

UPON the First-day after the Act came in force,[2] Friends met as they used to do in the morning, where every minister declared their going to the several meetings as they were moved. And Friends asked me to what meeting I would go and I told them, into the high fields to Gracious Street[3] meeting 〈where I expected the storm was most likely to begin〉. And this day all the train-bands were up and as I passed through the street to the meeting all the street was full of people, and a guard set to the meeting-house door to keep out Friends. And I went in the other passage that goes out of Lombard Street, and there was another guard set, of a company of watchmen, and the court full of people.

[1] Imperfect MS. copy in Fox Papers, Z, p. 25. In full, Ellwood, p. 338; Bicent., ii, 123.

[2] Sunday, 15th May, 1670. [3] i.e. Gracechurch St.

And William Warwick was speaking, but he had soon ended; and after he had done I stood up and spoke and was moved to say, ' Saul, Saul, why persecutest thou me ', and it was hard for him to kick against that which pricked him, and they that do persecute Christ in his members where he is made manifest kicked against that which pricked them now, so it was Saul's nature that persecuted still, and that it was the birth of the flesh that persecuted the birth of the Spirit; for we were a peaceable people and we did love them that persecuted us. And it was the nature of dogs to tear and devour the sheep, and we suffered as sheep that did not bite again, but others they might persecute that would bite again. Therefore all to stand still and see the salvation of God, and let the peace of God keep their hearts, for the bright morning star was risen.

And after I had spoken a pretty many more words, in came the constable with an informer, and an officer with a file of musketeers, and I cried, ' Blessed are the peacemakers.' Then they plucked me down and pulled me out and the officer said I was the man he looked for, he must carry me to the Lord Mayor's,[1] and he put me among his file of musketeers and bid them secure me, and took William Warwick and John Burnyeat[2] and haled us along the streets. And Thomas Lower and Gerard Roberts followed after me. The people cried to them, ' Have a care of him, he is a princely man ', and were mighty moderate. And we came along the streets to the Exchange and there they made a stand awhile, and then they had me on towards Moorfields. And as we were going alongst the streets this officer was laying his hand upon me, and some mocked at the constable and told him we would not run away. The informer was asking Will Warwick a question, how one might know the Scriptures, and William did not answer him; so I turned to him and said, ' By the

[1] The Lord Mayor of 1669-70 was Sir Samuel Starling.

[2] John Burnyeat (1631-1690), husbandman, of Cumberland, convinced 1653, travelled much, preaching, on both sides of the Atlantic.

same spirit that they were in that gave them forth.' 'Oh', said he, 'this is a rational man, I will talk with him.' Then said he, 'Where were all these new religions about two hundred years ago?' and that it would never be a good world until all people came to the good old religion that was two hundred years ago. 'What!' said I to him, 'art thou a Papist? what! a Papist informer? For two hundred years ago there was no other religion here but the popish!' But he would not be known nor discover it. And after he saw that he had insnared himself he was vexed, and as he went alongst in the streets I often spoke to him and manifested his wickedness to the people, that he was a Papist informer and was not only against us but against the Protestants.

So when I came to the Lord Mayor's house he was putting me forward with his hand, I said, 'What? Thou thinkest to get money? But I'll warrant thee.'

And when we came into the Lord Mayor's court there were several people got about me and asked how and for what I was taken. So I desired them to go and ask the informer and know what his name was, but he would not tell his name but began to gnaw his fingers' ends. And after a little while he went and whispered to the constable and said he would go his ways, he could do little more there, but the constable would not have had him go. And then one of the mayor's officers looking out a window spoke to him and said he should tell his name before he passed out of that house, for the Lord Mayor would know by what authority he intruded himself with his soldiers into the execution of those laws which belonged to the civil magistrate to execute, and not to the military. For aught he knew he was come to inform against his lord as much as against any other. And one of the officers called to him and said, 'Have you brought people here and now will you go away before the Lord Mayor comes?' 'Yes,' said he. After which he was restless till he got out, and came to the doorkeeper to let him forth, who was called unto not to let him go forth till the Lord Mayor came. But he forcibly pulled open the door and went out. And no sooner was he come out of the doors, the streets being full of people, but the people made such a shout that the streets rung with the noise, and cried, 'A Papist informer! A Papist informer!' and fell upon him and we thought would have torn him in pieces. So we desired the constable to go, who said he durst not go out, so the soldiers being there they rescued him from the people and brought him into the mayor's entry and kept him awhile and then he went forth again towards Moorgate. And they shouted after he came forth again, and then they fell upon him again and then the soldiers rescued him again and had him into an alley into a house and there he changed his periwig and vest, and passed away towards Moorfields unknown. It was judged he was gone to the mayor to inform him, the mayor not being come home.

So when the Lord Mayor came home I and William Warwick and John Burnyeat were brought before him. And some of the officers of his house would have taken off our hats, but he called to them and bid them let them alone and not to meddle with our hats, for, said he, 'They are not yet brought before me in judicature.'

So he called some of the Presbyterian and Baptist teachers before him and was somewhat sharp with them and convicted them.

After he was done with them I was brought up before him to his table, and the officers took off my hat. Then he swore the watchmen, that we were speaking at such a meeting.

I told him this Act did not concern us, which was made against seditious meetings that met under colour of religion to contrive insurrections, for we had been tried and were always found peaceable, and therefore he should put a difference betwixt the precious and the vile.

He said the Act was made against meetings and a worship not according to the liturgy.

I asked him whether the liturgy was according to the

Scriptures, whether they might not read Scriptures and speak Scriptures.

He said Yes.

Then I said, '"according to" is not the very same thing; and we ought to worship God in all times and all places'. And because this Act did take hold upon such as did meet and contrive as late experience had showed, they found no such experience by us. Because thieves were sometimes on the road, must not honest men travel; because plotters and contrivers of mischief had sometimes met, must not therefore peaceable people meet? We were not the people concerned in the Act, for if we were such as did meet to plot and contrive we did not believe five pounds, or ten, or twenty could clear us.

'Nay', said the mayor, 'that would reach further.'

'Yea', said I, 'to life and estate. Now if we had been the people that meet and contrive, then we might draw ourselves into fours; four might do more mischief than if there were a hundred, for they might speak out their minds, which they could not do so well before a hundred; therefore we being innocent and not the people this Act concerns, we keep our meetings as we used to do.'

Then the mayor very lovingly said, 'Mr. Fox, you are an eminent man amongst those of your profession, pray will you be instrumental to dissuade them from meeting in such great numbers? Seeing Christ hath promised that where two or three are met in his name, he will be in the midst of them, and the King and Parliament are graciously pleased to allow four to meet together to worship God, why will not you be content to partake both of Christ's promise of two or three and the King's indulgence to four?'

Unto which I answered that <Christ's promise was not to discourage many from meeting together in his name, but to encourage the few, that the fewest might not forbear to meet, because of their fewness. But> if Christ had promised to manifest his presence in the midst of such an assembly where but two or three were gathered in his name, then how much more where two or three hundred are gathered in his name. Would not this Act have taken hold upon Christ and his apostles and disciples in their day, who often met together above the number of four, who had seventy and twelve disciples, which was a considerable number ?

To which the mayor said, ' You speak too popular.'[1]

Then said I, ' Is it not true ? '

Thomas Moore said unto the Lord Mayor he thought that was a mistake, in saying that the King and Parliament in this Act allowed of four, for though the Act takes hold of all that are met together above that number yet it doth not allow of four, nor two to meet together to worship God in other manner than the liturgy allows; and though if two, three, or four so met together were not punishable by this Act, yet by several other Acts they are, and therefore there was no allowance for any to meet together to worship God in any other manner than the liturgy allows, which he thought was very hard and unchristian.

To which the Lord Mayor replied, ' Mr. Moore, I will talk with you upon this subject another time.'

Then the mayor said to John Burnyeat because he looked whitely,[2] ' Come, your countenance shows you have come lately from beyond seas and are some Jesuit.' But I said he was neither Jesuit nor Papist but an honest countryman, I knew him. The mayor said he would have a certificate from him. I said that he might give him one.

So he took our names and recorded where I lodged. I told him I was but a lodger in London and had been there much since the Independents and Presbyterians had brought me up in Oliver's time as a plotter, and finding nothing against me invented such a thing. So at last, seeing the informer was gone, he set us at liberty and said the Act did allow four of us might meet.

I said again, if it did allow four to meet it must be such as meet to contrive under a colour, and not such as are

[1] Perhaps 'You are making them out to be too numerous.'

[2] i.e. of pale complexion.

innocent. And as I was going away I spoke to the mayor and told him he knew in his own conscience we were an innocent people and that that Act did not concern us.

And after we were set at liberty Friends asked me whither I would go, and I told them to Gracechurch Street Meeting again, and when we came there the people were gone; only some people stood at the gate.

So we went into Gerard Roberts's house, and I sent out to know how all the meetings were. And some were kept out and some were taken but set at liberty again a few days after. And the Lord's power came over all, and a glorious time it was for the Lord's everlasting Truth, for as fast as some were taken down that were speaking, others were moved of the Lord to stand up and speak, to the admiration of people. And many Baptists and other sectaries forsook their meetings and came to see how the Quakers would stand both in city and country.

And this informer was so frightened that there durst hardly any informer appear in London for several years after.

And yet this Lord Mayor after this proved a very great persecutor of our Friends and cast many into prison: as you may see in the books of the trials of William Penn and William Meade and Thomas Rudyard.[1] And his name became a stink, and the Lord cut him off.

In the time of this persecution the Presbyterians and all other sectaries generally fled. And when the constables came to apprehend Priest Vincent[2] at Devonshire House, he would give the people a psalm and in the mean time get away; and some times ask leave of the constables to go and refresh himself and in the mean time fly away. And at Spitalfields they had a meeting, and some of the people said, 'They are coming ! they are coming ! ' and the priest and people fled away in such haste they had like to have spoiled one another, though it was but a false alarm, given by their own watchmen through a mistake. And

[1] *The People's Ancient and Just Liberties Asserted.* 1670. 2 parts.
[2] Thomas Vincent.

these were the Presbyterians and Independents that had persecuted us when they had power, because we would not follow their religion, which now durst not stand to it themselves.

Persecution after a time came to assuage again; and after I had visited Friends and things were pretty quiet in the city, I passed into the country; and several meetings I had amongst Friends in Middlesex, Buckinghamshire, and Oxfordshire; though in some places there was much threatening. And Friends much desired me for to come to Reading where most of Friends were in prison. And some of Reading Friends came to me to a place called Turville Heath where we had a quiet meeting though much threatened. And after, I came to Reading of a Seventh-day I went to the prison, and diverse Friends came in and sober people. And I was loath to go to meetings in prison, for I told them I would rather be taken in a public meeting than in prison. And Ann Curtis told me that John Story stayed there a great while, and had many meetings in prison; and I told her that was nothing to me.

So the prisoners being gathered together, and several other persons come in, I declared the word of life amongst them and encouraged them in the Truth, and they were refreshed in the Lord's power and presence. And after the meeting was ended, the gaoler understood that I was there. Then Friends were troubled as fearing how to get me out free again.

And after I had stayed with them and supped with them, I went down the stairs. And the gaoler was standing at the door, and Friends were very fearful; so I put my hand in my pocket, which he had such an eye unto, and the hope of some silver, that he forgot to question me. So I gave him some silver and bid him be kind and civil to my friends in prison whom I came to visit, and so I passed out, and the Lord's power came over him and chained them all. But the next that came to visit them he stopped, to wit Isaac Penington, ⟨and caused him to be made a prisoner⟩.

And the next morning I passed about fourteen miles into Hampshire: to a place called Baughurst, ⟨Thomas Briggs being with me,⟩ and when we came into the parish there were some sober people came to us and told us that the priest[1] of the town was an envious man and did threaten us.

But when our meeting, which was very large, was gathered, the priest had got a warrant, and sent the constables and officers; and they came into the house, but did not come into the meeting-room, and so they passed away again. And we knew not in the meeting that they were come and gone again. So after Thomas Briggs had done speaking, I was moved of the Lord to stand up, and I declared the word of Truth and life to the people, and a precious, fresh meeting we had. When I had done and stepped down, and ended the meeting, I heard a great clutter in the yard.

And after the meeting was ended we came forth, and the man of the house told us that the priest had sent the constables again, and his own servant with them, in a great rage; and they had been in the house, but came not into the meeting-room, but went their ways. Thus the Lord's power preserved us over the devilish design of the priest, and out of his snare. And after we passed away, many Friends passed by the priest's house, which set him in a great rage.

And so I came upon the edge of Berkshire to a Friend's house, where several Friends came to visit us: and the Lord's power was over all and we in it were preserved.

And from thence we passed into Surrey, visiting Friends, and had many precious meetings, and came to Stephen Smith's near Guildford,[2] where they had taken very much goods away from Friends for their meetings, and there were great threatenings, yet we had several blessed meetings there, and the Lord's power was over all.

And from thence I passed into Sussex by Richard Bax's

[1] The priest of Baughurst was William Woodward.

[2] Stephen Smith lived at Worplesdon.

where we had a large, precious meeting and quiet, though the constables had threatened.

And after, I had many meetings up and down that country, though there was much threatening, but quiet, for the Lord's power was over all. And Friends were refreshed and established upon the foundation of God, that stands sure.

After this I came into Kent and had many glorious meetings, and all was quiet; and I travelled most part of that county over, and at last came up to a great meeting near Deal beyond Canterbury. And after the meeting was done I came to Canterbury, and the next day visited Friends, and from thence I came into the Isle of Sheppey where I stayed two or three days, and Alexander Parker, and George Whitehead, and John Rous came to me there.

And the next day we passed away after I had finished my service for the Lord there; and as I was going towards Rochester I lighted and walked down a hill; and a great weight and oppression fell on my spirit. So I got on my horse again, but my weight and oppression remained so as I was hardly able to ride. So we came to Rochester; but I was very weak to ride, and very much loaden and burdened with the world's spirits, so that my life was oppressed under them.

I got to Gravesend and went to an inn but could hardly eat or sleep.

And the next day, John Rous and Alexander Parker went for London and I passed with John Stubbs over the ferry into Essex; and so we came to Hornchurch, where there was a meeting on the First-day, but I was so oppressed I could not go into it. After the meeting was done, I came down and spoke to Friends a few words, and after desired them to get me my horse ready. So I endeavoured to ride ten miles to Stratford, three miles off London, to an honest Friend's house, that had been a captain whose name was Williams; but I was exceeding weak. And several Friends came thither unto me from London.

But at last I lost my hearing and sight so as I could not see nor hear. And I said unto Friends that I should be as a sign to such as would not see, and such as would not hear the Truth. And in this condition I continued a pretty while. And several people came about me, but I felt their spirits and discerned, though I could not see them, who was honest hearted and who was not.

And several Friends that were doctors came and would have given me physic but I was not to meddle with their things. And under great sufferings and groans and travails, and sorrows and oppressions, I lay for several weeks.

And young Margaret Rous continued with me and I was sensible of her tenderness and love, and Edward Mann's wife,[1] and I saw that I had a travail to go through, and I spoke to Friends to let none but sober women be about me.

And one time, when they had given me up, several went away and said they would not see me die; and others said I would be still enough by such a time; and it was all over London and in the country that I was past hopes of recovery, and that I was deceased.

And the next morning I spoke to Friends to get a coach to carry me to Gerard Roberts about twelve miles off, and I called for my clothes, which put them into more fears and doubts, because people had used to desire a little before their departing to be changed; and so they said I had all the symptoms of death upon me and all their hopes were gone, except two or three. And when they thought to put me by concerning my clothes and made excuses, I perceived it and told them it was deceit, but at last they brought me my clothes and things and put them on. And so I spoke to the man and woman of the house and had a little glimmering sight, and I saw Edward Mann's wife putting up my clothes and told her she did well; and I felt the Lord's power was over all. So I went down a pair of stairs to the coach, and when I came to the coach I was like to have fallen down I was so weak and feeble, but I got up into the

[1] Elizabeth. Edward Mann, hosier, a prominent London Friend, was many times Fox's host.

coach and some Friends with me and I could discern the people and fields and that was all.

And it was noised up and down in London that I was deceased but the next news they heard I was gone twelve miles in a coach to Gerard Roberts who was very weak, which astonished them to hear it. And I was moved to speak to him and encourage him, though I could hardly hear or see. And there I was about three weeks, and many times I could not tell when it was day or when it was night; and once I lay twenty-four hours, and asked them what day it was, and they said I had missed a day.

And then it came to me I might go to Enfield, and they were afraid, that I should remove. But I told them I might go and they should get a coach. And when they had gotten one I was moved to speak to Gerard Roberts who was very weak, and to take leave of them. And when I came to Enfield I went to see Amor Stoddard who lay very weak and almost speechless. I was moved to tell him he had been faithful as a man and faithful to God and that the immortal Seed of life was his crown, and with many other words I was moved to speak to him though I was so weak I was hardly able to stand. And from thence I went to the widow Dry's,[1] and within a few days after Amor Stoddard died at Samuel Newton's hard by.

And there I lay at the widow Dry's all that winter, warring with the evil spirits, and could not endure the smell of any flesh meat.

And I saw all the religions and people that lived in them, and the priests that held them up, as a company of men-eaters, and how they ate up the people like bread, gnawing the flesh off their bones. And great sufferings I was under at this time beyond words to declare, for I was come into the deep, and the men-eaters were about me and I warred with their spirits.

And at this time there were great persecutions and there had been searching for me at London, and some meeting-houses plucked down and broken up with soldiers. Sometimes

[1] Elizabeth Dry, probably widow of Thomas Dry of Enfield.

they would come with a troop of horse and a company of foot, and they would break their swords and muskets, carbines and pikes, with beating Friends and wounding abundance, so that the blood stood like puddles in the streets. And Friends were made to stand, by the Lord's power. And some of the formalists would say if Friends did not stand the nation would run into debauchery.

And Colonel Kirkby he came to several meetings to break them up with a company of foot; and as he went over the passage to Horslydown there was some striving betwixt his soldiers and some of the boatmen and he commanded his men to shoot them and they did and killed some men of the world. And often he would enquire for me at the meetings he came to break up.

And at Droitwich there came John Cartwright to a Friend's house and being moved of the Lord to speak a few words before supper in praise to God there came an informer and hearkened under the window. And he went to Lichfield for an order to distrain the Friend's goods, of the house, under pretence that there was a meeting at the Friend's house, hoping to have got some prey and gain, whereas there was no one in the house at that time when he spoke before supper but the man of the house[1] and his wife and servant maid. So he got a warrant to distrain and as he returned in the night to Droitwich with his order he was coming up a bottom near the town and another man with him when an owl flew before him and screeched. And the other man cried, 'God bless him.' 'Oh', said the informer, 'why say you so? what, are you afraid of an owl?', but he presently after fell off his horse and broke his neck and there was the end of this wicked informer, who hoped to have spoiled Friends, but the Lord prevented him and cut him off in his wickedness and spoiled him.

And it was a cruel bloody persecuting time, but the Lord's power went over all, and his everlasting Seed. And as persecution began to cease I began to arise out of my sufferings.

[1] Said to be John Watts.

As for religion and worship and ministers of God, alack ! I saw there was none in the world amongst those that pretended it, but amongst such as were in the Truth. I saw the church as a company of men-eaters of cruel visages and of long teeth. Though they had cried against the men-eaters of New England, I saw they were in the same natures.

For the great professing Jews did eat up God's people like bread; and the false prophets and priests and others preached peace to people if they put into their mouths and fed them, but if not they gnawed their flesh off to the bone and chopped them for the cauldron. And these that profess themselves Christians now, both priests and professors, were in the same nature, men-eaters, who were not in the same power and spirit as Christ, the prophets, and apostles were in.

So in my deep misery I saw things beyond words to utter; and I saw a black coffin but I passed over it.

And at last I overcame these spirits and men-eaters though many times I was so weak that people knew not whether I was in the body or out. And many precious Friends came far and nigh to see me and attended upon me and were with me; and towards the spring I began to recover and to walk up and down, to the astonishment of Friends and others.

But they all saw and took notice that as the persecution ceased I came from under my travails and sufferings as by this following letter in part appears.

[1]Dearly beloved and ever honoured in the truth, Margaret Fox.

I am now with thy dear husband, who is recovering I hope; and yesterday in the afternoon, I had a fine opportunity to speak my mind to him, being alone in his chamber with him. I told him I expected to have a few lines from thee that night, but it's proved otherwise. He bid me write to thee, and his words were thus, ' Tell her I have been ill, and so I could not write but now I am better, blessed be the Lord, praises to the

[1] The letter, now separated from the MS. Journal, is Abraham MSS. 13.

Lord, and mind my love to them all.' He had better rest the last night than formerly. I continue here near him, for I see it is my place and I have peace in it—he enquires every post for letters, but few come. If thou please to write to him at any time, thou mayst direct them to me in a cover to Henry Salter's at the Black Lion in Bishopsgate or to Edward Mann's. I have not much to add at present, because the messenger cannot stay. Meetings were pretty peaceable in London the last First-day, and also at Horslydown—so being constrained to conclude, with a postscript,

Enfield at Widdow Dry's house the 25d. 8m. [Oct.] 1670. Thy servant in the truth J. Stubbs

Also he bid me tell thee that great have been the tenderness and care of Friends to him in this condition and *nothing wanting*. Two or three women sit up every night, and sometimes I and men Friends formerly,—but 2 good women Friends constantly. I would be glad to write to thee every week if thou would order me so to do.

So after I could stir up and down I went from Enfield to Gerard Roberts, and from thence to the women's school,[1] and so to London and went to the meeting at Gracechurch Street though I was but weak; yet the Lord's power upheld me to declare his eternal word of life.

⟨In the motion of life, I sent the following lines as an encouraging testimony amongst Friends.

My dear Friends,

The Seed is above all. In it walk, in which ye all have life. Be not amazed at the weather; for always the just suffered by the unjust, but the just had the dominion. And all along ye may see, by faith the mountains were subdued; and the rage of the wicked, and his fiery darts, were quenched. And though the waves and storms be high, yet your faith will keep you to swim above them, for they are but for a time, and the Truth is without time. Therefore keep on the mountain of holiness, ye who are led to it by the light where nothing shall hurt. And do not think that anything will outlast the Truth, which standeth sure, and is over that which is out of the Truth; for the good will overcome the evil; and the light, darkness; and the life, death; and virtue, vice; and righteousness, unrighteousness.

[1] The girls' school at Shacklewell, see p. 520 ante.

The false prophet cannot overcome the true, but the true prophet, Christ, will overcome all the false. So be faithful, and live in that which doth not think the time long.

G.F.〉

Whilst I was in my travails and sufferings I saw the state of the city New Jerusalem which comes out of heaven. And I and Richard Richardson and John Stubbs cast it up according to the account as it is written in the Revelations. According to the world's account of the measure of the earth, it was ten times bigger than the earth. Yet the professors had looked upon it to be like an outward city or some town that had come out of the elements.

[1]But all who are within the light of Christ, and in his faith which he is the author of, and in the Spirit, the Holy Ghost, . . . are members of this city. . . . But they that are out of the grace, out of the truth, out of the light, spirit, and power of God, such as resist the Holy Ghost, quench, vex, and grieve the Spirit of God and hate the light and turn the grace of God into wantonness . . . and despise prophesying, revelation, and inspiration, these are the dogs and unbelievers that are without the city. . . .

Many things more did I see concerning the heavenly city, the New Jerusalem, which are hard to be uttered, . . . Christ, who is the first and last, sets man free, and is the resurrection of the just and unjust and the judge of the quick and dead, and they that are in him are invested with everlasting rest and peace, out of all the labours and travail and miseries of Adam in the fall. So he is sufficient and of ability to restore man up into the state that man was in before he fell, and not into that state only, but up into that state also that never fell, even to himself.

Oh, this blessed city is appeared. Oh, glorious things will come to pass. You will see glorious things will come. I desire, I wish that these outward powers of the earth were given up. I can tell what to say to them. Oh, hypocrisy ! It makes me sick to think of them. I have given them a visitation and as faithful a warning as ever was. There is an ugly a slubbering hound, an ugly hound, an ugly slubbering hound. But the Lord forgive them—destruction, destruction. We have given them

[1] Discourse in full, *Camb. Jnl.*, ii, 172-5; Ellwood, pp. 345, 346; Bicent., ii, 135-6.

indeed a visitation and salutation and they will not hear, but refuse it and reject the Lord. But we shall be clear of all their blood.

[This next paper to the King is endorsed, ' given forth in the time of his great exercise and weakness ', but without further explanation.]

A few words to the King, if he should inquire after me.

We have all given them a visitation and have faithfully warned them of our innocency and uprightness and that we never did any hurt to the King nor to any of his people. We have nothing in our hearts but love and goodwill to him and his people and desire their eternal welfare. If that they will not hear nor forbear, then the day of judgment and sorrow, of torment and misery and sudden destruction will come from the Lord upon them, that have been the cause of the sufferings of many thousand simple, innocent, harmless people, that have done no hurt nor have had ill will towards him or them, but have desired their eternal good for the eternal Truth's sake. Destruction will come upon them that turn the sword backward. I have nothing but love and goodwill. G.F.

Postscript. Do not blind your eyes. The Lord will bring swift destruction and misery upon you, surely he will do it and relieve his innocent people who have groaned for deliverance and have also groaned for your deliverance out of wickedness.

Blessed be the Lord God that he hath a people in this nation that seeks the good of all men and of all people and of all women upon the face of the earth. It is not a sect nor opinion, but the good of all. We have the mind of the Lord Jesus Christ, that desires not the death of a sinner but the good of all people, blessed be the name of the Lord God for ever. G.F.

Let Esquire Marsh know this.

⟨Whilst I continued at Enfield, a sense came upon me of a hurt that sometimes happened by persons coming under the profession of Truth, out of one country into another, to take an husband or wife amongst Friends, where they were strangers, and it was not known whether they were clear and orderly, or no. And it opened in me to recommend the following method unto Friends for preventing such inconveniences.

All Friends that do marry, whether they be men or women, if they come out of another nation, island, plantation, or county, let them bring a certificate from the Men's Meeting of that country, nation, island or plantation from which they come, to the Men's Meeting where they do propound their intention of marriage. For the Men's Meeting being made up of the faithful, this will stop all bad and raw spirits from roving up and down. And then when any come with a certificate, or letter of recommendation from one Men's Meeting to another, one is refreshed by another, and can set their hands and hearts to the thing, and this will take away a great deal of trouble. And then what ye have to say to them in the power of God, in admonishing and instructing them, ye are left to the power and spirit of God to do it, and to let them know the duty of marriage, and what it is, that there may be unity and concord in the Spirit, and power, and light, and wisdom of God, throughout all the Men's Meetings in the whole world in one, in the life.

Let copies of this be sent to every county, and nation, and island where Friends are, that so all things may be kept holy and pure and righteous, in unity and peace, and God over all may be glorified among you, his lot, his people and inheritance, who are his adopted sons and daughters and heirs of his life. So no more, but my love in that which changeth not. G.F.

14th of 1st month, 1670/1 [Mar., 1671].

About this time I was moved to pray to the Lord as followeth:

O Lord God Almighty, prosper Truth, and preserve justice and equity in the land, and bring down all injustice and iniquity, oppression, and falsehood, and cruelty and unmercifulness in the land; and that mercy and righteousness may flourish !

And, O Lord God, establish and set up verity, and preserve it in the land ! and bring down in the land all debauchery and vice, and whoredoms and fornication, and this raping spirit, which causeth and leadeth people to have no esteem of thee, O God, nor their own souls or bodies, nor of Christianity, modesty, or humanity.

And, O Lord, put it in the magistrates' hearts to bring down all this ungodliness, and violence, and cruelty, profaneness, cursing, and swearing, and to put down all these whorehouses and playhouses, which do corrupt youth and people, and lead them from the Kingdom of God where no unclean thing can enter, neither shall come ! But such works lead people to hell. And the Lord in mercy bring down all these things in the nation, to stop thy wrath, O God, from coming on the land.

This prayer was writ, the 17th day at night, of the 2nd Month [Apl.], 1671. G.F.

And I had a vision about the time that I was in this travail and sufferings, that I was walking in the fields and many Friends were with me, and I bid them dig in the earth, and they did and I went down. And there was a mighty vault top-full of people kept under the earth, rocks, and stones. So I bid them break open the earth and let all the people out, and they did, and all the people came forth to liberty; and it was a mighty place. And when they had done I went on and bid them dig again. They did, and there was a mighty vault full of people, and I bid them throw it down and let all the people out, and so they did.

And I went on again and bid them dig again, and Friends said unto me, 'George, thou finds out all things,' and so there they digged, and I went down, and went along the vault; and there sat a woman in white looking at time how it passed away. And there followed me a woman down in the vault, in which vault was the treasure; and so she laid her hand on the treasure on my left hand and then time whisked on apace; but I clapped my hand upon her and said, 'Touch not the treasure.' And then time passed not so swift.

They that can read these things must have the earthy, stony nature off them. And see how the stones and the earth came upon man since the beginning, since he fell from the image of God and righteousness and holiness. And much I could speak of these things, but I leave them to the right eye and reader to see and read.

And I was moved of the Lord to speak to Martha Fisher and Hannah Stringer[1] to go to the King and his Council and to move them for Margaret's liberty. And they went in the Lord's power.

[1] Hannah Salter; she married Henry Salter in 1666.

And those two women got Margaret's discharge[1] under the broad seal, who had been ten years a prisoner and praemunired, of which the like was never heard in England.

And I sent down the discharge by John Stubbs with my horse and sent her word that if she came up to see me she might come up with John Stubbs for it was upon me to go beyond the seas into America and Barbados and those countries. ⟨And I therefore desired her to come to London, for the ship was then fitting for the voyage.⟩ So I went in a coach to Kingston, to John Rous's where I stayed till she came up.

And when I was at Kingston the King's discharge that cleared Margaret from her former praemunire came down into the country and she was cleared, so she came up to London. And after she came up to London a free woman, I began to prepare to go beyond sea after I had finished my service here in England for the Lord.

At the Yearly Meeting, many came up from all parts of the nation, and a mighty meeting it was and the Lord's power was over all and his glorious everlasting renowned Seed of life was set over all.

CHAPTER XXIII

ABOUT the 6th month [Aug.] I went down with Margaret and William Penn[2] and Mary Penington[3] and her daughter Guli,[4] and we got the King's barge,[5] and they carried us down ⟨from Wapping to the ship which lay⟩ three miles below Gravesend. And they went

[1] Dated 4th April, 1671. Her estate was granted to Susannah and Rachel Fell.

[2] William Penn (1644-1718), son of Admiral Sir Wm. Penn, founded Pennsylvania, 1682.

[3] Mary Penington (*c.* 1625-1682), formerly Springett, daughter of Sir John Proude, wife of Isaac Penington, early Quaker leader.

[4] Gulielma Springett (1644-1694), married Wm. Penn a year after this.

[5] i.e. a barge in the service of the King's navy.

with me to the Downs, a larger account whereof ye may see in the journal and in the several letters that give an account of passages.

[In the absence of a journal by George Fox himself of his voyage to America, the following diary or log kept by John Hull is used, ending on page 592. Those parts of it which Ellwood used in his edition were put by him into the first person, as though Fox were the author. Incidents related by Fox himself are printed after Hull's diary. About Hull himself very little else is known.]

A Journal of George Fox's, with other Friends who accompanied him from London in England towards America and some of the isles thereunto belonging, vizt: Thomas Briggs,[1] William Edmondson,[2] John Rous,[3] Solomon Eccles,[4] John Stubbs,[5] James Lancaster,[6] John Cartwright,[7] Robert Widders,[8] George Pattison,[9] John Hull, Elizabeth Hooton,[10] Elizabeth Miers, beginning the 11th day of the Sixth Month [Aug.] 1671.

The Sixth Month [Aug.] 11th. Most of those Friends before mentioned, after they had a very good meeting at Thomas Yoakley's, went by water to Gravesend that evening in order to go aboard the ketch then lying there,

[1] Thomas Briggs (*c.* 1610-1685), Quaker preacher in extensive journeys in England and America.

[2] William Edmondson (1627-1712), settled in and founded Quakerism in Ireland, was three times in America and W. Indies.

[3] John Rous (d. 1695), born in Barbados, merchant, Fox's stepson-in-law.

[4] Solomon Eccles (*c.* 1618-1683), of London, formerly a music teacher.

[5] John Stubbs, see p. 176 ante.

[6] James Lancaster, see p. 116 ante.

[7] John Cartwright of Stourbridge, settled in Jamaica where he d. 1683.

[8] Robert Widders of N. Lancashire (*c.* 1618-1686), see pp. 119, 140 ante.

[9] George Pattison (*c.* 1628-1678) of London, mariner, noted as the Quaker skipper who, in 1663, unarmed retook his ship from Moorish pirates off Majorca and put them ashore in Algeria.

[10] Elizabeth Hooton, see p. 43 ante.

called the *Industry*,[1] wherein we were to go, the master's name being Thomas Foster.

12th. George Fox, with his wife and several Friends, who had a desire to bear him company to the Downs, went from James Strutt's in Wapping in one of the King's barges to the said ship, where George Fox stayed aboard that night, but most of the company with William Penn and others lodged that night at Gravesend, to whom John Hull came likewise down that night, who after waiting upon the Lord in his chamber about two hours, vizt. the ninth and tenth in the morning, was moved to follow them in order to go the voyage with them.

13th [Sunday]. Early in the morning George Pattison, by George Fox's order, roused Friends up who lodged at Gravesend about the first hour, and about the sixth those Friends with some others of our passengers went a-ship-board, the anchor being weighed, and ship ready to sail. Then, after a little while, many of our Friends, having taken their leaves, passed away in very great tenderness; but George Fox's wife with several others sailed with us as far as the Downs, where that evening we arrived, having had a very fine and quick passage of it, having outsailed all such ships that were likewise outward bound. About the eleventh or twelfth hour that night George Fox's wife with some other Friends went a-shore to Deal and lodged there, where we were presently informed that some had an order from the Governor to take our names in writing.

14th. In the morning one came and took our names, though he was told they were taken at Gravesend. Having taken leave of Edward Mann and his wife (who in love came to the Downs with us) and several other Friends at Deal, about the afternoon we came aboard, where we met with some Dover Friends and country adjacent, who likewise came to visit George Fox and the others and who afterwards took their leaves and so departed. And then we were hindered from proceeding on our voyage some hours, by reason that one of the captains of the King's

[1] Probable tonnage between 80 and 100.

two men-of-war which lay in the Downs sent his press-master aboard us, who pressed and carried away three of our seamen, which might have proved very prejudicial unto us, even to the loss of our voyage, had not the captain of the other of the King's frigates being made sensible of the much leakiness of our ship and length of our voyage, out of compassion and much civility spared us two of his own men. And before this was over an officer of the custom-house came aboard to peruse packets and get fees, so that what between one and the other we were hindered from sailing on till about sunset, during which stop a very considerable number of merchant-men, bound outward thence, were got several leagues before us. But being now clear, we set sail that evening. We were in number of passengers about fifty.

15th. We overtook part of the aforesaid fleet about the height of Dover in the morning.

16th. We came as far as the Isle of Wight.

17th. In the morning we were as far as Topsham[1] in Devonshire. Note, as we overtook the fleet so we got and kept before them well nigh these two days past. We had this evening a very good meeting. We were in the afternoon as high as Dartmouth, the wind being scant, the fleet still not far from us; in all which time, through mercy, we have been generally pretty well. This evening we were within two or three leagues of the Eddystone, which had destroyed many ships, whereupon we bore away S.b.W. About the ninth or tenth hour that night we haled a ship we met with, which came from Ireland bound for London. A very fine gale all night.

18th. About the fifth hour in the morning we passed the Lizard, four leagues south of it, and in a little time saw the Land's End. And three leagues southward we saw, all in a range, a fleet of ships of Hollanders, most about forty, bound outwards, which came from the Downs a week before us. The fleet, that came from the Downs the morning before us, we left behind, and no sight of them.

[1] The MS. has *Apsum*.

We have a pretty fine gale. Wind being NE. we get ground of the fleet.

19th. In the morning we were about fifteen leagues west of Scilly, wind being SW. somewhat scant. We saw this morning but two or three of the fleet, leeward of us about three leagues distance. That evening we lost sight of the fleet which made towards the straits, leeward of us, only two of them singled themselves out and stood westward towards Virginia as was supposed.

20th [Sunday]. We saw those two ships early, windward of us, about four leagues distance. In the afternoon towards the evening the wind began to blow hard which made the billows mount aloft, so that the master by persuasion of Friends lowered the main topmast, which, if he had not done, it is very probable that it had broken. And at that instant George Pattison, casting his eye towards those two ships, he perceived the foremost had lost mainmast, foremast, if not the bowsprit, they could discern nothing but as it were the mizzen. His consort came up to him after a while, but, making little stay, left her. It began to grow dark, so that we never saw them more. This morning we met with a fleet of Hollanders and some English; one of them hailed us, who said he belonged to Lubeck but came out of the Straits and enquired whether there were war with France or no. We were that day about fifty leagues off Scilly and before the Bay of Biscay.

21st. Wind NW. Our shrouds were straightened, being too slack, and our mainmast fixed close to the deck.

22nd. We are still crossing the bay, being 100 leagues off of the Land's End of England about the twelfth hour. Towards the afternoon it was pretty calm, and seas somewhat smooth, to what they were before. Friends were sickish these two or three days, especially John Cartwright who was something feverish, and that evening George Fox was moved to pray for him and felt an intercession for his life.

23rd. Early our mainstay was cut sheer in two, by rubbing caused, which was mended ere night, in latitude

44° 41′. Sailed from noon to noon thirteen leagues, two miles, wind being NW.b.N. Friends mostly pretty well this day, also John Cartwright who told us he thought he should have died, but it was revealed to him he should not, but that he must go and preach the gospel. That evening we had in our cabin a very good meeting.

24th. This morning John Stubbs we found somewhat ill, and feverish, as the surgeon said; he was in a breathing sweat. We are past the northern Cape,[1] and are off of the coast of Portugal about eighty leagues. Wind NE. and a fresh gale, the sea somewhat lofty. We sailed about fifty-six leagues from noon to noon, steering our course SW. John Stubbs somewhat better this evening. We saw several grampuses sporting themselves in the briny ocean not far from us, and two great porpoises leapt a great height above water. We closed up this evening with a very fine and powerful meeting. In latitude 43° 3′ some of our company said they saw a great whale, and some said they saw a rainbow a good while after sunset.

25th. From noon to noon we ran twenty-nine leagues SW.b.S. in latitude 40° 11′. Wind variable and scant at ENE. to WNW., but a little fresher this afternoon. John Stubbs pretty well, and falls to his victuals. We took a dolphin, which made us good broth, and is a very good fish to eat, and lovely for variety of colours. It is very remarkable how several Friends were so soon raised up again that were very ill.

26th. Sailed WSW. thirty-six leagues, and a mile in latitude 40° 36′. Wind variable at E.b.N., a reasonable gale. We saw no fish to-day. George Fox, John Stubbs, and I spent two hours in our cabin in perusing some Scriptures.

27th [Sunday]. Sailed SSW. thirty-six leagues and one mile, wind variable at W. and WNW. Little wind this day, a very smooth sea. We took two dolphins. Friends generally pretty well. Two good meetings, the passengers seemed to be very attentive. We had a very fine meeting

[1] Cape Ortegal.

by ourselves in our cabin at night, wherein the power of the Lord was felt. Our ship so leaky ever since we came to the Downs that seamen and passengers do for the most part, day and night, pump. This day we observed that in two hours she sucked in sixteen inches of water in the well; some make it ten ton a day. It is well, however, for it is good to keep seamen and passengers in health.

28th. Course steered S.b.W. fifteen leagues and two miles from noon to noon; in latitude 39° 14′; wind variable at N.b.W. and at W. and at SW.b.W. This morning George Fox, John Stubbs, and I were employed about finding out the signification of the four rivers of Eden, according to the Hebrew, together with the mystical meaning of them. Bare wind this day; we were in latitude with the rock at Lisbon.

29th. Sailed SSW. seventy-five miles. Wind at WNW.; Friends very well; wind very scant; smooth seas; a very great shower of rain early in the morning.

30th. Course we steered SSW.; ten leagues and two miles; wind WSW. in latitude 37° 44′. Little wind this afternoon so as our vessel lay as in a millpond, very smooth, little motion. We are very hot, sweat exceedingly at night; it is very uncomfortable to lie two in a little hole or cabin.

31st. Course SSW.; wind NNE. very bare; distance run three leagues and a mile, from twelve to twelve, in latitude 37° 35′. We hooked a great albacore about an ell long, but through the hastiness of the hauler up, broke the hook and dropped the fish. Another rainbow was seen after sunset.

The Seventh Month [September].

1st. Steered SSW. fifteen leagues from twelve to twelve; wind WNW. and bare in latitude 36° 53′. I was very ill yesterday and also this. Water very smooth. In the afternoon we perceived by the cockling of the sea a fine breeze of wind approaching us. Friends generally in health through mercy, though it is a very hot time with us, especially in the cabin, being so many thronged and crowded together; and where we lay two together, we were forced to part. This morning a great dolphin was taken by Thomas Foster with a fisgig,[1] being likely companion to the last, for she followed the vessel ever since, having a flying fish and a young dolphin in her maw, with another pretty big fish.

2nd. Sailed four degrees and 30′ westerly; wind variable at W.b.S. and WSW. in latitude 36° 20′. About four in the afternoon we espied a vessel four leagues a-stern that seemed to give us a chase. To prevent her, when it began to be dark, we altered our course, who notwithstanding came up within a mile and a half of us by the eleventh hour following; whereupon as soon after as the moon did set, we steered NE. a while, and after that E. and SE. till break of day, and so saw no sight of her. Some conjectured, by her sails, among the mariners that it was likely a Sallee[2] man-of-war standing off the Azores Islands, which caused a great fear among some of the passengers, dreading to be taken by them; but Friends were well satisfied in themselves, having no fear upon their spirits. And when the master and George Pattison came to George Fox to advise with him and understand his judgement of it, in the power he made answer that the life was over all, and the power was between them and us.

3rd [Sunday]. Sailed SW.b.W. 1° 45′ southerly; distance run ten leagues; wind variable at W.b.S. and W. and SSW. In latitude 36° 2′ this morning we quite left the supposed Sallee man, and had a very good meeting.[3]

4th. Sailed ten leagues and two miles, wind variable at SSW. and S. in latitude 36° 3′; a great calm.

5th. Course 2° 50′ from noon to noon, westerly, four leagues and a mile; wind variable at SW.b.S. and SW. and WSW., but scant; in latitude 36° 5′ we took one bonito, and one pilot fish; many were about us; a fresh gale all night.

[1] A harpoon.

[2] A Moorish sea-port.

[3] Fox's own account of this escape is printed later, on pp. 592-4.

6th. Sailed S.b.W. 5° 30′ west; from twelve to twelve; distance run thirty-seven leagues and one mile. Wind variable at W.b.S. and WNW., latitude 34° 17′. A fresh gale this day, store of bonitoes.

7th. Made our way good SW. by S. 1° 4′ southerly; distance run thirty-four league. Wind variable at NW.b.W. and NNE. with a handsome fresh moderate gale; latitude 32° 54′.

8th. Sailed SW.b.S. thirteen leagues and a mile from twelve to twelve, in latitude 32° 22′. We are a little to the southward of the latitude of Bermudas. Wind somewhat scant.

9th. Sailed SSW. 4° 30′ westerly; distance run sixteen leagues; wind variable at ENE. by E.; fair and moderate weather in latitude 31° 37′.

10th [Sunday]. Sailed SW.b.S. fifteen leagues; wind variable at NNE. and NE.b.N. and NE. with a reasonable gale and fair weather, in latitude 30° 58′. We had a very fine meeting this morning; some dolphins and pilots seen.

11th. Sailed SW.b.S. fifteen leagues and one mile, wind variable at NE. and NNW., a little gale, and fair weather in latitude 30° 20′. Friends and passengers generally well, only myself.

12th. Sailed SW.b.S. thirty-two leagues; wind variable at NW. and NE. in latitude 29° 1′. Some pilots seen.

13th. Sailed SW.b.S. seventeen leagues; wind variable at NE. and NE.b.N. in latitude 28° 43′. No fish but pilots about us; fair and hot weather; very great shower early. We begin to come into the long reach.

14th. Sailed by the log board SW.b.S. thirty leagues; wind NE., a handsome fresh gale all night in latitude 27° 35′. Friends and passengers generally well. The sun begins to be exceeding hot; a very fresh gale all night, and by the log board run sometimes eight leagues a watch. George Fox's legs begin to swell very much and very pimply, itching and burning much.

15th. This morning a flying fish was taken upon the deck that flew in that night; we saw several of them flying.

Friends and passengers pretty well. Sailed SW.b.S. thirty-eight leagues and one mile, wind variable at NE. and ENE. in latitude 26° 26′.

16th. Sailed SW. thirty-four leagues; wind variable at NE. and SE. with some rain in latitude 35° 13′. We account ourselves within thirty leagues of the Tropic of Cancer, which lies in 23½°. Friends, etc., generally in health, only myself seldom well. A very fine fresh gale, which serves to qualify very much the burning heat of the sun.

17th [Sunday]. Sailed SW. twenty-eight leagues; wind ESE. in latitude 24° 19′. This afternoon we ran after four leagues an hour.

18th. Sailed SW. 5° 50′ westerly; distance run fifty-four leagues wind being at ENE. a very fresh gale in latitude 22° 36′. Southward of the Tropic fifty-six miles. Several flying fish I have seen on the wing, five or six at a time, some flying about 200 yards or more.

19th. Sailed SW.b.W. 1° 15′ southerly; run fifty-one leagues and two miles; wind ENE. in latitude 21° 7′. We had a very good meeting before we went to bed.

20th. Course by the compass SW.b.S. 5° 25′ westerly, run forty-six leagues and two miles, wind at NE. in latitude 19° 69′.

21st. Sailed SW. 5° westerly; run forty-one leagues, wind at NE.; a handsome fresh gale, in latitude 18° 40′. George Fox very ill this morning in his stomach. A tropic bird was seen, and many herring-hogs and grampuses.

22nd. Sailed SW.; run twenty-seven leagues; wind variable at NE. and ENE. an ordinary gale in latitude 17° 47′. Tropic birds were seen. George Fox very ill this night; he had been very much out of order for several days past, being very much in his bones. We were much becalmed most part of the night and next morning. George Fox met with such stinking meat, pork and beef, which caused him to loathe flesh a long time after, and lost his stomach with it.

23rd. Sailed SW.b.W. seventeen leagues, and 45′

westerly, in latitude 17° 18′. A seaman told me they pumped near 700 strokes in half an hour, indeed they were necessitated to keep it going still. We saw a ship this afternoon about three leagues off of us steering somewhat the same course with us. This day George Fox was somewhat better than before. And this evening Solomon Eccles's seven-days fast was out, having neither eaten nor drunk all the time, unless sometimes he washed his mouth with vinegar; neither did he go to bed nor hardly slept during the time prefixed, unless now and then he nodded a little at night-times as he sat up. This day I saw a tropic bird.

24th [Sunday]. Course twenty-six leagues in latitude 16° 39′. This morning we saw the ship again which we discovered last night, being come very near us, having it seems a desire to speak with us. She got near us towards the evening, so that we persuaded the master to stay for her; so she came side by side with us; our master hailed them, who answered that he came from London about the time we came away, the master's name being Barber, bound for Barbados. George Fox was very ill in his stomach so as at last he vomited very much cold waterish flegm, though he was never sea-sick.

25th. This morning we saw the ship again leeward of us about a league; but after a little while we met with a fresh gale we so outwent her, that before it was dark we run them out of sight. We sailed WSW. 1° westerly; run thirty-four leagues; wind at ENE. a fine handsome gale and fair weather in latitude 16° 2′.

26th. Course WSW. 4° 30′ southerly; run forty-nine leagues and a mile; wind at ENE. a very fresh gale, in latitude 14° 45′. Store of porpoises were seen and bonitoes playing about the ship this night and evening; several birds were seen this day. George Fox very ill to-day. I saw two birds called men-of-war, somewhat like a herne.

27th. Course SW. sailed half a point westerly; distance run forty-eight leagues and a mile, wind at ENE.; a fine handsome fresh gale, about five knots, in latitude 13° 41′.

George Fox pretty well. It lightened very much this night.

28th. Sailed WSW. 4° 50′ westerly. Distance, forty-six leagues and two miles; wind variable at E.b.N. and ENE. A fresh gale and fair weather; yea they are pretty temperate and cool most part of the long reach; the most sultry weather we had before, when we were somewhat becalmed and had but little wind for near a fortnight before we came into the reach. In latitude 12° 57′, three miles southward of Barbados, some supposed the water began to change, as usually it doth a good while ere they come near the island. A fresh gale all night.

29th. Some suppose we are about 100 leagues east of Barbados. Some saw a bird called booby, as big as a wild goose. A fresh gale also this morning. Friends generally well and so is George Fox. This day is called Michaelmas. No observations this day, by reason the sun was so clouded as it appeared not; a handsome fresh gale, sailed W. 5° northerly; run fifty-three leagues in latitude 13° 11′ at E.b.N.

30th. The sun not appearing this day, they could not well take any observation, we sailed west two degrees southerly; forty-four leagues, wind E.b.N. in latitude 13° 6′. Friends generally well. Many porpoises were seen, and a flock of birds at a distance. We are somewhat yare[1] in looking out for land: tomorrow or next day the master supposes we may see Barbados.

The Eighth Month [October].

1st [Sunday]. Sailed about thirty leagues W. in latitude 13°.

2nd. About thirty-two leagues in latitude 13° 20′.

3rd. We saw early in the morning the Island of Barbados, and about the ninth hour at night, or tenth, we anchored in Carlisle Bay, and about or after the tenth hour we came ashore. George Fox walked at that time of night with some others to Richard Forstall's house, a merchant,

[1] Quick, alert.

a Friend, above a quarter of a mile from the Bridge. Being ill before he came ashore and then by reason of so tiresome a walk at that time of night too, he was in a manner quite spent, and abode there very ill for several days, and could not sweat, no not for three weeks before, he was so dried and parched up.

5th. On the fifth we had a great meeting at the Bridge.

6th. He told me this island lay as a heavy load upon him, pointing at his breast. Abundance of Friends came daily to visit him.

7th. Early in the morning George Fox (being very restless that night) told me that the island was a very great weight upon him, reiterating the same. That afternoon John Rous brought Colonel Chamberlaine's coach for George Fox, but it was late ere we could get to Thomas Rous's, his father. But George Fox could take little or no rest that night. Some few days after, the said Colonel came to give him a visit, who seems to be a civil person.

Now to draw to a close, George Fox, though somewhat better at present, yet has not been well hardly ever since he came from England. While at sea his legs swelled so much and his feet, as if the skin would break, and but with much difficulty could one draw on his stockings, or slippers, for he coming weak from London aboard, did sweat exceedingly for the space of three weeks, so that his head was as if it were sodden, and all his body broke out into pimples, and afterwards struck in again on a sudden, and the swelling of his legs fell, so that what with his old pains, and former bruises in his joints, all struck up to his heart and stomach, so as that he became very weak beyond words, which was enough to have killed some others.

And then for the space of a month after, he could not sweat at all while at sea, and when he came on land it was the same, insomuch that they gave him several times some things to make him sweat, which was so far from working that effect that it dried up and parched up his body the more, so as it made him worse likely than it might otherwise have been, and so could drink hardly any thing but water all the time aboard and after, mixed with a little ginger, that did best agree with him.

And now this three weeks and upwards since he landed, he hath not sweated but hath still very much pains in his bones and joints and whole body, that he can hardly get any rest; and yet notwithstanding he is cheery and keeps above all.

This island, it is said, was all of a fire, as it were, when they heard of his coming. Divers considerable persons, besides abundance of our Friends, came to visit him from all quarters, which hath much abated and quenched it; and they are very desirous to hear him at meetings but as yet he hath not been able to go to any.

[End of John Hull's log.]

[1]And as we sailed to Barbados[2] there came out against us a Sallee man-of-war and pursued us. ⟨Our master said, 'Come, let us go to supper and when it grows dark we shall lose him.' This he spoke to please and pacify the passengers.⟩ For when they saw the pirate they said there were but two ways, either to outrun him or to steer the same course till night and then to alter our course. ⟨When it grew dark⟩ they changed their course. And that night the passengers and the master and the seamen were in a great care what to do. And he and two more that were masters of ships, that were passengers, came to ask my advice what they should do. And I told them I was no mariner; and I asked them what they thought was the best to be done. They said they had but two ways, to tack about and go our old course, or to out-run him. And I said, to out-run him they were not like, for he far over-went us; and to tack about and steer their old course, if he were a thief, sure he would turn up to us. So I told them the most was to me that they should tack about and

[1] The account of this incident is a conflation using three sources, the Spence MS. (*Camb. Jnl.*, ii, 214, 215), another MS. at Friends House by George Fox (Portfolio 10, 41), and Ellwood (Bicent., ii, 142, 143).

[2] Saturday, 2nd Sept., see p. 586 ante.

steer their own course, for I felt most of the power of God for them to turn up, so they turned up. And I told them then it was a matter of faith; the Lord's power and spirit was placed betwixt us and him.

And so about the eleventh hour at night, towards the setting of the moon, he was just upon us. I could see him out of my cabin on the other side of the ship. And they came down to me to my cabin, the master and other mariners; and then all the company and passengers were in a great fear; and as I was getting up I was made to lie still. And I charged them all to be still and quiet, ⟨and to put out all their candles but the one they steered by.⟩ And I remembered my words, how that the Lord's power and spirit was placed betwixt us and him. And I saw out of my cabin he was rather before us, but we being of the dark side of the moon, and it being upon going down, we missed him. And after midnight we discovered him about two miles or half a league off us as we supposed. ⟨The master and some of the seamen came again and asked me if they might not steer such a point, I told them they might do as they would.⟩

And the moon set and there came a fine gale, and we steered the compass off three points at large, and we saw him no more, which was the almighty hand of God that delivered us. To him alone be all glory, honour and praise for evermore. And the wild passengers were all humbled.

They said to me after that I said I did not understand sea affairs. They said if the mariners had taken Paul's counsel they had not suffered shipwreck. But they had boasted how their ketch would over-run all the ships in the world.

The next day, ⟨being the First-day of the week⟩ we had a meeting and the Lord's presence was amongst us. ⟨And I desired the people to mind the mercies of the Lord who had delivered them, for they might have been all in the Turks' hands by that time, had not the Lord's hand saved them.

About a week after, the master and some of the seamen endeavoured to persuade the passengers that it was not a

Turkish pirate that chased us but a merchantman going to the Canaries. When I heard of it I asked them why then did they speak so to me, why did they trouble the passengers, and why did they tack about from him and alter their course? I told them they should take heed of slighting the mercies of God.〉

And we passed on to Barbados, and when we came thither there came a merchant from Sallee and said there was a Sallee man-of-war had a ketch three days in pursuit, the biggest in the world, and once was upon her; and there was a spirit in that ship that he could not take her with all that he could do, and that the Lord by his eternal arm and power delivered us. And so that spirit that he spoke of was the Lord God and his word that stopped him, that I told the master and mate of before.

And our ship that brought us from London was very leaky. At the keel of the ship there was a long hole one might put his hand in, and when they stopped it, there were little fishes in the ship. It was a wonder and amazement to the people who saw it and heard of it, that the Lord had preserved us in our coming.

[Fox's time in Barbados is here presented through the letters which he and his companions wrote home to England (*Camb. Jnl.*, ii, 187-202). This method has been preferred to that employed by Ellwood, who built up from the information in the letters of Fox's companions a narrative as though written by Fox (Ellwood ed., 351-61; Bicent., ii, 145-59). Fox's own narrative, which deals only very briefly with Barbados, will be resumed on page 609.]

Barbados, 1st of 9th mo. [Nov.], 1671.

Dear Friends,

I have been very weak these seven weeks past and so not able to write myself. My desire is to you and for you all that you may live in the fear of God and in love one unto another, and be subject one to another in the fear of God.

I have been weaker in my body than ever I was in my life, yea my pains such as are beyond words or expressions, but yet my heart and spirit are as strong as ever. I have hardly sweat these seven weeks past, though I am come into a very hot climate where hardly any but are well nigh continually sweating. But as for me, my old bruises, colds, and numbness, and pains struck inwardly, even to my very heart, so that little rest have I taken; and the chiefest things that were comfort to me were a little water and powdered ginger, but now I begin to drink a little beer as well as water and a little wine and water mixed. Great pains and travails I have seen, and in measure am under, but it is well, my life is over all, for this island was to me all of a fire ere I came to it; but now it is somewhat quenched and abated since.

Many Friends and considerable persons have been with me, so I came in weakness among those that are strong and have so continued; but now am got a little cheery and over it. We have ordered men's meetings to be at Thomas Rous's and women's meetings next week.

I tired out my body much when amongst you in England. It's the power of the Lord that helps me, and so I desire you all to prize the power of the Lord and his Truth, for I was but a weak man in body when I came away, after I saw my great travail amongst you; but after that it struck all back again into my body which was not well fastened after so sore travails in England. Then so tired out at sea that I could not rest, and have had little or no stomach a long time. Since I came into this island my life hath been very much burdened, but I hope if the Lord give strength to manage his work. I shall work thoroughly and bring things that have been out of course into better order, but for the present am but in a weak capacity. So, dear Friends, live all in the peaceable Truth and in the love of it, serving the Lord in newness of life, for glorious things and everlasting truths have been manifested amongst you plentifully, and to you the riches of the kingdom have been reached.

I have been almost a month in this island but have not been able to go abroad or ride out; but very lately I rode twice abroad here a quarter mile at a time, which tired me and wearied me. G.F.

Let a copy of this be sent into the north, to Margaret my wife, and to Bristol to W. Yeamans, and to Thomas Lower in Cornwall, and show unto other Friends, to whom is my love and life in Truth. G.F.

John Hull, Barbados, to Edward Mann, London, about 1st of 9th mo. [Nov.], 1671.

. . . 'Tis well nigh a month since we came here and now G.F. grows somewhat better but as yet not very well, and doubtless was, and still is, far the worse by reason of the filth, dirt, and unrighteousness, which lie as a heavy load and weight upon his spirit, so as it pressed down the spirit of God in him as a cart with sheaves. George Fox, Robert Widders, and Elizabeth Miers, and myself reside at Thomas Rous's[1] these three weeks, William Edmondson, Thomas Briggs, John Stubbs, and Solomon Eccles at the Bridge, and are sometimes here and are up and down the island in service, thrashing, cutting, and hewing, and have very considerable numbers at their several meetings, which are many both as to place and time, and are the greater and fuller by reason that many of the world flock unto them, so that people begin to be awakened, both backsliders (as 'tis feared here are too many) and others not before convinced. And they are in an earnest and longing expectation of George Fox's appearing at meetings, querying, 'When will George Fox speak? When shall we hear him?' For as yet he hath not been at any, by reason of his much weakness, nor as yet like to be, and therefore George Fox appointed the women's meeting to be kept here at Thomas Rous's and so they met here yesterday accordingly, in which he, Solomon Eccles, and myself spent three or four hours at least, delivering himself as to their concerns very sweetly and very fully. There were, it is supposed, near a hundred women Friends, grave and sober. And the day before, being the First-day of the week, was the meeting for this part of the country, it removing from one particular family or house each First-day to another near adjacent, of another plantation. And a very great one it was, being in number about three or four hundred persons; to which Lewis Morris and his wife came, and with him a neighbour of his, one Ralph Fretwell,[2] one of the judges of this island, who liveth about fourteen miles off at least, on the windward side. Here, I say, we had a very good meeting, George Fox being very powerful, to the great satisfaction of the judge, yea

[1] A wealthy planter whose Quaker son John was married to Fox's stepdaughter Margaret.

[2] d. 1686. His adoption of Quakerism cost him much in position and estate.

also of most present. Though he was weak, he hath likewise appointed the men's meeting to be here tomorrow, so that I question not but the Lord will crown his great undertakings with blessed success, that so the isles may call him blessed of the Lord, in that the Lord hath and will make him a choice instrument in his hand for much good unto them, even unto the blacks as unto the whites, for the blacks (as 'tis said) expect some good by his coming here.

But more of that, it may be, hereafter, as occasion serves, although as yet he be not well able to appear abroad, yet most Friends have often visited him, besides some others of quality of the world. Many inhabitants of this isle are wise and sober and civil and many already reached and convinced. Meetings are very quiet, without disturbance or noise, so that here is like to be very great work and good service done for the Lord, in so much that it's the faith of some that the Lord hath not brought George Fox here for nought, and that the Lord will now make good in this his day to these western isles in the particular, as are recorded promises or prophesies or rather both in general, 'the isles', saith the Lord by his servants the prophets, 'shall wait for his law' (Isa. xlii. 1-4); and 'my righteousness is near; my salvation is gone forth, and mine arms [that is, the mighty power of the Lord] shall judge the people; the isles shall wait upon me, and on mine arm shall they trust' (Isa. li. 5).

While I was at sea I took from the mouth of George Fox two several papers. Them likewise I wrote out fair and intend to transmit them for London by Thomas Hudson with my letters; and it's George Fox's desire that thou hasten the well and careful printing of them and send back some of the printed books by the first opportunity, for they will savour exceeding well here. And more I am preparing, so that I may truly say I am not nor have been idle. No, the errand the Lord sent me upon is to do his work according to my capacity, for I must needs say, 'Praises, praises, be to his blessed name for ever more.' There is a spark of love from the altar of God kindled in me to all the Seed, the blessed Seed of God. George Fox's company is desired at L. Morris's; as yet we cannot go there, but may ere long. [He writes of a hurricane that hath done much hurt, two weeks since the writing of his letter, as to sugar canes, Indian corn, ships, and houses, etc.]

Once more desiring thee to mind my present condition and

likewise desire the prayers of all the faithful there, viz.: that the Lord would manifest his life, light, power, and love, to salvation and consolation in me more and more, and that he will keep me in a virgin state pure and clean and holy, and righteous and spiritually minded, out of all visibles to the one invisible, which is that state my soul breathes after and is pressing forward to.

As I hinted before, George Fox appointed the men's meeting to be here, and so accordingly they met, where came some of the world, among others one Lieutenant-Colonel Lyne, a sober person, belonging to the island, who was much troubled at first that he might not have admission, but after that, George Fox speaking to all, he was exceedingly well satisfied to this purpose, 'Now I can gainsay such as I have heard speak evil of you, that say you own not Christ nor that he died, but now I perceive you exalt Christ in all his offices as that I never heard so much before.' And seeing me taking the heads of what was spoken, desired me to give him a copy of it. He after stayed with us another day, even until eight at night. I believe we shall have more of his company at meetings.

After this, when clear of all of the world, Friends kept their meeting above in a large chamber, where George Fox gave some directions as to several things as to the well-ordering and managing their affairs, viz.: to get three distinct books, one for births, the second for marriages, the third for burials, as also distinct ones for blacks unconvinced; that were Friends' servants; also about convenient burying places for Friends, for in many places they bury their own in their gardens; and also for the blacks. Likewise concerning Friends taking one another in marriage, and also of kindred and how Christ the restorer was now bringing them to the beginning, namely one man and one woman, not many, as also when they take one another to have a certificate of their good behaviour, life and conversation, and of their coming in order to marriage twice to the women's meeting and twice to the men. And whereas there hath been upon several accounts much wickedness, both as to marrying kin and of two wives at once, or two husbands, and being unclean to married persons, to such he used very sharp reproof. Also concerning wills and legacies to Friends for public use; also concerning condemnations, after which two read their own condemnations for their uncleanness and abominations; also about training up their negroes in the fear of God, those bought with their money and such as were born in their families, so that all may come to the knowledge of the Lord that so with Joshua they may say, ' As for me and my house we will serve the Lord ', and that their overseers might deal mildly and gently with them and not use cruelty as the manner of some is and hath been, and to make them free after thirty years servitude; also concerning the hasty marrying of Friends after the death either of husband or wife, and of Friends' children when but thirteen or fourteen years old, admonishing them to purge the floor thoroughly and sweep their houses very clean; and that nothing be spoken out of their meetings to the blemishing one another. Many things more were spoken to and treated of.

So, dear Friends, farewell . . .   John Hull.

George Fox's love to all Friends, both male and female.

[E. Mann's Postscript; forwarding to Margaret Fox.]

John Hull's love is to thee and thinks meet to insert one remarkable passage that a Friend in whose house, and to whom it was spoken, told me, namely William Fuller.

One John Drakes, a person of quality in the world's account, understanding of George Fox's coming out of England, told him that, if it were possible to procure it, he would have him burnt.

One Friend queried of him what he had done against him that he was so violent against him, and he replied again he would have him burnt. Whereupon our Friend told him, ' Do not march on so furiously lest thou come too soon to thy journey's end.' And about ten days after he was struck with a fever and died burnt up, and so his body is laid in the dust.

[a]John Drakes, of Barbados, that would have burned George Fox because he would not suffer him to have Abia Trott, was a cruel swearer and a bad man, and was burned himself with a cruel fever, as black as a coal (as the people said), and so died, three or four days before George Fox came into Barbados.

Now George Fox being concerned with Abia Trott, ⟨left by her mother very young and with a considerable portion,⟩ and being entrusted with her by the will of her mother, could not answer Drakes's demand ⟨that he, who was out of the fear of God, should marry her,⟩ which made him in such a rage against George Fox.[a]

[a]. . . . . .[a] MS. *Epistles and Queries* (G.F. papers, Xx, p. 1), and Ellwood, p. 352; Bicent., ii, 146.

George Fox to Friends in England.

⟨Dear Friends and brethren, to whom is my love in that which never changeth, but remains in glory, which is over all, the top and corner-stone. In this all have peace and life, as ye dwell in the blessed Seed, wherein all is blessed; over that which brought the curse, where all shortness and narrowness of spirit is and brittleness and peevishness is. Therefore keep the holy order of the Gospel. And keep in this blessed Seed, where all may be preserved in temperance, in patience, in love, in meekness, in righteousness, and holiness, and in peace. . . . So let all minds and spirits, and souls, and hearts be bended down under the yoke of Christ Jesus, the power of God.

Much I could write, but am weak, and have been very weak mostly since I left you. Burdens and travails I have been under and have gone through many ways; but it is well. The Lord Almighty knows my work, which he hath sent me forth to do by his everlasting arm and power, which is from everlasting to everlasting, blessed be his holy name, which I am in, and in which my love is to you all. G.F.⟩[1]

John Stubbs to Margaret Fox, Barbados: 2nd 10th mo. [Dec.], 1671.

My dear and truly honoured in the Lord: Margaret Fox.

. . . I at this time thought it my duty to write unto thee to give thee an account of things here at present in this island, which take as followeth.

In the first place, thy husband is finely well, and pretty strong, and rides abroad to meetings, from one side of the island to another; and hath been so some weeks now by-past. I only give thee an account how things are at present, as also since the account I sent to William Dundas, which was ordered to be sent to thee, which I hope is come to thy hands some weeks since. So I omit mentioning anything that was contained in it, only give an account of things since, vizt, about three weeks ago thy husband went to visit the governor at his own house; and he was very civilly and kindly treated of him. Lewis Morris, Thomas Rous and I think his two sons and John Hull, with other Friends, went along with thy husband: and there they continued most part of the day and dined there also.

And that week thy husband came down to the Bridgetown, having not been there before but as he passed through it when

[1] In full, Ellwood, pp. 355, 356; Bicent., ii, 150, 151.

he came into the island. And it was so that the General Meeting happened to be the same week that thy husband was with the governor, and his kind reception with the governor did give a sound among the officers, both military and civil, throughout the island, insomuch as they came from all parts of the island, as it were, and that not of the least rank as colonels, and justices, and judges, and captains, etc., came to this General Meeting, hearing that thy husband would be at it. After thy son Rous, Thomas Briggs, and William Bayly had spoken, then thy husband spoke, and opened things to the great satisfaction of people, but he was straitened for time, and indeed, I was grieved from my very heart for it, and they cannot but suffer, that were the cause of it. Then after the meeting he passed to Lewis Morris's house that night, which was about nine or ten miles distant, partly performing his journey along the sea coast in a boat, and the rest upon horseback by land; and there he continued about a week. There is the finest air in the island about Lewis's plantation.

The next day after he went to Lewis Morris; Thomas Briggs and William Edmondson went to him to take their leave of him, being to pass to Antigua and Nevis. The following day, which was upon the seventh day of the week, just this day two weeks, they passed away from thy husband at that place and Lewis is gone along with them. So here are at present thy husband, and Solomon, and I; and upon First-days Meetings thy son Rous helps us: William Bayly is here.

The people in a manner generally affect him very much, and it's well. Here are mighty great meetings in the island, and a very great convincement in all parts; but we will leave the issue of all to the Lord. . . . He hath had two great First-day meetings at Thomas Rous's, it being the greatest meeting in the island except this General Meeting, at the town aforementioned.

Now tomorrow, being the First-day, I think he will have a meeting at one John Holder's, who is a justice of peace. Solomon and I have been there at two several meetings.

The Truth is freely preached, both to white people and black people. Solomon and I have had several meetings among the negroes in several plantations, and it's like must have more yet. But thy husband, it's like, hath had more than any of us; we feel the Lord's presence and power in that service, as well as when we speak among the white people, and that's enough.

Thy husband had the first meeting with them, and then after a while, it fell upon me and Solomon; and it was a great cross at the first, but now it's made more easy. Thus much I thought to write to thee, in as short a manner as ever I could. We have as much service as we are able to go through, and not above our strength given us, everlasting praises for ever; who renews our strength daily.

Thus with my dear and tender and true love to thyself and children, and Friends in thy house who are thy servants, and to dear Leonard Fell and his wife, and Robert and William Salthouse, and all other Friends as though I named them, farewell.

From thy friend and brother in the blessed light, life, and power made manifest, John Stubbs.

⟨We drew up a paper, to go forth in the name of the people called Quakers, thus.⟩

To the Governor and Assembly at Barbados, 1671.

To the Governor Codrington of Barbados and his Council and Assembly and all others in power both civil and military in this island, from the people called Quakers.

Whereas many scandalous lies and slanders have been cast upon us to the rendering us the more odious, (vizt) that we do deny God and Christ Jesus and the Scriptures of Truth, etc., this is to inform you that all our books and declarations (that for these many years have been published to the world) do clearly testify to the contrary, but yet for your sakes this is now given forth.

That God who is the only wise, omnipotent, and everlasting God we do own and believe in, who is the creator of all things both in heaven and in earth, and the preserver of all that he hath made, who is God over all, blessed for ever, to whom be all honour and glory and dominion and praise and thanksgiving both now and for evermore.

And that Jesus Christ is his beloved and only begotten son in whom he is well pleased, who was conceived by the Holy Ghost, and born of the virgin Mary, in whom we have redemption, through his blood even the forgiveness of sins, who is the express image of the invisible God, the first-born of every creature, by whom were all things created that are in heaven and that are in the earth, visible and invisible, whether they be thrones or dominions or principalities or powers; all things were created by him.

And we do own and believe that he was made sin for us, who knew no sin, neither was guile found in his mouth, and was crucified for us in the flesh without the gates of Jerusalem; and that he was buried and rose again the third day by his own power for our justification, and we do believe that he ascended up into heaven, and now sitteth at the right hand of God; and that this Jesus is the foundation of the prophets and apostles, and our foundation, so that there is no other foundation to be laid but what is laid, even Christ Jesus; and that he tasted death for every man, and shed his blood for all men; that he is the propitiation for our sins, and not for our sins only, but also for the sins of the whole world; for saith John the Baptist of him, 'Behold, the Lamb of God that taketh away the sins of the world' (John i. 29).

And we do believe that he is our alone redeemer and saviour, even the captain of our salvation, who saves us from sin, as well as from hell and the wrath to come, and destroys the Devil and his works; who is the seed of the woman that bruises the serpent's head, to wit, Christ Jesus who is alpha and omega, the first and the last; that he is, as the Scriptures of Truth say, our wisdom and righteousness, justification and redemption; neither is there salvation in any other, for there is none other name under heaven, given among men whereby we must be saved. He it is who is the shepherd and bishop of our souls; he it is who is our prophet, whom Moses long since testified of; as 'A prophet shall the Lord your God raise up unto you of your brethren, like unto me; him shall you hear in all things whatsoever he shall say unto you. And it shall come to pass that every soul that will not hear that prophet shall be destroyed from among the people' (Acts iii. 22, 23).

He it is that is now come and hath given us an understanding that we may know him that is true; and to rule in our hearts even with his law of love and of life in our inward parts which makes us free from the law of sin and death. And we have no life but by him, for he is the quickening spirit, the second Adam the Lord from heaven, by whose blood we are cleaned and our consciences sprinkled from dead works to serve the living God, by whose blood we are purchased, and so he is our mediator that makes peace and reconciliation between God offended and us offending, being the oath of God, the new covenant of light, life, grace, and peace, the author and finisher of our faith.

Now this Lord Jesus Christ, the heavenly man, Emanuel, God with us, we all own and believe in, whom the high priest raged against and said he had spoken blasphemy; and the chief priests and elders of the Jews took council together and put him to death; the same whom Judas betrayed for thirty pieces of silver which he had from the priests as a reward, and who gave a large sum of money to the soldiers to broach a horrible lie, namely that they should say that his disciples came and stole him away by night whilst they slept. And after he was risen from the dead, as you may see in the Acts of the Apostles, how that the chief priests and elders persecuted the disciples of this Jesus for preaching Christ and his resurrection, this, we say, is that Lord Jesus Christ whom we own to be our life and salvation.

Now concerning the Holy Scriptures, we do believe that they were given forth by the Holy Spirit of God through the holy men of God, who spoke, as the Scriptures of Truth saith, 'As they were moved by the Holy Ghost' (2 Peter i. 21); and that they are to be read, and believed, and fulfilled, and he that fulfills them is Christ; and they are 'profitable for doctrine, for reproof, for correction, for instruction in righteousness, that the man of God may be perfect, throughly furnished unto all good works' (2 Tim. iii. 16, 17) and are able to make us wise to salvation through faith in Christ Jesus. And we do believe that the Scriptures are the words of God, for it is said, 'God spake all these words' (Exod. xx. 1) meaning the ten commandments given forth upon Mount Sinai; and saith John, 'I testify unto every man that heareth the words of the prophecy of this book, if any man addeth unto these and if any man shall take away from the words' (not *word*) 'of the book', etc. (Rev. xxii. 18, 19). So in Luke i. 20: 'Because thou believest not my words'; and so in John v. 47, xv. 7, xiv. 23, xii. 47. So that we call the Scriptures, as Christ and the apostles called them, and as the holy men of God called them (vizt) the words not *word* of God.

Another slander and lie they have cast upon us is, namely, that we should teach the negroes to rebel, a thing we do utterly abhor and detest in and from our hearts, the Lord knows it, who is the searcher of all hearts and knows all things and so can witness and testify for us, that this is a most egregious and abominable untruth. For that which we have spoken and declared to them is to exhort and admonish them to be sober and to fear God, and to love their masters and mistresses, and to be faithful and diligent in their masters' service and business, and that then their masters and overseers will love them and deal kindly and gently with them; and that they should not beat their wives, nor the wives their husbands, nor multiply wives; and that they do not steal, nor be drunk, nor commit adultery, nor fornication, nor curse, nor swear, nor lie, nor give bad words to one another nor unto anyone else, for there is something in them that tells them that they should not practise those evils or any other before mentioned. If notwithstanding, they should do them, there are but two ways, the one that leads to heaven, where the righteous go, and the other that leads to hell, where the wicked and debauched, whoremongers and adulterers, murderers and liars go. To the one the Lord will say, 'Come, ye blessed of my Father, inherit the kingdom prepared for you from the foundation of the world', but to the other he will say, 'Depart, ye cursed, into everlasting fire, prepared for the Devil and his angels; the wicked into everlasting punishment but the righteous into life eternal' (Matt. xxv. 34, 41, 46).

Now consider, Friends, that it's no transgression for a master of a family to instruct his family himself or else some others in his behalf, but rather that it is a very great duty incumbent upon them, as Abraham did and Joshua did. As to the first, the Lord said, 'I know that Abraham will command his children and his household after him; and they shall keep the way of the Lord to do justice and judgement, that the Lord may bring upon Abraham the things that he hath spoken of him' (Gen. xviii. 19). And as for Joshua, said he, 'And if it seems evil unto you to serve the Lord, choose you this day whom you will serve, whether the gods which your fathers served that were on the other side of the flood, or the gods of the Amorite in whose land ye dwell; but as for me and my house we will serve the Lord' (Joshua xxiv. 15). And further consider this, that it is a duty incumbent upon us to pray, and to teach, instruct, and admonish those in and belonging to our families, it being the command of the Lord, the disobedience to which will incur the Lord's displeasure, as you may see where it's written, 'Pour out thy fury upon the heathen that know thee not, and upon the families that call not upon thy name' (Jer. x. 25).

Now negroes and tawny Indians make up a very great part of families here in this island for whom an account will be required by him who comes to judge both quick and dead at the great day of judgement, when every one shall be 'rewarded according to the deeds done in the body, whether they be good or whether they be evil'—at that day, I say, of the resurrection, both of the good and the bad, the just and the unjust, when 'the Lord Jesus shall be revealed from heaven with his mighty angels, in flaming fire, taking vengeance on them that know not God and obey not the Gospel of our Lord Jesus Christ; who shall be punished with everlasting destruction from the presence of the Lord and from the glory of his power, when he shall come to be glorified in his saints and admired in all them that believe' (2 Thess. i. 7-9). See also 2 Pet. iii. 3-5, 9.[1]

At Barbados the priest and the justice combined against me and the Truth, and stirred up the people against it. They came to the General Meeting, and then the Baptists began first and they bawled and railed till one of them foamed at the mouth, one of their teachers called Hatchman.[2] And when he had done, one Paul Gwyn[3] and his company fell on and they bawled and raged till they had spent themselves. They asked me whether I had the same spirit as the apostles had. And I said I had. And away they went.

And when they were gone stood up the lawyers, and they made a great noise and bawling, and when their mouths were stopped they went away. Then stood up others; and thus they relieved one another that the world [b]took notice of them and[b] made verses of them. And one of these disturbers, his name is Pearson[4] of Barbados, a wicked man who had two wives, as they said, railed against me in the meeting, and after was so bold that he railed against the governor; and he cast him into prison in irons, and so he had his reward. Afterwards we had a good meeting, and the power of the Lord and his blessed Seed were set over all. Blessed be his holy name for ever, Amen.

[1] The foregoing paper was also published in Fox's tract *To the Ministers, Teachers, and Priests . . . in Barbadoes.* 1672.

[2] Thomas Hatchman.

[3] Cf. p. 270-3 ante.

[4] Ben Pearson, 'an old apostate from Truth'.

[b]. . . . . .[b] *Camb. Jnl.*, ii, 252.

⟨Before I left the island I wrote the following letter to my wife.

Barbados, 6th of 11th mo. 1671/2 [Jan., 1672].

My dear heart,

To whom is my love, and to all the children, in the Seed of life that changeth not but is over all, blessed be the Lord for ever. I have gone under great sufferings in my body and spirit beyond words. But the God of heaven be praised, his truth is over all. I am now well, and, if the Lord permit, within a few days I pass from Barbados towards Jamaica; and I do think to stay but little there. I desire that you may be all kept free in the Seed of life, out of all cumbrances. Friends are generally well. Remember me to Friends that enquire after me. So no more but my love in the Seed and life that changeth not.

G.F.⟩

John Stubbs to Margaret Fox

Barbados, 20th of 11th mo. 1671/2 [Jan., 1672].

Dearly Beloved in the Lord, Margaret Fox.

After the salutation of my love to thee and thine remembered, I thus write unto thee to give thee a very short account of passages here in this island as relating to Truth, which prospers abundantly, at which the priests and professors rage much and stir up the magistrates against us, though hitherto we have not been molested in our meetings except twice or thrice by some professors, especially Baptists, who came in bawling against thy husband into the General Meeting in the town, occasioned by a malicious printed paper sent over to this island by John Pennyman.[1] The Baptists came into the meeting, where there was an exceeding great meeting of men and women of several ranks and qualities, and a Baptist speaker, when thy husband stood up to speak, asked him if his name were Mr. Fox, etc., and asked him whether he owned such and such titles as were given to him by Solomon Eccles in a certain paragraph contained in a paper of John Pennyman's,[2] etc.; and a great bawling they made. And a great company came with them and it's very probable intended wickedly. Thy husband answered things so in the pure wisdom of God that generally the auditory received satisfaction, so that the professors lost by their coming. So when they had wearied themselves with bellowing, they

[1] John Pennyman (1628-1706) erstwhile Quaker.

[2] This was *A Letter to John Bolton*. London, 21st Aug., 1671.

went away, and thy husband continued the meeting and brought the life and power over all. My time prevents me from being large, but I think it my duty to write to thee by every opportunity; now I have not time to be large, only so much as to speak of things in short.

Thy husband passed from this island towards Jamaica the eighth of this instant, exceeding well every way as ever he was since I knew him. After a very large and an heavenly meeting with the chief of Friends in the island that came to accompany him to the sea shore, he passed aboard, where several Friends accompanied him. The Friends that go with him are Robert Widders, William Edmondson, Solomon Eccles, and Elizabeth Hooton. Thomas Briggs is here with me left behind; his love is to thee; he is often very weakly. Here is a great addition to our meetings, the priests and others are very angry at present at this great loss of their children. The magistrates in this town have this week put several of our Friends into the common gaol for not putting off their hats, in their courts.

If the Lord give me an opportunity of writing again to thee, I hope I shall have more time, for I think, God willing, not to miss any opportunity in writing.

He hath left Friends in this island in a sweet frame every way, and we that are left here behind to do as well as we can. Thomas Briggs, who is very often ill, William Bayly, and thy son Rous help us in the service as much as their occasions will permit. I was at five meetings this week. Thy husband hath been twice with the Governor, once he went to him and the Governor came once since to Thomas Rous's to him. I desire thee to excuse me for my brevity for I have several miles to travel this night or tomorrow; so concluding with my tender respects to thee and thy family and to Friends that meet at thy house, farewell,

From thy friend and brother in a spiritual relation,

J. Stubbs.

[The narrative of the American travels from Barbados onwards reproduces the original travel diaries from page 609, October, 1671, until 11th April, 1673, when Cliffs, Maryland, was reached for the last time, page 655. Preserved in Bristol Friends MSS. V, which are described in the *Journal of the Friends Historical Society*, ix (1912), pp. 122, 189-98, are two small home-made notebooks without covers, in the handwritings of James Lancaster and Robert Widders, two of Fox's travelling companions. The style is Fox's own, and the occasional use of the present tense to describe his situation shows that he dictated to one of his companions at frequent intervals throughout the period covered, sometimes bringing the story right up to the moment of writing and recording the plan for the next day.

The narrative given in the Spence MSS. (*Camb. Jnl.*, ii, 221-45), from Rhode Island, 30th May, 1672, till Cliffs, Maryland, 11th April, 1673, is a recension, with but slight changes, of the relevant parts of these diaries.]

[Here begins Fox's first American travel diary, from the original MS. Interpolations from other sources are indicated.]

We came from London on the thirteenth day of the sixth month [Aug.] and we came to Barbados the third day of the eighth month [Oct.], where we had many and great meetings among the whites and blacks. And there was some opposition by the priests and Papists but the power of the Lord and his glorious Truth was over all and reached most in the island. And we stayed above a quarter of a year there and I went to visit the governor[1] and he was loving to me; and a few days before I passed from the island the governor with many more came to see me to Thomas Rous's house. [c]And many persons of quality were convinced and loving, and Judge Fretwell became a pretty Friend, and his family, and Judge Farmer was very loving.[c] And I was at several men's and women's meetings which was of great service for that island. And we set up meetings in families [d]in every Friend's house, among the blacks, some 200, some 300, in their houses[d] that the

[1] Colonel Christopher Codrington, Lieut. Governor.

[c]. . . . . .[c] *Camb. Jnl.*, ii, 255. Fox's discourse on this is printed in his *Gospel Family Order . . . of Whites, Blacks and Indians.* 1676.

[d]. . . . .[d] *Camb. Jnl.*, ii, 255.

masters and dames of families might admonish their families of blacks and whites, as Abraham did, which is a great service.

And when we had stayed about a quarter of a year there we passed to Jamaica and were about ten days passing thither, having a good wind. And a great love of God did we leave behind in Barbados, and several Friends that had good service in the ministry there. [e]Many hundreds of Friends accompanied us to the ship.[e]

And we came from Barbados the 8th day of the 11th month [Jan.]; and the 13th day sprang a leak in our ship [f]and we were in danger,[f] and the carpenter, being a seaman, dived in the sea [f]with his hammer, chisel, and oakum,[f] and groped out the hole with a maul[1] [f]and stopped it under water with oakum, and came up again and said he had made her as tight as a dish, and so she was, so the Lord preserved us.[f]

And the day before, the rope that stayed the main yard broke in a storm, but they made it fast again and all was well, praised be the Lord.

And we passed by St. Lucia and by the Island of Martinique and by the Island St. Eustatius and the 14th day of 11th month [Jan.] we are over against Hispaniola,[2] a great and an high country. And the 16th day of the 11th month [Jan.], we passed near the Island of Cones and so we came to Jamaica the 18th day of the 11th month [Jan.], which they say was 1,200 miles from Barbados, and from England to Barbados 4,500 miles. And in Jamaica I travelled about 300 miles and from Jamaica to the capes of Virginia 1,800 miles, and from the capes of Virginia to Patuxent in Maryland 200 miles,—8,000 miles. And we had meetings every First-day but one in all the ships among the seamen and passengers, and sometimes other days beside.

[g]We travelled many hundreds of miles up and down in

[1] A heavy mallet.
[2] Now called Ḥaiti.
[e]......[e] *Camb. Jnl.*, ii, 255. [f]......[f] MS. Portfolio 10.41.

Jamaica among Friends and the people of the world, and set up a matter of seven meetings and also there are men's meetings and a women's meeting,[g] many were convinced and loving and very tender. [g]And there is a justice of the peace and his wife and several others of account convinced. And not a mouth was opened against us, but people were mighty civil and respectful, and when we were to go away[g] they said it was a pity such men should go out of the land. And I was two times apiece with the governor[1] and the major called Banister by name; and they were loving to me in words.

[h]Elizabeth Hooton is deceased at Jamaica. She was well upon the Sixth-day of the week and deceased the next day about the eleventh hour, in peace like a lamb. James Lancaster was by her and can give an account of what word she spoke and of her testimony concerning Truth.[h]

Twelfth Month [Feb. 1672]

⟨Before I left Jamaica, I writ another letter to my wife, as follows:

Jamaica, 23rd 12th mo. 1671/2 [Feb. 1672].

My dear Heart,

To whom is my love, and to the children, in that which changeth not but is over all, and to all Friends in those parts. I have been at Jamaica about five weeks. And Friends here are generally well, and here is a convincement, but things would be too large to write of. Sufferings in every place attend me, but the blessed Seed is over all, the great Lord be praised, who is Lord of sea and land and of all things therein. We intend to pass from hence about the beginning of the next month; and we shall pass towards Maryland, if the Lord please. Dwell all of you in the Seed of God. In his Truth I rest in love to you all.

G.F.⟩

[1] Sir Thomas Lynch.
[g]......[g] *Camb. Jnl.*, ii, 206, 207. [h]......[h] *Camb. Jnl.*, ii, 213.

CHAPTER XXIV

AND after we had stayed seven weeks and a day in Jamaica we took shipping for Maryland on the sixth day of the week, the 8th day of the 1st month [Mar.].

[a]Intending to Virginia with six other Friends more, we sought for a vessel for our passages, and had choice of two, a frigate and a ketch. The owner of the frigate was unreasonable for our passages, as we did judge. The master of the ketch was willing to carry us ten shillings apiece cheaper than the other asked, so we shipped ourselves aboard the ketch, and came out together, intending both for Virginia, and intending to be consorts, and sailed together several days. But with calms and contrary winds we separated; and we came on our intended voyage. The frigate our consort was put back again towards Jamaica and then came on her intended voyage with much difficulty. They lost their way and fell among the Spaniards and by them were taken and robbed and the master and mate taken prisoner. She was retaken again by the English and sent home to her owners in Virginia; wherein we see the providence of God in all these things to preserve us out of our enemies' hands. And he who was covetous fell among the covetous. Some Friends would have had us come to the ship that was taken, but the Lord in his wisdom would have it to be otherwise.[a]

And we left Solomon Eccles in Jamaica to stay there awhile among Friends, who were generally well there. And there is a great convincement by the power of the Lord which is over all, and his blessed Seed. And here is a convincement in the east and in the west and in the north

[a]......[a] *Camb. Jnl.*, ii, 214.

and in the south of this land of Jamaica by the blessed power and his Truth. And after, many Friends did accompany us to the ship. And after we had set sail we passed windward two days, and the third day, not being able to pass against the winds we turned leewards and this day we are over against Alligator Pond in Manatee Valley, being the first day of the week and the 11th day of the 1st month [Mar.].

And we passed a week backwards and forwards before we passed out of the sight of Jamaica on the 15th of the 1st month [Mar.]. This day being the 16th of the month we passed by the Island of Little Cayman and Cayman Brac and by Grand Cayman, the island of turtles and alligators, and sharks and crocodiles, and chonasses about the bigness of a cat.[1] And on the 21st day of the 1st month [Mar.], we passed by the Island of Pines near Cuba and Cape St. Antonio.

And the same day [b]we were in great danger;[b] our mainstay of our ship's great yard fell down. And on the 23rd of the 1st month [Mar.], in the night we passed under the tropic; and the 27th of the 1st month [Mar.], we saw the table land on Cuba after a long calm and passing to and fro with contrary winds. And on the 29th day we saw the Island of Tortugas; and this day we [b]came to shoal water and[b] saw the bottom of the sea and the sands and rocks; [b]and being strangers they feared, seeing the sands,[b] which was about eight leagues from the Gulf of Florida.

And on the 2nd day of the 2nd month [Apr.], we saw the land [c]of Florida, and entered into the Gulf, leaving Florida upon the left hand, having had great winds and many storms that tossed us backwards and forwards; but the great God of the sea and of the land who rideth upon the wings of the wind gave us dominion. In the storm our boltsprit broke and blew the jibsail into the

[1] A corruption of *cunāhăs*, Spanish for any coney-like animal, of which there are several species in the W. Indies.

[b]. . . . . .[b] *Camb. Jnl.*, ii, 207.

sea to the great hazard of the ship, but all was well, praises be unto the Lord.

And the 3rd of the 2nd month [Apr.], we were in the Gulf of Florida and the winds and the seas were calm, praises be to the Lord for ever. And on the 4th day of the 2nd month [Apr.], we saw no land, having passed some days about Florida shore where the man-eaters live, and several days we sailed forwards and backwards. And the wind being against us, and an high storm, I was moved to pray to the Lord, and the Lord's power was over all and he caused the wind to cease as well as could be desired, praised be his name for ever

The 5th of the 2nd month [Apr.], we were come to 30° wanting 4′, and on the 6th of the 2nd month [Apr.], were in the 31st°.

And on the 9th of the 2nd month [Apr.], we had high winds and blustering weather and rain and great storms in the night so that it struck the company[c] in a sudden amazement, and a fright came upon the people and a great noise. And in the midst of it I prayed to the Lord and the wind immediately stopped, though there was much rain and our sails were taken down, and all of us much wet, [c]both company and passengers, with the rain and waves.[c] And all of us were much wrought; and it was in the night.

And on the 10th of the 2nd month [Apr.], we had a great storm so that they tied up the rudder bands and let the ship go as she would and whither she would, and towards night it ceased, praised be the Lord who hath power over the wind.

And on the 11th day we had contrary winds and partly a calm; and we are now in the latitude of 37° and 5′, and so are gone back again.

And this day being the 14th day of the 2nd month [Apr.], we are in the latitude of 36° 10′, blustering weather, but praised be the Lord all things are sanctified to me, sea and land and the winds and the sea-storms, the several sorts of weather and climates as they are called, knowing the

[c]. . . . . .[c] *Camb. Jnl.*, ii, 208.

foundation of man and the foundation of God, and many travails on the sea we have had; but praised be the Lord who hath carried us through over and above them all.

On the 16th day of the 2nd month [Apr.], we had a great storm and great rain almost all the day and we tied up the rudder bands and the helm and let the ship go herself which way she would, so all was given up to the Lord whose power ordered all things to his glory, yea the sea and land, praised be the Lord for ever.

And on the 17th day of the 2nd month [Apr.] was a great fog and mist but when it did clear we saw the land of Virginia, and the sea and wind were moderate. Praised be the Lord who with his mighty hand and power and by faith in it carried us and preserved us ever in it, praising and rejoicing in the Lord.

And this day being the 18th day of the 2nd month [Apr.], we came to Cape Henry on Virginia, within the sight of it; and this day there was a man that died, and his corpse was cast overboard, a seaman. Blessed be the Lord of heaven and earth [d]and of the great seas[d] that hath preserved us to this day.

And this day being the 19th of the 2nd month [Apr.], [d]we cast anchor in the bay of Patuxent River, and[d] we passed up the bay, and the 20th of the 2nd month [Apr.], we cast anchor again in Patuxent River, blessed be the Lord. And the master of the ship, a Boston man in New England, went to a ship of New England and came again, mad drunk, and threatened to cut down the mast and to do other mischiefs, but I had power over him. And at his best he was bad, for he said he mattered not for throwing twenty men overboard, no more than he did a dog.

And the 20th day of the 2nd month [Apr.], after we had cast anchor there was a great storm and there was a boat cast upon us for shelter in which there were men and women and children, and some of account in the country, and they were preserved in our ship. One of them had been high sheriff four years, and a lawyer, and a clerk of their court,

[d]. . . . . [d] *Camb. Jnl.*, ii, 209.

and some of their wives were there. On the 22nd day in the morning, all our boats being gone after four that were broken from the ship, and the seamen to look after them, those great persons' boat was lost and not found, with the value of £500 worth of things as they said. [e]And the people were fain to continue with us several days on shipboard, and could not get off to land, but we had a fine meeting with them on the sea.[e] And George Pattison ventured his life in a little boat to get to the ship of Samuel Groom, and came again [e]and none could believe, except Friends, but that he would be cast away.[e] That boat was driven away and he with a sloop went after it and the wind laid him and them up. [e]And our provision was gone,[e] and we did not know how to get on the shore. There came another boat from Francis Camfield's plantation, and they fell sick and could not help themselves.

In the morning I laid me down being not well and I fell in a slumber, and I had a vision that Friends were coming to fetch us away from the ship to land, and as I was in it a Friend came and wakened me and said Friend were come. [e]Then all were glad, as well the company as they that were cast upon us, for they had no provision and ours was gone also.[e] So they carried us about fourteen miles by water and we came to land with them, and the 23rd day of the 2nd month [Apr.] we came to James Preston's house.

Then there was a meeting appointed by John Burnyeat about three score miles off, which held four days,[1] which we went to though we were weary. And there came to it five or six justices of the peace and he that was Speaker of the Assembly and one of the Council and many considerable people of the world, and a glorious meeting we had. ⟨After the public meeting there were men's and women's meetings and I opened to Friends the service thereof⟩ and all were satisfied.

[e]......[e] *Camb. Jnl.*, ii, 209.

[1] This General Meeting, held at West River, Maryland, was the beginning of the present Baltimore Yearly Meeting of Friends. The place is still known as The Friends Meeting.

And when all was done we passed up and down by land and we came about forty miles by water, and a great storm came on us soon after we set out and our sloop was cast on ground, ready to be broken in pieces. That day I had been very hot in the meeting and all in a sweat, and was wet to the skin [f]with the water also without me;[f] but we got the boat off the sands and all was well. And we got to the place called the Cliffs, by the break of day, blessed be the Lord, where another general meeting was. And many of the world's people were there and did receive the Truth with gladness and reverence. And many or most of the backsliders came in [f]and a brave men's meeting and women's meeting we had; and we established several women's meetings and men's meetings.[f] ⟨After these meetings James Lancaster and John Cartwright went by sea for New England. William Edmundson and three Friends more with him sailed for Virginia where things were much out of order. John Burnyeat, Robert Widders, George Pattison and I with several Friends of the province⟩ came next day about forty miles by water ⟨to the Eastern Shore⟩ to another general meeting, and all Friends and people received the Truth with gladness and there was a very great heavenly meeting, near Great Choptank River, and there were two justices of the peace and several people of an account.

And it was upon [me] from the Lord to send for the Indian emperor and two of their kings to come to the First-day's meeting; and the emperor came and stopped all the meeting; [f]but the kings could not reach so far.[f] And when it was done he [f]was very courteous and loving and[f] came and took me by the hand, and [f]I bade Friends take him[f] from the meeting to a Friend's house where I was to lodge that night. And the two kings also came to meet with me and four of their nobles and they stayed all that night and I had two very good speeches to them and they heard the word of the Lord and did confess to it. [g]And what I said to the kings and emperor I desired them to speak to their

[f]......[f] *Camb. Jnl.*, ii, 210.

people, that God is setting up his tabernacle of witnesses in their wilderness countries and setting up his glorious ensign and standard of righteousness.[g] And they asked when we had meetings and they said they would come to them and were very loving. And they said they had a great dispute and a council before they came to me, about their coming.

The 6th of the 3rd month [May], Robert Widders, John Burnyeat, George Pattison and I with many Friends went towards New England by land, having two Indians to be our guides. [h]We passed by the head of Miles River[1] and so steered through the woods and then[h] we passed by the head of Wye River, and through the woods thence by the head of Chester River, but we took up our lodging in the woods before we came to Chester River head, and made us a fire and stayed all night. Thence we passed the next day through the woods and wilderness having no path and came to a plantation which was out of our way, called The World's End, [h]being very much tired.[h] And one swam our horses over Sassafras River and we went over ourselves in dangerous canoes. Thence we passed through the woods and came to Bohemia River and there we swam over our horses and went over ourselves in canoes. Thence we some of us came thirty miles ⟨and George Pattison and Robert Widders⟩ and the rest, their horses being weak, stayed in the woods by a fire. It being a great thunder and rain, I with some others [h]whose horses were stronger,[h] got to Delaware which is now called New Castle that night, being [h]wet to the skin,[h] a town of Dutch and Swedes. ⟨Robert Widders and George Pattison came to us next morning.⟩

The 9th day of the 3rd month [May] we passed over a great water and carried our horses over in a sloop [h]and were some of us in great danger of our lives,[h] and hired new guides with great trouble, which were very chargeable. When we were over the river Delaware we passed through the woods and sometimes we lay in the woods by a fire

[1] St. Michael's River, Talbot Co., Md.
[g]......[g] *Camb. Jnl.*, ii, 210. [h]......[h] *Camb. Jnl.*, ii, 211.

and sometimes at Indians' houses or cabins. A tedious journey we had through bogs, rivers, and creeks, and wild woods where it was said never man was known to ride. And I came to an Indian king's house and he and his queen were very loving, and the rest of his attendance, and received me and laid me on a mat for a bed, to lie by him, [i]a very pretty man.[i] ⟨But provision was very short with them having caught but little that day.⟩ Then we came to another Indian town where the king came to me and could speak some English and was very loving, and I spoke much to him and his people. And we did pass [i]with a second guide about 200 miles from New Castle,[i] through many Indian towns and they helped us over a great river in a canoe and swam our horses over. And so we passed through the woods and bogs, and had lain many nights in the woods, and came to Middletown, a place in New Jersey, and were very glad when we got to a highway. And we stayed there a while and refreshed ourselves. [i]We could not stay to have a meeting but[i] went to a Friend's house who is called Richard Hartshorne, [i]who is Hugh Hartshorne's brother, a Friend who is an upholsterer in Houndsditch in London, who received us gladly, where we were refreshed, for we were weary.[i] And he carried us and our horses over a great water [j]in his own boat,[j] where we were almost a whole day a-passing it; and we came to Gravesend on Long Island, and there were Friends.

[j]Next morning we set forward, though weary,[j] above forty miles to Oyster Bay ⟨and got to Flushing. And the day following we reached to Oyster Bay, several Friends of Gravesend and Flushing accompanying us⟩, where there was a General Meeting of men and women Friends that held six days, and large. There we met with some of the hat spirit[1] which was judged down and condemned. And the Truth was set over all.

And this General Meeting began on the 17th day of the 3rd month [May], which was of very great service to Friends

[1] See p. 549 ante.

[i]......[i] *Camb. Jnl.*, ii, 211. [j]......[j] *Camb. Jnl.*, ii, 212.

and to the people of the world, and did not part until the 23rd day of the month, so it was longer than used to be. ⟨On the first and second days we had public meetings for worship; on the third day were men's and women's meetings wherein the affairs of the church were taken care of. So the men's and women's meetings being over we had a meeting with some of those discontented people, and the Lord's power brake forth gloriously to the confounding of the gainsayers. And then some of them[1] began to fawn upon me and to cast the matter upon others, but the deceitful spirit was judged down and condemned and the glorious Truth was exalted and set over all; and they were all brought down and bowed under, which was of great service to Truth and satisfaction and comfort to Friends.⟩

And from thence we went to another meeting, and thence through the woods to Flushing where was a large meeting at John Bowne's house, [k]who was banished by the Dutch into England.[k] And many hundreds of the world were there and were much satisfied and desired to hear again and said that if I came to their town I should have their meeting place, they were so loving. And from thence we came to Oyster Bay again where we do wait for wind to go to Rhode Island. These meetings were in the Duke of York's dominions, and the governor heard of me and was loving and said that he had been in my company.

[k]And on the 28th of the 3rd month [May], we took boat again[k] and on the 30th day of the 3rd month [May], 1672, we came to Rhode Island. It was about 200 miles by water, and Friends and others received us very gladly. We were weary with travelling by land and water, [k]but the eminent arm and power of the Lord carried and preserved us through and over the fury of wild beasts and men, woods, storms, wildernesses, bogs, rivers, famine, and frosts.[k] And I came to Nicholas Easton's house,[2] he being made governor of that colony, where I lay. And we

[1] George Dennis was the chief instigator.

[2] On Farwell Street, Newport, Rhode Island.

[k]. . . . . .[k] *Camb. Jnl.*, ii, 212.

had two good meetings; and many justices, with the governor and the deputy governor[1] and captain, were there, and all were satisfied and did not think there had been such a man in the world.

[l]And the Fifth-day after, I went to the men's meeting in the island, and after to the women's meeting about the church affairs. And the next week after came up[l] the General Meeting where Friends came up out of all the rest of the colonies of New England, which meeting lasted six days together.

⟨And John Stubbs came from Barbados and James Lancaster and John Cartwright from another way. They have no priest in the island so there is no restriction as to worship this way or the other way.⟩ Most of the officers and justices with the governor and deputy governor were there and at most meetings, and Friends out of other jurisdictions, [l]and all mightily affected with Truth. And we had a general men's meeting and a general women's meeting, through which men's meetings and women's meetings were established in all other parts[l] ⟨to take care of the poor and other affairs of the church. And when it was ended it was hard for Friends to part, for the glorious power of the Lord which was over all and his blessed Truth and life flowing amongst them had so knit and united them together that they spent two days in taking leave of one another and Friends went away being mightily filled with the presence and power of the Lord. And yet by the continued coming in of people in sloops from divers other colonies and jurisdictions it continued longer, and for several days after we had large meetings.⟩ [m]John Burnyeat with John Cartwright and George Pattison are gone with them ⟨into the eastern parts of New England⟩ and John Stubbs and James Lancaster are to go after them into their several colonies. And Robert Widders stays with me to go into other parts.[m]

And I was at a marriage there for example's sake. It

[1] John Cranston.

[l]. . . . . .[l] *Camb. Jnl.*, ii, 212. [m]. . . . . .[m] *Camb. Jnl.*, ii, 212, 213.

was such a one as was never in New England and many of the world were there, and three justices of the peace. And the people and Friends never saw such a solemn assembly and so weighty and such order, so it was beyond words and the Truth was set over all. It was at a Friend's house that had formerly been governor[1] and was an example to all the rest of the jurisdictions. Some out of many places were there.

Then I had a great travail concerning the Ranters for they had been rude at a meeting where I was not at. I appointed a meeting among them and I knew that the Lord would give me power over them and he did, to his praise and glory, blessed be his name for ever. And there was a justice of the peace convinced that day there, who had been a justice twenty years. He said he did not think that there had been such a man in the world, and he never heard the like nor such things in all his life. Many Friends and other justices and officers were there and most of them did speak the like, beyond words for me to utter. And all was quiet, and many other meetings we had.

And on the 30th day of the 4th month [June], we had a meeting at Providence, very large, and all sorts and sects of people were there. I had a great travail concerning the meeting, in having and preserving it quiet, and for the bringing the Truth over them and in them, and so set the power of God and his Seed above all and in them and over them, for they were above the priests in high notions. And the Lord set his Seed over all and above all and they went away mightily satisfied and said that they never heard the like and did much desire another meeting. And some came a-purpose to dispute, but all were silent and the power of the Lord was over all, praised be the Lord. And many came to me for more meetings and people came far and near to it, and it was of great service and to the honour of God. And from Rhode Island it was about threescore miles by water backwards and forwards; and the governor

[1] William Coddington (1601-1678), founder of Newport, Rhode Island.

went with me, and many others. And there were two justices of the peace and other officers there, and the glorious power of the Lord shined over all, glory to the great Lord for ever.

A great barn was so full of people and I was so hot with sweat as though I had been sodden, but all was well. The blessed Seed was over all. There was a priest did threaten, but his mouth was stopped. There was a woman that was bad and scoffed, and she went away and was struck sick and sent for one to look to her; and she told of her scoffing and her badness and would not look to her, and this was at Providence. And Men's and Women's Meetings are established in all these colonies or jurisdictions and in the order of the gospel, and a general Women's Meeting is set up at Boston, and the power of the Lord is over all and his blessed Seed, blessed be his name for ever. And on the 13th day of the 5th month [July], I had a meeting at a justice's house where never was a meeting before, and all the country came and most that had never heard before. And all were quiet and mightily taken, and there were four justices of the peace there and the governor. And we went about forty miles backward and forward to it. And a great desire there is among the people. The meeting was at Narragansett and people came from Connecticut and far and nigh. It was of service beyond words blessed be the Lord for ever, Amen.

And many other meetings of men and women I was at, and passages there, which would be too large to mention. But I had a general men's meeting of all the colonies and jurisdictions; and after, a general women's meeting of all the colonies, etc., which once a year is to be kept, besides their own men's and women's in their several colonies, which be settled, blessed be the Lord to his glory, Amen.

And in Rhode Island we had ten glorious meetings together, one day after another [n]with only one Seventh-day in between,[n] blessed be the Lord. And all Friends were

[n]......[n] *Camb. Jnl.*, ii, 223.

filled with the love of God, and the glory of the Lord shineth over all. And at Narragansett where almost all the country came in to hear, in a justice's barn, there was another justice there, and they were all drawing up a paper to invite me to come again, for they were so taken with the Truth; but I was coming away towards Shelter Island. I desired John Stubbs, John Burnyeat, and John Cartwright ⟨whom they had left at Piscataway,⟩ to visit them.

And at another place they, with an ancient justice, said that if they had money enough they would hire me. So I said then it was time for me to go away, for then they would not come to their own teacher, for that (viz. hiring) did and had spoiled them and many for not improving their own talents, for we brought every one to their own teacher.

°In New England there was an Indian king that said he saw that there were many of their people of the Indians turned to the New England professors. He said they were worse since than they were before they left their own religion; and of all religions he said the Quakers were the best. And if they should turn to the New England professors' religion, that made the people worse than they were before, and if he should turn to the Quakers, which was the best, then the professors would hang him and put them to death and banish them as they did the Quakers, and therefore he thought it was the best to be as he was.

And an Indian said, before the English came, that a white people should come in a great thing of the sea, and their people should be loving to them and receive them; but if they did hurt or wrong the white people, they would be destroyed. And this hath been seen and fulfilled, that when they did wrong the English they never prospered and have been destroyed. So that Indian was a prophet and prophesied truly.°

We came to Rhode Island on the 4th day of the 4th month [June], and the people were loving and all the justices and governor, deputy governor and his wife, and

°......° *Camb. Jnl.*, ii, 250, 251.

captain were convinced and came to the meeting continually.

And after we had stayed two months in Rhode Island and thereabouts, we left [p]in a sloop about the 26th of the 5th month [July];[p] and ⟨Robert Widders, James Lancaster, George Pattison, and John Jay of Barbados went with me⟩. And the same day we passed by Point Juda and Block Island and came to Fisher's Island as before.

The man that carried us before up to Rhode Island, a Friend called Nicholas Davis, was cast away overboard and drowned, but not in our sloop that time. He had a great family; there was something in the thing.

We went at night on shore and we were not able to stay for the mosquitoes, so we went on the sloop again and put off from the shore and cast anchor and stayed all that night. The next day we went out into the sound but our sloop was not able to live in the water so we turned in again, for we could not pass, and came to anchor again at Fisher's Island, two nights, and there was exceeding much rain whereby we were much wet, being in an open boat. So we passed all day and night there, the 28th of 5th month [July]. And we passed the two Horse Races, waters so called, and passed by Garner's Island and Gull's Island and so came to Shelter Island which was 27 leagues from Rhode Island.

There we had a meeting on the 29th day, being First-day, so we were three days a-coming there. And I had a meeting at Shelter Island among the Indians [p]on the 1st day of the 6th month [Aug.]. Their king[p] and his council with about 100 more Indians with him, sat about two hours, and I spoke to them by an interpreter that was an Indian that could speak any English very well. They [q]sat down like Friends and[q] appeared very loving; they said all was truth and did make a confession of it after the meeting. So I have set up a meeting among them once a fortnight, and a

[p]......[p] Bodleian MS.; *Jnl. F.H.S.*, ix, 13.
[q]......[q] *Camb. Jnl.*, ii, 224.

Friend Joseph Silvester[1] is to read the Scriptures to them, negroes and Indians.

On the First-day after, the 4th day of the 6th month [Aug.], there was a great meeting at Shelter Island. Many of the world were there, and priests' people that never heard Friends before, and they were very much satisfied and could not go away until they had seen me and spoken to me after the meeting. And people came a great way to it from many places, and they said such a meeting had not been before. And I went down to them and they were taken with the Truth. A great desire there is and a great love and satisfaction were among the people, blessed be the Lord. His name spreads and will be great among the nations and dreadful among the heathen.[r]

William Edmondson to Margaret Fox.[2]

Dublin, 7.xi.1672 [Jan. 1673].

Dear M.F.

We were about seven weeks in sailing from England to Barbados; and after three days abiding there, James Lancaster, John Cartwright, and George Pattison went with the ship to Jamaica. The rest of our company stayed in Barbados where we had great service for the Lord, and many convinced of his blessed Truth. And when we had been about seven weeks there, Thomas Briggs and I, accompanied with Lewis Morris, sailed to Antigua and had several good meetings there and a great resort of people, and many convinced.

And from thence we sailed for Nevis, accompanied with Samuel Winthrop, Governor of Antigua, but Charles Wheeler, Governor of Nevis, would not suffer us to come on shore, but banished us to Barbados. And after about three weeks longer there we left Thomas Briggs and John

[1] Probably should be Nathaniel Silvester who was proprietor of Shelter Island, which he made a shelter for persecuted Friends, originally called Farret's Island.

[2] *Camb. Jnl.*, ii, 220-1. Letter used as a source for narrative by Ellwood. Cf. note on p. 594.

[r] Diary continued on p. 628.

Stubbs in Barbados, and thy dear husband and the rest of us sailed for Jamaica, and there met again with James Lancaster, John Cartwright, and George Pattison. We abode there seven weeks and odd days and had much service in that debauched wicked Sodom and brought Friends into pretty good order and settled five meetings, and several were convinced. And after seven weeks and three days we left Solomon Eccles there and the rest of us sailed for Maryland. And in the gulf of Florida we met with some trials through winds and storms, but by the help of the Lord, whose presence and power was plenteously with us in six weeks and three days we landed safe in Maryland, where we met with John Burnyeat, ready to sail for old England, but we stayed with him and abode together there two General Meetings and then we parted, thy husband accompanied by John Burnyeat, Robert Widders, and George Pattison for New England by land, though very tedious through the wilderness; James Lancaster and John Cartwright went for New England by sea, and myself accompanied with three Friends sailed for Virginia, where things were much mangled and scattered; and indeed I had a blessed service amongst them, the Lord's presence going along, which cut a way through all. From thence I travelled to Roanoke, through all the desert country and through difficulties and trials, but the Lord gave ability; and I met with a tender people there and am in hopes there may be a people gathered there. And after seven weeks spent in those parts I sailed to Maryland and from thence to New York and had two good meetings there and several eminent people came. From thence I came through Long Island and visited Friends, and to Shelter Island, and there I met with thy dear husband again, and he was very well, I have not seen him more healthy and cheery for some years, of which we were all very glad. He was going back to Maryland and Virginia accompanied with Robert Widders, James Lancaster, and George Pattison; I parted with them there and they were all very well. I came from thence to Rhode Island, there met with John Stubbs, John Burnyeat, and John Cartwright. Of our service there whilst we were together, I suppose the inclosed from John Stubbs gives you an account. I parted with them at Rhode Island, they were going to Virginia.

After I parted from them I visited Friends in New England and to Boston, where I had two peaceable meetings, and from thence I took shipping and landed well in Ireland in three weeks and two days and am very well, blessed be the Lord.

So, dear Margaret, with my true love to thee and thine in the everlasting Truth, I rest thy true friend and brother,

William Edmondson.

We buried Elizabeth Hooton in Jamaica about a week after we landed there. Solomon Eccles came from Jamaica and landed at Boston, and was there taken at a meeting and banished to Barbados.

[s]So we came from Shelter Island on the 5th day of the 6th month [Aug.] and on the 7th we came to Oyster Bay in Long Island. And we had a very rough way on the waters and as we passed Plum Island there was a very great fog. And the tide did run so strong for several hours I have not seen the like. Though we had a gale we could hardly get forwards and when we were gotten through it there came a great rain all the night. Our sloop was open, we were very wet and were driven a great way back again, near to Fisher's Island, for it was very dark. And towards the day a great storm arose so that we were fain to go over the Sound, and got over with much ado. When we had gotten from Fisher's Island we passed by Falcon Island and came to the main, where we cast anchor till the storm was over.

And then we came over the Sound about ten leagues or thirty miles, all being very much wet, and hard work we had to get the land, the wind being against us. But, blessed be the Lord God of heaven and earth and of the sea and waters, all was well and we came to Oyster Bay in the night of the 6th day of the 6th month [Aug.]; about 200 miles

[s] Diary continued from p. 626.

from Rhode Island, as they say, but we came about and were tossed backward and forward many hundreds of miles.

And we had a very large meeting at Oyster Bay. James Lancaster and Christopher Holder went over the bay from Oyster Bay in Long Island and had a meeting the same day at Rye on the continent in Winthrop's[1] government.

From Oyster Bay we passed about thirty miles to Flushing. Christopher Holder and others went to Jamaica,[2] and had a meeting there. And the other Friends we left in New England, and some in Rhode Island and some other places in the service of the Truth which is very great. At many places where there were never meetings are now established meetings.

The 17th of 6th month [Aug.] we had a very large meeting at Flushing with many hundreds of the people of the world, some came about thirty miles. And a justice of the peace was there and his family, and many considerable persons were there. A glorious and heavenly meeting it was, praised be the Lord God, and the people much satisfied.

At Flushing as soon as the meeting was done, there stood up a priest's son and laid down three things that he would dispute, the first was the ordination of ministers, the second women's speaking, and the third that we held a new way of worship. And I spoke to him and demanded what he had against what I had spoken and he could say nothing. Then I said it was like Christ's way of worship which he set up above 1,600 years ago, and was a new way of worship to him and his priests, it being in the spirit and in the truth. And as for women's speaking, such as the apostles did own I owned, and such as they did deny I did deny.

But what was the priests of New England's ordination ? For we do deny them to be as the apostles, for they have not the same spirit as the apostles had, as some of themselves say.

But this priest's son said that their priests had the same spirit as the apostles had.

Then I said to him that they would have the same fruits,

[1] John Winthrop, Governor of Connecticut.

[2] In Long Island.

and the apostles' spirit did not lead them to cut off people's ears, and to hang and banish them, and imprison, and to spoil people's goods, as they, the priests of New England, had done.

And the priest's son said that their priests' ministry was as Judas's was and as old Eli's son had.

Then I told him, then must they have their end and reward.

And the priest's son said, for the proof of his priests, that they must go into all nations and preach and give the Supper.

And then I said, 'When did any of the priests of New England go into all nations and give them the Supper? For do they go any further than they can have a great or a fat benefice? Or shall people have any Paternoster without the penny?'

Then the priest's son said the priests were of the tribe of Levi.

Then I said that Christ had cut off that tribe of priests of Levi and changed it, and changed and ended the law by which it was made; and Christ came not of the tribe of Levi, but after the order of Melchizideck, and is called the Lion of the tribe of Judah, 'And so thou hast cut off all thy priests from being Gospel ministers to be such as deny Christ come in the flesh.'

And from thence we passed by Jamaica to Gravesend [Long Island] about twenty miles and there had a very precious meeting on the 20th of 6th month [Aug.]. And we left John Stubbs and John Burnyeat who did travel several hundreds of miles by land and did visit Governor Winthrop's government and his people, who had good service, and so to come by sea to Maryland. For I do intend to pass by land another way than we came. And we had three precious meetings at Gravesend, and then we waited for wind, for many would have come from [New] York, but the weather hindered them.

And when the wind served we came to the sloop, and many Friends came with us, where we took water for the new country, Jersey, down the great bay twenty-one miles and we were much toiled to get in our horses; and the 27th day of the 6th month [Aug.], we landed in the morning by break of the day, in the new country at Middletown Harbour. As we passed down the bay we passed by Coney Island, and by Naton Island,[1] and by Staten Island, and we came to Richard Hartshorne's. And on the 28th day we passed about thirty miles in the new country through the woods, very bad bogs, one worse than all, where we and our horses were fain to slither down a steep place, and then let them lie and pant, and breathe themselves, and they call this place Purgatory. And so we came to Shrewsbury in East Jersey,[2] and on the first day of the week, the 1st day of the 7th month [Sept.], we had a very large and a precious meeting; and the blessed presence of the Lord was with us. And in that place a Friend is made a justice. Friends and other people came far to this meeting. And on the 2nd day of the 7th month [Sept.], we had a men's and women's meeting, out of most parts of the new country Jersey, which will be of great service in keeping the gospel order and government of Christ Jesus (the increase of which hath no end) and for them to see that all do live in the pure religion and to walk as becometh the Gospel; and there is a Monthly and a General Meeting set up, and they are building a meeting-place in the midst of them. I passed about six miles to Porback a mile by water [t]to visit a Friend,[t] and came back again to Shrewsbury.

And there a Friend, John Jay of Barbados, that was with me went to try a horse, and got on his back. And the horse ran and cast him on his head [u]and broke his neck as they called it,[u] and the people took him up dead, and carried him a good way, and laid him on a tree. And I came to him and felt on him, and saw that he was dead, and as I was pitying his family and him, for he was one that was to pass with me through the woods to Maryland that land journey, I took him by the hair of his head, and his head turned like a cloth it was so loose. I threw away

[1] Now Governor's Island.

[2] Shrewsbury Meeting, settled 1670, was said to be the first Meeting in New Jersey.

[t]. . . . . .[t] *Camb. Jnl.*, ii, 226. [u]. . . . . .[u] *Camb. Jnl.*, ii, 227.

my stick and gloves, and took his head in both my hands, and set my knees against the tree and wrested[1] his head and I did perceive it was not broken out that way. And I put my hand under his chin, and behind his head, and wrested his head two or three times with all my strength, and brought it in, and I did perceive his neck began to be stiff, and then he began to rattle, and after to breathe, and the people were amazed, and I bid them have a good heart and be of good faith, and carry him into the house, and then they set him by the fire, and I bid them get him some warm thing to drink and get him to bed. So after he had been in the house awhile, he began to speak, and did not know where he had been. [v]So we bound up his neck warm with a napkin,[v] and the next day we passed on and he with us, pretty well, about sixteen miles to a meeting at Middletown, [w]and many hundreds of miles afterwards,[w] through the woods and bogs. And we swam our horses over a river, and went over on a tree ourselves. And at the meeting was most of the town. And Friends were and are very well, blessed be the Lord, and a glorious meeting we had and the Truth was over all, blessed be the great Lord God for ever.. And after the meeting we passed to Middletown harbour about five miles, on the 9th day of the 7th month [Sept.], to take our long journey through the woods towards Maryland. So we hired Indians, for it was upon me to pass through the woods on the other side Delaware Bay, to head the creeks and rivers if it were possible. So the 9th of the 7th month [Sept.], we set forward, and passed through many Indian towns, and rivers, and bogs, and at night made us a fire, and lay by it. When we had passed about forty miles among the Indians, we declared the day of the Lord to them, and the next day we passed fifty miles and found an old house, [w]which the Indians had forced the people to desert,[w] and got us

[1] The original diary has *wrested*, spelt *rasted*; other 17th-century copies and the first edition all have *raised*.

[v]. . . . . .[v] Bodleian MS.; *Jnl. F.H.S.*, ix, 16.

[w]. . . . . .[w] *Camb. Jnl.*, ii, 227.

some fire, at the head of Delaware Bay. And the next day we swam our horses over a river about a mile, at twice,[1] first to an island called Upper Tineconk[2] and then to the mainland, and hired Indians to help us over in their canoes, and our horses.

The 12th day of the 7th month [Sept.], this day we passed about thirty miles and came at night to a Swede's house, and got a little straw, and lay there all night. And there we hired another guide; and next day we travelled about forty miles through the woods and rivers, and made us a fire at night and lay in the woods. And we were continually wet on our feet [x]in our travels by day,[x] but we dried us by our fires at night. On the 14th day of the 7th month [Sept.], we passed over a desperate river of rocks and broad stones,[3] very dangerous to us and our horses; and from thence we came to Christian River[4] and swam over our horses, and it was bad and miry, some were like to have lain bogged there. We came over in canoes.

From thence we came to New Castle, called Delaware or New Amsterdam, sixteen miles, and being very weary in the streets and enquiring to buy some corn for our horses, the governor came in to the street and invited me to his house and to lodge there, and said that he had a bed for me and I was welcome. I went to his house on the Seventh-day of the week, and he proffered his house for a meeting, and so I had a meeting at his house the First-day, a precious one, blessed be the Lord, and pretty large. The heads of the town were there and most of the town, the governor and his wife, and the sheriff,[5] and the scout, who is a man of great esteem amongst them. Many men and women were tender and confessed to the Truth and received it, blessed be the Lord for ever, Amen. Here had never been a meeting before,

[1] In two stages.
[2] Now Matineconk.
[3] Probably Brandywine River.
[4] Probably Christiana Creek.
[5] Captain Edmund Cantrell was high-sheriff.
[x]. . . . . .[x] *Camb. Jnl.*, ii, 228.

not within a great way of it till now, [y]by any of our Friends.[y]

[z]The Indians at Delaware lay in wait to cut off some of our company as they passed that way, but their design was discovered, one being hanged at Delaware two or three days before we came thither. The Lord gave us power over all, blessed be his name for ever.[z]

On the 16th day of the 7th month [Sept.], we travelled about fifty miles in the woods and through the bogs, and headed Bohemia River and Sassafras River, and some of the branches of the above said rivers, and at night made us a fire and lay all night in the woods. And in the night it rained but we got under trees, and after dried us. On the 17th day we waded through Chester River, a great river. And this day we passed through many bad bogs, and made us a fire and lay in the woods, and went above thirty miles.

On the 18th day we passed through many tedious bogs, and travelled hard about fifty miles, and came well through the woods to Maryland, to Robert Harwood's at Miles River, very weary. The next day, the 19th of 7th month [Sept.], all being weary and dirty through the bogs, yet we went this day to a meeting about a mile or half by water. From thence we passed about three miles by land and one mile by water to John Edmondson's, and from thence on the 22nd day, three or four miles by water to the First-day's meeting. And a judge's wife was there who was never at our meeting before, and many others there who were well satisfied, and the power of the Lord was over all, blessed be his name for ever. And she said after the meeting she had rather hear this man once than the priests a thousand times, and she is convinced. Then I passed about twenty-two miles, and had a meeting upon the Kentish shore[1] and one of the burgesses was there at it. A Friend went to invite him to the meeting, and he said that he would go to hear Mr. Fox, as far as any of them that desired him,

[1] Kent County, Maryland.

[y]......[y] *Camb. Jnl.*, ii, 228. [z]......[z] *Camb. Jnl.*, ii, 250.

for he was a grounded man. And a good meeting we had at Henry Wilcock's house on the 26th day of 7th month [Sept.].

And on the 27th day we passed by water twenty miles to a meeting, very large, some hundreds of the world, and an establishing meeting it was, and there were four justices of the peace and an Indian emperor, and one of his great men, and another great man of another nation of Indians, and they stayed all the meeting. And I had a good speech with them the night before; and I spoke by an interpreter, and they received the Truth, and were very loving; and the emperor said he did believe that I was a very honest man.

Blessed be the Lord, his Truth doth spread.

And after the meeting was done, the wife of a judge of that side of the country, one of the Assembly, being at the meeting that day sent to speak with me and desired me to go with her, home to her house, for her husband was sick and not like to live; and it was three miles. And after the meeting I was hot, but I got a horse and went with her; and he was finely raised up and after came to our meetings. And then I came three miles back to the house, the man being much refreshed when I left him. And the high sheriff of Delaware and some others from thence were at the meeting that day; and a blessed one it was beyond words.

On the 30th we passed five miles by water and then about fourteen miles by land through the woods to John Edmondson's at Tred Avon[1] Creek. And on the 3rd day of the 8th month [Oct.], we came to the General Meeting of all Maryland Friends; and it held from the Sixth-day to the Third-day of the next week, which was five days, that is three days were the General Meetings for public worship, and two days the men's and women's meetings. And many of the world were at the public meetings, some

[1] John Edmondson lived at Cedar Point. Tred Avon is now corrupted to *Third Haven*, situate near the present town of Easton, Talbot County, Maryland.

Papists, clerks of their courts, and there were eight justices of the peace, and one of the judges and his wife, and another judge's wife, and many considerable persons of quality. And they judged that there was a thousand people; and one of the justices said, that he never saw so many people together in the country, though it was rainy weather. And Friends and people were generally satisfied and convinced, and the blessed power of the Lord was over all, and a great convincement there is, and a great inquiring after the Truth among all sorts of people, and the Truth is of a good report and Friends are much established, and the world convinced. They said they had never heard the Scriptures so clearly opened before, for said they, 'He hath them at his fingers' ends, and as a man should read them in a book and hold it open before him.' And the people were satisfied beyond words, and a glorious powerful meeting there was, blessed be the Lord for ever. And when the General Meeting was done, we had some of all the choice of the men and women to meet together for I had something to inform them concerning the glory of God, and the order of the Gospel and the government of Christ Jesus and concerning the great meeting. I went every day by boat to the meeting, about four or five miles. And there was never seen there so many boats together. ⟨And one of the justices said⟩ it was almost like the Thames. There was one whose place is above a justice of the peace, a great man, he was much taken with the Truth, was at most of the meetings, and many others would have been there, but there was a general court that did prevent, [aa]and take up their time,[aa] and some of them sent a man to me, to know where they might come to hear me. Some of them were judges and justices. And there was never such a meeting the people said in Maryland, they had of late made the meeting place as big again as heretofore, and yet it would not hold them.

And on the 10th day of the 8th month [Oct.], we passed thence about thirty miles by water, by Cranes Island, and

[aa]......[aa] *Camb. Jnl.*, ii, 230.

by Swan Island, and by Kent Island, and we had very much rain and foul weather, in an open boat, insomuch that when we came [bb]on shore early the next morning[bb] to a house, one of the world said that he did think we had been cast away and did intend to go look for us in the morning; but blessed be the Lord we were very well. The season was very wet, and so we lay most of us by the fire in a little house, where we dried us. And the 11th day we had very foul weather, and sometimes we rowed and sometimes we sailed, and did not get above twelve miles, and at night we got to the land, and made us a fire, and some lay by it, and some lay by the fire in a house a little way off.

And the 12th day of the 8th month [Oct.], we sailed again and passed over the bay,[1] and passed by Swan Island. And this day we passed about forty miles, and in the night we came to an alehouse, and there lay on a bed; and some lay in the boat. And the 13th day we passed about six or seven miles to a Friend's house, who is a justice of the peace, where we had a meeting that day, it being the First-day of the week. And this place was a little above the head of the great bay, so we were almost four days on the water. And all were very well but weary with rowing, blessed and praised be the Lord. The 14th day of the 8th month [Oct.] we passed by water about seven miles to a Friend's house near the head of Hattons Island, and had service among Friends and others. And from thence we passed by water three miles to George Wilson's to a meeting: a precious one it was. And it was a place where the priest did wont to preach. And a great tenderness there was amongst the people. And from thence after the meeting we sailed and rowed about ten miles to James Frisby's, a justice of the peace. The next day being the 16th of the 8th month [Oct.], we had a very large meeting, which was a blessed, heavenly, powerful, and thundering one, and there were three justices of peace at it, and the under sheriff, and two that were captains, and many other persons of

[1] Chesapeake Bay.

[bb]......[bb] *Camb. Jnl.*, ii, 231.

quality and some Papists. And all went away satisfied, and the high sheriff came to the house. A great sense there was among the people, and some hundreds were at the meeting, and a great brokenness and tenderness there was. And after the meeting was done we stayed till about the 11th hour in the night, till the tide turned and was for us, and then we went and took boat and passed that night and the next day by water about fifty miles to a Friend's house the 17th day. The 18th day some of us passed by land and water about five miles, being the nearest way, and other of our company went about with our boat to Friends. And on the 19th day we passed three miles by water and two miles by land to a Friend's house, and thence about three miles by water to a great meeting at Severn;[1] and the meeting place would not hold the people by many. And it was a blessed and a heavenly one; there were three justices of the peace, and the Speaker of the Assembly[2] his wife, and many considerable people, and the people came generally to it, and were much satisfied, the 20th day of the 8th month [Oct.]. And on the 22nd day we had a meeting with some people that walked disorderly. And after, we came about eight miles by water down the bay in the night to a Friend's house. And on the 23rd day we passed by water eight miles. And on the 24th we passed by water nine miles to the Western Shore, and on the 25th day we had a precious and glorious meeting, and large, at William Coale's; and the Speaker of the Assembly was there and his wife, and another justice of the peace, and several people of quality. And on the 26th day of the 8th month [Oct.], we had a meeting [cc]six or seven miles further[cc] at Abraham Birkhead's[3] in his tobacco-house. There were two of their assembly-men, the Speaker was one, who is convinced; and a blessed meeting it was, and a

[1] Now Annapolis.

[2] Thomas Notley was then the Speaker of the Lower House of the Maryland Assembly.

[3] Birkhead is said to have lived at Herring Creek.

[cc]......[cc] *Camb. Jnl.*, ii, 232.

heavenly one, praised be the Lord, and there were many people of account. And on the 28th day we had a meeting at Peter Sharpe's on the Cliffs, a very large one and a precious and heavenly one it was, and there were three or four justices of the peace, and one out of Virginia who is convinced, and since hath had a meeting at his house. And the wife of one of the governor's Council is convinced; and her husband is loving, and many people of account and of the world were very well satisfied. And some Papists were there, and merchants, and this meeting was between thirty and forty miles from the other. Blessed be the Lord, the Truth is reached in the hearts of people beyond words, and it is of a good report in the hearts of people. A great Papist there threatened before, that he would dispute with G.F. but when he came he was reached and then said that G.F. was a notable man and would shake the foundations of them that were not established. And then after the meeting we came about eighteen miles to James Preston's on Patuxent. We passed about 300 miles, and as many down from the Capes, besides crossing it and the many rivers and creeks. And at James Preston's there came an Indian king and his brother, and I spoke and they did understand the thing. And on the 4th of the 9th month [Nov.], we had a large meeting at Patuxent at the meeting place, and many of the world were there of all sorts, and a powerful meeting it was.

[Here begins Fox's second American travel diary. The MS. is headed *James Lancaster's book, 1673, made in Virginia that part called Maryland*, of which the first three words and the date are in Fox's own hand.]

And on the 5th day of the 9th month [Nov.], being the Third-day of the week, we[1] set sail towards Virginia, and the 6th day we rowed and sailed about eighty miles. The weather being stormy, and wind and fog and rain, at night we put to the shore; and in the woods we made us a

[1] Fox's companions were Robert Widders, James Lancaster, and George Pattison.

fire with much ado, all things being wet, and there stayed all the night by it. And the next day in the morning, we went on the water, and sailed all the day, and at the night, being very dark and much rain, we came to a ship that came from Plymouth, and there I with some Friends stayed all that night, and some lay in our sloop, and when it was day we got into our sloop, and sailed till we came to Nancemond, and there went on shore to a Friend's house, the widow Wright's, about 200 miles, as they account, from Patuxent, the 7th of 9th month [Nov.]. And on the 10th day at Nancemond there was a great meeting of Friends and people; and there came Colonel Thomas Dewes and a justice and a captain with other officers, and many of account, and they were much taken with the Truth.

And the 12th day we passed over the water called Nancemond and went about four miles by land, where we had a precious meeting, and men's and women's meetings settled. And from thence we passed twelve miles and boated over a creek called Pagan's Creek to William Yarrow's house, and on the 17th day we had a very large meeting and two justices of the peace and their wives; and a lieutenant-colonel's wife was there. We were put to meet without the doors, for there were so many people, and a great openness in them to receive the Truth, and after the meeting was done we passed by water about a mile and, ten miles by land to one Thomas Jordan's house[1] and there came an old man, a justice, to a Friend, and said that George Fox was a very famous man, the noise of the Truth did sound abroad in the hearts of people, the Lord have the glory for ever. And the 18th day we passed about eight miles to the Western Branch, where we met with Friends and [dd]we were refreshed in one another's company.[dd] And on the 19th day we passed about thirty miles through the woods towards Carolina, and a flashy and a wet way, and at the night we came to a place called Somerton, to a poor house, and there we found a woman that had a sense

[1] At Chuckatuck, Nancemond Co., Virginia.
[dd] . . . . . . [dd] Bodleian MS.; *Jnl. F.H.S.*, ix, 23.

of God, and most of us lay by the fire all the night and it was very cold. And the next day we passed all the day, and saw neither house nor man through the woods, and swamps, and many cruel bogs and watery places, that we were wet to the knees most of us, and at the night we took up our lodging in the woods and made us a fire, all of us being weakly horsed. Some people beyond Somerton had heard of me, and had been at the house where we lay, and had a great desire to hear and see us, but missed us. The Truth sounds abroad every way, ⟨so acceptable was the sound of Truth in that wilderness country⟩. This is the 20th of the 9th month [Nov.].

And the next day we passed through the woods, and over many bogs and swamps, and at the night we came to Bonner's Creek,[1] and there we lay. And the woman of the house lent us a mat, and we lay on it by the fire-side and this was the first house in Carolina. We came the 21st of the 9th month [Nov.]; and there we left our horses, all being very weary.

And the 22nd day we passed in a canoe down the creek to Macocomocock River[2] and came to Hugh Smithwick's house, about a mile and a half; and the people of the world came to see us, for there were no Friends in those parts. And many people of the world did receive us gladly, and they came to us at one Nathaniel Batts, formerly Governor of Roanoke, who goeth by the name of Captain Batts, who hath been a rude desperate man [ee]who hath a great command over the country, especially over the Indians.[ee] He came to us and said that a captain told him that in Cumberland G.F. bid one of his friends go to a woman that had been sick a long time, and all the physicians had left her, and could not heal her, and G.F. bid his friend to lay his hands upon her and pray by her; and G.F.'s friend did go to the woman, and did as he bad him, and

[1] Or Bennett's Creek.
[2] Now Chowan River.
[ee]......[ee] Bodleian MS.; *Jnl. F.H.S.*, ix, 24.

the woman was healed that time. And this Captain Batts told me and had spread it up and down among the people in the country, and he asked me of it and I said many things had been done by the power of Christ. On the 24th day of the 9th month [Nov.], we had a meeting among the world's people, and there were no Friends in that side on the country, and the people were taken with the Truth, blessed be the Lord.

And from thence, we passed on the 25th of the 9th month [Nov.], down the River Maratick[1] in a canoe, and went down Cone-oak Bay[2] to a captain's house who was loving, and lent us his boat, for we were much wet in the canoe, the water came upon us in waves; and in that boat from thence we came to the governor's[3] house; but the boat being deep and the water shoal that our boat would not swim, I was fain to put off my shoes and stockings and wade through the water a pretty way to the governor's house, who with his wife received us lovingly. And there was a doctor that did dispute with us, which was of great service and occasion of opening much to the people concerning the Light and the Spirit. And he so opposed it in every one, that I called an Indian because he denied it to be in them, and I asked him if that he did lie and do that to another which he would not have them do the same to him, and when he did wrong was not there something in him, that did tell him of it, that he should not do so, but did reprove him. And he said there was such a thing in him when he did any such a thing that he was ashamed of them. So we made the doctor ashamed in the sight of the governor and the people; and he ran so far out that he would not own the Scriptures. And the next morning we passed away and sent our boat about, and the governor went afoot two miles through the woods with us, and set us in our way to the boat. And on the 26th day of the 9th month [Nov.] we came to one Joseph Scott's

1 Now Roanoke River.
2 Now Edenton Bay, North Carolina.
3 Probably Peter Carteret, who lived at Edenton.

house by Perquimans River, who was one of the burgesses of the country, and this was about thirty miles by water.

And now they say we are 1,000 miles from Boston southward, they that have travelled it; all which we have travelled by land, and down bays, and over rivers, and creeks, and bogs, and wildernesses. At the first house we came to in Carolina we met with an Indian king, a pretty, sober man. The Truth spreadeth, and as we passed down, we passed by Batts Island and by Kickwold Youpen, and Perquimans River, where there are some friendly people, and where we had a meeting at Joseph Scott's house who is one of their burgesses. And many of the people were there, and were tender, and a sound precious meeting there was, blessed be the Lord; and the people much desired after meetings. And on the 28th day of the 9th month [Nov.] we passed by water four miles to Henry Phillips's[1] house, and at the meeting there was the governor's secretary, who is secretary of the province, which formerly had been convinced. On the 29th day of the 9th month [Nov.], I went among the Indians. Their young king and others of their chief men were very loving, and received what I said to them. And I showed them how that God made all things in six days, and made but one man and a woman and how that God did drown the old world, because of their wickedness, and so along to Christ, and how that he did die for all and for their sins, and did enlighten them; and if they did do evil he would burn them, and if they did well, they should never be burned. ⟨Now having visited the north part of Carolina and made a little entrance for Truth upon the people there, we began to return towards Virginia.⟩ Then I went back about two miles by water and land to the house that I came from. The 1st of the 10th month [Dec.], we went down by water five miles, and I was fain to put off my shoes and stockings, and so did the rest, and waded through the water, it was so shoal that the boat could not go. And there this day we had a blessed meeting, and a large one,

[1] Henry Phillips (Phelps) lived by Perquimans River.

and several of the Indians were there and their wives, and some of their great men of the king's council, and one that is to be king, and they were very tender and loving, and so were all people. After the meeting I passed by land and water about five or six miles to Joseph Scott's, where we had a day of washing [ff]and sweeping of some that had defiled themselves.[ff] On the 2nd day of the 10th month [Dec.], we passed by water about five miles, and I lay by the fire on a mat all the night; and the next day we had a glorious and a precious meeting, and pretty large for that country. And after the meeting we passed away to the secretary's house, ten miles by water, and we were very wet, it being much rain, and in a rotten boat very dangerous. [gg]The water being shallow we could not get the boat to the shore,[gg] and the secretary's wife came in a canoe, barefooted and barelegged, to get us to land out of our boat, and so we stayed at their house all that night. And the next day in the morning, our boat was sunk and full of water, and we [hh]turned out the water and[hh] mended her, and that day we passed about twenty-four miles, the sea being troublesome and rough and the winds high; but the great power of God was seen in carrying us in that rotten boat. So we left our boat where we had borrowed her, and took our canoe and came to Captain Batts, and there we lay most of us by the fire that night. And after, we came half a mile to Hugh Smithwick's, and on the 8th day we had a precious meeting, praised be the Lord God for ever. And there was the Indian priest ⟨whom they call a powaw⟩[1] sat among the people of the world, and the people were very tender and desirous after Truth and there came an Indian captain, and was very loving, and did confess to the Truth which was spoken to him, and with many others we had good service. And after the meeting was done we passed about half a mile by water

[1] i.e. Medicine-man.

[ff]. . . . .[ff] *Camb. Jnl.*, ii, 236, and Bodleian MS., *Jnl. F.H.S.*, ix, 26.

[gg]. . . . .[gg] *Camb. Jnl.*, ii, 236.

[hh]. . . . .[hh] Bodleian MS.; *Jnl. F.H.S.*, ix, 26.

to a sober man's house where I lay all the night on a couch.

And the 9th day of the 10th month [Dec.], we passed by water about half a mile in a canoe to Bonner's, where our horses were, and then we passed through the woods and bogs towards Virginia, ⟨having spent a matter of eighteen days in the north of Carolina⟩. In that country as in Carolina they keep many great dogs, and as we came to a house, there was a woman of the world said to her son that he might keep up their dogs, but her son replied that they did not use to meddle with us. When we were come to the house she said to us before others that we were like to the children of Israel whom the dogs did not move their tongues against.

So we passed all the day through the woods and bogs, and sometimes in to the knees, and at the night we made us a fire to lie by, and dried us. And the next day we passed through the woods and bogs and were sorely wet and flashed in them and so travelled all the day, and at night we came to Somerton, for we had a sore journey through the bogs and were all dirty and wet all the day. And at night we dried us, it was fair over head, and that night lay by the fire all night in our clothes, as we had done many nights before. And the next day we had a precious meeting, for the people of that country had heard of me and us and had a great desire to hear me, and so we had a good meeting among them (where never was any before), praised be the Lord for ever. And after the meeting was done, we passed in the woods about twenty miles, and in the night we came to a sober man's house to query the way, and they desired us to stay all night, which we did, and the next day we passed away about eight miles. And the 12th day we came among Friends [ii]at Nancemond[ii] when we had travelled about 100 miles from Carolina to Virginia to Friends through the woods. We passed so far till the country was warm and a-spring, and from a warm country thence to a cold country and very cold. But the power of the Lord is over

[ii]. . . . .[ii] Bodleian MS.; *Jnl. F.H.S.*, ix, 27.

all, and it doth reach the good in all, praised be the Lord for ever. [jj]At Newport News we bought provision, where we were almost frozen and starved in the woods for three or four nights, our provision short.[jj] And the 13th day we came two miles by land and six miles by water to widow Wright's—about 200 miles going and coming to Carolina besides what we passed in that country—and on the 15th day we had a very large meeting and precious and reverent with a heavenly dread, praised be the Lord. And all was chained, for the priest had threatened to a major who was his kinsman that he would be there; and the major told him that I would convince him, but the power of the Lord is over all; and his Seed of life stopped him. And the major was at the meeting and the high sheriff of the county, and another major and a justice, and many people of quality, and all were reached with the Truth, blessed be the Lord. And there was a woman so reached that she said, 'He is a worthy man and worthy to be heard.' And on the 16th day we passed sixteen miles by water to the widow Norton's, and on the 17th day we passed twelve miles by water, and two by land to a meeting at Crickatrough and a precious and blessed one it was. And there were many considerable people, and they were much refreshed, praised be the Lord, and many people that never had heard before. And many others would have been there, and several justices and their wives, but there being much rain hindered. The house was full and one justice's wife was there, a tender woman. After meeting we returned back again; and on the 18th day we passed about twenty miles by water, and rowed [kk]part of the way[kk] against tide and wind and we passed by Kiketan, and in the night came to Elizabeth River, where we went on shore and called up the people at a house, where we lodged that night, some lay by the fireside and some on a bed in our clothes, and it was so cold, that I felt no warmth by my lodging. And the 19th day we passed up a branch of Elizabeth River and at night came to a Friend's house whose name is

[jj]. . . . .[jj] *Camb. Jnl.*, ii, 250. [kk]. . . . .[kk] *Camb. Jnl.*, ii, 238.

John Porter,[1] when we had rowed about ten miles. And on the 22nd day we had a meeting, a very precious and glorious one, very living and fresh, and most of them of the world, and it brought the Truth above all bad walkers and talkers, blessed be the Lord.

And on the 23rd day we passed to a Friend's house, being the farthest in Virginia. And two Friends went to a justice's house to visit him, who was very loving and very tender to Friends. Then we returned back again being two miles, and the 24th day we passed by water about twelve miles up Elizabeth River to a Friend's house, and the 25th day we passed by water six miles to a Friend's house called Thomas Goode where we had service. And on the 28th day we came about four miles where we had a meeting pretty large. Now this last week we were among Friends ‖where some bad spirits had entered and we were‖ sweeping away that which should not be, and working down the bad spirit; but blessed for ever be the name of the Lord, who over all gives victory. And there in this county they said the high Sheriff had an order to take me; but I met him by chance, and he took me by the hand and was very civil and courteous. And we passed about six miles by land and water to take in Friends for Maryland.

On the 30th day we passed towards Maryland, and had a very great storm. And being very much wet we got to land, and went about two miles to a house at Willoughby's Point, where we lodged all that night. The woman of the house was a very tender widow woman of the world, received us with tears kindly. And the next day we passed the two miles back again through the woods and by the seaside to our boat, and sailed on. But the storm and wind being high, towards evening we had much ado to get to the shore, and our boat being open the water flashed in and over, and when we had got to the shore, we made us a fire to warm us, and there lay by it all that night in the woods, and the wolves roaring about us.

[1] John Porter, pioneer colonist, of Norfolk Co., Virginia.

‖. . . . . .‖ Bodleian MS.; *Jnl. F.H.S.*, ix, 28.

The 1st day of the 11th month [Jan., 1673] we sailed, but the wind being against us we sailed backwards and forwards and we got to the shore called Point Comfort ⟨where yet we found but small comfort⟩ and got to the wood and made us a fire, and lay by it all night. It was so cold that it froze our water that we had got by the fire-side. And on the 2nd of the 11th month we came up with a sloop that came from Barbados, on which sloop I had letters from Judge Fretwell. The sloop being laid up as we were, for the wind was contrary, we went by land backwards about ten miles to look for a house to buy some provisions. And we lay in the woods this night, it being very cold; and it snew and blew so that it was hard for some to abide it. And on the 3rd day of the 11th month [Jan.], the wind was pretty fair, and we passed on our way, sailing and rowing. That night we lay in Milford Haven at Richard Long's near Quince's Island, the weather being very cold. I lay on a bed in my clothes. And on the 4th day of the 11th month [Jan.], we passed by Rappahannock River, where there is much people, and Friends had a meeting thereaways at a justice's house, that had been with me at a meeting, and were refreshed, and we passed Potomac River, and thataways, and there came some people of the world to meeting and were convinced, and some of our company went among them. And when we parted thence, we passed over Potomac and the water was very rough, and the sea high and our sloop open, and the weather cold. I was moved to sit at the helm most part of the day and night. And about the first hour in the night we came to James Preston's in Patuxent River which is about 200 miles from Nancemond in Virginia and very weary we were. And the next day being the First-day of the week, the 5th day of 11th month [Jan.], we went to the meeting, about half a mile, all being weary, having been tossed by the water, with hard lodging in the woods. And on the 7th of 11th month [Jan.] I went to an Indian king's cabin about a mile from our lodging, where we met with several Indians and they were loving. And on the 9th of the 11th month

[Jan.], we went to a General Meeting, about a mile backwards and forwards, and from thence we passed eighteen miles to John Gary's[1] and had a precious meeting. And the 12th day the weather was very cold, so that the people could hardly endure, frost and snowy weather as hath not been a great while, it was so deep. All this week we are kept in it, and travelled not, only two miles, I went one on foot, and the other on horseback. And on the 19th day we had a precious meeting, praised be the Lord God for ever; and the 22nd of 11th month [Jan.], the frost and snow kept us so in that there was hardly any stirring, though we rode through it six miles to John Mayor's house and six miles back again, where Friends from New England, whom we left behind, came to us. And glad we were to see them, after our long travels. In New England they left John Veres who took ship for Jamaica, and William Edmondson for Ireland, and Solomon Eccles and Nicholas Alexander for Jamaica and Barbados and the rest of the Leeward Islands, and John Stubbs and John Baker among Friends in New Jersey the new country. And Nathaniel Milner died in one of the Leeward Islands, where he had done good service for the Lord.

And on the 27th day we had a precious and a glorious meeting in a tobacco house. And it was very cold weather; yet one day, in the midst of the cold a gust of hot weather broke out so hot we could hardly abide for heat, and the next night and day for cold. And we passed eighteen miles to James Preston's, whose house was burned, where we left our boxes and our things. And when we came my great chest was burned, and James Lancaster's and some other Friends' things, and all the clothes in our chests burned, and the house burned to the ground, by means of a careless wench. And there we lay three nights by the fire on the ground, being very cold weather. And the 30th day of the 11th month [Jan.], we passed three miles, and the creek being frozen up, the next day we came three miles back. And the next day we went two miles [mm]and

[1] John Gary lived at the Cliffs in Md.

endeavoured to pass at another creek, but that was also frozen up.[mm]

And the 2nd day of 12th month [Feb.], we had a glorious meeting at Patuxent, at the meeting place half a mile from the house, and after it was done we passed about eighteen miles to John Gary's where we do wait for a boat.

And on the 6th day of the 12th month [Feb.] was the Monthly Meeting at the Cliffs, a living one, praised be the Lord, and on the 9th day of the 12th month [Feb.], we had a glorious meeting and the glory of the Lord shined over all, blessed be his name for ever, Amen. And on the 12th day of the 12th month [Feb.], we passed by water in an open boat about seventy miles, and most of it was in the night. And they ran her on the ground near Manoco[1] River in a creek. And the weather being bitter and very cold with hard frost, some had like to have lost the use of their hands, they were so frozen and benumbed; but in the morning, when the tide came we got to land and made us a fire to warm us, and then we came to the water to our boat again and passed about ten miles and came to a Friend's house. And on the 14th day we had a very precious meeting, one of the justices and a justice's wife were there, and when the meeting was done I passed four miles by land to a justice's house in Annamessicks,[2] that is near the head of Annamessicks River and on the 15th day the judge of the county came to me and was very loving and much satisfied with Friends' order; and they did desire that the same might be spoken again there. And on the 16th day we had a large and a precious meeting at a justice's in his barn; the house would not hold them. And the people were much taken with Truth. And the clerk of the county and another justice's wife and one that had been a justice were there, and an opposer, but all was quiet, blessed be the Lord. And on the 17th day we passed eight miles to a captain's house who is a justice, whose name is

[1] Manokin, Somerset Co., Maryland.

[2] In Somerset Co., Maryland.

[mm]......[mm] Bodleian MS.; *Jnl. F.H.S.*, ix, 30.

William Colebourne, where we had service. And on the 19th we passed about nine miles among Friends and on the 20th day of the 12th month [Feb.], we had a very precious and a glorious meeting at the same justice's house before mentioned. And there were many people of account, the judge of that country and the captain and the high sheriff of last year and the head secretary at whose house the priest preached. And they were all much taken with the Truth and a large meeting it was and the Lord's power was much seen, and there were four New England men, masters of ships and merchants; the Truth spreads, blessed be the Lord.

And on the 22nd we passed through the woods and bogs about sixteen miles and we headed Annamessicks River and we headed Amoroca River and went over part of it in a canoe and a man got our horses over and we came to Manoco to a friendly woman's house, and on the 24th day we had a glorious meeting in a barn and the Lord's living presence was with us and among the people, blessed be his name for evermore. And there was never a meeting before in that part of the country. And on the 26th day of the 12th month [Feb.], we passed about nine miles and passed in a boat over a great river called Wicomico,[1] to a Friend's house called James Jones who is a justice. And on the 27th of the 12th month [Feb.], we had a very glorious meeting at James Jones's, and large, praised be the Lord God for ever, Amen. And on the 28th of the 12th month [Feb.], we passed over the water in a boat and carried our horses over in it and rode through the woods and swamps and creeks a tedious way, by water about twenty-four miles to a justice's house where we had a precious meeting. And John Cartwright went with another Friend[2] to Accomack in Virginia where there were desires after the Truth.

And on the 3rd day of the 1st month [Mar., 1673] we had a precious and a glorious meeting and the living

[1] On the Eastern Shore, of Chesapeake Bay.

[2] John Jay.

presence of the Lord was amongst us, praised be the Lord. And there were many people of an account and some came far to it, and it was at the justice's house as before; and the judge and the captain came to it and there were three justices' wives and many others of an account and a very large meeting it was. And after the meeting was done we passed four miles to a Friend's house. And there was a woman at Annamessicks who had been many years in trouble and would sometimes sit moping two months together and hardly speak, nor mind any thing. So I was moved to go to her and tell her that salvation was come to her house and did speak other words to her and for her; and that hour she mended and passed up and down with us to meetings and is well, blessed be the Lord. And on the 5th of the 3rd month we had a heavenly and a living meeting at Annamessicks and there were two justices of the peace and their wives and many others—blessed be the Lord God over all, whose truth is over all and doth rule. And now we are clear we wait for wind.

We went from Annamessicks on the 7th of the 1st month [Mar.], and passed by water about fifty miles and came to Hunger River, to a friendly woman's house. And in our passage the weather was something rough, and the jybing of the sails over the boat struck off my hat and cap. And we had like to have turned the boat over, but at the last we got them again with much ado. And on the 10th day of the 1st month [Mar.], we had a meeting where never was any before, and two Papists were at it. The man was very tender and the woman confessed to the Truth. And many others would have been there but the weather was very rough, and rain and snow, that they could not get over the water. Two justices of the peace and their wives had a desire to have been there but they were hindered. And now we do wait for the wind, it being against us, and the weather foul; and none is with me but Robert Widders: all the rest are abroad in their service.

On the 14th day we passed about forty miles by water and rowed most part of the way, and in the night came to the head of Little Choptank River, to Doctor Winsmore's, a justice of the peace, who was lately convinced, where we met with Friends. And from thence we passed two miles by land, and he lent me his horse and went afoot to guide me the way through the woods to one William Stephens. And on the 16th day of the 1st month [Mar.], we passed by water about four miles to a meeting, which was without the doors, the house being too little. And a justice and the judge of that county and their wives were there and many people, blessed be the Lord who is making his name known.

And on the 18th day of the 1st month [Mar.], we passed four miles by water to a Friend's house, William Stephens, where Friends met that had been abroad; and on the same day we went a mile or two and visited some Friends. On the 23rd day of the 1st month [Mar.], we had a glorious meeting, blessed be the Lord for ever, and an established and a settled one. And the judge of that country and his wife and three other officers, justices, were at it, and the high sheriff and his wife were there and the Indian emperor and another Indian king and their speaker. And all were very loving and sat all the meeting.

And John Cartwight and John Jay are gone towards Barbados; and he[1] had a good savour in Accomack. Several justices and colonels and lieutenant-colonels received him and were very loving to him. And he had several meetings among them and Truth spreads, blessed be the Lord God for ever.

And on the 24th of the 1st month [Mar.], we went by water ten miles to the Indian town where the heathen emperor of them dwells. And I had sent to him before that he should send for the rest of their kings and their council. And the emperor came himself in the morning and had me to the town, and they came together generally and their head speaker with them and their other officers, and the old empress that sat in their council with them. They were very attentive and sober and loving and sat all

[1] In this paragraph Fox is referred to in the third person.

the meeting, grave and soberly beyond many. I had two of the justices of the peace and some others with me to interpret; and it was of great service and we had a very good meeting with them, blessed be the Lord for ever, Amen.

On the 25th day of the 1st month [Mar.], we went five miles by land, and a justice of peace helped to row us over a broad creek called Fisher's Creek in a canoe to a Dutchman's house, a Friend. And on the 26th day we went back again five miles through the woods, being very wet under foot, and on the 27th day we had a blessed meeting and large at William Stephens's, at Great Choptank, where were four justices of the peace and the judge of the country and a justice of another court and the high sheriff of the county, a Papist, and his wife. And it was a general monthly meeting and there were many people of an account, blessed be the Lord whose fresh power is plenteous among his people.

And when the meeting was done we went by water about four miles and about one by land to a Friend's house; and on the 28th day we passed about by land fourteen miles to Tred Avon Creek. And on the 30th day we had a glorious meeting and it was very precious and we passed by land and water six miles and came to Miles River[1] and then about sixteen miles forward and backward to Wye River and crossed over a branch in a boat and back in a canoe. And on the 1st of 2nd month [Apr.], at Wye we had a very precious meeting, blessed be the Lord. And the judge of that country and his wife were there and they were very tender. And many other people. Thereaways the Truth is of a good savour. Upon the 3rd of 2nd month [Apr.], we passed about six miles by water and five by land to Tred Avon River and came back again to Reconow Creek where we left our boat, and had there a glorious meeting at a Friend's house where the glory of the Lord did shine over all to the edifying of people, and it was large, praised be the Lord for ever, Amen. And on the 4th of the

[1] St. Michael's River.

2nd month [Apr.], we passed by water fourteen miles, and two by land on foot, to the Island of Kent, and on the 6th day of 2nd month [Apr.], we had a precious meeting at Kent at Thomas Taylor's. Many more would have been there but the rain hindered them. And on the 7th day of 2nd month [Apr.], we went over a creek in a boat, and about a mile by land, to a Friend's house and on the 8th day of 2nd month [Apr.], we passed in a boat over the Bay to the Western Shore about fourteen miles to a Friend's house where we met with [nn]some of our Friends that we had parted from before, that had been abroad in service;[nn] and I sent for Thomas Thurston,[1] to bring the Truth over his actions, and had meetings with him.

And on the 9th day of 2nd month [Apr.], I went about seven miles to the speaker of the Assembly's house, who is the judge of that country, who had much desired me before, and he and his wife are very loving. And on the 10th day of 2nd month [Apr.], we had a very living meeting, blessed be the Lord forever; it was in a school house and there were several people of account, a judge's wife and one of the Council's wife and one of the Assembly were there, and very loving; the glory of the Lord and his Truth is over all. And on the 11th day we passed by water about thirty miles down the bay to a Friend's house on The Cliffs.

[This is the end of the original MS. travel diaries. At the end in George Fox's hand are the words *To the Capes of Virginia of our travels 12873 miles.* The narrative is now continued from the Spence MS., *Camb. Jnl.*, ii, 245.]

On the 20th day of 2nd month [Apr.], we had a meeting at Patuxent meeting place, about a mile over a creek from our Friend's house where we lodged; and this week we had much writing and answering, and on the 27th day we went a mile to meeting and the heavenly presence was felt among us, glory to the Lord for ever, Amen. And on the 28th of the 2nd month [Apr.], I passed over the creek in a canoe,

[1] Extravagant spiritual claims put him out of unity with Friends.
[nn]......[nn] Bodleian MS.; *Jnl. F.H.S.*, ix, 34.

and thence to Leonard's Creek about three miles to see for a ship °°to take our passage for England.°°

And on the 29th we went down a creek called Hopper's Creek two miles in a boat; and on the 30th day I had a good speech with an Indian that could speak English and their king was by. And on the 1st of the 3rd month [May], I went a mile to an Indian's cabin where the king and his company were and stayed awhile with them and returned, and on the 4th of 3rd month [May], we had a very precious meeting and to it we went about a mile. And on the 5th day we passed through the woods about eight miles and on the 6th we passed ten miles, and at night had a precious meeting at the house that was Peter Sharpe's, and on the 8th of 3rd month [May], there came one of the governor's council to a house where I was and I had discourse with him; he is a great Papist. He was civil but dark, in Egypt.

On the 11th of 3rd month [May], we had a glorious meeting at The Cliffs, and on the 15th day there came a justice from Potomac in Virginia, a pretty man, and had been under persecution and threatened by the priest and others. He and his man came forty miles on foot; he hath a great love to the Truth. On the 15th day we passed through the woods about twenty-two miles; and on the 16th we passed about thirteen miles. On the 17th day began the General Meeting of the province of Maryland,[1] which held four days. The first day were the men's and women's meetings where we discoursed about the affairs of the Church of God. On the 18th and 19th days was the general public meeting and a wonderful and glorious meeting it was and the mighty presence of the Lord over all was seen, blessed and praised be his name for ever, Amen. And there were two of the governor's council and their wives and two of the Assembly and their wives and two justices of the peace and many considerable people of account, and all were very much reached and satisfied and parted in the life and power of the Lord. And

[1] This General Meeting was held at Petty's Cove on Miles River.

°°......°° Bodleian MS.; *Jnl. F.H.S.*, ix, 35.

the Lord's power is over all, blessed be his name for ever who over all giveth dominion. So after the meeting was done, we in the power of the Lord parted and passed away and went by water and land fifty miles, and at the night the boat came for us, to carry us to the ship; so we went on ship-board[1] and many Friends went down with us in another boat. The ship is called the *Society of Bristol*.[2] It was the 21st day that we came on ship-board, and many Friends stayed with us all the night. And on the 22nd day of the 3rd month [May] we drew anchor and sailed but about one mile to Point Patience PPand there cast anchor, the wind being against us. And there came on board us a doctor, a man of note and esteem, who did acknowledge and confess to the Truth and said he had never heard G.F. before. On the 23rd we drew anchor again and sailed about one mile more; and on the 24th drew anchor again and sailed about six or seven miles near Cedar Point, and there cast anchor again.PP This day came Richard Covell on our ship; his ship was taken from him by the Dutch. On the 25th day we drew anchor again and set sail down the bay. It being the First-day of the week we had a very precious meeting on board the ship. And towards night we cast anchor in the bay, the wind being against us; and on the 26th of the 3rd month [May], we drew anchor and sailed over against Potomac River, and the wind being against us we cast anchor again.

On the 27th day in the morning the wind came pretty fair, then we drew anchor and set sail and sailed over Potomac River which is about twenty miles; and by the Point called Little Wicomico we lay at anchor again, and the 28th day we drew anchor and sailed again till night, then cast anchor again. The weather being foul and the wind against us, we lay near Great Wicomico and the 29th day we drew anchor and sailed backwards and forwards and cast anchor again near Peanke Danke and rode in

[1] George Fox, James Lancaster, and Robert Widders.
[2] Probable tonnage between 150 and 200.
PP......PP Bodleian MS.; *Jnl. F.H.S.*, ix, 36.

Rappahannock River. And on the 30th day we drew anchor and sailed by Stinger Island and by the 8th hour the next morning being the 31st of the 3rd month [May], we left the Capes of Virginia and came into the main ocean, about 200 miles from Patuxent in Maryland. At the Capes of Virginia I first espied a ship and said, ' Yonder is a sail ', which put a question in the seamen's minds what she should be, but I felt from the Lord she was not an enemy and would do us no hurt, and so at some distance she passed by up the bay and we on to the sea. On the 1st of the 4th month [June], we had a very precious meeting on the ship with the seamen, and on the 2nd day of the 4th month [June], we had high winds and our bolt-sprit was loose, that we were forced to turn the ship to lie upon the stays for some time, to mend it, and in the night we had much thunder and rain and high winds, so that they took in most of the sails. And on the 3rd of the 4th month [June], the wind was west and not so high, blessed be the Lord. The 4th of the 4th month [June], we had little wind, and the 5th of the 4th month [June], we had a very good wind but could take no observation for the sun did not shine clear this two days. This day we saw another ship and it did put many thoughts into the seamen, but I felt the power of the Lord over all, and said nothing, for I saw in a vision two ships on the west side that did pass by us and did us no hurt. And the 6th day we had a fair wind and the ship passed away leeward of us southeast. The 7th day of the 4th month [June], we had a very fair wind, and are on our voyage from the Capes of Virginia near 700 miles. And the 8th day of the 4th month [June], we had a blessed meeting on our ship with the seamen, praised be the Lord. And on the 9th day we sailed about seventy-five miles and we had a calm in the night after a storm and much rain. And on the 10th day we sailed about ninety-seven miles, and on the 11th day we sailed about 100 miles, and the 12th day in the night we had a calm, but in the day a good wind, and sailed about eighty miles, then were distant from the Capes 1,239 miles.

On the 13th day we had a tempestuous wind that made the sea like mountains, the waves like mountains in the sea were so big, and, as it were, stood upright upon her sometimes. And the master and men wondered and said they never saw the like before, especially that being a great ship, and long, and of that bigness, but it blew fair for us, blessed be the Lord. We sailed this day 155 miles, a great storm we had, and it lasted all the night, that it made the sea like mountains, and roar like cannons in the ship; and we in our beds sat up, the seamen said they never saw such seas in their lives. But the Lord preserved us over all, who rideth on the wings of the wind, and who is Lord of the heaven, and the seas, and the earth, blessed be his name, his wonders are seen in the deep. This day we sailed 150 miles, being the 14th of the 4th month [June]; and though it was a storm yet it was for us, so that we sailed before it, blessed be the Lord. And on the 15th day we sailed 150 miles, and this day we had a precious meeting and the presence of the Lord was among us, blessed be his name for ever.

And now we have left America and that ocean, and are on the ocean of Europe; and the 16th day we sailed 110 miles and are in the latitude of 44°. And on the 17th day we sailed 125 miles and had a good wind, blessed be the Lord, who steered our course. And on the 18th day, praised be the Lord God, we had a very precious meeting and open to the people, and the Lord was among us, blessed be the Lord God, and we sailed fifty-six miles and are in the latitude of 46° 50′. And on the 19th of the 4th month [June], we sailed 120 miles, and are in the latitude of 47° 47′, and have a good wind, blessed be the Lord. And on the 20th day we sailed 143 miles, and are in latitude 48° 40′, and the weather is and hath been cold several days and nights. The 21st day we sailed 150 miles; the weather being close, we could not take observation to know the latitude. And the 22nd day of the 4th month [June], we sailed ninety-three miles, and being the First-day of the week we had a precious meeting, blessed be the Lord God for ever, Amen. And on the 23rd day we sailed fifty-five miles, and the 24th day we sailed 120 miles and the weather being clear we took an observation and found we were in the latitude of 50° 5′. And we have a good wind but so tossed that we cannot rest, but are safe and well, blessed be the Lord of heaven and earth. And the 25th of the 4th month [June], we sailed 154 miles, the weather having been very foggy, blessed be the Lord it is well; this day we sounded and laid out about 100 fathom but found no bottom. And on the 26th day we sailed about 140 miles, and are in the latitude of 51° 6′, and this day we had a precious meeting, blessed be the Lord, being the Fifth-day of the week; and at night we sounded and found ground at sixty fathom. And on the 27th day we sailed 150 miles, and had a good wind SSW.; and at night we sounded and found ground at thirty-five fathom. And it being a great storm and windy, we took down our sails and mizzen, and let her drive northwards, fearing the land, and at midnight they did discern the Island of Lundy, and then they were greatly glad, for all were upon the watch.

And the 28th day of the 4th month [June] we cast anchor about the first hour in the afternoon at King's Road, the harbour of Bristol. And there lay a man-of-war, and the press masters came on board us, to press our men, and took four. And we had a precious meeting with the seamen, and the press masters stayed the meeting, and liked it very well. And one of them said that he was refreshed more by hearing of us than any other people. And after the meeting was done I spoke to him that he would leave two men that he had pressed, one was lame and the other was the mate; and he said, for my words he would. So we came off the ship in a boat to land and it was rainy and dirty, and walked about a mile, and a Friend got me a horse, and brought me to the town called Shirehampton, and there we stayed a while and got horses, and rode that night to Bristol being the 28th day of the 4th month [June], blessings and praises and thanks be to the Lord for ever and ever, Amen.

So we were 28 days from the Capes of Virginia to Bristol, and we were 10 days on the ship in Maryland and Virginia on the water, before we cleared the Capes, so in all we were on the water 38 days.

[qq]The great Lord God of heaven and earth and creator of all, who is over all, carried us by his high hand and mighty power and wisdom over all, and through many dangers and perils by sea and land; and perils of deceitful professors without possession, who were as the raging waves of the sea, but made a calm; and perils of wolves, bears, tigers, and lions; and perils of rattlesnakes and other venomous creatures of like poisonous nature; and perils through great swamps, and bogs, and the wilderness, where no way was, but for such-like creatures, where we travelled and lodged in the nights by fires; and perils over great bays, creeks, and rivers, in open small boats and small canoes; and perils in great storms and tempests in the ocean, which many times were beyond words to utter; and great perils through the Indian countries in the woods or wildernesses by man-eaters, some whereof lay in wait for some of our company that passed from us, but they were discovered, for the Lord's power gave them dominion over all; and great perils by night through the cold, rain, frosts, snow, in lying in the woods and wilderness several nights together until some of our company had their hands and fingers benumbed, whenas some of the world at such times have had some their noses and some their fingers and toes frozen off (I was an eye witness of some of these things); and perils of robbers by land and pirates by sea, these troublesome times, whereof the sea abounds.

The blessed Lord God, in his blessed power, who by his power stretched over all these workers of death his line of life, the Lord God made all easy by his spirit and power, and gave his people dominion over all and made all plain and low as a meadow, and made his great power and glory in his Light and Truth known over all in the hearts of people, blessed be his name forever, Amen.

[qq] See note [rr] on p. 664.

The Lord was our convoy; the Lord God steered our course; the Lord God, who rides upon the wings of the wind, ordered our winds for us; who raiseth a storm and makes a calm and makes his chambers in the deep and makes the clouds his chariots to send his rain abroad, who, when we were in danger of the enemy, he raised mists and fogs to blind them and storms to scatter them, both evenings and mornings, but at noon-time he cleared up the heavens that the sun might be seen for a quarter of an hour, little more or less, to take our observations, and shut up the heavens again, insomuch that we might have passed through a fleet of pirates.

The Lord brought over such a mist that we could see so little distance from us, that the very seamen confessed that if the Lord God was ever in any ship he was in this ship and that they were blessed for this man's sake, for the Lord made darkness our pavilion and so the presence of the Lord God was with us all along.

When we were in Virginia there was an embargo[1] and a convoy, for the fleet lay in Virginia; so the master and the men held a council together and their joint consent was to set sail without the convoy for England. We heard of Dutch men-of-war towards New York; a master of a ship that came from England came aboard of us bringing us news that he was taken, besides another sloop, and that the same men-of-war had taken eleven ships more besides his, and that several ships were taken about Scilly and the coasts of Ireland. But notwithstanding all this dark and black news we set sail and in the power of the Lord we passed on. Now several Londoners sent to me to go in their ships, and also several Bristol men, but I was moved by the power of the Lord to go in this, though I said little to any till the time.

And when we came near Cape Henry, about the 8th hour, in the morning, we espied a ship on the coast where the pirates used to be, which occasioned some fear and trouble to fall upon the seamen. But the Lord God, whose

[1] On account of war with the Netherlands.

I am and we are, let me see in a vision two ships to the westward that should make towards us but should do us no hurt. So when about three or four days after we espied another ship westward, which occasioned some fear to the seamen, the Lord opened it unto me that was the other ship he showed me in the vision, which was no enemy. And then I desired of the Lord God that if it was his will we might see no more ships until we came to England, to keep the fear out of the people, and the Lord answered me, so that we saw none until we came into King's Road, the Bristol harbour, and so I desired of the Lord God that he, who was able, would clear our coasts of all thieves and pirates, God, whose power and life was over all such workers of death and darkness, who had power over all the heavens and the earth, the sea and the winds, to steer our course and scatter all the pirates, confound them and drive them back, who did it, blessed be his name for ever.

The Lord God said, 'Into thy hand and power I have given thee the ship and all that is in it', that it should come safe, and Paul's words came into my mind. And I told the company I believed in God. And when we came near home the Lord God said unto me, after he had given the ship into my hand, 'Canst thou give up thy self, ship, and all that is in it now, to be taken by the pirates so that all the ships that are behind in Virginia and Maryland might come safe to England?' And I freely did it. And in the twinkling of an eye it was given again, and the blessed God brought us well and safe home.

When there were any storms or fogs, that they could not take observation, I was moved of the Lord to bid them be content and have a good faith and keep over all for it was all good, and was in the will of God and stood in his will; and it was the will of God that things should be so. We had many precious living meetings on the First-days, and other days of the week, and the Lord's living presence was felt there as well as on the land.

Many places the Lord carried us through, Barbados, Jamaica; I was with the Governors, and precious meetings we had in those places, and through the Government of Plymouth and Rhode Island and the King's province, New York Government, Boston, New Jersey Governments and the Government of Delaware, and Maryland, Virginia, Carolina, and some to Antigua and Nevis and many other places which would be too large to mention, through which the blessed Truth did answer the witness of God, and was received in many to the glory of the great God, blessed be his name for ever. So blessed be the great God for ever who is over all the heavens, the earth and winds, and all evil spirits, who orders all to his glory, who rides upon the wings of the wind and makes the clouds his chariots, and stretcheth forth the line of the righteous over the wicked and keeps them in their bound and sets bounds to all things, and preserved his people as the apple of his eye. Blessed be his name for ever.

And when we were come in the harbour I called the master and mate and merchant, and declared to them what the Lord had showed me, and that now the ship, which the Lord had given me and had preserved it and us by his power, I delivered up to them again.[rr]

So on the 28th of 4th month [June], 1673 (as aforesaid) we came safe to Bristol, where we stayed some time to refresh ourselves till the fair.[1]

⟨In the evening I wrote a letter to my wife, to give her notice of my landing: as follows:

Bristol 28th of 4th mo. [June], 1673.

Dear Heart,

This day we came into Bristol near night, from the seas; glory to the Lord God over all for ever, who was our convoy, and steered our course; the God of the whole earth, of the seas and winds; who made the clouds his chariots beyond all words, blessed be his name for ever ! He is over all in his great power and wisdom, Amen.

Robert Widders and James Lancaster are with me, and we are well; glory to the Lord for ever, who hath carried us through

[1] The fair began 25th July and lasted a week.

[rr] This passage from [qq] on p. 661 has been corrected by the original in Bristol MSS., v, 56.

many perils, perils by water, and in storms, perils by pirates and robbers; perils in the wilderness and amongst false professors! praises to him whose glory is over all for ever, Amen! Therefore mind the fresh life, and live all to God in it. I intend (if the Lord will) to stay a while thisaway; it may be till the fair. So no more, but my love to all Friends. G.F.⟩

And Margaret, and Thomas Lower ⟨her son-in-law, with two of her daughters,⟩ Sarah Fell and Rachel Fell, came up to Bristol to me out of the north, and John Rous, and William Penn and his wife, and Gerard Roberts came down from London to see us; and many Friends from several parts of the nation came to see us at the fair.

Glorious, powerful meetings we had there, and the Lord's infinite power and life was over all. I was moved to declare

⟨ . . . . God was the first teacher, in Paradise; and whilst man kept under his teaching he was happy. The serpent was the second, and when man followed his teaching he came into misery, into the fall from the image of God, from righteousness and holiness, and from the power that they had over all that God made, even the serpent. Christ Jesus was the third teacher; of whom God saith, 'This is my beloved Son, in whom I am well pleased, hear ye him'; and who himself saith, 'Learn of me'; he bruises the head of the serpent that is the false teacher, who is the head of all false teachers, and of all false religions, ways, worships and false churches. Now Christ saith, 'Learn of me, I am the way to God, I am the Truth, and the Life, and the Light.' So that man and woman come up again to God, and are renewed up into his image and righteousness and holiness by Christ, by which he comes up into the Paradise of God, as man was before he fell; and into a higher state than that, to sit down in Christ that never fell. So the Son of God is to be heard in all things, who is the Saviour and the Redeemer; and hath laid down his life, and bought his sheep with his blood.

We can challenge all the world. Who hath anything against our way, our Saviour, our Redeemer, who is our prophet, whom God hath raised up, whom we must hear in all things?

. . . Now, many would force us to hear the hirelings who plead for sin and the body of death to the grave; which savours of the Devil's teaching, not Christ's; but we resolve to hear the Son, as both he and the Father command, and in hearing the Son we hear the Father also, as the Scripture testifies. . . . And whereas some have objected, that, although Christ did speak both to his disciples and to the Jews in the days of his flesh, yet since his resurrection and ascension he doth not speak now; the answer is, that as God did then speak by his Son in the days of his flesh, so the Son, Christ Jesus, doth now speak by his Spirit. . . . They who neglect or refuse to hear the voice of Christ, now speaking from heaven in this his gospel day, harden their hearts. . . .

They that come to be renewed up again into the divine, heavenly image, in which man was at first made, will know the same God, that was the first teacher of Adam and Eve in Paradise, to speak to them now by his son who changes not. Glory be to his name for ever !

Many deep and precious things were opened in those meetings by the eternal Spirit which searcheth and revealeth the deep things of God.〉[1]

And much more I could write of what was spoken in the meetings there and other places upon this subject, but it would be too large to write thereof here.

CHAPTER XXV

After I had finished my service for the Lord in Bristol, I came into Gloucestershire where we had many large and precious meetings; and the Lord's everlasting power flowed over the nation.

And after I had finished my service there I came into Wiltshire where we had many precious meetings, though some opposition by one Nathaniel Coleman against the women's meetings at Slaughterford. But as he went out of the house in a rage and passion, he saw the angel of the Lord stand ready with his drawn sword to cut him off. And he came in again, like a dead man, and besought me

[1] In full. Ellwood, pp. 384-6; Bicent., ii, 199-202.

to pray for him, and said he was a dead man and desired me to forgive him. And I told him if he felt forgiveness from the Lord whom he had opposed, I should freely forgive him.

Then he came and proffered his service to me to assist in the settling of women's meetings, but I bid him wait till he felt remission by the Lord's power, for the Lord had no need of him in the condition he was in.

But after, he gave forth a paper of condemnation, ⟨wherein he declared that he did wilfully oppose (although I often warned him to take heed), until the fire of the Lord did burn within him; etc.⟩ this Coleman and others, in their opposition, asked me whether it was not the command of God that a man must rule over his wife, and he would rule over his wife. And did not the apostle say, 'I permit not a woman to teach'? And where did we read of women elders and women disciples? And it was an abuse to the elders to set up a women's meeting.

But I told them that he and they were but elders in the Fall, ruling over their wives in the Fall, but neither he nor they must rule over widows and young women, and other men's wives.

And I showed him that Dorcas was a disciple, and the apostle commands that the elder women should be teachers of good things to the younger; and though the apostle said, 'I permit not a woman to teach nor usurp authority over the man', as also saith the law (for Eve was first in transgression, and such teaching as Eve taught her husband, and usurped authority over the man, is forbidden); yet the apostle also says that daughters and handmaids should prophesy, which they did both in the time of the law and the Gospel; and man and woman were meet-helps (before they fell) and the image of God and righteousness and holiness; and so they are to be again in the restoration by Christ Jesus.

And thy ruling over thy wife and eldership is in the Fall, for thou art in the transgression and not an elder in the image of God and righteousness and holiness, before transgression and the Fall was; nor in the restoration where they are helpsmeet in the righteousness and image of God, and in the dominion over all that God made.

<I was moved of the Lord to recommend to Friends, for the benefit and advantage of the Church of Christ, that the faithful women who were called to the belief of the Truth, being made partakers of the same precious faith, and heirs of the same everlasting Gospel of life and salvation as the men are, might in like manner come into the possession and practice of the Gospel order, and therein be meet-helps unto the men in the restoration, in the service of Truth, in the affairs of the Church, as they are outwardly in civil, or temporal things. That so all the family of God, women as well as men, might know, possess, perform, and discharge their offices and services in the house of God, whereby the poor might be the better looked after and the younger sort instructed, informed, and taught in the way of God; the loose and disorderly reproved and admonished in the fear of the Lord; the clearness of persons proposing marriage more closely and strictly inquired into in the wisdom of God; and all the members of the spiritual body, the Church, might watch over and be helpful to each other in love.>

And after the women's meetings were settled in those countries and I had had many precious meetings amongst Friends, I passed to Marlborough where some of the magistrates came to the meeting and were civil and moderate.

And from thence I passed to Bartholomew Maylin's[1] where I had a precious meeting. And from thence I passed beyond Oare where we had a large precious meeting; and from thence we passed to the borders of Hampshire where we had another large precious meeting, and thence into Oxfordshire, visiting Friends, and thence to Reading where we had a very large and precious meeting.

From thence we passed into Buckinghamshire where I had many precious meetings, and so through the country visiting Friends till I came to Kingston on Thames, where Margaret and Rachel Fell met me.

And after I had visited Friends there I came to London where the Baptists and Socinians and old apostates were

[1] Bartholomew Maylin lived at Lambourne Woodlands, Berkshire.

very rude and had given forth many books against us; and a great travail I had in the Lord's power before I went to meetings in London; but the Lord's power came over all and all their lying, wicked, scandalous books were answered.

And after I had visited the meetings in London, and all was generally quiet and the Lord's everlasting power and seed was set over all, I went to visit Esquire Marsh, whom the king had knighted and had made Master of the Armoury in the Tower, who was very loving and tender, and who shortly after died. But he had been very serviceable to the Truth and had his dependence upon the Lord.

And after a while I went into the country, into Essex and Middlesex, and visited Friends in their meetings and their children in their schools, and after returned up to London again.

And having set all things straight amongst Friends in London I went down to Kingston again, and from thence to Stephen Smith's, where there were many hundreds of people to a meeting. And after I was clear of the service of the Lord in those parts I returned to Kingston and so to London again.

And I had a vision when I was lying in my bed at Kingston; I saw that I was taken prisoner and I saw also that I rid down into a deep steep water three times and up again.

And many Friends were imprisoned and had before the magistrates up and down in the cities and nation for opening their shop windows upon holy days and fast days and bearing their testimony against all such observations of days, knowing that the true Christians did not observe the Jews' holy days in the apostles' days. Neither could we observe the heathens' and Papists' holy days which have been set up amongst Christians since the apostles' days. For we were redeemed out of days by Christ Jesus and brought into his day that hath sprung from on high, and are come into him who is Lord of the Jewish Sabbath, and is the substance of the Jews' signs.

And after I had stayed a while in London I passed with Margaret and Rachel Fell into the country to Hendon and from thence to William Penn's ⟨at Rickmansworth in Hertfordshire⟩, where Thomas Lower came to us the next day ⟨to accompany us on our journey northward⟩. And after we had visited Friends there we passed to a Friend's house near Aylesbury, and from thence to Bray D'Oyly's[1] in Oxfordshire and there I set up in the country two or three more meetings, Friends being very plenty in those countries and the Truth very much increasing.

And as I was sitting at supper the night before the morning I went away, I felt I was taken, ⟨yet said nothing to anybody of it then,⟩ and the next morning we got up before day and rid through the country into Worcestershire to John Halford's house at Armscote[2] in Tredington parish, where we had a very large and precious meeting in his barn and the Lord's powerful presence was amongst us.

And after the meeting was done and Friends many of them gone, as I was sitting in the parlour with some Friends, discoursing, there came one Justice Parker[3] and a priest called Rowland Harris,[4] priest of Honington, to the house. This justice came to the knowledge of the meeting through a woman Friend that was nurse to his child, who asked leave of her mistress to come to the meeting to see me. And she speaking to her husband, he, together with the priest, complotted to come and break up the meeting and to apprehend me. But, through their long sitting to dinner (it being the day when his child was christened) they came not till the meeting was ended and Friends mostly gone and going.

⟨But though there was no meeting when they came, yet Henry Parker took me, and Thomas Lower for company with me; and though he had nothing to lay to our charge,

[1] Bray D'Oyly lived at The Manor House, Adderbury West.

[2] 17th Dec., 1673.

[3] Probably Henry Parker, recorder of Evesham.

[4] MS. has Haines, and on p. 672.

sent us both to Worcester gaol by a strange sort of mittimus, a copy of which here follows :〉

Worcestershire Sessions.

To the constables of Tredington, in the said county of Worcester, and to all constables and tithing-men of the several townships and villages within the said parish of Tredington, and to the keepers of the gaol for the county of Worcester.

Complaint being made to me, being one of His Majesty's justices of the peace for the said county of Worcester, that within the said parish of Tredington in the said county, there has of late been several meetings of divers persons, to the number of four hundred persons and upwards at a time, upon a pretence of exercise of religion otherwise than what is established by the laws of England, and many of the said persons, some of which were teachers and came from the north, and others from remote parts of the kingdom, which tends to the prejudice of the reformed and established religion and may prove prejudicial to the public peace; and it appearing to me that there was, this present day, such a meeting as aforesaid, to the number of two hundred or thereabouts, at Armscott, in the said parish of Tredington, and that George Fox of London, and Thomas Lower of the parish of Creed, in the county of Cornwall, were present at the said meeting, and the said George Fox was teacher or speaker at the said meeting; and no satisfactory account of their settlement or place of habitation appearing to me, and forasmuch as the said George Fox and Thomas Lower refused to give sureties to appear at the next Sessions of the peace, to be holden for the said county, to answer the breach of the common-laws of England, and what other matters should be objected against them; these are, therefore, in His Majesty's name, to will and require you, or either of you, forthwith to convey the bodies of the said George Fox and Thomas Lower to the county gaol of Worcester aforesaid, and there safely to be kept, until they shall be from thence delivered by due course of law; for which this shall be your sufficient warrant in that behalf.

Dated the 17th of December in the 25th year of His Majesty's reign over England,[1] &c. Henry Parker.

〈Being thus made prisoners, without any probable appearance of being released before the Quarter Sessions

[1] 1673.

at soonest, we got some Friends to accompany my wife and her daughter into the north, and we were conve- ' to Worcester gaol.

When we had been some time in the gaol we thought fit to lay our case before the Lord Windsor,[1] who was lord-lieutenant of Worcestershire, and before the deputy-lieutenants and other magistrates, which we did by the following letter:⟩

These are to inform you, the lord-lieutenant and the deputy lieutenants and the justices of the county of Worcester, how unchristian and inhumanly we have been dealt withal by Henry Parker, a justice (so called), in our journey or travel towards the north.

We coming to our Friend John Halford's house at Armscott on the 17th of 10th month [Dec.], 1673, and some friends bringing us on the way, and others coming to see us there, towards night there came the aforesaid justice, and a priest called Rowland Harris of Honington in Warwickshire and demanded our names and places of abode. And we not being in any meeting but discoursing together when they came in, yet he took our names and made a mittimus to send us to Worcester gaol, taking the names of others but only sent us two to the gaol.

Now he says in his mittimus that complaint had been made unto him of several by-past meetings of many hundreds at a time, concerning which we know nothing. And he farther says that no satisfactory account of our settlement or place of habitation appeared unto him, both of which he contradicts in his own mittimus, therein mentioning the places of our abode and habitation, the account of which we satisfactorily and fully gave him.

Thomas Lower told him that he was going down with his mother-in-law the wife of George Fox and his sister to fetch home his wife and child from the north into his own country. And George Fox said he was setting forward his wife on her journey towards the north, who had been at London to visit one of her daughters that had lately lain in. Having received word from his mother, an ancient woman in Leicestershire who desired earnestly to see him before she died, he intended to

[1] Thomas Hickman, seventh Baron Windsor and first Earl of Plymouth (*c.* 1627-1687).

accompany his wife in her journey as far as Coleshill in Warwickshire and then to have turned over into Leicestershire to have seen his mother and relations there and so to have returned to London again.

But by his interrupting of us in our journey, taking the husband from his wife, the son from his mother, and sister, and from visiting his wife and child so remote off, we were forced to get strangers or whom we could to help them on their journey, to our great damage and their hindrance. So that we were forced to say, was this to do as they would be done by, and asked the priest whether this was his gospel and their entertainment of strangers.

The justice said, he had said it and he would do it; and whereas he says they refused to give sureties, he only asked George Fox for sureties, and he replied he was an innocent man and knew no law he had broken. But he did not ask Thomas Lower for any, as if it had been crime and cause enough for his commitment that he came out of Cornwall. And if we were at a meeting as he says in his mittimus, he might have proceeded otherwise than by sending us to gaol, to answer the breach of the common laws. Yet he mentions no breach of any, as may be seen in the mittimus. So we thought fit to lay before you the substance of his proceedings against us, hoping there will be more moderation and justice appear in you towards us so that we may prosecute our intended journey as aforesaid.

George Fox.
Thomas Lower.

[a]His mother, an ancient woman above seventy years old, who greatly desired to see him before she died, being weak and aged as aforesaid, when she heard that he was stopped and sent to prison it struck her to her heart and killed her, as he received a letter from a doctor of that country.[a]

[b]And when I heard she was dead, it struck me, for I did in verity love her as ever one could a mother, for she was a good, honest, virtuous and a right-natured woman. And when I had read the letter of her death it struck a great weight upon my spirit, and it was in a travail for a

[a]......[a] From a paper by Fox in Spence MSS. (*Camb. Jnl.*, ii, 294) describing the errors in Parker's indictment.

quarter of an hour. And there being people in the room they saw some sudden travail upon me, though they said nothing. And when my spirit had gotten through I saw her in the resurrection and the life, everlastingly with me over all, and father in the flesh also. So these wicked justices God will judge, who hindered me from visiting her according to her motherly and tender desire.[b]

⟨But no enlargement did we receive by our application to the Lord Windsor. And although Thomas Lower received several letters from his brother Dr. Richard Lower[1] who was one of the King's physicians, concerning his liberty, and one by his procurement from Henry Savile who was of the King's bed-chamber, to his brother called the Lord Windsor, to the same effect, yet seeing it related only to his enlargement, not mine, so great was his love and regard to me that he would not seek his own liberty singly but kept the letter by him unsent. So we were continued prisoners till the next general Quarter Sessions of the Peace.⟩

[George Fox to George Whitehead and others in London.]

Worcester gaol this 17th day of the 11th mo.,
1673 [Jan., 1674].

Dear George Whitehead, Ellis Hookes, Thomas Moore,

To whom is my love in the Seed of God that is over all, from everlasting to everlasting, in whom all hath life and blessings and peace with the everlasting God.

Now concerning the present matters about us, we were called the last day of the sessions. And the days before, divers eminent Friends being here did speak to the justices, and the justices spoke very fair to them and said we should be discharged; and it was the general discourse. ⟨For many of the justices seemed to dislike the severity of Parker's proceedings against us and did declare an averseness to ensnare us by the tender of the oaths.⟩

Some Friends had spoken with the Lord Windsor who also promised fair, and also we understood that a letter came from

[1] Richard Lower, M.D., F.R.S.

[b]. . . . . .[b] MS., *Jnl. F.H.S.*, vii, 79, xvi, 61.

one Colonel Sands from London to some of the justices, procured by Dr. Lower. What were the contents of the letter we know not fully, only we heard it was for both our discharges.

⟨When we came in they were stricken with paleness in their faces; and it was some time before anything was spoken, insomuch that a butcher in the hall said, 'What! Are they afraid? Dare not the justices speak to them?'⟩

After we were called they began with Thomas Lower, to examine him of the cause of his travel, concerning which he gave them an account as you have heard before.

But Parker first made a long speech in the court, much to the same effect in his mittimus, only with this addition, that he thought it a milder course to send us two to gaol than to put his neighbours to the loss of £200, which they must have suffered if he had put the law in execution against conventicles. All which was a mere piece of deceit, for he had no evidence to convict us and them by, he coming after the meeting was ended. And he spoke of the common laws but instanced none. And then when Thomas Lower had given them a full account, and as he was speaking, I spoke sometimes. And they said they were upon his examination now; when it came to my turn I should have free leave to speak and they would not hinder me nor ensnare us, but I should have time to speak.

So then they asked me an account of my travelling and I told them, as I have formerly mentioned, but more at large. Only whereas he said there were some there from Bristol and from the north and from London and Cornwall, my answer was that these all were but one company or family, ⟨for there was none from London but myself, none from the north but my wife and her daughter, none from Cornwall but my son-in-law Thomas Lower,⟩ and that it was a providence that the Friend of Bristol, a merchant, was there to assist Margaret and her daughter in their journey towards the north. So the chairman, one Leonard Simpson ⟨an old Presbyterian⟩, said, 'Your relation or account is very innocent.'

Then they sat down and whispered together and the chairman stood up and said, 'You Mr. Fox are a famous man and all this may be true that you have said. But, that we may be better satisfied, will you take the Oath of Allegiance and Supremacy?' Then I told them it was a snare; and then they caused the oath to be read. And when they had done I told them, I never took oath in my life, and that I was cast in the dungeon at Derby and kept six months there because I would not take up arms against King Charles at Worcester fight, and was carried up to London to Oliver Cromwell as a plotter to bring in King Charles, because I went to meetings. And 'You know in your own consciences that we cannot take an oath nor swear in any case because Christ forbids it. But this I can speak concerning the oaths, that I do own and acknowledge the King of England to be lawful heir and successor to the realm of England', and that I had nothing but love and good will in my heart to him and all men and desired his and their prosperity (the Lord knows it), who am an innocent man. 'And as to the Oath of Supremacy I deny the Pope and his power and religion, and abhor it with my heart.'

And when I was speaking what I could say instead of the oath they cried, 'Give him the book.' And I said, 'The book says, "Swear not at all"'; and then they cried, 'Take him away gaoler, ⟨take him away, we shall have a meeting here; why do you not take him away ?⟩ That fellow loves to hear him preach.'

Then I stretched out my arm and said, 'The Lord forgive thee, who casts me in prison for obeying the doctrine of Christ.' And though they promised we should have liberty to speak and they would not snare us, yet when it came to be tried they made no conscience of lying.

Now some of the justices had spoken to Friends desiring them to acquaint us that we should speak little and not provoke them and they would warrant we should be discharged. All people said we were as lambs before them, which people took notice of. And they are the more inexcusable and have manifested their unjust and wicked proceedings against us. And some said it was like Bonner's[1] proceedings. Also I asked them what I had been imprisoned for, this month, that now they had nothing else to charge me with but tendering the oath, to ensnare me by, knowing I could not swear. So they did not discharge me from my first imprisonment, but as the keeper informed us, returned me for not finding sureties to appear at the next Assizes.

Then ⟨after I was had away⟩ Thomas Lower began to speak again unto them but they said they would not hear a word more from him, saying, 'You may be gone about your business;

[1] Edmond Bonner, Bishop of London, persecutor under Mary, d. 1569.

we have nothing to say to you more, you are discharged.' Then Thomas Lower told them by their recommitting of his father, they did necessitate his staying also; for he was obliged to attend and wait upon his father as he was in duty bound. They said they commended his love, respect, and duty to his father, and if he would give security for his father's return to the Assizes, he should be at liberty till then. He replied he was a stranger to the country. They said, 'You have good friends.' Then he said he was not willing to engage them upon that affair. Then they said I might take my choice, and if I liked their offer, come to them again, and they would do as they had said, which was but a farther snare. So now there is something for Thomas Moore to move the King upon, seeing they have not proceeded against us according to law, and did not nor could not produce any law which we had broken, but only tendered the oath as a snare. And let the King know what I said unto them instead of the oath, which they would not hear.

And if that my liberty cannot be procured by two or three words from him, you may inform yourselves otherwise as touching my removal, which if the first take not effect you may obtain the other as privately and suddenly as may be, before Parker get up to prevent it, which some think he may endeavour.

So this is the substance of our trial here.

Now as touching that paper thou desires to know of me, which was presented to the Parliament, it was that John Whitehead and I drew up. So remember me to all Friends as Alexander Parker and the rest as though I named. The Truth is over all; and these things have made a stir and work in people's minds concerning it, and it loses nothing. Blessed be the Lord for ever. And Thomas Lower, though he is at liberty, won't leave me, but stays with me in prison till he see what may be done concerning me. Let Friends see the substance of this at their men's meeting, so you may see what can be done and send us word by the next.

So no more but my love,

George Fox.

Thomas Lower's dear love is remembered to you and he would have Ellis Hookes send him the King's speeches, and keeper's, and what the proceedings are in Parliament.

And after Thomas Lower was discharged from his imprisonment by the Bench, who never was examined what he had been committed for, and had lain in prison six or seven weeks, he went to the justices to their chamber to know of them what cause they had to discharge him and detain his father, and whether this was not partiality and would be a blemish to them.

Then Simpson threatened and, said he, 'If you are not content we will tender you the oath also and send you to your father.' Unto which Thomas Lower replied he might if he thought fit, but whether he sent him to his father or no, he intended to go and wait upon him in prison, for that was his business in that country.

Then said Justice Parker, 'But Mr. Lower, do you think that I had not cause to send you to prison when your father and you had such a great meeting, in so much that the parson of the parish complained to me that he hath lost the greatest part of his parishioners, and when he comes amongst them he hath scarce any auditors left.'

Unto which Thomas Lower replied that he had heard by some of the parishioners that the priest of the parish did so seldom come to visit his flock (but once or twice in the year to gather up tithes), that it was but charity in his father to visit such a forlorn and scattered flock, and therefore he had no cause to send his father to prison for visiting them, or teaching or instructing, and directing them to Christ their true teacher, who had so little comfort or benefit from their pretended pastor, who came only to seek for his 'gain from his quarter' amongst them. Whereupon the justices laughed, for it seems Dr. Crowder[1] who was the priest they spoke of was in the room sitting amongst them, whom Thomas Lower knew not. But he never opened his mouth. And after some other words to the justices, Thomas Lower came away to the prison to his father. The said Dr. Crowder was pitifully ashamed, the justices did so play upon him afterwards, as we heard.

But he was so exceeding provoked thereby, after a short time this Dr. Crowder came to the prison under pretence to dispute with me and to talk with Thomas Lower about

[1] Joseph Crowther, B.D., d. 1689.

this business, ⟨and he brought another with him, he himself being then a prebendary at Worcester.⟩ And when he came in he asked me what I was imprisoned for.

So I said unto him, 'Knowest thou not? Wast not thou upon the Bench when Simpson and Parker tendered the oath to me, and hadst thou not a hand in it?'

Then said he, 'It's lawful to swear, and Christ did not forbid swearing before a magistrate but swearing by the sun and the like. Which I bid him prove by the Scriptures. But he could not, but brought that saying of Paul's where he said all things were lawful to him, etc., and 'If', said he, 'all things were lawful to him, then swearing, etc.'

Then said I unto him, 'By this argument thou mayst also affirm that drunkenness and adultery and all manner of sin and wickedness are lawful also, as well as swearing.'

To which Dr. Crowder said, 'Do you hold that adultery is unlawful?'

And then I replied unto him, 'Yes, I do.'

'Why then', said Crowder, 'this contradicts the saying of St. Paul.' Upon which I called to the prisoners and the gaoler to hear what doctrine Dr. Crowder had laid down for orthodox—that drunkenness, swearing, adultery, and such like were lawful. So then Crowder said he would put it under his hand, but he took a pen and writ another thing than he had spoken. And then he spoke to Thomas Lower and asked him whether he would answer it, who said he might send him an answer to it. So he threatened Thomas Lower for speaking so abusively of him before the justices, and said he would bring action for defamation against him in the Bishop's Court.

Thomas Lower bid him begin when he pleased, he would answer him and bring his parishioners in evidence against him; so he went away in a great fret in his mind and grumbling all the way as he went. And after a few days Thomas Lower sent him an answer to the paper he had written whereupon he put his name,[1] ⟨and a Friend of Worcester carried it to him and he read it and said he would reply

[1] In *Camb. Jnl.*, ii, 277-83.

to it but never did, though he often sent him word he would do it⟩.

A letter from George Fox to his wife.[1]

Worcester Gaol,
21st of 11th mo., 1673 [Jan., 1674].

Dear Heart,

To whom is my love and the rest of Friends and thy children, Sarah and Susan and dear Rachel. I desire their growth in the Truth and in the wisdom of God, that by it you may all be ordered to his glory, and to touch nothing but the life in any and to be separated from the evil and to stand as Nazarites consecrated to God, that in the life all may be a good savor to God. I received thy letter by Leonard Fell and another from Rebecca Travers from London, and she strangeth that thee hath not written to her, for she and the rest of London Friends generally thinks that thou art with me in prison, and did stay, and not gone into the north, and therefore thou should write to her and them, for they oft remember their love as though thou wast here, and do not think that thou art gone.

We have sent all passages to London, and T. Lower hath given you account of the Sessions. All people disliketh the justices' proceeding and saith it is like to Bonner; and some clapped their hands and said it was a snare. So be over all and out of all, free and not in bondage under outward things. Bring things even and straight that thou may be free. So no more but my love. G.F.

Wheat was the last Seventh-day at seven and sixpence a bushel, and four shillings pease and barley, and oats two shillings a bushel. The poor people are ready to mutiny in the market, here is such a cry for corn to make them bread. Here was a great stir with the mayor and the people; some sacks were cut, but the Lord's power is over all. G.F.

And rye at seven; and this Fourth-day there was a great uproar, likes that the mayor and constables were fain to appease the people, for they cut the bags.

⟨By the time I thought my wife could be got home, I wrote her the following letter:[2]

[1] Hist. Soc. Penna. MSS., *Jnl. F.H.S.*, xi, 98.
[2] Abraham MSS., *Jnl. F.H.S.*, xi, 157, 158.

8th of 12th mo. 1673 [Feb., 1674].

Dear Heart,

Thou seemed to be much grieved when I was speaking of prisons, and when I was taken thou began to fall upon me with blaming of me, and I told thee that I was to bear it, and why could not thee be content with the will of God? And thou said some words and then was pretty quiet. And thou was loath to go to Parker, but it was well thou did, and it had been well thou had been more over it to me; for when I was at John Rous's I saw that I was taken prisoner, and when I was at Bray D'Oyly's as I sat at supper, I saw I was taken the night before I was.

The three pound thou sent up to me, in love, for it I did speak to a Friend to send thee as much Spanish black cloth as will make thee a gown and it did cost us a pretty deal of money.

And I saw I had a winepress to tread and the Lord's power is over all, blessed be his name for ever; and not only so but the winepress is to be trodden among Friends where the life is not lived in.

I hear of a ship of Thomas Edmondson's is cast away, which I had a part in, but let it go; and Thomas can give you or thee an account of all things. G.F.

After I had been a prisoner at Worcester, ⟨soon after the Sessions were over⟩ I was removed to London by a *habeas corpus* for the sheriff to bring me up to the King's Bench bar. ⟨The under-sheriff made Thomas Lower his deputy to convey me to London, and we set forth out of Worcester on the 29th of 11th month, 1673 [Jan., 1674], and came to London the 2nd of 12th [Feb.], the ways being very deep and the waters out. Next day notice being given that I was brought up, the sheriff was ordered to bring me into court. So I went and did appear before Judge Wilde,[1] and both he and the lawyers were pretty fair so that I had time to speak to clear my innocency and show my wrong imprisonment. After the return of the writ was entered, I was ordered to be brought into court again next day.

So I went in the morning and walked in the Hall[2] till

[1] Sir William Wilde (1611?-1679), member of the Convention Parliament, 1660, for the City of London.

[2] Westminster Hall.

the sheriff came to me (for he trusted me to go whither I would), and it being early we went into the Court of the King's Bench and sat there among the lawyers almost an hour till the judges came in. When the judges came in the sheriff took off my hat; and after a while I was called, and the Lord's presence was with me and his power was over all. I stood and heard the King's attorney, whose name was Jones, who indeed spoke notably on my behalf, as also did another counsellor after him, and the judges, who were three, were very moderate, nor casting any reflecting words at me. So I stood still in the power and spirit of the Lord, seeing how the Lord was at work and the earth was helping the woman. When they had done, I applied myself to the chief justice, desiring that I might speak, and he said I might. Then I told him the cause of our journey, the manner of our being taken and committed, and the time of our imprisonment until the Sessions; with a brief account of our trial at the Sessions, and what I had offered to the justices then, as a declaration that I could make or sign, instead of the Oaths of Allegiance and Supremacy. When I had done, the Chief Justice said I was to be turned over to the King's Bench, and the sheriff of Worcester to be discharged of me. He said also they would consider further of it; and if they found any error in the record, or in the justice's proceedings, I should be set at liberty. So a tipstaff was called to take me into custody, and he delivered me to the keeper of the King's Bench, who let me go to a Friend's house, where I lodged, and appointed to meet me at Edward Mann's in Bishopsgate Street next day.

But after this Justice Parker, or some other of my adversaries, moved the court that I might be sent back to Worcester. So another day was appointed for another hearing, and they had four counsellors that pleaded against me. And there was one George Stroude, a counsellor, pleaded for me, and was pleading before I was brought into court; but they bore him down, and prevailed with the judges to give judgement that I should be sent down to

Worcester Sessions. Only they told me I might put in bail to appear at the Sessions, and to be of good behaviour in the meantime. But I told them I never was of ill behaviour in my life, and that they, the four judges, might as well put the oath to me there as send me to Worcester to be ensnared by the justices, in their putting the oath to me, and then praemuniring me, who never took an oath in my life. But I told them if I brake my ' yea ' and ' nay ', I was content to suffer the same penalty that they should who break their oaths. This alteration of the judges' minds in my case proceeded (as was thought) from some false informations that my adversary, Justice Parker, had given against me; for between the times of my former appearance and this, he had spread abroad a very false and malicious story, viz. that there were many substantial men with me, out of several parts of the nation, when he took me, and that we had a design or plot in hand, and that Thomas Lower stayed with me in prison, long after he was set at liberty, to carry on our design. This was spoken in the Parliament-house, insomuch that if I had not been brought up to London when I was I had been stopped at Worcester, and Thomas had been recommitted with me. But although these lies were easily disproved, and laid open, to Parker's shame, yet would not the judges alter their last sentence, but remanded me to Worcester gaol. Only this favour was granted, that I might go down my own way, and at my own leisure, provided I would be without fail there by the Assize, which was to begin on the 2nd day of the 2nd month [Apr.] next following.〉

George Fox to the King, when they were about to send him to Worcester.

This is a matter that hath been laid before the King and his Council before already, how that George Fox was going down with his wife, towards the north, to see his ancient mother before she died, and so to return to London again. . . . So we desire the King will be pleased to take this innocent man into consideration, for they do intend to send him down [to Worcester] within four days, because in tenderness he cannot take an oath.[1]

George Fox to Margaret Fox.[2]

Dear Love, London. 6th of 1st mo. [Mar.], 1674.

to whom is my love and to Thomas Lower and his Mary and Sarah, Rachel, and Isabel and the rest of Friends, in that which is over all and changeth not.

There hath been a book[3] given to the King and Council, and both Houses of Parliament; and they do generally acknowledge the reason of the thing: and Friends did attend the Parliament; and they were so taken with the thing that they intended to have done something, had they sat longer. And Friends gave some of them to the Mayor and Aldermen and Common Council; and they called them into the Mayor's Court, and were very civil and did generally confess the reason of the thing. I have sent them to Barbados and Scotland and Ireland and Virginia for Friends to take the substance and give to their Parliaments, Assemblies, and governors; and they sing them about the streets. And I desire that you at your Monthly and Quarterly Meetings would send for some of them and give them on assizes to all the justices, and them that be in power and bailiffs or mayors; for they do give a great light to dark people. And it was given to the judges and the men of the jury; and Friends have distributed many of them to under-officers. That which Sarah writes, of some of them coming up to me, I can say little how I may be ordered, for they moved the court to have me down to Worcester, and have got a *habeas corpus* and a warrant for the same purpose, and a great jumble and work there hath been about it. The King can do nothing, it being in the judges' and the sheriffs' hands; so they do suppose that I must go to Worcester Assizes or Sessions.

The salmon thou speaks of is not yet come, neither do they know by what carrier, nor where he inns. I had written to you before, but there hath been a great jumble about me and is still. But the Lord is at work among them and it will be well, blessed be the Lord.

So in haste, my love to you all. G.F.

[1] In full, *Camb. Jnl.*, ii, 274. Repeats the events, charges, defence, and protestations already given on pp. 674-7.

[2] From John Barclay: *Letters of Early Friends*, p. 195.

[3] Probably *The Case of the People called Quakers relating to Oaths or Swearing*. 1673.

⟨I stayed in and about London till toward the latter end of the 1st month [Mar.], 1674, and then went down leisurely (for I was not able to abide hasty and hard travel), and came into Worcester on the last day of the First Month, the day before the judges came to town. On the 2nd of the Second month [Apr.] I was brought from the gaol to an inn near the hall, that I might be in readiness if I should be called. But I was not called that day and the gaoler came to me at night and told me I might go home (meaning to the gaol). Whereupon, Gerard Roberts of London being with me, he and I walked down together to the gaol without any keeper. Next day I was brought up again and they set a little boy of about eleven years old to be my keeper. I was told that Justice Parker and the Clerk of the Peace had given order that I should not be put into the calendar, that so I might not be brought before the judge; but I got the judge's son to move in court that I might be called, and thereupon I was called, and brought up to the Bar before Judge Turner, my old persecutor, who had formerly put the oath to me and praemunired Margaret once before at Lancaster.

After silence made, he asked me what I did desire. I said, 'My liberty, according to justice.' He said I lay in prison upon the matter of the oath; and asked me if I would take it. I desired he would hear the manner of my being taken and committed, and he being silent, I gave him an account thereof at large. When I had done speaking, he again asked me to take the oaths; I told him I could not take any oath, for conscience sake, and that I did believe he and they all knew in their consciences that it was for conscience sake I could not swear at all. But I did declare amongst them what I could say and what I could sign in owning of the King's right to the government and in denying the Pope and his pretended power, and all plotters, plots and conspiracies against the government. Parker, who committed me, endeavoured to incense him against me, telling him that I was a ringleader; that many of the nation followed me, and he knew not what it might come to; with many more envious words, which some that stood near took notice of; who also observed that the judge gave him never a word in answer to it.〉

But he turned me off to the Sessions and would not meddle with me, but said the Sessions must try it, before whom I was first brought.

George Fox to Margaret Fox.[1]

4th of 2nd mo. [Apr.], 1674.

I came to Worcester on the last day of the first month. On the third I was brought into the court, and Turner my old persecutor asked me what I did desire and I said, ' My liberty ', and he said that I lay concerning the oath, and I spoke to them as I used to do and asked him who the oath was to, was it not to the King and against the Pope, and he said, ' Yes.' And I said, ' I was cast into Derby dungeon six months because I would not be a captain against the King, at this town of Worcester.' And the gentry was all astonished and startled, and exceeding moderate; and the judge said that I was a rational man. And I gave them account of my first commitment, and how my mother had a desire to see me before she died, and I sent her word of my coming; and when she heard of my being stopped by their imprisoning me, it struck her to the heart that she died.

The judge said I might put in bail, and I said that was another snare, and many of us had been snared by it, but if it was this for my appearance at the Sessions, if the Lord gave me health and life and liberty, I should appear. And he said that I must get bail, but I did forewarn all Friends of that. The power of the Lord was over all. And Parker and his company, that had brought me on their own heads, were tormented; and he had engaged to Richard Cannon at London of setting me at liberty; and when he came into the country, he boasted that he was too nimble for the Quakers. And some people said that if I had had my liberty, I would tread the judge and all them as dirt and a-trampled them under his feet. The Lord be praised, the Seed was over all and the press was trodden as at London.

And some that were in the court, that were in power, said that Parker was the worst enemy that we and I had, in incensing

[1] From original in possession of Robin A. Hodgkin, printed *Jnl. F.H.S.*, xi, 100.

the judge against me, and some of the justices that were above him stopped him and opposed him; and here you may see Richard Cannon and Ellis Hookes who had such a confidence in deceitful Parker, were lugging at the tail of Parker and plucked me into the ditch. But the Lord's power was over all, beyond words. And Bray D'Oyly and G. Roberts and Ed. Brookes were with me, and very much refreshed in the Lord's power which was over all.

And the judge's son said that Parker said sometimes one thing and sometimes another, that is, I should have my liberty and another time not, that he could not tell what for to make of his words. And the judge said that they had nothing against me, and it was his mind to set me a-liberty, but they desire to put it off unto the Sessions. And he gave order that then I should have my liberty and not for to trouble the Assizes with it. And the justices were generally willing and loving—this was in private—and the people were loving, and the justices have promised that I should have my liberty in the town and lodge at a Friend's house till Sessions.

I could write much but the bearer cannot stay. My love to you all and all Friends.

G.F.

〈Between this time and the Sessions (having the liberty of the town for my health's sake) I had some service for the Lord with several people that came to visit me. For at one time there came three nonconformist priests and two lawyers to discourse with me; and one of the priests undertook to prove that the Scriptures are the only rule of life. Whereupon, after I had plunged him about his proof, I had a fit opportunity to open unto them the right and proper use, service, and excellency of the Scriptures; and also to show that the spirit of God, which was given to every one to profit withal, and the grace of God, which bringeth salvation, and which hath appeared unto all men, and teacheth them that obey it to deny ungodliness and worldly lusts, and to live soberly, righteously, and godly in this present world: that this is the most fit, proper, and universal rule, which God hath given to all mankind to rule, direct, govern, and order their lives by.

Another time came a Common-Prayer priest, and some people with him, and he asked me if I was grown up to perfection.

I told him what I was, I was by the grace of God.

He replied, it was a modest and civil answer. Then he urged the words of John, 'If we say that we have no sin, we deceive ourselves, and the truth is not in us.' And he asked, what did I say to that.

I said, with the same apostle, 'If we say that we have not sinned we make him a liar and his word is not in us'; who came to destroy sin, and to take away sin. So there is a time for people to see that they have sinned, and there is a time for them to see that they have sin; and there is a time for them to confess their sin, and to forsake it, and to know 'the blood of Christ to cleanse from all sin'. Then the priest was asked whether Adam was not perfect before he fell, and whether all God's works were not perfect.

The priest said, there might be a perfection, as Adam had, and a falling from it.

But I told him, 'There is a perfection in Christ, above Adam and beyond falling; and that it was the work of the ministers of Christ to present every man perfect in Christ; and for the perfecting of whom they had their gifts from Christ; therefore, they that denied perfection denied the work of the ministry, and the gifts which Christ gave for the perfecting of the saints.'

The priest said, we must always be striving.

But I told him it was a sad and comfortless sort of striving, to strive with a belief that we should never overcome. I told him also that Paul, who cried out of the body of death, did also thank God who gave him the victory, through our Lord Jesus Christ. So there was a time of crying out for want of victory, and a time of praising God for the victory. And Paul said, 'There is no condemnation to them that are in Christ Jesus.'

The priest said, Job was not perfect.

I told him, God said, Job was a perfect man, and that

he did shun evil; and the Devil was forced to confess that God had set a hedge about him, which was not an outward hedge but the invisible heavenly power.

The priest said, Job said, 'He chargeth his angels with folly, and the heavens are not clean in his sight.'

I told him that was his mistake; for it was not Job who said so, but Eliphaz, who contended against Job.

'Well, but', said the priest, 'what say you to that Scripture, "The justest man that is, sinneth seven times a day"'?

'Why, truly', said I, 'I say, there is no such Scripture'; and with that the priest's mouth was stopped. Many other services I had with several sorts of people between the Assizes and the Sessions.

The next Quarter Sessions began the 29th day of the 2nd month [April], and I was called before the justices. The chairman's name was Street[1] who was a judge in the Welsh circuit, and he misrepresented me and my case to the country, telling them that we had a meeting at Tredington from all parts of the nation, to the terrifying of the King's subjects, for which we had been committed to prison; that for the trial of my fidelity the oaths were put to me. And having had time to consider of it, he asked me, if I would now take the oaths. I desired liberty to speak for myself, and having obtained that, began first to clear myself from those falsehoods he had charged on me and Friends, declaring that we had not any such meeting from all parts of the nation, as he had represented it; but that (except the Friend from whose house we came, and who came with us to guide us hither, and one Friend of Bristol who came accidentally or rather providentially, to assist my wife homewards, after we were taken) they that were with me were in a sense part of my own family, being my wife and her daughter, and her son-in-law.

And we did not meet in any way or manner that would occasion terror to any of the King's subjects, for we met peaceably and quietly, without arms. And I did not

[1] Sir Thomas Street (1626-1696), M.P. for Worcester.

believe there could any one be produced, that could truly say, he was terrified with our meeting. Besides, I told them, we were but in our journey, the occasion whereof I now again related, as before. Then as to the oaths, I showed why I could not take them (seeing Christ had forbidden all swearing), and what I could say or sign in lieu of them, as I had done before. Yet they caused the oaths to be read to me again, and afterwards read an indictment also, which they had drawn up in readiness, having a jury ready also.

When the indictment was read, the judge asked me if I was guilty.

I said, nay, for it was a great bundle of lies, which I showed and proved to the judge in several particulars which I instanced; asking him if he did not know in his conscience that they were lies.

He said, it was their form.

I said, it was not a true form.

He asked me again whether I was guilty.

I told him nay, I was not guilty of the matter, nor of the form, for I was against the Pope and popery, and did acknowledge and should set my hand to that.

Then the judge told the jury what they should say, and what they should do, and what they should write on the backside of the indictment; and as he said, they did.

But before they gave in their verdict I spoke to them and told them that it was for Christ's sake, and in obedience to his and his apostle's command, that I could not swear; and 'Therefore', said I, 'take heed what ye do, for before his judgement-seat ye shall all be brought.'

The judge said, 'This is canting.' I said, 'If to confess our Lord and Saviour, and to obey his command, be called "canting" by a judge of a court, it is to little purpose for me to say more among you; yet ye shall see that I am a Christian, and shall show forth Christianity, and my innocency shall be manifest.' So the gaoler led me out of the court; and the people were generally tender, like as if they had been in a meeting. Soon after I was brought in again, and the jury found the bill against me, which I traversed; and then I was asked to put in bail till the next Sessions, and the gaoler's son offered to be bound for me. But I stopped him, and warned Friends not to meddle; for I told them there was a snare in that; yet I told the justices that I could promise to appear if the Lord gave health and strength and I were at liberty. Some of the justices were loving, and would have stopped the rest from indicting me, or putting the oath to me; but Judge Street, who was the chairman, said he must go according to law. So I was sent back to prison again; yet within two hours after, through the moderation of some of the justices, I had liberty given me to go at large till next Quarter Sessions. These moderate justices, it was said, desired Parker to write to the King for my liberty, or for a *noli prosequi* (as they called it), because I was not such a dangerous person as I had been represented. This, it was said, he promised them to do; but did it not.

After I had got a copy of the indictment, I went up to London, in the 3rd month [May], visiting Friends as I went.〉

George Fox to Margaret Fox.[1]

Adderbury, Bray D'Oyly's, Oxfordshire.
4th of 3rd mo. [May], 1674.

Dearly loved,

I received Thomas's letter the one of the 6th day of the 1st month [Mar.], and thine on the 13th day of the 2nd mo. [Apr.], and another from thee which, [as] I was going out of London, I left Margaret to answer you for they came to me when I was going. And I received your last on the 28th day of 2nd mo. [Apr.].

And I had the liberty of the town before the Sessions, and all the people were respectful to me and very civil to me, and there came three nonconformist priests and others, and they were wicked but confounded and after, a Common-Prayer priest which was civil, and them that were with him.

And I write myself and I desire that thou would do nothing to provoke to strife, but rather in the love and power to lay thee. Write to William Penn of them at Kendal. I desire that thee

[1] From original in Friends House, London; (Gibson Collection, i, 123).

would rather forbear and be over such things. A Friend that came to Worcester told me a word that I had said to some of you, and it was gotten into Westmorland. I desire you may be wise and if you do leave Westmorland Women's Meeting to themselves a while and let their spirits cool and not strive for the power, life will arise over all. And so be still in the power and life and do as it moves.

The money you may return to E. Mann and the papers you may send to London; and so keep out of all strife and over it, for God is a God of peace and love.

Many Friends were at the Sessions from London, Bristol, and many other parts, and queried after you and Thomas. And the Sessions was like a meeting, and things were beyond words, blessed be the Lord. I have gone through much towing,[1] but all was gladded greatly for the Lord's power.

So my love to Thomas and all the children and all Friends as though I named them, and you may hear more after the term.

In haste, G.F.

And the black cloth Edward Reynolds of Worcester will look after and write to you.

⟨When I came there, some that were earnest to get me out of the hands of those envious justices that sought to praemunire me at Worcester, would needs be tampering again, to bring me before the judges of the King's Bench; whereupon I was brought again by a *habeas corpus* before them. I tendered them a paper, in which was contained what I could say instead of the Oaths of Allegiance and Supremacy, as follows:⟩

This I do in the truth, and in the presence of God declare:

That King Charles is lawful King of this realm, and all other his dominions, and he was brought in, and set up King over this realm by the power of God; and I have nothing but love and goodwill to him and all his subjects, and desire his prosperity and eternal good.

And I do utterly abhor and deny the Pope's power and supremacy, and all his superstitions and idolatrous inventions, and affirm that he hath no power to absolve sin. And I deny his murdering of princes or other people, by his plots or contrivances. And likewise all plotters and contrivers against

[1] *Tow* means to comb or card wool and flax.

the King and his subjects; knowing them to be the works of darkness, and the fruits of an evil spirit, and against the peace of the kingdom, and not from the spirit of God, the fruit of which is love.

And I dare not take an oath, because it is forbidden by Christ and the Apostle; but if I break my Yea or Nay, then let me suffer the same penalty as they that break their oaths.

From me who desire the peace and eternal welfare of the King and his subjects.

George Fox.

This was tendered to the judges before I was praemunired.

And I was cast into Derby dungeon and there kept six months together because I refused to take up arms at Worcester fight against King Charles. And also I was carried up a plotter to bring in King Charles, before Oliver Cromwell, by the Presbyterians and Independents, and there kept prisoner a long while. And now this oath was tendered to me in envy by one Simpson, a turncoat Presbyterian.

G.F.

⟨But the business being so far proceeded in at Worcester, they would not meddle in it, but left me to appear again before the justices at the next general Quarter Sessions at Worcester.

Meanwhile the Yearly Meeting of Friends came on, at which (through the liberty granted me till the Sessions) I was present, and exceeding glorious the meetings were beyond expression; blessed be the Lord.⟩

George Fox to Margaret Fox.[1]

London, 9th of 4th mo. [June], 1674.

My dear love,

To whom is my love, and to Thomas Lower and his wife and all the rest of the children and Friends.

This day and yesterday we had the General Meeting and quiet blessed be the Lord God, whose power is over all and his Seed. I received thy letter and the £50 of Walter Miers, and I got £50 more and paid Martha Fisher, for she said she was to take up money of interest to build a house on the meeting-place in the Strand, and because I put you to borrow of her I could not

[1] From a copy in Friends House, London. (Portfolio 36: 35.)

but in conscience see her paid; and so she is paid her hundred pound and here is her bond with the seals off and the date when. So for the use and other reckonings I leave to you to make amend; and so come no more in debt in London, and get out of debt that you may be free and on the top of such things.

Here are many Friends and of many places, and here were two from Norway and some from Holland, Scotland, and Ireland, and three men banished from Dantzig, pretty, sober men. And here many queried after thee, and you and Thomas, and thought some of you had been here.

So concerning your debts, clear them and this city.

So in haste, I am now come from the meeting and left Friends in it together. So dwell in the Seed of life in which you have life everlasting.

G.F.

⟨After the Yearly Meeting I set forward for Worcester, the Sessions drawing near, which were held in 5th month.⟩[1]

At the Quarter Sessions for the County of Worcester, I was called to the bar and an indictment read against me for my not taking the Oath of Allegiance at the last Sessions. There being a jury impanelled upon me before whom the indictment was read, and there being some jumble among the jury, some being scrupulous in their minds concerning it, Judge Street caused the oath to be read and tendered to me again.

I said I came thither to traverse my indictment and to answer it and said to them, was not this a second snare, to tender the oath to me, because they knew in their own consciences I could not take any oath. I said I had a question to ask him, whether the oath was to be tendered to the King's subjects or to the subjects of foreign princes?

Judge Street said, to the subjects of this realm.

'Then', I said, 'You have left me out as a subject in the indictment, and therefore you have made me uncapable of the oath, and therefore the court should take notice of it, and the jury cannot bring me in guilty according to this indictment.'

[1] He left London 9th July.

The judge cried, 'Read the oath to him.'

I said, 'I require justice according to the indictment,' and asked the judge whether the trial was not between the King and the body of the County and George Fox.

And Judge Street said, 'Yes.'

Then I said they had left the King out of the indictment, so how could I be made the King's prisoner and the King left out of the indictment, to which the Judge said, 'He was in before.'

Then the Judge did not deny but there were errors in the indictment, but said I might take my remedy in their proper place.

I said, 'You know we are a people that suffer all things and bear all things, and therefore you thus use us because we cannot revenge ourselves, but we leave our cause to the Lord.' And I said they had put George Fox in the indictment 'of Tredington', and in the mittimus 'of London'

Then the judge said the oath had been tendered to me several times and they would have some satisfaction from me concerning the oath.

And I told them what I had said and what I could say against popery and for the King, instead of the oath, viz. that if I did break my 'Yea' and 'Nay' according to Christ's command, then let me suffer as they that break the oath. And this I offered under my hand, but it would not be accepted; and I told them this was more than did they that swore and brake their oaths.

And the judge cried to the jury, 'You may go out,' but some of them were not satisfied; and the judge said, 'You hear a man which did swear that the oath was tendered to him at the last sessions.' And he told them what they should do.

Then I said I should leave the jury to their own consciences, and said, 'Seeing you put the oath to me afresh, is my indictment quashed? Yea or Nay? And must the jury go upon my indictment? They cannot bring me in guilty according to my indictment. Therefore you put it to me as a snare. I am to answer to my indictment.' So the jury brought me in guilty. And I asked the jury how they could bring me in guilty of the indictment in which I was left out as a subject; and how could they bring me in guilty for the King, and the King left out of the indictment; and how could they bring in George Fox of London guilty of the offence of George Fox of Tredington. For these were two George Foxes and I knew no George Fox of Tredington.

And the judge told me how favourable they had been to me.

And I said, how could he say so. Was ever any man worse used than I had been, being stopped in my journey, who was travelling with my wife and going to see my mother? I told the judge it was said in the indictment the oath was offered to me on such a day and I was not in the court that day.

To this the judge said all the days were as one, as to the Sessions.

So I told them I knew that, but my trial was not that day. And the judge said that I rambled away to London. But I said that I scorned that, I abhorred it, he should not say so; I did not run away to the King's Bench; I was removed by a *habeas corpus*.

Then I asked him a question, in the presence of the Lord God, in whose presence we are all, viz. whether this oath was not tendered to me in envy; to which the judge said he would I had never come there to trouble them and the country. So I said I was travelling on my journey, they had brought it on themselves for I troubled them not.

Then the judge told me what a sad sentence he had to tell me.

So I said to the judge I had something to say before he gave sentence, viz. whether or no he could pass the sentence on me as a subject and the word subject left out of the indictment, and for the King and the King left out of the indictment, and how could I be made the King's prisoner, and so went on with many words, how the oath was made only against Papists. And I bid them read the preamble to the Act which said the oath was for the discovering of Popish Recusants. But they would not read it.

Then he told me what a sad sentence a praemunire was, that I must forfeit my liberty and all my goods and chattels and endure imprisonment for term of life. So they looked wishfully on me, and the Truth and Life was over all.

So I asked him whether he spoke that by way of admonition or whether it was his sentence. For, I said, I had much to say to him before he passed sentence, and reasons that he could not pass sentence according to the indictment.

So he said it was not the sentence and bid the gaoler take me away and keep me a safe prisoner.

And I desired the Lord to forgive them and spoke several words to the jury who were gathered about him. And one of the worst of them would have taken me by the hand but I would not give my hand but said to him 'How now Judas, hast thou betrayed me and dost thou now come with a kiss?' So I bid him and them repent and so was brought away to the prison, where I am.

When I was gone the Clerk of the Court, Thomas Twitty, asked Street whether that was his sentence and he and the justices considered together; and Street told the Clerk of the Peace that was his sentence and should stand; and here a lie was found in his mouth. And this was done behind my back to save himself from the shame in the face of the country, for I looked to be called again.

Notwithstanding, Judge Street said in the morning before my trial to Bray D'Oyly and Edward Bourne that if he had been upon the Bench the first Sessions, he would not have tendered the oath to me; but if I had been convicted of being at a conventicle, he would have proceeded against me according to that law, and that he was sorry that ever I came before him. And yet he maliciously tendered the oath to me in the court again, when I was traversing my indictment. And generally all the justices and people were civil and quiet, and none of the justices spoke a word as I heard, but the judge and Thomas Twitty, and the lawyer, John Ashley, who was friendly the last time, and spoke for me now, and spoke and pleaded the errors of the indictment. But the judge of the court would not regard, but would over-rule all.

And some said that Judge Street said I had removed myself to the King's Bench for justice, but now they had done me justice. And I do hear that the people are much dissatisfied with their proceedings.

So you may read this in the men and women's meetings that they may be satisfied concerning things with me who desire the same. Worcester prison the 16th of 5th mo. [July]. G.F.[1]

⟨But the Lord pleaded my cause, and met with both him and Justice Simpson, who first ensnared me with the oath at the first Sessions; for Simpson's son was arraigned not long after, at the same bar, for murder.⟩ And betwixt the time of Street's causing me to be indicted and the Sessions where he passed sentence upon me, his only daughter, whom he so doted on she was called his idol, was brought down dead from London to Broadway, to the same inn where he had boasted what he would do against me, and thence to Worcester to be buried, which struck a great damp upon people. ⟨People took notice of the hand of God upon him; but it rather hardened than tendered him, as his conduct afterwards showed.

After I was returned to prison, several came to see me; and amongst others, the Earl of Salisbury's son,[2] who was very loving, and troubled that they had dealt so badly by me. He stayed about two hours with me, and took a copy of the errors in the indictment himself in writing.

The Sessions being now over, and I fixed in prison by a praemunire, my wife came up out of the north to be with

[1] This communication, included in the Journal MS., begins at [1] on p. 694.

[2] Fox in a letter to William Penn, 10 Oct., 1674, says ' the Earl of Salisbury's younger son '.

me. The Assizes coming on soon after, in the Sixth month [Aug.], the state of my case was drawn up in writing, and she and Thomas Lower delivered it to Judge Wilde. In it were set forth the occasion of my journey, the manner of my being taken and imprisoned, the proceedings of the several Sessions against me and the errors in the indictment by which I was praemunired. When the judge had read it he shook his head, and said we might try the validity or invalidity of the errors if we would; and that was all they could get from him.

While thus I lay in prison, it came upon me to state our principle to the King; not with particular relation to my own sufferings, but for his better information concerning our principle, and us as a people.

To the King.

The principle of the Quakers is the Spirit of Christ, who died for us, and is risen for our justification; by which we know that we are his. He dwelleth in us by his Spirit; and by the Spirit of Christ we are led out of unrighteousness and ungodliness. It brings us to deny all plottings and contrivings against the King, or any man. And the Spirit of Christ brings us to deny all manner of ungodliness, as lying, theft, murder, adultery, fornication, and all uncleanness, and debauchery, malice, and hatred, deceit, cozening, and cheating whatsoever, and the Devil and his works. The Spirit of Christ brings us to seek the peace and good of all men, and to live peaceably; and leads us from such evil works and actions as the magistrates' sword takes hold upon. Our desire and labour is, that all who profess themselves Christians may walk in the Spirit of Christ; that they, through the Spirit, may mortify the deeds of the flesh, and by the sword of the Spirit cut down sin and evil in themselves. Then the judges and other magistrates would not have so much work in punishing sin in the kingdom; neither then need kings or princes fear any of their subjects; if they all walked in the Spirit of Christ; for the fruits of the Spirit are love, righteousness, goodness, temperance, etc.

And if all that profess themselves Christians did walk in the Spirit of Christ, and by it did mortify sin and evil, it would be a great ease to the magistrates and rulers, and would free them from a great deal of trouble; for it would lead all men and women to do unto all others as they would have others do unto them; and so the royal law of liberty would be fulfilled. For if all that are called Christians did walk in the Spirit of Christ, by it to have the evil spirit and its fruit mortified and cut down in them, then, not being led by the evil spirit, but by the good Spirit of Christ, the fruits of the good Spirit would appear in all men and women. For as people are led by the good Spirit of Christ, it leads them out of sin and evil, which the magistrates' sword takes hold upon, and so would be an ease to the magistrates. But as people err from this good Spirit of Christ, and follow the evil spirit, which leads them into sin and evil, that spirit brings the magistrate into a great deal of trouble, to execute the law upon the sinners and transgressors of the good Spirit . . .

Now we are a people, who, in tenderness of conscience to the command of Christ and his Apostle, cannot swear; for we are commanded in Matt. v. and James v. to keep to 'Yea' and 'Nay', and not to swear at all; neither by heaven, nor by the earth, nor by any other oath, lest we go into evil, and fall into condemnation . . .

If we could take any oath at all, we could take the oath of allegiance, as knowing that King Charles was by the power of God brought into England, and set up King of England, etc., over the heads of our old persecutors; and as for the Pope's supremacy, we do utterly deny it. But Christ and the apostle having commanded us not to swear, . . . we desire, therefore, that the King would take this into consideration, and how long we have suffered in this case. This is from one who desires the eternal good and prosperity of the King and of all his subjects in the Lord Jesus Christ. G.F.[1]

About this time I had a fit of sickness, which brought me very low and weak in my body; and I continued so a pretty while, insomuch that some Friends began to doubt of my recovery. I seemed to myself to be amongst the graves and dead corpses; yet the invisible power did secretly support me, and conveyed refreshing strength into me, even when I was so weak that I was almost speechless. One night, as I was lying awake upon my bed in the glory of the Lord which was over all, it was said unto me that

[1] In full, Ellwood, pp. 402-404; Bicent., ii, 225-7.

the Lord had a great deal more work for me to do for him before he took me to himself.

Endeavours were used to get me released, at least for a time, till I was grown stronger; but the way of effecting it proved difficult and tedious; for the King was not willing to release me by any other way than a pardon, being told he could not legally do it; and I was not willing to be released by a pardon, which he would readily have given me, because I did not look upon that way as agreeable with the innocency of my cause.

A Friend, one Edward Pitway, having occasion to speak with Justice Parker, upon some other business, desired him to give order to the gaoler, that, in regard of my weakness, I might have liberty to go out of the gaol into the city. Whereupon Justice Parker wrote the following letter to the gaoler, and sent it to the Friend to deliver.

Mr. Harris,

I have been much importuned by some friends to George Fox to write to you. I am informed by them, that he is in a very weak condition, and very much indisposed; what lawful favour you can do for the benefit of the air for his health, pray show him. I suppose, the next term they will make application to the King. I am, Sir, your loving friend,

Evesham, the 8th of October, 1674. Henry Parker.

After this, my wife went to London, and spoke to the King, laying before him my long and unjust imprisonment, with the manner of my being taken, and the justices' proceedings against me in tendering me the oath as a snare, whereby they had praemunired me; so that I being now his prisoner, it was in his power and at his pleasure to release, which she desired. The King spoke kindly to her, and referred her to the lord-keeper, to whom she went, but could not obtain what she desired; for he said the King could not release me otherwise than by a pardon; and I was not free to receive a pardon, knowing I had not done evil. If I would have been freed by a pardon, I need not have lain so long, for the King was willing to give me pardon long before, and told Thomas Moore that I need not scruple being released by a pardon, for many a man that was as innocent as a child had had a pardon granted him. Yet I could not consent to have one. For I had rather have lain in prison all my days than have come out in any way dishonourable to truth; wherefore I chose to have the validity of my indictment tried before the judges.

And thereupon, having first had the opinion of a counsellor upon it (one Thomas Corbett, of London), whom Richard Davies, of Welshpool, was well acquainted with and recommended to me, an *habeas corpus* was sent down to Worcester to bring me up once more to the King's Bench Bar, for the trial of the errors in my indictment.〉

George Fox in Worcester to Margaret Fox in London.[1]
30th of 11th mo. 1674 [Jan., 1675].

Dear Heart,

My love unto thee and Susan and the rest of Friends as though named. I received thy letter wherein thou mentionest that I might have come up by the stage coach, but we told thee in our last it was fully taken up for two weeks, for Thomas went forthwith, as soon as we received thy letter, to take a place in the coach, and sent into the country and went to Wich[2] to have gotten one, but their horses were dead, and weak that were alive, and the coach out of order, and this he did before he spoke with the sheriff; nevertheless I sent for my own horse but he was sold, though I durst not to have adventured on him. And as for all those mistakes and neglects at London they must be looked over, which cannot be helped now they are past; and as for diligence and care, here there was as much used as could be done, for Thomas went the 6th day to speak with the sheriff in the country, with an attorney, though it was rainy and blustering weather, but could not speak with him, being gone upon executing a commission in the country, and he told the attorney that rid to the sheriff that he could do nothing then, being upon the commission, but he would be in Worcester the next day, being 7th day, in the afternoon, where Thomas spoke with him and served him with the writ; and he said he was required by the writ to certify the whole cause of my imprisonment and detention, which would require time to do it,

[1] Original in Spence MSS., iii, 168 ; at Friends House.
[2] i.e. Droitwich.

and that he could not do it till the Second-day. Thomas told him the whole cause was already certified upon the writ of error. He said that was nothing to him, he must do as the writ required him and so would certify; and farther said if Thomas would enter into bond of a £100 to bring me up by the time required in the writ he would make him my keeper. Then Thomas told him I was not able to ride up so soon. He replied that was not his fault but our Friends that had not made the return more large. And therefore now judge how was it possible, my present condition considered, that I could have come up within the time, for if you did look into the writ you might have seen the writ did require the ground and cause of my imprisonment to be certified, and as for *pro rege* and *ad subjaciendum*, it was sufficiently understood, both the one and the other; but as the attorney says, though the writ be *pro rege*, yet the sheriff ought to be paid for his certificate and return, which the court would allow him, though for the King. But the attorney was grieved upon my account and that made him express himself so as he did, that things were not managed as they might have been, nor that my condition was not considered, how I was.

But I desire that you will all keep the Prince of Princes' peace, that in the wisdom of God you may be all preserved and be acted in his power.

I do not know how I shall get up except it be by coach, which Thomas has partly engaged for the next 4th day. Thomas is to speak with the sheriff tomorrow and he will give a further account. I am not very well if I walk but out.

So no more but my love to you all. G.F.

[An addition by Thomas Lower states that a place in the stage coach was secured and that, accompanied by the sheriff, George Fox would be in London by the end of the week. He justifies coach travel, in spite of the delay, rather than horseback as Margaret Fox seems to have suggested, in these words, ' it was the most needful work, for if the sheriff had been never so ready and all things done to our minds, without a coach my father could not have travelled without hazard of his life, that is tired with walking a little in the garden; but I am better satisfied he is here and pretty well than to have him upon the road, sick and in danger of a relapse, which such a sudden push might have cast him into '.]

⟨The under-sheriff set forward with me the 4th day of

the Twelfth month [Feb.], there being with us in the coach the Clerk of the Peace and some others. The clerk had been my enemy all along, and now sought to ensnare me in discourse; but I saw, and shunned him. He asked me what I would do with the errors in the indictment.

I told him they should be tried, and every action should crown itself.

He quarrelled with me for calling their ministers priests.

I asked him if the law did not call them so.

Then he asked me what I thought of the Church of England; were there no Christians among them.

I said, 'They are all called so, and there are many tender people amongst them.'

We came to London on the 8th of the Twelfth month [Feb.], at the latter end of the term called Hilary Term and on the 11th I was brought before the four judges at the King's Bench.⟩

And Counsellor Corbett pleaded and said that they could not imprison any man upon a praemunire.

And Judge Hale, the Chief Justice, said, 'Mr. Corbett, you should have come sooner, at the beginning of the term, with this objection.'

And Corbett said, 'We could not get a copy of the return and of the indictment.'

Then said the judge, 'You should have told us, and we would have forced them to make a return sooner.'

And Judge Wilde said, 'Mr. Corbett, you go upon general terms and if it be so, as you say, we have committed many errors in the Old Bailey and other courts, and we must have time to look in our books and consider the statutes.'

And Counsellor Corbett affirmed again they could not imprison any man upon a praemunire.

But the judge said, 'There is summons.'

'Yes', said Corbett, 'but summons is not imprisonment, for summons is in order to a trial.' So it was deferred till the next day.

The next day they considered the errors of the indictment and meddled no more concerning my imprisonment.

And they found errors enough to quash the sentence of praemunire against me. There were several great men, lords and others, that were tendered the Oaths of Allegiance and Supremacy that day; and some moved to the judges that the oath might be again tendered unto me, and that I was a dangerous man to be at liberty. Judge Hale said he had heard some such reports of me, but he had heard also many more good reports of me. So he declared me in the open hall to be a free man and that I might go whither I would. So that I was set at liberty the 12th day of the 12th month 1674 [Feb., 1675] by the Lord Chief Justice Hale, ⟨upon a trial of the errors in my indictment, without receiving any pardon or coming under any obligation or engagement at all. And the Lord's everlasting power went over all to his glory and praise, and to the magnifying of his name for ever, Amen.⟩ Thus from the 17th of 10th month [Dec.], 1673, was I kept a prisoner and tossed to and from Worcester to London and from London to Worcester again three times, and so kept a prisoner till the 12th of 12th month 1674 [Feb., 1675], being one year and near two months.

And a judge came to Counsellor Corbett after this trial and said unto him, 'You have attained to a great deal of honour for pleading George Fox's cause so in the court.' And many lawyers came to him and said he had brought to light in the nation that which never was known before concerning their not being able to imprison any man upon a praemunire, which spread over the nation and was of great service.

⟨During the time of my imprisonment in Worcester, notwithstanding my illness and want of health, and my being so often hurried to and fro to London and back again, I writ several books for the press, one whereof was called *A Warning to England*. Another was *To the Jews proving by the prophets that the Messiah is come*; another *Concerning inspiration, revelation and prophesy*; another *Against all vain disputes*. Another was *For all bishops and ministers to try themselves by the Scriptures*; another *To such as say we love none but ourselves*; another on *Our testimony of what we believe of Christ*. Another little book *Concerning swearing* was the first of those two that were given to the Parliament. Besides these I writ many papers and epistles to Friends to encourage and strengthen them in their services for God; which some (who had made profession of Truth, but had given way to a seducing spirit, and were departed from the unity and fellowship of the Gospel in which Friends stand) endeavoured to discourage them from, especially in their diligent and watchful care for the well-ordering and managing of the affairs of the Church of Christ; which may be read amongst the rest of my Epistles.⟩

And so when I was set at liberty, having been very weak, I passed to Kingston after I had visited Friends in London. And after I had stayed a while there and visited Friends I came to London again. And I writ a paper to the Parliament and sent several books to them. And several papers out of divers parts of the nation were sent up to the King and Parliament from Friends. And a great book against swearing was given to them, ⟨which so influenced many of them it was thought they would have done something for our relief therein if they had sat longer⟩. And I went down into Middlesex and visited Friends and after came to London again to the Yearly Meeting, 1675, where there were several Friends from most parts of the nation and some from beyond seas, and a glorious meeting in the everlasting power of God it was.

And so then I stayed at London till the Parliament was broken up, and after they were broken up, who had done nothing for Friends nor against Friends, I was clear of my service for the Lord at London. At John Elson's[1] I had a glorious meeting the morning before I came out. And so I took coach ⟨towards the north⟩ with Margaret and her daughter Susan ⟨for I was not able to travel on horseback⟩. And many Friends accompanied us to Highgate, and after to Dunstable. And the next day we came to Newport Pagnell where many Friends came to

[1] John Elson lived at the Peel near St. John's Gate in the city.

visit us. Thence we came to Northampton where many Friends came to visit us, and from thence to Coventry where Friends visited us. And from thence to Coleshill where Friends came in at night and visited us. And there was a woman brought her daughter to show me how well she was, which had had the King's evil. For when I was there before, she desired me to lay my hands on her and pray for her, which I did, and it was immediately made well. And so from thence we came to Whitchurch and from thence to John Simcock's,[1] on the First-day, where Friends came to visit us. Thence we came to William Gandy's and from thence to Warrington, where we lodged all night, where several Friends came to visit us. Thence we came to Preston; where we stayed all night; and from thence the next day we came to Lancaster, where several Friends came to visit us. I had not been at Lancaster since I was carried away by the undersheriff and gaoler towards Scarborough Castle.

It was their fair time and their trained bands were gathered there to a general muster at that time, and when I came to the Kings Arms and went into the parlour there were many of the colonels and officers gathered together; and seeing it full, I went out again into a chamber. And many Friends, being come out of several places of the country, came to visit us. And it being the general Quarterly Meeting the day after, I stayed in town one day and two nights and went to both their meetings, both the men's and women's, which were very full, large and peaceable. And the Lord's power was over them all, and none meddled with us.

At Lancaster Thomas Lower and his wife, and Sarah Fell met us and Leonard Fell and James Lancaster; and the next day we came over the Sands with several other Friends and came to Swarthmoor, the 25th day of the Fourth month [June], 1675.

And after I had been a while at Swarthmoor several Friends from divers places came to visit me—from London

[1] John Simcock lived at Stoke, in Cheshire.

and out of Scotland and divers other parts of the nation and from beyond seas. At last Colonel Kirkby came to visit me, and to bid me welcome into the country, as he said, who had been one of my old great persecutors, and was seemingly very loving.

And in Scotland this year there were four young priests convinced at Aberdeen by Robert Barclay and George Keith at a dispute[1] that they had with some of the University there.

And after I had been at Swarthmoor a pretty while, and Colonel Kirkby was come again into the country, he sent for the constables of Ulverston and charged them to come up to Swarthmoor, and bid them tell me that we must not have any more meetings at Swarthmoor, for if we had, they were commanded by him to break them up. And they were to come the next First-day after. This was noised over all the country. And the next First-day I went into the meeting and we had a precious meeting, and the Lord's presence was amongst us. After the meeting was done one came up and told me the churchwardens were in the meeting, but it was a mistake; and the constables did not come to disturb us. And so the meetings have been quiet ever since and have increased.

[Fox's autobiography ends at this point. The chapter on 'George Fox's Later Years', which follows, has been written by Henry J. Cadbury to complete the account of Fox's life, in place of the narrative compiled in autobiographical form by Thomas Ellwood the first editor, which appeared in his edition of 1694 and its numerous reprints. Ellwood's concluding passage follows on p. 757.]

[1] The dispute took place on 14th April, 1675. The students were Robert Sandilands, James Alexander, Alexander Seaton, and Alexander Patersone.

[Among the various memoranda which are appended to the MS. Journal is the following passage which very briefly dates the first rise of Quakerism in different places. It is the latest dated part of the MS. in Thomas Lower's hand, and it suggests a latest date for Fox's conclusion of his autobiography. It did not appear in the first edition of the *Journal*, but was first printed in Fox's *Epistles*, 1698, p. 2. It has appeared in several modern editions of the Journal. (Cf. *Camb. Jnl.*, ii, 338 and note 3; Bicent., ii, 251.)]

The Truth sprang up first, ⟨to us so as to be a people to the Lord⟩, in Leicestershire in 1644, in Warwickshire in 1645, in Nottinghamshire in 1646, in Derbyshire in 1647, and in the adjacent counties in 1648, 1649, and 1650; and in Yorkshire in 1651, and in Lancashire and Westmorland in 1652, and in Cumberland, Bishoprick[1] and Northumberland in 1653, in London and most parts of the nation and Scotland and Ireland in 1654. And in 1655 many went beyond seas, where Truth also sprang up. And in 1656 Truth broke forth in America and in many other places.

And the Truth stood all the cruelties and sufferings that were inflicted upon Friends by the Long Parliament, and then by Oliver Protector, and all the Acts that Oliver Protector made, and his Parliaments, and his son Richard after him, and the Committee of Safety.

And after, it withstood and lasted out all the Acts and Proclamations, since 1660 that the King came in. And still the Lord's Truth is over all and his Seed reigns and his Truth exceedingly spreads unto this year 1676.

[1] i.e. Durham.

GEORGE FOX'S LATER YEARS

GEORGE FOX'S LATER YEARS

By HENRY J. CADBURY, Ph.D.

FOR the last fifteen and a half years of the life of George Fox we are dependent on scattered and in a sense inferior sources.[1] We lack his own dictated narrative with its inimitable freshness. That narrative, as reprinted in the preceding pages, has recounted his life from his birth in July, 1624, until he was nearly 51 years old. It shows how a religious seeker was turned into a finder and became the 'chief instrument' in the founding of the Society of Friends. It is a story of great activity, interspersed with periods of imprisonment due to the

[1] BIBLIOGRAPHICAL NOTE. For this period our primary sources are the diaries kept for him. They are preserved for less than nine of these years and were published in the *Short Journal and Itinerary Journals of George Fox* (Cambridge, 1925) with valuable notes by Norman Penney. For a few other months similar materials were evidently available to Thomas Ellwood and all these are summarized by him in the *Journal* as he first published it in 1694. This and subsequent editions generally included the valuable preface of William Penn and the testimony of Margaret Fox. In contrast to these external data the inner thoughts of Fox can be gleaned from his *Epistles* (London, 1698) and other writings of the period preserved in manuscript or in print. Many not preserved are listed sufficiently to be suggestive and tantalizing in the *Annual Catalogue of George Fox's Papers* (edited by the present writer in 1939).

Useful in various ways are also the following: *The Household Account Book of Sarah Fell of Swarthmoor Hall*, edited by Norman Penney (Cambridge, 1920), which ends, however, in August, 1678; *Margaret Fell, Mother of Quakerism*, by Isabel Ross (Longmans, 1949), which supersedes the older books by Maria Webb and Helen G. Crosfield; *The Personality of George Fox*, by A. Neave Brayshaw (Allenson, 1933); *The Second Period of Quakerism*, by William C. Braithwaite (Macmillan, 1921); *The London Friends' Meetings*, by William Beck and T. Frederick Ball (Kitto, 1869). Since all these except the last are well indexed, footnote references to them have here generally been omitted. The text will usually suggest the source of the information. The biographies of Fox are particularly inadequate for these later years.

hostility which authorities in church and state felt towards the unconventional and nonconformist persistence of these 'Children of the Light'. The activity included, at least since 1649, twenty years of strenuous itinerant preaching in Great Britain followed by a short journey to Ireland and a long one to the British colonies extending from Barbados to Rhode Island. Fox had something of a genius for friendship and for organization, and by correspondence and consultation he was occupied wherever he went. He was one of the most prolific writers of pamphlets at a time and in a movement when as was said pamphlets were 'as thick as butterflies'. He was engaged in the absorbing religious controversy of the day. He suffered eight imprisonments, four of them brief, but totalling nearly six years out of twenty-five. He had also at least three extended illnesses.

He had married in October, 1669, at the age of 45. His wife, who was ten years his senior, was Margaret, the widow of Judge Thomas Fell (d. 1658) of Lancashire and the mother of nine children, of whom six daughters outlived both the mother and the step-father. Fox had first visited the family in 1652 at their home in Swarthmoor Hall on the edge of the Fells in Furness, north Lancashire. The women and servants all yielded to his message and the home became for half a century a stable northern centre for Quakerism, and Margaret Fell 'the mother of Quakerism'. Since her second marriage her husband had been little with her; he was either travelling or in prison.

SWARTHMOOR 1675-77

The dictated narrative of Fox's life ends when he arrived from London with his wife at Swarthmoor Hall on June 25th, 1675, four months after his liberation from his long last imprisonment. It was a dozen years since he had been there and over five and a half years since he and Margaret Fell, the owner of the Hall during her widowhood, had been married.

There were four or five of the Fell daughters at home in 1675. Sarah, Susannah, more often called Susan, and Rachel were still unmarried. Mary and her husband from Cornwall, Thomas Lower, and one child were living at the Hall, and when they moved to the other ancestral property at Marsh Grange they were only a few miles away. Also Isabel, widow of William Yeamans of Bristol, came to the Hall with two children to live. Before Fox left in March, 1677, two more children were born to the Lowers. Two of the five children there died in this time, Margaret Lower, aged twenty months, and Rachel Yeamans, ten years old. The family included many servants, and George Fox was immersed in a large household whose intimate details for precisely this period are disclosed to us with remarkable fullness in the very business-like account book kept by Sarah Fell for the whole family.[1]

Fox, however, was busy with matters also of his own and with the wider concerns of the Society of Friends. It seems probable that the long continuous narrative in the handwriting of Thomas Lower which formed the basis of his published Journal was dictated during these months.[2] Many of the included documents had probably already accumulated at Swarthmoor Hall. There also were hundreds of letters addressed to him or to Margaret Fell in the early days of Quakerism which he now read over, to be engrossed as source for some future history of Quakerism, and still known as the Swarthmore Manuscripts. Though he was still at Swarthmoor and so absent from the Yearly Meeting in June, 1676, we know that then were started the official questionnaires which were to collect from each county a record of the first publishing of Truth. William Penn as well as Fox was interested in this undertaking, and we learn from a letter of this time to Fox that

[1] Unfortunately leaves for five and a half of the early months of this time are missing. Compare I. Ross, *op. cit.*, chapter 18, 'Life at Swarthmoor Hall, 1673-8.'

[2] Rather than during their common imprisonment in 1674. See *Camb. Jnl.*, i, xxxiv-xxxviii. Some of his letters dated in this period are in the handwriting of Lower, or are dated from Marsh Grange.

he was seeking from London 'Friends' letters and papers, which were written in the beginning of the spreading of Truth; but could find none, they being burnt in the firing of London.'[1] Other collections no longer extant were made or at least started in this period, and there was much personal correspondence. Several pamphlets written earlier were now printed and others were both written and printed before he left Swarthmoor.

Much of his writing consisted of general epistles to individuals or to Quaker groups in specific parts of the world, including now the colonies he had visited in America. Few of his letters to individuals are extant, but a full index of one collection of copies of 150 letters written during this stay at Swarthmoor gives us a better indication of the scope of this kind of correspondence than anything else we possess. Names well known to Quaker history, like Robert Barclay, William Dewsbury, William Edmondson, Isaac Penington and William Penn occur as well as many less known.[2] There were also Quaker visitors to him at Swarthmoor. 'Several Friends came from London to visit me and out of Scotland and divers other parts of the nation and from beyond seas,' he writes.[3]

As far as the authorities were concerned they little disturbed the Swarthmoor household or the local meetings of Friends which Fox attended. As he noted in his Journal, many of his old persecutors in Lancashire were

[1] A. R. Barclay, *Letters, &c. of Early Friends*, No. 99. (November, 1676.)

[2] See items marked M in *Annual Catalogue of George Fox's Papers* under 1675 and 1676. An indication of the many letters *to* Fox is the expense item so common in the Account Book: 'To Higgins for letters for father,' showing that nearly every Thursday when John Higgins, the carrier, made his weekly trip from Lancaster to Ulverston on market day he brought letters for Fox and sometimes boxes containing gifts from afar.

[3] *Camb. Jnl.*, ii, 311. The visitors included John Swinton and his wife from Scotland, Alexander Parker, William Penn, and John Banks. Their errands were various, but the last came explicitly to have Fox cure his withered hand and arm, as related in Banks's own journal and in George Fox's *Book of Miracles*.

now dead.[1] In spite of his threats to break up meetings at Swarthmoor Hall Colonel Richard Kirkby, their hostile neighbour, showed the courtesy of a friendly welcome to Fox upon his arrival, a visit which Fox returned some months later when he and the Colonel were both in London. Another ' old opposer ' in the neighbourhood died in 1677, William Lampitt, minister of Ulverston in the Commonwealth days but now long in retirement, though relentless against the Quakers until near the end. Yet even in these relatively peaceful months one member of the household, Sarah Fell, suffered an imprisonment of perhaps a month at Dalton and was in danger of being imprisoned again, while from afar came news of the revival of persecution in New England, and of trouble in Bermuda, Barbados and Nevis.

New problems were involved on which even from those distant colonies Fox was asked for advice. In New England King Philip's War had begun and the Friends in Rhode Island who controlled the government were unwilling to join the neighbouring colonies in their warlike measures. Fox urged them to ' seek all manner of ways to make peace with the Indians '. In Barbados a law had been passed specifically forbidding the taking of Negroes to Quaker meetings. Fox continued to encourage ' civil disobedience '. On the island of Nevis the Friends were puzzled by the demands made of them to watch, that is, to do guard duty. Fox encouraged them to do it, but without weapons, though some of the Friends had scruples against even unarmed patrolling.[2]

The most serious matter that claimed his attention was the dissension that had arisen over the establishing of women's Monthly and Quarterly meetings. This development of local organization had been initiated by Fox himself a few years before and met with general approval,

[1] Above, pp. 504-5.

[2] *Epistles*, No. 319. For this and the fuller and later correspondence on the matter see M. E. Hirst, *The Quakers in Peace and War*, 1923, pp. 315 ff, 322 ff.

but two Westmorland men, John Story and John Wilkinson, faithful 'publishers of Truth' in an earlier day, strongly objected to this innovation and found supporters in their own county and later elsewhere, especially in Wiltshire and Bristol. As this controversy developed, it inevitably merged into personal attacks upon George Fox and perhaps even more upon Margaret Fox.

At first, whether because of physical limitations or out of strategy, Fox himself kept in the background. An important conference of the leaders on both sides was held in April, 1676, at John Blaykling's house at Draw-well near Sedbergh, only 24 miles away. Margaret Fox, Sarah Fell, Thomas Lower, and William Penn, then a visitor at the Hall, all went to it from Swarthmoor, but Fox remained behind. The leadership of the Society generally shared with Fox his continued advocacy of the women's meetings along with his tender and tactful efforts at reconciliation. With these leaders as well as with the 'separates' as they were called and with Friends who tended to support them, Fox communicated by letter and occasionally by their visits to him. He also wrote many circular letters on the subject.[1]

Compared with the strain and discomfort of his earlier life of travel or imprisonment these days at Swarthmoor must have been a time of relief for Fox. Though a man of strong physique still in his early fifties he was obviously no longer as well as formerly. Speaking of this period his wife says, 'We got him home to Swarthmoor where he had a long time of weakness before he recovered.' In December, 1675, he writes in response to Lady Conway's urgent request to see him, 'I have not been able to stir or travel a pretty while as formerly'; in March to Gervase Benson and Mabel Benson only 25 miles away, 'I had a desire to see you here not being so fit to travel, as I have formerly been'; to Dennis Hollister in July, 'As I was

[1] See *Annual Catalogue*, especially pp. 2 f. under M. For the whole subject see W. C. Braithwaite, *op. cit.*, chapters 10 and 11, and I. Ross, *op. cit.*, chapter 19.

lying on my hammock (not very well) my love and life ran towards thee and would not have thee to be lost . . .'[1] Of the occasional purchases noted by Sarah Fell which were probably for medicinal use for man or beast, only brandy, camphor, juniper berries and mastick are entered as 'for father'.

Fox had probably realized that the earlier chapter of his life might be closing. Only a few months before (September, 1674), writing while ill in Worcester Prison to his 'dear friends in England and all parts of the world', he reviewed his life:

You have known the manner of my life the best part of thirty years since I went forth and forsook all things. I sought not myself: I sought you and his glory that sent me; and when I turned you to him that is able to save you, I left you to him. And my travels have been great, in hungers and colds, when there were but few, for the first six or seven years that I often lay in woods and commons in the night, [so] that many times it was a by-word, that I would not come into houses and lie in their beds. And the prisons have been made my home a great part of my time, and in danger of my life, and in jeopardy daily. And amongst you I have made myself of no reputation, to keep the Truth up in reputation, as you very well know it, that be in the fear of God. With the low I made myself low, and with the weak and feeble I was as one with them, and condescended to all conditions, for the Lord had fitted me so before he sent me forth; and so I passed through great sufferings in my body as you have been sensible.[2]

TRAVELLING AGAIN, 1677

In spite of his physical limitations, towards the end of 1676 George Fox made plans for travelling again. His horse was bought and brought home out of Cheshire and just before the journey began it was shod, his saddle was mended, and a male pillion and braces and three girths were bought for him. On March 26th, the day after the old style New Year, Fox left his home in easy stages for

[1] *Annual Catalogue*, 25, 37F; 25, 36F; 76F.
[2] *Epistles*, No. 308.

London. As far as Draw-well in Yorkshire his wife and Rachel Fell went with him. Then Leonard Fell became his companion. Also with him was, as servant, Edward Haistwell, a lad of about twenty, to whom we are indebted for a daily record of the journey of eight weeks to London, and for more than a year longer. The route taken was via York, Doncaster, Nottingham. At dozens of places he met with local Friends who had not seen him since before his American journey, his route northwards when, in 1675, he drove in a coach from London to Swarthmoor, having taken him, at least from Northampton, further to the west through Warrington and Lancaster. Haistwell gives us the host for each night and the distance travelled, which averaged only five miles per day for forty days of actual riding, while for the remaining days they did not travel at all. Before his wife left him at Draw-well she reports to her daughters—the letter is in Haistwell's handwriting—' Your father is not altogether so weary as he was, but he cannot endure to ride but very little journeys and [a]lights often: but he is pretty well and hearty, praised be the Lord '. From York Fox himself writes to his wife in his own hand:

> In the power of the Lord I am brought to York and had many meetings by the way, and the way was many times very bad and deep with snow that our horses some[times] were down and we were not able to ride and sometimes we had great storms and rain but by the power of the Lord I went through all.

He refers also to the large meetings of Friends which he attended. Haistwell reports his ' declaring some hours ' at regular or appointed meetings as well as long conferences with Friends, and Fox continues, ' So I am in my holy element and holy work in the Lord, glory to his name for ever though I cannot ride as in days past, but praised be the Lord for ever.'[1] In spite of threats by authorities

[1] See Brayshaw, *op. cit.*, pp. 139-140. Ellwood adds: ' that I can travel so well as I do '. Ellwood also composed a summary of the situation upon Fox's arrival in London, referring to late hours due to conferences at the houses of his hosts on the journey and to the pains in his head and teeth as due to riding in the rain.

the meetings suffered no worse disturbance than that at Dingley, Northants, where, after Fox had explained that Christendom had departed from the pure religion that is undefiled, a man went out of the meeting in a furious manner, crying 'I deny it'.

Arriving in London on May 23rd, a fortnight before Yearly Meeting, he visited or consulted not only local Friends but those who had 'come from all parts of the nation and from beyond seas in order to be at the Yearly Meeting'. He had a large number of friends in or near the city, at whose houses he stayed[1] and where he received other visitors. After Yearly Meeting he continued several days longer in London, when besides his visits with Friends he went to see Colonel Kirkby, as already mentioned, and Counsellor Thomas Corbett, who had successfully pleaded Fox's case in February, 1675. He received also a visit from 'one Dr. Moor', perhaps the famous Dr. Henry More, who 'came to dispute with G.F.' What Fox thought of the interview is not recorded. More is said to have reported 'that in conversing with him, he felt himself, as it were, turned into brass. So much did the spirit, crookedness or perverseness of that person move and affect his mind.'

Then he went down to William Penn's home at Worminghurst in Sussex, for nearly a month. Robert Barclay and George Keith, the Scotch Friends, were also there and doubtless discussed their projected trip together to the continent of Europe. Roger Williams's famous anti-Quaker book, *George Fox Digg'd out of his Burrows*, had recently come to hand dealing with the debate held between Williams and Fox's companions in Rhode Island five years before. John Burnyeat who was one of the debaters was now at Worminghurst, and he together with Fox and others prepared the answer of over 500 pages, *A New England Fire-Brand Quenched.* They then went up together to London where 'George Fox passed to Edward Mann's to prepare for his journey into Holland

[1] See below, p. 742 ff.

and to put his books and epistles and things concerning Truth's account in order before he went'.

OFF FOR THE CONTINENT

The trip to Europe which occupied the next three months was probably the most significant single incident in this later period of Fox's life. Like many of his earlier missionary travels it was not undertaken alone. It represented a joint mission by a group of the leaders of Quakerism, some of whom had already seen service in Holland or had connexions there. The original founders of Quakerism there were no longer living, but Fox had known them well and he had living contacts with the Quaker groups in Holland. In a letter written the preceding autumn[1] to Friends there, ten of whom he mentions by name, Fox said that as long ago as 1651 he had seen that 'the Lord has a great people to come out in those parts', but heretofore he had never visited them in their homes and meetings, nor arranged as he now could do personally for the organizing of Yearly, Quarterly and Monthly Meetings. News had come of small cells of like-minded persons in more remote places, or tender individuals like Princess Elizabeth of the Palatinate, a cousin of Robert Barclay. There were reports of persecution being suffered, and it was natural that Friends in England should be eager to bring to bear their influence in countering the misrepresentation of Quakerism so common abroad and in declaring its true tenets. Holland as the home of religious toleration was already admired by liberal Protestants of England.

On July 25th, 1677, the party assembled at Harwich for the packet boat to Briel. Fox had stopped for a day or two at Colchester. William Penn and George Watts arrived the following day. Other prospective voyagers included Robert Barclay, George Keith and his wife

[1] *Epistles*, No. 337 (2nd Sept., 1676). The names are given in the entry of the original *Annual Catalogue*, 110F.

Elizabeth from Scotland, Isabel Yeamans, Fox's step-daughter, and William Talcot and John Furly of Colchester. In his *Account of Travails in Holland and Germany, in 1677*, William Penn mentions two servants, one of whom was almost certainly Fox's attendant and amanuensis, Edward Haistwell. This Westmorland lad, the Neddy Haistwhistle of the *Household Account Book*, had been at or near Swarthmoor before Fox left and had copied sundry records of Fox's travels there in his neat hand. That experience was a good apprenticeship for the strenuous travel in Europe which he records so fully, more fully than did William Penn in his parallel account.

It was a large and effective party and they wisely did not long remain together but divided their forces, so as to cover more ground. Without overlapping the territory travelled by Fox, Penn made two excursions into Germany. The women rendered special service with women like Elizabeth Princess Palatine of the Rhine, granddaughter of James I of England. No doubt Isabel Yeamans kept a filial eye on her stepfather. Conditions of travel were difficult. Long distances had to be traversed, and lodging, not everywhere to be found in the congenial atmosphere of a Quaker home, was perforce in local inns, except when as sometimes happened the travellers reached a city after the gates were closed and had to lie in a boat.

In most of Holland they travelled by boats when in inland waters, or by wagon. The former were probably horsedrawn boats used on canals. Through the cities they often had to walk, sometimes as much as two miles. The distances, still carefully noted by Haistwell, were much greater than Fox was now used to in England and the hours much longer. Outside of Holland with its happy federal union, travellers had to contend with the bothersome formalities of frontiers.

The Colchester members of the party, like most people of that town, could probably speak some Dutch, and so perhaps could William Penn who had Dutch ancestry. He and Keith and Barclay were also able to use Latin when writing or talking to learned persons. Several Dutch Friends served the visitors as interpreters, not only in Holland but when they travelled east, south or north into German and Danish territory. Fox at least was fully dependent on interpreters. Though there is still extant the Dutch New Testament which he owned, secured from Peter Hendricks, it is not apparent that he used it easily.

Arriving at Briel after a quiet voyage of some thirty hours in the packet boat the party was met by Benjamin Furly and other Rotterdam Friends and taken to their homes. But in a few days they passed on to Amsterdam where in a busy week they held meetings with Friends and with the public and established meetings for discipline. The Holland Yearly Meeting dates its foundation from this visit. Shortly after his English companions had left for the south, Fox started out through north Holland with Jan Claus, crossed the Zuyder Zee into Friesland and so on until he left the country and crossed the Ems to Emden. Not even Thomas Ellwood keeps in his edition all the names or events of the full itinerary recorded in our source. Suffice it to say that at Alkmaar and Harlingen and Leeuwarden they had Quaker hosts and small Quaker communities to visit, while at Emden, from which Friends had been banished, Jan Claus and his wife (who is now mentioned as with him) stayed with her father, a merchant of the city. Here Edward Haistwell was taken ill and was cared for in the merchant's home, while Fox and Claus proceeded to Friedrichstadt and back. But the circumstance of Haistwell's illness means that for three weeks he is copying Fox's own account which again shows the freshness of Fox's style.[1]

GERMANY

As they travelled eastward through Oldenburg, Bremen, Hamburg, and many other places named and unnamed,

[1] *S.J.*, pp. 241-7.

they stopped little on the way. They were making for Friedrichstadt. This was in the Duke of Holstein's country and contained ' a fine meeting of Friends '. Here they remained a few days and set up in the city a men's and women's Monthly Meeting. The return journey, begun toward the end of August, followed much the same route. At Hamburg they were joined by John Hill, apparently an English Quaker preacher, and stayed two days. Travelling onward as usual in a wagon they had two near mishaps in crossing swollen rivers, which Fox vividly describes, but they came safe to Bremerhaven and so to Bremen, Oldenburg, ' a great city lately burned down ', and back to Emden. Haistwell's marginal estimates of mileage add up to over 250 miles one way. Rarely even in his younger years had Fox experienced such long days of travel, though he could have characterized them as Thomas Chalkley did his journey over the same route a few years later, ' all in wagons and vessels. We came not on a horse's back all the time.' Fox records interviews with a Levite that was a Jew at Friedrichstadt, with a Swede who was banished out of his own country for his religion at Hamburg, and with innkeepers, with frontier soldier guards and with all sorts of people on the way. He says, ' Many times in mornings, noons and nights and as I travelled, I spoke to the people the Truth and warned them of the day of the Lord and exhorted them to the Light and Spirit of God '. Presumably Jan Claus interpreted for him to these astonished and sometimes appreciative German audiences.

At the moment of his visit persecution was not rife in any of these places, though at Emden ' Friends had been cruelly persecuted and banished ', and at Friedrichstadt the efforts of the Duke in the same direction had been neutralized by the friendliness of the city magistrates. But at other times and in others of these places Fox was engaged to plead by letter or essay for tolerance from the civil authorities and to engage in controversy with the religious authorities.

HOLLAND

From Emden, on the 5th of September, Fox continued to retrace his steps to Amsterdam, except for a side journey by river and lakes to Gorredyk. He had again the company of young Haistwell, and for a time of William Penn. Thomas Rudyard and Isabel Yeamans came back to join him for ten days and then preceded him to England, as did also John Hill. For a month he stayed at Amsterdam, except for brief excursions to Landsmeer in Waterland, 'in which town there is above a hundred bridges', and to Haarlem. His hostess at Amsterdam was Gertrude Dericks Nieson, a widow with two children who lived 'on the Keysersgracht by the house with the heads' and who later crossed to England with her children and the returning group of Friends. Much of his time here when not in meetings or interviews was spent in writing. Amsterdam was the most famous resort on the Continent for sightseers and for seekers who wished to make contact with Friends. There as well as elsewhere on this journey the English visitors had discourse with notable persons, priests and doctors, including some from Germany and Poland, representatives of the Socinians, Collegiants and Baptists (or Mennonites) and persons eminent in political and social life. When Penn finally came back to Amsterdam from Germany, on 8th September, he and George Keith had two disputes with Galenus Abrahams, one of the greatest Baptists in all Holland. Fox took little part, but William Penn and William Sewel the historian, who may well have been present, both give some account of the affair.

For two other gatherings at this time it is possible to quote Fox's own account:

On the 26th day [of September], there being a fast through all the provinces of Holland, I was moved to stay a meeting the same day at Amsterdam, whither resorted many great persons as also a great concourse of people, and the Lord's power was over all. And I was moved to open to them that no man by all his wit and study, nor by reading history in his own will could declare or know the generation of Christ who was not begotten by the will of man but by the will of God; and this was largely opened. And then I did open to them the true fast from the false, showing them that the Christians, Jews and Turks were out of the true fast, and fasted for strife and debate, and the bands and fists of iniquity were over them, and oppression; and with that they were smiting one another, and the pure hands were not lifted up to God, and how that they did all appear to men to fast and did hang down their heads for a day like a bullrush, which fast God did not accept and in that state all their bones were dry, and when they called upon the Lord he did not answer them, neither did their health grow, for they kept their own fast and not the Lord's. And therefore all were to come and keep the Lord's fast. This with many other things were opened to the astonishment of the fasters. And all parted in peace, the Lord's power being over all.

And I having appointed a meeting at Haarlem city to be on the 27th day I and Peter Hendricks and Gertrude Dericks Nieson took waggon and passed thither, where we had a blessed meeting. Several professors and a high priest of the Lutherans were at the meeting, and the priest sat and heard G.F. declare some hours and then he went away and said that he had heard nothing but what was according to the word of God, and desired that the blessing of the Lord might rest upon us and our assemblies. Gertrude did interpret for me. So the meeting did end in peace and in the power of the Lord, others confessing to the Truth, saying they had never heard things so plainly opened to the understanding before.[1]

Leaving Amsterdam with William Penn and George Keith, Fox passed through Leiden, the Hague, 'which is accounted the greatest village in the world', and Delft, and arriving at Rotterdam spent a week there probably again under the hospitable roof of the learned Dutch Friend, Benjamin Furly. Here also there were epistles to write, great men to interview, Friends' Meetings to attend and farewells to be said. Finally, on 20th October they went down to Briel to take the English packet boat for Harwich.

[1] *S.J.*, pp. 250-1.

The passage was a very rough one, taking three days and two nights, and the vessel so leaky that it was believed they pumped more water than twice the vessel full. Penn and Keith took horse and passed at once to Colchester. Fox and his Dutch companions, requiring a coach, were delayed and cheated in getting one and finally hired a Friend's wagon and laid some straw in it and so went to Colchester.

SUNDRY PARTS OF ENGLAND, 1678-81

Haistwell's account of day by day doings of Fox continues until Midsummer Day, 24th June, 1678, when his term of service with his ' dear master ' came to a close. For the rest of Fox's life, with the possible exception of his second and last stay at Swarthmoor from September, 1678, to March, 1680, other attendants kept records of similar character, some of which are extant in a clean copy made apparently by John Field. For parts of the periods now missing similar records seem to have been available to Thomas Ellwood,[1] who displays the same pattern of summarizing in his own language but in the first person detailed records written in the third person. The modern editor without taking the same liberties must perforce also summarize. For detailed though the available materials are they are monotonous and without the vigour of Fox's own dictated journals. Much that we should

[1] It is evident that he had a fuller account of the month in Holland in 1684 than that given below, and of other short periods of travel in England, since he gives the bare itinerary. When he had details of life in and near London he vigorously condenses them and offers instead many longer papers of Fox with his own editorial explanation of the occasion for them. Beside his sources printed in the *Short Journal* a piece of ' Foul Journal ', as it is called, is extant in Friends House, London (Portfolio 10.44) partly overlapping and partly preceding the printed account for the winter of 1682-3. The modern reader who can now sample Fox's epistolary and expository style from later volumes of his collected works may regret Ellwood's substitution of such material for crisp, though not autobiographical diary.

like to know is not recorded and we must piece together and interpret what we gratefully possess.

Fox's life had, with some exceptions, become somewhat of a routine, centred in London and not taking him far away. The exceptions may be described first, so far as our sources of information permit.

Upon his return from Holland, after staying nearly a week each at Colchester and about Felstead, George Fox remained over a month in London, attending meetings, writing, and consulting on sundry problems. The last half of December he spent at Kingston-on-Thames in which time ' his book in answer to Roger Williams was examined and prepared ready for the press '. The next four months were spent out of London, about one month at Bristol at Fair time and the rest slowly passing from place to place in very short journeys. Nearly everywhere he stayed with Friends; other Friends came to see him. While he was at Bristol an unsuccessful effort was made to end the differences with William Rogers, the local leader of the Wilkinson-Story faction there. William Penn took the lead but Fox was there and involved, and indeed a chief object of criticism. John Story was also in Bristol but would not attend any public discussion. In Buckinghamshire also, where he visited Isaac Penington and Thomas Ellwood as he came and went, he tried to reconcile John Raunce and Charles Harris who had come into conflict with the main body of Friends. In March, 1678, a long anticipated visit was paid to Lady Conway's home at Ragley, with two extended interviews with the noble invalid herself. Her learned mentor, Francis Mercurius van Helmont, was there having recently turned Quaker, and with Keith, he helped Fox in answering some anti-Quaker publications. In May Fox attended the Yearly Meeting in London.

The second long stay at Swarthmoor began probably in September, 1678, and lasted about a year and a half. The members of the family at the Hall or at Marsh Grange were much the same as when he left fifteen months before. There was a new baby in the Lower family, and another grandchild at the Hall, twelve-year-old Bethiah Rous, who had been left there with her aunts and grandmother while John and Margaret Rous and the younger children went on a visit to John's home in Barbados. Except for the formal papers which Fox dated from that time and place we have almost no knowledge of his life and thought during this period. Early in March 1680, he left his home for the last time and travelled again by easy stages to London. He began through Westmorland and Lancashire into Yorkshire where his visit coincided with Quarterly Meeting and also with the Assizes in which many Quaker prisoners were involved. Later he visited Friends in Lincolnshire, Nottinghamshire, Derbyshire, Leicestershire, Warwickshire, Oxfordshire, Gloucestershire, Northamptonshire, Buckinghamshire, and Bedfordshire. Ellwood mentions his visit at Warwick with his old friend William Dewsbury and a very large meeting at Biddlesden, Bucks, in an old abbey house that a Friend rented and occupied. He reached London a week before Yearly Meeting.

During the summer of 1680 he made a tour of parts of Surrey and Sussex and in the summer of 1681 a similar visit in those counties and also in Buckinghamshire and Berkshire. For the rest he was either in London or in one of the several neighbouring places which served him as retreats from the city proper.

HOLLAND, 1684

The only distant journey from London in the last decade of Fox's life was his second visit to Holland in 1684. His associates were Alexander Parker, George Watts and Nathaniel Brassey, all from London. William Bingley and Samuel Waldenfield were also with him, though they travelled separately in Holland after the Yearly Meeting there concluded. Fox's actual time in Holland was just over a month, from 5th June to 6th July, compared with about three months in 1677, but the distance travelled in Holland is estimated at 420 miles, which is more than Fox's first journey (about 358) there when, however, he had taken the additional strenuous journey to Friedrichstadt and return.

The figures are calculated from an early summary of the journey which lists

> 18 meetings, viz. at Rotterdam 3, at Haarlem 1, at Amsterdam the Yearly Meeting and others 7, at Knipe 2, at Gorredyk, at Leeuwarden 1, at Harlingen 1, in Friesland 3, at Landsmeer 1, at Alkmaar 1, besides other private meetings and discourses relating to religion and Truth. Two earls came to the meeting at Amsterdam and also several considerable persons and great persons came to several of the meetings.[1]

Evidently so far as persons and places were concerned this visit to Holland in 1684 repeated much that Fox had done seven years before. The Yearly Meeting that occurred in Amsterdam while he was there now included Germany as well as Holland. He also met again Galenus Abrahams who, according to Ellwood's account, was now very tender and loving, and attentive to the testimony of Truth, whereas earlier he had been very high and shy and would not let Fox touch him or look upon him, because as he said his eyes pierced him. Among the papers Fox wrote during this journey was one to the Jews which was printed in Hebrew. Brief though the visit was, it helped to maintain Fox's contact with Friends across the Channel.

MEETINGS IN LONDON

The detailed diaries kept for Fox in and about London give us a quite clear picture of his activities there during most of his last years.[2] No doubt many personal details are omitted, for the diarists had their own emphases.

[1] Swale MSS., iii, 150, printed in *Jnl. F.H.S.*, vi, 1909, p. 37. Ninety-six miles each way between Rotterdam and Harwich is allowed in accordance with Haistwell's figures. The arithmetic for the number of meetings is puzzling. Ellwood evidently had access to a full itinerary which in its tourist comments resembled the record of Haistwell in 1677.

[2] The gaps occur especially in 1680, 1681, 1682, and from 9th Sept., 1687, to 22nd June, 1688.

One of these, and inevitably so, was Fox's attendance of meetings. The central meetings of the Society of Friends had just been organized, partly under Fox's own influence, in the early 70's. There was the Yearly Meeting, a body of delegates, held in London annually in Whitsun week. It included three or four business sessions preceded on Monday by the General Meeting for ministers from all over the nation. Fox was twice absent, in 1676 and 1679, both years at Swarthmoor, whence he sent the meeting a general letter of advice. Other years he attended not only the business sessions but the large week-day meetings for worship, not to mention the many informal conferences, which we should call committee meetings, and the opportunities to meet the visitors from out of town. It was his custom to write when present at Yearly Meeting a brief Epistle of his own which was appended to the Epistle sent out to all Friends' meetings by the Yearly Meeting.

The Meeting for Sufferings was established in 1675 with London correspondents for the several counties of England as well as for Quaker communities overseas. It dealt primarily as its name implies with the sufferings of Friends, though it was not, even at that time, occupied only with these. It was the principal executive body representing the wider concerns of the Society of Friends and increasingly became important as it is to-day. It met weekly, on Thursdays, later on Friday afternoons, and often required adjourned sessions or sub-committees. Fox, when in London, appears rarely to have missed this weekly engagement.

Nearly as regular was his attendance in London on Mondays at what was known as the Second Day's Morning Meeting. It was a meeting of the men ministers, though once a month it appears to have included a devotional period with the women ministers. One of its heaviest duties was the examination, rejection, revision or authorization of Quaker books or pamphlets submitted in manuscript for publication. In 1673 it founded the present Library of the Society of Friends in London. It had also a local concern, to consider the attendance and service of ministers at the London Sunday meetings. Each week were recorded on a blank schedule, sometimes in autograph, the names of those who gave notice what meeting they expected to attend on the following Sunday. Fox's name appears there from time to time.[1]

These ministering Friends met also at eight o'clock Sunday morning for a devotional period, from which they proceeded to the several meetings.

Frequent, though less regular was Fox's attendance at the strictly local business meetings—the Six Weeks Meeting which met eight times a year on Tuesdays and according to Fox was 'the prime meeting of the city', the Quarterly Meeting which met four times a year on Monday afternoons and included both London and suburban Middlesex Friends, and the smaller local units or Monthly Meetings of which six were in London and four in the suburbs. The Six Weeks meeting was a limited joint meeting of men and women which had important financial functions and still continues. There was also a Two Weeks meeting on Monday afternoons which had care of marriages. The Quarterly and Monthly Meetings included public occasions for worship and when Fox attended these he often spoke. Men and women met for business separately in Monthly and Quarterly Meetings. At them Fox apparently spoke often 'admonitionwise' to both women and men separately.

There were also the meetings for worship held regularly at the several Friends' meeting houses on Sunday morning and also on one of the week days. Fox was frequently at these and there is no mention I believe of his having remained silent throughout, though he usually spoke only after others had done so, and the meeting closed after he was through. His addresses were long and extempore. They were often followed by prayer and brief exhortation.

[1] The earliest of these books is extant, with a note under date of 6 mo. 13, 1683, 'G.F. seeing this book approved of it and ordered it to be kept as a record.'

A few taken down in ' characters ' or shorthand are extant, transcribed but not published. Sometimes, especially in the last year, the diarist has left on record some of the topics on which he spoke.

The meetings attracted strangers, referred to usually as ' many of the world's people '; but one notes with interest how much more abundant and respectable the visitors seem to become after the ban upon conventicles was withdrawn. Then in London, as before at Amsterdam, we hear of attendance of ' several great persons, one said to be a lord and another a knight ', or of ' two great persons from the Court ' or of ' the Earl of Ancrum and his nephew and two nieces '.

The laws employed against Friends' meetings were in force until almost the end of Fox's life, and in London as elsewhere the danger of arrest was always present to attenders, depending on the current attitude of the local authorities and on the activity of informers. There was reason for the diariest to note each time whether a meeting was peaceable or disturbed and whether it was held ' within the doors ' or without, that is, whether or not the authorities locked the Friends out of the meeting house so that they met in the yard or the street. Fox deliberately exposed himself again and again where arrests were expected, but it was noted that he was only once apprehended and then soon released.[1] His experiences of immunity were recorded with satisfaction as well as with unusual fulness of detail.

PERSECUTION, TOLERATION, AND OTHER PROBLEMS

In London and elsewhere Fox occasionally visited the prisoners, consulted with them and others for their release and appealed to the authorities for moderation and justice. In Bristol the persecution was even more severe than in

[1] October, 1683. The records for 1682 and 1683 are partly in the first person singular and hence derive from Fox himself. See ' Foul Journal ' mentioned above p. 728 note and *S.J.*, pp. 77, 78, 81, 84-7.

London, but no part of England was at this time immune. Nor was the Fell family. Thomas Lower was imprisoned at Launceston in Cornwall for three years, Isabel Yeamans who travelled in the ministry was a sufferer and testimony bearer, and at Swarthmoor itself Margaret Fell, her family and neighbours were under constant threats. The 'Justices Kirkby' of Kirkby Hall and Sir Daniel Fleming of Rydal Hall never really were reconciled to her holding meetings in Swarthmoor Hall. There were fines and distraints and at least one brief imprisonment for Margaret Fell and extended imprisonment for Daniel Abraham, who after his marriage to Rachel Fell in March, 1683, made his home in the Hall. In 1684 Fox was involved in a local suit for small tithes along with his wife and some other Friends in the north and the case was transferred to London, where Fox actively defended himself with the help of Rowland Vaughan, an attorney employed by Friends.[1] The testimony of William Meade that at his marriage Fox had renounced all claim to his wife's property evidently contributed to his defence.

There were other legal problems which required the professional assistance of an attorney. Some were individual like the dispute concerning Richard Preston's plantation in Maryland. Others had to do with efforts through the Attorney-General to secure relief of suffering Friends at Bristol or in Yorkshire. That concerning West Jersey was more inclusive. It was submitted to a group of London Friends, with whom Fox was associated in long conference through many months in 1684 and 1685. Less trouble but still of great interest to Fox was the grant to William Penn in 1681 of the American colony known as Pennsylvania. Penn was already involved in the proprietorship of both East and West Jersey and Fox often saw him on these and other matters in London—

[1] Ellwood gives this under 1681. His source is not known, perhaps an autobiographical account that Fox wrote of his imprisonments and being before magistrates, now lost except for a postscript. For the correct date see *S.J.*, p. 100 note 5; cf. p. 93.

at committees, at his lodgings in Charing Cross, at the houses of other Friends. On August 13th, 1682, William Penn on the eve of his departure to Pennsylvania stopped to say farewell to Fox at Enfield where Fox had been ill, and in March, 1683, Fox went fifty miles out to Worminghurst on purpose to see Gulielma Penn who had a new baby.[1] At that time and at many others Fox wrote letters to his numerous Friends in Pennsylvania.

Fox was interested in the 'Holy Experiment' not simply because he owned over a thousand acres in Pennsylvania, the gift of William Penn; he recognized also the opportunities as well as the difficulties and dangers of the new venture. He was aware that some of the best ministers in the Society of Friends had died there. He knew that after all their criticisms of other rulers, Friends, when they controlled the government, would be critically watched with jealous eyes. Did they, now that they were in office, bear consistently their testimony against flattering titles, against capital punishment and against war? And did some Friends who went to America do so merely to escape the punishments and the imprisonment that came to those who bore witness faithfully in England, Scotland and Wales? He urged the setting up of meetings for worship and for business, including women's meetings throughout the American colonies, with frequent visitation between them and with a common printing house for Friends in the whole continent.

There were many other places overseas which Fox kept in his heart, as letters, some extant, but many now missing, bear witness. The last letter from him, dated the day before he died, was addressed to Friends in Ireland, who unlike Friends in England were still in great suffering. His concern for Rhode Island and New Jersey has already been mentioned. There is unconfirmed evidence that at one time he had an ownership interest in a large tract in West Jersey. He was in correspondence with Friends in the more southern colonies which he had visited, Maryland,

[1] *Pennsylvania Magazine of History and Biography*, 74 (1950), 110-12.

Virginia and Carolina, as well as those in the Caribbean, and with Friends in Holland and Germany.

From these places from time to time visitors came to him in London like ' James Harding of Jamaica and other two from Rhode Island ', ' some German Friends that were going to Pennsylvania ' and two Friends from Holland, all in 1685. From Holland also came his former interpreters Jan Roeloffs with his wife and Jan Claus, in April and September, 1686, and from Barbados Richard Sutton and his daughter, in September, 1688.

He also made contacts with persons from abroad who were not Friends, very often in connection with the problems of local persecution. It is not altogether coincidence that a few days before Fox wrote his learned letter to the King of Poland we read that he sent for a great doctor that came from Poland and had discourse with him, in January, 1686. Two months later he went on foot about six o'clock in the morning to call on the former governor of Barbados at his lodgings in Pall Mall. This was soon followed by a series of conferences with London Friends about delivering to the King an account of Friends' sufferings in Barbados. So Fox's deep concern for some of the smaller groups and more unfortunate Quaker sufferers is constantly reflected in his writings to the sufferers themselves and to the civil and religious authorities overseas. Among these were the groups of Friends at Mequinez and at Algiers taken prisoner by the pirates of the Barbary Coast. At Algiers they were even allowed to hold a Friends' meeting. This liberality of their captors impressed Fox, though he entered vigorously into theological polemic against the Turks and Moors. Probably it was on one of these subjects that Fox spoke when on the morning of 8th February, 1682, he went with three Friends to see the Ambassador of the Emperor of Morocco, then in London.[1]

[1] See *Epistles*, Nos. 366, 388, 391, 420. The account of the interview (*Annual Catalogue*, 10, 11G) is unfortunately not now available. The ambassador was probably Mohammed ibn Haddu who was shortly after elected Fellow of the Royal Society in London. See *Friends Quarterly*, January, 1950, pp. 55-9.

Until the very end of Charles II's reign persecution of dissenters in England continued. Perhaps it was at its height in 1683 when Fox wrote to Friends in Charleston, South Carolina:

> We here are under great persecution, betwixt thirteen and fourteen hundred in prison, an account of which hath lately been delivered to the King, besides the great spoil and havoc which is made of Friends' goods by informers, and besides the great spoil upon two thirds of our estates and upon the twenty pound a month acts, and for not going to the steeple-house. And besides many are imprisoned and praemunired for not swearing allegiance, both men, women, widows and maids. And many are fined and cast into prison as rioters for meeting to worship God. And we are kept out of our meetings in streets and highways in many places of the land, and beaten and abused . . . and many are cast into prison because they cannot pay the priests' tithes, and also many are cast into prison by the bishops' writs, *De Excommunicato Capiendo.*[1]

The services which Fox could render varied with the country, the county, the individual, and the times. The local cases came under review at the Quarter Sessions which for London and Middlesex were held at Guildhall and at Hicks Hall. Fox and other London Friends helped in the preparation of the defendants' cases and were usually in close touch with the proceedings at both places.

On the national scale there were appeals to be presented to King and Parliament either in writing or by delegations, and these required consultation. An additional office or ' chamber ' was rented by Friends in Palace Yard adjoining Westminster Hall convenient for lobbying. When at last on 8th February, 1685, Charles II died and was succeeded by James II, new efforts were made. The very

[1] *Epistles*, No. 386, London, 23rd February, 1683-4. For the laws applied to Friends see Braithwaite, *op. cit.* The situation was at this time made more acute by the activity of informers, by the discovery of the Rye House Plot, and by the very severe weather in the winters of 1683 and 1684.

next day Fox ' for five hours had a meeting with several Friends about drawing up a paper to the King '. In March a petition was presented to the King showing 1,460 Quaker prisoners then in jail. Application for their release was not immediately successful partly because of Monmouth's rebellion. When thereafter the Chief Justice was proceeding on the Western Circuit a certificate was prepared to clear Friends in Somerset from any complicity in the event. When Parliament sat in May a new account of Friends' sufferings was quickly prepared and printed, to be sent to King and Parliament.

In March, 1686, the King issued a General Pardon and a royal warrant releasing certain lists of Friends from prison and cancelling all fines levied on any of them for not coming to church. Fox wrote to the King expressing gratitude, and to Friends advising them how not to abuse their new relief, and he joined with others in consulting about sending a special delegation to the Attorney-General, then out of London in the country, to secure his signature on the individual warrants.

Similar activities were employed by Fox and other Friends in London when the Declaration of Indulgence was issued in April, 1687; and when, on the fall of James II, William and Mary were welcomed to the throne, Friends were greatly concerned to have the wording of the Toleration Act suit their needs, especially in the obtaining of relief from oaths and in legalizing marriages. Fox joined Friends in these discussions ' reading and fitting their amendments upon the bill of indulgence '. He apparently never served as a member of any of the official delegations, since there were several other Friends personally in a better position to do so, but he had the satisfaction of seeing legally withdrawn before his death the majority of the grounds on which Friends had suffered so far as England was concerned.

The more local or individual concerns that occupied Fox's attention were so numerous that we can hardly exaggerate their variety. The minutes still extant of the central London meetings[1] would give some impression of the official matters considered. It should be remembered that George Fox was himself not an appointed member of any of the delegated bodies, not even of the Yearly Meeting. His influence was great however, as chance references or hostile ones clearly indicate. William Penn said of him: 'He held his place in the church of God with great meekness and a most engaging humility and moderation—his authority was inward not outward, and he got it and kept it by the love of God and power of an endless life.' It is rather in the informal discussions held at the Chamber, in his lodgings, at a Friend's inn or coffee-house and in the homes of Friends, that the variety was greatest.

In a single day Fox had as many concerns to turn to as the many houses to which the day took him. We may take for example one day, 1st June, 1683. According both to the 'itinerary journal' and to 'the foul journal' Fox's engagements included that day:

A meeting about the 5th hour in the morning at William Crouch's with some Friends from Scotland, Ireland, Holland, Friesland, Danzig and America.

A meeting at Benjamin Clark's about business.

A meeting of the physicians at James Wasse's.

Two meetings at Richard Richardson's chamber about business.

Baffling as such brevity is, it also invites to expansion and to detection of details from other sources. The 'chamber' was the central Quaker office off Lombard Street, and Richardson was now the official secretary. Neither Crouch, the upholsterer in Gracechurch Street, nor Clark, the bookseller and printer of Friends' books, was far away. Since 1680 two or three items a year by George Fox bore the imprint 'Printed for Benjamin Clark in

[1] Those of the Second Day's Morning Meeting from 1673, of the Meeting for Sufferings from 1675, of the Six Weeks Meeting from 1671, the Two Weeks Meeting from 1671, the Yearly Meeting from 1672.

George-yard in Lombard Street'. We can only guess what was discussed there, or among the Quaker physicians met with James Wasse, 'citizen and barber chirurgeon'. Fox was a great promoter of groupings of Friends by occupation—tailors, teachers, shoemakers, innkeepers, etc., to consider the implications of Quakerism for a special trade or profession. Already in Barbados there were special meetings of chirurgeons and of midwives.

As for the very international group, William Crouch was we know especially in touch with Dutch Friends. Many of those present so early that Friday morning in June had doubtless come to London for the Yearly Meeting, which was just over. By his own record[1] we happen to know that Francis Daniel Pastorius, the pioneer of Dutch immigration to Pennsylvania, was in London precisely on this date. He was lodging on Lombard Street, and two days later went to Gravesend to sail for Philadelphia in the ship *America*, Joseph Wasey master. He does not mention Fox by name but he does mention in London at that time the German Quaker physicians Tobias Ludwig Kohlhans of Rotterdam, and van Helmont. Many of his eighty fellow passengers must have been in London too. They were so varied that he likens the ship to Noah's Ark. Thomas Lloyd, the Welsh Quaker and Pennsylvania statesman, with his family, was among them. Both Lloyd and Pastorius might qualify also as physicians. Doubtless research and imagination could do much more to fill in the outline of this single day of Fox.

The diary usually contents itself with such a phrase as 'Friends business' or 'the service of Truth amongst Friends', but from its more definite references and other sources we know that individual matters—legal, professional, financial, matrimonial and what not—were discussed with him. He was asked to settle differences between individual Friends, to inspect a disputed right of way to a meeting house, to give his judgment on a house being

[1] M. D. Learned, *The Life of Francis Daniel Pastorius*, Philadelphia, 1908, 116-19, 123.

considered for a Friends' school, to comfort the sick or bereaved or ' distracted ' (i.e. mentally afflicted).

The unhappy separation begun by Wilkinson and Story was fortunately not spreading, though small schismatic groups of Friends maintained themselves in several places, as at Reading, at York and in the areas already mentioned, a few until even after the turn of the century. Fox, however, in these later years makes no direct reference to them, not even to the short-lived separate meeting set up at Harp Lane, London. It was just after Fox's death that his old Friend George Keith became the leader of a separate ' Christian-Quaker ' movement, first in America and then in England. Even though he was spared this sorrow, other aberrations of Friends caused him concern. One of these was the cabbalistical publications of van Helmont in which he found something to criticize. Francis Bugg, another Friend, became disaffected in 1680, but his published attacks on Friends, especially on Fox, began only later.[1]

HOMES AND HAUNTS IN LONDON

Though Fox is legally referred to during these years now as ' George Fox of London, gentleman ' and now as ' gentleman of Swarthmoor ', he really had no home in the south. He could still claim, as in 1670,[2] that he was ' but a lodger in London '. In 1683 he is listed among the ' country Friends ' who attended London meetings. Margaret Fox explains their separation during these years:

> And though the Lord had provided an outward habitation for him yet he was not willing to stay at it, because it was so remote and far from London, where his service most lay. And my concern for God, and his holy eternal Truth, was then in the north, where God had placed and set me, and likewise for the ordering and governing of my children and family: so that we

[1] See Braithwaite, *op. cit.*, pp. 469-88. Against van Helmont one of two manuscripts by Fox is at Friends House, London, in Portfolio 10-3.

[2] Above, p. 565.

were very willing, both of us, to live apart for some years upon God's account and his Truth's service, and to deny ourselves of that comfort which we might have had in being together, for the sake and service of the Lord and his Truth. And if any took occasion, or judged hard of us because of that, the Lord will judge them; for we were innocent. And for my own part, I was willing to make many long journeys for taking away all occasion of evil thoughts.[1]

After Fox's last visit to Swarthmoor three such journeys to London were undertaken by Margaret Fox, not, however, necessarily for the reason suggested. One was in the spring of 1681. It included her attendance at London Yearly Meeting and at the marriage thereafter in London of her daughter Sarah to William Meade. The second was in the winter of 1684-5. She arrived on 19th November and evidently divided most of her time, with or without her husband, between the homes of her daughters Sarah Meade and Margaret Rous. Thomas and Mary Lower were in London at the time and so was her daughter Susanna Fell. As usual Margaret Fox made efforts on her own to intercede directly on behalf of Friends both with Charles II, then on his death bed, and with the new king James II. On March 16 George Fox, accompanied by 'William Meade and his wife and Thomas Lower and Margaret Rous and Susanna Fell, took coach with Margaret Fox and Mary Lower to the *Swan with Two Necks* in Lad Lane to see them take coach to New Castle [under-Lyme] and so to Swarthmore '.

The third visit was in the spring of 1690. Apparently it was for but a few weeks, and she took coach with the Lower family for the north the last day of June. She says of it: 'Of all the times that I was at London, this last time was most comfortable, that the Lord was pleased to give me strength and ability to travel that great journey, being seventy six years of age, to see my dear husband . . . for he lived about half a year after I left him.'

For Fox himself in London many houses were like home.

[1] The Testimony of Margaret Fox. Ellwood, p. ix; Bicent., ii, 519.

There is scarcely a reference to his lodging in any inn in England, unless perchance it was that his normal Quaker host was also an innkeeper. But certain places were his repeated resort. Central to all his London activities was the Friends' Chamber in Three Kings Court off Lombard Street. In this suite of offices were the employed clerks of Friends, Ellis Hookes and after his death in 1681, Richard Richardson, with an assistant, Mark Swanner, after 1684. Here Fox participated in the many meetings which these clerks served, including the weekly Second Day's Morning Meeting and Meeting for Sufferings, and here were many minor or less regular conferences. The property had been secured by Friends after the Great Fire, and in the court of the former White Hart Inn had been built Gracechurch Street Meeting House and several private houses of Friends. Near here Andrew Sowle published and sold Quaker books, and here now lived Gerrard Roberts, John Osgood, Henry Gouldney and others. Nearby were Nathaniel and Elizabeth Bland, Nathaniel and Elizabeth Brassey, Mary Foster, William Crouch, Theodore Eccleston and other Friends who received Fox to dinner, or after or between meetings. Nathaniel Brassey and Mary Foster predeceased Fox in 1686. There was another large colony of Friends' houses in George Yard in many of which Fox visited. I may mention Edward Mann's hosiery warehouse, the homes of Edward Bathurst, Walter Benthall and Alexander Parker, and the shop and house of Daniel Wharley, woollen draper.

As for night's lodging, London supplied Fox with many hospitable homes. There was William Meade's city house on 'Fancy' (Fenchurch) Street at the Sign of the Ship. After Meade's marriage to Sarah Fell in 1681, Fox often went there for the night, almost regularly on Fridays after Meeting for Sufferings, which often lasted until 6 or 7 p.m. At the Savoy, in the property where the Friends' Meeting was held, lived Gilbert Latey and his wife and the widows Martha Fisher and Jane Woodcock. Fox lodged with Martha Fisher often, and not merely before or after attending Savoy Meeting. So at the Peel, that is, the Sign of the Baker's Peel, in Clerkenwell, John and Mary Elson in whose premises Peel Meeting was held, were his frequent overnight hosts. At one time he had a trunk with some of his things in it in their house and also his saddle, bridle, spurs and boots.[1] He was not infrequently at the Peel Monthly Meeting held on Wednesday afternoons. Every quarter when Friends' cases were pending at the Quarter Sessions at Hicks Hall, Clerkenwell, Fox's itinerary was likely to bring him for a night or two to the Elsons or to the city house of Francis Camfield nearby and in the daytime to the King's Head at Smithfield Bar, where the innkeeper was a Friend. Near Ratcliff Meeting his hosts were usually James and Mary Strutt. There were two meetings there on Sundays, the morning one being ' retired ' and intended for Friends. Near Wheeler Street Meeting House in Spitalfields one frequent host was a weaver (typical for this district) named Ezekiel Woolley with his wife Mary. Longer and quieter visits were with Mary Stott, a widow who lived at Dalston and later at Bethnal Green; and several of his letters indicate one of these as the place of writing. But in few if any homes in London was George Fox to be found more often, whether in the daytime or overnight, than in that of Benjamin Antrobus, linen-draper at the Plough and Harrow in Cheapside. Letters to him in later years usually bore this address. Here, at least a few years before his death, he kept another trunk, a hammock, some of his papers and other possessions, and a chest with some gold in it. Benjamin and Mary Antrobus had on deposit £100 of his money and another £100 which was ' for his daily charge '. Here Fox spent many a day and many more nights. On a Sunday, if because ' he was unfit to go forth ' or for other reasons he did not go to meeting, he would stay ' at B.A.'s ', often dictating or having his writings corrected with the help of the German Quaker scrivener, Mark

[1] This and similar data are taken from his testamentary papers, printed in the *Camb. Jnl.*, ii, 347-61.

Swanner. At an earlier time perhaps Edward Mann's house was his headquarters; so at least in the time of Haistwell's Journal, when Edward Mann must have had a house as well as a hosier's shop in town. Letters were addressed to Fox or his wife 'to be left with Edward Mann at his house next door to the Golden Lion in Bishopsgate Street'. But when in 1683 a London justice found himself unable to collect a fine from Fox because though he had means to pay he was a lodger, it would be perhaps safest to guess that his lodging would be regarded as at the home of Benjamin and Mary Antrobus. Fourteen years later, when Fox's widow registered for the administration of his estate, he was referred to (in Latin) as late of Swarthmoor in the County of Lancaster, but most recently of All Hallows [Parish], Lombard Street, London.

It is hard to know just what this hospitality involved of hosts and especially of hostesses. Some of the latter were remembered by token gifts in Fox's will. They were probably quite ready for his unexpected visits or for his longer stay. There was a blessing in his presence that they recognized, as is clear from statements made by Gulielma Penn and James Claypoole of his visit to Worminghurst in 1683. Many of his hostesses were widows with sufficient means, like Rebecca Travers of Watling Street, who wrote to his wife in 1671, 'I was never better pleased with my house than when he was in it and employed it for the service of Truth or any of his.'[1]

Fox himself was easily able to pay his own expenses, for the constant use of hackney coaches in and about London, and for what would have seemed to us the very modest rates current for board and lodging. The sources of his capital are not known. Not only his wife's money, but that inherited from his parents he seems to have left untouched. We learn incidentally of 24 head of cattle at Swarthmoor which were distrained in 1684 as belonging to Margaret Fox, though they really belonged to her husband. Earlier there was the purchase of bullocks there.

[1] Swarthmore MSS., i, 395.

In fact the largest single entry in the Account Book at Swarthmoor is, if I mistake not, a receipt of £94 'returned from Helen Dundas . . . father's account ' in December, 1676. His critics said of him that ' he lived in as much plenty as any knight in England ', and that he had twelve to thirteen hundred pounds a year ![1]

COUNTRY RETREATS

Alternating with the busy weeks in London Fox spent other periods in places which, though not more than a dozen miles from the City, were spoken of by Ellwood and in his sources as ' the country '. There was the household of John and Margaret (Fell) Rous at Kingston-on-Thames. Here Fox often stayed visiting Friends in the neighbourhood, attending the regular local meeting, writing or resting. There were frequent illnesses in the household and Fox's presence was sought more than once in such emergencies. Here Fox in December, 1677, finished off for the press his answer to Roger Williams[2] and from here many of his later smaller writings are dated. Both he and his wife were together here, probably for a month, in the winter of 1684-5. Three winters later Fox was at Kingston four months.

Another of his wife's daughters provided also a suburban home for Fox on the other side of the City. William Meade soon after his marriage to Sarah Fell in 1681 did not abandon his city house but obtained a place in Essex not far from Romford called Gooses (Gooseyes). Here also Susannah Fell made her home. Besides visits of six to eight weeks in earlier years, in 1689-90 Fox spent the whole winter here from mid-November to mid-April. He usually travelled little in the neighbourhood, though there were

[1] I have cited only evidence additional to that given in abundance in Brayshaw, *op. cit.*, ' Financial Position ', pp. 29-31. For the last two quotations see F. Bugg, quoted in A. Docwra, *An Apostate-Conscience Exposed*, 1699, p. 44, and *Truth the Defense and Shield of the Children of Light*, by William Rogers and others, 1679 (in MS. at Queen's College, Oxford, MS. 265), p. 780.

[2] See pp. 721 and 729 ante.

some meetings a few miles away held in weekly rotation as well as that held in the household. Either here or at their city house the Meades cared for a trunk with some of his business papers; and still in 1694 ' G.F. Library at W. Mead's House ', containing 335 books, is mentioned and partly listed.

To the north of London Fox also made longer or shorter visits. At Ford Green beyond Edmonton and near Winchmore Hill Meeting his host would be Edward Mann. At Enfield he stayed with Widow Dry, or with George Watts at the Chase Side, or with Thomas Hart. Bridget Austill often entertained him at South Street (now Southgate) and later, when she moved her school, at Tottenham High Cross. Less often he visited friends at Waltham Abbey, or at Epping Forest, and twice[1] he went on further to his friend Henry Stout's at Hertford. To this area he withdrew from London each of his last six summers for long retreats, including in turn, for days at a time, several of these habitual friendly homes.

The mention of Bridget Austill's school is not the only evidence of Fox's interest in education in this period. For he visited also Jane Bullock's school at Shacklewell, and Ann Travers' school at Chiswick. All these were ' womens schools '. At Waltham Abbey there was a Quaker co-educational boarding school, which Fox visited when in the neighbourhood, as he did also at Edmonton when Christopher Taylor the master moved it there.

HEALTH

Of his state of health in these last dozen years we can learn something from specific references in the rather impersonal diary kept for him, but we can perhaps infer more from his manner of life. Margaret Fox in her Testimony says explicitly that after his last visit to Swarthmoor ' he grew weakly, being troubled with pains and aches, having had many sore and long travels, beatings and hard

[1] 2nd-4th July, 1687, and 5th-9th Sept., 1690.

imprisonments'. Thomas Ellwood later in editing the Journal gives the same explanation and similar frequent diagnosis, and at the time itself he writes, 'Sure none that knows G.F. and understandingly considers how unwieldy and stiff his limbs are become through extreme cold and other hardships sustained in prisons . . . but will think he hath need enough to have some or other to travel with him.'[1] Ellwood was answering the criticism that Fox travelled in somewhat aristocratic style, with a man to wait on him. We have seen that he did have a young companion in 1677-8. The later record is less explicit, but a few casual uses of 'I' or 'we' by the original writer of the Itinerary Journals rather imply that Fox had still both in London and elsewhere a combined secretary and attendant generally with him.

Evidently Fox was never again in perfectly robust health, but there are no reasons to suppose that he was ever as ill as when he was in the London area in the winter of 1670-1, or when he arrived in Barbados in October, 1672, or when he was a prisoner at Worcester in the winter of 1674-5. As before, his powers of recuperation repeatedly asserted themselves. Less than a year before his death, his wife found him 'better in his health and strength than many times I had seen him before'. Just prior to his death he was quite as active as usual. But in addition to earlier evidences already mentioned, from 1683 on there are short notices of his being weary, weakly, unwell, or unfit to go forth, of lying down after meetings (very unusual in London), or staying where he was throughout the day. These references are ominously frequent after the Yearly Meeting of 1686 and during that of 1687. Dr. Edward Bourne of Worcester was much with him at the former time but probably not as attending physician. Except for a single reference to his being blooded by the horse leeches[2]

[1] T. Ellwood, *An Antidote against the Infection of William Rogers's Book*, 1682, p. 203.

[2] 14th May, 1685. Cf. his visit to the spectacle makers, 22nd August, 1685.

there is no evidence of his receiving medical attention. He was himself active and frequent in visiting the sick, sometimes at risk to his own health.[1] His visit to Gulielma Penn at Worminghurst occurred in that notoriously bad winter of 1683, a journey of fifty miles, of which he says, ' we went almost ten miles about, the ways being bad '. We know that a Friend with him had at the time a very severe attack of the stone and Gulielma herself was weak and soon so ill as to summon Thomas Ellwood to her bedside. There is no hint here of Fox's indisposition.

The long walks and nights spent in the open were now things of the past. Not only to London's suburbs but also within London he constantly used coaches or, in the case of Hammersmith, Chiswick and Kingston-on-Thames, river boats. The Seedsman's in Bishopsgate Street is often mentioned, evidently as the coach rendezvous convenient to the Chamber. In the country he went often to nearby meetings on horseback, and there are sections of the diary when it is frequently noted that he went on foot, a mile or less and up to three miles.

Thomas Ellwood explains Fox's withdrawals to the country as made for purposes of health, to escape ' the closeness of the city ' or ' the want of fresh air ', but I find no confirmation of this in the original sources. It is true that his occupation with committees was relaxed when he was out of London, but he was not idle, for as Willem Sewel remarks he was a diligent man. The diarist, who was perhaps also his secretary and had reason to know, says of six weeks at Gooses early in 1689, ' he writ a great deal touching many things '. Perhaps writing was less tiring and exacting. There is reason to think preaching was the most exhausting of all his occupations. In his later years he often rested after meeting in a neighbour's house on a bed or couch or even left the meeting before it was concluded. Speaking still put him in ' a great sweat '. Perhaps that was not unusual for the London meetings

[1] See *S.J.*, Index, ' Fox, George, visits to invalids ', and his *Book of Miracles*.

provided wine at the meeting's expense for the speakers after meeting. One notes that often Fox did not attend Sunday meeting at all. Sometimes when in London on Sunday he went only to the First Day Morning Meeting of ministers at 8 a.m. and not to any of the public meetings to which they subsequently scattered. Again and again he spent most of Sunday at home or in the office writing or dictating with one or even two secretaries; for Fox's correspondence and other writing in this period was still very great.

More than a thousand pages of his writing in this period can be read in his posthumously collected works or in over a hundred original separate publications (1675-1690). Some of these were translated and published also in Hebrew, Latin or continental languages. Others were published only in Dutch (or German) or were answers in manuscript to criticisms of Quakerism by German writers. Much other material is extant unprinted, and still more is known of.[1]

The longest and most famous of his later works has already been referred to, *A New England Fire Brand Quenched*, printed in 1678 and 1679. A good selection of typical short pieces from this period was included in the first edition of his published *Journal*, for want of satisfactory autobiographical data. The variety of his writing, hinted at already, can hardly be realized—personal, practical, pastoral, doctrinal, controversial, historical. Though it has little permanent value it adds to the picture of his versatile mind and of his energy. It was an integral and apparently effective part of his total service. His most prolific periods appear to have been the decades 1652-1661 and 1669-1679; the final years had, however, a substantial output and a wider range of subjects and correspondents. No picture of Fox in prison or out, in London or in the country, in England or overseas, in sickness or in health, is complete

[1] Joseph Smith, *Descriptive Catalogue of Friends' Books*, London, 1867, i, 674-90, 695-7. *Annual Catalogue of George Fox's Papers*, pp. 132-204, cf. summary by years, p. 2.

without including his ever ready capacity to put in writing, usually by dictating to a willing Friend, the current concern of his mind.

DEATH, BURIAL AND LEGACIES

With very little warning, death came at last on 13th January, 1691, or if we adopt both Quaker and Old Style reckoning, Eleventh Month 13, 1690. The circumstances of his illness, death and burial are familiar, being known to us from at least eight different contemporary accounts.[1] He had returned from the country on Monday, 29th December, and for a fortnight in the course of his usual activities he attended meetings on Mondays, Wednesdays, Fridays and Sundays. On the second Sunday he was at Gracechurch Street Meeting where 'he declared a long time very preciously and very audibly and went to prayer'. But after meeting, returning to the house of Henry Gouldney in the adjacent White Hart Court, he complained of cold, went to bed, grew worse, and finally expired—the time is variously stated as about 9.15, 9.30 or 10.00 p.m.—on Tuesday. No physician was present and no medicine taken. I do not know that even a lay diagnosis of his illness is preserved. According to the witnesses, his going was contented and appropriate to his life. 'I am clear, I am fully clear.' Appropriate also was the funeral, on Friday, where testimony was borne to his memory in the hearing of many persons who filled the meeting house, court and passage at Gracechurch Street and followed the body as it was carried by London Friends in six relays to the Friends' burial ground at Chequers Alley, very near to Bunhill Fields. Both the coffin and the headstone carried the initials of the name, the birthplace and the

[1] *S.J.*, p. 222, which Ellwood expanded, also the five letters mentioned in the note in *S.J.*, and another from Penn to Thomas Lloyd, printed in the *Friend* (Philadelphia), vi (1833), 210, and of course the official Epistle from the Second Day's Morning Meeting, printed with the *Journal*. For Ellwood's account see p. 759 of this edition.

age of the deceased. The age would have been 66 years, or more exactly 66½. About 66 years afterwards the coffin was disinterred in connection with some building changes and even opened but later sealed and buried in another location. The headstone was not replaced but a smaller one set in the wall. The earlier stone was subsequently deliberately destroyed. More recently a new stone has been erected.[1]

Margaret Fox survived her second husband eleven years. Except for one more visit to London in 1697-8 at the age of 83 she remained at Swarthmoor Hall, where her daughter Rachel Abraham had her home. She died on 23rd April, 1702, in the eighty-eighth year of her age. Beside his wife and her family Fox left a few relatives of his own. Shortly before his death he mentions, as though living, his brother John Fox of Polesworth, who had a son George, his sister Katharine, and a nephew Thomas Poultney, who was perhaps one of the children of his deceased sister Dorothy.

Fox's testamentary papers written from 1685 to 1688 were three of them proved in lieu of a will, late in 1697 when Margaret Fox was in London, and copies were deposited in the Prerogative Court of Canterbury. Fox left property to his own relatives and to his wife's progeny, and small amounts to some individual Friends including his London hosts, Edward Mann, Mary Elson, Mary Antrobus, Mary Woolley and Bridget Austill. His assets in cash, on loan, or invested, as listed or partly listed in 1685,

[1] For the history of Fox's grave I follow accounts in Webb, *Fells of Swarthmoor Hall*, 1865, 395 f., Beck and Ball, *op. cit.*, p. 331.

Of the erection in 1876 of the present grave stone no account is forthcoming, but at that time the location of the grave long forgotten was exactly identified through an old chart and was marked for the benefit of visitors. See *The Friend* (London), iv (1877), 105; v (1878), 99. Shortly afterwards was sold for housing by the Six Weeks Meeting a second portion of the Bunhill Fields burying ground, but not that part containing Fox's grave. In 1940-41 the neighbouring houses were mostly destroyed by enemy action, but the grave and marker were not disturbed.

came to perhaps £700. Evidently he expected some of this to be applicable to printing his *Journal.* A property known as Pettys near Swarthmoor, bought in 1687 and transferred to trustees, he gave to Friends to provide a meeting house, with endowment from its land. He said of it, 'It is all the house and land I have in England.' A grant of 1,250 acres in Pennsylvania made to him by William Penn in 1681 was willed to three of his sons-in-law and their heirs, with the exception of 16 acres given to Friends in Philadelphia for a meeting house, school house with botanical garden, a burial place and 'a close to put Friends' horses in when they come to meeting'. While the former of these plans was promptly carried out and the construction of a meeting house close to Swarthmoor Hall accomplished with volunteer help from the community, his Pennsylvania property was long unclaimed and then not all applied as he intended.

Above all Fox left earnest instructions for the collection and publication of all his writings. He had listed, arranged and endorsed some of them and he left memoranda where they were to be found.[1] The Second Day's Morning Meeting at once undertook the task, and under their direction Thomas Ellwood began transcribing and editing the manuscript materials for his *Journal.* Within a year he had gone as far as 1666. When he had finished, the manuscript was reviewed by a larger group of Friends. William Penn prepared an extended and valuable preface, and the whole was printed in a handsome folio volume of over eight hundred pages in 1694. A copy was presented to each Friends' meeting, and often methodically circulated among its members. Already the collecting of many other writings of Fox had made progress, and a list in very elaborate

[1] A few years before his death he thought they would make three volumes: 1. his epistles and letters and travels and books without controversy that are answers. 2. all the answers and controversy by themselves. 3. all the books of notes, and [doctrinal books] and the general papers to the men's and women's meetings by themselves. See the holograph memorandum, cited in *George Fox's Book of Miracles*, p. 39.

form arranged by years and with an index of first and last words was constructed by Mark Swanner, with whose help the Morning Meeting selected and prepared for the press over four hundred of Fox's Epistles. This was printed in 1698. The next category of writings was doctrinal. The Meeting limited itself to items already printed, and it excluded, for a possible later volume, the controversial pieces. Over a number of years those entrusted with this task read this large body of matter, rejecting much of it as duplicating what was elsewhere printed or as otherwise 'not meet to be reprinted'. The printing was done as they progressed, and in 1706 there was issued the 1,090-page volume entitled *Gospel-Truth Demonstrated*, often referred to as *Doctrinals*. Beyond these three large folios no further printing or reprinting of his works was undertaken. The reasons for this are not stated and can only be conjectured. The *Journal* as published in 1694 has often been republished, the last time in 1891, with reprints in 1901 and 1902. Once, in Philadelphia in 1831, not only the *Journal* but the other two large collections were reprinted in an eight-volume octavo edition of his works, with two early controversial pieces beside. Much of the unprinted collected manuscript material is still available, though some other parts of special interest have unfortunately disappeared.

Fox's death brought sorrow but not upheaval to the Society which he founded. Though few of his first associates long survived him, he had made himself dispensable. 'He had settled authority in the Church upon a basis which gave scope for the gifts of government of all and knew himself to be no hierarch. The best proof of this lies in the fact that his death made no disturbance in the life of the Church. Indeed, the only succession he had to provide for was that with respect to foreign correspondence . . . He remained to the last in close touch with affairs, but only as a revered elder among many brethren.'[1] The provision mentioned is in a letter written in his own

[1] Braithwaite, *op. cit.*, p. 432, part of a fine summary, pp. 427-44.

hand and brought in sealed after his death to the Morning Meeting:

All Friends in all the world, that used to write to me of all manner of things and passages, and I did answer them—let them all write to the Second-day's Meeting in London, directing them first to their correspondents there; and the Second-day's Meeting in London for them to answer them in the wisdom of God. And let a copy of this be sent to all places in the world among Friends, that they may know and understand this.

THOMAS ELLWOOD'S CONCLUSION

THOMAS ELLWOOD'S CONCLUSION

Thomas Ellwood's epilogue to the original edition of the Journal is notable for some of Fox's last sayings and for the picture of his taking leave of this life. In order to preserve it to readers of this edition, it is printed here, slightly abridged. Part has been taken direct from Ellwood's source for it, viz. *S.J.*, p. 222.

The 11th day of the 11th month [January, 1691], and the first day of the week, he was at Gracechurch Street meeting, where he declared a long time very preciously and very audibly and went to prayer. And the meeting after departed, which was large. Thence he went to Henry Gouldney's, a Friend's house in Whitehart Court near the meeting-house. And he said he thought he felt the cold strike to his heart as he came out of the meeting, but was pretty cheery with Friends that came to him there, and said, 'I am glad I was here. Now I am clear, I am fully clear.' And after they were gone he lay down upon the bed (as he was wont to do after a meeting) twice. And at his risings, which were but for a little space, he still complained of cold. The latter time he was worse and groaned much, so that after a very little, being much out of order he was forced to go to bed, where he lay in much contentment and peace, and very sensible to the last.

And in about two hours after, his strength failed him very much, and so he continued spending. And as in the whole course of his life, his spirit in the universal love of God was set and bent for the exalting of Truth and righteousness, and the making known the way thereof to the nations and peoples afar off, so now in the time of his outward weakness, his mind was intent upon, and (as it were) wholly taken up with that. And some particular Friends he sent for, to whom he expressed his mind and desire for the spreading Friends' books, and Truth thereby in the world, and through the nations thereof. Divers Friends came to visit him in his illness, unto some of whom he said, 'All is well. The Seed of God reigns over all, and over death itself. And though I am weak in body, yet the power of God is over all, and the Seed reigns over all disorderly spirits.'

Thus lying in an heavenly frame of mind, his spirit wholly exercised towards the Lord, he grew weaker and weaker in his natural strength; and on the third day of that week, between the hours of nine and ten in the evening, he quietly departed this life in peace, and sweetly fell asleep in the Lord . . . on the 13th day of the 11th month, 1690 [January, 1691], being then in the 67th year of his age.

Upon the 16th day of the same month a very great concourse of Friends, and other people of divers sorts, assembled together at the meeting-house (the house and yard well peopled) in Whitehart Court near Gracechurch street, about the middle time of the day, in order to attend his body to the grave. The meeting was held about two hours, with great and heavenly solemnity, manifestly attended with the Lord's blessed presence and glorious power; in which a great many testimonies were given concerning him.

After the meeting was ended, his body was borne by Friends, and accompanied by very great numbers of Friends, and other people,[1] to Friends burying ground near Bunhill Fields, where, after a solemn waiting upon the Lord, and several living testimonies borne concerning him, his body was decently committed to the earth; but his memorial shall remain, and be everlastingly blessed among the righteous.

[1] It was estimated that above four thousand people were present at the burial. (Robert Barrow's account in Thirnbeck MSS. at Friends House, London.)

INDEX

Note.—The following composite entries collect numerous headings which do not occur elsewhere in the index:

AMERICA: All place names on the American mainland.
FOX, GEORGE: Chronology.
—— Topics and incidents.
—— Journeys and visits, grouped regionally.
—— Teaching, various heads.
FRIENDS: Organized Quakerism, various heads.
LONDON: Localities, etc., in.
WEST INDIES.